HISTORY

OF THE

CHURCH OF JESUS CHRIST

OF

LATTER-DAY SAINTS.

PERIOD I.

History of Joseph Smith, the Prophet.

BY HIMSELF.

VOLUME III.
REVISED

AN INTRODUCTION AND NOTES
BY
B. H. ROBERTS.

PUBLISHED BY THE CHURCH.

DESERET BOOK COMPANY
Salt Lake City, Utah
1980

Lithographed by
DESERET PRESS
in the United States of America

TABLE OF CONTENTS.

VOLUME III.

INTRODUCTION.

CHAPTER I.

THE PROPHET JOSEPH'S DEPARTURE FROM KIRTLAND AND ARRIVAL IN MISSOURI.

CHAPTER II.

EXCOMMUNICATION OF OLIVER COWDERY AND DAVID WHITMER—THE WORK IN ENGLAND.

CHAPTER III.

READJUSTMENT AND SETTLEMENT OF AFFAIRS AT FAR WEST.

CHAPTER IV.

SELECTION OF LANDS IN CALDWELL AND DAVIESS COUNTIES FOR SETTLEMENT—ADAM-ONDI-AHMAN.

CHAPTER V.

INDEPENDENCE DAY AT FAR WEST—SUNDRY EVENTS AND REVELATIONS—EPISTLE OF DAVID W. PATTEN.

CHAPTER VI.

THE BEGINNING OF TROUBLE IN CALDWELL AND DAVIESS COUNTIES.

CHAPTER VII.

INCREASING DIFFICULTIES BETWEEN THE SAINTS AND THE MOBS OF DAVIESS AND CALDWELL COUNTIES.

CHAPTER VIII.

MOB MOVEMENTS IN CALDWELL, DAVIESS AND CARROLL COUNTIES—ARRIVAL OF KIRTLAND CAMP AT FAR WEST.

CHAPTER IX.

THE ORGANIZATION AND JOURNEY OF KIRTLAND CAMP.

CHAPTER X.

THE JOURNEY OF KIRTLAND CAMP (CONTINUED).

CHAPTER XI.

EXPULSION OF THE SAINTS FROM DE WITT, CARROLL COUNTY, MISSOURI.

CHAPTER XII.

MOVEMENTS OF THE MOB UPON DE WITT—BATTLE OF CROOKED RIVER —EXTERMINATING ORDER OF GOVERNOR BOGGS.

CHAPTER XIII.

MOB MOVEMENTS ABOUT FAR WEST—TREACHERY OF COLONEL HINKLE—SORROWFUL SCENES.

CHAPTER XIV.

RIVALRY AMONG THE MILITIA GENERALS FOR POSSESSION OF THE PRISONERS—"TRIAL" AT RICHMOND.

CHAPTER XV.

THE CASE OF THE SAINTS PRESENTED TO THE MISSOURI LEGISLATURE—THE PROPHET'S COMMUNICATION TO THE SAINTS FROM LIBERTY PRISON.

CHAPTER XVI.

CASE OF THE "MORMONS" BEFORE THE MISSOURI LEGISLATURE—CLOSE OF THE YEAR 1838.

CHAPTER XVII.

PREPARATIONS FOR LEAVING MISSOURI—ACTION OF THE STATE LEGISLATURE.

CHAPTER XVIII.

THE EXILED SAINTS GATHER AT QUINCY—PROPOSITION TO SETTLE AT COMMERCE.

CHAPTER XIX.

LETTERS TO THE PROPHET—AFFAIRS IN ENGLAND—PETITIONS.

CHAPTER XX.

SUNDRY MOVEMENTS IN THE INTEREST OF THE EXILED SAINTS—THE PROPHET'S LETTERS FROM LIBERTY PRISON.

CHAPTER XXI.

STIRRING SCENES ABOUT FAR WEST—THE EPISTLE OF THE PROPHET AND HIS FELLOW PRISONERS.

CHAPTER XXII.

THE PROPHET'S ACCOUNT OF HIS EXPERIENCES IN MISSOURI—FULFILLMENT OF A PROPHETIC REVELATION—COMPLETE EXODUS OF THE SAINTS FROM MISSOURI.

CHAPTER XXIII.

SETTLEMENT IN COMMERCE, ILLINOIS.

CHAPTER XXIV.

ADVENTURES OF THE PRISONERS REMAINING IN MISSOURI—THE PROPHET'S NARRATIVE OF PERSONAL EXPERIENCES IN MISSOURI.

CHAPTER XXV.

COMMERCE—THE PROPHET'S HISTORY—DOCTRINAL DEVELOPMENT.

CHAPTER XXVI.

THE PROPHET'S MINISTRY IN THE VICINITY OF COMMERCE—ADDRESS TO THE TWELVE.

CHAPTER XXVII.

BAPTISM OF ISAAC GALLAND—EPISTLE OF THE TWELVE TO THE CHURCH.

CHAPTER XXVIII.

THE ESCAPE OF PARLEY P. PRATT AND HIS FELLOW PRISONERS FROM MISSOURI—THE CLOSE OF AN EPOCH.

APPENDIX TO VOLUME III.

AFFIDAVITS OF HYRUM SMITH *et al.* ON AFFAIRS IN MISSOURI, 1831-39; OFFICIALLY SUBSCRIBED TO BEFORE THE MUNICIPAL COURT OF NAUVOO THE FIRST DAY OF JULY, 1843.

INTRODUCTION TO VOLUME III.

Enlightenment a Factor in Determining Responsibility for Conduct.

VOLUME THREE concludes,for the present, the history of the Church in Missouri. I think it proper, therefore, that here should be considered the causes of the Missouri persecutions, which resulted in the expulsion of the entire Church from that state.

There have been, of course, more extensive persecutions than those inflicted on the Saints in Missouri; but I doubt if there has ever been a persecution more cruel or terror-laden in its character. Viewed from the standpoint of its net results there were some fifty people, men, women, and children, killed outright; about as many more were wounded or cruelly beaten, and many more perished indirectly because of the exposure to which they were subjected through the winters of 1833-4 and 1838-9.

In round numbers it is estimated that between twelve and fifteen thousand people, citizens of the United States, after being dispossessed of their lands, were forcibly driven from the state. It is known that they paid to the United States government for land alone, three hundred and eighteen thousand dollars, which, at the minimum price of one dollar and a quarter per acre, would give them land holdings of over two hundred and fifty thousand acres, which represented for that day very large interests.*

To this list of results must be added the more horrible one of several cases of ravishment at Far West; and also, after barely escaping from the sentence of death pronounced by a court martial, the cruel imprisonment through weary months of a number of Church leaders.

In passing judgment upon such matters as these account must be taken of the age and country in which they occurred; likewise the pretensions to right views of life, and devotion to freedom on the part of the perpetrators of the injustice. Undoubtedly a heavier debt is incurred to history, to humanity and to God, when the parties who resort to such acts of mob violence and injustice live in an enlightened age, and where the free institutions of their country guarantee both the freedom and security of its citizens.

* See "American Commonwealths," Missouri, (Houghton, Mifflin & Company, 1888), p. 181.

If in the jungle a man meets a tiger and is torn to pieces, no one thinks of holding the tiger to any moral accountability. Perhaps the hunt will be formed to destroy the beast, but that is merely to be rid of a dangerous animal, and prevent the repetition of the deed. If another meets a cruel death among savages in heathen lands, while some moral responsibility would hold against them, according to their degree of enlightenment, yet the fact that it was an act of savages would be held to reduce the degree of moral turpitude. And likewise even in civilized states, in localities to which the vicious may gravitate, when acts of violence are committed there, some allowance may be, and generally is, made for the ignorance and general brutality of the particular neighborhood.

By this process of reasoning I think it will appear quite clear that moral responsibility, both on the part of individuals and communities or nations, increases in proportion to their enlightenment. If, therefore, this principle be kept in view, the persecution of the Latter-day Saints by the people of Missouri was a very heinous offense.

True it may be said that the worst acts of cruelty were perpetrated by low, brutish men among the mob or in the militia—for these bodies were convertible from one to the other on shortest possible notice, and wholly as the exigencies of the enemies of the Saints demanded—but these were led and abetted by quite a different order of men: by lawyers, members of the state legislature, by county and district judges, by physicians, by professed ministers of the gospel, by merchants, by leading politicians, by captains, majors, colonels, and generals—of several grades—of the militia, by many other high officials of the state including the Governor and Lieutenant Governor, and finally by the action of the state legislature which appropriated two hundred thousand dollars to defray the expenses incurred by the mob-militia in carrying out the Governor's order, exterminating the Saints from the state. These facts are made apparent in the pages of this and the two preceding volumes of the HISTORY OF THE CHURCH. The facts cannot be questioned. They are written out most circumstantially in the Prophet's story. Times, places, and names are given of the incidents related, and the more important of these may be corroborated by histories of these events other than our own.

The persecutions then of the Latter-day Saints in Missouri, and their final expulsion from that state, were crimes against the enlightenment of the age and of the state where the acts occurred; a crime against the constitutions and institutions both of the state of Missouri and of the United States; as also a crime against the Christian religion. All this we have in mind when speaking of the severity and cruelty of these compared with other persecutions. The state of Missouri was guilty of a greater crime when it persecuted the Latter-day Saints than states were which in the barbarous times of the dark ages persecuted their people; though when estimated in net results there may have been more murders and robberies, greater destruction of property, and more wide-spread suffering in the latter than in the former.

It is in the light of the principle here laid down that I propose to review the causes of the persecutions of the Latter-day Saints in Missouri.

The People of Missouri and the Saints.

The people of the state of Missouri, and especially those living in western and upper Missouri, in the early decades of the nineteenth century, were chiefly from the states of the South—from Kentucky, Tennessee, Virginia, and the Carolinas. This is not stated as a matter of reproach, for among the American people there have been no better or nobler citizens of the Republic than the people of the states enumerated. I merely make the statement in order to present a fact, and because other facts grow out of it. To say that Missouri was settled by emigrants from the states of the South carries with it the explanation why Missouri was one of the slave states, and her people attached to the social and industrial methods of life attendant upon that circumstance. That is to say, they looked with contempt upon manual labor; regarding it as menial and proper only for slaves to perform. With that idea is closely related another; namely, that white people who from circumstances were compelled to perform manual labor, or who followed it from principle, in the eyes of the people of the South were of an inferior class; contemptuously characterized by some as "white trash," and by others, inclined to be more polite, as "poor whites."

Freedom from manual labor gave to those of active dispositions in such communities an opportunity to follow the more desirable vocations of professional life; the law, medicine, the Christian ministry, merchandizing and general business; or leisure for political or military activities; or the pursuit of pleasure, fishing, hunting, horse racing, and social life generally. These conditions naturally resulted in pride, often in arrogance, and a desperate sort of courage, which held honor high and weakness and cowardice in contempt; also something of intolerance for those disposed to set themselves against such an order of things.

The reader will recognize, of course, that I have so far in mind only the better element of the population, the least of the evils and some of the advantages resulting from such industrial and social conditions. There were, however, quite different and more serious results than any yet noted arising from this system of society. While those disposed to activity and inclined to honorable pursuits might enjoy certain advantages from the system, on the other hand, it fostered man's natural inclination to idleness and love of ease that comes of idleness; and fostered jealousy and bitterness against those more industrious and successful. In such a class the system led to ignorance, irreligion, and criminal tendencies; constituting them a dangerous element in the community. It was doubtless this class the Prophet Joseph had in mind when he said soon after his first arrival in western Missouri: "Our reflections were great, coming as we had from a highly cultivated state of society in the East, and standing now upon the confines or western limits of the United States, and looking into the vast wilderness of those that sat in darkness. How natural it was to observe the degradation, leanness of intellect, ferocity and jealousy of a people that were nearly a century behind the times, and to feel for those who roamed about without the benefit of civilization, refinement, or religion!"

Many of the positions in the higher walks of life, in western Missouri, were sought by the unworthy, the corruptible and the vicious—men who sought all the advantages of the southern ideals of life without possessing the refining virtues which for generations in the older states of the south made some of the evils of the social system that obtained there at least tolerable. Such were the Brazeales, the Wilsons, the Hunters, the Kavanaughs, the Likens, the Loveladys, the McCartys, the McCoys, the Pixleys, the Simsons, the Silvers, the Westons, the Gilliams, the Birches, the Blacks, the Bogarts, the Clarks, the Liveseys, and the Penistons.

Another circumstance which influenced somewhat the character of western Missouri's population in the early decades of the nineteenth century, was the fact that these sections of the state constituted part of the frontiers of the United States, and here had gravitated a more or less lawless class which sought the security of proximity to the boundary lines of the United States, from whose confines they could make their escape in the event of being hard pressed for violations of law in the older states whence they had come, or in their new habitat. Such were the Lovels, the Hawkins, the Heatherleys and many others.

The Latter-day Saints who settled in Missouri from 1831 to 1839 had come for the most part from the New England States and New York. There were, therefore, marked differences in character between them and the old settlers of Missouri; differences of ideas as to industrial and social life; of moral and religious life. The Saints were descendants chiefly of the Puritans, and both by inheritance and training had fallen heirs to the Puritan's strict views of industry, religion and morality. The Puritans taught that all labor was honorable, and industry a duty. Religion occupied a large share of their attention—entered in fact into all the affairs of life—though its duties meant largely a regular attendance upon church service; a strict observance of the proprieties while there; a rigid observance throughout of the Sabbath day. Neither work nor amusements were tolerated on that day. In the olden time among some of their forefathers it had been unlawful to sit in Boston Common on the Sabbath or to walk in the streets of Boston, except to church. Once a man was publicly whipped for shooting a fowl on Sunday. A woman was threatened with banishment for smiling in church. A person absent from church for more than one Sunday was in danger of being fined, whipped, or set in the stocks. Swearing was prohibited in nearly all the New England colonies, and a split stick was sometimes placed on the swearer's tongue.*

Both food and dress were plain, and the latter, in some instances, was regulated by law. Amusements were few. Dancing and card-playing were forbidden, and there was little music. The state sought to take entire charge of the individual, and supposed that tendency toward immorality could be stemmed by legislation. In early Connecticut no one under twenty was allowed to use tobacco, and none to use it more than once a day. The laws were severe and the penalties cruel. The stocks and whipping-post and pillory were in frequent requisition to correct moral delinquents. An offender might be made to stand on a stool in church with the name of his misdemeanor displayed on his breast. Among the common punishments were cropping or boring the ears and branding with a hot iron.†

Of course in later years there was a general relaxation from these severities, and many of these customs and laws, by the time our generation of Saints came on the scene, were obsolete. Still, the moral and spiritual atmosphere in which the Saints and their fathers had been reared was austere in its moral character, and stood in marked contrast to the moral atmosphere of the South, where, in respect of such things as church attendance, religious observances, personal liberty in eating, drinking and amusements, there was wider freedom.

In the sparsely settled country of western Missouri, the descendants of the old cavaliers and their following, who settled the South, and the descendants of the Puritans, who settled the North, were to meet: and very naturally one may see in these antagonistic elements—aside from the cause of antagonism which will be found in the newly revealed religion of the Latter-day Saints—natural causes of irritation between them founded in the differences of character, and their respective conceptions of industrial, moral, and religious duties. That the old settlers

* "History of the United States," (Morris) p. 132.

† Ibid, pp. 135-7.

in Missouri, even those friendly disposed towards the Saints, recognized the incompatibility of the two classes is evident from the public utterances of a mass meeting held at Liberty, in Clay county, when the Saints were urged to seek a new locality where they could live by themselves. "They are eastern men," said the address, "whose manners, habits, customs, and even dialect, are essentially different from our own. We earnestly urge them to seek some other abiding place, where the manners, the habits, and customs of the people will be more consonant with their own."*

This difference of character between the Saints and the old settlers I account one of the causes of the Missouri persecutions.

The Question of Slavery.

The question of slavery in Missouri was a delicate one. It will perhaps be remembered that it was the application of the territory of Missouri for admission into the Union, 1818-19, that brought the question of slavery into one of its acute stages before the country; and inaugurated a long series of debates in the National Congress on the subject. It was upon the admission of Missouri into the Union in 1821 that the great Compromise which bears the state's name settled, not the question of slavery itself, but, for the time, the agitation of it.

That Compromise consisted finally in this: that while Missouri herself was admitted with a clause in her constitution permitting slavery, and also prohibiting free people of color from immigrating into the state, slavery was forever to be prohibited in all territory of the United States north of the line thirty-six degrees and thirty minutes north latitude (the southern boundary line of the state of Missouri); and Missouri was required "by a solemn, public act" of her legislature, to declare that the clause in her constitution relating to the immigration of free negroes into the state, should never be construed to authorize the passage of any law by which any citizen of either of the states in this Union shall be excluded from the enjoyment of any of the privileges and immunities to which he is entitled under the Constitution of the United States.

These historical facts are referred to here that the reader may be reminded that slavery was a delicate question in Missouri; that her people were super-sensitive about it since she was the first territory upon which the National Congress sought to impose the prohibition of slavery as a condition precedent to her admission into the Union, which, up to that time, had been a matter left to the people of the territory seeking admission to determine for themselves. Of course this attempt at re-

* HISTORY OF THE CHURCH, Vol. II, p. 450.

striction of slavery was made by northern members of the national Congress.* All the sentiment for the restriction of slavery was in the North. In 1831 the sentiment for the positive abolition of slavery had made such progress in Massachusetts, that William Lloyd Garrison established in Boston "*The Liberator*," a paper which advocated "the immediate and unconditional emancipation of every slave in the United States." As a result of this agitation anti-slavery societies were formed and active measures taken to advocate these opinions by means of lectures and pamphlets. These extreme measures against slavery did not meet with the approval of all or even the majority of the people of New England, much less with the approval of the people of other northern states. Still this agitation arose and was chiefly supported in New England. It will not be difficult to understand, therefore, that any considerable number of people from that section of the Union immigrating into a slave state would arouse suspicion; especially when that immigration was into a slave state upon which, when as a territory she had made application for admission into the Union, prohibition of slavery was sought to be enforced by the northern members of the National Congress. Nor will it be sufficient to dispel this suspicion to aver that these particular immigrants from New England, and other northern states are not abolitionists; that they take no part with, and do not share the fanatical sentiments of, the abolitionists; that their objects and purposes are of an entirely different and larger character.

The answer to all this was given in a public document drawn up to voice the sentiment of a great mass meeting of the people of Clay county—a people, be it remembered, who at the time (1836) were not unfriendly towards the Saints, but a people who a few years before had received the Saints into their homes, and given them shelter when they were exiles from Jackson county, and who, at the time of the utterance I am about to quote was published, were in a covenant of peace with the Saints, and the Saints in a covenant of peace with them—I say the answer to all disclaimers on the part of the Saints respecting their not being abolitionists was found in this public utterance: "They are eastern men, whose manners, habits, customs and even dialect are essentially different from our own. They are non-slaveholders, and opposed to slavery, which in this peculiar period, when abolitionism has reared its deformed and haggard visage in our land, is well calculated to excite deep and abiding prejudices in any community where slavery is tolerated and protected."

I call attention to these facts that the student of the history of the Church may appreciate the weight of influence they would have in cre-

* Mr. Tallmadge, a representative from the state of New York, offered the restricting provision.

ating popular sentiment against the Saints; a matter which hitherto, if I may be permitted to say so, has not been fully appreciated. One can readily see what a potent factor this sentiment against New England and other northern states people would be in the hands of political demagogues and sectarian priests seeking to exterminate what they would respectively consider an undesirable element in politics and a religious rival. That both political demagogues and sectarian priests made the most of the opportunity which hostile sentiment in Missouri against abolition and abolitionists afforded, abundantly appears in the pages of the first volume of the Church History. That sentiment was appealed to from the first; indeed in the very first manifesto of the mob —known as "The Secret Constitution,"*—issued against the Saints in Missouri, it was a prominent feature. This was at Independence, in July, 1833. In that "Manifesto" the following passage occurs: "More than a year since, it was ascertained that they [the Saints] had been tampering with our slaves, and endeavoring to sow dissensions and raise seditions amongst them. Of this their Mormon leaders were informed, and they said they would deal with any of their members who should again in like case offend. But how specious are appearances. In a late number of the *Star*, published in Independence by the leaders of the sect, there is an article inviting free negroes and mulattoes from other states to become Mormons, and remove and settle among us. This exhibits them in still more odious colors. It manifests a desire on the part of their society, to inflict on our society an injury that they know would be to us entirely insupportable, and one of the surest means of driving us from the country; for it would require none of the supernatural gifts that they pretend to, to see that the introduction of such a caste amongst us would corrupt our blacks, and instigate them to bloodshed."

The article on "Free People of Color" referred to appeared in the *Evening and Morning Star* for July. The charge of sowing dissensions and inspiring seditions among the slaves, and inviting free negroes to settle in Missouri, had no foundation in truth. Concerning such people the Missouri laws provided that: If any negro or mulatto came into the state of Missouri, without a certificate from a court of record in some one of the United States, evidencing that he was a citizen of such state, on complaint before any justice of the peace, such negro or mulatto could be commanded by the justice to leave the state; and if the colored person so ordered did not leave the state within thirty days, on complaint of any citizen. such person could be again brought before the justice who might commit him to the common jail of the county, until

* HISTORY OF THE CHURCH, vol. 1, p. 374, et seq.

the convening of the circuit court, when it became the duty of the judge of the circuit court to inquire into the cause of commitment; and if it was found that the negro or mulatto had remained in the state contrary to the provisions of this statute, the court was authorized to sentence such person to receive ten lashes on his or her bare back, and then order him or her to depart from the state; if the person so treated should still refuse to go, then the same proceedings were to be repeated and punishment inflicted as often as was necessary until such person departed.

And further: If any person brought into the state of Missouri a free negro or mulatto, without the aforesaid certificate of citizenship, for every such negro or mulatto the person offending was liable to a forfeit of five hundred dollars; to be recovered by action of debt in the name of the state.

The editor of the *Star* commenting upon this law said: "Slaves are real estate in this and other states, and wisdom would dictate great care among the branches of the Church of Christ on this subject. So long as we have no special rule in the Church as to people of color, let prudence guide; and while they, as well as we, are in the hands of a merciful God, we say: shun every appearance of evil."

Publishing this law and the above comment was construed by the old settlers to be an invitation to free people of color to settle in Jackson county! Whereupon an extra was published to the July number of the *Star* on the sixteenth of the month, which said: "The intention in publishing the article, "Free People of Color," was not only to stop free people of color from immigrating to Missouri, but to prevent them from being admitted as members of the Church. * * * * * To be short, we are opposed to having free people of color admitted into the State."*

But in the face of all this the Missourians still claimed that the article was merely published to give directions and cautions to be observed by "colored brethren," to enable them upon their arrival in Missouri, to "claim and exercise the rights of citizenship." "Contemporaneous with the appearance of this article"—the above article in the *Star*

* In making the statement that it was the intention of the *Star* article not only to stop "free people of color" immigrating to Missouri, but also to "prevent them from being admitted as members of the Church," the editor of the *Star*, of course went too far; if not in his second article, explaining the scope and meaning of the first, then in the first article; for he had no authority to seek to prevent "free people of color" from being admitted members of the Church. But as a matter of fact there were very few if any "free people of color" in the Church at that time. The "fears" of the Missourians on that head were sheer fabrications of evil dis posed minds.

—continued the charge published in the *Western Monitor*—"was the expectation among the brethren, that a considerable number of this degraded caste were only waiting this information before they should set out on their journey."* And this base falsehood was used to inflame the minds of the old settlers against the Saints.

I do not refer to this question of slavery in connection with the persecution of the Saints in Missouri in order to set it down as one of the causes of that persecution; because, as a matter of fact, the views of the Saints, and especially of the leading Elders of the Church on that question were such that they could never be truthfully charged with being a menace to that institution. The Prophet Joseph himself, at the time of the Jackson county troubles and subsequently, held very conservative views on the subject of slavery, surprisingly conservative views when his own temperament and environment are taken into account, of which fact any one may convince himself by reading his paper on the subject of abolition in Volume II of the Church History, pages 436-40.

Finally, it was given by the inspiration of God to the Prophet first to utter the most statesman-like word upon this vexed question of slavery, and had the nation and people of the United States but given heed to his recommendations it would have settled the question in harmony with the convictions of the people of the North, and without injustice to the South. Here follows his statesman-like word, published throughout the United States in 1844—eleven years before Ralph Waldo Emerson made substantially the same recommendation, and for which the philosopher received no end of praise:—

"Petition, also, ye goodly inhabitants of the slave states, your legislators to abolish slavery by the year 1850, or now, and save the abolitionist from reproach and ruin, and infamy and shame. Pray Congress to pay every man a reasonable price for his slaves out of the surplus revenue arising from the sale of the public lands, and from the deduction of pay from the members of Congress. Break off the shackles from the poor black man, and hire him to labor like other human beings; for an hour of virtuous liberty is worth a whole eternity of bondage."†

But now to return to the course of the Missourians in misrepresenting the views of the Saints on the subject of slavery. Notwithstanding the explicit denials through the "*Evening and Morning Star*," that the article on "Free People of Color" was intended to invite such a class into the state; and the further declaration that the Saints were opposed to such persons coming into the state; as also the fact that it is

* *Western Monitor* for the 2nd of August, 1833.

† Joseph Smith's "Views of the Powers and Policy of the Government of the United States," *Mill. Star*, Vol. XXII. p. 743.

doubtful if there were any free negroes who were members of the Church—notwithstanding all this, their enemies continued to misrepresent them, and their views on the subject of slavery. They saw in the fact that many of them were from New England, where abolition sentiment was rife, their opportunity to charge them with abolition sentiments and intention to interfere with slavery, with every prospect of having it quite generally believed—hence the charge was made and became a pretext if not a cause of acts of aggression upon the Saints, and as such is a factor that must be taken account of in these pages.

Political Fears.

I know of no circumstances which developed what the political faith of the Saints really was during their sojourn in the state of Missouri; and doubt if any data exists from which it could be determined whether a majority of them were Whigs or Republican-Democrats, as the party now designated as the Democratic party was then called. In fact, politics, local or national, concerned the Saints but very little during their stay in Missouri. Their minds were occupied by quite other, and I may say, larger and higher things; and their activities were concerned with other issues than those political. They were concerned about the redemption of Zion, her establishment, the proclamation of the Gospel, the salvation of men, the preparation of the earth for the incoming of that Kingdom whose King is the Lord. Their mission encompassed the whole world, it was not confined to the state of Missouri and her petty political affairs; nor even to the political affairs of the United States, important as they were. "Mormonism" was a world-movement, not merely a national one. It concerned itself with the deeper and broader subject of religion, rather than with the principles and methods of the administration of government, state or national. Still, in common with other people of the county, state and nation of which they were citizens, they possessed civil and political rights and privileges, accompanied as such rights and privileges always are in a republic with certain duties both to the state and themselves, among which the exercise of the elective franchise. As this made them a power in the community, their actual and prospective influence in the affairs of the counties where they resided, and in the state, was a matter of frequent discussion among the old settlers in Missouri. I do not know that it was ever charged that they were Whigs, and that by acting with that party in Missouri they could wrest the control of the state from the Republican-Democratic party then in power; though that they were Whigs might have been inferred from the fact of their being chiefly from New England and other northern states; yet this was not charged.

There was repeatedly expressed, however, a fear of their political power. In the document issued by the mob meeting at Independence on the 20th of July, 1833, it is said: "When we reflect on the extensive field in which the sect is operating, and that there exists in every country a leaven of superstition that embraces with avidity, notions the most extravagant and unheard of, and that whatever can be gleaned by them from the purlieus of vice and the abodes of ignorance, is to be cast like a waif into our social circle, it requires no gift of prophecy to tell that the day is not far distant when the civil government of the county will be in their hands; when the sheriff, the justices, and the county judges will be Mormons, or persons wishing to court their favor from motives of interest or ambition."

It was an effort to prevent members of the Church from voting at an election at Gallatin, Daviess county, in August, 1838, which led to the commencement of those acts of hostility against the Saints which ended ultimately in their expulsion from that state. There was no political offense even charged against the Saints; only that if permitted to exercise the franchise they would in time obtain control of the counties where they resided, so rapidly were they increasing in numbers; and the old settlers would lose the offices; and as these old settlers were dear lovers of office, it was political jealousy born of fear which prompted in part the acts of aggression against the Saints. When such jealousy is awakened, pretexts for the justification of its existence are not difficult to find, and in this instance the old settlers in Missouri relied upon the false charges of ignorance, superstition, and general unworthiness of the Saints to be considered good citizens of the state. The charge was not that they were all of one political faith; or that they voted solidly; or that they were under the political dictation of their religious leaders; or that religious influence was dragged into political affairs. None of these charges were made: it was simply a fear that the old settlers would lose the offices, and the new settlers, the Saints, being in the majority, would hold them. How much justification there was for this "fear" may not be determined, since it was based upon no accomplished fact, but regarded as the natural outcome of the operation of the political system obtaining in the United States; namely, the right of the majority to choose the public officers; and if the Saints happened to be in the majority it was regarded as likely that they would elect their friends to office, among whom, at least, would have been some members of their own faith. How the matter would have terminated in the event of the Saints having been permitted to remain in Missouri—what would have been the political alignment of the members of the Church I mean, no one can say. The only political utterance made by any Church leader was that given out by the Prophet Joseph soon after his arrival in Missouri, and called at the time "*The Political Motto of the Church.*" I quote it:

"*The Constitution of our country formed by the Fathers of Liberty; peace and good order in society; love to God, and good will to man. All good and wholesome laws; virtue and truth above all things, and Aristarchy* [a government by good men] *live for ever; but woe to tyrants, mobs, aristocracy, anarchy and toryism, and all those who invent or seek out unrighteous or evasive law suits, under the pretext and color of law or office, either religious or political. Exalt the standard of Democracy! Down with that of priestcraft, and let all the people say Amen! That the blood of the fathers may not cry from the ground against us. Sacred is the memory of that blood which bought for us our liberty.*"

This surely is sufficiently non-partisan, cosmopolitan and patriotic. Is it not of the essence of Americanism? And under such sentiments would not every member of the Church be able to perform his political duty in either of the great American parties then existing or afterwards to arise?

It is not necessary to pursue this subject further. It is enough to say that the political fears of the old settlers of Missouri, though based upon conjecture as to what could or might happen, were real fears, and became one of the causes of the Missouri persecutions.

The Saints and the Indians.

The interest of the Saints in the American Indians grows out of the knowledge they have of their forefathers, revealed through the Book of Mormon. From the historical parts of that book they learned the origin of these Indians; that they are of the house of Israel: from the prophetic parts of the book they learn of their future, that it is to be glorious; that fallen as their fortunes now are, they will not always remain so; extinction is not their fate, but before many generations shall pass away they will become a white and a delightsome people, favored of God, and prominent in bringing to pass His purposes in the land of Zion—the two Americas. It was a mission to the Lamanites or Indians which first brought several of the Elders of the Church of Christ to western Missouri. When the people of Missouri learned in what esteem the Saints held the forefathers of the Indians, and also the Indians themselves, both on account of their forefathers and the promises of God to them, it was but reasonable that they should conclude there was—as indeed there is—a strong sympathy on the part of the Saints towards the Indians; and there was great reason to believe that this sympathy might become mutual.

It was in this substratum of truth that the false accusations against the Saints were founded to the effect that they were seeking to enter into an alliance with the Indian tribes of the west for the purpose of driving the old settlers from their possessions in western Missouri, in order that the Saints with the Indians might possess the land to the exclusion of the "Gentiles."

To appreciate the seriousness of this charge, it should be remembered that the Indian tribes formerly residing east o the Mississippi, about this time—during President Jackson's two presidential terms, 1829-1837—were being transplanted into the country immediately west of Missouri, so that there were great numbers of these people—amounting to many thousands—being massed just beyond the boundaries of the state. Many of the tribes were in no amiable mood either. In some instances the terms of the treaties by which they accepted lands in the Indian territory west of Missouri, for lands that constituted their old homes in the East and South, were forced upon them after—to them—disastrous wars; so that it might well be suspected that they would be ready to follow any leader who would hold out promise of regaining their lost possessions, or who would give them the hope of revenge upon their despoilers.

Let these facts be considered and given their due weight, and the reader will not find it difficult to perceive what a potent factor against the Saints this charge of holding communication with the Indians for the purpose of dispossessing the people of western Missouri of their homes would be; and, as in the case of the slavery question, their enemies were not slow to see the advantage, and made the most of it. It was not until the agitation for the removal of the Saints from Clay county began, however, 1836, that this charge of holding communication with the Indians for the purposes already set forth, was publicly made. Then in the document adopted at the mass meeting setting forth the several reasons of the old settlers for asking the Saints to remove from Clay county, this passage occurs:

"In addition to all this, they are charged, as they have hitherto been, with keeping up a constant communication with our Indian tribes on the frontiers; with declaring, even from the pulpit, that the Indians are a part of God's chosen people, and are destined by heaven to inherit this land, in common with themselves. We do not vouch for the correctness of these statements; but whether they are true or false, their effect has been the same in exciting the community. In times of greater tranquility, such ridiculous remarks might well be regarded as the offspring of frenzied fanaticism; but at this time, our defenseless situation on the frontier, the bloody disasters of our fellow citizens in Florida and other parts of the South, all tend to make a portion of our citizens regard such sentiments with horror, if not alarm. These and many other causes have combined to raise a prejudice against them, and a feeling of hostility, that the first spark may, and we deeply fear will, ignite into all the horrors and desolations of a civil war, the worst evil that can befall any country."

Governor Dunklin, shortly after this, in answer to appeals made to him by the Saints for protection, by the execution of the law, on this charge of holding communication with the Indians, said: "Your neighbors accuse your people with holding illicit communication with the Indians, and of being opposed to slavery. You deny. Whether the charge or the denial is true, I cannot tell. The fact exists, and your neighbors seem to believe it true; and whether true or false, the consequences will be the same (if your opponents are not merely gasconnading), unless you can, by your conduct and arguments, convince them of your innocence. If you cannot do this, all I can say to you is that in this Republic the *vox populi* is the *vox Dei.*"

Of course this false accusation was emphatically denied by the Saints. In a public meeting held by the members of the Church to draw up a reply to the request of the people of Clay county, that the Saints remove from that county, they said: "We deny holding any communication with the Indians, and mean to hold ourselves as ready to defend our country against their barbarous ravages as any other people. We believe that all men are bound to sustain and uphold the respective governments in which they reside, while protected in their inherent and inalienable rights by the laws of such governments; and that sedition and rebellion are unbecoming every citizen thus protected, and should be punished accordingly."

In a communication signed by the Prophet Joseph and several other presiding officers of the Church, and addressed to the leading men of Clay county, referring to the Indian charge, this was said: "Another charge of great magnitude is brought against our friends in the west, that of keeping up a constant communication with the Indian tribes on the frontier; with declaring, even from the pulpit, that the Indians are a part of God's chosen people, and are destined by heaven to inherit this land, in common with themselves. We know of nothing under the present aspect of our Indian relations calculated to arouse the fears of the people of the Upper Missouri more than a combination of influences of this nature; and we cannot look upon it as being other than one of the most subtle purposes of those whose feelings are embittered against our friends, to turn the eye of suspicion upon them from every man who is acquainted with the barbarous cruelty of rude savages. Since a rumor was afloat that the western Indians were showing signs of war, we have received frequent private letters from our friends, who have not only expressed fears for their own safety, in case the Indians should break out, but a decided determination to be among the first to repel any invasion and defend the frontier from all hostilities. We mention the last fact because it was wholly uncalled for on our part, and came previous to any excitement on the part of the people of Clay county against our friends, and must definitely show that this charge is untrue."

But all these denials went for nothing. As remarked by Governor Dunklin, whether the denial or the charge was true, people at a distance, at least, might not tell; quite generally, however, the charge was believed, and helped to swell the volume of prejudice—already too great—against the Saints. Indeed, so potent a factor was this charge of holding illicit communication with the Indians, in arousing prejudice against the Saints, that it was used against them with great effect after their settlement in Utah. It was one of the charges made against them at the time the general government of the United States was induced by their enemies to send out an army to suppress a rebellion in Utah that had no existence except in the hate-frenzied minds of the detractors of the Saints.

"It is charged," said Stephen A. Douglas in a speech at Springfield, Illinois, on the 12th of June, 1857*—"It is charged * * * * that the Mormon government, with Brigham Young at its head, is now forming alliances with Indian tribes in Utah and adjoining territories, stimulating the Indians to acts of hostility, and organizing bands of his own followers, under the name of Danites or destroying angels, to prosecute a system of robbery and murders upon American citizens who support the authority of the United States, and denounce the infamous and disgusting practices and institutions of the Mormon government."

The army came only to find the foregoing with other charges that had induced the general government to send it to Utah, untrue. But this is digression.

Mormon communication with the American Indians for the purpose of despoiling the Gentiles and taking possession of their lands can never be set down as one of the causes of the Missouri persecution; for such communication never took place—the charge of it was untrue. It was, however, one of a number of pretexts, and became a factor in creating public prejudice, which alone made possible the expulsion of the Saints from Missouri.

The Unwisdom of the Saints.

I come now to one of the most delicate subdivisions of this Introduc-

* The speech appears in the *Missouri Republican* of June 18th, 1857.

tion; namely, the unwisdom of the Saints. To appreciate this as a factor in the Missouri persecutions one needs to take into account not only human nature, but also human nature under the stress of religious impulse and influence. First, however, as to the facts involved.

To the Saints of those times had been given a dispensation of the Gospel—a new revelation of it. They had been blessed with the spirit of faith to receive it. To them it was made known that God had again spoken from heaven; He had again conferred divine authority upon men to act in His name—many of the brethren, the majority of the male membership of the Church in fact, held that divine authority, the priesthood of God; the terms of man's salvation were restated; the spiritual powers and gifts of the Gospel were guaranteed anew and plenteously enjoyed by the Saints. To them was made known the truth of a new volume of scripture, the Book of Mormon. The knowledge imparted by that book was in itself, and especially to them, wonderful. From it they learned that the ancient inhabitants of the American continents, the ruins of whose civilization challenged the curiosity of men and excited their wonder, were of the house of Israel; the American Indians were their fallen descendants and, of course, also of the house of Israel and heirs to the general promises made to that people, to say nothing of special promises made to them as direct descendants of the house of the patriarch Joseph, son of Jacob. Messiah in his resurrected and glorified state had visited America and its inhabitants shortly after His resurrection at Jerusalem,and established the Christian institution,—a Christian ministry, and a Christian Church, followed by a veritable golden age of peace, prosperity, and righteousness; and although the descendants of that ancient God-favored people were now fallen from the high estate of their fathers, yet were the promises and prophecies great concerning them. God would again visit them by His grace, they should be redeemed from their ignorance and barbarism, and they should yet be important factors in establishing a "New Jerusalem," the Zion of God on this land of America, given to the descendants of the ancient patriarch Joseph, whose descendants principally the Indians are. The Saints had been even so far favored as to have the place for the chief city of refuge and safety pointed out to them by revelation; as also the site of its temple—Independence, Missouri; and they were required by the commandments of God to bear witness to the world of these things. In view of all this—the fact that they were made at once the depository and witnesses of these great revelations, is it not likely that they would regard themselves as a people peculiarly favored of God? And is it matter of astonishment if some among them, not possessed of the soundest judgment, should run into an excess of zeal and give expression to unwise, as also to unwarranted conclusions?

Moreover, the Lord had spoken of the future glory of Zion—of the city, the location of which the Elders were to testify; also of the glory of the temple, with its future cloud by day and pillar of fire by night; of the future union of this New-World Zion with the ancient Zion of Enoch, where the Lord will make His abode, "and for the space of a thousand years shall the earth rest;"* also of his covenant with them concerning Zion, both as pertaining to time and eternity, wherein He said: "I have made the earth rich; and behold it is my footstool, wherefore, again I will stand upon it; and I hold forth, and deign to give unto you greater riches, even a land of promise, a land flowing with milk and honey, upon which there shall be no curse when the Lord cometh: and I will give it unto you for the land of your inheritance, if you seek it with all your hearts. And this shall be my covenant with you,you shall have it for the land of your inheritance, and for the inheritance of your children forever,while the earth shall stand,and you shall possess it again in eternity, no more to pass away."†

The Lord said again concerning Zion: "Wherefore I, the Lord, have said, gather ye out from the eastern lands, assemble yourselves together ye elders of my Church; go ye forth into the western countries, call upon the inhabitants to repent, and inasmuch as they do repent, build up churches unto me; and with one heart and with one mind, gather up your riches that ye may purchase an inheritance which shall hereafter be appointed unto you, and it shall be called the New Jerusalem, a land of peace, a city of refuge,a place of safety for the Saints of the Most High God; and the glory of the Lord shall be there, insomuch that the wicked will not come unto it, and it shall be called Zion. And it shall come to pass, among the wicked, that every man that will not take his sword against his neighbor, must needs flee unto Zion for safety. And there shall be gathered unto it out of every nation under heaven; and it shall be the only people that shall not be at war one with another. And it shall be said among the wicked, Let us not go up to battle against Zion, for the inhabitants of Zion are terrible; wherefore we cannot stand."‡

These promises to the Saints respecting Zion; these descriptions given to them of her future sanctified and glorified state; their connection with a work so exalted and far-reaching, was apt to fire their minds with a zeal not always tempered with wisdom. It was in vain that limitations of time and conditions were placed upon these general descriptions of the future greatness and glory of the city of God; nor could they understand that their own relationship to these great things

* Pearl of Great Price, pp. 44, 45, 1902 edition.

† Doc. & Cov. Sec. 38.

‡ Doc. and Cov. Sec. 45.

was merely to lay the foundation of them, to locate the site of the future city and temple, and then bear witness of it to the world. Yet that their work in connection with the founding of Zion was chiefly this, is clearly to be seen in the revelations of God to them.

The immediate and triumphant establishment of Zion, though expected by many of the Saints, was nowhere contemplated in the revelations of God to the Church. That hope of immediate establishment and glorification of Zion was the result of faulty deductions from the revelations of God; but the Lord was not blind respecting the events about to take place on the land of Zion, nor did He hold out any false hope to His people had they but read His revelations aright. A few days before the first conference held by the Elders on the land of Zion, the Lord said to them through His Prophet:

"Hearken, O ye elders of my Church, and give ear to my word, and learn of me what I will concerning you, and also concerning this land unto which I have sent you: For verily I say unto you, blessed is he that keepeth my commandments, whether in life or in death; and he that is faithful in tribulation, the reward of the same is greater in the kingdom of heaven. Ye cannot behold with your natural eyes, for the present time, the design of your God concerning those things which shall come hereafter, and the glory which shall follow *after much tribulation. For after much tribulation comes the blessings.* Wherefore the day cometh that ye shall be crowned with much glory; the hour is not yet, but is nigh at hand. Remember this, which I tell you before, that you may lay it to heart, and receive that which shall follow. Behold, verily I say unto you, for this cause I have sent you that you might be obedient, and that your hearts might be prepared to bear testimony of the things which are to come; and also that you might be honored of laying the foundation, and of bearing record of the land upon which the Zion of God shall stand; * * * * and that the testimony might go forth from Zion, yea, from the mouth of the city of the heritage of God. * * * * And now, verily, I say, concerning the residue of the elders of my Church, *the time has not yet come, for many years*, for them to receive their inheritance in this land, except they desire it through the prayer of faith, only as it shall be appointed unto them of the Lord. For, behold, they shall push the people together from the ends of the earth."*

These statements, when rightly considered, dispel all notion of the immediate establishment of Zion. The Lord distinctly warns His servants against any such supposition. He predicts "tribulation" before the glory shall come. It is only after "much tribulation" that the blessings are

* Doc. & Cov. Sec. 58.

promised. He reminds them that He has "told them before" of this, and asks them "to lay it to heart," and gives them to understand that it will be "*many years*" before some of the Elders of His Church will receive their inheritance in the goodly land.

The Lord still further foreshadowed the trouble which afterwards overtook His people by urging them to make arrangements for the purchase of the whole region that had been designated as the center place of Zion. "For, behold, verily I say unto you, the Lord willeth that the disciples, and the children of men should open their hearts, even to purchase this whole region of country, as soon as time will permit. Behold, here is wisdom. Let them do this lest they receive none inheritance, save it be by the shedding of blood."*

In this same month of August the Lord again said: "Behold, the land of Zion, I, the Lord, hold it in mine own hands; nevertheless, I, the Lord, render unto Cæsar the things which are Cæsar's: wherefore, I, the Lord, will that you should purchase the lands that you may have advantage of the world, that you may have claim on the world, that they may not be stirred up unto anger; for Satan putteth it into their hearts to anger against you, and to the shedding of blood; wherefore the land of Zion shall not be obtained but by purchase or by blood, otherwise there is none inheritance for you. And if by purchase behold you are blessed; and if by blood, *as you are forbidden to shed blood, lo, your enemies are upon you, and ye shall be scourged from city to city, and from synagogue to synagogue, and but few shall stand to receive an inheritance.*"†

About a month after this word, the Lord said: "Behold the Lord requireth the heart and a willing mind; and the willing and obedient shall eat the good of the land of Zion in these last days; and the rebellious shall be cut off out of the land of Zion, and shall be sent away, and shall not inherit the land; for, verily, I say that the rebellious are not of the blood of Ephraim, wherefore they shall be plucked out."‡

All this makes it very clear that while great things were promised concerning the establishment of Zion and the glory that is to be hers, yet all was predicated upon the faithfulness of the Saints in keeping the commandments of the Lord—in purchasing the lands that constituted the center place of Zion, and living upon them in all righteousness.

This they failed to do. In a revelation given in November, 1831, a few months after the land had been dedicated unto the Lord for the gathering of His people, He thus complained of those who had assembled in western Missouri:

---

* Doc. and Cov., Sec. 58, verses 52-3.

† Doc. and Cov., Sec. 63, verses 25-31.

‡ Doc. and Cov., Sec. 64, verses 34-36.

"And the inhabitants of Zion shall also observe the Sabbath day to keep it holy. And the inhabitans of Zion also shall remember their labors, inasmuch as they are appointed to labor, in all faithfulness; for the idler shall be had in remembrance before the Lord. Now, I, the Lord, am not well pleased with the inhabitants of Zion, for there are idlers among them; and their children are also growing up in wickedness; they also seek not earnestly the riches of eternity, but their eyes are full of greediness. These things ought not to be, and must be done away from among them: wherefore let my servant, Oliver Cowdery carry these sayings unto the land of Zion. And a commandment I give unto them, that he that observeth not his prayers before the Lord in the season thereof, let him be had in remembrance before the judge of my people. These sayings are true and faithful; wherefore transgress them not, neither take therefrom."*

In addition to these evils there were jealousies and bickerings among some of the brethren in Zion, and also between some of the Elders in Zion, and leading Elders in Kirtland. In the spring of 1832 the Prophet visited the Saints in Jackson county, and there were reconciliations among the brethren, and forgiveness of sins obtained from the Lord;† but shortly after the Prophet's departure for Kirtland these ill feelings broke out again with renewed bitterness; carelessness as to keeping the commandments of God characterized the conduct of the Saints in Zion, and there arose some confusion also in the government of the Church there, owing to conflicting claims of authority between traveling Elders and the standing ministry in the branches of the Church. This led to the following reproof from the Lord in a revelation given on the 22nd and 23rd of September, 1832:

"And your minds in times past have been darkened because of unbelief, and because you have treated lightly the things you have received, which vanity and unbelief hath brought the whole Church under condemnation. And this condemnation resteth upon the children of Zion, even all: and they shall remain under this condemnation until they repent and remember the new covenant, even the Book of Mormon, and the former commandments which I have given them,‡ not only to say, but to do according to that which I have written, that they may bring forth fruit meet for their Father's kingdom, *otherwise there remaineth a scourge and a judgment to be poured out upon the children of Zion:* for shall the children of the kingdom pollute my holy land? Verily, I say unto you, Nay."§

* Doc. and Cov., sec. 68, verses 29-34.

† See "History of the Church," Vol. I, ch. 19.

‡ Including of course, and I may say especially including, the commandment to purchase the lands of Jackson county.

§ Doc. and Cov., sec. 84, verses 54-59.

When this revelation, given early in January, 1833, was sent to the Elders in Zion, it was accompanied also by a letter from the Prophet, sharply reproving the brethren and Saints in Zion, in which the following passage occurs:

"Let me say unto you, seek to purify yourselves, and also the inhabitants of Zion, lest the Lord's anger be kindled to fierceness. *Repent, repent, it is the voice of God to Zion;* and strange as it may appear, yet it is true, mankind will persist in self-justification until all their iniquity is exposed, and their character past being redeemed, and that which is treasured up in their hearts be exposed to the gaze of mankind. I say to you (and what I say to you, I say to all), hear the warning voice of God, *lest Zion fall, and the Lord swear in His wrath, 'The inhabitants of Zion shall not enter into my rest.'* "*

Hyrum Smith and Orson Hyde were appointed by a Council of the High Priests in Kirtland at this time, to write a letter of reproof and warning to the brethren in Zion. In this communication the conduct of the Saints in Zion was reviewed in great plainness. The whole spirit of the communication may be judged by the following paragraph:

"We feel more like weeping over Zion than rejoicing over her, *for we know that the judgments of God hang over her, and will fall upon her except she repent,* and purify herself before the Lord, and put away from her every foul spirit. We now say to Zion, this once, in the name of the Lord, Repent! repent! awake! awake! put on thy beautiful garments, before you are made to feel the chastening rod of Him whose anger is kindled against you. Let not Satan tempt you to think we want to make you bow to us, to domineer over you, for God knows this is not the case; our eyes are watered with tears, and our hearts are poured out to God in prayer for you, that He will spare you, and turn away His anger from you. * * * Therefore, with the feelings of inexpressible anxiety for your welfare, we say again, Repent, repent, *or Zion must suffer, for the scourge and judgment must come upon her.*"†

All this reproof and warning, however, only produced a partial repentance, and in July following acts of violence began to be perpetrated upon the Saints by the old settlers of Missouri, and in the month of November, under circumstances of great cruelty, all the Saints were driven from Jackson county, and later more than two hundred of their homes, together with their public improvements, were destroyed.

When the Lord revealed to the Prophet Joseph why this affliction had befallen the people, He said: "Verily I say unto you concerning your

---

* History of the Church, Vol. I p 316.

† *Ibid,* pp 317-21.

brethren who have been afflicted, and persecuted, and cast out from the land of their inheritance, I, the Lord, have suffered the affliction to come upon them wherewith they have been afflicted, in consequence of their transgressions; yet I will own them, and they shall be mine in that day when I shall come to make up my jewels. Therefore, they must needs be chastened and tried, even as Abraham, who was commanded to offer up his only son; for all those who will not endure chastening, but deny me, cannot be sanctified. Behold, I say unto you, there were jarrings, and contentions, and envyings, and strifes and lustful and covetous desires among them; therefore, by these things they polluted their inheritances. They were slow to hearken unto the voice of the Lord their God, therefore the Lord their God is slow to hearken unto their prayers, to answer them in the day of their trouble. In the day of their peace they esteemed lightly my counsel; but in the day of their trouble, of necessity they feel after me. Verily I say unto you, notwithstanding their sins my bowels are filled with compassion towards them; I will not utterly cast them off; and in the day of wrath I will remember mercy.*

From this it is very clear that the reason why the Saints were prevailed against by their enemies and driven from the center place of Zion, was because of their failure to live up to the high requirements made of them by the Lord. In subsequent efforts to redeem Zion, by attempting to return the exiles to Jackson county, the Saints in all parts of the land again failed to respond with sufficient promptness and fulness to the requirements of the Lord, for He commanded them again to consecrate money to purchase lands in Jackson county and in the counties round about, saying to the Church: "There is even now already in store a sufficient, yea even abundance, to redeem Zion, and establish her waste places, no more to be thrown down, were the churches who call themselves after my name willing to hearken to my voice."†

The Lord also commanded them to gather up their forces and to go in sufficient strength to possess the land, and maintain their inheritance against their enemies. This, however, they failed to do. Instead of raising five hundred men, as they were commanded to do,‡ they started from Kirtland in "Zion's Camp" with a company of only about one hundred and thirty men ,and twenty baggage wagons. This number was increased by additions *en route* to one hnndred and eighty-two men,but even this number fell far short of the strength required to accomplish the purpose for which the camp was organized. In the matter of rais-

* Doc. and Cov., sec. 101, vereses 1-9.

† Ibid, verse 75.

‡ Ibid, sec. 103.

ing money for the purchase of lands the failure was more conspicuous than in raising men to take possession of them, and hence this effort to redeem Zion failed.

Here let me pause in pointing out the unwisdom of the Saints, to make an explanation, lest there should be a misunderstanding of what is thus far set down respecting their transgressions, by reason of which they were prevailed against by their enemies. These transgressions, be it understood, were no violations of the laws of the land, nor did they consist in any acts of aggression or of trespass upon their Missouri neighbors. The old settlers of Missouri themselves are our witnesses here; for in all their procedure in this Jackson county persecution there is no accusation made against the Saints of violations of the law. On the contrary, in their public utterances against the Saints and in justification of their own course, the old settlers declare—after expressing their determination to rid their society of the Saints, peacefully if they could, but forcibly if they must—"*that the arm of the civil law does not afford us a guarantee, or at least a sufficient one, against the evils which are now inflicted upon us, and seem to be inreasing by the said religious sect.*"* A more emphatic acknowledgement that the alleged offenses of the Saints were not cognizable by the laws, that the Saints had not violated the laws of the land, could not be made.

In their second manifesto the mob said: "*The evil is one that no one could have foreseen, and is therefore unprovided for by the laws; and the delays incident to legislation would put the mischief beyond remedy.*"† Another admission that amounts to a declaration, that the Saints, whatever the nature of the complaints made against them were, had not violated any of the laws of the state, that their offending was not cognizable by the laws of the land.

The transgressions and sinfulness referred to in the revelations and letters of reproof and warning quoted, and for which transgressions the Saints were left in the hands of their enemies, were sins against each other and the Lord—unbelief in the word of God, hardness of heart towards each other, rejection of the servants of God, fault-finding, bickerings, jealousies, covetousness, pride, idleness, boastfulness, levity of thought and conduct, disregard of the scriptures, especially of the Book of Mormon, neglecting to instruct their children in sacred things and to bring them up in the fear and admonition of the Lord; all of which were displeasing to the Lord, contrary to His commandments, and a violation of the conditions upon which He had promised to redeem Zion and preserve His people from their enemies. "Ye call

* First Manifesto of the Mob, History of the Church, Vol. I, p. 374.

† History of the Church, Vol. I, p. 396.

upon my name for revelations;" said the Lord to the Elders in Zion, "and I give them unto you; and inasmuch as ye keep not my sayings, which I give unto you, ye become transgressors, and justice and judgment are the penalty which is affixed to my law. * * * I, the Lord, am bound when ye do what I say; but when ye do not what I say, ye have no promise."*

This, then, was the nature of their offenses; they sinned against the Lord in the particulars named; they sinned against each other in the manner described; they did not trespass against their non-Mormon neighbors, nor break the laws of the land; but they failed to live in accordance with the high moral and spiritual law of the Gospel; they failed to meet the conditions on which God was pledged to their maintenance upon the land of Zion, and hence were left in the hands of their enemies.

At the commencement of this subdivision of the Introduction I called attention to the great things which God had revealed to the Saints, the greatness of the dispensation committed unto them, accompanied by the promise to establish Zion and give unto the Saints the land thereof as an everlasting inheritance. It would be marvelous indeed, and past all human experience, if these great things did not turn the heads of some of the weak-minded, and make them vain-glorious and boastful. I doubt not for a moment that many vain and foolish things were said by such characters in the presence of, and perhaps directly to, the old settlers of Jackson county, about the Saints taking possession of the land, and the wicked being driven away. There was doubtless enough of this kind of talk to give color to what the Missourians charged on this head, viz., "They [the Saints] declare openly that their God hath given them this county of land, and that sooner or later they must and will take possession of our lands for an inheritance."

The Missourians made much of, and attached a sinister meaning to the following expression in one of the revelations to the Saints: "*The land of Zion shall not be obtained but by purchase or by blood, otherwise there is none inheritance for you.*"† This the Missourians pretended to regard as a threat to take possession of their land by armed conquest. Had they read the context of the passage they would have known how entirely groundless were their fears, if indeed they had any fears, for I am convinced that all their expressed apprehensions on this head were mere pretense. The passage and its context are: "Wherefore the land of Zion shall not be obtained but by purchase or by blood, otherwise there is none inheritance for you. *And if by purchase, behold you*

---

* Doc. and Cov., sec. 83.

† Doc. and Cov., sec. 63.

are blessed; and if by blood, as you are forbidden to shed blood, lo, your enemies are upon you, and ye shall be scourged from city to city, and from synagogue to synagogue and but few shall stand to receive an inheritance."*

Clearly this is a warning to the Saints, not a threat to the Missourians. If the Saints obtained the land by purchase they were blessed. If by blood—since the Saints were forbidden to shed blood, lo their enemies would be upon them and they would be driven from city to city—not the Missourians, but the Saints. In consequence of the agitation of this matter by the foolish, the following passage occurred in *The Evening and Morning Star* for July, 1833, addressed to the churches scattered abroad: "To suppose that we can come up here and take possession of this land by the shedding of blood, would be setting at nought the law of the glorious Gospel, and also the word of our great Redeemer. And to suppose that we can take possession of this country without making regular purchases of the same according to the laws of our nation, would be reproaching this great Republic, in which the most of us were born, and under whose auspices we all have protection."†

Of this the Missourians said that whether they were to be dispossessed of their lands "by the hand of the destroying angel, the judgments of God, or the arm of power, they [the Saints] are not fully agreed among themselves. Some recent remarks in the *Evening and Morning Star*, their organ in this place, by their tendency to moderate such hopes, and repress such desires, show plainly that many of this deluded and infatuated people have been taught to believe that our lands were to be won from us by the sword!"‡

Thus the very efforts of the Church to correct the misconceptions and silence the utterances of the over-zealous and foolish members, were made to contribute as proof that the Saints contemplated the very armed conquest of the land which they disclaimed. History, however, will do the Saints justice, and it will say, and now says, that neither their general principles, nor the special commandments under which they moved into the land of Zion, nor any act of theirs warranted the least suspicion that they at any time contemplated taking possession of the land by force, or in any other manner whatsoever except by purchase and possession under the laws of the state of Missouri and the United States. And while history will do them this justice it will at the same time say that the "fears" of the Missourians on this head were simulated; that to the foolish boasts of a few ignorant persons they attached an undue importance because it happened to give a coloring to their pretended fears in the eyes of those at a distance who had no oppor-

* Doc. and Cov., sec. 63: 29-31.

† Evening and Morning Star, p. 220.

‡ "History of the Church," Vol. I, p. 396.

tunity to learn the truth, and tended to prejudice the public mind against the Saints, and thus served the purpose of their enemies.

In like manner there may have been some talk among the same class of people—the ignorant and over-zealous Church members—respecting the Indians, and their future union with the Saints in redeeming the land of Zion; a circumstance which led the good people of Clay county and Governor Dunklin,to refer to the charge of the Saints holding illicit communication with the Indians, designing to employ them in taking possession of the land of Zion. Of this charge also history will and does vindicate the Saints. It will, and does say, that they disclaimed holding any such communication; that neither their general principles nor any special commandment from God, and particularly that no action of theirs warranted any suspicion on the subject, much less justified the charge of such a diabolical purpose.

After the Saints withdrew from Clay county and at the suggestion of her citizens—including some of the most influential men in western Missouri, some of whom afterwards attained national reputations—located in the sparsely settled counties of Caldwell and Daviess, the situation became somewhat changed. For two years the work of purchasing lands, locating settlements, opening farms, establishing merchantile houses, and preparing for manufacturing and commercial enterprises went steadily on. In Caldwell and adjoining counties, by the autumn of 1838, the Saints had opened two thousand farms, and paid to the general government three hundred and eighteen thousand dollars for land, which at the minimum price for government land would give them over two hundred and fifty thousand acres.* One hundred and fifty houses had been erected in Far West; there were four dry goods stores, three family groceries, half a dozen blacksmith's shops, and two hotels.† The excavation for a temple 120 by 80 feet had been made, and a large commodious schoolhouse had been erected on the public square.‡ The town of Adam-Ondi-Ahman was also making rapid progress.

---

* These estimates are by the late President George A. Smith, Church Historian, and hence are entirely reliable. They are quoted by Lucien Carr in his History of Missouri, "American Commonwealths," p. 181, and are also to be found in an Historical Address by George A. Smith, Journal of Discourses, Vol. XIII, pp. 103, *et seq.*

† "History of Caldwell county" (National Historical Company, 1886) p. 121.

‡ "In the fall of 1836, a large and comfortable schoolhouse was built and here courts were held after the location of the county seat until its removal to Kingston. The Mormons very early gave attention to educational matters. There were many teachers among them and schoolhouses were among their first buildings. The schoolhouse in Far West was used as a Church, as a town hall and as a court house, as well as for a schoolhouse. It first stood in the southwest quarter of town, but upon the establishment of the county seat it was removed to the center of the square." ("History of Caldwell County," p. 121.—National Historical Company, 1886).

By this time the Prophet Joseph and other leading men of the Church had left Kirtland and located with the Saints in Missouri, and everything looked propitious for the permanent establishment of the Saints in the borders of Zion. The Saints had now been driven bodily from Jackson county; and their homes, store houses and printing establishment had been destroyed. The courts of Missouri had proven powerless to restore to them their homes, their lands and other property. The executive of the state confessed himself powerless to return them to their possessions in Jackson county, and maintain them there against the wishes of the people of that county. Indeed, Governor Dunklin had weakly given up the vindication of the outraged laws of the state, as we have seen, saying that whether the charges of their enemies or the denials by the Saints were true he could not tell; their neighbors seemed to believe them true, and whether true or false the consequences would be the same, unless the Saints by their conduct and argument could convince the Missourians of their innocence. "If you cannot do this," said the governor, "all I can say to you is that in this Republic the *vox populi is the vox Dei!*" The Saints at some considerable sacrifice had withdrawn from Clay county at the request of her citizens, in the interests of peace, and had settled in the new counties of Caldwell and Daviess, where settlers were few and the country less desirable than in Jackson and Clay counties. In doing these things they had repeatedly sacrificed their rights as citizens, both of Missouri and of the United States. Smitten on the one cheek—speaking figuratively—they had turned the other; sued at the law for their coat, they had given their cloak also; compelled to go one mile with their enemy, they had gone with him twain. After doing all this for the sake of peace and the friendship of the Missourians, when the Saints saw forming again those elements which threatened their peace; when old enemies appeared upon the new scene of the Saints' activities, and openly threatened their peace and boasted that they would again prosper by despoiling them of their new possessions; when they saw the red right hand of a relentless persecution arming again to plague them, it is small wonder if righteous anger flushed their cheek, made bright their eyes with indignation and led them instinctively to form the resolution that they would submit no more to such acts of despoliation, injustice and outrage.

It was this sense of outraged justice and humanity which led to the deliverance of a very noted "Oration" by Sidney Rigdon at Far West, on the Fourth of July, 1838, in the course of which there was expressed a strong determination to no more submit quietly to mob violence, and acts of pillage. At this distance of time from that occasion, and balancing against the heated utterances of the speaker the subsequent uses made of them to incite the public mind to that series of acts which culminated in the expulsion of the Saints from the state, we say those utterances were untimely, extreme, and unwise. So indeed they were. The speaker seems to have thrown discretion to the winds, and in the fervor of his rhetoric made threats of retaliation on behalf of the Saints, if assailed, that went beyond all bounds of reason and humanity, and proved a very damaging as also a very potent factor against the Saints in the subsequent movements of their enemies against them.

But while this oratorical outburst against injustice was unwise, it was a very natural thing. The marvel is not that it came at the time it did, but that it did not come earlier, more vehemently, and that some of the things it threatened were not effectively carried out. What the Prophet thought, and how he felt respecting the repeated acts of injustice heaped upon himself and the Saints in Missouri; how he felt and what he proposed for the future is made clear in his journal entry for September 1st, 1838; and, fortunately, is more temperately expressed than in the oration of July the fourth. He said:

"There is great excitement at present among the Missourians, who are seeking if possible an occasion against us. They are continually chafing us, and provoking us to anger if possible, one sign of threatening after another, but we do not fear them, for the Lord God, the Eternal Father is our God, and Jesus the Mediator is our Savior, and in the great I Am is our strength and confidence.

"We have been driven time after time, and that without cause; and smitten again and again, and that without provocation; until we have proved the world with kindness, and the world has proved us, that we have no designs against any man or set of men, that we injure no man, that we are peaceable with all men, minding our own business, and our business only. We have suffered our rights and our liberties to be taken from us; we have not avenged ourselves of those wrongs; we have appealed to magistrates, to sheriffs, to judges, to government and to the President of the United States, all in vain; yet we have yielded peaceably to all these things. We have not complained at the great God, we murmured not, but peaceably left all, and retired into the back country, in the broad and wild prairies, in the barren and desolate plains, and there commenced anew; we made the desolate places to bud and blossom as the rose; and now the fiend-like race is disposed to give us no rest. Their father the devil, is hourly calling upon them to be up and doing, and they, like willing and obedient children, need not the second admonition; but in the name of Jesus Christ, the Son of the living God, we will endure it no longer, if the great God will arm us with courage, with strength and with power, to resist them in their persecutions. We will not act on the offensive, but always on the defensive; our rights and our liberties shall not be taken from us, and we peaceably submit to it as we have done heretofore, but we will avenge ourselves of our enemies, inasmuch as they will not let us alone."

No one can marvel at the conclusion here arrived at if he will but pay attention to and give due weight to the enumerated wrongs which precede it. It would be asking the Saints to be more than human if we say they ought not to have indulged, much less to have expressed, such feelings of resentment.

Meantime, however, we may not close our eyes to the fact that there was unwisdom manifested on the part of a few of the Saints, which gave advantage to their enemies, by affording pretexts for some of their accusations. That unwisdom, as we have seen, consisted of boasting as to what the Lord would do in the immediate future in giving them possession of western Missouri as an inheritance; perhaps some unwise allusions to the supposed part the Lamanites would take in the establishment and redemption of Zion; and the vehement threats of retaliation in the event of their being further assailed. These unwise utterances, however, were made, for the most part, by the overzealous and ignorant. Men who had no grasp of the real genius of the great work whose foundations were then being laid; men who, in common with men of like nature in all ages and in all great movements, have been trouble-breeders; who, in their contemplation of ultimate results to be achieved, overleaped the intervening space through which the movement must pass, the difficulties it must encounter and overcome, the experiences its adherents must gain, the great and varied labors they must perform. They seem not to undestand that great movements require time for the achievement of their ends; that time with God is one thing, with man quite another thing; that the thing which is "nigh at hand" with the Lord may be to men afar off; and overlooking these important facts leads such men into many errors of thought and action. It was wholly reprehensible, unwarranted, and cowardly, however, on the part of the Missourians to take advantage of the unwise utterances of such characters and charge their sentiments and folly to the whole body religious, that never entertained such sentiments nor contemplated the actions such sentiments suggest. And this is to be said even of those who were unwise enough to give the advantage here noted to the enemies of the Saints, they at no time or place were ever guilty of attempting in any manner to carry into effect by any action of their own the unwise and unwarranted opinions they entertained and expressed. Their boastings and vain speculations were in relation to what the Lord was going to do, not what they themselves purposed doing. These utterances were merely the effervescence of overwrought minds, of overzealous, foolish, but well meaning and harmless people. Unhappily, however, what they said gave the enemy an advantage that he was not slow to avail himself of, and the unwisdom of some of the Saints is a factor that must be reckoned with in dealing with the causes of the persecutions of the Saints in Missouri.

The Real Cause of the Missouri Persecutions.

Having considered those facts and circumstances which may be regarded as the minor causes and pretexts of the Missouri persecutions, let us now come to the heart of the matter, to the real cause of the persecution of the Saints.

It was against the Saints as a religious sect that the Missourians first complained. It was "in consequence of a pretended religious sect of people" that had settled, and was still settling in their country, "styling themselves Mormons," that led the Missourians of Jackson county to pretend to believe that an important crisis regarding their civil society was at hand. "It is more thant wo years," they said, "since the first of these fanatics, or knaves (for one or other they undoubtedly are), made their first appearance amongst us, and pretended as they did, and do now, to hold personal communication and converse face to face with the Most High; to receive communications and revelations direct from heaven; to heal the sick by laying on hands; and, in short, to perform all the wonder-working miracles wrought by the inspired apostles and prophets of old. We believed them deluded fanatics, or weak and designing knaves, and that they and their pretensions would soon pass away; but in this we were deceived. * * * They openly blaspheme the Most High God, and cast contempt on His holy religion, by pretending to receive revelations direct from heaven, by pretending to speak unknown tongues by direct inspiration, and by divers pretenses derogatory to God and religion, and to the utter subversion of human reason."*

The foregoing is quoted from the first "Manifesto," or "Secret Constitution" of the mob. Somewhat later, in a second manifesto issued to the public in justification of their contemplated acts of violence against the Saints, they say: "What would be the fate of our lives and property, in the hands of jurors and witnesses, who do not blush to declare, and would not upon occasion hesitate to swear, that they have wrought miracles, and have been the subjects of miraculous and supernatural cures, have conversed with God and His angels, and possess and exercise the gifts of divination and of unknown tongues, and fired with the prospect of obtaining inheritances without money and without price—may be better imagined than described. * * * Of their pretended revelations from heaven—their personal intercourse

* "History of the Church," Vol., 1, pp. 375-6.

with God and His angels—the maladies they pretend to heal by the laying on of hands—and the contemptible gibberish with which they habitually profane the Sabbath, and which they dignify with the appellation of unknown tongues, we have nothing to say: vengeance belongs to God alone."*

Yet it was because the Saints entertained these religious beliefs that the mob of Jackson county issuing this "manifesto," proceeded to take "vengeance" into their own hands, and wreak it upon the Saints. All their other accusations against them,—namely, idleness, ignorance, inviting "free negroes" into the state, inciting the slaves to insubordination to their masters, claiming Jackson county as their inheritance to be obtained by force if not bloodshed, and poverty—all these charges, except, perhaps the last (for some of the Saints were very poor, though I have yet to learn that that is a crime), were absolutely untrue. The Saints, however, did claim the existence of spiritual power in their religion; that the channel of communication between God and men by means of revelation, the visitation of angels, and the inspiration of the Holy Ghost, had been opened anew; that gifts of the Gospel—tongues, interpretations, visions, inspired dreams, healings—that all the spiritual powers and graces of the Gospel, in fact, were manifested in the religion they had accepted. By this religion, also, they were admonished to righteousness of life; to the strict observance of the Sabbath; to respect for the name of Deity; to temperance; to industry; to true speaking and true acting; to patience—in a word, to godliness; all of which but to live was to place themselves in marked contrast to those about them, and their righteous lives were a great rebuke to the general dissolute conduct of the Missourians. It was this effort at a godly walk and conversation, and the religion which commanded it, that was offensive in the eyes of the Missourians, and which led them to form their strong determination to be rid of a people and a religion which made their own lives a reproach.

That this was regarded as the chief, if not the sole cause of their persecution, appears in the subsequent discussion of the Jackson county difficulties, both *pro et con*. All other questions, all the minor causes and pretexts were lost sight of in that discussion. Governor Dunklin, in a communication to Colonel J. Thornton, in answer to a letter written by that gentleman proposing a compromise between the Saints and their enemies in Jackson county, recognizes what he calls "the eccentricity of the religious opinions of the Mormons" as being the cause of their persecution. "I am fully persuaded," he remarks, "that the eccentricity of the religious opinions and practices of the Mormons is at the bottom of the outrages committed against them."

---

* "History of the Church," Vol. I, p. 397.

In this important communication he no where considers anything else as the cause of their persecution, but argues at length in favor of their right to the entertainment of their religious views, eccentric howsoever they might be, so long as they did not interfere with the rights of others. "They have the right constitutionally guaranteed to them," he remarks, "and it is indefeasible, to worship Joe Smith as a man, an angel, or even as the only true and living God, and to call their habitation Zion, the Holy Land, or even heaven itself. Indeed, there is nothing so absurd or ridiculous that they have not a right to adopt as their religion, so that in its exercise they do not interfere with the rights of others."*

The people of Clay county when they called upon the Saints to peaceably remove from their borders and seek a locality where they could form a community that should be largely, if not exclusively, made up of their own Church membership, indicated very clearly that it was the religion of the Saints that was the chief cause of complaint against them. In a document they published setting forth the reasons why they suggested such removal, they said: "The religious tenets of this people are so different from the present churches of the age, that they always have, and always will, excite deep prejudices against them in any populous country where they may locate. We, therefore, in a spirit of frank and friendly kindness, do advise them to seek a home where they may obtain large and separate bodies of land, and have a community of their own."*

Again, after the surrender at Far West, when the Church leaders had been betrayed into bondage; after the Saints had delivered up their arms; after they had signed over their properties to defray the expenses of the "war;" and when the whole body of the Church was making hasty preparations to depart from the state, a number of the brethren were assembled on the temple square at Far West, and in the course of a long speech, which he read† to them, General John B. Clark said:

"I am sorry, gentlemen, to see so great a number of apparently intelligent men found in the situation you are; and oh! that I could invoke that Great Spirit, the Unknown God, to rest upon you, and make you sufficiently intelligent to break that chain of superstition, and liberate you from those fetters of fanaticism with which you are bound—that you no longer worship a man! I would advise you to scatter abroad, and never again organize yourselves with Bishops, Presidents,

* "History of the Church," Vol. II, p. 85.

* "History of the Church," Vol. II, p. 450.

† "History of Caldwell and Livingston Counties," compiled by the St. Louis National and Historical Company, 1886, p. 140.

etc., lest you excite the jealousies of the people, and subject yourselves to the same calamities that have now come upon you."

This to a people whose leaders had been betrayed into the hands of their enemies; who themselves had been disarmed, though acting only in defense of their homes and families; who had been compelled at the muzzle of the musket to sign away their property to defray the expenses of the militia mobs that had brought their calamities upon them; who were then under an order of expulsion from the state and making hurried preparations for their enforced departure—this to men who had sacrificed or had been robbed of the most sacred rights of American citizenship! And he who thus addressed the brethren impudently told them in the very speech from which I quote, that he approved of all that had been done to them! But the foregoing quotation is not made in order to point out the mockery of the speech; or the mixture of hypocrisy and blasphemy in it; or the utter contemptibility of him who delivered it. I quote the passage merely to point out the fact that it was hatred of their alleged "superstition" and "fanaticism," in other words the religion of the Saints that was the cause of their persecution. The crimes against which the Saints are warned for the future—under penalty of having their present troubles revisited upon them—is gathering together in large bodies, and organizing themselves with Bishops, Presidents, etc. In other words it was the religion of the people and the organization which was both the depository of its doctrines, and the instrumentality by which they were promulgated—the Church—which was the object of the Missourians' animosity, the thing they were determined to destroy.

Later, when the Prophet Joseph and other leading brethren were under examination before Judge Austin A. King at Richmond, Ray county, special inquiry was made as to the belief of the witnesses in the declaration of the Prophet Daniel: "And in the days of these kings shall the God of heaven set up a kingdom, which shall never be destroyed: and the kingdom shall not be left to other people, but it shall break in pieces and consume all these kingdoms, and it shall stand for ever."*

The judge on being answered that the Saints believed the prophecy, turned to the clerk and told him to write the answer down as it was "*a strong point for treason*!"† I call it another evidence that it was the religious beliefs of the Saints that constituted their offense. True the Prophet and several other brethren were technically held for trial on

* Daniel 2: 44.

† Autobiography of Parley P. Pratt, p. 230, also History of the Church, Vol. III p. 212.

the charge of "treason, murder, arson, burglarly, robbery, larceny and perjury," but no one in Missouri ever seriously believed the charges since they were wholly untrue or grew out of those acts of self defense, and defense of their families against the aggressions of mob violence—a course which all men have a right to take in the protection of their own lives and the preservation of their homes from the hand of the despoiler.

The meeting of discordant elements of society—New England people and people from the Southern States, descendants of Puritans and descendants of Cavaliers—may have been a cause of dislike, and, on the part of the Missourians, a cause of irritation against the Saints; the suspected existence of anti-slavery sentiments among the Saints may have been to the Missourians a cause of distrust; the interest of the Saints in the Indians and the beliefs of the former in the future rehabiliation of the latter as a people favored of God, may have been, under all the circumstances, a cause of uneasiness to the Missourians; and the desire to plunder the Saints and to profit by dispossessing them of their lands and homes might have been, and doubtless was, an incentive to many of the mob who participated in the events which culminated in the expulsion of the Saints from the state; but, at bottom, I repeat, it was the destruction of the religion of the Saints, and of the organization that taught its doctrines, and controlled its membership in ecclesiastical affairs, that were the objectives of all that agitation, violence and injustice, which make up the persecution of the Latter-day Saints in Missouri. But how shall the truth of this be established beyond reasonable doubt? Listen:—

The author of the "*Decline and Fall of the Roman Empire*" gives the following pen-picture of conditions with reference to religious toleration which obtained in the empire under the reign of the Antonines, Adrian and Marcus Aurelius, second century, A. D. "The firm edifice of Roman power was raised and preserved by the wisdom of ages. The obedient provinces of Trajan and the Antonines were united by laws, and adorned by arts. They might occasionally suffer from the partial abuse of delegated authority; but the general principle of government was wise, simple, and beneficent. They enjoyed the religion of their ancestors, whilst in civil honors and advantages they were exalted, by just degrees, to an equality with their conquerors. The policy of the emperors and the senate, as far as it concerned religion, was happily seconded by the reflections of the enlightened, and the habits of the superstitious, part of their subjects. The various modes of worship, which prevailed in the Roman world, were all considered by the people as equally true; by the philosopher, as equally false; and by the magistrate, as equally useful. And thus toleration produced not only mutual indulgence, but even religious concord. The superstition of the people was not embittered by any mixture of theological rancor; nor was it confined by the chains of any speculative system. The devout polytheist, though fondly attached to his national rites, admitted with implicit faith the different religions of the earth. Fear, gratitude, and curiosity, a dream or an omen, a singular disorder, or a distant journey, perpetually disposed him to multiply the articles of his belief, and to enlarge the list of his protectors. The thin texture of the Pagan mythology was interwoven with various but not discordant materials. As soon as it was allowed that sages and heroes, who had lived or who had died for the benefit of their country, were exalted to a state of power and immortality, it was universally confessed that they deserved, if not the adoration, at least the reverence, of all mankind. The deities of a thousand groves and a thousand streams possessed in peace their local and respective influence: nor could the Roman who deprecated the wrath of the Tiber, deride the Egyptian who presented his offering to the beneficent genius of the Nile. The visible powers of nature, the planets, and the elements, were the same throughout the universe. The invisible governors of the moral world were inevitably cast in a similar mould of fiction and allegory. Every virtue, and even vice, acquired its divine representative; every art and profession its patron, whose attributes, in the most distant ages and countries, were uniformly derived from the character of their peculiar votaries. A republic of gods of such opposite tempers and interests required, in every system, the moderating hand of a supreme magistrate, who, by the progress of knowledge and flattery, was gradually invested with the sublime perfections of an eternal parent, and an omnipotent monarch. Such was the mild spirit of antiquity, that the nations were less attentive to the difference, than to the resemblance, of their religious worship. The Greek, the Roman, and the Barbarian, as they met before their respective altars, easily persuaded themselves, that under various names, and with various ceremonies, they adored the same deities. * * * * Rome, the capital of a great monarchy, was incessantly filled with subjects and strangers from every part of the world, who all introduced and enjoyed the favorite superstitions of their native country. Every city in the empire was justified in maintaining the purity of its ancient ceremonies; and the Roman senate, using the common privilege, sometimes interposed to check this inundation of foreign rites. The Egyptian superstition, of all the most contemptible and abject, was frequently prohibited; the temples of Serapis and Isis demolished, and their worshipers banished from Rome and Italy. But the zeal of fanaticism prevailed over the cold and feeble efforts of policy. The exiles returned, the proselytes multiplied, the temples were restored with increasing splendor, and Isis and Serapis at length assumed their place among the Roman deities. * * * * Rome gradually became the common temple of her subjects; and the freedom of the city was bestowed on all the gods of mankind."*

Some Christian editors of Gibbon's great work, in their annotations, hold that the author of the "Decline and Fall" gives in the foregoing a too favorable view of pagan-religious toleration; but after giving due weight to the instances of intolerance they cite in evidence of their contention, and viewing them in connection with the extent of the empire and the period of time covered by Gibbon's description, I do not regard them as of sufficient importance to warrant any change in the representation made by our author of conditions as to religious toleration in the Roman empire at the time of which he writes. Especially, since Gibbon himself in a foot note admits that "some obscure traces of an intolerant spirit appears in the conduct of the Egyptians," the case chiefly relied upon by his critics to disprove his description of universal religious toleration in the empire; and in the same note he refers to the Christians and the Jews as forming an important exception; so important an exception indeed that he promises, and subsequently gives, a distinct chapter to the discussion of the subject.†

It is to Christianity as the chief exception to the Roman policy of universal religious toleration that I wish now to direct attention. Let it be borne in mind that the spirit of universal religious toleration within the Roman empire claimed for the second century of our era, largely obtained also in the first century. It was in this reign of universal religious toleration that the Christian religion was brought forth and developed. Christ was born in the eighteenth year of the reign of Tiberius Cæsar, in the Roman province of Palestine, in which, also, His personal labors as religious teacher and reformer were chiefly confined. In the villages of Galilee, and subsequently in Samaria and Judea and in the ancient city of Jerusalem, He went about doing good; speaking words of encouragement to the oppressed and the poor; healing the sick; opening the eyes of the blind; cleansing the lepers; teaching, as no one ever taught before, the fatherhood of God, the brotherhood of men, and proclaiming Himself the Son of God and the Redeemer of the world. He gathered about Him a few devout followers, and from their number He established a priesthood and organized a Church to perpetuate the gentle doctrines He Himself taught. Strangely enough, notwithstanding the beauty and purity of His moral precepts, and the gentleness of His own deportment, proclamation of His doctrines everywhere incited hostility. The people of the village in which He was reared rejected Him.

* "Decline and Fall of the Roman Empire," Vol. I, Chapter II.

† "This is Chapter XVI of the "Decline and Fall."

His own people, the Jews, were so hostile that they at last clamored for His execution; and so deep was their hatred that they were willing that responsibility for the shedding of His blood should be upon their heads and upon the heads of their children after them, if only the Roman authorities would sanction His execution! He was finally crucified amid the rejoicings of His enemies.

After His resurrection He appeared among His disciples and commissioned them to evangelize the world. As they went about this work they encountered the same spirit of opposition that had met their Master. Whippings, imprisonment, and martyrdom confronted them on every hand, and when they extended their labors beyond the borders of Palestine, notwithstanding the general religious tolerance that obtained in the Roman empire, the Christians were everywhere spoken against, and their ministers everywhere opposed and persecuted.

Passing by the persecutions inflicted upon the Christians by the Jews —the whipping of Peter and John, under the order of the Jewish Sanhedrim, the martyrdom of Stephen, the execution of Saint James, the repeated mobbing and whippings of Paul—I call attention to the first great pagan persecution under the cruel edict of the Emperor Nero, in the second half of the first Christian century. The emperor having set on fire the city of Rome in order that he might view a great conflagration, and wishing to divert suspicion from himself, he first accused and then tried to compel the Christians to confess the crime. At this point I summon Tacitus, the renowned Roman annalist, to tell the remainder of the story:

"With this view he inflicted the most exquisite tortures on those men who, under the vulgar appellation of Christians, were already branded with deserved infamy. They derived their name and origin from Christ, who, in the reign of Tiberius, had suffered death by the sentence of the procurator Pontius Pilate. For awhile this dire superstition was checked, but it again burst forth, and not only spread itself over Judea, the first seat of this mischievous sect, but was even introduced into Rome, the common asylum, which receives and protects whatever is impure, whatever is atrocious. The confessions of those that were seized discovered a great multitude of their accomplices, and they were all convicted not so much for the crime of setting fire to the city, as for their hatred of human kind. They died in torments, and their torments were embittered by insults and derision. Some were nailed on crosses; others sewn up in the skins of wild beasts and exposed to the fury of dogs; others, again, smeared over with combustible materials, were used as torches to illuminate the darkness of the night. The gardens of Nero were destined for the melancholy spectacle, which was accompanied with a horse race, and honored with the presence of the emperor, who mingled with the populace in the dress and attitude of a charioteer. The guilt of the Christians deserved indeed the most exemplary punishments, but the public abhorrence was changed into commiseration from the opinion that those unhappy wretches were sacrificed, not so much to the public welfare as to the cruelty of a jealous tyrant."*

This first great persecution of the Christians under the authority of the Roman emperor, is sufficiently characteristic to describe the other persecutions which were intermittingly perpetrated upon the Christians through the two succeeding centuries. What seems to be the most incongruous circumstance connected with these persecutions is, that they occurred not only under such wretches as Nero and Domitian, but under such virtuous emperors as Trajan, Adrian, Marcus Aurelius and Diocletian. Intermittingly, then, through three troubled centuries, and under circumstances of the utmost cruelty, persecution raged against the Christians. As the highest authority on Roman history remarks: "If the empire had been afflicted by any recent calamity, by a plague, a famine, or an unsuccessful war; if the Tiber had, or the Nile had not risen above its banks; if the earth had shaken, or if the temperate order of the seasons had been interrupted, the superstitious pagans were convinced that the crimes and impurities of the Christians, who were spared by the excessive lenity of the government, had at length provoked the divine justice."† And however virtuous the emperors were,or however mild and equitable in character the governors of the provinces, it is certain that they did not hesitate to appease the rage of the people by sacrificing the obnoxious Christian victims. All this at a time, too, when religious tolerance and in large measure even religious freedom were enjoyed by those of all other religions within the empire, and in fact we may say that the persecution of the Christians was the only circumstance which broke in upon the religious concord of the world. From the apologies of the early church fathers, addressed to some of the emperors of the second and third centuries, we find them making the most pathetic complaints to the effect, "that the Christians who obeyed the dictates, and solicited the liberty of conscience, were alone, among all the subjects of the Roman empire, excluded from the common benefits of their auspicious government."

Why was this? Surely it did not arise from any vicious principle inherent in the Christian religion itself. "If we seriously consider the purity of the Christian religion," remarks Gibbon, in the opening paragraph of his great treatise on the "*Conduct of the Roman Government Toward the Christians*," "the sanctity of its moral precepts, and the

* Tacitus Annal., lib. XV, ch. 44.

† "Decline and Fall," Vol. I, ch. 15.

innocence as well as the austere lives of the greater number of those who, during the first ages, embraced the faith of the gospel, we should naturally suppose that so benevolent a doctrine would have been received with due reverence even by the unbelieving world; that the learned and polite, however they might deride the miracles, would have esteemed the virtues of the new sect; and that the magistrates, instead of persecuting, would have protected an order of men who yielded the most passive obedience to the laws, though they declined the active cares of war and government. If, on the other hand, we recollect the universal tolerance of polytheism, as it was invariably maintained by the faith of the people, the incredulity of philosophers, and the policy of the Roman senate and emperors, we are at a loss to discover what new offense the Christians had committed, what new provocation could exasperate the mild indifference of antiquity, and what new motives could urge the Roman princes, who beheld without concern a thousand forms of religion subsisting in peace under their gentle sway, to inflict a severe punishment upon any part of their subjects who had chosen for themselves a singular but an inoffensive mode of faith and worship."*

What, then, I again ask, was the cause of the singular departure from the enlightened policy of the empire in granting religious toleration and even large religious freedom to its subjects? I am sure that modern Christians will scarcely be satisfied with the various causes assigned for this strange conduct on the part of the Roman emperors who persecuted the Christians. These causes, or at least the principal ones, are conceded by both infidel and Christian authorities to be:

First, the Christians were a sect and not a nation, and were open to the charge that they had deserted the faith of their forefathers, a thing inexplicable to the Roman mind. It could be claimed on the part of the Christians, of course, that this was not true; that so far were they from deserting the faith of their fathers, that their present Christian faith was but the complement of their fathers' faith, the fulfillment alike of its prophecies and symbols—in a word, the gospel was the fulfillment of the law. This, however, was a refinement of explanation to which the haughty Romans could not be expected to give attention.

Second, the Christians condemned and abhorred the public religion of the state, so closely connected with the affairs of the government, and hence they were judged to be enemies of the state, a circumstance which made them objects of detestation to those intrusted with the administration of the laws.

* "History of the Decline and Fall of the Roman Empire," ch. 16.

Third, the Christians in their worship employed no images, nor temples, nor incense, nor sacrifices; neither did they represent their God by any corporeal figure or symbol, therefore they were adjudged to be atheists, and accordingly detested.

Fourth, the gloom and austere aspect of the Christians, and their thorough abhorrence of the common business and pleasures of life, their denunciation of war, together with their frequent predictions of impending divine judgments, caused them to be regarded as the enemies of mankind.

Fifth, the secrecy in which they conducted their religious services (a policy first born of necessity, because of the fear of their adversaries, and afterwards continued under the false notion that it would render their sacred institutions more respectable) drew upon them the suspicion that they only "concealed what they would have blushed to disclose;" and this left them open to the misrepresentation and calumny of their enemies, by which the fury of the multitude was aroused against them.

Sixth, the severe simplicity of the Christian mode of worship, employing as it did neither sacrifices nor an elaborate priesthood—excited the animosity of the pagan priests and their servitors, in exact proportion as the Christians became a menace to their occupation; for it was painfully apparent to them that if Christianity was successful there would be no need of the pagan priesthood—its occupation would be gone.

All these alleged causes for the persecution of the Christians within the Roman empire may be allowed, though some of them may be more properly regarded as pretexts for, than causes of the persecution. But back of all the assigned causes—which are at best but secondary in their nature—one may see moving a force, the primary cause of the persecution, of which the apprehensions of magistrates, the hatred of the pagan priesthood, and the clamor of the multitude were but the outward manifestations. That primary cause of the persecution of the Christians is to be found in the bitter hatred of that dark spirit who in heaven, before he fell from his high estate, was known under the splendid appellation of "The Light Bearer," "Lucifer," "Son of the Morning," as high in favor as in station, before his sin of rebellion against the Father-God.*

Beyond the mere fact that he impiously did rebel in heaven against God, and that he was impelled thereto by a vaulting ambition which overleaped itself, the Hebrew scriptures give us little information concerning Lucifer. No cause for the rebellion is assigned, though evidence

* Isaiah 14: 12-15. Doc. and Cov., sec. 76: 25-9.

of the fact and reality of the rebellion is abundant.* In some ancient scripture revealed to Joseph Smith, however, the cause of that Lucifer-led rebellion is stated. It was immediately connected with man's earth-life, and the means and conditions of his salvation.

In order that the reader may appreciate the force of the truth to be presented, it is necessary to remind him that the spirit of man had an existence before he dwelt in his body of flesh and bones—a self-conscious existence, in which he possessed all the faculties and attributes that the spirit or mind of man now possesses; that the time had come when the present earth-life became necessary to his continued progress; that all that would take place in that earth-life was known to God—the fall of man, the wickedness of the human race, the redemption through the atonement of a sinless sacrifice—all was known, and for all these events ample provisions were to be made; one chosen to open the series of dispensations that should make up the history of man's earth-life; one chosen to redeem man from his fallen state. It was at this point that Lucifer came before the grand council in heaven saying: Behold—here am I, send me, I will be Thy son, and I will redeem all mankind, that one soul shall not be lost, and surely *I will do it;* wherefore give me Thine honor. "But, behold," said the Lord, "My Beloved Son, which was My Beloved and Chosen from the beginning, said unto Me—Father, Thy will be done, and the glory be Thine forever. Wherefore, because that Satan rebelled against Me, and sought to destroy the agency of man, which I, the Lord God, had given him; and also that I should give unto him Mine own power; by the power of Mine Only Begotten, I caused that he should be cast down; and he became Satan, yea, even the devil, the father of all lies, to deceive and to blind men, and to lead them captive at his will, even as many as would not hearken unto My voice."†

This discloses the reason of Lucifer's rebellion—opposition to the plan of man's redemption—a counter plan that involved the destruction of the agency of man. Then what?

"I beheld Satan," says Jesus, "as lightning fall from heaven."‡

"And the angels which kept not their first estate, but left their own habitation, He hath reserved in everlasting chains, under darkness, unto the judgment of the great day."§

"And there was war in heaven: Michael and his angels fought

* See Luke 10: 17, 18. John 8: 44. Rev. 12. In the light of these references consider also Isaiah 14: 12-5, and Doc. and Cov. section 76: 25-9.

† Pearl of Great Price, chapter 4: 1-4.

‡ Luke 10: 18.

§ Jude 1: 6

against the dragon; and the dragon fought and his angels, and prevailed not; neither was their place found any more in heaven. And the great dragon was cast out, that old serpent, called the devil, and Satan, which deceiveth the whole world; he was cast out into the earth, and his angels were cast out with him. And I heard a loud voice saying in heaven, Now is come salvation, and strength, and the kingdom of our God, and the power of His Christ: for the accuser of our brethren is cast down, which accused them before our God day and night. And they overcame him by the blood of the Lamb, and by the word of their testimony; and they loved not their lives unto the death. Therefore rejoice, ye heavens, and ye that dwell in them. Woe to the inhabiters of the earth, and of the sea! for the devil is come down unto you, having great wrath, because he knoweth that he hath but a short time."*

Lucifer, then, becomes a factor to be reckoned with in the persecution of the Saints. In heaven he opposed the gospel of Jesus Christ; cast out into the earth will he not oppose it there? Herein lies the real cause of the persecution of the Christians within the Roman empire. So long as the inhabitants of the earth were content with the pagan superstitions, wherein there was no power of God unto salvation; so long as they were content with conflicting pagan philosophies, wherein was no power of God unto salvation, it was a matter of indifference to Lucifer whether they worshiped Jupiter Olympus, or Isis; Apollo, or Minerva; or bowed at the philosopher's shrine of the Unknown God—all were equally barren of saving power and left the kingdom of Lucifer undiminished in its strength and numbers; left all nations in his thraldom. But when the Christ and His apostles came preaching repentance and the coming of the kingdom of heaven; making known the origin of man and his relationship to Deity; making known the purpose of God to redeem him from his fallen state; establishing His Church as the depository of divine truth, and the instrumentality for conveying to man divine instruction—then Lucifer saw cause for alarm, for it was evident that the days of his dominion were numbered; his kingdom must decline if Christianity prevailed; his sway over the kingdoms of the earth must be broken if Christ was preached: and hence in all the bitterness of hatred, with all the strength of his cunning, with all the power of his resourcefulness, and using every instrumentality he could command—corrupted human nature over which he had influence; the apprehension of magistrates; the jealousy of pagan priesthoods—all were employed to destroy that institution wrought out in the wisdom of God to bring to pass the salvation of man; and hence the fire, the

* Rev. 12: 7-12.

sword and the rack; the lions, the dungeons,—in a word, the pagan persecutions of the Saints of God; Lucifer and his hatred of the truth the primary cause of all, all other causes and pretexts but secondary, mere instrumentalities used by him to impede the progress of and destroy, if possible, the truth, the gospel, wherein lies the power of man's salvation.

* * * * * * * *

It is said that history repeats itself; and this in matters of religion as in other things. In the introduction to the first volume of the Church History, the paganization of Christianity was discussed at some length, and when the Lord would again prepare the way for the incoming of the last dispensation of the Gospel—the dispensation of the fullness of times—as part of that preparation, He established a great republic in the New World, the chief corner stone of whose temple of liberty was religious freedom. The Congress of the United States, by express provision of the Constitution, is prohibited from making any law respecting an establishment of religion, or prohibiting the free exercise thereof.* Similar guarantees of religious freedom are provided for in the constitutions of all the states. The clause in Missouri's constitution on the subject was as follows:

"All men have a natural and indefeasible right to worship Almighty God according to the dictates of their own consciences; that no man can be compelled to erect, support or attend any place of worship, or to maintain any minister of the gospel or teacher of religion; that no human authority can control or interfere with the rights of conscience; that no person can ever be hurt, molested or restrained in his religious professions or sentiments, if he do not disturb others in their religious worship: that no person, on account of his religious opinions, can be rendered ineligible to any office of trust or profit under this state; that no preference can ever be given by law to any sect or mode of worship; and that no religious corporation can ever be established in this state."

Under these guarantees of religious liberty, in both state and national constitutions, infidels, Jews, and all sects of the Christian religion lived in unbroken peace. In the colonial history of the country there had been some intolerance and acts of violence practiced by the sects of Christians on one another, but in the main, and especially since the establishment of the republic of the United States, under its present Constitution, there had been absolute religious freedom. But now a strange thing occurred. A youth, yet in his early teens, startled the neighborhood in which he resided with the announcement that he had received a revelation from God; a new dispensation of the Gospel of Christ had been committed to him; he is authorized to found again the very

* First Amendment, Constitution of the United States.

Church of Christ; men are to teach once more by divine authority; and the world is to be made ready for the incoming of the glorious kingdom, whose king shall be the resurrected, glorified Christ; and peace and truth and righteousness are to abound. Strangely enough, notwithstanding all the guarantees of religious freedom in the state and national constitutions, this proclamation is resented by the people, and those who advocate it are persecuted in various ways, until at the last, as set forth in the three volumes of the Church History now published, it culminated in the death and misery of many souls, and the final expulsion of from twelve to fifteen thousand Saints from the state of Missouri, under all the circumstances of cruelty detailed in this history.

Why is this violence done to the principle of religious freedom, a principle that is both the pride and boast of the American people? Why are constitutions and institutions violated in efforts made by the authorities of the sovereign state of Missouri to destroy this religion and this Church of Christ? What is the cause of these Missouri persecutions? In view of the principles already set forth in these pages, the primary cause of these persecutions in Missouri will not be difficult to find. In them, as in the Roman persecutions of the Christians, the cunning and power of Lucifer will be apparent. So long as only apostate forms of Christianty obtained; so long as men adhered to mere forms of godliness and denied the power thereof, so long Lucifer cared not with what devotion they clung to these lifeless forms of religion. He laughed; his kingdom was undiminished; the nations were held in his thraldom. But when the Prophet of the dispensation of the fulness of times announced his revelation; when God again stood revealed once more before a witness; when the divine plan of life and salvation was again communicated to men through an inspired prophet; when the Church of Christ in all its completeness and power was restored to the earth, then it behoved Lucifer to look to his dominions, to strengthen his forces, and to prepare for the final conflict for possession of this world; for now God had taken it in hand to complete His work of redeeming the earth, of saving men, and overthrowing Lucifer and his power so far as this earth is concerned; and hence when Joseph Smith announced his new revelation, the incoming of the dispensation of the fulness of times, Lucifer with all the cunning and power at his command, and setting in motion every force—the fears and jealousies of men, misrepresentation and calumny, hatred of righteousness and truth, in a word, every force that he could summons, every pretext that he could suggest to men of evil disposed minds was employed to destroy the inauguration of that work which was to subdue his power, conquer his dominions, and render men free from his influence. Lucifer's bitterness, then, his hatred, his cunning, his devisements were the cause of the Missouri persecutions. All else was secondary, pretext, his instrumentalities, nothing more.

Retribution.

But what of Missouri? Missouri, who had violated her constitution which guaranteed religious freedom to all who came within her borders! Missouri, whose officers from the Governor down entered into a wicked conspiracy, contrary to all law and righteousness, and drove the Saints from the state! Missouri, who had violated not only her own constitution by becoming a party to a religious persecution, but had also violated the spirit of our times, and outraged the civilization of the nineteenth century—what of Missouri? Did she pay any penalty for her wrong-doing? Are states such entities as may be held to an accounting for breaches of public faith and public morals—constitutional immoralities? Is there within the state a public conscience to which an appeal can be made; and in the event of the public conscience being outraged is there retribution?

I answer these questions in the affirmative; and hold that Missouri paid dearly for the violations of her guarantees of religious freedom, and her lawlessness and her cruelties practiced towards the Latter-day Saints.

I have already referred to the relationship which the state of Missouri sustained to the great question of slavery. By the political compromise which bore her name, Missouri became a "cape of slavery thrust into free territory." Except for the state of Missouri alone, her southern boundary line was to mark the furthermost point northward beyond which slavery must not be extended into the territory of the United States. In 1854, however, the Missouri compromise was practically overthrown by the introduction into Congress of the "Kansas-Nebraska Act," by Stephen A. Douglas, United States senator from Illinois. This act provided for the organization of two new territories from the Louisiana purchase, west of Missouri and Iowa. The act proposed that the new territories should be open to slavery, if their inhabitants desired it. This left the question of slavery in the status it occupied previous to the Missouri Compromise, and left the people in the prospective states to determine for themselves whether slavery should or should not prevail in their state. This opened again the slavery question, and there was begun that agitation which finally resulted in the great American Civil War.

As soon as it became apparent that the people of new territories were to determine for themselves the question of slavery, very naturally each party began a struggle for possession of the new territory according as its sentiments or interests dictated. The struggle began by the abolition party of the north organizing "Emigrant Aid Societies," and sending emigrants of their own faith into Kansas. The slave holders of Missouri also sent settlers representing their faith and interests into the new territory in the hope of bringing it into the Union as a slave state. This brought on a border warfare in which the settlements of western Missouri and eastern Kansas alternately suffered from the raids and counter raids of the respective parties through some six years before the outbreak of the Civil War. As to which were the more lawless or cruel, the fanatical abolitionists or the pro-slavery party, the "jayhawkers," as the organized bands of ruffians of the former party were called, or the "bushwhackers," as the similarly organized bands of the pro-slavery men were called, is not a question necessary for me to discuss here. Both held the laws in contempt, and vied with each other in committing atrocities. The western counties of Missouri, where the Latter-day Saints had suffered so cruelly at the hands of people of those counties some eighteen or twenty years before, were in this border warfare laid desolate, and all the hardships the Missourians had inflicted upon the Saints were now visited upon their heads, only more abundantly.

Speaking of the situation in Missouri in 1861,the out-going Governor, Robert M. Stewart, in his address to the legislature, and referring to Missouri and her right to be heard on the slavery question, said:

"Missouri has a right to speak on this subject, because she has suffered. Bounded on three sides by free territory, her border counties have been the frequent scenes of kidnapping and violence, and this state has probably lost as much, in the last two years, in the abduction of slaves, as all the rest of the Southern States. *At this moment several of the western counties are desolated, and almost depopulated, from fear of a bandit horde, who have been committing depredations—arson, theft, and foul murder—upon the adjacent border*"*

Brigadier-General Daniel M. Frost, who had been employed in repressing lawlessness in the western counties of Missouri, in reporting conditions prevailing there in November, 1860, said:

"The deserted and charred remains of once happy homes, combined with the general terror that prevailed amongst the citizens who still clung to their possessions, gave but too certain proof of the persecution to which they had all been subjected, and which they would again have to endure, with renewed violence, so soon as armed protection should be withdrawn."* "In view of this condition of affairs," continues the historian of Missouri I am quoting, "and in order to carry out fully Governor Stewart's order to repel invasions and restore peace to the border, General Frost determined to leave a considerable force in

* "The Fight for Missouri," (Snead) p. 14.

the threatened district. Accordingly, a battalion of volunteers, consisting of three companies of rangers and one of artillery, was enlisted, and Lieutenant-Colonel John S. Bowen, who afterwards rose to high rank in the Confederate service, was chosen to the command."*

"With the organization of this force, and perhaps owing also, in some degree, to the inclemency of the season, 'jayhawking,' as such, came to an end, though the thing itself, during the first two or three years of the Civil War, and, in fact, as long as there was anything left on the Missouri side of the border worth taking, flourished more vigorously than ever. The old jayhawking leaders, however, now came with United States commissions in their pockets and at the head of regularly enlisted troops, in which guise they carried on a system of robbery and murder that left a good portion of the frontier south of the Missouri river as perfect a waste as Germany was at the end of the Thirty Years' War."†

While this description confines the scenes of violence and rapine to the border counties south of the Missouri river,—it included Jackson county, however, which was one of the heaviest sufferers both in this border warfare and subsequently during the Civil War—still, the counties north of that stream also suffered from lawlessness and violence.

At the outbreak of the Civil War Missouri was peculiarly situated. She was surrounded on three sides by free states. The great majority of her own people were for the Union, but her government, with Clairborne Jackson as the state executive, was in sympathy with the South. As the extreme Southern States one after another seceded from the Union, Missouri was confronted with the question: What position she ought to assume in the impending conflict. The question was referred to a state convention in which appeared no secessionists. Indeed, the people of Missouri in this election by a majority of eighty thousand decided against secession. The convention, in setting forth the attitude of the state on the subject, said that Missouri's position was, "Evidently that of a state whose interests are bound up in the maintenance of the Union, and whose kind feelings and strong sympathies are with the people of the Southern States, with whom we are connected by ties of friendship and blood. We want the peace and harmony of the country restored, and we want them with us. To go with them as they are now * * * * is to ruin ourselves without doing them any good."‡

While this doubtless voiced the sentiment of a great majority of Mis-

* "American Commonwealths, Missouri," p. 258.

† "American Commonwealths, Missouri," p. 259.

‡ "American Commonwealths, Missouri," (Carr) p. 288.

souri's people, the government of the state and many thousands of its inhabitants sympathized with the South. The general assembly of the state authorized the raising and equipment of large military forces held subject, of course, to the orders of the governor, under the pretense of being prepared to repel invasion from any quarter whatsoever, and enable the state to maintain a neutral attitude. The governor refused to raise Missouri's quota of four regiments under President Lincoln's first call for seventy-five thousand men to suppress the rebellion, on the ground that these regiments were intended to form "part of the President's army, to make war upon the people of the seceded states." This he declared to be illegal, unconstitutional, and therefore could not be complied with. This precipitated a conflict between the state and national forces that resulted in a civil war within the state since some of her citizens sided with the general government and some with the state.

On the 20th of April, 1861, the state militia under the governor's orders captured the Federal arsenal at Liberty, Clay county, and in the nineteen months following that event "over three hundred battles and skirmishes were fought within the limits of the state," and it is assumed that in the last two years of the war, there were half as many more; "and it may be said of them," continues our historian, "that they were relatively more destructive of life, as by this time the contest had degenerated into a disgraceful internecine struggle."*

In the fall of 1864, General Sterling Price penetrated the state at the head of twelve thousand men; captured Lexington, in Ray county, and Independence, in Jackson county, and thence made his escape into Arkansas. "In the course of this raid he marched 1,434 miles, fought forty-three battles and skirmishes, and according to his own calculation destroyed upwards of 'ten million dollars' worth of property,' a fair share of which belonged to his own friends."†

In August, 1863, the celebrated Military Order No. 11 was issued from Kansas City, by General Thomas Ewing, by which "all persons living in Cass, Jackson, and Bates counties, Missouri, and in that part of Vernon included in this district, except those living within one mile of the limits of Independence, Hickman's Mills, Pleasant Hill, and Harrisonville, and except those in that part of Kaw township, Jackson county, north of Brush creek and west of the Big Blue, embracing Kansas City and Westport, are hereby ordered to remove from their present places of residence within fifteen days from the date hereof.

* "American Commonwealths, Missouri." p. 342.

† History of Missouri, Carr, p. 360. General Price was the Colonel Sterling Price, who held the Prophet Joseph in custody at Richmond in 1838, who shackled the brethren and whose scurrilous guards were so severely rebuked by the Prophet.—History of the Church, Vol. III, p. 208, Note.

Those who, within that time, establish their loyalty to the satisfaction of the commanding officer of the military station nearest their present place of residence, will receive from him certificates stating the fact of their loyalty, and the names of the witnesses by whom it can be shown. All who receive such certificates will be permitted to remove to any military station in this district, or to any part of the state of Kansas, except the counties on the eastern borders of the state. All others shall remove out of this district. Officers commanding companies and detachments serving in the counties named will see that this paragraph is promptly obeyed."*

The admonition in the last clause to commanding officers was rigidly followed; and within the district named scenes of violence and cruelty were appalling. This order with its cruel execution has been more severely criticized than any other act during the entire Civil War. The justification for it has been urged on the ground that Jackson county afforded a field of operations for Confederates; that here the bushwhacking marauders recruited their forces, and found the means of support; that the policy was necessary on the ground of putting an end to that kind of warfare. On the other hand, it is contended that "tried by any known standard," the people in that section of Missouri were as loyal to the Union as were their neighbors in Kansas. "They had voted against secession; they had not only, thus far, kept their quota in the Union army full, and that without draft or bounty, but they continued to do so; and if they did not protect themselves against the outrages alike of Confederate bushwhackers and Union jayhawkers, it was because early in the war they had been disarmed by Federal authority and were consequently without the means of defense."†

By the execution of the order, however, the people in the districts named "were driven from their homes, their dwellings burned, their farms laid waste, and the great bulk of their movable property handed over, without let or hindrance, to the Kansas 'jayhawkers.' It was a brutal order, ruthlessly enforced, but so far from expelling or exterminating the guerrillas, it simply handed the whole district over to them." "Indeed," continues Lucien Carr, "we are assured by one who was on the ground, that from this time until the end of the war, no one wearing the Federal uniform dared risk his life within the devatasted region. The only people whom the enforcement of the order did injure were some thousands of those whom it was Ewing's duty to protect."‡

* "History of Caldwell and Livingston Counties," p. 51.

† "American Commonwealths, Missouri," p. 351.

‡ Ibid. p. 351.

Whether justified or not by the attitude of the Jackson county people in the Civil War, the execution of Order No. 11 certainly was but a re-enactment, though upon a larger scale, of those scenes which the inhabitants of that section of the country thirty years before had perpetrated upon the Latter-day Saints in expelling them from Jackson county. The awful scenes then enacted inspired the now celebrated painting by G. C. Bingham, bearing the title "Civil War," and dedicated by the artist "to all who cherish the principles of civil liberty."

Connected with the scenes of civil strife in Missouri, is a prophecy uttered by Joseph Smith many years before they began, and recently published in a very able paper by Elder Junius F. Wells, in the November number of the *Improvement Era* for 1902. Elder Wells, it appears, had the pleasure of an interview with the Hon. Leonidas M. Lawson, of New York city, formerly a resident of Clay county, Missouri, and a brother-in-law of General Alexander W. Doniphan, whose name so frequently occurs in our pages, dealing with events in the history of the Church while in Missouri.

In the course of the interview, which took place at the University Club, New York city, Mr. Lawson referred to an incident connected with a visit to General Doniphan in 1863. General Doniphan, it will be remembered by those acquainted with his history, took no part in the Civil War beyond that of a sorrowful spectator. On the occasion of Mr. Lawson's visit to him, just referred to, they rode through Jackson county together, and in a letter to Elder Wells, under date of February 7, 1902, Mr. Lawson relates the following incident, which is part of a biographical sketch of General Doniphan, prepared by Mr. Lawson:

"In the year 1863, I visited General A. W. Doniphan at his home in Liberty, Clay county, Missouri. This was soon after the devastation of Jackson county, Missouri, under what is known as 'Order No. 11.' This devastation was complete. Farms were everywhere destroyed, and the farmhouses were burned. During this visit General Doniphan related the following historical facts and personal incidents:

"About the year 1831-2, the Mormons settled in Jackson county, Mo., under the leadership of Joseph Smith. The people of Jackson county became dissatisfied with their presence, and forced them to leave; and they crossed the Missouri river and settled in the counties of De Kalb, Caldwell and Ray. They founded the town of Far West, and began to prepare the foundation of a temple. It was here that the troubles arose which culminated in the expulsion of the Mormons from the state of Missouri according to the command of Governor Lilburn W. Boggs. This was known in Missouri annals as the Mormon War. There were many among those who obeyed the order of the governor, in the state militia, who believed that the movement against the Mormons was unjust and cruel, and that the excitement was kept up by those who coveted the homes, the barns and the fields of the Mormon people. The latter, during their residence in the state of Missouri, paid, in entry fees for the land they claimed, to the United States government land office, more than $300,000, which, for that period represented a tremendous interest. During their sojourn in Missouri the Mormons did not practice or teach polygamy, so that question did not enter into it.

"Following the early excitement, Joseph Smith was indicted for treason against the state of Missouri, and General Doniphan was one of the counsel employed to defend him, he having shown a friendly interest in Smith, whom he considered very badly treated. Joseph Smith was placed in prison in Liberty, Missouri, to await his trial. This place was the residence of General Doniphan. His partner in the practice of law was James H. Baldwin.

"On one occasion General Doniphan caused the sheriff of the county to bring Joseph Smith from the prison to his law office, for the purpose of consultation about his defense. During Smith's presence in the office, a citizen of Jackson county, Missouri, came in for the purpose of paying a fee which was due by him to the firm of Doniphan and Baldwin, and offered in payment a tract of land in Jackson county.

"Doniphan told him that his partner, Mr. Baldwin, was absent at the moment, but as soon as he had an opportunity he would consult him and decide about the matter. When the Jackson county man retired, Joseph Smith, who had overheard the conversation, addressed General Doniphan about as follows:

"'*Doniphan, I advise you not to take that Jackson county land in payment of the debt. God's wrath hangs over Jackson county. God's people have been ruthlessly driven from it, and you will live to see the day when it will be visited by fire and sword. The Lord of Hosts will sweep it with the besom of destruction. The fields and farms and houses will be destroyed, and only the chimneys will be left to mark the desolation.*'"

"General Doniphan said to me that the devastation of Jackson county forcibly reminded him of this remarkable prediction of the Mormon prophet." (signed) L. M. LAWSON.

"There is a prediction of the Prophet Joseph," remarks Elder Wells, in commenting upon Mr. Lawson's story, "not before put into print, and history has recorded its complete fulfillment."

That a just retribution overtook the entire state, as well as the inhabitants of Jackson county, and other western counties, I think must be conceded by all who are familiar with the events of her history in the Civil War. That which she did to an inoffensive people was done to her inhabitants, especially to those living within the districts formerly occupied by the Latter-day Saints; only the measure meted out to the Missourians was heaped up, pressed down, and made to run over.

The Missourians had complained that the Latter-day Saints were eastern men, whose manners, habits, customs, and even dialect were different from their own;* but the Missourians lived to see great throngs of those same eastern men flock into an adjoining territory and infest their border, so that the settlers of western Missouri became accustomed to, and learned to endure the strange manners, customs and dialect so different from their own.

The Missourians complained of the rapidity with which the Saints were gathering into the state to establish their Zion; but the Missourians lived to see hordes of the detested easterners gather into their region of country by continuous streams of emigrant trains, sent there by "Emigrant Aid Companies" of New England.

The Missourians falsely charged that the coming of "Zion's Camp" into western Missouri to aid their brethren to repossess their homes in Jackson county, was an armed invasion of the state; but the Missourians lived to see formidable hosts of eastern and northern men gather upon their frontiers and frequently invade the state. "The character of much of this emigration may be gathered," says one historian, "from the fact that the Kansas Emigration Societies, Leagues and Committees * * * *sent out men only*;" and that in some of their bands Sharp's rifles were more numerous than agricultural implements."† Of course the "Blue Lodges" of Missouri were organized largely on the same principle as the "Emigrant Aid Companies" of New England, and adopted practically the same methods, expecting to add Kansas to the list of slave states. But "certainly," remarks Lucien Carr, "if a company of so-called northern emigrants, in which there were two hundred and twenty-five men and only five women, whose wagons contained no visible furniture, agricultural implements or mechanical tools, but abounded in all the requisite articles for camping and campaigning purposes, were considered as *bona fide* settlers and permitted to vote, there could not have been a sufficient reason for ruling out any band of Missourians who ever crossed the border and declared their intention of remaining, even though they left the next day."‡

Among the men sent to the borders of Missouri by the "Emigrant Aid Companies" of New England were some of the most desperate adventurers; and the Missourians who had pretended to be alarmed at the coming of "Zion's Camp," and feigned to regard it as an armed invasion

* Minutes of Citizen Meeting, Liberty, Clay county, Church History Vol. III, p. 450.

† History of Missouri, Carr, p. 343, Note.

‡ History of Missouri, Carr, 245.

of the state, saw their state repeatedly invaded—especially Jackson county—by the bands of Union "jayhawkers" organized from among these desperate eastern and northern men, who ruthlessly laid waste their homes and farms.

The Missourians had falsely charged the Saints with abolition madness, with tampering with their slaves, with inviting free negroes into the state to corrupt their blacks, whose very presence would render their institution of slave labor insecure; but they lived to see their system of slave labor abolished by the setting free of some one hundred and fifteen thousand slaves, valued at $40,000,000, eight thousand of whom were "martialed and disciplined for war" in the Federal armies, and many of them marched to war against their former masters.

Governor Dunklin and his advisors in the government of Missouri claimed that there was no warrant of authority under the laws and constitution of the state for calling out a permanent military force to protect the Saints in the peaceful possession of their homes until the civil authority proved itself competent to keep the peace and protect the citizens in the enjoyment of their guaranteed rights; but the people in the western part of Missouri saw the time come when they themselves prayed for the same protection; and Governor Stewart, unlike Governor Dunklin, approved the appointment of a battalion of volunteers consisting of three companies of rangers and one of artillery, all of which were placed under command of Lieutenant-Colonel John L. Bowen, to do the very thing the Saints had prayed might be done in their case.* But even this provision for their protection did not avail; for their old jayhawking enemies soon reappeared under new conditions —which will be stated in the next paragraph—under which they renewed their incursions of rapine and murder.

The state authorities of Missouri converted the mobs which had plundered the Saints, burned their homes and laid waste their lands, into the state militia, which gave the former mob a legal status, under which guise they plundered the Saints, compelled them to sign away their property and agree to leave the state. To resist this mob-militia was to be guilty of treason; but the people of western Missouri lived to see a like policy pursued towards them. They suffered much in Jackson and other western counties in the border war, previous to the opening of the Civil War, from the inroads of abolition "jayhawkers" in the interest of anti-slavery. For a time this was in part suppressed by the state militia under General Frost and by the permanent force stationed on the border under Lieutenant-Colonel Bowen. But later, and when the Civil War broke out, these old "jayhawking" leaders "now came with United States commissions in their pockets, and at the head of regularly enlisted troops, in which guise they carried on a sys-

* History of Missouri, Carr, p. 158.

tem of robbery and murder that left a good portion of the frontier south of the Missouri river as perfect a waste as Germany was at the end of the Thirty Years' War."*

Such wretches as Generals Lane and Jennison, though Union officers, and denounced alike by Governor Robinson of Kansas—of course a strong Union man—and General Halleck,† commander-in-chief of the western armies of the Union, were permitted to disgrace alike the Union cause and our human nature by their unspeakable atrocities. But they were retained in office, nevertheless. It was the outrages committed by these men and their commands, and the Kansas "Red Legs" that led to the equally savage reprisals on the people of Kansas. In revenge for what western Missouri had suffered, outlawed Missourians sacked Lawrence, Kansas, a Union city, massacred one hundred and eighty-three of its inhabitants, and left it in flames. In justification of their act of savagery, they declared: "Jennison has laid waste our homes, and the 'Red Legs' have perpetrated unheard of crimes. Houses have been plundered and burned, defenseless men shot down, and women outraged. We are here for revenge—and we have got it."‡ How nearly this language of the Missourians—and there can be no question that it describes what had been done in Missouri by Lane, Jennison, and their commands, and the Kansas "Red Legs"§—follows the complaint justly made by the Latter-day Saints years before against the Missourians! But thank God, there is recorded against the Saints no such horrible deeds of reprisal.

The Missourians falsely charged that the Saints held illicit communication with the Indian tribes then assembled near the frontiers of the state, and pretended to an alarm that their state might be invaded by the savages, prompted thereto by "Mormon" fanaticism; but these same Missourians lived to see cause for real fear of such an invasion when the Governor of an adjoining state—Arkansas—authorize Brigadier General Albert Pike to raise two mounted regiments of Choctaw and Chickasaw Indians to actually invade the state. These regiments of savages were engaged in the battle of Pea Ridge, on the southwest

* History of Missouri, Carr, p. 259.

† General Halleck when he learned that the "jayhawking" leader, Lane, had been promoted to the command of a brigade, declared that such an appointment was "offering a premium for rascality and robbing generally;" and that it would "take twenty thousand men to counteract its effect in the state." History of Missouri, Carr, p. 348.

‡ Spring's Kansas, p. 287.

§ These were bands of Kansas robbers, whose custom it was at intervals to dash into Missouri, seize horses and cattle—not omitting other and worse crimes on occasion—then to repair with their booty to Lawrence, where it was defiantly sold at auction." History of Missouri, Carr, p. 348.

borders of Missouri. General Pike, who led them in that battle, dressed himself in gaudy, savage costume, and wore a large plume on his head —*a la Niel Gilliam* at Far West—to please the Indians. It is also charged that before the battle of Pea Ridge, he maddened his Indians with liquor "that they might allow the savage nature of their race to have unchecked development. In their fury they respected none of the usages of civilized warfare, but scalped the helpless wounded, and committed atrocities too horrible to mention."* The "fear" expressed by the Missourians respecting the alleged illicit communication of the Saints with the Indians was mere feigning, but with this example before them, and knowing that there were many thousands of Indians on their frontiers that might be similarly induced to take up arms, their former feigned fears became real ones.

The Missourians instead of demanding the execution of the law in support of the liberties of the Saints, expressed the fear that the presence of the Saints would give rise to "Civil War," in which none could be neutrals, since their homes must be the theatre on which it would be fought,† so they drove the Saints away; but the Missourians lived to see the outbreak of a civil war in their state that was one of the most appalling men ever witnessed; and Missouri, when all things are considered, and especially western Missouri, suffered more than any other state of the Union. In other states the war lasted at most but four years; but counting her western border warfare in the struggle for Kansas, the war was waged in western Missouri from 1855 to 1865, ten years; and for many years after the close of the Civil War, a guerrilla warfare was intermittently carried on by bands of outlaws harbored in western Missouri—especially in Jackson, Ray, Caldwell and Clay counties—that terrorized the community and shocked the world by the daring and atrocity of their crimes—including bank robberies in open day, express train wrecking and robberies, and murders. Not until 1881 was this effectually stopped by the betrayal and murder of the outlaw chief of these bands.

Missouri sent into the Union Armies one hundred and nine thousand of her sons, including eight thousand negroes. About thirty thousand enlisted in the confederate army. According to official reports the percentage of troops to population in the western states and territories was 13.6 per cent, and in the New England states 12 per cent; whilst in Missouri, if there be added to her quota sent to the northern army the thirty thousand sent to the confederate army, her percentage was fourteen per cent, *or sixty per cent of those who were subject to military duty*. Of the deaths among these enlisted men, only approximate esti-

* History of the United States, Lossing, p. 592—*note*.

† History of the Church, Vol. II, p. 450-1.

mates may be made, since of the mortality among the Confederates no official records were kept. But of those who entered the Union service, thirteen thousand eight hundred and eighty-five deaths are officially reported. The rate of mortality in the Confederate forces, owing to the greater hardships they endured, and the lack of medical attendants to care for the wounded, was much higher, and is generally estimated at twelve thousand, (most of whom were from western Missouri), which added to the deaths of those in the Union army would aggregate the loss among the troops from Missouri to twenty-five thousand eight hundred and eighty-five. "This estimate," says Lucien Carr, "does not cover those who were killed in the skirmishes that took place between the home guards and the guerrillas; nor does it include those who were not in either army, but who were shot down by "bushwhackers" and "bushwhacking" Federal soldiers. Of these latter there is no record, though there were but few sections of the state in which such scenes were not more or less frequent. Assuming the deaths from these two sources to have been 1,200, and summing up the results, it will be found that the number of Missourians who were killed in the war and died from disease during their term of service amounted to not less than 27,000 men."*

The loss in treasure was in full proportion to the loss in blood. The state expended $7,000,000 in fitting out and maintaining her Union troops in the field.† She lost $40,000,000 in slave property; and four years after the close of the war—two of which, 1867-8, were remarkably prosperous—the taxable wealth of the state was $46,000,000 less than it was in 1860. "In many portions of the state," says the historian to whom I am indebted for so many of the facts relating to Missouri in these pages, "especially in the southern and western borders, whole counties had been devastated. The houses were burned, the fences destroyed, and the farms laid waste. Much of the live stock of the state had disappeared; and everywhere, even in those sections that were comparatively quiet and peaceful, the quantity of land in cultivation was much less than it had been at the outbreak of the war. Added to these sources of decline, and in some measure a cause of them, was the considerable emigration from the state which now took place, and particularly from those regions that lay in the pathway of the armies, or from those neighborhoods that were given over to the "bushwhackers." The amount of loss from these different sources cannot be accurately gauged, but some idea may be formed of it, and of the unsettled condition of affairs, from the fact that only 41 out of the 113 counties in the state

* History of Missouri, Carr, p. 358.

† It is but proper, however, to say that the state was afterwards reimbursed for this amount by the general government.

receipted for the tax books for 1861; and in these counties, only $250,000 out of the $600,000 charged against them were collected."*

This only in a general way indicates the losses in property sustained by the state during the period under consideration, but it assists one to understand somewhat the enormity of those losses.

It is in no spirit of gloating exultation that these facts in Missouri's history are referred to here. It gives no gratification to the writer to recount the woes of Missouri, and his hope is that it will give none to the reader. These facts of history are set down only because they are valuable for the lesson they teach. It may be that visible retribution does not always follow in the wake of state or national wrong-doing; but it is well that it should sometimes do so, lest men should come to think that Eternal Justice sleeps, or may be thwarted, or, what would be worst of all, that she does not exist. I say it is well, therefore, that sometimes visible retribution should follow state and national as well as individual transgressions, that the truth of the great principle that "as men sow, so shall they reap," may be vindicated. Missouri in her treatment of the Latter-day Saints during the years 1833-9, sowed the wind; in the disastrous events which overtook her during the years 1855-65, she reaped the whirlwind. Let us hope that in those events Justice was fully vindicated so far as the state of Missouri is concerned; and that the lessons of her sad experience may not be lost to the world. May the awful and visible retribution visited upon Missouri teach all states and nations that when they feel power they must not forget Justice; may it teach all peoples that states and nations in their corporate capacity are such entities as may be held accountable before God and the world for their actions; that righteousness exalteth a nation, while injustice is a reproach to any people. May the retribution that was so palpably visited upon the state of Missouri satisfy and encourage the Latter-day Saints; not that I would see them rejoice in the suffering of the wicked; but rejoice rather in the evidence that Justice slumbereth not; that their wrongs are not hidden from the All-seeing eye of God; that they are within the circle of His love; that they cannot be unjustly assailed with impunity, however humble and weak they may be. From all these considerations may they be established in peace, hope, confidence and charity; knowing that God is their friend; that His arm is strong to protect; or, if in the course of God's economy in the management of the affairs of the world it must needs be that for a time they suffer at the hands of oppressors, that He will avenge them of their enemies; and amply reward them for their sufferings in His cause.

* History of Missouri, Carr, p. 359.

HISTORY

OF THE

CHURCH OF JESUS CHRIST OF LATTER-DAY SAINTS.

VOL. III.

HISTORY

OF THE

CHURCH OF JESUS CHRIST

OF

LATTER-DAY SAINTS.

PERIOD I.

HISTORY OF JOSEPH SMITH, THE PROPHET.

CHAPTER I.

THE PROPHET JOSEPH'S DEPARTURE FROM KIRTLAND AND ARRIVAL IN MISSOURI.

January, 1838.—A new year dawned upon the Church in Kirtland in all the bitterness of the spirit of apostate mobocracy; which continued to rage and grow hotter and hotter, until Elder Rigdon and myself were obliged to flee from its deadly influence, as did the Apostles and Prophets of old, and as Jesus said, "when they persecute you in one city, flee to another." On the evening of the 12th of January, about ten o'clock, we left Kirtland, on horseback, to escape mob violence, which was about to burst upon us under the color of legal process to cover the hellish designs of our enemies, and to save themselves from the just judgment of the law.

Flight of the Prophet and Sidney Rigdon from Kirtland.

We continued our travels during the night, and at eight o'clock on the morning of the 13th, arrived among the brethren in Norton Township, Medina county, Ohio, a distance of sixty miles from Kirtland. Here we tarried about thirty-six hours, when our families arrived; and on the 16th we pursued our journey with our families, in covered wagons towards the city of Far West, in Missouri. We passed through Dayton and Eaton, in Ohio, and Dublin, Indiana; in the latter place we tarried nine days, and refreshed ourselves.

About January 16, 1838, being destitute of money to pursue my journey, I said to Brother Brigham Young: "You are one of the Twelve who have charge of the kingdom in all the world; I believe I shall throw myself upon you, and look to you for counsel in this case." Brother Young thought I was not earnest, but I told him I was. Brother Brigham then said, "If you will take my counsel it will be that you rest yourself, and be assured you shall have money in plenty to pursue your journey."

Brigham Young to the Prophet's Rescue.

There was a brother living in the place who had tried for some time to sell his farm but could not; he asked counsel of Brother Young concerning his property; Brother Young told him that if he would do right, and obey counsel, he should have an opportunity to sell. In about three days Brother Tomlinson came to Brother Brigham and said he had an offer for his place; Brother Brigham told him that this was the manifestation of the hand of the Lord to deliver Brother Joseph Smith from his present necessities. Brother Brigham's promise was soon verified, and I got three hundred dollars from Brother Tomlinson, which enabled me to pursue my journey.*

The weather was extremely cold, we were obliged to secrete ourselves in our wagons, sometimes, to elude the

* This incident occurred at Dublin, Indiana, where, and after, the Prophet had sought for a job at cutting and sawing wood to relieve his necessities.—"Life of Brigham Young, (Tullidge), p. 85.

grasp of our pursuers, who continued their pursuit of us more than two hundred miles from Kirtland, armed with pistols and guns, seeking our lives. They frequently crossed our track, twice they were in the houses where we stopped, once we tarried all night in the same house with them, with only a partition between us and them; and heard their oaths and imprecations, and threats concerning us, if they could catch us; and late in the evening they came in to our room and examined us, but decided we were not the men. At other times we passed them in the streets, and gazed upon them, and they on us, but they knew us not. One Lyons was one of our pursuers.

The Bitterness of the Prophet's Enemies.

I parted with Brother Rigdon at Dublin, and traveling different routes we met at Terre Haute, where, after resting, we separated again, and I pursued my journey, crossing the Mississippi river at Quincy, Illinois.

The Prophet's Arrival in Missouri.

TRIAL OF THE FAR WEST PRESIDENCY OF THE CHURCH.

Minutes of the Proceedings of the Committee of the whole Church in Zion, in General Assembly, at the following places, to-wit: At Far West, February 5, 1838; Carter's Settlement on the 6th; Durphy's Settlement, on the 7th; Curtis' Dwelling-house on the 8th; and Haun's Mills on the 9th. Thomas B. Marsh, Moderator, John Cleminson, Clerk.

After prayer, the Moderator stated the object of the meeting, giving a relation of the recent organization of the Church here and in Kirtland. He also read a certain revelation given in Kirtland, September 3, 1837, which made known that John Whitmer and W. W. Phelps, were in transgression, and if they repented not, they should be removed out of their places;* also read a certain clause contained in the appeal published in the old *Star*, on the 183rd page as follows:

"And to sell our lands would amount to a denial of our faith, as that is the place where the Zion of God shall stand, according to our faith and belief in the revelations of God."

Elder John Murdock then took the stand and showed to the congregation, why the High Council proceeded thus was that the Church

* See Vol. II, p. 511.

might have a voice in the matter; and that he considered it perfectly legal according to the instructions of President Joseph Smith, Jun.

Elder George M. Hinkle then set forth the way in which the Presidency of Far West had been labored with, that a committee of three, of whom he was one, had labored with them. He then read a written document, containing a number of accusations against the three presidents. He spoke many things against them, setting forth in a plain and energetic manner the iniquity of Elders Phelps and Whitmer, in using the monies which were loaned to the Church. Also David Whitmer's wrong-doing in persisting in the use of tea, coffee, and tobacco.

Bishop Partridge then arose and endeavored to rectify some mistakes of minor importance, made by Elder Hinkle; also the Bishop spoke against the proceedings of the meeting, as being hasty and illegal, for he thought they ought to be had before the Common Council, and said that he could not lift his hand against the Presidency at present. He then read a letter from President Joseph Smith, Jun.

A letter from William Smith was then read by Thomas B. Marsh, who made some comments on the same, and also on the letter read by Bishop Partridge.

Elder George Morey, who was one of the committee sent to labor with the Missouri Presidency, spoke, setting forth in a very energetic manner, the proceedings of that Presidency, as being iniquitous.

Elder Thomas Grover, also, being one of the committee, spoke against the conduct of the Presidency, and of Oliver Cowdery, on their visit to labor with them.

Elder David W. Patten spoke with much zeal against the Presidency, and in favor of Joseph Smith, Jun., and that the wolves alluded to, in his letter, were the dissenters in Kirtland.

Elder Lyman Wight stated that he considered all other accusations of minor importance compared to Brothers Phelps and Whitmer selling their lands in Jackson county; that they had set an example which all the Saints were liable to follow. He said that it was a hellish principle on which they had acted, and that they had flatly denied the faith in so doing.

Elder Elias Higbee sanctioned what had been done by the Council, speaking against the Presidency.

Elder Murdock stated that sufficient had been said to substantiate the accusations against them.

Elder Solomon Hancock pleaded in favor of the Presidency, stating that he could not raise his hand against them.

Elder John Corrill then spoke against the proceedings of the High Council and labored hard to show that the meeting was illegal, and that the Presidency ought to be arraigned before a proper tribunal, which he considered to be a Bishop and twelve High Priests. He labored in favor of the Presidency, and said that he should not raise his hands against them at present, although he did not uphold the Presidents in their iniquity.

Simeon Carter spoke against the meeting as being hasty.

Elder Groves followed Brother Carter in like observations.

Elder Patten again took the stand in vindication of the cause of the meeting.

Elder Morley spoke against the Presidency, at the same time pleading mercy.

Titus Billings said he could not vote until they had a hearing in the Common Council.*

Elder Marsh said that the meeting was according to the direction of Brother Joseph, he therefore considered it legal.

Elder Moses Martin spoke in favor of the legality of the meeting, and against the conduct of the Presidency, with great energy, alleging that the present corruptions of the Church here, were owing to the wickedness and mismanagement of her leaders.

The Moderator then called the vote in favor of the Missouri Presidency; the negative was then called, and the vote against David Whitmer, John Whitmer, and William W. Phelps was unanimous, excepting eight or ten, and this minority only wished them to continue in office a little longer, or until Joseph Smith, Jun., arrived.

THOMAS B. MARSH, Moderator,
JOHN CLEMINSON. Clerk.

Minutes of Proceedings in Other Settlements than Far West.

In Simeon Carter's settlement the Saints assembled on the 6th instant, when they unanimously rejected the three above-named Presidents. On

* The question raised here several times by the brethren, and hereafter alluded to by the defendants in the case, concerning the illegality of the Council attempting then to try David Whitmer, John Whitmer, and William W. Phelps, constituting the local Presidency of the Church in Missouri, grew out of a misapprehension of a council provided for in the revelations of God for the trial of a President of the High Priesthood, who is also of the Presidency of the whole Church. The said revelation provides that if a President of the High Priesthood, shall transgress, he shall be brought before the Presiding Bishop, or bishopric, of the Church, who are to be assisted by twelve counselors chosen from the High Priesthood. Here the President's conduct may be investigated, and the decision of that council upon his head is to be the end of controversy concerning him. (See Doc. and Cov., sec. 107: 76, 81, 82, 83). But the Presidency of the Church in Missouri was a local presidency, hence they could not plead the illegality of a local council of the Church to try them.

the 7th, the Saints assembled at Edmond Durphy's, agreeable to appointment, where the above-named Presidents were unanimously rejected; also on the 8th at Nahum Curtis' dwelling-house, they were unanimously rejected by the assembly; also at Haun's Mills, on the 9th, the Saints unanimously rejected them.

At a meeting of the High Council the Bishop and his counsel, February 10, 1838, it was moved, seconded, and carried, that Oliver Cowdery, William W. Phelps, and John Whitmer, stand no longer as chairman and clerks to sign and record licenses.

Voted that Thomas B. Marsh and David W. Patten be authorized to attend to such business for the time being.

Also voted that Thomas B. Marsh and David W. Patten be presidents, pro tempore, of the Church of Latter-day Saints in Missouri, until Presidents Joseph Smith, Jun., and Sidney Rigdon, arrive in the land of Zion.

J. MURDOCK, Moderator,
T. B. MARSH, Clerk.

High Council Meeting at Far West.

The High Council of Zion met in Far West, on Saturday, March 10, 1838, agreeable to adjournment; when after discussion it was resolved,

First—That the High Council recommend by writing to the various branches of this Church, that all those who wish to receive ordination, procure recommends from the branches to which they belong, and have such recommends pass through the hands of the different quorums for inspection, previous to the applicants' ordination.

Second—Resolved that the High Council recommend to all those who hold licenses, between the ages of eighteen and forty-five, and do not officiate in their respective offices, be subject to military duty.*

A charge was then preferred against William W. Phelps and John Whitmer, for persisting in unchristian-like conduct.

Six councilors were appointed to speak, viz., Simeon Carter, Isaac Higbee, and Levi Jackman, on the part of the accuser; and Jared Carter, Thomas Grover, and Samuel Bent, on the part of the accused; when the following letter, belonging to Thomas B. Marsh, was read by

* The law of Missouri excused from military duty all licensed ministers of the Gospel, and as nearly all the adult members of the Church who were worthy had received ordination to the Priesthood, it left the community in Far West, then a frontier country and liable to be raided by warlike tribes of Indians, without militia companies and state arms for its protection; hence the recommendation of the Council that the brethren within the ages specified, and not actively employed in the ministry, place themselves in a position to accept militia service.

Brother Marcellus F. Cowdery, bearer of the same, previous to giving it to its rightful owner:

"FAR WEST, March 10, 1838.

"Sir—It is contrary to the principles of the revelations of Jesus Christ and His gospel, and the laws of the land, to try a person for an offense by an illegal tribunal, or by men prejudiced against him, or by authority that has given an opinion or decision beforehand, or in his absence.

"Very respectfully we have the honor to be,
"DAVID WHITMER,
"WILLIAM W. PHELPS,
"JOHN WHITMER,
"Presidents of the Church of Christ in Missouri.

"To Thomas B. Marsh, one of the [Twelve] Traveling Councilors."

Attested: OLIVER COWDERY,
Clerk of the High Council of the Church of Christ in Missouri.

I certify the foregoing to be a true copy from the original.
OLIVER COWDERY,
Clerk of the High Council.

All the effect the above letter had upon the Council, was to convince them still more of the wickedness of those men, by endeavoring to palm themselves off upon the Church, as her Presidents, after the Church had by a united voice, removed them from their presidential office, for their ungodly conduct; and the letter was considered no more nor less than a direct insult or contempt cast upon the authorities of God, and the Church of Jesus Christ; therefore the Council proceeded to business.

A number of charges were sustained against these men, the principal of which was claiming $2,000 Church funds, which they had subscribed for building a house to the Lord in this place, when they held in their possession the city plat, and were sitting in the presidential chair; which subscription they were intending to pay from the avails of the town lots; but when the town plat was transferred into the hands of the Bishop for the benefit of the Church, it was agreed that the Church should take this subscription off the hands of W. W. Phelps and John Whitmer: but in the transaction of the business, they bound the Bishop in a heavy mortgage, to pay them the above $2,000, in two years from the date thereof, a part of which they had already received, and claimed the remainder.

The six councilors made a few appropriate remarks, but none felt to plead for mercy, as it had not been asked on the part of the accused, and all with one consent declared that justice ought to have her demands.

After some remarks by Presidents Marsh and Patten, setting forth the iniquity of those men in claiming the $2,000 spoken of, which did not belong to them, any more than to any other person in the Church, it was decided that William W. Phelps and John Witmer be no longer members of the Church of Christ of Latter-day Saints, and be given over to the buffetings of Satan, until they learn to blaspheme no more against the authorities of God, nor fleece the flock of Christ.

The Council was then asked if they concurred with the decision, if so, to manifest it by rising; they all arose.

The vote was then put to the congregation, and was carried unanimously.

The negative was called, but no one voted.

Brother Marcellus F. Cowdery arose and said he wished to have it understood that he did not vote either way, because he did not consider it a legal tribunal. He also offered insult to the High Council, and to the Church, by reading a letter belonging to Thomas B. Marsh, before giving it to him, and in speaking against the authorities of the Church.

A motion was then made by President Patten, that fellowship be withdrawn from Marcellus F. Cowdery, until he make satisfaction, which was seconded and carried unanimously.

THOMAS B. MARSH,
DAVID W. PATTEN,
Presidents.
EBENEZER ROBINSON,
Clerk of High Council.

The Prophet's Reception in Zion.

When I had arrived within one hundred and twenty miles of Far West, the brethren met me with teams and money to help me forward; and when eight miles from the city, we were met by an escort, viz., Thomas B. Marsh and others, who received us with open arms; and on the 13th of March, with my family and some others I put up at Brother Barnard's for the night. Here we were met by another escort of the brethren from the town, who came to make us welcome to their little Zion.

On the 14th of March, as we were about entering Far West, many of the brethren came out to meet us, who also with open arms welcomed us to their bosoms. We were immediately received under the hospitable roof of Brother George W. Harris, who treated us with all possible kindness, and we refreshed ourselves with much satisfaction, after our long and tedious journey, the brethren bringing in such things as we had need of for our comfort and convenience.

After being here two or three days, my brother Samuel arrived with his family.

Shortly after his arrival, while walking with him and certain other brethren, the following sentiments occurred to my mind:

The Political Motto of the Church of Latter-day Saints.

The Constitution of our country formed by the Fathers of liberty. Peace and good order in society. Love to God, and good will to man. All good and wholesome laws, virtue and truth above all things, and aristarchy, live for ever! But woe to tyrants, mobs, aristocracy, anarchy, and toryism, and all those who invent or seek out unrighteous and vexatious law suits, under the pretext and color of law, or office, either religious or political. Exalt the standard of Democracy! Down with that of priestcraft, and let all the people say Amen! that the blood of our fathers may not cry from the ground against us. Sacred is the memory of that blood which bought for us our liberty.

JOSEPH SMITH, JUN.,
THOMAS B. MARSH,
DAVID W. PATTEN,
BRIGHAM YOUNG,
SAMUES H. SMITH,
GEORGE M. HINKLE,
JOHN CORRILL,
GEORGE W. ROBINSON.

*The Prophet's Answers to Questions on Scripture.**

Who is the Stem of Jesse spoken of in the 1st, 2nd, 3rd, 4th, and 5th verses of the 11th chapter of Isaiah?

Verily thus saith the Lord, it is Christ.

What is the rod spoken of in the first verse of the 11th chapter of Isaiah that should come of the Stem of Jesse?

* Doctrine and Covenants, sec. cxiii.

Behold, thus saith the Lord, it is a servant in the hands of Christ, who is partly a descendant of Jesse as well as of Ephraim, or of the House of Joseph, on whom there is laid much power.

What is the root of Jesse spoken of in the 10th verse of the 11th chapter?

Behold, thus saith the Lord, it is a descendant of Jesse, as well as of Joseph, unto whom righty belongs the Priesthood, and the keys of the Kingdom, for an ensign, and for the gathering of my people in the last days.

Questions by Elias Higbee:

"What is meant by the command in Isaiah, 52nd chapter, 1st verse, which saith, put on thy strength O Zion? And what people had Isaiah reference to?"

He had reference to those whom God should call in the last days, who should hold the power of Priesthood to bring again Zion, and the redemption of Israel; and to put on her strength is to put on the authority of the Priesthood, which she (Zion) has a right to by lineage; also to return to that power which she had lost.

"What are we to understand by Zion loosing herself from the bands of her neck; 2nd verse?"

We are to understand that the scattered remnants are exhorted to return to the Lord from whence they have fallen, which if they do, the promise of the Lord is that He will speak to them, or give them revelation. See the 6th, 7th and 8th verses. The bands of her neck are the curses of God upon her, or the remnants of Israel in their scattered condition among the Gentiles.

The Prophet's Letter to the Presidency of the Church of Jesus Christ of Latter-day Saints in Kirtland.

FAR WEST, March 29, 1838.

Dear and Well Beloved Brethren—Through the grace and mercy of our God, after a long and tedious journey of two months and one day, my family and I arrived safe in the city of Far West, having been met at Huntsvills, one hundred and twenty miles from this place, by my brethren with teams and money, to forward us on our journey. When within eight miles of the city of Far West, we were met by an escort of brethren from the city, viz.: Thomas B. Marsh, John Corrill, Elias Higbee, and several others of the faithful of the West, who received us with open arms and warm hearts, and welcomed us to the bosom of their society. On our arrival in the city we were greeted on every hand by the Saints, who bid us welcome to the land of their inheritance.

Dear brethren,you may be assured that so friendly a meeting and reception paid us well for our long seven years of servitude, persecution, and affliction in the midst of our enemies, in the land of Kirtland; yea, verily our hearts were full; and we feel grateful to Almighty God for His kindness unto us. The particulars of our journey, brethren, cannot well be written, but we trust that the same God who has protected us will protect you also, and will, sooner or later, grant us the privilege of seeing each other face to face, and of rehearsing all our sufferings.

We have heard of the destruction of the printing office, which we presume to believe must have been occasioned by the Parrish party, or more properly the aristocrats or anarchists.

The Saints here have provided a room for us, and daily necessaries, which are brought in from all parts of the country to make us comfortable; so that I have nothing to do but to attend to my spiritual concerns, or the spiritual affairs of the Church.

The difficulties of the Church had been adjusted before my arrival here, by a judicious High Council, with Thomas B. Marsh and David W. Patten, who acted as presidents *pro tempore* of the Church of Zion, being appointed by the voice of the Council and Church, William W. Phelps and John Whitmer having been cut off from the Chuch, David Whitmer remaining as yet. The Saints at this time are in union; and peace and love prevail throughout; in a word, heaven smiles upon the Saints in Caldwell. Various and many have been the falsehoods written from Kirtland to this place, but [they] have availed nothing. We have no uneasiness about the power of our enemies in this place to do us harm.

Brother Samuel H. Smith and family arrived here soon after we did, in good health. Brothers Brigham Young, Daniel S. Miles, and Levi Richards arrived here when we did. They were with us on the last part of our journey, which ended much to our satisfaction. They also are well. They have provided places for their families, and are now about to break the ground for seed.

Having been under the hands of [men who urged against me] wicked and vexatious law suits for seven years past, my business [in Kirtland] was so deranged that I was not able to leave it in so good a situation as I had anticipated; but if there are any wrongs, they shall all be noticed, so far as the Lord gives me ability and power to do so.

Say to all the brethren, that I have not forgotten them, but remember them in my prayers. Say to Mother Beaman that I remember her, also Brother Daniel Carter, Brother Strong and family, Brother Granger and family; finally I cannot enumerate them all for want of room, I will just name Brother Knight, the Bishop, etc.; my best respects to them all, and I commend them and the Church of God in Kirtland to our Heavenly Father, and the word of His grace, which is able to make you wise unto salvation.

I would just say to Brother Marks, that I saw in a vision while on the road, that whereas he was closely pursued by an innumerable concourse of enemies, and as they pressed upon him hard, as if they were about to devour him, and had seemingly obtained some degree of advantage over him, but about this time a chariot of fire came, and near the place, even the angel of the Lord put forth his hand unto Brother Marks and said unto him, "Thou art my son, come here," and immediately he was caught up in the chariot, and rode away triumphantly out of their midst. And again the Lord said, I will raise thee up for a blessing unto many people." Now the particulars of this whole matter cannot be written at this time, but the vision was evidently given to me that I might know that the hand of the Lord would be on his behalf.

I transmit to you the Motto of the Church of Latter-day Saints.

We left President Rigdon thirty miles this side of Paris, Illinois, in consequence of the sickness of Brother George W. Robinson's wife.

On yesterday Brother Robinson arrived here, who informed us that his father-in-law (Sidney Rigdon) was at Huntsville, detained on account of the ill health of his wife. They will probably be here soon.

Choice seeds of all kinds of fruit, also choice breeds of cattle, would be in much demand; and best blood of horses, garden seeds of every description, and hay seeds of all sorts, are much needed in this place.

Very respectfully I subscribe myself your servant in Christ, our Lord and Savior.

JOSEPH SMITH, JUN.,
President of the Church of Christ of Latter-day Saints.

CHAPTER II.

EXCOMMUNICATION OF OLIVER COWDERY AND DAVID WHITMER —THE WORK IN ENGLAND.

PRESIDENT RIGDON arrived at Far West with his family, Wednesday, April 4th, having had a tedious journey, and his family having suffered many afflictions.

Arrival of Sidney Rigdon at Far West.

Minutes of a General Conference of the Church at Far West.

FAR WEST, April 6, 1838.

Agreeable to a resolution passed by the High Council of Zion, March 3, 1838, the Saints in Missouri assembled in this place to celebrate the anniversary of the Church of Jesus Christ of Latter-day Saints, and to transact Church business, Joseph Smith, Jun., and Sidney Rigdon, presiding.

The meeting was opened by singing, and prayer by David W. Patten, after which President Joseph Smith, Jun., read the order of the day as follows: Doors will be opened at 9 o'clock a. m., and the meeting will commence by singing and prayer. A sexton will then be appointed as a door keeper, and other services in the House of the Lord. Two historians will then be appointed to write and keep the Church history; also a general recorder to keep the records of the whole Church, and to be the clerk of the First Presidency. And a clerk will be appointed for the High Council, and to keep the Church records of this Stake. Three presidents will be appointed to preside over this Church of Zion, after which an address will be delivered by the Presidency. Then an intermission of one hour, when the meeting will again convene, and open by singing and prayer. The Sacrament will then be administered, and the blessing of infants attended to.

The meeting proceeded to business. George Morey was appointed sexton, and Dimick Huntington assistant; John Corrill and Elias Higbee, historians; George W. Robinson, general Church recorder and clerk to the First Presidency; Ebenezer Robinson, Church clerk and recorder for Far West and clerk of the High Council; Thomas B. Marsh, President *pro tempore* of the Church in Zion, and Brigham Young and David W. Patten, his assistant Presidents.

After one hour's adjournment, meeting again opened by David W. Patten. The bread and wine were administered, and ninety-five infants were blessed.

JOSEPH SMITH, JUN., President.
EBENEZER ROBINSON, Clerk.

Minutes of the First Quarterly Conference at Far West.

Agreeable to a resolution of the High Council, March 3, 1838, the general authorities of the Church met, to hold the Quarterly Conference of the Church of Latter-day Saints, at Far West, on the 7th of April, 1838.

President Joseph Smith, Jun., Sidney Rigdon, Thomas B. Marsh, David W. Patten, and Brigham Young, took the stand, after which the several quorums, the High Council, the High Priests, the Seventies, the Elders, the Bishops, the Priests, Teachers and Deacons, were organized by their Presidents.

President Joseph Smith, Jun., made some remarks and also gave some instructions respecting the order of the day. After singing, prayer by Brigham Young, and singing again, President Smith then addressed the congregation at considerable length, followed by President Rigdon.

Adjourned twenty minutes.

Opened by David W. Patten, who also made some remarks respecting the Twelve Apostles. He spoke of Thomas B. Marsh, Brigham Young, Heber C. Kimball, Orson Hyde, Parley P. Pratt, and Orson Pratt, as being men of God, whom he could recommend with cheerfulness and confidence. He spoke somewhat doubtful of William Smith, for something he had heard respecting his faith in the work. He also spoke of William E. McLellin, Luke S. Johnson, Lyman E. Johnson, and John F. Boynton, as being men whom he could not recommend to the conference.

President John Murdock represented the High Council. The report was favorable. The seats of Elisha H. Groves, Calvin Bebee, and Lyman Wight were vacant in consequence of their having moved so far away they could not attend the Council.

Thomas B. Marsh nominated Jared Carter, to fill the seat of Elisha H. Groves; John P. Greene that of Calvin Bebee, and George W. Harris that of Lyman Wight; which nominations were severally and unanimously sanctioned.

George W. Harris was ordained a High Priest.

On motion, conference adjourned to the 8th, 9 o'clock a. m.

Sunday, April 8th, 9 o'clock a. m., conference convened and opened as usual, prayer by Brigham Young.

President Joseph Smith, Jun., made a few remarks respecting the Kirtland Bank. He was followed by Brigham Young, who gave a short history of his travels to Massachusetts and New York.

President Charles C. Rich represented his quorum of High Priests, and read their names. The principal part were in good standing.

President Daniel S. Miles and Levi W. Hancock represented the Seventies.

The quorum of Elders were represented by their President, Harvey Green, numbering one hundred and twenty-four in good standing.

President Joseph Smith, Jun., made a few remarks on the Word of Wisdom, giving the reason of its coming forth, saying it should be observed.

Adjourned for one hour.

Conference convened agreeable to adjournment, and opened as usual, after which Bishop Partridge represented his Council and the Lesser Priesthood, and made a report of receipts and expenditures of Church funds which had passed through his hands.

It was then moved, seconded and carried, that the First Presidency be appointed to sign the licenses of the official members of the Church.

Conference adjourned until the first Friday in July next.

JOSEPH SMITH, JUN., President.
EBENEZER ROBINSON, Clerk.

Demand on John Whitmer for the Church Records.

The following letter was sent to John Whitmer, in consequence of his withholding the records of the Church in the city of Far West, when called for by the clerk.

Mr. John Whitmer, Sir: We were desirous of honoring you by giving publicity to your notes on the history of the Church of Latter-day Saints, after making such corrections as we thought would be necessary, knowing your incompetency as a historian, and that writings coming from your pen, could not be put to press without our correcting them, or else the Church must suffer reproach. Indeed, sir, we never supposed you capable of writing a history, but were willing to let it come out under your name, notwithstanding it would really not be yours but ours. We are still willing to honor you, if you can be made to know your own interest, and give up your notes, so that they can be corrected and made fit for the press; but if not, we have all the materials for another, which we shall commence this week to write.

Your humble servants,
JOSEPH SMITH, JUN.,
SIDNEY RIGDON,
Presidents of the whole Church of Latter-day Saints.
Attest: EBENEZER ROBINSON, Clerk.

Wednesday, April 11, Elder Seymour Brunson preferred the following charges against Oliver Cowdery, to the High Council at Far West:*

Charges Against Oliver Cowdery.

To the Bishop and Council of the Church of Jesus Christ of Latter-day Saints, I prefer the following charges against President Oliver Cowdery:

"First—For persecuting the brethren by urging on vexatious law suits against them, and thus distressing the innocent.

"Second—For seeking to destroy the character of President Joseph Smith, Jun., by falsely insinuating that he was guilty of adultery.

"Third—For treating the Church with contempt by not attending meetings.

"Fourth—For virtually denying the faith by declaring that he would not be governed by any ecclesiastical authority or revelations whatever, in his temporal affairs.

"Fifth—For selling his lands in Jackson county, contrary to the revelations.

"Sixth—For writing and sending an insulting letter to President Thomas B. Marsh, while the latter was on the High Council, attending to the duties of his office as President of the Council, and by insulting the High Council with the contents of said letter.

"Seventh—For leaving his calling to which God had appointed him by revelation, for the sake of filthy lucre, and turning to the practice of law.

Eighth—For disgracing the Church by being connected in the bogus business, as common report says.

"Ninth—For dishonestly retaining notes after they had been paid; and finally, for leaving and forsaking the cause of God, and returning to the beggarly elements of the world, and neglecting his high and holy calling, according to his profession."

The Bishop and High Council assembled at the Bishop's

* The charges were drawn up and dated the 7th of April, and handed to Bishop Partridge.

office, April 12, 1838. After the organization of the Council, the above charges of the 11th instant were read, also a letter from Oliver Cowdery, as will be found recorded in the Church record of the city of Far West, Book A. The 1st, 2nd, 3rd, 7th, 8th, and 9th charges were sustained. The 4th and 5th charges were rejected, and the 6th was withdrawn. Consequently he (Oliver Cowdery) was considered no longer a member of the Church of Jesus Christ of Latter-day Saints.* Also voted by the High Council that

Trial of Oliver Cowdery.

* The following letter from Oliver Cowdery respecting his difficulties at this time in the Church, is copied from the Far West Record of the High Council, and is an interesting document for several reasons: First, it shows the spirit of Oliver Cowdery at that time, also his misapprehensions of the policy of the authorities in the government of the Church, for it is to be noted that the two principal points covered in this letter, numbers four and five of Elder Brunson's charges, were rejected by the Council as not being proper to be considered, and the sixth charge also is withdrawn, so that Oliver Cowdery was not disfellowshiped from the Church on the points raised in his letter at all, but on the first, second, third, seventh, eighth and ninth charges in Elder Brunson's formal accusation, and since these charges were sustained upon testimony of witnesses, as the minutes of the High Council proceedings in the Far West Record clearly show, it is to be believed that the Church had sufficient cause for rejecting him.

Elder Cowdery's Letter.

FAR WEST, MISSOURI, April 12, 1838.

Dear Sir:—I received your note of the 9th inst., on the day of its date, containing a copy of nine charges preferred before yourself and Council against me, by Elder Seymour Brunson.

I could have wished that those charges might have been deferred until after my interview with President Smith; but as they are not, I must waive the anticipated pleasure with which I had flattered myself of an understanding on those points which are grounds of different opinions on some Church regulations, and others which personally interest myself.

The fifth charge reads as follows: "For selling his lands in Jackson County contrary to the revelations." So much of this charge, "for selling his lands in Jackson County," I acknowledge to be true, and believe that a large majority of this Church have already spent their judgment on that act, and pronounced it sufficient to warrant a disfellowship; and also that you have concurred in its correctness, consequently, have no good reason for supposing you would give any decision contrary.

Now, sir, the lands in our country are allodial in the strictest construction of that term, and have not the least shadow of feudal tenures attached to them, consequently, they may be disposed of by deeds of conveyance without the consent or even approbation of a superior.

The fourth charge is in the following words, "For virtually denying the faith

Oliver Cowdery be no longer a committee to select locations for the gathering of the Saints.

Charges against David Whitmer.

April 13.—The following charges were preferred against David Whitmer, before the High Council at Far West, in council assembled.

"First—For not observing the Word of Wisdom.

"Second—For unchristian-like conduct in neglecting to attend meet-

by declaring that he would not be governed by any ecclesiastical authority nor revelation whatever in his temporal affairs."

With regard to this, I think I am warranted in saying, the judgment is also passed as on the matter of the fifth charge, consequently, I have no disposition to contend with the Council; this charge covers simply the doctrine of the fifth, and if I were to be controlled by other than my own judgment, in a compulsory manner, in my temporal interests, of course, could not buy or sell without the consent of some real or supposed authority. Whether that clause contains the precise words, I am not certain—I think however they were these, "I will not be influenced, governed, or controlled, in my temporal interests by any ecclesiastical authority or pretended revelation whatever, contrsry to my own judgment." Such being still my opinion shall only remark that the three great principles of English liberty, as laid down in the books, are "the right of personal security, the right of personal liberty, and the right of private property." My venerable ancestor was among the little band, who landed on the rocks of Plymouth in 1620—with him he brought those maxims, and a body of those laws which were the result and experience of many centuries, on the basis of which now stands our great and happy government; and they are so interwoven in my nature, have so long been inculcated into my mind by a liberal and intelligent ancestry that I am wholly unwilling to exchange them for anything less liberal, less benevolent, or less free.

The very principle of which I conceive to be couched in an attempt to set up a kind of petty government, controlled and dictated by ecclesiastical influence, in the midst of this national and state government. You will, no doubt, say this is not correct; but the bare notice of these charges, over which you assume a right to decide, is, in my opinion, a direct attempt to make the secular power subservient to Church direction—to the correctness of which I cannot in conscience subscribe—I believe that principle never did fail to produce anarchy and confusion.

This attempt to control me in my temporal interests, I conceive to be a disposition to take from me a portion of my Constitutional privileges and inherent right—I only, respectfully, ask leave, therefore, to withdraw from a society assuming they have such right.

So far as relates to the other seven charges, I shall lay them carefully away, and take such a course with regard to them, as I may feel bound by my honor, to answer to my rising posterity.

I beg you, sir, to take no view of the foregoing remarks, other than my belief in the outward government of this Church. I do not charge you, or any other person who differs with me on these points, of not being sincere, but such difference does exist, which I sincerely regret.

With considerations of the highest respect, I am, your obedient servant,

[Signed.] OLIVER COWDERY.

Rev. Edward Partridge, Bishop of the Church of Latter-day Saints.

ings, in uniting with and possessing the same spirit as the dissenters.

"Third—In writing letters to the dissenters in Kirtland unfavorable to the cause, and to the character of Joseph Smith, Jun.

"Fourth—In neglecting the duties of his calling, and separating himself from the Church, while he had a name among us.

"Fifth—For signing himself President of the Church of Christ in an insulting letter to the High Council after he had been cut off from the Presidency."

After reading the above charges, together with a letter sent to the President of said Council,* the Council held that the charges were sustained, and consequently considered David Whitmer no longer a member of the Church of Latter-day Saints.

* The letter referred to is to be found in the Far West Record. It is as follows

"FAR WEST, MO., April 13, 1838.

"JOHN MURDOCK:

"Sir:—I received a line from you bearing date the 9th inst., requesting me as a High Priest to appear before the High Council and answer to five several charges on this day at 12 o'clock.

"You, sir, with a majority of this Church have decided that certain councils were legal by which it is said I have been deprived of my office as one of the Presidents of this Church. I have thought, and still think, they were not agreeable to the revelations of God, which I believe; and by now attending this Council, and answering to charges, as a High Priest, would be acknowledging the correctness and legality of those former assumed councils, which I shall not do.

"Believing as I verily do, that you and the leaders of the councils have a determination to pursue your unlawful course at all hazards, and bring others to your standard in violation of the revelations, to spare you any further trouble I hereby withdraw from your fellowship and communion—choosing to seek a place among the meek and humble, where the revelations of heaven will be observed and the rights of men regarded.

"DAVID WHITMER."

In the minutes of the council in which this letter was read appear also the following paragraphs:

"After the reading of the above letter it was not considered necessary to investigate the case, as he [David Whitmer] had offered contempt to the Council by writing the above letter, but it was decided to let the councilors speak what they had to say upon the case, and pass decision.

"The councilors then made a few remarks in which they spoke warmly of the contempt offered to the Council in the above letter, therefore, thought he [David Whitmer] was not worthy a membership in the Church.

"Whereupon President Marsh made a few remarks, and decided that David Whitmer be no longer considered a member of the Church of Jesus Christ of Latter-day Saints."

The Council sustained the decision of President Marsh and David Whitmer was excommunicated. The letters of both Oliver Cowdery and David Whitmer to the High Council, setting forth their position respecting matters involved, are here

The same day three charges were preferred against Lyman E. Johnson, which were read, together with a letter from him, in answer to the one recorded in Far West Record.* The charges were sustained, and he was cut off from the Church.

Charges against Lyman E. Johnson.

The work continued to prosper in England, and Elders Richards and Russell having previously been called to Preston, to prepare for their return to America, a general conference was held in the Temperance Hall, (Cock Pit) Preston, on Sunday, April 1st, for the purpose of setting in order the churches, etc. Brother Joseph Fielding was chosen President over the whole Church in England, and Willard Richards and William Clayton† were chosen his Counselors, and were ordained to the High Priesthood and to the Presidency. This was the first notice given Elder Richards that he would be required to continue in England. At this conference eight Elders were ordained, among whom was Thomas Webster, and several Priests, Teachers and Deacons; about forty were confirmed, who had previously been baptized; about sixty children were blessed, and twenty baptized that day. Conference continued without intermission from 9 a.m. to 5 p.m. About fifty official members met in council in the evening.

The Work in England—Conference in Preston.

presented that I might call attention to this fact: neither of them deny or even slight the great facts in which Mormonism had its origin—the coming forth of the Book of Mormon, and the ministration of the angels of heaven to both Joseph Smith and themselves. Had there been any fraud or collusion entered into between Joseph Smith and Oliver Cowdery and David Whitmer, I take it that it would have been a very natural thing for men smarting under what they regarded as injustice, to have manifested that fact in one way or another in these communications. Their silence at this critical time of their experience, and in the experience of the Church, constitutes very strong presumptive evidence of the reality of those facts which brought Mormonism into existence.

* A copy of which may be found in Far West Record, Book A, p. 128.

† William Clayton was born in Penworthan, Lancashire, England, July 17, 1814. He was baptized soon after the arrival of the Mormon Elders in England in 1837. Soon after his ordination to the Holy Priesthood and Presidency of the British mission he abandoned all other business and gave himself to the ministry, in which he was remarkably successful.

From the 1st to the 8th of April Presidents Kimball and Hyde visited the churches a short distance from Preston, and on the 8th attended meeting in the "Cock Pit." After preaching by Elder Richards, they bore their farewell testimony to the truth of the work. After they had closed, and while Elder Russell was speaking, the enemy severed the gas pipes which lighted the house, and threw the assembly into darkness in an instant. The damage was soon repaired, and the design of breaking up the meeting frustrated.

Farewell Meetings with the Saints.

On Tuesday, the 10th of April, at 12 o'clock, Elders Kimball and Hyde left Preston by coach for Liverpool.

While the Elders were in Liverpool they wrote as follows:

A Prophecy.

LIVERPOOL, GOOD FRIDAY, April 13, 1838.

DEAR BROTHERS AND SISTERS IN PRESTON:—It seemeth good unto us, and also to the Holy Spirit, to write you a few words which cause pain in our hearts, and will also pain you when they are fulfilled before you, yet you shall have joy in the end. Brother Thomas Webster will not abide in the Spirit of the Lord, but will reject the truth, and become the enemy of the people of God, and expose the mysteries that have been committed to him, that a righteous judgment may be executed upon him, unless he speedily repent. When this sorrowful prediction shall be fulfilled, this letter shall be read to the Church, and it shall prove a solemn warning to all to beware.

Farewell in the Lord,

HEBER C. KIMBALL,
ORSON HYDE.

The foregoing letter was written and sealed in the presence of Presidents Joseph Fielding and Willard Richards, who had gone to Liverpool to witness the brethren sail, and, by the writers, committed to their special charge, that no one should know the contents until the fulfillment thereof.

Previous to this period, very few of the foolish and wicked stories which filled the weekly journals and pamphlets in America concerning the "Mormons," as the Saints were termed, had found their way into the English prints; but immediately after Elders Kimball and Hyde left Preston, on or about the 15th of April, one Livesey (a Methodist priest, who had previously spent some years in America, and said he heard nothing about the Saints in America) came out with a pamphlet, made up of forged letters, apostate lies, and "walk on the water" stories, he found in old American papers, which he had picked up while in America. But he stopped the circulation of his own pamphlet by stating to a public congregation, that he had accidentally found the contents of his pamphlet in old papers in his trunk, which was quite providential, to stop such abominable work as the Saints were engaged in; and in the same lecture said he "wished the people to purchase his pamphlet, as he had been at a great expense to procure the materials for writing it!" His hearers retired.

American Slanders Reach England.

On the 20th of April Elders Kimball and Hyde sailed from Liverpool on the ship *Garrick*.

CHAPTER III.

READJUSTMENT AND SETTLEMENT OF AFFAIRS AT FAR WEST.

April 17.—I received the following:

*Revelation Given at Far West.**

1. Verily thus saith the Lord, it is wisdom in my servant David W. Patten, that he settle up all his business as soon as he possibly can, and make a disposition of his merchandise, that he may perform a mission unto me next spring, in company with others, even twelve, including himself, to testify of my name, and bear glad tidings unto all the world;

2. For verily thus saith the Lord, that inasmuch as there are those among you who deny my name, others shall be planted in their stead, and receive their bishopric. Amen.

I also received the following:

Revelation Given to Brigham Young at Far West.

Verily thus saith the Lord, let my servant Brigham Young go unto the place which he has bought, on Mill Creek, and there provide for his family until an effectual door is opened for the support of his family, until I shall command him to go hence, and not to leave his family until they are amply provided for. Amen.

April 26.—I received the following:

Revelation Given at Far West making known the will of God concerning the building up of that place, and of the Lord's House.†

1. Verily thus saith the Lord unto you, my servant Joseph Smith, Jun., and also my servant Sidney Rigdon, and also my servant Hyrum Smith, and your counselors who are and shall be appointed hereafter;

2. And also unto you my servant Edward Partridge, and his counselors;

* Doctrine and Covenants, sec. cxiv.

† Doctrine and Covenants, sec. cxv. It will be observed that in verses three and

3. And also unto my faithful servants, who are of the High Council of my Church in Zion (for thus it shall be called), and unto all the Elders and people of my Church of Jesus Christ of Latter-day Saints, scattered abroad in all the world;

4. For thus shall my Church be called in the last days, even the Church of Jesus Christ of Latter-day Saints.

5. Verily I say unto you all, Arise and shine forth, that thy light may be a standard for the nations,

6. And that the gathering together upon the land of Zion, and upon her stakes, may be for a defense, and for a refuge from the storm, and from wrath when it shall be poured out without mixture upon the whole earth.

7. Let the city, Far West, be a holy and consecrated land unto me, and it shall be called most holy, for the ground upon which thou standest is holy;

8. Therefore I command you to build an house unto me, for the gathering together of my Saints, that they may worship me;

9. And let there be a beginning of this work, and a foundation, and a preparatory work, this following summer;

10. And let the beginning be made on the 4th day of July next, and from that time forth let my people labor diligently to build an house unto my name,

11. And in one year from this day let them re-commence laying the foundation of my house:

12. Thus let them from that time forth labor diligently until it shall

four of this revelation the Lord gives to the Church its official name, "The Church of Jesus Christ of Latter-day Saints." Previous to this the Church had been called "The Church of Christ," "The Church of Jesus Christ," "The Church of God,"and by a conference of Elders held at Kirtland in May, 1834, (see Church History, vol. 2, pp. 62-3), it was given the name"The Church of the Latter-day Saints." All these names, however, were by this revelation brushed aside, and since then the official name given in this revelation has been recognized as the true title of the Church,though often spoken of as"The Mormon Church," the "Church of Christ," etc. The appropriateness of this title is self evident, and in it there is a beautiful recognition of the relationship both of the Lord Jesus Christ and of the Saints to the organization. It is "The Church of Jesus Christ." It is the Lord's; He owns it, He organized it. It is the Sacred Depository of His truth. It is His instrumentality for promulgating all those spiritual truths with which He would have mankind acquainted. It is also His instrumentality for the perfecting of the Saints, as well as for the work of the ministry. It is His in all these respects; but it is an institution which also belongs to the Saints. It is their refuge from the confusion and religious doubt of the world. It is their instructor in principle, doctrine, and righteousness. It is their guide in matters of faith and morals. They have a conjoint ownership in it with Jesus Christ, which ownership is beautifully recognized in the latter part of the title. "The Church of Jesus Christ of Latter day Saints," is equivalent to "The Church of Jesus Christ," and "The Church of the Latter-day Saints."

be finished, from the corner stone thereof unto the top thereof, until there shall not any thing remain that is not finished.

13. Verily I say unto you, let not my servant Joseph, neither my servant Sidney, neither my servant Hyrum, get in debt any more for the building of an house unto my name;

14. But let an house be built unto my name according to the pattern which I will show unto them.

15. And if my people shall build it not according to the pattern which I shall show unto their Presidency, I will not accept it at their hands.

16. But if my people do build it according to the pattern which I shall show unto their Presidency, even my servant Joseph and his counselors, then I will accept it at the hands of my people.

17. And again, verily I say unto you, it is my will that the city of Far West should be built up speedily by the gathering of my Saints,

18. And also that other places should be appointed for stakes in the region round about, as they shall be manifested unto my servant Joseph, from time to time;

19. For behold, I will be with him, and I will sanctify him before the people, for unto him have I given the keys of this kingdom and ministry. Even so. Amen.

The Teachers' quorum voted today [April 26th] not to hold any member of the quorum in fellowship, who would not settle his own difficulties in the Church, and show himself approved in all things; and that they would not hold any member of the quorum in fellowship who would take unlawful interest.

April 27.—This day I chiefly spent in writing a history of the Church from the earliest period of its existence, up to this date.

Minutes of the High Council.

Saturday, April 28, 1838. This morning Presidents Joseph Smith, Jun., and Sidney Rigdon attended the High Council, by invitation.

The business before the Council was an appeal case, from the branch of the Church near Guymon's Mill. A Brother Jackson was accuser, and Aaron Lyon accused. Thomas B. Marsh and David W. Patten presiding.

It appeared, in calling the Council to order, that some of the seats were vacant, which the Council proceeded to fill, but as there were not a sufficient number present who were eligible for the station, Presidents

Smith and Rigdon were strongly solicited to act as Councilors, or to preside and let the presiding officers act as Councilors.

They accepted the former proposal, and President Smith was chosen to act on the part of the defense, and to speak upon the case, together with George W. Harris.

President Rigdon was chosen to speak on the part of the prosecution, together with George M. Hinkle.

After some discussion as to whether witnesses should be admitted to testify against Aaron Lyon, or whether he should have the privilege of confessing his own sins, it was decided that witnesses should be admitted, and also the written testimony of the wife of a brother of the name of Jackson.

[This trial is written up at great length in the minutes of the Far West Record, and also in G. W. Robinson's summary of the proceedings heretofore printed. Condensed, the account of the fault of Brother Aaron Lyon was this: He claimed to have had a revelation that a Sister Jackson, who was a married woman, and whose husband was still living, was to become his wife. Lyon claimed that it had been revealed to him that the woman's husband was dead. He exerted undue influence in persuading her of these things, and she consented to be his wife; but before they were married the woman's husband appeared on the scene, with the result, of course, that the prospective marriage did not take place. The witnesses were permitted to testify, although Brother Lyon confessed the facts and admitted his error. The conclusion of the matter follows as stated by G. W. Robinson, clerk of the Council].

Council decided that, inasmuch as this man had confessed his sins, and asked forgiveness, and promised to make well the paths of his feet, and do, as much as lies in his power, what God should require at his hands, he should give up his license as High Priest, and stand as a member in the Church; and this in consequence of his being considered incapable of magnifying that office.

G. W. ROBINSON.

Sundry Employments of the Prophet.

Sunday, 29.—I spent the day chiefly in meeting with the Saints, ministering the words of life. *Monday, 30.*—The First Presidency were engaged in writing the Church history and in recitation of grammar lessons, which recitations at this period were usually attended each morning before writing.

May 1st, 2nd, 3rd, and 4th.—The First Presidency were engaged in writing Church history and administering to the sick. Received a letter from John E. Page on the 4th.

Saturday, 5.—The Presidency wrote for the *Elders' Journal;* also received intelligence from Canada by Brother Bailey, that two hundred wagons, with families, would probably be here in three weeks; also listened to an address on political matters delivered by General Wilson, Federal candidate for Congress.

Sunday, *May 6*.—I preached to the Saints, setting forth the evils that existed, and that would exist, by reason of hasty judgment, or decisions upon any subject given by any people, or in judging before they had heard both sides of a question. I also cautioned the Saints against men who came amongst them whining and growling about their money, because they had kept the Saints, and borne some of the burden with others, and thus thinking that others, who are still poorer, and have borne greater burdens than they themselves, ought to make up their losses. I cautioned the Saints to beware of such, for they were throwing out insinuations here and there, to level a dart at the best interests of the Church, and if possible destroy the character of its Presidency. I also gave some instructions in the mysteries of the kingdom of God; such as the history of the planets, Abraham's writings upon the planetary systems, etc.

The Prophet's Discourse on Evils of Hasty Judgment.

In the afternoon I spoke again on different subjects: the principle of wisdom, and the Word of Wisdom.

The Teachers' quorum at Far West numbered twenty-four members.

Monday, 7.—I spent the day in company with Judge Morain, one of our neighboring county judges, and Democratic candidate for the state senate.

I also visited with Elders Reynolds Cahoon and Parley P. Pratt, who had this day arrived in Far West, the former from Kirtland, the latter from New York City, where he had been preaching for some time; and our hearts were made glad with the pleasing intelligence of the gatering of the Saints from all parts of the earth to this place, to avoid

Arrival of Elder Parley P. Pratt at Far West.

the destructions which are coming upon this generation, as spoken by all the holy prophets since the world began.

Death of Jas. G. Marsh.

James G. Marsh, son of Thomas B. Marsh, aged fourteen years, eleven months, and seven days, died this day, in the full triumph of the everlasting Gospel.

The Prophet's Answers to Sundry Questions

Tuesday, *8*.—I spent the day with Elder Rigdon in visiting Elder Cahoon at the place he had selected for his residence, and in attending to some of our private, personal affairs; also in the afternoon I answered the questions which were frequently asked me, while on my last journey but one from Kirtland to Missouri, as printed in the *Elders' Journal*, vol. I, Number II, pages 28 and 29, as follows:

First—"Do you believe the Bible?"

If we do, we are the only people under heaven that does, for there are none of the religious sects of the day that do.

Second—"Wherein do you differ from other sects?"

In that we believe the Bible, and all other sects profess to believe their interpretations of the Bible, and their creeds.

Third—"Will everybody be damned, but Mormons?"

Yes, and a great portion of them, unless they repent, and work righteousness.

Fourth—"How and where did you obtain the Book of Mormon?'"

Moroni, who deposited the plates in a hill in Manchester, Ontario county, New York, being dead and raised again therefrom, appeared unto me, and told me where they were, and gave me directions how to obtain them. I obtained them, and the Urim and Thummim with them, by the means of which I translated the plates; and thus came the Book of Mormon.

Fifth—"Do you believe Joseph Smith, Jun., to be a Prophet?"

Yes, and every other man who has the testimony of Jesus. For the testimony of Jesus is the spirit of prophecy.—Revelation, xix: 10th verse.

Sixth—"Do the Mormons believe in having all things in common?"

No.

Seventh—"Do the Mormons believe in having more wives than one?"

"No, not at the same time. But they believe that if their companion dies, they have a right to marry again. But we do disapprove of the custom, which has gained in the world, and has been practiced among us, to our great mortification, in marrying in five or six weeks, or even in two or three months, after the death of their companion. We believe that due respect ought to be had to the memory of the dead, and the feelings of both friends and children.

Eighth—"Can they [the Mormons] raise the dead?"

No, nor can any other people that now lives, or ever did live. But God can raise the dead, through man as an instrument.

Ninth—"What signs does Joseph Smith give of his divine mission?"

The signs which God is pleased to let him give, according as His wisdom thinks best, in order that He may judge the world agreeably to His own plan.

Tenth—"Was not Joseph Smith a money digger?"

Yes, but it was never a very profitable job for him, as he only got fourteen dollars a month for it.

Eleventh—"Did not Joseph Smith steal his wife?"

Ask her, she was of age, she can answer for herself.

Twelfth—"Do the people have to give up their money when they join his Church?"

No other requirement than to bear their proportion of the expenses of the Church, and support the poor.

Thirteenth—"Are the Mormons abolitionists?"

No, unless delivering the people from priestcraft, and the priests from the power of Satan, should be considered abolition. But we do not believe in setting the negroes free.

Fourteenth—"Do they not stir up the Indians to war, and to commit depredations?"

No, and they who reported the story knew it was false when they put it in circulation. These and similar reports are palmed upon the people by the priests, and this is the only reason why we ever thought of answering them.

Fifteenth—"Do the Mormons baptize in the name of 'Joe' Smith?"

No, but if they did, it would be as valid as the baptism administered by the sectarian priests.

Sixteenth—"If the Mormon doctrine is true, what has become of all those who died since the days of the Apostles?"

All those who have not had an opportunity of hearing the Gospel, and being administered unto by an inspired man in the flesh, must have it hereafter, before they can be finally judged.

Seventeenth—"Does not 'Joe' Smith profess to be Jesus Christ?"

No, but he professes to be His brother, as all other Saints have done and now do: Matt., xii; 49, 50, "And He stretched forth His hand toward His disciples and said, Behold my mother and my brothren; for whosoever shall do the will of my Father, which is in heaven, the same is my brother, and sister, and mother."

Eighteenth—"Is there anything in the Bible which licenses you to believe in revelation now-a-days?"

Is there anything that does not authorize us to believe so? If there is, we have, as yet, not been able to find it.

Nineteenth—"Is not the canon of the Scriptures full?"

If it is, there is a great defect in the book, or else it would have said so.

Twentieth—"What are the fundamental principles of your religion?"

The fundamental principles of our religion are the testimony of the Apostles and Prophets, concerning Jesus Christ, that He died, was buried, and rose again the third day, and ascended into heaven; and all other things which pertain to our religion are only appendages to it. But in connection with these, we believe in the gift of the Holy Ghost, the power of faith, the enjoyment of the spiritual gifts according to the will of God, the restoration of the house of Israel, and the final triumph of truth.

I published the foregoing answers to save myself the trouble of repeating the same a thousand times over and over again.

Wednesday, 9.—I attended the funeral of James G. Marsh, and complied with the request that I should preach on the occasion.

Elder Rigdon's Political Address.

Thursday, 10.—I listened to an address on the political policy of our nation, delivered by President Rigdon, at the school house, in the southwest quarter of the city, to a large concourse of people from all sections of the county, and from other counties also. Although President Rigdon was suffering under a severe cold and great hoarseness, yet being assisted by the Spirit of God, he was enabled clearly to elucidate the policy of the Federal and Democratic parties from their rise in our country to the present time, to the understanding of all present, giving an impartial review to both sides of the question. This address was delivered in consequence of a partial electioneering Federal speech of General Wilson at the same place a short time previously, and the politics of the Church of

Latter-day Saints, generally being Democratic,* it seemed desirable to hear an elucidation of the principles of both parties, with which I was highly edified.

Friday, 11.—I attended the trial of William E. McLellin and Dr. McCord, for transgression, before the Bishop's court.

Trial of Wm. E. McLellin and Dr. McCord.

McCord said he was sorry to trouble the Council on his account, for he had intended to withdraw from the Church before he left the place; that he had no confidence in the work of God, or His Prophet, and should go his way. He gave up his license and departed.

William E. McLellin stated about the same as McCord, and that he had no confidence in the heads of the Church, believing they had transgressed, and had got out of the way, consequently he quit praying and keeping the commandments of God, and indulged himself in his lustful desires, but when he heard that the First Presidency had made a general settlement, and acknowledged their sins, he began to pray again. When I interrogated him, he said he had seen nothing out of the way himself, but he judged from hearsay.†

Saturday, 12.—President Rigdon and myself attended the High Council for the purpose of presenting for their cosideration some business relating to our pecuniary concerns.

Remuneration of the Prophet and Sidney Rigdon for Temporal Labors in the Church.

We stated to the Council our situation, as to maintaining our families, and the relation we now stand in to the Church, spending as we have for eight years, our time, talents, and property, in the service of the Church: and being reduced as it were to beggary, and being still detained in the business and

* Of course what is meant by this statement is that the individuals composing the Church were quite generally Democrats, not that the Church as an organization was democratic or had any politics.

† It will be observed that the text is silent in relation to what action was taken respecting William E. McLellin, and the Far West Record is silent upon the subject also. In fact the minutes of the trial before the Bishop are not written in that record at all. It is known, however, from other sources that William E. McLellin was finally excommunicated from the Church at Far West. Thence for-

service of the Church, it appears necessary that something should be done for the support of our families by the Church, or else we must do it by our own labors; and if the Church say to us, "Help yourselves," we will thank them and immediately do so; but if the Church say, "Serve us," some provision must be made for our sustenance.

The Council investigated the matter, and instructed the Bishop to make over to President Joseph Smith, Jun., and Sidney Rigdon, each an eighty-acre lot of land from the property of the Church, situated adjacent to the city corporation; also appointed three of their number, viz., George W. Harris, Elias Higbee and Simeon Carter, a committee to confer with said Presidency, and satisfy them for their services the present year; not for preaching, or for receiving the word of God by revelation, neither for instructing the Saints in righteousness, but for services rendered in the printing establishment, in translating the ancient records, etc., etc. Said committee agreed that Presidents Smith and Rigdon should receive $1,100 each as a just remuneration for their services this year.

Sunday, 13.—Elder Reynolds Cahoon preached in the forenoon. In the afternoon President Rigdon preached a

ward he took an active part in the persecution of the Saints in Missouri, and at one time expressed the desire to do violence to the person of Joseph Smith, while the latter was confined in Liberty prison. Subsequently he attempted what he called a reorganization of the Church, and called upon David Whitmer to take the presidency thereof, claiming that he was ordained by Joseph Smith on the 8th of July, 1834, as his (the Prophet Joseph's) successor. The Prophet himself, according to the minutes of the High Council held in Far West, on the 15th of March, 1838, referred to his ordaining of David Whitmer in July, 1834, and this is the account of what he said:

"President Joseph Smith, Jun., gave a history of the ordination of David Whitmer which took place in July, 1834, to be a leader or a Prophet to this Church, which (ordination) was on conditions that he (Joseph Smith, Jun.,) did not live to God himself. President Joseph Smith, Jun., approved of the proceedings of the High Council after hearing the minutes of the former councils."—Far West Record, page 108.

The minutes of the councils here referred to, and which the Prophet approved, gave the account of deposing David Whitmer from the local Presidency of the Church in Missouri.

funeral sermon on the death of Swain Williams, son of Frederick G. Williams.

Monday, 14.—I spent in plowing my garden, while Elder Rigdon was preparing and correcting some matter for the press. Elder Harlow Redfield arrived from Kirtland, Ohio.

CHAPTER IV.

SELECTION OF LANDS IN CALDWELL AND DAVIESS COUNTIES FOR SETTLEMENT—ADAM-ONDI-AHMAN.

The Prophet Leaves Far West to Locate Settlements.

Friday, May 18.—I left Far West, in company with Sidney Rigdon, Thomas B. Marsh, David W. Patten, Bishop Partridge, Elias Higbee, Simeon Carter, Alanson Ripley, and many others, for the purpose of visiting the north country, and laying off a stake of Zion; making locations, and laying claim to lands to facilitate the gathering of the Saints, and for the benefit of the poor, in upholding the Church of God. We traveled to the mouth of Honey Creek, which is a tributary of Grand river, where we camped for the night. We passed through a beautiful country the greater part of which is prairie, and thickly covered with grass and weeds, among which is plenty of game, such as deer, turkey, and prairie hen. We discovered a large, black wolf, and my dog gave him chase, but he outran us. We have nothing to fear in camping out, except the rattlesnake, which is native to this country, though not very numerous. We turned our horses loose, and let them feed on the prairie.

The Prophet and Party Reach Tower Hill.

Saturday, 19.—This morning we struck our tents and formed a line of march, crossing Grand River at the mouth of Honey Creek and Nelson's Ferry. Grand River is a large, beautiful, deep and rapid stream, during the high waters of Spring, and will undoubtedly admit of navigation by steamboat and other water craft. At the mouth of Honey Creek is a good landing. We pursued our course up the river, mostly through timber, for about eighteen miles, when we arrived at Colonel Lyman Wight's home. He lives at the foot of Tower Hill (a name I gave the place in consequence of the remains of an old Nephite altar or tower that stood there), where we camped for the Sabbath.

Adam-ondi-Ahman.

In the afternoon I went up the river about half a mile to Wight's Ferry, accompanied by President Rigdon, and my clerk, George W. Robinson, for the purpose of selecting and laying claim to a city plat near said ferry in Daviess County, township 60, ranges 27 and 28, and sections 25, 36, 31, and 30, which the brethren called "Spring Hill," but by the mouth of the Lord it was named Adam-ondi-Ahman,* because, said He, it is the place where Adam shall come to visit his people, or the Ancient of Days shall sit, as spoken of by Daniel the Prophet.†

* See Doctrine and Covenants, sec. 116. This is not the first time that the name or phrase "Adam-ondi-Ahman" is used in the revelations of the Lord. Some six years before this, viz., in the year 1832, it is used incidentally in one of the revelations where the Lord in addressing a number of the brethren who had been ordained to the High Priesthood, said that notwithstanding the tribulations through which they should pass, He had so ordered events that they might come unto the crown prepared for them, "and be made rulers over many kingdoms, saith the Lord God, the Holy One of Zion, who hath established the foundations of *Adam-ondi-Ahman.*" (Doctrine and Covenants, sec. lxxviii: 15). Some years afterwards, viz., in 1835, W. W. Phelps composed his beautiful hymn bearing the name of Adam-ondi-Ahman, which was first published in the *Messenger and Advocate* (No. 9, vol. I); see also History of the Church, Vol. II, p 365.

This hymn was a great favorite among the early Saints, although they, perhaps, did not understand at that time the significance of the name, nor even now do they understand its full significance. All that is known of its meaning is what the Lord revealed to the Prophet, viz., that it is significant of the fact that it designates the place where the Lord will come and meet with His people as described by Daniel the Prophet.

† Daniel's description of the events here referred to is found in the 7th chapter of his prophecies. The description is very imposing, hence I quote it: "I beheld till the thrones were cast down, and the Ancient of Days did sit, whose garment was white as snow, and the hair of his head like the pure wool: his throne was like the fiery flame, and his wheels as burning fire. A fiery stream issued and came forth from before him: thousand thousands ministered unto him, and ten thousand times ten thousand stood before him: the judgment was set, and the books were opened. * * * * * * I saw in the night visions, and, behold, one like the Son of man came with the clouds of heaven, and came to the Ancient of Days, and they brought him near before Him. And there was given Him dominion, and glory, and a kingdom, that all people, nations, and languages,

Sunday, *20*.—This day was spent by our company principally at Adam-ondi-Ahman; but near the close of the day, we struck our tents, and traveled about six miles north and encamped for the night with Judge Morin and company, who were also traveling north.

Monday, *21*.—This morning, after making some locations in this place, which is in township 61, ranges 27 and 28, we returned to Robinson's Grove, about two miles, to secure some land near Grand River, which we passed the day previous; and finding a mistake in the former survey, I sent the surveyor south five or six miles to obtain a correct line, while some of us tarried to obtain water for the camp.

Council called to determine Location of Settlements.

In the evening, I called a council of the brethren, to know whether it was wisdom to go immediately into the north country, or tarry here and hereabouts, to secure land on Grand River, etc. The brethren spoke their minds freely on the subject, when I stated to the council that I felt impressed to tarry and secure all the land near by, that is not secured between this and Far West, especially on Grand River. President Rigdon concurred, and the council voted unanimously to secure the land on Grand River, and between this and Far West.

Elders Kimball and Hyde this day (21st May) arrived at Kirtland from England.

American Antiquities Discovered.

Tuesday, *22*.—President Rigdon went east with a company, and selected some of the best locations in the county,* and returned with a good report of that vicinity, and with information of

should serve Him: His dominion is an everlasting dominion, which shall not pass away, and His kingdom that which shall not be destroyed."

The Prophet Daniel also saw in this connection that earthly powers would make war upon the Saints and prevail against them—until the Ancient of Days should come. "And [then] the kingdom and dominion, and the greatness of the kingdom under the whole heaven, shall be given to the people of the Saints of the Most High, whose kingdom is an everlasting kingdom, and all dominions shall serve and obey Him."

* This most likely was Livingstone county, which borders both Daviess and Caldwell counties on the east.

valuable locations which might be secured. Following awhile the course of the company, I returned to camp in Robinson's Grove, and thence went west to obtain some game to supply our necessities. We discovered some antiquities about one mile west of the camp, consisting of stone mounds, apparently erected in square piles, though somewhat decayed and obliterated by the weather of many years. These mounds were probaby erected by the aborigines of the land, to secrete treasures. We returned without game.

Wednesday, 23.—We all traveled east, locating lands, to secure a claim, on Grove Creek, and near the city of Adam-ondi-Ahman. Towards evening I accompanied Elder Rigdon to Colonel Wight's, and the remainder of the company returned to their tents.

Varied Movements of the Prophet's Company.

Thursday, 24.—This morning the company returned to Grove Creek to finish the survey, accompanied by President Rigdon and Colonel Wight, and I returned to Far West.

Friday, 25.—The company went up Grand River and made some locations. In the afternoon they struck their tents and removed to Colonel Wight's.

Saturday, 26.—The company surveyed lands on the other side of the river opposite Adam-ondi-Ahman.

Sunday, 27.—The company locating lands spent the day at Colonel Wight's.

Monday, 28.—The company started for home (Far West), and I left Far West the same day in company with Brother Hyrum Smith and fifteen or twenty others, to seek locations in the north, and about noon we met President Rigdon and his company going into the city, where they arrived the same evening.

President Hyrum Smith returned to Far West on the 30th, and I returned on the 1st of June, on account of my family, for I had a son born unto me.*

Birth of Alexander Hale Smith.

*The birth of the son took place on the 2nd of June. It was Alexander Hale Smith.

Monday, June 4.—I left Far West with President Rigdon, my brother Hyrum and others for Adam-ondi-Ahman, and stayed at Brother Moses Dailey's over night; and on the morning of the 5th, went to Colonel Lyman Wight's in the rain. We continued surveying, building houses, day after day, for many days, until the surveyor had completed the city plat.

The Prophet's Return to Adam-ondi-Ahman.

Monday, June 11.—President Joseph Fielding was married to Hannah Greenwood, Preston, England.

June 16.—My uncle, John Smith, and family, with six other families, arrived in Far West, all in good health and spirits. I counseled them to settle at Adam-ondi-Ahman.

Minutes of the Meeting which Organized the Stake of Zion called Adam-ondi-Ahman.

Adam-ondi-Ahman, Missouri, Daviess county, June 28, 1838. A conference of Elders and members of the Church of Jesus Christ of Latter-day Saints was held in this place this day, for the purpose of organizing this Stake of Zion, called Adam-ondi-Ahman.

The meeting convened at 10 o'clock a. m., in the grove near the house of Elder Lyman Wight.

President Joseph Smith, Jun., was called to the chair. He explained the object of the meeting, which was to organize a Presidency and High Council to preside over this Stake of Zion, and attend to the affairs of the Church in Daviess county.

It was then moved, seconded and carried by the unanimous voice of the assembly, that John Smith* should act as President of the Stake of Adam-ondi-Ahman.

Reynolds Cahoon was unanimously chosen first counselor, and Lyman Wight second counselor.

After prayer the presidents ordained Elder Wight as second counselor.

Vinson Knight was chosen acting Bishop *pro tempore* by the unanimous voice of the assembly.

President John Smith then proceeded to organize the High Council. The councilors were chosen according to the following order, by a unanimous vote: John Lemon, first; Daniel Stanton, second; Mayhew Hillman, third; Daniel Carter, fourth; Isaac Perry, fifth; Harrison Sagers, sixth; Alanson Brown, seventh; Thomas Gordon, eighth; Lorenzo D.

* The Prophet's uncle, who had but recently arrived at "Diahman.'

Barnes, ninth; George A. Smith, tenth; Harvey Olmstead, eleventh; Ezra Thayer, twelfth.

After the ordination of the councilors who had not previously been ordained to the High Priesthood, President Joseph Smith, Jun., made remarks by way of charge to the presidents and counselors, instructing them in the duties of their callings, and the responsibility of their stations, exhorting them to be cautious and deliberate in all their councils, and be careful and act in righteousness in all things.

President John Smith, Reynolds Cahoon, and Lyman Wight then made some remarks.

Lorenzo D. Barnes was unanimously chosen clerk of this Council and Stake. After singing the well known hymn, Adam-ondi-Ahman, the meeting closed by prayer by President Cahoon, and a benediction by President Joseph Smith, Jun.

LORENZO D. BARNES,
ISAAC PERRY,
Clerks.

Description of Adam-ondi-Ahman.

Adam-ondi-Ahman is loated immediately on the north side of Grand River, in Daviess county, Missouri, about twenty-five miles north of Far West. It is situated on an elevated spot of ground, which renders the place as healthful as any part of the United States, and overlooking the river and the country round about, it is certainly a beautiful location.*

* Perhaps the following more detailed description of Adam-ondi-Ahman, as also the allusion to at least one stirring event which occurred there in the past, may not be without interest: Adam-ondi-Ahman, or "Diahman," as it is familiarly known to the Saints, is located on the north bank of Grand River. It is situated, in fact, in a sharp bend of that stream. The river comes sweeping down from the northwest and here makes a sudden turn and runs in a meandering course to the northeast for some two or three miles, when it as suddenly makes another bend and flows again to the southeast. Grand River is a stream that has worn a deep channel for itself, and left its banks precipitous; but at "Diahman" that is only true of the south bank. The stream as it rushes from the northwest, strikes the high prairie land which at this point contains beds of limestone, and not being able to cut its way through, it veered off to the northeast, and left that height of land standing like palisades which rise very abruptly from the stream to a height of from fifty to seventy-five feet. The summit of these bluffs is the common level of the high rolling prairie, extending off in the direction of Far West. The bluffs on the north bank recede some distance from the stream, so that the river bottom at this point widens out to a small valley. The bluffs on the north bank of the river are by no means as steep as those on the south, and are covered with a light growth of timber. A ridge runs out from the main line of the bluffs into the river bottom some two or three hundred yards, approach-

June 28.—This day Victoria was crowned queen of England.

ing the stream at the point where the bend of the river is made. The termination of the bluff is quite abrupt, and overlooks a considerable portion of the river bottom. On the brow of the bluff stood the old stone altar, and near the foot of it was built the house of Lyman Wight. When the altar was first discovered, according to those who visited it frequently, it was about sixteen feet long, by nine or ten feet wide, having its greatest extent north and south. The height of the altar at each end was some two and a half feet, gradually rising higher to the center, which was between four and five feet high—the whole surface being crowning. Such was the altar at "Diahman" when the Prophet's party visited it. Now, however, it is thrown down, and nothing but a mound of crumbling stones mixed with soil, and a few reddish boulders mark the spot which is doubtless rich in historic events. It was at this altar, according to the testimony of Joseph Smith, that the patriarchs associated with Adam and his company, assembled to worship their God. Here their evening and morning prayer ascended to heaven with the smoke of the burning sacrifice, prophetic and symbolic of the greater sacrifice then yet to be, and here angels instructed them in heavenly truths.

North of the ridge on which the ruins of the altar were found, and running parallel with it, is another ridge, separated from the first by a depression varying in width from fifty to a hundred yards. This small valley with the larger one through which flows Grand River, is the valley of Adam-ondi-Ahman. Three years previous to the death of Adam, declares one of the Prophet Joseph's revelations, the Patriarchs Seth, Enos, Cainan, Mahalaleel, Jared, Enoch, and Methuselah, together with all their righteous posterity, were assembled in this valley we have described, and their common father, Adam, gave them his last blessing. And even as he blessed them, the heavens were opened, and the Lord appeared, and in the presence of God, the children or Adam arose and blessed him, and called him Michael, the Prince, the Archangel. The Lord also blessed Adam, saying: "I have set thee to be the head—a multitude of nations shall come of thee, and thou art a prince over them for ever." So great was the influence of this double blessing upon Adam, that, though bowed down with age, under the outpouring of the Spirit of God, he predicted what should befall his posterity to their latest generation. (Doctrine and Covenants, sec. cvii). Such is one of the great events which occurred on this old historic land of Adam-ondi-Ahman.

CHAPTER V.

INDEPENDENCE DAY AT FAR WEST—SUNDRY EVENTS AND REVELATIONS—EPISTLE OF DAVID W. PATTEN.

July 4.—The day was spent in celebrating the Declaration of Independence of the United States of America, and also by the Saints making a "Declaration of Independence" from all mobs and persecutions which have been inflicted upon them, time after time, until they could bear it no longer; having been driven by ruthless mobs and enemies of truth from their homes, and having had their property confiscated, their lives exposed, and their all jeopardized by such barbarous conduct. The corner stones of the Houses of the Lord, agreeable to the commandments of the Lord unto us, given April 26, 1838, were laid.

Celebration of Independence Day at Far West.

Joseph Smith, Jun., was president of the day; Hyrum Smith, vice-president; Sidney Rigdon, orator; Reynolds Cahoon, chief marshal; George M. Hinckle and J. Hunt, assistant marshals; and George W. Robinson, clerk.

The Officers.

The order of the day was splendid. The procession commenced forming at 10 o'clock a. m., in the following order: First, the infantry (militia); second, the Patriarchs of the Church; the president, vice-president, and orator; the Twelve Apostles, presidents of the stakes, and High Council; Bishop and counselors; architects, ladies and gentlemen. The cavalry brought up the rear of the large procession, which marched to music, and formed a circle, with the ladies in front, round the excavation. The southeast corner stone of the Lord's House in Far West, Missouri, was then laid by the

The Procession.

presidents of the stake, assisted by twelve men. The southwest corner, by the presidents of the Elders, assisted by twelve men. The northwest corner by the Bishop, assisted by twelve men. The northeast corner by the president of the Teachers, assisted by twelve men. This house is to be one hundred and ten feet long, and eighty feet broad.

The Oration.

The oration was delivered by President Rigdon,* at the close of which was a shout of Hosanna, and a song, composed for the occasion by Levi W. Hancock, was sung by Solomon Hancock. The most perfect order prevailed throughout the day.†

* The oration soon afterwards appeared in *The Far West*, a periodical published at Liberty, Clay County, Missouri. It was also published in pamphlet form from the office of the "*Elders' Journal.*" (See statement of Ebenezer Robinson in *The Return*, vol. 1, p. 170). This oration by Sidney Rigdon has always been severely criticised as containing passages that were ill-advised and vehemently bitter. Especially those passages which threatened a war of extermination upon mobs should they again arise to plague the Saints. But when such criticism is made, the rank injustice, the destruction of property and the outrages committed upon the persons of many of the members of the Church, by the Jackson county mob, should also be remembered. Also the failure on the part of the officers of the State to protect the Saints in the enjoyment of their civil and religious liberties or even to return them to their homes in Jackson county—from which failure to magnify the law the Saints were still suffering. When, therefore, they saw mobocracy again threatening them, it is small wonder if they gave way for a moment to anger, and denounced in strong terms those who were likely to disturb their peace and repeat the outrages under which they had so long suffered.

† Following this account of the 4th of July celebration at Far West the Prophet in his history, as heretofore published, takes up the account of the organization of "Kirtland Camp," an organization effected by the First Seven Presidents of the Seventies, assisted by Elder Hyrum Smith. The object of the organization was to move the Saints, who desired to go, in a body, from Kirtland to Missouri. The Prophet in his history gives an account, as already stated, of the organization of this camp and its departure from Kirtland. Then from day to day as more or less important events took place in the camp, he records such events in his own personal history, with the result that his narrative is frequently interrupted by brief paragraphs from the camp's Journal. But as we have the full daily journal of the camp's progress from Kirtland to Far West, written in a most careful and commendable style by the camp's Historian, Elias Smith, it has been decided to publish the history of the camp from the time it met for organization in Kirtland (March, 1838), until its arrival at Far West, (on the 2nd day of October, 1838), without other interruptions; and then omit from the narrative of the Prophet those occasional paragraphs taken from the said journal of the camp. This arrangement will relieve the Prophet's narrative of so many interruptions, and on the other hand it will give an unbroken narrative from an original document of one of the most remarkable organizations and journeys in the early history of the

July 6.—This day I received a letter from Heber C. Kimball and Orson Hyde, dated at Kirtland, Ohio, expressing their good feelings, firmness in the faith and prosperity.

A Word from Elders Kimball and Hyde

Also another letter from my brother Don Carlos Smith, as follows:

NINE MILES FROM TERRE HAUTE, INDIANA.

Brother Joseph:—I sit down to inform you of our situation at the present time. I started from Norton, Ohio, the 7th of May, in company with father, William, Wilkins Jenkins Salisbury, William McClary and Lewis Robbins, and families, also Sister Singly. We started with fifteen horses, seven wagons, and two cows. We have left two horses by the way sick, and a third horse (our main dependence) was taken lame last evening, and is not able to travel, and we have stopped to doctor him. We were disappointed on every hand before we started in getting money. We got no assistance whatever, only as we have taken in Sister Singly, and she has assisted us as far as her means extended. We had, when we started, $75 in money. We sold the two cows for $13.50 per cow. We have sold of your goods to the amount of $45.74, and now we have only $25 to carry twenty-eight souls and thirteen horses five hundred miles.

We have lived very close and camped out at night, notwithstanding the rain and cold, and my baby only two weeks old when we started. Agnes* is very feeble; father and mother are not well and very much fatigued; mother has a severe cold, and in fact it is nothing but the prayer of faith and the power of God, that will sustain them and bring them through. Our courage is good, and I think we shall be brought through. I leave it with you and Hyrum to devise some way to assist us to some more expense money. We have unaccountably bad roads, had our horses down in the mud, and broke one wagon tongue and thills, and broke down the carriage twice, and yet we are all alive and encamped on a dry place for almost the first time. Poverty is a heavy load, but we are all obliged to welter under it.

It is now dark and I close. May the Lord bless you all, and bring us together, is my prayer. Amen. All the arrangements that brother Hyrum left for getting money failed; they did not gain us one cent.

DON C. SMITH.

Church. This promised history will be inserted at the point of the Prophet's narrative where the camp arrives at Far West.

* This refers to Don Carlos Smith's wife, who before her marriage to him in Kirtland, on July 30, 1835, was Agnes Coolbirth.

The three revelations* which I received January 12, 1838, the day I left Kirtland, were read in the public congregation at Far West; and the same day I inquired of the Lord, "O Lord! Show unto thy servant how much thou requirest of the properties of thy people for a tithing," and received the following answer, which was also read in public:

Missing Revelations.

Revelation, Given at Far West, July 8, 1838.†

1. Verily, thus saith the Lord, I require all their surplus property to be put into the hands of the Bishop of my Church of Zion,

2. For the building of mine house, and for the laying of the foundation of Zion and for the Priesthood, and for the debts of the Presidency of my Church;

3. And this shall be the beginning of the tithing of my people;

4. And after that, those who have thus been tithed, shall pay one-tenth of all their interest annually; and this shall be a standing law unto them forever, for my holy Priesthood, saith the Lord.

5. Verily I say unto you, it shall come to pass, that all those who gather unto the Land of Zion shall be tithed of their surplus properties, and shall observe this law, or they shall not be found worthy to abide among you.

6. And I say unto you, if my people observe not this law, to keep it holy, and by this law sanctify the land of Zion unto me, that my statutes and my judgments may be kept thereon, that it may be most holy, behold, verily I say unto you, it shall not be a land of Zion unto you;

7. And this shall be an ensample unto all the stakes of Zion. Even so. Amen.

Also I received the following:

Revelation, given July 8, 1838, making known the disposition of the properties tithed as named in the preceding revelation.‡

Verily, thus saith the Lord, the time is now come that it shall be disposed of by a council composed of the First Presidency of my Church, and of the Bishop and his council, and by my High Council, and by mine own voice unto them, saith the Lord. Even so. Amen.

* The three revelations here referred to do not appear in the Doctrine and Covenants nor in any other publication. Diligent search also has been made for them through the several packages of Church documents in the Historian's Office, but they have not been found.

† Doctrine and Covenants, sec. cxix.

‡ Doctrine and Covenants, sec. cxx.

Also I received the following:

*Revelation given to William Marks, Newel K. Whitney, Oliver Granger and others, at Far West, July 8, 1838.**

1. Verily thus saith the Lord unto my servant William Marks, and also unto my servant N. K. Whitney, let them settle up their business speedily and journey from the land of Kirtland, before I, the Lord, send again the snows upon the earth;

2. Let them awake, and arise, and come forth, and not tarry, for I, the Lord, command it;

3. Therefore if they tarry it shall not be well with them.

4. Let them repent of all their sins,and of all their covetous desires, before me, saith the Lord, for what is property unto me, saith the Lord?

5. Let the properties of Kirtland be turned out for debts, saith the Lord. Let them go, saith the Lord, and whatsoever remaineth, let it remain in your hands, saith the Lord;

6. For have I not the fowls of heaven, and also the fish of the sea, and the beasts of the mountains? Have I not made the earth? Do I not hold the destinies of all the armies of the nations of the earth?

7. Therefore will I not make solitary places to bud and to blossom, and to bring forth in abundance, saith the Lord?

8. Is there not room enough upon the mountains of Adam-ondi-Ahman, and on the plains of Olaha Shinehah, or the land where Adam dwelt, that you should covet that which is but the drop, and neglect the more weighty matters?

9. Therefore come up hither unto the land of my people, even Zion.

10. Let my servant William Marks be faithful over a few things, and he shall be ruler over many. Let him preside in the midst of my people in the city of Far West, and let him be blessed with the blessings of my people.

11. Let my servant N. K. Whitney be ashamed of the Nicholatine band and of all their secret abominations, and of all his littleness of soul before me, saith the Lord, and come up to the land of Adam-ondi-Ahman, and be a Bishop unto my people, saith the Lord, not in name but in deed, saith the Lord.

12. And again, I say unto you, I remember my servant Oliver Granger, behold, verily I say unto him, that his name shall be had in sacred remembrance from generation to generation, for ever and ever, saith the Lord.

13. Therefore let him contend earnestly for the redemption of the

* Doctrine and Covenants, sec. cxvii.

First Presidency of my Church, saith the Lord, and when he falls he shall rise again, for his sacrifice shall be more sacred unto me, than his increase, saith the Lord;

14. Therefore let him come up hither speedily, unto the land of Zion, and in the due time he shall be made a merchant unto my name, saith the Lord, for the benefit of my people;

15. Therefore let no man despise my servant Oliver Granger, but let the blessings of my people be on him for ever and ever.

16. And again, verily I say unto you, let all my servants in the land of Kirtland remember the Lord their God, and mine house also, to keep and preserve it holy, and to overthrow the money changers in mine own due time, saith the Lord. Even so. Amen.

Also I received the following:

*Revelation given at Far West, July 8, 1838, in answer to the question, Show unto us thy will O Lord concerning the Twelve.**

1. Verily, thus saith the Lord, let a conference be held immediately, let the Twelve be organized, and let men be appointed to supply the place of those who are fallen.

2. Let my servant Thomas remain for a season in the land of Zion, to publish my word.

3. Let the residue continue to preach from that hour, and if they will do this in all lowliness of heart, in meekness and humility, and long-suffering, I, the Lord, give unto them a promise that I will provide for their families, and an effectual door shall be opened for them, from henceforth;

4. And next spring let them depart to go over the great waters, and there promulgate my gospel, the fullness thereof, and bear record of my name.

5. Let them take leave of my Saints in the city Far West, on the

* Doctrine and Covenants, sec. cxviii. This date, the 8th of July, 1838, is remakable for the many revelations given. In addition to the foregoing which are printed in the Doctrine and Covenants, in the sections indicated in the foot notes, the following was also received, which is not published in the Doctrine and Covenants nor elsewhere. It is found on file in Package XVI at the Historian's Office: Revelation given July 8, 1838, making known the duty of William W. Phelps and Frederick G. Williams.

"Verily, thus saith the Lord, in consequence of their transgressions their former standing has been taken away from them, and now, if they will be saved, let them be ordained as Elders in my Church to preach my Gospel and travel abroad from land to land and from place to place, to gather mine elect unto me, saith the Lord, and let this be their labors from henceforth. Amen.

26th day of April next, on the building spot of my house, saith the Lord.

6. Let my servant John Taylor, and also my servant John E. Page, also my servant Wilford Woodruff, and also my servant Willard Richards, be appointed to fill the places of those who have fallen, and be officially notified of their appointment.

Minutes of a Meeting of the Twelve.

Far West, July 9, 1838, a conference of the Twelve Apostles assembled at Far West, agreeable to the revelation, given July 8, 1838. Present, Thomas B. Marsh, David W. Patten, Brigham Young, Parley P. Pratt and William Smith: T. B. Marsh, presiding.

Resolved 1st. That the persons who are to fill the places of those who are fallen, be immediately notified to come to Far West; as also, those of the Twelve who are not present.

Resolved 2nd. That Thomas B. Marsh notify Wilford Woodruff, that Parley P. Pratt notify Orson Pratt, and that President Rigdon notify Willard Richards, who is now in England.

Voted that President Marsh publish the same in next number of *The Elders' Journal.*

President Rigdon gave some counsel concerning the provisions necessary to be made for the families of the Twelve, while laboring in the cause of their Redeemer, advising them to instruct their converts to move without delay to the places of gathering, and there to strictly attend to the law of God.

T. B. MARSH, President.
G. W. ROBINSON, Clerk.

Tuesday, 10.—About this time I visited Adam-ondi-Ahman in company with President Rigdon, Brother Hyrum, and George W. Robinson.

Thursday, 26.—The First Presidency, High Council, and Bishop's court assembled at Far West to dispose of the public properties of the Church in the hands of the Bishop, many of the brethren having consecrated their surplus property according to the revelations.

The Disposition of Public Church Properties.

It was agreed that the First Presidency should keep all their properties that they could dispose of to advantage, for their support, and the remainder be put into the hands of the Bishop or Bishops, according to the commandments.

Moved, seconded, and carried unanimously:

"First—That the First Presidency shall have their expenses defrayed in going to, and returning from Adam ondi-Ahman; equally by the Bishop of each place.

"Second—That all the traveling expenses of the First Presidency shall be defrayed.

"Third—That the Bishop be authorized to pay orders coming from the east, inasmuch as they will consecrate liberally, but this is to be done under the inspection of the First Presidency.

"Fourth—That the First Presidency shall have the prerogative to direct the Bishop as to whose orders shall or may be paid by him in this place, or in his jurisdiction.

"Fifth—That the Bishop of Zion receive all consecrations from those living east, west, and south, who are not in the jurisdiction of a Bishop of any other stake.

"Sixth—That we use our influence to put a stop to the selling of liquors in the city Far West, or in our midst, that our streets may not be filled with drunkenness; and that we use our influence to bring down the price of provisions.

"Seventh—That Brother William W. Phelps be requested to draw up a petition to locate the county seat at Far West."

Arrival of Saints from Canada.

Saturday, *28*.—I left Far West for Adam-ondi-Ahman, in company with President Rigdon, to transact some important business, and to settle some Canadian brethren in that place, as they are emigrating rapidly to this land from all parts of the country.

Elder Babbitt, with his company from Canada has arrived, and Brother Theodore Turley is with him.

Sunday, *29*.—Elders Kimball and Hyde having just returned from England, preached in Far West.

Monday, *30*.—The circuit court sat in Far West, Judge King presiding.

I returned this evening from Adam-ondi-Ahman to Far West, with President Rigdon.

Tuesday, *31*.—Attended the circuit court awhile, and received a visit from Judge King.

Some time in July we succeeded in publishing the third

number of the *Elders' Journal;* Joseph Smith, Jun., editor; Thomas B. Marsh, printer and publisher. In this number of the *Journal* was published the following Epistle of David W. Patten, one of the Twelve Apstles of the last days:

Publication of the *Elders' Journal.*

The Epistle of Elder David W. Patten.

To the Saints Scattered Abroad:

DEAR BRETHREN:—Whereas many have taken in hand to set forth the kingdom of God on earth, and have testified of the grace of God, as given unto them to publish unto you, I also feel it my duty to write unto you, touching the grace of God given unto me, to you-ward, concerning the dispensation we have received, which is the greatest of all dispensations, and has been spoken of by the mouth of all the holy Prophets since the world began.

In this my communication to you, I design to notice some of these prophecies. Now, the Apostle Paul says on this wise: "For I would not, brethren, that ye should be ignorant of this mystery, lest ye should be wise in your own conceits; that blindness in part is happened to Israel, until the fullness of the Gentiles be come in. And so all Israel shall be saved: as it is written, There shall come out of Sion the Deliverer, and shall turn away ungodliness from Jacob." What is it that he says? "For I would not have you ignorant." Ignorant of what? Why of this mystery, that blindness in part had happened unto Israel. And to what end? Why, that salvation might come unto the Gentiles. "Now if the fall of them be the riches of the world, and the diminishing of them the riches of the Gentiles; how much more their fullness!" "For I speak to you Gentiles, inasmuch as I am the Apostle of the Gentiles, I magnify mine office." (See Rom., xi: 12, 13). Now we are to understand the Apostle, as speaking of the return of Israel, when he said, "How much more their fullness," in their return. "For I would not have you ignorant concerning this matter," that blindnesss will depart from them in the day that the fullness of the Gentiles is come in. And the reason is very obvious, because it is said, that "Out of Sion shall come the deliverer;" and for what cause? Why? That the word of God might be fulfilled, that this deliverer might, through the grace and mercy of God, "turn away ungodliness from Jacob." This work evidently commences at the time God begins to take the darkness from the minds of Israel, for this will be the work of God by the deliverer, for He shall turn away ungodliness from the whole family of Jacob, "for this is my covenant unto them, when I shall take away their sins."

Now, then, we can see that this deliverer is a kind of harbinger or forerunner, that is, one that is sent to prepare the way for another, and this deliverer is such a one, for he comes to turn away ungodliness from Jacob, consequently he must receive a dispensation and an authority suitable to his calling, or he could not turn away ungodliness from Jacob, nor fulfill the Scriptures. But the words of the prophets must be fulfilled, and in order to do this, to this messenger must be given the dispensation of the fullness of times, according to the prophets. For Paul says again, in speaking of the dispensation of the fullness of times, "Having made known unto us the mystery of His will, according to His good pleasure, which He hath purposed in Himself: that in the dispensation of the fullness of times, He might gather together in one all things in Christ, both which are in heaven, and which are on earth; even in Him." (Ephesians, i: 9). And Isaiah says, "And it shall come to pass in that day, that the Lord shall set His hand again the second time to recover the remnant of His people." (chapter xi: 11). Now is the time that the deliverer shall come out of Zion and turn away ungodliness from the house of Israel. Now the Lord has said that He would set His hand the second time, and we ask, for what, but to recover the house of Jacob? For what have they fallen? Most assuredly they have broken the covenant that God had made with their fathers, and through their fathers with them. For Paul says, "Thou wilt say then, The branches were broken off, that I might be grafted in. Well; because of unbelief they were broken off, and thou standest by faith. Be not highminded, but fear."—Rom., xi: 18, 20.

Now it is evident that the Jews did forsake the Lord, and by that means they broke the covenant, and now we see the need of the Lord setting His hand the second time to gather His people according to Eph., i: 10, "That in the dispensation of the fullness of times, he might gather together in one all things in Christ, both which are in heaven, and which are on earth." Now, I ask, what is a dispensation? I answer, it is power and authority to dispense the word of God, and to administer in all the ordinances thereof. This is what we are to understand by it, for no man ever had the Holy Ghost to deliver the Gospel, or to prophesy of things to come, but had liberty to fulfill his mission; consequently the argument is clear; for it proves itself; nevertheless I will call on the Scriptures to prove the assertion: "If ye have heard of the dispensation of the grace of God, which is given me to you-ward: how that by revelation he made known unto me the mystery;(as I wrote afore in few words)." (Ephesians, iii: 2.) And also, Colossians, i: 25. "Whereof I am made a minister, according to the dispensation of God which is given to me for you, to fulfill the word of God." It is evident, then, that the dispensation given to the Apostle. came to him by revelation from God. Then by this we may understand, in some degree, the power by which he spake, and also the dispensation of the fullness of times.

Now this, at first thought, would appear very small to some who are not acquainted with the order of God from the beginning; but when we take under consideration the plan of God for the salvation of the world, we can readily see that plan carried out most faithfully in all its bearings. Soon after the fall of Adam, the plan of salvation was made known to him of God Himself; who in like manner, in the meridian of time, revealed the same in sending His first begotten Son Jesus Christ, who also revealed the same to the Apostles; and God raised him from the dead to perfect the plan, and the Apostles were made special witnesses of that plan, and testified that in the dispensation of the fullness of times, God would gather together in one all things in Christ, whether they be things in heaven, or things on the earth.

Now the thing to be known is, what the fullness of times means, or the extent or authority thereof. It means this, that the dispensation of the fullness of times is made up of all the dispensations that ever have been given since the world began, until this time. Unto Adam first was given a dispensation. It is well known that God spake to him with His own voice in the garden, and gave him the promise of the Messiah. And unto Noah also was a dispensation given; for Jesus said, "As it was in the days of Noah, so shall it be also in the days of the Son of man;" and as the righteous were saved then, and the wicked destroyed, so it will be now. And from Noah to Abraham, and from Abraham to Moses, and from Moses to Elias, and from Elias to John the Baptist, and from then to Jesus Christ, and from Jesus Christ to Peter, James, and John, the Apostles—all received in their time a dispensation by revelation from God, to accomplish the great scheme of restitution, spoken of by all the holy prophets since the world began; the end of which is the dispensation of the fullness of times, in the which all things shall be fulfilled that have been spoken of since the earth was made.

Now the question is, unto whom is this dispensation to be given? Or by whom to be revealed? The answer is, to the deliverer that is to come out of Zion, and be given to him by the angel of God. "And I saw another angel, fly in the midst of heaven, having the everlasting Gospel to preach unto them that dwell on the earth, and to every nation. and kindred, and tongue, and people, saying with a loud voice, Fear God, and give glory to Him: for the hour of His judgment is come: and worship Him that made heaven, and earth, and the sea, and the fountains of waters." (Revelation, xiv: 6, 7). Now observe, this angel delivers the everlasting Gospel to man on the earth, and that, too, when the hour of the judgments of God had come on the generation in which the Lord should set His hand the second time to gather His people, as stated above. Now we have learned that this deliverer must be clothed with the power of all the other dispensations, or his dispensation could not be called the dispensation of the fullness of times, for this it means, that all things shall be revealed both in heaven and on earth; for the Lord said there is nothing secret that shall not be revealed, or hid that shall not come abroad, and be proclaimed upon the house top, and this may with propriety be called the fullness of times.

The authority connected with the ordinances, renders the time very desirable to the man of God, and renders him happy amidst all his trials and afflictions. To such a one through the grace of God we are indebted for this dispensation, as given by the angel of the Lord. But to what tribe of Israel was it to be delivered? We answer, to Ephraim, because to him were the greater blessings given. For the Lord said to his father Joseph, A seer shall the Lord thy God raise up of the fruit of thy loins, and he shall be a choice seer unto the fruit of thy loins. Yea, he truly said, Thus saith the Lord, a choice seer will I raise up out of the fruit of thy loins, and he shall be esteemed highly, and unto him will I give commandment that he shall do a work for the fruit of thy loins, his brethren, which shall be of great worth unto them, even to the bringing of them to the knowledge of the covenants which I have made with their fathers. And I will give unto him a commandment that he shall do none other work save the work which I shall command him, and I will make him great in mine eyes, for he shall do my work, and he shall be great like unto Moses; and out of weakness he shall be made strong, in that day when my work shall commence among all people, unto the restoring of the house of Israel, saith the Lord.

And thus prophesied Joseph, saying—Behold, that seer will the Lord bless, and they that seek to destroy him shall be confounded. Behold, I am sure of the fulfillment of this promise, and his name shall be called after the name of his father, and he shall be like unto me, for the thing which the Lord shall bring forth by his hand, by the power of the Father, shall bring forth my people unto salvation.

And thus prophesied Joseph, "I am sure of this thing, even as I am sure of the promise of Moses." (II Nephi, iii: 6-16). And again, Jesus says, as recorded in the Book of Mormon, page 526: "Behold my servant shall deal very prudently; he shall be exalted and extolled, and be very high. As many as were astonished at thee. * * * So shall he sprinkle many nations; the kings shall shut their mouths at him, for that which had been told them shall they see; and that which they had not heard shall they consider." Upon this servant is bestowed the keys of the dispensation of the fullness of times, that from him the Priesthood of God, through our Lord Jesus Christ, might be given to many, and the order of this dispensation established on the earth. And to the Church He has said by commandment, "Wherefore, meaning the Church, thou shalt give heed unto all his words and commandments, which he shall give unto you as he receiveth them, walking in all holiness before me; for his word ye shall receive as if from my own mouth, in all patience and faith; for by doing these things, the gates of hell shall not prevail against you."—Doctrine and Covenants, sec. xxi.

Now, my readers, you can see in some degree the grace given to this man of God, to us-ward: that we, by the great mercy of God, should receive from under his hands, the Gospel of Jesus Christ, having the promise of partaking of the fruit of the vine on the earth with him, and with the holy Prophets and Patriarchs, our fathers. For those holy men are angels now; and these are they who make the fullness of times complete with us; and they who sin against this authority given to him (the aforementioned man of God), sin not againt him only, but against Moroni, who holds the keys of the stick of Ephraim [Book of Mormon], and also Elias, who holds the keys of bringing to pass the restitution of all things, and also John, the son of Zacharias, which Zacharias Elias visited, and gave promise that he should have a son, and his name should be John, and he should be filled with the spirit of Elias, which John I have sent unto you, my servants Joseph Smith, Jun, and Oliver Cowdery, to ordain you to this first Priesthood, even as Aaron; and also Elijah who holds the keys of committing the power to turn the hearts of the fathers to the children, and the hearts of the children to the fathers, that the whole earth may not be smitten with a curse; and also Joseph and Jacob and Isaac and Abraham, your fathers, by whom the promises remain; and also Michael, or Adam, the Father of all, the Prince of all, the Ancient of Days; and also Peter and James and John, whom I have sent unto you, by whom I have ordained you, and confirmed you to be Apostles and especial witnesses of my name, and bear the keys of your ministry, and of the same things I revealed unto them, unto whom I have committed the keys of my kingdom, and a dispensation of the Gospel for the last times, and for the fullness of times, in the which I will gather together in one all things, both which are in heaven, and which are on earth. (Doctrine and Covenants, sec. xxvii.)

Therefore, brethren, beware concerning yourselves, that you sin not against the authority of this dispensation, nor think lightly of those whom God has counted worthy for so great a calling, and for whose sake He hath made them servants unto you, that you might be made the heirs of God to inherit so great a blessing, and be prepared for the great assembly, and sit there with the Ancient of Days, even Adam our father, who shall come to prepare you for the coming of Jesus Christ our Lord; for the time is at hand, therefore gather up your effects, and gather together upon the land which the Lord has appointed for your safety.

DAVID W. PATTEN.

CHAPTER VI.

THE BEGINNING OF TROUBLE IN CALDWELL AND DAVIESS COUNTIES.

Wednesday, August 1.—I tarried at home with my family, also the 2nd and 3rd, to refresh myself after my many late fatigues and arduous duties which I had been called upon to perform.

The Prophet Rests.

Sunday, 5.—I attended meeting. Elder Erastus Snow* preached, after which I addressed the congregation, and particularly the Elders, on the principle of wisdom, etc. President Rigdon preached in the afternoon, and several were confirmed, among whom was Frederick G. Williams, who had recently been re-baptized.

Monday, 6.—This morning my council met me at my house, to consider the conduct of certain Canada brethren, who had settled on the forks of Grand river, contrary to counsel. On investigation, it was resolved that they must return to Adam-ondi-Ahman, according to counsel, or they would not be considered one with us.

Reproof of Canadian Brethren.

This day the citizens of Caldwell county assembled at Far West, and organized by calling Elias Higbee to the chair, and appointing George W. Robinson secretary.

* Erastus Snow was the son of Levi and Lucina Snow. His ancestors were among the early settlers of the Massachusetts colony. He was born on the 9th of November, 1818, and converted to the Gospel in the Spring of 1832, through the ministry of Elders Orson Pratt and Luke S. Johnson. Though converted to the Gospel by these Elders he was baptized by his elder brother, William, on the 3rd of February, 1833, and soon afterwards was ordained a teacher and commenced his work in the ministry. Previous to his arrival at Far West he had been active in the ministry for several years, preaching extensively in Ohio, New York and Pennsylvania. He was a member of the second quorum of Seventies, and had already given evidence of his sterling integrity and untiring efforts as a minister of the Lord Jesus Christ which so characterized all the subsequent years of his long life.

W. W. Phelps having resigned the office of postmaster, it was voted unanimously that Sidney Rigdon be recommended to the Postmaster General, as the person of our choice to fill the place of W. W. Phelps, as postmaster in this city.

A Citizens' Meeting at Far West.

In the afternoon, the citizens of Far West assembled in the school house and organized the meeting by calling Judge Elias Higbee to the chair, and appointing George W. Robinson, secretary. I stated to the meeting, that the time had come when it was necessary that we should have a weekly newspaper, to unite the people, and give the news of the day. It was unanimously agreed that such a paper be established, and that President Sidney Rigdon should be the editor. It was also voted that a petition be circulated to locate the county seat at Far West. I addressed the meeting on the propriety of the measure, and also on the duty of the brethren to come into cities to build and live, and carry on their farms out of the cities, according to the order of God. President Rigdon and Brother Hyrum Smith spoke upon the same subject.

Some two weeks previous to this, Judge Morin, who lived at Mill Port, informed John D. Lee* and Levi Stewart, that it was determined by the mob to prevent the "Mormons" from voting at the election on the sixth day of August, and thereby elect Colonel William P. Peniston, who led the mob in Clay county. He also advised them to go prepared for an attack, to stand their ground, and have their rights.

Judge Morin's Friendly Warning.

The brethren, hoping better things, gave little heed to Judge Morin's friendly counsel, and repaired to the polls at Gallatin, the shire town of Daviess county, without weapons.

About eleven o'clock a. m., William P. Peniston mounted a barrel, and harangued the electors for the pur-

* John D. Lee was born on the 6th of September, 1812, in the town of Kaskaskia, Randolph County, Illinois; and was the son of Ralph Lee, of Virginia, and the daughter of John Doyle, of Nashville, Tennessee.

pose of exciting them against the "Mormons," saying, "The Mormon leaders are a set of horse thieves, liars, counterfeiters, and you know they profess to heal the sick, and cast out devils, and you all know that is a lie." He further said that the members of the Church were dupes, and not too good to take a false oath on any common occasion; that they would steal, and he did not consider property safe where they were; that he was opposed to their settling in Daviess county; and if they suffered the "Mormons" to vote, the people would soon lose their suffrage; "and," said he, addressing the Saints, "I headed a mob to drive you out of Clay county, and would not prevent your being mobbed now."

Peniston's Harangue.

Richard (called Dick) Welding, the mob bully, just drunk enough for the occasion, began a discussion with Brother Samuel Brown, by saying, "The Mormons were not allowed to vote in Clay county no more than the negroes," and attempted to strike Brown, who gradually retreated, parrying the blow with his umbrella, while Welding continued to press upon him, calling him a liar, etc., and meanwhile trying to repeat the blow on Brown. Perry Durphy sought to suppress the difficulty by holding Welding's arm, when five or six of the mobbers seized Durphy and commenced beating him with clubs, boards, and crying, "*Kill him, kill him*, when a general scuffle commenced with fists and clubs, the mobbers being about ten to one of the brethren. Abraham Nelson was knocked down, and had his clothes torn off, and while trying to get up was attacked again, when his brother, Hyrum Nelson, ran in amongst them, and knocked the mobbers down with the butt of his whip. Riley Stewart struck Welding on the head, which brought him to the ground. The mob cried out, "Dick Weldin's dead; who killed Dick?" And they fell upon Riley, knocked him down, kicked him, crying, "Kill him, kill him; shoot him," and they would have killed him, had not

"Dick" Welding's Row.

John L. Butler sprung in amongst them and knocked them down. During about five minutes it was one succession of knock downs, when the mob dispersed to get fire arms.

Very few of the brethren voted. Riley, escaping across the river, had his wounds dressed, and returned home.

John L. Butler's speech.

John L. Butler called the brethren together and made a speech, saying, "We are American citizens; our fathers fought for their liberty, and we will maintain the same principles." The authorities of the county finally came to the brethren, and requested them to withdraw, stating that it was a premeditated thing to prevent the "Mormons" from voting.

Gathering of the Mob

The brethren held a council about one-fourth of a mile out of town, where they saw mob recruits coming in, in small parties, from five and ten, to twenty-five in number cursing and swearing, and armed with clubs, pistols, dirks, and some guns. The brethren not having arms, thought it wisdom to return to their farms, collect their families, and hide them in a thicket of hazel bush, which they did, and stood guard around them through the night, while the women and children lay on the ground in the rain.

Reports of Gallatin Trouble Reach Far West.

Tuesday, 7.—A report came to Far West this morning, by way of those not belonging to the Church, to the effect that at the election at Gallatin, yesterday, two or three of our brethren were killed by the Missourians, and left upon the ground, and not suffered to be interred; that the brethren were prevented from voting, and a majority of the inhabitants of Daviess county were determined to drive the Saints from that county.

The Departure of the Prophet for Gallatin.

On hearing this report, I started for Gallatin, to assist the brethren, accompanied by President Rigdon, Brother Hyrum Smith, and fifteen or twenty others, who were armed for their own protection; and the command of the company was given to George W. Robinson.

On our way we were joined by the brethren from different parts of the county, some of whom were attacked by the mob, but we all reached Colonel Wight's that night in safety, where we found some of the brethren who had been mobbed at Gallatin, with others, waiting for our counsel. Here we received the cheering intelligence that none of the brethren were killed, although several were badly wounded.

The Prophet Commends the Brethren for Standing for Their Rights.

From the best information, about one hundred and fifty Missourians warred against from six to twelve of our brethren, who fought like lions. Several Missourians had their skulls cracked. Blessed be the memory of those few brethren who contended so strenuously for their constitutional rights and religious freedom, against such an overwhelming force of desperadoes!

Interview with Adam Black.

Wednesday, 8.—After spending the night in counsel at Colonel Wight's, I rode out with some of the brethren to view the situation of affairs in that region, and among others, called on Adam Black, justice of the peace, and judge elect for Daviess county, who had some time previous sold his farm to Brother Vinson Knight, and received part pay according to agreement, and afterwards united himself with a band of mobbers to drive the Saints from, and prevent their settling in, Daviess county. On interrogation, he confessed what he had done, and in consequence of this violation of his oath as magistrate, we asked him to give us some satisfaction so that we might know whether he was our friend or enemy, whether or not he would administer the law in justice; and politely requested him to sign an agreement of peace, but being jealous, he would not sign it, but said he would write one himself to our satisfaction, and sign it, which he did, as follows—

Adam Black's Agreement.

I, Adam Black, a Justice of the Peace of Daviess county, do hereby

Sertify to the people, *coled Mormin*, that he is bound to *suport* the Constitution of this State, and of the United State, and he is not attached to any mob, nor will not attach himself to any such people, and so long as they will not molest me, I will not molest them. This the 8th day of August, 1838.

ADAM BLACK, J. P.*

Hoping he would abide his own decision, and support the law, we left him in peace, and returned to Colonel Wight's at Adam-ondi-Ahman.

Interview with Citizens of Mill Port.

In the evening some of the citizens from Mill Port called on us, and we agreed to meet some of the principal men of the county in council, at Adam-ondi-Ahman the next day at twelve o'clock, noon.

Thursday, 9.—The Committee assembled at Adam-ondi-Ahman at twelve, according to previous appointment, viz., on the part of Mill Port citizens, Joseph Morin, senator elect: John Williams, representative elect; James B. Turner, clerk of the circuit court, and others: on the part of the Saints, Lyman Wight, Vinson Knight, John Smith, Reynolds Cahoon, and others. At this meeting both parties entered into a covenant of peace, to preserve each other's rights, and stand in each other's defense; that if men did wrong, neither party would uphold them or endeavor to screen them from justice, but deliver up all offenders to be dealt with according to law and justice. The assembly dispersed on these friendly terms, myself and friends returning to Far West, where we arrived about midnight and found all quiet.

Friday, 10.—Being somewhat fatigued I spent the day with my family, transacting but little business.

Treaties of Peace of Little Avail.

The spirit of mobocracy continued to stalk abroad, notwithstanding all our treaties of peace, as will be seen by the following affidavit—

* The original orthography and composition of this note are preserved in the above copy.

Peniston's Affidavit.

STATE OF MISSOURI, }
RAY COUNTY. } ss.

Personally appeared before me, the undersigned, judge of the Fifth Judicial Circuit, William P. Peniston, and makes oath that he has good reason to believe, and that he verily does believe, that there is now collected and embodied in the County of Daviess, a large body of armed men, whose movements and conduct are of a highly insurrectionary and unlawful character; that they consist of about five hundred men, and that they, or a part of them, to the number of one hundred and twenty, have committed violence against Adam Black, by surrounding his house, and taking him in a violent manner, and subjecting him to great indignities. by forcing him, under threats of immediate death, to sign a paper writing of a very disgraceful character, and by threatening to do the same to all the old settlers and citizens of Daviess county; and that they have, as a collected and armed body, threatened to put to instant death this affiant on sight; and that he verily believes they will accomplish that act without they are prevented; and also that they have threatened the same to Wm. Bowman and others; and this affiant states that he verily believes all the above facts to be true, and that the body of men now assembled do intend to commit great violence to many of the citizens of Daviess county, and that they have already done so to Adam Black; and this affiant verily believes, from information of others, that Joseph Smith, Jun., and Lyman Wight are the leaders of this body of armed men, and the names of others thus combined are not certainly known to this affiant; and he further states the fact to be that it is his opinion, and he verily believes, that it is the object of this body of armed men, to take vengeance for some injuries, or imaginary injuries, done to some of their friends, and to intimidate and drive from the county all the old citizens, and possess themselves of their lands, or to force such as do not leave, to come into their measures and submit to their dictation.

WILLIAM P. PENISTON.

Sworn to and subscribed before me the undersigned judge, as aforesaid, this 10th day of August, 1838.

AUSTIN A. KING.

Reflections of the Prophet

The above was also sworn to by William Bowman, Wilson McKinney, and John Netherton. So it is that when men's hearts become hardened and corrupt, they will more readily swear to lies than speak the truth.

At this time some of the brethren had removed with

their families from the vicinity of Gallatin, to Diahman and Far West, for safety.

Saturday, 11.—This morning I left Far West, with my council and Elder Almon W. Babbitt, to visit the brethren on the Forks of Grand river, who had come from Canada with Elder Babbitt, and settled at that place contrary to counsel.

Inquiry at Far West concerning Gallatin Affair.

In the afternoon, after my departure, a committee from Ray county arrived at Far West, to inquire into the proceedings of our society in going armed into Daviess county, complaint having been entered in Ray county by Adam Black, William P. Peniston, and others. The committee from Ray county requested an interview with a committee of Caldwell, and a general meeting was called at the city hall, at six in the evening, when it was stated that they were assembled to take into consideration the doings of the citizens of Ray county, wherein they have accused the "Mormons" of this place of breaking the peace, in defending their rights and those of their brethren in the county of Daviess. The meeting was organized by appointing Bishop Edward Partridge, chairman; and Geo. W. Robinson, clerk. The meeting adopted the following—

Resolutions.

"Resolved 1st. That a committee of seven be appointed to confer with the committee from Ray county.

"Resolved 2nd. That this committee, with their secretary, be authorized to answer such questions as may be offered by the committee from Ray county, and as are named in the document presented to this meeting, purporting to be the preamble and resolutions of the citizens of Ray county.

"Resolved 3rd. That whereas the document referred to has no date or signature, our committee judge of the fact, and act accordingly.

"Resolved 4th. That our committee report their proceedings to this meeting as soon as possible.

"EDWARD PARTRIDGE, Chairman,
"GEO. W. ROBINSON, Clerk."

Sunday, 12.—I continued with the brethren at the Forks

of Grand river, offering such counsel as their situation required.

Monday, 13.—I returned with my council to Far West. We were chased ten or twelve miles, by some evil designing men, but we eluded their pursuit. When within about eight miles of home, we met some brethren who had come to inform us that a writ had been issued by Judge King, for my arrest, and that of Lyman Wight, for attempting to defend our rights against the mob.*

Chased by a Mob.

Tuesday and Wednesday, 14 and 15.—I spent principally at home, engaged in domestic affairs.

Thursday, 16.—I spent principally at home.

The sheriff of Daviess county, accompanied by Judge Morin, called and notified me, that he had a writ to take me to Daviess county, for trial, for visiting that county on the seventh instant.

The Prophet's Interview with the Sheriff of Daviess County.

It had been currently reported that I would not be apprehended by legal process, and that I would not submit to the laws of the land; but I told the sheriff that I intended always to submit to the laws of our country, but I wished to be tried in my own county, as the citizens of Daviess county were highly exasperated at me, and that the laws of the country gave me this privilege. Upon hearing this, the sheriff declined serving the writ, and said he would go to Richmond, and see Judge King on the subject. I told him I would remain at home until his return.

The sheriff returned from Richmond, and found me at home (where I had remained during his absence), and informed me very gravely, that I was out of his jurisdiction, and that he could not act in Caldwell county, and retired.

August 20.—Nothing peculiar transpired at Far West, from the sixteenth to this day, when the inhabitants of the different parts of the county met to organize

* The warrant was issued on the misrepresentations of what the Prophet and Lyman Wight did on their visit to Adam Black on the 8th of August.

themselves into Agricultural Companies. I was present and took part in their deliberations. One company was formed, called the "Western Agricultural Company," which voted to enclose one field for grain containing twelve sections, seven thousand six hundred and eighty acres of land. Another company was also organized, called the "Eastern Agricultural Company," the extent of the field not decided.

Organization of Agriculture Companies.

Tuesday, 21.—Another company was formed, called the "Southern Agricultural Company," the field to be as large as the first mentioned.

Wednesday, 22.—I spent part of the day in counseling with several brethren upon different subjects.

The brethren continued to gather to Zion daily.

Some time this month the Saints were warned by the mob to leave De Witt, Carroll county.

Thursday, 23.—This day I spent transacting a variety of business about the city.

Friday, 24.—I was at home. Also on the 25th, 26th, 27th, 28th, 29th, and 30th.

Affidavit of Adam Black.

STATE OF MISSOURI, }
COUNTY OF DAVIESS. } SS.

Before me, William Dryden, one of the justices of the peace of said county, personally came Adam Black, who being duly sworn according to law, deposeth and saith: that on or about the 8th day of August, 1838, in the county of Daviess, there came an armed force of men, said to be one hundred and fifty-four, to the best of his information, and surrounded his house and family, and threatened him with instant death if he did not sign a certain instrument of writing, binding himself, as a justice of the peace for said county of Daviess, not to molest the people called Mormons; and threatened the lives of himself and other individuals, and did say they intended to make every citizen sign such obligation, and further said they intended to have satisfaction for abuse they had received on the Monday previous, and that they could not submit to the laws: and further saith, that from the best information and his own personal knowledge, that Andrew [Alanson] Ripley, George A. Smith, Ephraim Owens, Harvey Humstead, Hiram Nelson, A. Brown, John L.

Butler, Cornelius [P.] Lott, John Wood, H. Redfield, Riley Stewart, James Whitaker, Andrew Thor, Amos Tubbs, Dr. Gourze, and Abram Nelson was guilty of aiding and abetting in committing and perpetrating the above offense.

ADAM BLACK.

Sworn to and subscribed this the 28th of August, 1838.

W. DRYDEN,
Justice of the Peace of the County aforesaid.

This document, with that of the 8th of August, of said Black, shows him in his true light—a detestable, unprincipled mobocrat and *perjured man*.

Comment on Adam Black.

Thursday, *30*.—This day Governor Boggs issued the following order to General Atchison—

Proclamation of Governor Boggs.

HEADQUARTERS OF MILITIA, ADJUTANT GENERAL'S OFFICE,
August 30th, 1838.

General David R. Atchison, 3rd Division, Missouri Militia.

SIR—Indications of Indian disturbances on our immediate frontier, and the recent civil disturbances in the counties of Caldwell, Daviess, and Carroll, render it necessary, as a precautionary measure, that an effective force of the militia be held in readiness to meet either contingency. The Commander-in-Chief therefore orders that you cause to be raised immediately, within the limits of your division, to be held in readiness, and subject to further orders, four hundred mounted men, armed and equipped as infantry or riflemen, and formed into companies according to law, under officers already in commission. The Commander-in-Chief suggests the propriety of your causing the above to be carried into effect, in a manner calculated to produce as little excitement as possible, and report your proceedings to him through the Adjutant General.

By order of the Commander-in-Chief,
B. M. LISLE, Adjutant-General.

A similar letter was also addressed to Major Generals John B. Clark, Samuel D. Lucas, David Willock, Lewis Bolton, Henry W. Crawther, and Thomas D. Grant.

I spent considerable time to day in conversation with Brother John Corrill, in consequence of some expressions made by him, in presence of several brethren who had not been long in the place. Brother Corrill's conduct for some time had been very unbecoming, especially in a man in whom so much confidence had been placed. He said he would not yield his judgment to anything proposed by the Church, or any individuals of the Church, or even the Great I Am, given through the appointed organ, as revelation, but would always act upon his own judgment, let him believe in whatever religion he might. He stated he would always say what he pleased, for he was a Republican, and as such would do, say, act, and believe what he pleased.

Conduct of John Corrill Reproved.

Mark such republicanism as this! A man to oppose his own judgment to the judgment of God, and at the same time to profess to believe in that same God, who has said: "The foolishness of God is wiser than man; and the weakness of God is stronger, than man."

President Rigdon also made some observations to Brother Corrill, which he afterwards acknowledged were correct, and that he understood things different after the interview from what he did before.

CHAPTER VII.

INCREASING DIFFICULTIES BETWEEN THE SAINTS AND THE MOBS OF DAVIESS AND CALDWELL COUNTIES.

Saturday, September 1, 1838.—The First Presidency, with Judge Higbee, as surveyor, started this morning for the half-way house, as it is called, kept by Brother Littlefield, some fourteen or fifteen miles from Far West, directly north—for the purpose of appointing a city of Zion, for the gathering of the Saints in that place, for safety, and from the storm which will soon come upon this generation, and that the brethren may be together, and that they may receive instructions to prepare them for that great day which will come upon this generation as a thief in the night.

The Prophet Leaves Far West to Found a City of Zion.

There is great excitement at present among the Missourians, who are seeking if possible an occasion against us. They are continually chafing us, and provoking us to anger if possible, one sign of threatening after another, but we do not fear them, for the Lord God, the Eternal Father is our God, and Jesus the Mediator is our Savior, and in the great I Am is our strength and confidence.

Excitement Among the Missourians.

We have been driven time after time, and that without cause; and smitten again and again, and that without provocation; until we have proved the world with kindness, and the world has proved us, that we have no designs against any man or set of men, that we injure no man, that we are peaceable with all men, minding our own business, and our business only. We have suffered our rights and our liberties to be taken from us; we have not avenged ourselves of those wrongs; we have appealed to magistrates, to sheriffs, to judges, to

The Prophet's Review of the Wrongs of the Saints.

government and to the President of the United States, all in vain; yet we have yielded peaceably to all these things. We have not complained at the Great God, we murmured not, but peaceably left all; and retired into the back country, in the broad and wild prairies, in the barren and desolate plains, and there commenced anew; we made the desolate places to bud and blossom as the rose; and now the fiend-like race is disposed to give us no rest. Their father the devil, is hourly calling upon them to be up and doing, and they, like willing and obedient children, need not the second admonition; but in the name of Jesus Christ the Son of the living God, we will endure it no longer, if the great God will arm us with courage, with strength and with power, to resist them in their persecutions. We will not act on the offensive, but always on the defensive; our rights and our liberties shall not be taken from us, and we peaceably submit to it, as we have done heretofore, but we will avenge ourselves of our enemies, inasmuch as they will not let us alone.

Site for a City Selected.

But to return again to our subject. We found the place for the city, and the brethren were instructed to gather immediately into it, and soon they should be organized according to the laws of God. A more particular history of this city may be expected hereafter, perhaps at its organization and dedication. We found a new route home, saving, I should think, three or four miles. We arrived at Far West about the close of day.

The High Priests met at Brother Pea's at Far West, and received Levi Richards into their quorum.

Rumors of Mobs Gathering.

Sunday, 2.—The First Presidency attended meeting as usual in the morning. I tarried at home in the evening to examine the Church records, and spent a part of the time in company with a gentleman from Livingston county, who had become considerably excited, on account of a large collection of people, as he said, to take Joseph Smith, Jun., and Lyman Wight, for going to one Adam Black's in Daviess county; and as the said

President Smith and Colonel Wight had resisted the officer who had endeavored to take them, accordingly these men are assembling to take them—as they say. They are collecting from every part of the country, to Daviess county. Report says that they are collecting from eleven counties, to help take two men who had never resisted the law or officer, nor had they thought of doing so, and this their enemies knew at the same time, or many of them at least knew it. This looks a little too much like mobocracy, it foretells some evil intentions. The whole of upper Missouri is in an uproar and confusion.

An Appeal to Gen. Atchison.

This evening I sent for General Atchison, of Liberty, Clay county, who is the major general of this division—to come and counsel with us, and to see if we could not put a stop to this collection of people, and to put a stop to hostilities in Daviess county. I also sent a letter to Judge King containing a petition for him to assist in putting down and scattering the mob collecting in Daviess county.

Monday, 3.—Nothing of importance occurred today. Reports come in concerning the collection of a mob in Daviess county, which has been collecting ever since the election in Daviess county, on the sixth of August last. I was at home most of the day.

This evening General Atchison arrived in Far West.

Consultation with General Atchison.

Tuesday, 4.—This day I spent in council with General Atchison. He says he will do all in his power to disperse the mob. We employed him and Alexander Doniphan (his partner) as our counsel in law. They are considered the first lawyers in upper Missouri.

The Prophet and Sidney Rigdon Study Law.

President Rigdon and myself commenced this day the study of law, under the instruction of Generals Atchison and Doniphan. They think, by diligent application, we can be admitted to the bar in twelve months.

The result of our consultation with our lawyers was

that myself and Colonel Wight volunteer to be tried by Judge King in Daviess county. Colonel Wight was present, having been previously notified to attend the consultation. Accordingly, Thursday next, was appointed for the trial, and word to that effect was sent to Judge King (who had previously agreed to try the case). All are to meet at Brother Littlefield's, near the county line in the southern part of Daviess county. I was at home in the evening after six o'clock.

The Prophet and Lyman Wight to submit to Trial.

Wednesday, *5*.—I gave the following affidavit, that the truth might appear before the public in the matter in controversy:

The Prophet's Affidavit on the Adam Black Incident.

STATE OF MISSOURI,
CALDWELL COUNTY. } ss.

Before me, Elias Higbee, one of the justices of the county court, within and for the county of Caldwell aforesaid, personally came Joseph Smith, Jun., who, being duly sworn according to law, deposeth and saith: That on the seventh day of August, one thousand eight hundred and thirty-eight, being informed that an affray had taken place in Daviess county, at the election, in the town of Gallatin, in which two persons were [reported] killed, and one person badly wounded, and fled to the woods to save his life; all of which were said to be persons belonging to the society of the Church of Latter-day Saints; and further, said informant stated that those persons who committed the outrage would not suffer the bodies of those who had been killed to be taken off the ground and buried.

These reports, with others, one of which was that the Saints had not the privilege of voting at the polls as other citizens; another was that those opposed to the Saints were determined to drive them from Daviess county, and also that they were arming and strengthening their forces and preparing for battle; and that the Saints were preparing and making ready to stand in self defense—these reports having excited the feelings of the citizens of Far West and vicinity, I was invited by Dr. Avard and some others to go out to Daviess county, to the scene of these outrages; they having previously determined to go out and learn the facts concerning said reports.

Accordingly some of the citizens, myself among the number, went out, two, three, and four, in companies, as they got ready. The reports and excitement continued until several of those small companies through the day were induced to follow the first, who were all eager to learn the facts concerning this matter. We arrived in the evening at the house of Lyman Wight, about three miles from Gallatin, the scene of the reported outrages. Here we learned the truth concerning the said affray, which had been considerably exaggerated, yet there had been a serious outrage committed. We there learned that the mob was collected at Millport, to a considerable number; that Adam Black was at their head; and that they were to attack the Saints the next day, at the place we then were in, called Adam-ondi-Ahman. This report we were still inclined to believe might be true, as this Adam Black, who was said to be their leader, had been, but a few months before, engaged in endeavoring to drive those of the society who had settled in that vicinity, from the county. This had become notorious, from the fact that said Black had personally ordered several of said society to leave the county.

The next morning we dispatched a committee to said Black's, to ascertain the truth of these reports, and to know what his intentions were; and as we understood he was a peace officer, we wished to know what we might expect from him. They reported that Mr. Black, instead of giving them any assurance of peace, insulted them and gave them no satisfaction. Being desirous of knowing the feelings of Mr. Black for myself, and being in want of good water, and understanding that there was none nearer than Mr. Black's spring, myself with several others mounted our horses and rode up to Mr. Black's fence.

Dr. Avard, with one or two others who had ridden ahead, went into Mr. Black's house; myself and some others went to the spring for water. I was shortly after sent for by Mr. Black, and invited into the house, being introduced to Mr. Black by Dr. Avard. Mr. Black wished me to be seated. We then commenced a conversation on the subject of the late difficulties, and present excitement. I found Mr. Black quite hostile in his feelings toward the Saints; but he assured us he did not belong to the mob, neither would he take any part with them; but said he was bound by his oath to support the Constitution of the United States, and the laws of the State of Missouri. Deponent then asked him if he would make said statement in writing, so as to refute the statement of those who had affirmed that he (Black) was one of the leaders of the mob. Mr. Black answered in the affirmative. Accordingly he did so, which writing is in possession of the deponent. The deponent further saith, that no violence was offered to any individual in his presence, or within his knowledge; and that no insulting language was given by either party, except on the part of Mrs. Black, who, while Mr. Black was engaged in making out the above-named writing, (which he made with his own hand), gave to this deponent, and others of his society, highly insulting language and false accusations, which were calculated in their nature to greatly irritate, if possible, the feelings of the bystanders belonging to said society, in language like this—being asked by the deponent if she knew anything in the "Mormon" people derogatory to the character of gentlemen, she answered in the negative, but said she did not know but the object of their visit was to steal something from them. After Mr. Black had executed the writing, deponent asked Mr. Black if he had any unfriendly feelings towards the deponent, and if he [the deponent] had not treated him genteelly. He answered in the affirmative. Deponent then took leave of said Black and repaired to the house of Lyman Wight. The next day he returned to Far West, and further this deponent saith not.

JOSEPH SMITH, JUN.

Sworn to and subscribed this fifth day of September, A. D. 1838.

ELIAS HIGBEE, J. C. C. C.

Judge King at Far West.

Judge King arrived at Far West, on his way to Daviess to meet the proposed trial. General Atchison had gone before Judge King arrived, and the judge tarried all night. I was at home after six o'clock in the evening.

Start for the Place of Trial.

Thursday, 6.—At half-past seven this morning, I started on horseback, accompanied by several brethren, among whom were my brother Hyrum and Judge Elias Higbee, to attend my trial at Brother Littlefield's. I thought it not wisdom to make my appearance before the public at the county seat of Daviess county, in consequence of the many threats made against me, and the high state of excitement. The trial could not proceed, on account of the absence of the plaintiff, and lack of testimony, and the court adjourned until tomorrow at ten o'clock in the morning, at a Mr. Raglin's, some six or eight miles further south, and within half a mile of the line of Caldwell. Raglin is a regular mob character. We all returned to Far West, where we arrived before dark.

The Trial at Raglin's.

Friday, 7.—About sunrise I started with my friends, and arrived at Mr. Raglin's at the appointed hour. We did not know but there would be a disturbance among the mob characters today; we accordingly had a company of men placed at the county line, so as to be ready at a minute's warning, if there should be any difficulty at the trial.

The trial commenced; William P. Peniston, who was the prosecutor, had no witnesses but Adam Black, but he contrived to swear to a great many things that never had an existence, and I presume never entered into the heart of any other man, and in fine, I think he swore by the job, and that he was employed so to do by Peniston.

The witnesses on the part of the defense were Dimick B. Huntington, Gideon Carter, Adam Lightner, and George W. Robinson.

The Prophet and Lyman Wight Bound Over.

The judge bound Colonel Wight and myself over to court in a five hundred dollar bond. There was no proof against us to criminate us, but it is supposed he did it to pacify, as much as possible, the feelings of the mobbers. The judge stated afterwards, in the presence of George W. Robinson, that there was nothing proven against us worthy of bonds, but we submitted without murmuring a word, gave the bonds, with sufficient securities, and all returned home the same evening.

A Committee of Inquiry from Chariton County.

I found two persons in Daviess county at the trial, who were sent from Chariton county as a committe, to inquire into all this matter, as the mobbers had sent to that place for assistance, they said,to take Smith and Wight; but their real object was to drive the brethren from the county of Daviess, as had been done in Jackson county. They said the people in Chariton county did not see proper to send help without knowing for what purpose they were doing it, and this they said was their errand. They accompanied us to Far West, to hold a council with us, in order to learn the facts of this great excitement, which is, as it were, turning the world upside down. We arrived home in the evening.

The Presidency met in council with the committee from

Chariton county, together with General Atchison, where a relation was given of our affairs in general, the present state of excitement, and the cause of all this confusion. The gentlemen from Chariton expressed their fullest satisfaction upon the subject, and considered they had been outrageously imposed upon in this matter. They left this afternoon apparently perfectly satisfied with the interview.

Rumors of an Attack upon "Diahman."

News came this evening that the mob were to attack Adam-ondi-Ahman, and a few of the brethren from Far West started to assist the brethren to defend themselves.

Sunday, *9*.—This morning a company in addition to that which went last evening went to Adam-ondi-Ahman to assist the brethren there in their defense against the mob.

Capture of Arms Intended for the Mob

Captain William Allred took a company of ten mounted men and went to intercept a team with guns and ammunition, sent from Richmond to the mob in Daviess county. They found the wagon broken down, and the boxes of guns drawn into the high grass near by the wagon; there was no one present that could be discovered. In a short time two men on horseback came from towards the camp of the mob, and immediately behind them was a man with a wagon; they all came up and were taken by virtue of a writ on the supposition that they were abetting the mob, by carrying guns and ammunition to them. The men were taken together with the guns to Far West; the guns were distributed among the brethren, for their defense, and the prisoners were held in custody. This was a glorious day indeed, the plans of the mob were frustrated in losing their guns, and all their efforts appeared to be blasted. Captain Allred acted under the civil authorities in Caldwell, who issued the writ for securing the arms and arresting the carriers. The prisoners were brought to Far West for trial.

The mob continue to take prisoners at their pleasure; some they keep, and some they let go. They try all in their power to make us commit the first act of violence. They frequenty send in word that they are torturing the prisoners to death, in the most cruel manner, but we understand all their ways, and their cunning and wisdom are not past finding out.

The Mob Take Prisoners.

Monday, 10.—This day the prisoners taken by Captain Allred on Sunday, viz., John B. Comer, William L. McHoney, and Allen Miller, were brought before Albert Petty, justice of the peace, for examination. The prisoners asked for bail, to allow time to get counsel. The law allowed no bail, but the court adjourned till Wednesday to give time to the prisoners to get counsel.

Allred's Prisoners.

After the arrest the facts were communicated to Judge King by letter, under date of Richmond, September 10th, asking his advice how to dispose of the guns and prisoners.

Judge King advised by letter to turn the prisoners loose, and let them receive kind treatment; that the guns were government property, in the care of Captain Pollard of his vicinity, but whether they went by his authority or permission he could not say, he was at a loss to give any advice about them; but said that they should not, through any agency of his, be taken from us to be converted and used for illegal purposes. The letter was signed by A. A. King (directed to Messrs. Smith and Rigdon).

Advice from Judge King.

Under the same date Judge King advised General Atchison "to send two hundred or more men, and dispel the forces in Daviess county and all the assembled armed forces in Caldwell, and cause those 'Mormons' who refuse to give up, to surrender, and be recognized, for it will not do to compromise the law with them." What compromise need there be, Judge King, for no "Mormons" had refused to surrender to the requisitions of the law? It is mob violence, alone, that the "Mormons" are contending against.

Judge King's Apparent Double Dealing.

Petition from Ray County.

A petition was this day made out by the citizens of Ray county, directed to General Atchison, asking him to call out the militia to suppress the insurrection in Caldwell and Daviess counties, and save the effusion of blood, which must speedily take place unless prevented. Signed by Jesse Coates and twenty-eight others.

The Trial of Allred's Prisoners.

Wednesday, 12.—This day the prisoners, [Allred's] John B. Comer and his comrades, were put upon trial. It was proven to the court that the guns were taken by one of the prisoners and that he with the others were taking them to Daviess county to arm the mob. It was also proved that the mob was collecting for the purpose of driving the Saints from their homes. The prisoners were held to bail for their appearance at the circuit court, Comer as principal, the others were merely in his service.

The Citizens of Daviess County to the Governor.

This day also a communication was sent to Governor Boggs, dated Daviess county, containing all the falsehoods and lies that the evil genius of mobocrats, villains, and murderers could invent, charging the "Mormons" with every crime they themselves had been guilty of, and calling the "Mormons" impostors, rebels, Canadian refugees, emissaries of the prince of darkness, and signed, "The Citizens of Daviess and Livingston Counties."

Atchison Orders Out the Militia.

Under this date, General Atchison informed the Governor, by letter from headquarters at Richmond, that on the solicitation of the citizens and the advice of the judge of the circuit, he had ordered out four companies of fifty men each from the militia of Clay county, and a like number from Ray; also four hundred men to hold themselves in readiness if required, all mounted riflemen, except one company of infantry. The troops were to proceed immediately to the scene of excitement and insurrection.

CHAPTER VIII.

MOB MOVEMENTS IN CALDWELL, DAVIESS AND CARROLL COUNTIES—ARRIVAL OF KIRTLAND CAMP AT FAR WEST.

ABOUT this time [September 12th] sixty or more mobbers entered De Witt* and warned the brethren to leave that place.

Trouble at De Witt Begins.

Friday, 14.—I was at home after three o'clock in the evening.

William Dryden, Justice of the Peace in Daviess county, stated to the Governor, in a long communication, that he had issued a writ against Alanson Ripley, George A. Smith, and others, for assaulting and threatening Adam Black, on the eighth of August last; and that the officer, with a guard of ten men, in attempting to serve the writ, was forcibly driven from the town where the offenders were supposed to be, and that the "Mormons" were so well armed and so numerous in Caldwell and Daviess, that the judicial power of those counties was wholly unable to execute a writ against a "Mormon," and that the "Mormons" held the "institutions of the country in utter contempt," with many more such falsehoods of the blackest kind. Upon this representation Governor Boggs issued an order to General David R. Atchison, of the third Division of Missouri militia, through the Adjutant General, B. M. Lisle, to raise a sufficient force of troops under his command, and aid the civil officers in Daviess county, to execute all writs and other processes, in their charge, and especially assist the officer

Dryden's Report to the Governor.

* De Witt is located in the southeast corner of Carroll county, about fifty miles southeast of Far West, and near the point where Grand river empties into the Missouri. During the summer of 1838 a number of the Saints settled there, some of whom, when the above warning was given, were still encamped in their wagons and tents.

charged with the execution of a writ issued by William Dryden, Justice of the Peace, on the twenty-ninth of August last, for the arrest of Alanson Ripley, George A. Smith and others, and bring the offenders to justice.

The following letter gives a tolerably fair view of the movements of the militia for a few days past:

Doniphan's Report to Atchison.

HEADQUARTERS, FIRST BRIGADE, 3RD DIVISION MISSOURI MILITIA, CAMP AT GRAND RIVER, September 15, 1838.

Major General David R. Atchison, Commanding 3rd Division Missouri Militia:

SIR:—In pursuance of your orders, dated 11th instant, I issued orders to Colonel William A. Dunn, commanding the 28th regiment, to raise four companies of mounted riflemen, consisting of fifty men each; also to Colonel John Boulware, commanding 70th regiment, to raise two companies of mounted riflemen, consisting each of like number to start forthwith for service in the counties of Caldwell and Daviess.

On the same day, Colonel Dunn obtained the four companies of volunteers required from the 28th regiment, and on the morning of the 12th I took the command in person, and marched to the line of Caldwell, at which point, I ordered the colonels to march the regiments to the timber of Crooked river. I then started for Far West, the county seat of Caldwell, accompanied by my aid alone.

On arriving at that place, I found Comer, Miller, and McHoney, the prisoners mentioned in your order. I demanded of the guard, who had them in confinement, to deliver them over to me, which was promptly done. I also found that the guns that had been captured by the Sheriff and citizens of Caldwell, had been distributed and placed in the hands of the soldiery, and scattered over the country; I ordered them to be immediately collected and delivered up to me. I then sent an express to Colonel Dunn to march the regiment by daylight, for that place, where he arrived about seven a. m., making forty miles since ten o'clock, a. m., on the previous day.

When my command arrived, the guns were delivered up, amounting to forty-two stand, three stand could not be produced, as they had probably gone to Daviess county. I sent these guns under a guard to your command in Ray county, together with the prisoner Comer, the other two being citizens of Daviess I retained, and brought with me to this county, and released them on parol of honor, as I conceived their detention illegal.

At eight o'clock a. m., we took up the line of march, and proceeded through Millport in Daviess county, thirty-seven miles from our former encampment, and arrived at the camp of the citizens of Daviess and other adjoining counties, which amounted to between two and three hundred, as their commander, Dr. Austin, of Carroll county, informed me. Your order requiring them to disperse, which had been forwarded in advance of my command, by your aid, James M. Hughes, was read to them, and they were required to disperse. They professed that their object for arming and collecting was solely for defense, but they were marching and counter marching guards out; and myself and others who approached the camp were taken to task and required to wait the approach of the sergeant of the guard. I had an interview with Dr. Austin, and his professions were all pacific. But they still continue in arms, marching and counter marching.

I then proceeded with your aid, J. M. Hughes, and my aid, Benjamin Holliday, to the Mormon encampment commanded by Colonel Lyman Wight. We held a conference with him, and he professed entire willingness to disband and surrender up to me every one of the Mormons accused of crime, and required in return that the hostile forces, collected by the other citizens of the county, should also disband. At the camp commanded by Dr. Austin, I demanded the prisoner, demanded in your order, who had been released on the evening after my arrival in their vicinity.

I took up my line of march, and encamped in the direct road between the two hostile encampments, where I have remained since, within about two and a half miles of Wight's encampment, and sometimes the other camp is nearer, and sometimes further from me. I intend to occupy this position until your arrival, as I deem it best to preserve peace, and prevent an engagement between the parties, and if kept so for a few days, they will doubtless disband without coercion. I have the honor to be, yours with respect,

A. W. DONIPHAN,
Brig-General 1st Brigade, 3rd Division Missouri Militia.

The Prophet's Comment.

By this it is clearly seen that the officers and troops acting under the Governor's orders had very little regard for the laws of the land, otherwise Comer, Miller, and McHoney would not have been discharged by them.

I was at and about home this day, attending to my business as usual.

Sunday, 16.—Held meeting in the afternoon, had

preaching and breaking of bread. I was at home all day with my family.

Monday, 17.—I was counseling with the brethren at home and about the city.

Atchison's Report to the Governor.

HEADQUARTERS 3RD DIVISION, MISSOURI MILITIA,
GRAND RIVER, Sep. 17, 1838,

To His Excellency the Commander-in-Chief:

SIR:—I arrived at the county seat of this county, Daviess, on the evening of the 15th instant, with the troops raised from the militia of Ray county, when I was joined by the troops from Clay county under the command of General Doniphan. In the same neighborhood I found from two to three hundred men in arms, principally from the counties of Livingston, Carroll and Saline. These men were embodied under the pretext of defending the citizens of Daviess county, against the Mormons, and were operating under the orders of a Dr. Austin from Carroll county. The citizens of Daviess, or a large portion of them, residing on each side of Grand river, had left their farms, and removed their families either to the adjoining counties, or collected them together at a place called the Camp Ground. The whole county on the east side of Grand river appears to be deserted, with the exception of a few who are not so timid as their neighbors. The Mormons of Daviess county have also left their farms, and have encamped for safety at a place immediately on the east bank of Grand river, called Adam-ondi-Ahman. The numbers are supposed to be about two hundred and fifty men, citizens of Daviess county, and from fifty to one hundred men, citizens of Caldwell county; both parties have been scouting through the country, and occasionally taking prisoners, and threatening and insulting each other, but as yet no blood has been shed. I have ordered all armed men from adjoining counties to repair to their homes; and Livingston county men, and others, to the amount of one hundred men, have returned, and there remain now about one hundred and fifty, who will, I am in hopes, return in a few days. I have been informed by the Mormons, that all of those who have been charged with a violation of the laws will be in today for trial; when that is done, the troops under my command will be no longer required in this county, if the citizens of other counties will return to their respective homes. I have proposed to leave two companies of fifty men each, in this county, and discharge the remainder of the troops; said two companies will remain for the preservation of order, until peace and confidence are restored. I also enclose to your Excellency the report of General Doniphan, and refer you for particulars to Major Rogers.

I have the honor to be your obedient servant,

D. R. ATCHISON,

Major General 3rd Division Missouri Militia.

Tuesday, 18.—I have been at home all day, considerably unwell, but am somewhat better this evening.

Marching Orders to the Militia.

This day the Governor ordered Captain Childs to have the Boonville Guards mounted, with ten days' provisions, and in readiness to march on his arrival at the end of the week. The Governor also ordered General S. D. Lucas, of the fourth division to march immediately with four hundred mounted men to the scene of difficulty, and co-operate with General Atchison. Similar orders were issued to Major Generals Lewis Bolton, John B. Clark, and Thomas D. Grant.

Wednesday, 19.—I was at and about home.

Thursday, 20.—I was at home until about ten o'clock, when I rode out on horseback. I returned a little before sunset, and was at home through the evening.

Movements of the Militia.

The following extracts from General Atchison's letter of this date, to the Governor, from Liberty, will give a pretty correct view of the movements of the militia:

Excerpts of Atchison's Letter to the Governor.

SIR:—The troops ordered out for the purpose of putting down the insurrection supposed to exist in the counties of Daviess and Caldwell, were discharged on the 20th instant, with the exception of two companies of the Ray militia, now stationed in the county of Daviess, under the command of Brigadier General Parks. It was deemed necessary in the state of excitement in that county that those companies should remain there for a short period longer, say some twenty days, until confidence and tranquility should be restored. All the offenders against the law in that county, against whom process was taken out, were arrested and brought before a court of inquiry, and recognized to appear at the Circuit Court. Mr. Thomas C. Birch attended to the prosecution on the part of the State. The citizens of other counties who came in armed, to the assistance of the citizens of Daviess county, have dispersed and returned to their respective homes, and the Mormons have also returned to their respective homes, so that I consider the insurrection, for the present at least, to be at an end. From the best information I can get, there are about two hundred and fifty Mormon families in Daviess county, nearly one half of the population, and the whole of the Mormon forces in Daviess, Caldwell, and the adjoining counties, is estimated at from thirteen to fifteen hundred men, capable of bearing arms. The Mormons of Daviess county, as I stated in a former report, were encamped in a town called Adam-ondi-Ahman, and are headed by Lyman Wight, a bold, brave, skillful, and I may add, a desperate man; they appeared to be acting on the defensive, and I must further add, gave up the offenders with a good deal of promptness. The arms taken by the Mormons, and prisoners were also given up upon demand, with seeming cheerfulness.

The mob this day again threatened De Witt.

Friday, 21.—I was about home.

Saturday, 22.—I went out early in the morning, returned to breakfast at half past seven, and took an airing on horseback at nine in the morning.

Petition of the Saints of De Witt to Governor Boggs.

DE WITT, CARROLL COUNTY, STATE OF MISSOURI,
September 22, 1838.

To His Excellency Lilburn W. Boggs, Governor of the State of Missouri:

Your Petitioners, citizens of the county of Carroll, do hereby petition your Excellency, praying for relief: That whereas, your petitioners have on the 20th instant, been sorely aggrieved, by being beset by a lawless mob, certain inhabitants of this and other counties, to the injury of the good citizens of this and the adjacent places; that on the aforesaid day, there came from one hundred to one hundred and fifty armed men, and threatened with force and violence, to drive certain peaceable citizens from their homes, in defiance of all law, and threatened then to drive said citizens out of the county, but, on deliberation, concluded to give them, said citizens, till the first of October next, to leave said county; and threatened, if not gone by that time, to exterminate them, without regard to age or sex, and destroy their chattels, by throwing them into the river. We therefore pray you to take such steps as shall put a stop to all lawless proceeding; and we, your Petitioners, will ever pray, &c.

Benj. Kendrick. John Tillford,
Dudley Thomas, H. G. Sherwood,

William P. Lundow,	John Murdock,
Jno. Kendrick,	G. M. Hinkle,
Thos. Dehart,	James Valance,
Francis Brown,	Jabez Lake,
Albert Loree	H. M. Wallace,
Samuel Lake,	D. Thomas, (non-(Mormon,
Asa Manchester,	
Wm. Winston,	Nathan Harrison,
John Clark,	Elizabeth Smith,
Thos. Hollingshead,	Henry Root,
Asa W. Barnes,	A. L. Caldwell,
Elijah T. Rogers,	Rufus Allen,
John Dougherty,	Ezekiel Barnes,
Moses Harris,	D. H. Barnes,
Perry Thayer,	Wm. S. Smith,
B. B. Bartley,	James Hampton,
Jonathan Harris,	Robert Hampton,
Wm. J. Hatfield,	Jonathan Hampton,
Oliver Olney,	George Peacock,
John Thorp,	Daniel Clark,
H. T. Chipman,	John Proctor,
David Dixon,	James McGuin,
Benj. Hensley,	Smith Humphrey,

Franklin N. Thayer.

Sunday, 23.—I attended meeting both forenoon and afternoon, and was at home in the evening.

Monday, 24.—I was at home until half-past eight a. m., when I rode out on horseback, and returned about five in the evening.

The governor, having heard that peace had been restored in Daviess and Caldwell counties, ordered Generals Clark, Crowther, Lewis, and Bolton to discharge their troops. The order was dated at Jonesborough.

General Parks' Report to Governor Boggs.

Tuesday, 25.—General Parks wrote the governor from Mill Port, that he had been in the upper part of Daviess county to assist the constable in bringing offenders to justice, and that the major-general, with the troops from Ray and Clay counties on the 18th instant, (except two companies from

Ray under his command) were disbanded. In this letter General Parks said:

Whatever may have been the disposition of the people called Mormons, before our arrival here, since we have made our appearance they have shown no disposition to resist the laws, or of hostile intentions. There has been so much prejudice and exaggeration concerned in this matter, that I found things entirely different from what I was prepared to expect. When we arrived here, we found a large body of men from the counties adjoining, armed and in the field, for the purpose, as I learned, of assisting the people of this county against the Mormons, without being called out by the proper authorities.

P. S.—Since writing the above, I received information that if the committee do not agree,* the determination of the Daviess county men is to drive the Mormons with powder and lead.

The same day, General Parks wrote General Atchison as follows:

I am happy to be able to state to you, that the deep excitement existing between the parties, has in a great degree ceased; and so far I have had no occasion to resort to force, in assisting the constables. On tomorrow, a committee from Daviess county meets a committee of the Mormons at Adam-ondi-Ahman, to propose to them to buy or sell, and I expect to be there.

Wednesday, 26.—Fifteen or twenty of the Mormons were cited to trial at Gallatin where Lyman Wight has pledged himself to me that they will attend.

I was at home until ten or eleven o'clock in the morning, when I rode out, and returned home and spent the evening.

The mob committee met a committee of the brethren, and the brethren entered into an agreement to purchase all the lands and possessions of those who desired to sell and leave Daviess county. The High Council of Adam-ondi-Ahman was immediately called and Elders Don C. Smith, George A. Smith, Lorenzo D. Barnes and Harrison Sagers were appointed to go immediately to the churches in the south and east and raise men and means to fulfill the contract. The commit-

Agreement to Buy Out the Mob.

*This has reference to the committee appointed by the respective parties to negotiate terms for buying or selling on the part either of the mob or the Saints.

tee arrived at Far West late in the evening, and called upon me and gave me the foregoing information. I approved of the action of the brethren.

Thursday, *27*.—I was home and about the city.

Extract of a Letter from General Atchison to Governor Boggs, Dated—

LIBERTY, September 27th, 1838.

The force under General Parks is deemed sufficient to execute the laws and keep the peace in Daviess county. Things are not so bad in that county as represented by rumor, and, in fact, from affidavits I have no doubt your Excellency has been deceived by the exaggerated statements of designing or half crazy men. I have found there is no cause of alarm on account of the Mormons; they are not to be feared; they are very much alarmed.

Friday, *28*.—I was about home until near sundown, when I rode out.

Elder John E. Page arrived at De Witt with his Canada company sometime this week.

Saturday, *29*.—I rode out on horseback, returning about three in the afternoon and spent the evening at home.

Sunday, *30*.—I left home about ten o'clock in the morning.

Monday, *October 1*.—I returned home about five o'clock where I tarried the remainder of the evening. The mob having left Daviess county (after they were organized into a militia by Atchison, Doniphan and Parks and disbanded) went to Carroll county and gathered at De Witt, threatening vengeance to the Saints without regard to age, sex or condition; but Daviess county was for a season freed from those peace disturbers.

Mob Activities Shifted to De Witt.

Tuesday, *2*.—The mob pressed harder upon De Witt and fired upon the Saints.

The Kirtland Camp arrived in Far West from Kirtland. I went in company with Sidney Rigdon, Hyrum Smith, Isaac Morley and George W. Robinson, and met them some miles out, and escorted them into the city, where they encamped on the

Arrival of Kirtland Camp at Far West.

public square directly south, and close by the excavation for the Lord's House. Here friends greeted friends in the name of the Lord. Isaac Morley, Patriarch at Far West, furnished a beef for the camp. President Rigdon provided a supper for the sick, and the brethren provided for them like men of God, for they were hungry, having eaten but little for several days, and having traveled eleven miles this day; eight hundred and sixty miles from Kirtland, the way the camp traveled.

CHAPTER IX.

THE ORGANIZATION AND JOURNEY OF KIRTLAND CAMP.*

At a meeting of the Seventies in the House of the Lord in Kirtland, on the sixth day of March, 1838, the moving of the Saints from Kirtland to the land of Missouri, in accordance with the commandments and revelations of God, was spoken of and also the practicability of the quorum of the Seventies locating in as compact a body as possible in some stake of Zion in the west, where they could meet together when they were not laboring in the vineyard of the Lord; and also could receive counsel from the Twelve and the First Presidency in matters pertaining to their mission to the nations with greater facilities than they would if scattered here and there over all the face of the land.

The Meeting of the Seventies.

The subject was discussed at some length, and a resolution was passed requesting the Councilors to consult together and make a report on the subject at the next meeting of the quorum. The meeting was then adjourned to Saturday, the 10th instant, at one o'clock p. m.

At that time the quorum met again and the Presidents reported that they had consulted together on the subject referred to them at the last meeting, and that they were of the opinion that the subject should be laid before the First Presidency of the Church for their counsel and advice; and also if it would be thought expedient to appoint the place for their location in Far West or some other place where it should seem good unto them.

The Report of the Presidents.

The measures proposed by the Councilors were unanimously approved of by the members of the quorum pres-

* This chapter and the one following contain the uninterrupted history of Kirtland camp promised at p. 42, and is taken from the camp's daily journal, kept by the late Judge Elias Smith.

ent. The Presidents further stated that they had taken into consideration the extreme poverty of the Seventies in Kirtland and vicinity, and that it seemed to them almost an impossible thing for the quorum [as such] to move from this place under existing circumstances; that the measures entered into by the High Council and High Priests for removing the Saints had failed and they had given up making any further attempts after their scheme of going by water had fallen through, and that they had further advised every individual of the Church wishing to go up unto Zion to look out for himself individually and make the best of it he could.

To Move in a Body not Thought Practicable.

Much was said on the subject; and while the subject of going up in a body—which seemed to be the prevailing desire of the members present—was under discussion, the Spirit of the Lord came down in mighty power, and some of the Elders began to prophesy that if the quorum would go up in a body together, and go according to the commandments and revelations of God, pitching their tents by the way, that they should not want for anything on the journey that would be necessary for them to have; and further that there should be nothing wanting towards removing the whole quorum of Seventies that would go in a body, but that there should be a sufficiency of all things for carrying such an expedition into effect.

The Subject Discussed.

President James Foster arose in turn to make some remarks on the the subject, and in the course of his address he declared that he saw a vision in which was shown unto him a company (he should think of about five hundred) starting from Kirtland and going up to Zion. That he saw them moving in order, encamping in order by the way, and that he knew thereby that it was the will of God that the quorum should go up in that manner.

Foster's Vision.

The Spirit bore record of the truth of his assertions for

it rested down on the assembly in power, insomuch that all present were satisfied that it was the will of God that the quorum should go up in a company together to the land of Zion, and that they should proceed immediately to make preparations for the journey. The Councilors were requested to devise the best course to be pursued to carry the plan into effect, and the meeting adjourned to Tuesday, 13th, at one p. m.

"God Wills It."

In the forenoon of that day the Council of the Seventies met and invited President Hyrum Smith, and sent for President William Marks, but he was not at home, and consequently did not attend. Benjamin S. Wilber, in absence of the clerk, was invited to act as clerk *pro tem.* After the meeting was opened by President Hyrum Smith by prayer, they proceeded to draw up under the supervision of President Smith the outlines of the following Constitution for the organization and government of the camp, which was adopted at the meeting in the afternoon.*

Meeting of the 13th of March.

At the time appointed in the afternoon the quorum met according to adjournment. Several of the High Council and High Priests attended the meeting. The Spirit of God was manifested as before. The subject was discussed and the Constitution presented, which was approved by the quorum and by the visiting Elders who testified that the movement was of God and recommended it to the brethren of the Church; and said that they should lay the subject immediately before their own quorums. On motion it was resolved that two of the quorum should be appointed to act as members of the Council, *pro tem*, in the place of Daniel S. Miles and Levi Hancock—who were then in the west—till the camp should arrive at Far West. This to be in accordance with the first article of the Constitution, which recognized the whole seven [First Seven Presidents of the Seventy] as councilors of the camp.

Presidents *pro tem.* Appointed.

* See page 90.

On motion it was resolved that the President of Seventies should have the right of nominating the two assistant councilors and all other officers of the camp required by the Constitution, or on the journey, up to the land of Zion. In accordance with the above resolution Elias Smith, clerk of the Council, and Benjamin S. Wilber, were nominated and received the unanimous vote of the quorum as Councilors of the camp. The Constitution was read and explained to the meeting item by item, that there might be no misunderstanding concerning any part of it or of the motives and designs of the Seventies in the movement then in agitation; and those who subscribed to the Constitution were exhorted to make all preparations in their power to carry into effect the object of the camp, and the meeting was adjourned to Saturday, 17th, at one p. m.

Power of Nominating Officers Vested in First Council.

The Constitution.

The council of the Seventies met this day in the attic story of the Lord's House and took into consideration the propriety and necessity of the body of the Seventies going up to the land of Zion in a company together the present season, and adopted the following rules and laws, for the organization and government of the camp:

First—That the Presidents of the Seventies, seven in number, shall be the Councilors [i. e. leaders] of the camp; and that there shall be one man appointed as treasurer, who shall by the advice of the Councilors manage the financial concerns during the journey, and keep a just and accurate account of all monies received and expended for the use of the camp.

Second—That there shall be one man appointed to preside over each tent, to take charge of it; and that from the time of their appointment the tent-men shall make all necessary arrangements for the providing of teams and tents for the journey; and they shall receive counsel and advice from the Councilors; and furthermore, shall see that cleanliness and decency are observed in all cases, the commandments kept, and the Word of Wisdom heeded, that is, no tobacco, tea, coffee, snuff or ardent spirits of any kind are to be taken internally.

Third—That every man shall be the head of his own family, and shall see that they are brought into subjection according to the order of the camp.

Fourth—That all those who shall subscribe to the resolutions, rules and regulations, shall make every exertion, and use all lawful means to provide for themselves and their families, and for the use and benefit of the camp to which they belong; and also to hand over to the Seven Councilors all monies appropriated for that purpose on or before the day the camp shall start.

Fifth—That the money shall be retained in the hands of the Councilors, being divided proportionately among them for safety and to be paid over to the Treasurer as circumstances may require.

Sixth—That any faithful brethren wishing to journey with us can do so by subscribing to, and observing these rules and regulations.

Seventh—That every individual shall at the end of the journey—when a settlement is to be made, or as soon thereafter as their circumstances will admit—pay their proportional part of the expenses of the journey. By expenses it is understood all that is necessarily paid out for the use of a team, wagon or cow, if they safely arrive at the place where the camp shall finally break up.

Eighth—That these rules and laws shall be strictly observed, and every person who shall behave disorderly and not conform to them shall be disfellowshiped by the camp and left by the wayside.

Ninth—That this shall be the law of the camp in journeying from this place up to the land of Zion, and that it may be added unto or amended as circumstances may require by the voice of those who shall subscribe unto it.

[The names of the persons and number in their respective families, who subscribed to the foregoing constitution].

NAME	NO. IN FAMILY	NAME	NO. IN FAMILY
James Foster	6	Eleazer King, Jun.	3
Josiah Butterfield	4	Thomas G. Fisher	4
Zerah Pulsipher	7	Alfred Brown	2
Joseph Young	5	Stephen Headlock	2
Henry Harriman	2	John R. Folger	4
Elias Smith	3	Nathan K. Knight	9
W. S. Wilbur	2	Joel Judd	3
Joshua S. Holman	8	Thomas Nickerson	4
J. D. Parker	3	Brother Nickerson's family	5
Duncan McArthur	9	David D. Demming	2
Stephen Starks	6	Nancy Richerson	3
Anson Call	3	Joseph McCaseland	4
Amos B. Fuller	3	Hiram H. Byington	4
Jeremiah Willey	4	David Gray	8

Hiram Dayton......................12
Truman O. Angell................ 4
Dominicus Carter................. 6
Jonathan H. Holmer............. 3
J. B. Noble.......................... 7
Levi B. Wilder..................... 6
James S. Holmon................. 7
Amos Nickerson.................... 6
Lewis Eager......................... 3
Stephen Shumway 3
Enoch S. Sanborn................ 5
Jonathan Crosby.................. 2
Jonathan Hampton............... 4
Otis Shumway...................... 7
Frederick M. Vanleuven......... 6
Benjamin Butterfield 7
Eleazer King. 7
John Tanner.........................10
Alanson Pettingill................ 5
William Perry 4
Warren Smith....................... 7
Samuel Barnet...................... 5
William Carpenter................ 5
John Greabble...................... 8
Arnold Healey...................... 3
Joel Harvey......................... 5
Justin Blood......................... 5
Reuben Daniels.................... 7
Jonas Putnam............... 6
Daniel Pulsipher.................. 4
Charles Thompson................ 2
Nathan B. Baldwin................ 2
Michael Griffith.................... 6
Henry Stevens...................... 3
Levi Osgood......................... 5
Cyrus B. Fisher.................... 6
Elijah Merriam...................... 2
Samuel Hale......................... 3
Martin Hanchet.................... 5
Orin Cheney......................... 9
George Stringham................. 6
Mary Parker 4
Julia Johnson....................... 8
Alexander Wright................. 1
Adonijah Cooley................... 5
Elijah Cheney........................ 2
Jesse Baker........................... 2
Elias Pulsipher..... 8
Jason Brunett........................ 7
E. B. Gayland........................ 6
Samuel Fowler...................... 8
David K. Dustin. 2
Charles Bird.......................... 7
Thomas Butterfield............... 3
William Field..................... .. 5
William Shuman.................... 7
Cornelius Vanleuven............. 3
Benjamin K. Hull....... 6
Oliver Olney............... 9
William Bosley...................... 2
Joseph Pine........................... 6
Noah Packard........................ 9
John M. King........................ 4
Jonathan Dunham.................. 4
Joel H. Johnson..................... 6
Austin W. Cowles................... 9
Jonathan H. Hale.................. 5
George W. Brooks.................. 4
Abraham Wood..................... 4
Shearman A. Gilbert............. 3
William B. Pratt.................... 4
Samuel Parker....................... 4
Daniel Bowen........................ 7
Richard Brasier...................... 4
John Pulsipher. 2
Alba Whittle.......................... 6
Joel Drury............................. 5
Jonathan Fisher..................... 5
Benjamin Baker 6
Amasa Cheney....................... 6
Josiah Miller..........................10
Amos Baldwin........................12
John Sweat........ 10
Daniel Allen, Jun.................. 4
Stephen Richardson............... 8
Martin H. Peck......... 6

Zemira Draper...................... 6
Isaac Rogers........................ 4
Abram Boynton...................... 7
Michael McDonald................. 5
James Brown......................... 7
Alexander Campbell..............
Joseph C. Clark..................... 6
Jared Porter.......................... 3
William Earl.........................11
Daniel Bliss........................... 2
Isaac W. Pierce 5
Jabez Lake............................ 5
Samuel Mulliner..................... 5
Aaron M. York....................... 4
James Strop.......................... 6
Reuben Hedlock..................... 8
Andrew Lamereaux............... 7
William Wilson....................... 3
John Carter........................... 2
Samuel Parker....................... 4
Isaac Dewitt.......................... 8
Hiram Griffiths...................... 3
John Hamond........................ 6
Arnold Stevens...................... 6
Gardner Snow........................ 3
George Snow......................... 2
Thomas Draper.....................
Abram Bond.......................... 3
John Lameraux....................... 6
Jesse P. Harmon 6
John Vanleuven, Jun............ 9
Aaron Cheney........................ 6
Nathan Cheney...................... 4
Edwin P. Merriam.. 3
Henry Munroe....................... 3
Ira P. Thornton..................... 7
Oliver Rowe.......................... 6
Stephen Rowe....................... 6
John Thorp 7
Daniel L. Nuptire.................. 3
William Gribble..................... 3
Charles N. Baldwin............... 2
William Draper, Sen.............. 2
Laban Morris........................ 2
Lucius N. Scovil................... 4
Aaron Johnson...................... 4
Joseph Coon 4
Nathan Staker....................... 6
Asa Wright...........................10
Zephaniah W. Brewster......... 9
Munro Crosier....................... 2
Asaph Blanchard.................. 1
Ethan A. Moore.................... 8
William Carey.......................
James Lethead......................
John Rulison......................... 8

March 17.—Met again agreeable to adjournment in the attic story of the Lord's House, at 1 p. m. A general attendance of those belonging to the camp and many others belonging to the different quorums of the Church came in. The room was full to overflowing. Elder Josiah Butterfield, presided. After opening by prayer the object of the meeting was stated by the chairman, viz., the removing of the Saints to Zion. Elder James Foster next laid before the meeting the movements of the Seventies in relation to that desired object and was followed by Elders Joseph Young, Henry Harriman, Zera Pulsipher, and by others of the different quorums, who highly ap-

The Movement Commended.

proved of the proceedings of the quorum of Seventies in relation to the order of removing and of the organization of the camp. The Constitution was read by the clerk, which was spoken of in terms of commendation by all who spoke. Much of the Spirit of God was manifested on this occasion and the hearts of all made glad in anticipation of their deliverance from Kirtland.

Hyrum Smith on Previous Movements.

President Hyrum Smith came in and addressed the meeting at some length on the movements of the Saints in Kirtland in relation to their emigration to the land of Zion since the commandment had gone forth for the honest in heart to rise up and go up unto that land. He stated that what he had said and done in reference to chartering a steamboat, for the purpose of removing the Church as a body, he had done according to his own judgment without reference to the testimony of the Spirit of God; that he had recommended that course and had advised the High Council and High Priests to adopt that measure, acting solely by his own wisdom, for it had seemed to him that the whole body of the Church in Kirtland could be removd with less expense in the way he had proposed than in any other. He said further that the Saints had to act oftentimes upon their own responsibility without any reference to the testimony of the Spirit of God in relation to temporal affairs, that he has so acted in this matter and has never had any testimony from God that the plan of going by water was approved of by Him, and that the failure of the scheme was evidence in his mind that God did not approve of it.

Hyrum Smith Commends the Seventies.

He then declared that he knew by the Spirit of God that the movements that were making by the quorum of the Seventies for their removal and the plan of their journeying was according to the will of the Lord. He advised all who were calculating to go up to Zion at present, whose circumstances would admit, to join with the Seventies in their plan and go up with them; and if he were so situated that he could join the camp himself and go with them, he would do so, and strictly comply with the rules which had been adopted for the regulation of the camp on the journey. It would be his delight to go as an individual without having any concern whatever in the management of affairs, either directly or indirectly, during the journey.

Advantage of a Large Company.

In answer to an inquiry that was made about the difficulties that might attend the movements of so large a body, he observed that no fears need be entertained by any on that score, for there would no difficulty attend the camp, if there should be 5,000 persons in it. The more the better; and the advantages of their going altogether would be greater than they could possibly be if they should go in small companies, as provisions and other necessities could be purchased in large quantities much cheaper than they could by small squads who would be under the necessity of buying at great disadvantage.

Caution as to the Word of Wisdom.

After advising the camp not to be too particular in regard to the Word of Wisdom and advised them to have the assistance of the High Council in carrying the plan into execution, and giving other advice about organizing the camp, President Hyrum Smith retired.

The Constitution being read again, about forty who did not belong to the quorum of Seventies came forward and subscribed their names to it, making in all about eighty. The meeting was then adjourned to Tuesday, March 20th, at 1 p. m.

Practical Steps.

March 20.—In the afternoon the Seven Councilors met to consult on the best measures to be pursued for procuring teams and tents and other things necessary for the journey. After considering the subject carefully it was thought that two good teams and one tent, if no more could be obtained, would suffice for eighteen persons; and that it would be advisable to appoint the overseers of tents at the meeting to be held in the afternoon, whose duty according to the Constitution would be to form their companies of eighteen, or as near that number as circumstances will admit of, and proceed immediately to procure teams and a tent for the same, and to make all necessary arrangements for the journey.

Elders Oliver Granger, Mayhew Hillman and Harvey Redfield and some others attended who were requested to express their views of the expedition, as a rumor had gone forth that they considered it an impracticable undertaking and one that would never be accomplished. Elder Granger said that he considered it would be the greatest thing ever accomplished since the organization of the Church or even since the exodus of Israel from Egypt if the Saints in Kirtland, considering their poverty, should succeed in going from that place in a body, and that it would require great wisdom and prudence and the most determined perseverance to effect such a measure, though he considered it possible to do it and believed God would bless them in so doing.

Views of Oliver Granger *et al.*

Elder Redfield spoke at some length and said that in consequence of the rumors which were afloat he had thought the Seventies were taking unwarrantable ground, and had expressed his views freely on the subject, and rather justified himself on that score, though he condemned the principle of believing reports which were put in circulation without first considering their foundation and the source from which they came. He said he was convinced that the things he had heard were untrue concerning some movements which he had heard the Seventies were making, and the declarations and denunciations they gave some of the other quorums, which had come to his ears, were likewise without foundation. He said he was heart and hand with the Council of the Seventies in their endeavors to remove the Saints in Kirtland to the land of Zion, and the Spirit testified to him that the movements were in righteousness and according to the will of God.

Elder Hillman spoke in confirmation of what his brethren had said, approved of the movement and said that the High Priests and High Council had at a meeting held a day or two previous passed a resolution to uphold and support the Seventies in their undertaking.

A selection of names for overseers of tents was made and the meeting adjourned.

Admonitions.

At one p. m. the members of the camp and others who attended met in the upper court of the Lord's House. Elder Henry Harriman presided, and opened by prayer. He also addressed the meeting, followed by Elder Foster, both setting forth the greatness of the undertaking in hand, of the necessity of every individual bestirring himself and making every exertion to prepare for the journey. The names of those who had signed the Constitution were read over, that if there were any objection against their going in the camp in consequence of any difficulty that might exist or of disobedience to the commandments of the Lord it might be made manifest by those who might know of the existence of any such thing.

The names of those selected for overseers of tents were read over one by one and were voted in by the voice of the camp, and Jonathan H. Hale was appointed treasurer, and the meeting was then adjourned.

Sundry Meetings and the Object of Them.

After the 20th of March the Council met often to counsel on the things which from time to time pressed themselves upon their attention relative to the preparation necessary for the journey, things both spiritual and temporal; and to ask counsel and give their advice that they might decide in righteousness all things pertaining to their calling and the affairs of the camp, and to implore their heavenly Father to provide means to soften the hearts of the enemies of the Saints, in Kirtland, and in the region round about:

that His people might be delivered from their power, as they have fallen into the hands of their enemies like Israel of old, in consequence of disobedience and their slowness of heart to obey the commandments of the Lord which He had given unto them; and that He would have mercy upon them and deliver them from bondage in this land, that they might go up to the land of Zion according to the commandments and revelations of the Lord by His servant Joseph Smith, Jun., and according to the pattern given unto them.

In these meetings for counsel and prayer God truly verified His promises; for when His servants asked they received, and His Spirit was poured out upon them abundantly, from time to time manifesting the will of the Lord concerning the movements necessary to be made in order to carry the arduous undertaking into effect, in removing the quorum of Seventies, and those that joined with them, from Kirtland to the land of Zion.

Difficulties Encountered.

The extreme poverty of the majority of those belonging to the camp and the depression of their spirits in consequence thereof and the downfall of Kirtland; the opposition of those who had dissented from the Church and of those who from the beginning had opposed the commandments of God which He had established in the last days among the children of men, and last of all, though not least, the opposition of many who called themselves Saints, were obstacles which presented themselves in formidable aspect against the exertions of the Council to bring about the order of things to be entered into in order to accomplish the work, and to unite the feelings of the brethren and to restore their confidence in each other, which had in a great measure been lost during the past year, or since the failure of their imaginary means of speculation, of grandeur and wealth.

Thursday, July 5.—The camp commenced organizing on a piece of land in the rear of the house formerly occupied by Mayhew Hillman, about one hundred rods south of the

House of the Lord, in Kirtland. The morning was beautiful. At an early hour the heavens were overspread with a cloud which continued to hide the scorching rays of the sun till towards evening, when it moved away. The horizon at every point that was unobstructed by intervening objects was clear, and everything seemed to indicate that the God of heaven has His all-searching eye upon the camp of the Saints, and had prepared the day for the express purpose of organizing the camp, that the Saints might start on their journey in the order which had been shown in the beginning. About twenty tents were pitched in the course of the day and several other companies came on late who had not time to pitch their tents. Many spectators from the towns round about came to behold the scene, and, with few exceptions, they behaved with the greatest decorum. The day was solemn to all concerned and the greatest solemnity was visible on the countenances of the Saints who expected to tarry for a season in Kirtland, and also on the countenances of many of the unbelievers in the everlasting Gospel of Jesus Christ and of the great work of the gathering of the Saints of the Most High in these last days of wickedness before God's judgments shall have been poured out without measure upon the wicked, to sweep them off from the face of the earth.

Assembling of the Camp.

Between four and five hundred of the camp tented on the ground during the night. The spectators retired at a late hour and left the camp in quietude. The night was clear and the encampment and all around was solemn as eternity; which scene, together with the remembrance of those other scenes through which the Saints in Kirtland had passed during the last two years all presented themselves to the thinking mind; and, together with the greatness of the undertaking, the length of the journey, and many other things combined, could not fail to awaken sensations that could be better felt than described.

Solemn Reflections.

Friday, July 6.—At an early hour in the morning the

people began to assemble to witness the exodus of the camp, and several hundred persons had gathered together before all things could be arranged in order to move off from the ground without confusion, all of which consumed most of the forenoon. At twelve o'clock, noon, the camp began to move, and at half-past twelve the whole company had left the ground in order, and took up their line of march towards Chester, south from Kirtland, where they encamped at six o'clock p. m., a distance of seven miles from Kirtland.

The Start.

After the tents were pitched and all things arranged an enumeration of the camp was taken, when it was ascertained that there were in the camp 529 souls present—a few necessarily absent—of which 256 were males, and 273 females. There were 105 families, all on the ground excepting five, which had not time to get ready in season to start with the camp, two of which came up in the evening; of the others Elder Martin H. Peck joined at Petersburgh; the other two, Elders S. Shumway and Brother Charles Wood, joined the camp at the same place a few hours after. President William Marks and some other brethren from Kirtland accompanied the camp to Chester, and on parting with the Councilors blessed them, in the name of the Lord, and left his blessing with them, and with the camp, covenanting to uphold them by the prayer of faith and required the same of the Councilors and of the brethren of the camp.

Number in the Camp.

The feelings of the brethren on leaving Kirtland and parting with those who were left behind were somewhat peculiar, notwithstanding the scenes they had passed through in Kirtland; but the consciousness of doing the will of their heavenly Father, and obeying His commandments in journeying to Zion, over balanced every other consideration that could possibly be presented to their minds, and buoyed up their spirits, and helped them to overcome the weaknesses and infirmities

Sorrow at Parting.

of human nature which men are subject to here on the earth.

Saturday, July 7.—Started from Chester about half-past six in the morning, and camped in Aurora, Portage county—thirteen miles from Chester—at four p. m., on the farm of Mr. Lacey. The road between Chester and Aurora, through Russell and Bainbridge, in Geauga county, was bad and somewhat hilly. The weather being extremely warm and the camp not being sufficiently accustomed to moving and acting in concert, all contributed to make some confusion in the camp during the latter part of the day. One wagon, Andrew Lamereaux's, broke down twice and some other small accidents happened, but nothing very serious. During the day several children were sick, some dangerously so, and some adults were attacked by the destroyer.

First Experiences.

Sunday, July 8.—Public worship at eleven o'clock, Elder Joseph Young preached. Many came in the course of the day to visit the camp. They generally treated us with great civility, though there were some exceptions. In the afternoon about half-past five the heads of families were called together and were instructed by Elders Foster, Pulsipher, Butterfield and Dunham to keep their families in more strict subjection to the laws of God, and to adhere strictly to the Constitution of the camp. They were told that the destroyer was in the camp and some would fall victims to his power if they did not comply with the requisitions of the Lord.

A Renewal of Covenants.

A vote was called and the camp covenanted anew strictly to observe the laws of the camp and the commandments of the Lord. Soon after night-fall a company of marauders were heard about the camp, but we were not molested during the night.

Monday, July 9.—At seven in the morning the camp began to move, passed through the village of Aurora, through the corner of Streetsborough to Hudson, a handsome village, in which is situ-

Incidents of a Day.

ated the "Western Reserve College." Stopped at one o'clock near the south line of that town. David Elliot broke his wagon down near Streetsborough, and Samuel Hale's wagon tongue was broken a little south of the village of Hudson. The fourth division of the camp came up about two o'clock, at which time the first moved on and passed through Stowe Corners, so called, across the Pittsburgh and Akron canal (which is yet in an unfinished state at the falls on the Cuyahoga river, which empties into Lake Erie at Cleveland), and encamped for the night on Mr. Camp's farm, at Talmadge, at half-past six in the evening. The first, second and third divisions came on to the grounds together, the fourth, composed chiefly of ox teams, did not come up till ten o'clock. The roads were generally good, the country level, with few exceptions, the weather extremely warm, but nearly all withstood the fatigue of the day with fortitude and patience, feeling thankful for the blessings which the Lord bestowed upon the camp of His Saints.

The country through which we passed this day was better adapted to pasturage than tillage, the grass generally looked well, some fine fields of wheat were seen which had began to whiten for the harvest.

Joel H. Johnson's oxen failed and were left behind, and some others were very much fatigued and did not arrive at the encampment until late at night. Traveled twenty miles, which was three or four more than we should have done if accommodations for the teams could have been obtained short of that distance.

Tuesday, *Juld 10.*—Before starting the Council drew up the following resolutions for the further organization of the camp, which were unanimously adopted:

Additional Camp Regulations.

Resolved—First. That the engineer of the camp shall receive advice from the Councilors concerning the duties of his office, and that he shall call on his assistants to perform those duties which he cannot attend to himself, and that he shall be relieved from the arduous task of [personally] superintending the movements of the camp during the journey.

Second—That the horn shall be blown for rising at four o'clock, and at twenty minutes past four for prayer every morning, at which time each overseer shall see that the inmates of his tent are in order, that worship may commence throughout the camp at the same time, immediately after the blowing of the horn.

Third—That the head of each division shall keep a roll of all able-bodied men, and that he shall call out as many men each night as the engineer shall require of his division to stand on guard. One-half of which guard shall stand the fore part of the night, and the other the latter part, being regularly relieved by the engineer or one of his assistants at one o'clock in the morning.

Fourth—That every company in the camp is entitled to an equal proportion of the milk whether the cows are owned by the individuals of the several tents or not, and that it shall be so distributed, as near as may be, among the several companies in the camp.

Fifth—That Thomas Butterfield shall be appointed herdsman of the camp, whose duty it shall be to superintend the driving of the cows and other stock, and to see that they are well taken care of on the journey, and that he shall call on as many as shall be necessary to assist him in performing those duties.

Sixth—That in no case at present shall the camp move more than fifteen miles in one day, unless circumstances shall absolutely require it.

Joel H. Johnson sold one of his oxen for ten dollars, the other came up with the camp.

The First Deserter.

The camp began to move at nine o'clock and passed through the village of Talmadge, one mile, then turned southwest to Middleburg, a fine village situated on a branch of the Cuyahoga, three miles from Talmadge, and encamped for the night in the town of Coventry, about one mile from the village of Akron, which is situated on the Ohio and Erie canal. At twelve o'clock, for the purpose of lightening our loads, we left some of our goods on the canal boats to be conveyed by water. The wind rose high and the roads were dusty which made it hard traveling on account of the dust. In the afternoon we had a small shower of rain, the first that had fallen since the camp started Benjamin Butterfield left the camp in the morning and started off by himself. Traveled this day six miles. Brother John Hammond broke his wagon, the only accident.

Wednesday, July 11.—After the goods that were to be sent by water were conveyed to Akron, the camp moved on, all but the first division which waited to attend to the burial of Brother and Sister Wilbur's little son, aged six months and twelve days, who died at 11 o'clock a. m. and was interred in an orchard on the farm of Israel Allen in Coventry, at 2 p. m. He had been sick two or three days, and some other children in the camp had also been sick, but all recovered excepting Brother Wilbur's son. Passed this day through New Portage on the Ohio canal, which we crossed two or three miles below that place, and encamped on the farm of Mr. Bockmans, in Chippeway township, county of Wayne. A heavy shower of rain fell in the afternoon and the whole company got thoroughly wet for the first time since we started; but very few complained, however, and all retired to rest wet and weary after the usual duties of the evening were ended.

The First Death.

The country through which we passed this day was somewhat uneven and swampy. Near New Portage it is low and to all appearance must be quite unhealthful. The crops of wheat, corn and grass look well, the wheat being generally about ripe and ready to harvest. John Hammond broke his wagon again today and was left behind to repair it, and did not get up to the encampment at night. Traveled this day eleven miles.

Thursday, July 12.—Left the encampment at half-past eight; passed through the village of Doylestown, situated on a hill in the township of Chippeway. Crossed Chippeway creek; some of the headwaters of the Muskingum river came through the township of Milton, where we stopped at one p. m. to feed. Then passed through the township of Green into Wayne, and encamped on the farm of Mr. ———,

Nature of the Country Traversed.

two miles from Wooster, at seven in the evening. The road was rough in some places, in some places stony, and, in consequence of the shower of rain which fell the day before, in some places muddy.

The country through which we passed today is somewhat hilly, the soil productive and the crops of wheat, corn and oats look fine and beautiful. Timber, principally of oak, with some chestnut and some other kinds of forest trees, is scattered here and there.

Difficulties by the way.

John Hammond overtook us in the morning on horseback, his wagon had broken again, the third time, so it could not be easily mended. The Council advised him to go back and get the brethren residing near New Portage to assist him in exchanging it for another, or let him have one to go up to Zion with, and have it returned to them, as he had now fallen so far behind that we could not well assist him without hindering many others.

Nathan B. Baldwin broke one of his wagon tires, and Henry Harriman one of his axle-trees, and stopped near Chippeway creek to have them mended. Brother Baldwin came up in the evening and Henry Harriman the next morning.

It rained a little in the course of the day, the air was cool and the horses and oxen performed the journey with greater ease than any other day since the camp started. Traveled in the course of the day about seventeen miles.

Descriptions of Country.

Friday, July 13.—The fourth division left the encampment about eight o'clock, the third and second followed, and the first left at nine. Passed through Wooster, the county seat of Wayne county, a large and beautiful village surrounded by a fertile country and is a place of considerable business. There are eight or ten public houses and several synagogues for worship, and many other commodious and elegant buildings in the village which is in Wayne township.

At Wooster we took the road to Mansfield, west from

Wooster thirty-three miles. Passed through the village of Jefferson, a small place in the township of Plain, thence to Reedsborough in Mohican township, and encamped a little after five p. m. on the farm of William Crothers, in Mohican, thirteen miles from Wooster, making this day sixteen miles.

The country west of Wooster is rather hilly, some beautiful flats on the creeks, though not in so good a state of cultivation as in many other places. Crossed Apple creek east of Wooster, and Killbuck west of the town, a branch of the White Woman and Mohican creek, which fall into the same stream in Coshocton county. The roads were somewhat better than between New Portage and Wooster, though more hilly. On the flats of Mohican the road was bad, being muddy and stony. The country west of Wooster is not so productive as it is north of that place through which we passed on the twelfth inst., yet some beautiful fields of grain were seen. Two wagons failed this day, Joseph C. Clark's and Edwin P. Merriam's. The first was mended at Wooster, the other broke down just at the entrance of the field in which we pitched our tents. Bought four barrels of flour, the first provisions we purchased after the camp started. The people between Kirtland and Wooster were generally apprised of our coming before we arrived, and were not so much surprised to see us as they were west of that place. After we left the main road to Columbus, as we followed along, they seemed astonished and filled with wonder and amazement at seeing so large a body moving together, and some did not fail to express their feelings with warmth to the brethren as they passed along, declaring against the "fallacy", as they called it, of "Jo Smith's" prophecies, and expressing their pity for the deluded believers in modern revelation. We saw this day the first harvesting of grain of any kind, though many of the farmers in Wayne county had done most of their haying.

Sorrow for the "Deluded" Saints.

Saturday, July 14.—Struck our tents at seven a. m. and

the fourth division left the encampment followed by the third and second, the first left at eight. We passed through Jeromeville, a small village situated on a branch of the Mohican, thence through the village of Haysville in Vermillion township, county of Richland, and pitched our tents on the farm of Mr. Solomon Braden, in the town of Petersborough. The country we passed through this day is beautifully diversified with hills and valleys. The timbered lands were covered principally with oak, the roads good, the weather warm and dry. Brother William Perry turned over his wagon and his wife and children were hurt, though not dangerously. A young woman, a daughter of John Vanleuven, Jun., came very near being killed by having a wagon run over her, these were the only accidents that occurred during the day. This was the first day since we left Kirtland that we traveled without breaking down one or more wagons. Pitched our tents at two p. m. on a hill near the east line of Petersburg township and washed and prepared for the Sabbath. In the afternoon a complaint was prepared by N. B. Baldwin against Abram Bond for murmuring and other unchristian-like conduct. The Council, after hearing the complaint and the defense, referred the case to the company in their own tent to settle among themselves. This was the second complaint made to the Council of any consequence on the way from Kirtland. Traveled this day ten miles.

Preparations for the Sabbath.

Sunday, July 15.—The Council met in the morning and made some arrangements about the order of the day. Elder Josiah Butterfield and Joseph Young were appointed to preside during the day.

Public Worship.

At eleven o'clock public worship commenced. Many of the citizens of the town attended, most of whom behaved well, and treated us with respect. Elder Jonathan Dunham delivered a discourse on the first principles of the Gospel, from Mark, 16th chapter, followed by several others of the Elders.

Martin H. Peck came up and joined the camp about noon, and Stephen Shumway and Charles Wood came up in the afternoon.

Some left by the Way Rejoin the Camp.

John Hammond, who was left behind at New Portage in consequence of breaking his wagon, also joined us again. Benjamin Butterfield, who left the camp at Talmadge, Portage county, found his way into camp again in the course of the day.

Monday, July 16.—Started in our usual order in the morning, traveling west toward Mansfield, through which we passed in the afternoon about four o'clock. Passed through the village of Petersburg two miles from our encampment, then through Mifflic township, three or four miles east of Mansfield. In Madison township we were met by the sheriff and a deputy, and a Mr. Stringer, who had taken out a warrant for several of the brethren for Kirtland Safety Society money, and took Josiah Butterfield, Jonathan Dunham and Jonathan H. Hale for Joseph Young, and committed them to jail. As we came to Mansfield we were *honored* by the discharge of artillery, but as the Lord would have it we were not enjoined nor molested more than by insulting language from some of the numerous crowd of persons that thronged the streets. From Mansfield we came through Newcastle, in the township of Springfield, and encamped on the farm of Frederick Cassel over night. Mansfield is a fine village, the county seat of Richland, situated on a hill surrounded by a fertile country. Traveled this day sixteen miles.

Prominent Elders Arrested.

Benjamin Butterfield left the camp again before night in ill humor and went off by himself.

Tuesday, July 17.—Started at eight in the morning; passed through the village of Ontario in Springfield, thence through the town of Sandusky into Jackson, in Crawford county, and encamped six miles east of Bucyrus, the county seat of Crawford county. Traveled sixteen miles.

On the Headwaters of the Sciota and Sandusky.

The country we passed through between Mansfield and Bucyrus is the highest in the State of Ohio, being on the headwaters of the Sciota which falls into the Ohio, and of the Sandusky that falls into Erie, the country though high is generally level.

Just at dark the brethren who had been committed to prison came up. They were discharged by the court at 12 o'clock, noon, after which they traveled twenty-two miles.

The court for Richland county was in session and would have been adjourned the evening the brethren, Josiah, Butterfield Jonathan Dunham and Jonathan H. Hale, were arrested, had it not been for that occurrence. Their case was called on the same evening and adjourned till eight o'clock next morning. Dominicus Carter went back from our camp and staid with them till they were liberated. We were all glad and thanked the Lord for their deliverance out of the hands of our enemies.

Instructions to Overseers.

Wednesday, July 18.—The Council met in the morning and called together the overseers of tents and gave them some instructions concerning their duty in presiding over their tents, and Dominicus Carter was appointed commissary of the camp, and Aaron M. York chosen overseer of tent No. 3, third division, in his place; and the tent removed to No. 5, first division. About eight the camp started, passed through Benjamin and took the road to upper Sandusky, and stopped at one p. m. on the edge of a prairie to rest. For the first time we had the privilege of encamping without pay. The road in the afternoon in some places was rather bad in the groves between the openings of the grand prairie, the edge of which bordered on the right of our road from our encampment east of Bucyrus till we encamped at night in the town of Grand Prairie, county of Marion, on the line between that county and Crawford, ten miles southwest from Bucyrus. Passed through the township of Antrim, in Crawford county, in the afternoon. Traveled this day sixteen miles. As we passed through Bucyrus the people seemed much agitated and made many remarks concerning us. One man said he had received a liberal education and had prepared himself for the ministry, but it now availed him nothing. The movements of the "Mormons" were actions and not words, and looked more like love and like the spirit of union than anything that had come under his observation.

Thursday, *July 19*.—The second, third and fourth divisions started about eight o'clock, the first stayed on the ground, some of them until afternoon, to repair wagons. Traveled through a prairie country to Little Sandusky, a little north of west from the place of our encampment on the night of the eighteenth. Then turned west and pitched our tents on the west side of the prairie, about a mile and a half from the village of Sandusky. Traveled this day seven and one-half miles. No particular occurrence through the day worthy of notice. Encamped for the first time in a straight line, and being on a prarie the tents and wagons presented a beautiful picture to a distant beholder, and could not fail to bring to the mind of anyone familiar with the history of the journeyings of Israel from Egypt, the prophecy of Balaam, concerning Israel's prosperity, and his pathetic exclamation, when he beheld them abiding in their tents from the top of Peor: "How goodly are thy tents, O Jacob, and thy tabernacles, O Israel! As the valleys, as they spread forth, as gardens by the river side, as the trees of lign-aloes which the Lord hath planted, and as cedar trees beside the waters."

Friday, *July 20*.—The Council met in the morning to attend to another complaint preferred by E. B. Gaylord,* superintendent of the fourth division, against Abram Bond, for murmuring and complaining, and for personal abuse. Elder Zera Pulsipher, who presided, gave him a severe reprimand for his conduct in general on the journey and for abusing others without

Reproofs Administered.

*By typographical error this name, in the list of those who signed the camp's constitution (p 92), is given as E. B. Gayland.

any provocation, and he was informed that he would be left by the wayside if he did not reform, and behave more like a man of God than he had of late, or for a few days past. Some other business relative to our circumstances and situation in journeying was talked over and the Council unanimously decided that the camp should be called together before we started and some instructions given to them concerning their duties, and also to reprimand some for indulging themselves in covetousness and murmuring against the Council, and also others of the camp who held important stations as captains of divisions or overseers of tents.

The camp was accordingly called together and such instructions given them as the Spirit of the Lord dictated, by Elders Pulsipher, Young, Butterfield, Foster and Harriman, which had the desired effect in restoring good order and the spirit of union in the camp.

The Council Relieved of Guard Duty.

On motion of Samuel Parker it was unanimously resolved that the Councilors should be excused from standing on guard during the journey, that they might have more time to counsel together and to attend to those duties which necessarily devolved upon them as Councilors of the camp. James A. Clark, Jared Porter and Daniel Bliss were appointed to assist the herdsman in taking care of the herds, as it was found too arduous for one. The camp started about nine and traveled westwardly two miles to Bowsherville, which is one hundred and forty-three miles from Detroit; thence four miles in the same direction, and then turned south and came through the village of Burlington, situated on Taymockty creek, a branch of the Sandusky, and pitched our tents in the highway near a schoolhouse, about one-half mile from Burlington, in the township of Grand, Marion county, between three and four o'clock p. m.

A heavy shower of rain fell soon after we encamped and it continued to rain most of the night. Most of the company got thoroughly wet. Distance this day nine and one-half miles.

Saturday, July 21.—Started about eight a. m.; traveled southwesterly through the township of Goshen, Hardin county to the Sciota river, in the township of Dudley, where we stopped to refresh ourselves and teams, at Judge Wheeler's. From thence we came to Mr. Bosman's, in township of Jackson, where we encamped in the highway, seven miles from Sciota, making in all sixteen miles. It was quite cool and comfortable traveling, but the road was extremely bad, being in some places almost impassable, but the Lord attended us and His blessings were multiplied upon us so that no accident of any account happened to us during the day. Newel K. Knight broke an axle-tree out of his wagon which was mended in a short time.

Sunday, July 22.—On account of forage we were under the necessity of traveling about five miles through Rush creek, and pitched our tents on a rise of ground, by the wayside, on the farm of Mr. Partial, inn-keeper in the town of Rush Creek, Logan county, and held public meeting at five p. m. Attended to offering our sacraments to the Most High, breaking bread for the first time on our journey. The first two Sabbaths after we started on our journey we were so circumstanced and thronged with visitors that we omitted attending to the ordinance of the Lord's Supper. At our meeting in the afternoon the Lord blessed us by the outpouring of His Spirit, our hearts were comforted and most of the camp felt thankful for the blessings conferred upon us by our heavenly Father, thus far on the journey to the land of Zion.

As we passed along the road in the morning, molesting no one, some of the company were saluted in modern style by having eggs thrown at them by some ruffians from their dwellings near the road, but on seeing some of our company stop, they desisted from their course fearing the consequences from appearances, and even showed three or four bayonets, intimating that they would defend themselves in case of assault. No one, however, intended doing any harm to them, and only wished them to understand that we noticed their intrusion upon our privileges as citizens to travel the high road unmolested. Sometime in the night a luminous body about the size of a cannon ball came down from over the encampment near the ground then whirled round some forty or fifty times and moved off in a horizontal direction, soon passing out of sight.

Monday, July 23.—The camp began to move at a quarter past seven a. m., and came through the village of Rushsylvania, where we were threatened before our arrival with prosecution for "Kirtland Bank Money," signed by F. G. Williams, president, and Warren Parrish, cashier. Some of the company passed on from our encampment in the morning to find out what was intended against us, but no person made any attempt to stop any one, and we passed on in safety. From Rushsylvania we came through the village of Bellefontaine, the county seat of Logan county; twelve miles thence to McKee's creek, a branch of the Miami, in the township of Union, and camped at the side of the creek at seven o'clock. Traveled this day sixteen miles.

Threats of Arrest Made.

On the road near Bellefontaine one of the sons of Martin H. Peck, had a wagon wheel run over his leg, but as the Lord would have it, and to the astonishment of all—considering the weight of the load on the wagon—he received no particular injury, although the wheel ran over the boy's leg on a hard road without any obstruction whatever. The wheel made a deep cut in the limb, but after hands were laid on him in the name of the Lord, the boy was able to walk considerable in the course of the afternoon. This was one, but not the first, of the wonderful manifestations of God's power unto us on the journey.

A Case of Healing.

After we left Bucyrus hill we came to Bellefontaine,

the road was in many places very bad, especially in the backwoods. In Marion and Hardin counties provisions were scarce and could not be obtained, consequently we were obliged to do with what we had; and here was another manifestation of the power of Jehovah, for seven and a half bushels of corn sufficed for the whole camp, consisting of six hundred and twenty souls, for the space of three days, and none lacked for food, though some complained and murmured because they did not have that to eat which their souls lusted after.

Scarcity of Food.

Tuesday, July 24.—We lay in our encampment at McKee's creek through the day to wash our clothes and refresh our teams, as they were very much fatigued by traveling for several days on a rough and muddy road. We took two jobs, one of chopping cord wood, and one of shoemaking, and earned about twenty dollars, besides mending and repairing several wagons and putting things in order in the camp.

A Day of Rest.

Wednesday, July 25.—Started on our journey and came through West Liberty, situated on Mad river, thence into the township of Salem, Champaign county, and encamped about two miles north of Terbana, on the farm of Joseph Vance, Governor of the state of Ohio. The encampment was formed near his residence, at six o'clock, having traveled twelve miles this day. The country in the valley of Mad river is level and beautiful and very fertile. We saw extensive fields of wheat on each side of the way, mostly reaped, and crops of all kinds were far better than any we had seen elsewhere on our journey.

Camp at the Farm of the Governor of Ohio.

In the evening the camp was called together by the Council, and some of them severely reprimanded in general terms for their unchristian-like conduct, and much instruction given concerning our duties to God, and to one another, in order to move on our journey in righteousness, that we might obtain the favor of the Lord, and have His blessings attend us from day to day.

After the assembly was dismissed, the Council returned and listened to a complaint presented by B. S. Wilbur against Stephen Starks, for some unchristian-like conduct during the day. The trouble was amicably settled to the satisfaction of all concerned. The Council adjourned, after transacting some other business, at eleven o'clock p. m. From Kirtland to our encampment in Salem, is two hundred and fifteen miles.

Thursday, July 26.—Camp began to move at eight o'clock; the first division, however, did not leave the grounds until after eleven. Several of the brethren went out to labor both yesterday and today, in order to procure means to further us on our journey, and they did not come up with us at night. We traveled south through the village of Urbana, the county seat of Champaign county; thence into the township of Moneyfield, Clark county, and camped on the farm of Mr. A. Breneman, four and one half miles off the National road at Springfield. Traveled twelve miles, plus two hundred and fifteen miles from Kirtland, equals two hundred and twenty-seven miles.

Camp Labors.

The camp was called together in the evening and a timely lecture was given by Elder Pulsipher, on our situation, and all were exhorted to be united in heart and hand in order to join together. The Spirit of the Lord was manifested and we returned to our tents feeling thankful for the blessings of the Lord upon us.

Admonitions.

Friday, July 27.—Continued our journey to Springfield on the National road, one hundred and seventy-one miles from Wheeling, in Virginia. Crossed Buck creek, a branch of Mad river, just before entering the village on the north. Springfield is a large and beautiful village, the county seat of Clark county, containing about three thousand inhabitants. There are many elegant buildings of brick, and it seems to be a place of considerable trade.

Through Springfield.

A little west of Springfield we left the National road and took the road to Dayton, distance from Springfield twenty-five miles, and passed through the township of Mad river, and a small village called Washington in the same township, and pitched our tents just at dark in a grove near Lenox, in Mad river township. The day was excessively warm and the road dusty, but we all arrived safely at our encampment in the evening, except some of those who stopped to labor. Many of the people all along the road seemed quite astonished to see so many in the company. Some judging there were three hundred teams, and made some curious remarks concerning us and "Jo Smith;" and one man threatened to shoot Elder Dunham if he did not immediately leave his premises when he called to procure forage for our teams at noon. After we encamped a stage went by and the passengers behaved as they passed us more like the savages of the west than anything we have seen since the commencement of our journey. Distance traveled today, fifteen miles. J. D. Parker, who had left Kirtland some time after we did, overtook us at our encampment this evening and staid with us till Monday morning.

Astonishment Created by the Camp.

Saturday, July 28.—We removed from Mad river township and came to Fairfield, three miles, thence to Bath township and encamped about noon half a mile from the road on the banks of Mad river in Green county, five and one half miles from Dayton. Distance this day nine miles. Distance from Kirtland, two hundred and fifty-one miles.

Sunday, July 29.—We held a public meeting in a grove on a farm of Mr. Houghman, about one fourth of a mile from our encampment, at eleven o'clock, Elder Zera Pulsipher preached.

In the afternoon we had a sacrament meeting on the camp grounds. Elder Duncan McArthur, after the administration of the Lord's Supper, bore testimony of the truth of the revelations of the Lord in these last days to the numerous spectators who were present, and in a brief way made known unto them some of those things that the Lord was doing in the earth; and others that would shortly come to pass among the inhabitants thereof. The Spirit of God attended his testimony and we had a joyful meeting.

The Sacrament Administered.

The Council met in the morning to regulate some things relative to the duties of the day, and adjourned till five p. m. At that time they met again and took into consideration the case of Abram Bond, and unanimously resolved that for his murmuring and not giving heed to the regulations of the camp, he should be disfellowshiped by the camp and left to the care of himself, which decision was made known unto him and approbated by those who were present at the time. He accordingly left the camp the next day. Warren Smith, who left Kirtland about the first of June, came into the camp with his family and joined us. William Gribble—whose wife accompanied us from Kirtland—also joined the camp this day. We found many of the Saints from Kirtland and other places, and Elder John E. Page, with a part of his company that started from Oak Point, in St. Lawrence county, New York, whither they had fled in the course of the past winter, from the commotions and rumors of war in Canada.* They were scattered along the

Abram Bond Disfellowshiped.

John E. Page's Company.

* The war rumors here mentioned have reference to what is known in Canadian history as the "Canadian Rebellion." It was the culmination of agitation begun as early as 1831, on the part of the people of Canada, under popular leaders, such as Papineau, Brown, Nielson, McKenzie and others, for enlarged measures of home rule for the Dominion. The popular leaders marshaled their forces against the government during the winter of 1837-8, and a number of skirmishes took place. Canadian independence was much talked of, and the people in the United States along the Canadian border were much excited, and volunteers began to flock in considerable numbers to aid the cause of the "patriots," as the insurgents were called. "But," to quote a Canadian historian, "the American President, Mr. Van-Buren, issued two successive proclamations warning the people of the penalties to which they would expose themselves by engaging in hostilities with a friendly power, and also appointed General Scott to take command of the disturbed fron-

road from Springfield to Dayton, some of them laboring for means to prosecute their journey and some had stopped to recruit their teams as well as their purses, that they might continue their journey after the warm season had passed. Many of them came to visit us and were received with feelings of gratitude for the goodness of our heavenly Father for the preservation of our lives and for the privilege of meeting each other in this land of strangers.

The weather has been extremely hot and dry in the land, and in the southwestern part of the state of Ohio, for many weeks: and rain was much needed, and supplication was made to the God of Israel for rain on the land in this region of country, at the meeting in the forenoon, and at the close of the service in the afterpart of the day. Elder Dunham and Elder Charles Thompson each held a meeting in the afternoon, about two miles from camp.

Prayer for Rain.

Monday, July 30.—We remained in our encampment during the day and were visited by several gentlemen, and were solicited to tarry in this place for a season and take a job on the Springfield and Dayton turnpike. Some of the brethren went out to make what discoveries they could relative to labor, and partly engaged some small jobs on condition that we tarried here for a few days. In the afternoon and evening it rained on each side of us, that is, to the north and to the south, and at no great distance from us quite hard, to all appearances; and we also had a small shower in the afternoon, though not enough to water the earth sufficiently, yet it cooled the air and greatly revived both the animal and vegetable kingdoms, for which we thank that

Rain.

tier and enforce a strict neutrality." After the arrival of General Scott on the frontiers, effective measures were taken to prevent further supplies and recruits from reaching the "patriots," and the militia ordered out by the Canadian government, after some severe fighting, dispersed the insurgents, many of whom fled to the United States. The British parliament subsequently granted some of the legislative reforms demanded by the people.

Being that rules the armies of heaven and the inhabitants of the earth, and sendeth rain both upon the just and upon the unjust.

Elder John E. Page, who preached about one mile from us in the evening, tarried with us over night and left us in the morning to go to his family at Fairfield, five miles and one half distant, where they had resided for a few weeks since the Canada camp (John E. Page's company) had stopped.

Tuesday, *July 31.*—A part of our company went off to work on a job of raising a levee for Mr. Hushman, and some one way and some another to labor during the day. In the morning all the men in the camp were called out and were made acquainted with our pecuniary circumstances, and an inquiry made who, if any, wished to leave the camp and look out for themselves. One man, Brother Asa Wright, said that his wife had always been opposed to going in the camp, and that he had told some of the brethren in the camp that in consequence of that and some other things it was his choice to leave. Elder Stephen Headlock also complained of the murmuring of some of the camp, and said that he had rather leave the camp—though he desired with all his heart to go in it up to the land of Zion—than to hear so much complaining as he had for a few days past, and had freely expressed his mind before to that effect to some of the brethren.

Some Leave the Camp.

He was reprimanded by Elder Pulsipher for his own neglect of duty and told to set his own tent in order, and then if he knew of any infringement on the rules of the camp by others, to try, as the law of God required, to reclaim the offenders and restore them to order that the blessings of God might be poured out upon the camp during the long and tedious journey which still lay before it. A vote was taken to see how many were desirous of stopping and laboring, if the Council thought advisable to do so. Some further inquiries were

A Reproof.

made concerning the conditions that had been or might be offered to the camp to make a piece of turn pike road or do any other work that might be obtained by the Council, and under their superintendency, when all, with a few exceptions,—and they were persons unable to labor—voted to abide by the advice of the Council, and would stay or go, as they should advise or direct.

Elder Page Exhorts the Camp.

Elder John E. Page made a short speech, exhorting all to fulfill their covenants, let what would come, life or death, inasmuch as they were in righteousness before God; and said that all our deeds would be had in remembrance; that we would be rewarded for them, whether good or evil, both in time and in eternity; and further observed that the journeying of the Saints to Zion in obedience to the commandments of the Lord afforded an opportunity for them to become what they desired; either to be as great and as noble as they could or to sink into obscurity in the eyes of God and His Saints and be the least in this last kingdom which God has set His hand to build up upon the earth. After making many appropriate remarks he implored the blessings of heaven upon us, which was responded to by a hearty amen, and then all dispersed to attend to the duties of the day.

Work on the Turnpike.

In the course of the day we took a job of making half a mile of turnpike, and removed our encampment into a beautiful grove near the edge of a prairie about one-fourth of a mile, and about the same distance from Mad river. Here we began to make preparations to commence work, but made little progress, for most of the laboring men were absent, and we did not get our tents pitched till nearly night.

Wednesday, *August 1.*—Began at an early hour to make arrangements to commence our job. Sent off part of the men to finish the levee and some to build a fence around our camp, and about twelve o'clock made a beginning on the road. A few sick in the camp this day, but most of us were in good health and satisfied with our situation.

Thursday, *August 2*.—Very warm and dry as it had been for many days, with the exception of the showers on Monday evening.

Progressed with our labors on the road rather slowly, for we were not in condition to work to good advantage, as we had not tools enough, and had been on our journey so long that it was rather fatiguing to labor hard in the commencement. Some sickness in the camp, but no more than would be expected, owing to our change of climate, and the extreme heat and drouth in the land.

Renewed Diligence.

Friday, *August 3*.—Made great progress in the turnpike, and the desponding spirits of some began to revive, for laboring had looked to some to be rather a hard way to procure means to prosecute our journey, though but few complained. Some new cases of sickness, but many of those who were unwell the day before were recovering fast. The men and boys in camp were called together in the evening and instructed by the Council as the Spirit of the Lord manifested unto them concerning cleanliness and decency and the importance of being industrious in laboring with their hands to procure means to go on our way. The covenant to put our strength, our properties and monies together for the purpose of going together in the camp to Zion, and of delivering the poor from their poverty and oppression in the land of Kirtland was adverted to by Elders Pulsipher and Foster, and all exhorted and entreated to give heed to it if they wished to enjoy the blessings of the Lord.

An Assistant Council Appointed.

The Council at a meeting held in the afternoon had taken into consideration the propriety of appointing three men to sit as councilors or judges [known as an Assistant Council, see p. 128] to settle matters and difficulties between brethren, that the Council might be relieved in some measure from the arduous duties of settling controversies and have more time to devote to other things that devolved upon them as Presidents of the camp. Duncan McArthur, Gordon Snow and George Stringham were nominated, and the subject was laid before the meeting in the evening to receive the unanimous approbation of all present. The many blessings conferred on us by our Heavenly Father since He first made known His will unto the Council of Seventies, that it was His will that the Seventies should go to Zion in a camp together, were recapitulated and our hearts were made glad and we rejoiced in the Rock of our salvation whose mercies had been extended unto us, notwithstanding our murmurings against Him and slowness of heart to believe His words, and the many promises which He had made unto us. At the close of the meeting our united prayers ascended to God in the name of His Son, Jesus Christ, for the recovery of Elder Jacob Chapman's family who resided near the city of Dayton, and had sent unto us for some of the Elders to go and lay hands on them in the name of the Lord, as they were sorely afflicted with disease, and for the recovery of the sick in our own camp, and that the destroyer might cease to make inroads among us.

Saturday, August 4.—Our circumstances about the same as on the day previous. A heavy shower towards evening cooled the air and greatly revived the vegetation which was suffering for want of rain in the country round about. In the evening the camp was called together again and the names of those who had absented themselves from labor were read over and those who had no excuse for their absence were severely reprimanded, and the overseers of tents instructed by the Council to withhold the usual rations allotted from such individuals as could but would not labor, that the idler should not eat the bread of the laborer, according to the commandments of the Lord.—Doctrine and Covenants, sec. xlii.

CHAPTER X.

THE JOURNEY OF KIRTLAND CAMP. (CONTINUED).

Sunday, August 5.—One month had passed away since the camp was organized and we were all present in the camp with few exceptions. Elder Joseph Young preached from Acts xvi, and 30th verse, on the principles of salvation through the Gospel of Jesus Christ. A respectable congregation of strangers assembled with us and gave the best attention to what was declared unto them. The sacrament of the Lord's supper was administered in the afternoon by Elders Foster and Wilbur and the services of the day were closed by singing and imploring the blessings of God upon us and upon the Saints of the Most High in every land, and for the triumph of Christ's kingdom on the earth. The Council met after the public services of the day were ended, to transact some business of the camp which seemed to be necessary; and after that was disposed of Elder Zera Pulsipher suggested the propriety of ordaining George Stringham to the office of an Elder, and said that the Spirit had borne witness to him for some time that it was the will of the Lord that he should be ordained to that office. The subject was taken into consideration and the Council decided that he should be ordained if it was congenial to his own feelings. On being interrogated he said that he was willing to be ordained and would do anything the Lord required of him for the building up of His kingdom on the earth. Elder James Foster with some others then proceeded to ordain him according to the rules of the Church of Latter-day Saints, an Elder in said Church. The Council then adjourned.

Preaching of Elder Young.

Monday, August 6.—Some complaining in the camp and some sick, principally children and aged persons. We progressed finely in our labors on the road, and a greater interest seemed to be manifested for the welfare of the whole body than had been since the camp stopped. John Hammond lost one of his horses in the night, the first one that had died during our journey.

An Increase of Interest in the Camp.

Tuesday, August 7.—No occurrence worthy of note during the day. The destroyer continued to afflict us with sickness as a body, and many of the men were unable to labor. In the evening the laborers were called together and some instructions were given to them concerning our labors and the necessity of diligence impressed upon those who manifested an indifference to the general interest of the whole camp.

Exhortations.

Wednesday, August 8.—This morning found another of our horses dead, one that had been bought for the benefit of the camp, and before noon we had to kill another that had his leg broken. It belonged to John Matthews who had left the camp a few days before without the consent of the Council. Sickness still prevailed among us though the laboring men were in better health than usual and the spirit of love and union was manifested by most of the camp and all that were able labored cheerfully without a murmur during the day. In the evening a child of Hiram H. Byington died, which was the second time death had entered our camp on the road from Kirtland to this place.

Death of Horses.

Thursday, August 9.—Brother Byington's child was buried at twelve o'clock. Some sickness in the camp this day, but not quite so much as there has been for a few days past. A little shower about noon cooled the air though enough did not fall to water the earth which was suffering from want of rain and had been for some time, insomuch that the shower that fell on the 4th instant did not suffice to water it enough to restore

A Burial.

vegetation to its natural state, and the crops of corn and other grains were suffering almost beyond description in the region of country round about.

Friday, August 10.—The weather continued extremely hot and dry. Elder James Foster took his tent in company with J. S. Holman, S. Shumway of the 3rd division and Joel Harvey of the 4th, with the inmates of their tents and went to work on a job of building a levee for Mr. Hushman about two miles from the camp, where E. B. Gaylord of the 4th division had moved his tent a few days before, and was digging a ditch for the same individual. In the evening a daughter of Thomas Carico, aged one year and five months, died, and was buried the next day.

More Employment.

Saturday, August 11.—One or two showers of rain cooled the air and revived the languid and drooping spirits of those in the camp, and symptoms of better health were visible on the countenances of the afflicted. In the fore part of the night Sarah Emily, daughter of Dominicus Carter, aged about two years and three months, died, being the fourth one the destroyer took from our midst.

Showers.

Sunday, August 12.—Elder Pulsipher preached in the forenoon to a large congregation of strangers most of whom gave the best attention. At two p. m. the funeral of Elder Carter's child was attended, and at four Elder John E. Page, who had been invited, preached a sermon on the gathering of Israel and the location of Mount Zion,* after which the Council met

Charles Thompson Corrected.

*In speaking of the services this 12th day of August, and the discourse of Elder John E. Page, Brother Samuel D. Tyler, who, as well as Judge Elias Smith, kept a most excellent journal of the camp's proceedings day by day, says: "Elder John E. Page of the Canada camp preached at three o'clock to us, and many spectators. Text. Jer. 31: 6. In his discourse he proved that America was the land given to Joseph's posterity, and that the Indians are the descendants of Joseph, and that they would be gathered to Zion and the Jews to Jerusalem and that the watchmen shall lift up their voices on Mount Zion, etc. In short, he preached the truth with power. At the close he said he had been preaching in Fairfield and had the confidence and good feeling of the people, and he advised that none of less talent

to regulate and set in order some things that seemed to be necessary in the camp, in order to preserve harmony and union among us. Elder Charles Thompson was called in question for something he had taught concerning the order of moving of the camp. After being shown the impropriety of his conduct, and the fallacy of some of his views and the effect the promulgating of them had and would have in the camp, he made ample retraction before the Council, and before the camp which was called together for that purpose in the evening.

Several brethren from Elder Page's camp and others that resided in this region of country spent the Sabbath with us. Among the number were Elder Nelson and Brother Ide, who resided near the city of Dayton. Several of the brethren who had resided in Kirtland, being now on the way to the land of Zion, had stopped to labor near us and they were also present, and met with us at communion which was administered by Elders John E. Page and Jonathan H. Hale at the close of the meeting in the afternoon.

Spirit of Union Manifested.

Monday, August 13.—Richard D. Blanchard joined the camp by the consent of the Council. Somewhat cooler towards evening than it had been for some time. About twenty sick in the camp, mostly women and children, but none are dangerously ill. The laborers were called together again in the evening and some instructions given them concerning our labors and prospects in relation to means to prosecute our journey, and a spirit of union was manifested which cheered our hearts and made us thankful to the God of Israel for that and the many other blessings we daily received from His liberal hand.

Tuesday, August 14.—The day passed away as usual.

than himself, should venture to preach to them, lest they should injure the cause. He said he did not say this to boast, but I think he had better not [have] said it, for I think it was not according to scripture and the Spirit of God; for God has chosen the weak and foolish things of the world to confound the wisdom of the wise and prudent. Now, if the Lord will send poor, weak Elders to any people to preach to them, I doubt not that He will risk them, yea, and risk His cause with them also.

For some time past most of the laborers were able to perform the work assigned them, and but few comparatively were sick in the camp, and these generally were growing better.

Wednesday, August 15.—It rained most of the afternoon which hindered us from our labors a considerable part of the time.

Jonas Putnam Commended.

Brother Jonas Putnam and family by the advice of the Council left the camp and moved about twelve miles on to a farm belonging to Brother Ide to take charge of it while he [Brother Ide] went to prepare a place for himself and the small branch of the Church in this vicinity in some of the Stakes of Zion in the west. We were not willing that Brother Putnam should leave the camp upon any other principle than that of mutual consent of all concerned, for he was esteemed by all as a just man, and devout, and one that was worthy of the fellowship of the Saints. Elder Elijah Cheney who had left Kirtland before the camp with his family came into our encampment in the forenoon having been blessed of the Lord on his journey and was received with a hearty welcome by the brethren of the camp.

Thursday, August 16.—Elder B. S. Wilbur took about twenty men with Elder George Stringham and his tent and company and went to the city of Dayton to do a job of work which had been engaged by the advice of the Council.

Expulsion from the Camp.

In the evening G. W. Brooks and wife were called before the Council and inquiry made into some things which had been in circulation for some days respecting them, and in the course of the investigation it was acknowledged that Brother Brooks' wife had used tea most of the time on the road, and had used profane language, and she declared she would still pursue the same course, and it was not in the power of her husband or the Council to stop it. She further said that she was not a member of the Church and did not expect to come under the rules of the camp.

The decision of the Council was that they must leave the camp, and Brother Brooks was severely reprimanded for not keeping his tent in order according to the Constitution of the camp, and not keeping his family in subjection, as a man of God, especially as an Elder of Israel.

Further Investigation of Camp Members.

Friday, August 17.—Elders J. Foster and Henry Harriman, having finished the job of embankment [levee], came back into the encampment themselves but did not bring back their tents. In the afternoon the Council met and several of the members of the camp were tried for breach of the Constitution, and Nathan K. Knight presented an appeal from a decision of the Assistant Council on a charge preferred against himself and wife by Amos Jackson, overseer of his tent, for some misdemeanor in respect to the order of the camp and unchristian-like conduct on the journey, which decision was that they had violated the Constitution of the camp and disregarded their covenant to observe and keep it, and consequently must be left by the wayside. After an inquiry into the affair the decision made [by the Assistant Council] was confirmed by the Council of the camp.

Josiah Miller was advised, in consequence of the conduct of his son-in-law, Aaron Dolph, who was not a member of the Church, and would not conform to the order of the camp, to take his family and go by himself.

Expulsions from Camp.

Nathan Staker was requested to leave the camp in consequence of the determination of his wife, to all appearances, not to observe the rules and regulations of the camp. There had been contentions in the tent between herself and Andrew Lamereaux, overseer of the tent, and also contentions with his family several times on the road, and after the camp stopped in this place. The Council had become weary of trying to settlethese contentions between them. Andrew Lamereaux having gone to Dayton to labor, taking his family with him, was not present at the Council, neither was there any new complaint made, but the impossibility of Brother Staker to keep his family in order was apparent to all, and it was thought to be the best thing for him to take his family and leave the camp. Some other things were brought before the Council and inquiry made into the conduct of several individuals, and the Council had come to the determination to put iniquity from the camp wherever it could be found, that God's anger might be turned away and His blessings rest down upon us.

Saturday, August 18.—Josiah Miller, agreeable to the counsel given him, took his family and left the camp with the best of feelings existing between him and the Council of the camp; he left it only in consequence of the disposition of his son-in-law, Aaron Dolph, to set at naught the Constitution by which the camp were bound by agreement to put their strength, properties and monies together in order to move the camp to the land of Zion.

Another child died this day, aged about three years, a daughter of Martha Higby, who was in company with Z. H.* Brewster. Sister Higby's husband had left her some time before the camp started. The brethren finished their job at Mr. Harshman's on Friday, and at Dayton on Saturday. The health of the camp was much better than usual since we stopped here.

Sunday, August 19.—As usual a large congregation met with us and gave good attention to the services of the day. Elder Joel H. Johnson, by the request of Elders Young and Harriman, who presided, preached on the first principles of the Gospel from Galatians i, in the forenoon. In the afternoon the sacrament was administered agreeable to the commandments of the Lord.

Religious Service.

Monday, August 20.—Nathan K. Knight and George W. Brooks, who had been excluded from the camp as before stated, left the camp. Daniel Bliss went with George W. Brooks by the consent of the Council—at his own request—

* By an error this initial in the list of names is given as W.

as he was not well provided for as to a place for his family to ride on the road.

Births in Camp.

Tuesday, *August 21.*—Two boys born in the camp in the morning. One, the son of Gardner Snow, the other of Frederick M. Vanleuven. The Council held a consultation in the afternoon and concluded to make preparations to start on our journey as soon as possible, if the Lord did not open the way clearly before us to tarry longer in this place. J. A. Clark was excluded from the camp.

Turnpike Contract finished.

Wednesday, *August 22.*—Finished our job of grading in the morning and the remainder of the day most of us rested ourselves, and made some preparation to start again on our way. Extremely hot, and the earth parched with drought to a greater degree than has been known for many years in this region of country.

Andrew J. Squires called on us on his way to Kirtland on Tuesday afternoon, and left again after having some consultation with the Council of the Seventies about his standing in the Church, and went on his way to Kirtland.

Arrangements for Renewal of the Journey.

Thursday, *August 23.*—The Council met to regulate some things and concluded to start on Monday, the 27th instant, and to labor all the time we could till that time. Several resolutions were passed among which was the following: That those of the camp who were absent should come back to the encampment and that the vacancies in overseers of tents be filled and then all called together and instructed more particularly concerning the duties of their office before the camp shall start again; that the camp shall be reorganized, inasmuch as some have left since its organization.

John Hammond was expelled by the assistant Council from the camp for not standing at the head of his family, his wife making much disturbance in the tent, of which Brother Hammond was the overseer.

Friday, *August 24.*—Most of the brethren who

were absent came into the camp during the day to make preparations to go on our journey.

Gathering of the Absent.

Elder Joseph Young went to Dayton to attend the funeral of William Tenny, late of Kirtland, who died yesterday.

Saturday, August 25.—In the afternoon the overseers of the tents were called together by the Council, and inquiry made into the affairs of each tent to see if there were any difficulties existing among them or any other persons in the camp. The inquiry resulted in discovering much that was not as it should be. Several tents were in disorder, and the Council proceeded to make inquiry and to set in order the inmates of those tents that were in a state of confusion. Most of the difficulties were amicably settled, one exception. John Rulison was turned out of the camp by the assistant Council. The same Council were directed to go to Brother Nickerson's tent and set it in order; breaking the Word of Wisdom and disbelief in some of the revelations constituted the difficulties in this tent.

Sunday, August 26.—As usual a public meeting was held in the forenoon and a sacrament meeting in the afternoon. The Spirit of the Lord was poured out on the assembly and some were convinced of the truth of what was declared unto them.

Monday, August 27.—Having finished our turnpike contract, we made every possible exertion to continue our journey on the morrow, by shoeing horses and fixing wagons. We had a blacksmith shop in operation in the camp for several days, doing the necessary work. In the evening a heavy shower of rain fell which was greatly needed, and it seemed for some time past that it would be almost impossible for us to travel in consequence of the drought, and the dust that flew on the highway; but as the Lord had been merciful to us before, so He was in this instance, for which we felt thankful in very deed.

Preparations for the Journey.

Tuesday, August 28.—Made every exertion in our power to start, but found it impossible about noon, as we had to make provisions for several families who had been deprived of a team by those who were turned out of the camp taking their teams with them.

Charles Wood was expelled from the camp by two of the Council, James Foster and Henry Harriman, on the 27th. Brother Wood was tenting about two miles from our encampment with two or three other families, who for some misdemeanor had been expelled from the camp. Brothers Foster and Harriman, by the consent of all concerned, acted in this matter without a majority of the Council being present, but this was not the practice of the Council, as a majority was considered necessary to have a trial or council concerning any matter relating to the affairs of the camp; but in this instance no exceptions were made by any. In the evening the brethren in the camp were called together and our labors and tribulations were talked over. The Spirit of God rested down upon the camp with power, and after singing the hymn, "The Spirit of God like a fire is burning," we concluded by a song, "Hosanna to God and the Lamb," and retired with joyful hearts to our tents.

The Camp Resumes its Journey.

Wednesday, August 29.—Early in the morning we began to leave the ground, having the previous day reorganized as far as possible.

Z. H. Brewster and his father-in-law, J. Higby who was with him, were left behind for want of a team to carry them with their families.

We passed through the city of Dayton, situated near the junction of Mad river with the Great Miami, and took the road to Eaton and traveled through the township of Jefferson and put up in the township of Jackson, near the village of Johnsville, twelve miles from Dayton, and pitched our tents in the highway, having traveled eighteen miles. Having been at work one month we all were thankful for the privilege of again marching on our way.

Our labors in Bath and its vicinity amounted to about ——.*

Thursday, *August 30*.—Traveled through Twin township on the north line, and through Washington township, in Preble county; passed through the village of Alexander, in Twin township, and then through the village of Eaton, twelve miles from Johnsville, and pitched our tents on the line of Indiana and Ohio, eleven miles from Eaton, having traveled twenty-four miles, and are now two hundred and ninety-three miles from Kirtland.

On the Indiana Line.

The land from Dayton to the Ohio line is generally bad, and covered with maple, beach, elm, ash, whitewood and other northern timber; and the soil after leaving the bottoms of the Miami is not so fertile as the lands on that [Miami] and Mad river. The road was generally good, and the weather extremely fine. Our teams stood the journey much better than when we first started from Kirtland.

On Thursday a daughter of Otis Shumway died, at Eaton, on the road, and was buried in the woods near where we camped at night, in the township of Jackson, Preble county, Ohio.

Friday, *August 31*.—Started early, crossed the line of Indiana a few rods from our encampment into the township of Wayne, Wayne county, Indiana. We came to the village of Richmond, on the east branch of Whitewater, four miles. Richmond is a flourishing place on the national road, which we came to soon after we passed the line, or between there and Richmond. From Richmond we came to Centerville, the county seat of Wayne county, six miles; and thence we came to the village of Germantown, eight miles, and encamped for the night near that village, about sunset. Crossed during the day several tributary streams of the

Camp Enters the State of Indiana.

* The amount is not stated in the camp journal.

Whitewater, the principal of which was Nolands Fork, west of Centerville. Traveled fourteen miles.

Course of Journey.

September 1.—The camp started at eight a. m. We came through a small village called Cambridge, one mile from Germantown; then through Dublin three miles; through Louisville, nine miles; then to Flatrock, in Franklin township, Henry county; thence to Roysville, on the east side of Blue river, and Knight's Town, on the east side ten miles, and encamped by the side of the way one mile west of Knight's Town, just at dark. The air was cool in the evening and after the fires were built, which was necessary for our comfort and convenience, our encampment looked beautiful, and we attracted the attention of all who passed by, and of the citizens of the neighborhood who declared that our company exceeded any they had before seen in all their lives. Distance from Kirtland three hundred and thirty-five miles

A Sunday Journey.

Sunday, *September 2.*—Frost seen in the morning. It being quite cool, we thought it our duty to go on our way, so we started at eight o'clock, and came through the small villages of Liberty and Portland, and stopped at noon in Center township, Hancock county, at Mr. Caldwell's, about nine miles from our encampment. Here the son of E. P. Merriam died; the body was carried on to our place of encampment at night. In the afternoon we came through Greenfield, the county seat of Hancock county. Crossed Sugar creek, nine miles, and encamped at night on Buck creek on the west line of Hancock county, and east line of Marion county, having traveled twenty-one miles through a low, level country of clay soil and hard road. The crops of corn were small, and all grain scarce. The weather is cool and the roads good, but from appearances they had been almost impassable. Three hundred and fifty-six miles from Kirtland.

Monday, *September 3.*—Cold and frosty in the morning.

We arose at four, as usual, and at half-past five Sister Bathsheba Willey, who was sick when we started from Kirtland, died and was buried together with Brother Merriam's child in the northeast corner of T. Ruther's orchard, Jones township, Hancock county, about one-fourth of a mile east from Buck creek. The stage broke Lucius N. Scovil's wagon down.* We came this day to Indianapolis, on the east side of White river, the metropolis of the state of Indiana, and pitched our tents at night six and one-sixth miles west of the city, in Wayne township, on the farm of Brother Miller. Distance from Kirtland, three hundred and seventy-three miles.

Death of Bathsheba Willey.

Tuesday, September 4.—In the morning B. S. Wilbur, who had been left behind in Dayton, Ohio, to transact some business, came up in the stage about four o'clock. The camp was called together in the morning, and warned by the Council of the displeasure of our heavenly Father with some for their wickedness, and that His judgments would fall upon them with greater weight than they had if there was not a speedy repentance. The Council also entreated all to be humble and pray much, for the destroyer was in our midst and many were afflicted. Ira Thornton, overseer of tent No. eight, third division, by leave of the Council, stayed behind to go up to the land of Zion with his father-in-law, who resided near our encampment, and was going to start in a few days. Brother Thornton during the journey had been a faithful brother, and stopped now merely on his wife's account, and not that he was or had been disaffected with the movements in the camp or with the management of the Council.

Warning and Exhortation.

Josiah Butterfield stopped to get a wagon wheel made, and the camp started at a late hour. We came through

* This incident is related by Samuel D. Tyler, under date of Sunday, September 2nd, as follows: "This afternoon a miserable drunken stage driver maliciously ran aside out of his course and struck the fore wheel of one of our wagons and stove it in and dropped it; then drove off exulting in his mischief. The stage he drove was marked "*J. P. Voorhees.*"

Cumberland village, two miles; thence through Plainfield, in Guilford township, Hendricks county, five miles; and stopped at noon in Liberty township, two miles east of Bellville, five miles from Plainfield, through which we passed in the afternoon; thence through the village of Bellville eight miles, and encamped late in the evening about three miles west of Bellville, having traveled twenty-three miles. David Elliot left the camp this morning. Distance from Kirtland, three hundred and ninety-six miles.

Wednesday, *September 5*.—Thomas Nickerson's child died in the night, and was buried where we stopped at noon on the farm of Noal Fouts, west of the village of Putnamville. Passed this day through Mt. Meridian, Putnamville, and Manhattan. Crossed Walnut and McCray creek and encamped by the side of the way just west of Clay county, having traveled twenty miles. Distance from Kirtland, four hundred and sixteen miles.

Thursday, *September 6*.—Traveled thirteen miles through a fine country, good road, and pitched our tents between two and three miles east of Terre Haute, the county seat of Vigo county, situated on the west side of the Wabash, on a swell of land in a beautiful prairie surrounded by a fruitful and fertile country. Distance from Kirtland, four hundred and thirty-three miles.

Arrival at Terre Haute.

Friday, *September 7*.—Sometime in the night a daughter of Otis Shumway died; and in the morning a child of J. A. Clark died. Both were buried in the graveyard in Terre Haute through which we passed, and crossed the Wabash about twelve o'clock at both ferries, and left the national road and turning to the right, took the North Arm Prairie road to Paris. Traveled nine miles, and encamped in LaFayette township, three-fourths of a mile east of the Illinois line. The distance from Kirtland, the way we came, to Terre Haute is four hundred and thirty-six miles. E. Cherry did not come up, and was left behind; his family was sick.

Saturday, *September 8*.—Crossed the Illinois line in the

morning into Edgar county; crossed the North Arm Prairie, so-called; crossed Sugar creek and came through Paris, the county seat of Edgar county, and traveled fourteen miles on a prairie, and put up for the night at a late hour, pitching our tents on the prairie near the house of Mr. Keller, who appeared friendly and obliging. Traveled today twenty-five miles. Distance from Kirtland, four hundred and seventy miles.

In Illinois.

Sunday, September 9.—Started early, and came to Ambro creek, in a grove, two miles, and encamped during the day. The fourth division came up just as we started in the morning; for they were unable to travel as fast as the other divisions owing to the heat of the day on Saturday. Distance from Kirtland, four hundred and seventy-two miles.

Serious Difficulties Considered.

The Council met after we encamped, and after much consultation concluded to call the heads of families together and lay before them our situation with respect to means and the prospects before us and the apparent impossibility of our obtaining labor for ourselves and for the support of our families in the city of Far West during the coming winter; and to advise them, especially those that did not belong to the Seventies, to commence looking for places for themselves where they could procure a subsistence during the Winter and procure means sufficient to remove them to Missouri in the Spring. Accordingly in the afternoon the camp were called together and those things laid before them for their consideration, which seemed to meet with the approval of a large majority of the heads of families in the camp. Distance from Kirtland, four hundred and seventy-two miles.

Dissatisfaction in Camp.

Monday, September 10.—Considerable anxiety seemed to be manifested by some concerning the advice of the Council, and some complained, like ancient Israel, and said that they did not thank the Council for bringing them so far, and had rather been left in Kirtland, and some said one thing and some another. Among the number were Aaron Cheney, Nathan Cheney, William Draper and Thomas Draper and Henry Munroe, who were sent for, to come and settle with the clerks and look out for quarters immediately. Themira Draper, Alfred Draper and Cornelius Vanleuven left the camp with them. Reuben Daniels, whose wife was sick and had a son born in the night, together with Ethan A. Moore and Joel Harvey, also left the camp to stop for a few days and then pursue their journey by themselves. After the camp started Joseph Coon stopped because his wife was sick. We traveled five or six miles west of the little Ambarras, where we encamped. We passed through a small place called Independence, which is in an oak opening, in which we had encamped. It was about six miles through it, and then we crossed through a prairie fifteen miles, and encamped on the west side of the East Ocha or Kaskaskias, some of the teams not coming up to the encampment till twelve o'clock. Traveled twenty-two miles. Distance from Kirtland, four hundred and ninety-four miles.

Tuesday, September 11.—Crossed another prairie, fourteen miles, and encamped at four p. m. on the west side of the West Ocha, in Macon county, having traveled sixteen miles. Distance from Kirtland, five hundred and ten miles.

Increased Sickness.

Many in the camp at this time were sick and afflicted. Some with fever and ague, and some with one thing and some with another. The most dangerous were Elder Josiah Willey and John Wright, son of Asa Wright, aged about fourteen years.

Wednesday, September 12.—Started at eight o'clock and crossed another prairie twelve miles, then through a piece of timber land on the headwaters of San Juan river, then over a three-mile prairie, and stopped to refresh our teams in the edge of the wood a little after noon, sixteen miles from our encampment of the night before. In the afternoon crossed over a prairie four miles, then through a piece of timbered land, then another prairie two miles, and encamped by the side of a small creek, having traveled this day twenty-two miles. Distance from Kirtland, five hundred and thirty-nine miles.

Thursday, September 13.—In the morning it was ascertained that George Stringham and Benjamin Baker, with Joseph C. Clark had stopped behind, or could not come up because of the failure of their teams. Asa Wright did not come up at night, but came up in the morning by himself before we started, to settle his accounts. His son being sick was the reason of his staying behind. Alba Whittle and Joel H. Johnson also settled their accounts, as they expected to stop at Springfield or sooner if they could find a place.

Started at a late hour and traveled fourteen miles through a prairie country down the Sangamon river, which ran on the right of the road in a westerly course to the Illinois. We encamped about three p. m. on a piece of land laid out for a village called Boliva or Bolivar. Here Ira Thornton's child died. Distance from Kirtland, five hundred and fifty-three miles.

Camp Passes Through Springfield.

Friday, September 14.—Before the first division left the ground Elder Stringham and Benjamin Baker came up, but we left them there. We came this day to Springfield, eighteen miles, crossing several small creeks and passing through a small place called Rochester. From Springfield we came four miles, and encamped for the night. We could not procure anything for our teams to eat and were obliged to fasten them to our wagons and give them a little corn or turn them onto dry prairie almost destitute of vegetation. Springfield is destined to be the seat of government of Illinois and the state house is now in course of building. It is situated on a beautiful prairie and looks like a flourishing place though it is yet in its infancy. Elder J. H. Johnson and his mother and their families, together with

Alba Whittle, Jonathan and Cyrus B. Fisher, Edwin P. Merriam and Samuel Hale—who was sick—and wife, also stopped at Springfield or near there, and Richard Brasher went to Huron, three miles west from Springfield to stop with his friends for a short season. Traveled twenty-two miles. Distance from Kirtland, five hundred and seventy-five miles.

Saturday, September 15.—William Gribble left the camp in the morning to stop at Springfield during the winter, and Ira Thornton left and went on with Allen Wait.

We started before breakfast and traveled fourteen miles. Passed through a small village called Berlin and camped on Spring creek in Island Grove. Here T. P. Pierce's child died, and was buried on Sunday, near Elder Keeler's house. Elder Keeler was late from New Portage, Ohio. Here we tarried till Monday morning. Distance from Kirtland, five hundred and eighty-nine miles.

Sunday, September 16.—We held a meeting in the afternoon and attended to communion. We had but few spectators in the camp during the day. A spirit of union rarely manifested was felt at the meeting, and our souls rejoiced in the Holy One of Israel.

More Departures from the Camp.

Monday, September 17.—This morning Elias Pulsipher, Daniel Pulsipher, Steven Starks, Hiram H. Byington and Monro Crosier settled their accounts and stopped behind. Traveled this day through Jacksonville, a fine village, the county seat of Morgan county, which we entered about fourteen miles east of Jacksonville. From thence we came to Geneva, a small, dusty place, and encamped near David Orton's, on a prairie, having traveled twenty-five miles. Most of the camp was late in arriving on the ground, and some did not come up till morning. Distance from Kirtland, six hundred and fourteen miles.

Tuesday, September 18.—Warren Smith, Jonas Putnam, Stephen Shumway and D. C. Demming and Joseph

Young stopped at Geneva, Morgan county, and in the course of the day, Asaph Blanchard, Stephen Headlock and B. K. Hall also stopped near Exeter, and James C. Snow, whom we found near Geneva, joined us. We came through Exeter to Philip's ferry on the Illinois river, four miles below Naples, which is on the same river, on the straight road from Jacksonville to Quincy on the Mississippi, which we left and traveled six miles east of the ferry. We arrived at the ferry about four p. m., and some of the teams went over and encamped on the west side of the river in Pike county. In the night David Elliot, whom we had left in Putnam county, Indiana, came up on horseback, having arrived with his family within fifteen miles of us in the evening and left us again to hasten on his team that he might overtake us at Louisville, Missouri. Distance from Kirtland, six hundred and twenty-nine miles.

Wednesday, September 19.—We all got over the Illinois at half-past one p. m. and came to Griggsville, then to Pittsfield, the county seat of Pike county, twelve miles, and encamped on a small hill one mile west of the village. While we were crossing the river two brethren arrived from Far West and brought us the first direct information from that place or from any of the brethren in the West since we started on our journey. The country between the Illinois river and Pittsfield is more rolling than it is on the east of that river, especially east of Springfield. Distance traveled from Kirtland, six hundred and forty-two miles.

First Tidings from Far West.

Thursday, September 20.—Started on our journey and came to Atlas, a small village, the former county seat of Pike county, twelve miles through a rolling prairie country, then to the Snye, a branch of the Mississippi, about six miles from the river where we crossed in the afternoon, all but three wagons, into the town of Louisiana, in the state of Missouri; and encamped about three-fourths of a mile west of the town. Traveled twenty miles. Distance from Kirtland, six hundred and sixty-two miles.

A Missouri Storm.

Friday, September 21.—Traveled about seventeen miles throug a hot country and encamped in a wood near a prairie in a heavy rain which fell all the afternoon, and was the first that had fallen on us since we left Bath, Ohio, and was the most tedious time we had passed through. In the evening it thundered and rained powerfully, most of us went to bed without our supper, and tied our horses to our wagons. We thought it a perilous time, but few complained, nearly all bore it patiently. Duncan McArthur broke down his wagon in the forenoon and did not come up at night.

Bad Roads.

Saturday, September 22.—Traveled this day eighteen miles, eight miles of which was the worst road we had on the journey. The other ten miles prairie. Thomas Carico broke down his wagon and stopped and mended it, and did not overtake the camp at night. Eleaser King and sons, who left Kirtland before the camp, came up and encamped with us at night. The air was cool and chilly and towards night uncomfortably cold. We encamped about one-half mile east of Lick creek, in Monroe county. Distance from Kirtland, six hundred and ninety-seven miles.

Sunday, September 23.—A heavy frost in the morning, but after the sun arose it was pleasant and warm. We thought it our duty to travel and accordingly started on our way. The road very rough and bad part of the way, especially in the timbered land. Duncan McArthur and Thomas Carico, who had been left behind in consequence of breaking down their wagons, overtook us in the morning before we all started, some having to stay behind to find their horses, which went back across the prairie about nine miles in the night. E. B. Gaylord broke down his wagon and got badly hurt, and did not overtake us till Monday night. We traveled to Paris, the county seat of Monroe county, twenty miles, and encamped one mile west of the town late in the evening near a prairie. Crossed south fork of Salt river, five miles east of Paris, and several other tributary streams of the same river, most of which were dry by reason of the extreme drought which had prevailed in this land during the summer. Traveled today twenty-one miles. Distance from Kirtland, seven hundred and eighteen miles.

Monday, September 24.—Reorganized the camp which had become rather disorganized by reason of so many stopping by the way. The third division was put into the first and second, as that division had become quite small. The Council called the camp together and laid before them the scanty means in their hands, and wanted the brethren to furnish such things as they had to dispose of to purchase corn, etc., for our cattle and horses, that we might continue our journey. Traveled twenty miles before sunset, most of the way prairie, and encamped on the Elk fork of Salt river. We found the inhabitants in commotion and volunteering, under the order of Governor Boggs, as we were repeatedly told, to go up and fight the "Mormons" in Far West and that region of country. We were very correctly informed that one hundred and ten men had left Huntsville in the morning on that expedition; and that the govenor had called on five thousand from the upper counties ,and if we went any farther we should meet with difficulty and even death as they would as leave kill us as not.

Reorganization of the Camp.

We had been saluted with such reports every day after we came through Jacksonville, Illinois; but we paid little attention to it, trusting in that God for protection which had called upon us to gather ourselves together to the land of Zion, and who had thus far delivered us out of the hands of all our enemies, on every hand, not only in Kirtland, but on all our journey. Traveled this day twenty miles. Distance from Kirtland, seven hundred and thirty-eight miles.

Tuesday, September 25.—Thomas Nickerson lost his

horses and could not find them before the camp started, and did not overtake us at night.

We came through Huntsville, the county seat of Randolph county, eleven miles, where we were told before we arrived there, that we should be stopped, but nothing of the kind occurred when we came through the town, and we even heard no threats whatever, but all appeared friendly. A mile and a half west of Huntsville we crossed the east branch of Chariton, and one and a half miles west of the river we found Ira Ames and some other brethren near the place where the city of Manti is to be built, and encamped for the night on Dark creek, six miles from Huntsville. Traveled this day seventeen miles. Distance from Kirtland, seven hundred and fifty-five miles.

Wednesday, September 26.—In the morning Elder James Foster at a late hour proposed to disband and break up the camp in consequence of some rumors he had heard from the west which he said he believed. Elder Pulsipher being away only five of the Councilors could be present. The other four objected to this proposal, but so far yielded as to consent to have the camp stop till an embassy could be sent to Far West to see the state of things in that region and ascertain whether it would be wisdom or not for us to go into that or any of the western states this winter.

Proposition to Disband the Camp.

The camp was called together and the subject was partially laid before them by Elder Foster, which produced a sadness of countenance seldom seen in the course of our journey. While we were talking over the subject Elder Pulsipher came up, just as a gentleman by the name of Samuel Bend, of Pike county, Missouri, came along, and without knowing our intentions or destination, told us of the state of affairs in Far West, and Adam-ondi-Ahman, and everything we desired to know concerning some particular things. On being told that our intentions were to stop for a while, he advised us to go right along. He told us about the Daviess county mob and that the volunteers called for by the governor, which had rendezvoused at Keatsville, would be discharged at twelve o'clock, noon.

On reconsidering the subject a motion was made to go on which was carried unanimously. Accordingly we moved on and came to Chariton river in Chariton county, sixteen miles, and encamped about four p. m. on the west side of the river. In the afternoon before we started from the place where we stopped to feed on the seven mile prairie, near Brother Kellog's, the militia volunteers began to go by on their return home, and we continued to meet them most of the afternoon. Most of them passed us civilly, but some of them were rather saucy, few replies, however, were made to them. We met some brethren from Far West during the day which confirmed what we had been told in the morning by Mr. Bend. Brother Nickerson overtook us having found his horses, and eight or ten wagons of brethren from Huron county, Ohio, and other places, also Ira O. Thompson, who had formerly been with us as a member of the camp, stayed with us at night. Traveled sixteen miles this day. Distance from Kirtland, seven hundred and seventy-one miles.

Proposition Rejected.

Thursday, September 27.—Started in the morning in some confusion, owing to some misunderstanding, and came to Keatsville on a branch of the Chariton, two miles, and about half a mile west of the town, which is the county seat of Chariton county. We left the state road and took the road to Chillicothe and went up on the east side of Grand river, crossed a prairie about eighteen miles, beautifully diversified with valleys and rolling swells which give it a truly picturesque appearance. It has been surveyed and allotted for military purposes, and for that reason is still unoccupied. We encamped at night at the confluence of the forks of Yellow creek, having traveled twenty-two miles.

On Grand River.

Elder James Foster left us at Keatsville to go by the

way of De Witt, to see his son-in-law, Jonathan Thompson. In the evening the Council met to settle some difficulties and set in order some things that seemed to require attention to enable us to move in order and in peace the remainder of the journey. Traveled twenty-two miles today. Distance from Kirtland, seven hundred and ninety-three miles.

Friday, September 28.—Crossed Turkey creek, seven miles; Locus, four; and pitched our tents on the east side of Parson's creek, in Linn county, six miles from Locus creek, making seventeen miles. Distance from Kirtland, eight hundred and ten miles.

Saturday, September 29.—Came to Mr. Gregory's on Madison creek, six miles; thence to Chillicothe, a town lately laid out for the county seat of Livingston county, eight miles; and encamped about a mile west toward Grand river.

Thomas Carico's and J. H. Holmes' wagons were turned over in the course of the day, but no particular injury was done to any person. The road was new, and in some places rough, especially in the timbered land on the creeks. Traveled fifteen miles today. Distance from Kirtland, eight hundred and twenty-five miles.

Sunday, September 30.—Came to Grand river, two and one-half miles, crossed over and came to a small collection of houses, called Utica; two and one-half miles, here we found Brother Sliter from Kirtland, and some other brethren. From Utica we came through a rough and rolling country for ten miles to Brother Walker's, on Shoal creek, crossed the creek and camped on the west side near the prairie. Richard Blanchard, who joined the camp at Bath, left the camp and went to join his friends who lived near Chillicothe. Traveled fifteen miles today. Distance from Kirtland, eight hundred and forty miles.

Monday, October 1.—Came from Elder Walker's across the prairie, about nineteen miles, and encamped on

Brushy creek. Joshua S. Holman, by permission of one or two of the Council, went on Sunday evening to visit Elder Jacob Myers, formerly from Richland county, Ohio, and early in the morning started on his way without waiting for the camp, disregarding the advice of the Council, and in the evening, at a meeting of the camp, his proceedings were condemned by a unanimous vote. Traveled twenty miles and encamped on Brushy fork of Shoal creek, on the prairie. The entire distance from Kirtland, eight hundred and sixty miles.

Tuesday, October 2.—Crossed Long, Log, and Goose creeks, and arrived in Far West about five p. m. Here we were received with joyful salutations by the brethren in that city. Five miles from the city we were met by the First Presidency of the Church of Latter-day Saints, Joseph Smith, Jun., Sidney Rigdon and Hyrum Smith, together with Isaac Morley, Patriarch of Far West, and George W. Robinson, and by several other brethren between there and the city, who received us with open arms, and escorted us into the city. We encamped on the public square round the foundation of the Temple. Traveled this day ten miles. Whole distance from Kirtland, eight hundred and seventy miles.

[Here the camp journal's narrative ends. The two following entries which complete the history of this remarkable journey are taken from the Prophet's account of the proceedings relative to the camp on its arrival.]

Wednesday, October 3.—The camp continued their journey to Ambrosial creek, where they pitched their tents. I went with them a mile or two, to a beautiful spring, on the prairie, accompanied by Elder Rigdon, brother Hyrum and Brigham Young, with whom I returned to the city, where I spent the remainder of the day.

Thursday, October 4.—This is a day long to be remembered by that part of the Church of Jesus Christ of Latter-day Saints, called the Camp, or Kirtland Camp No. 1, for they arrived at their destination and began to pitch their tents about sunset, when one of the brethren living in the place proclaimed with a loud voice:

"*Brethren, your long and tedious journey is now ended; you are now on the public square of Adam-ondi-Ahman. This is the place where Adam blessed his posterity, when they rose up and called him Michael, the Prince, the Arch-angel, and he being full of the Holy Ghost predicted what should befall his posterity to the latest generation.*"—*Doctrine and Covenants.*

CHAPTER XI.

EXPULSION OF THE SAINTS FROM DE WITT, CARROLL COUNTY, MISSOURI.

Wednesday, October 3.—Sister Alice Hodgin died at Preston on the 2nd of September, 1838. And it was such a wonderful thing for a Latter-day Saint to die in England, that Elder Willard Richards was arraigned before the Mayor's Court at Preston, on the 3rd of October, charged with "killing and slaying" the said Alice with a "black stick," etc., but was discharged without being permitted to make his defense, as soon as it was discovered that the iniquity of his accusers was about to be made manifest.

Vexatious Persecution of Willard Richards.

The mob continued to fire upon the brethren at De Witt.

Mob Movements at De Witt.

The following is an extract from General Parks' express to General Atchison:

DEAR SIR:—I received this morning an affidavit from Carroll county. The following is a copy: "Henry Root, on his oath, states that on the night of the first of October, there was collected in the vicinity of De Witt, an armed force, consisting of from thirty to fifty persons, and on the morning of the second of October they came into the town of De Witt and fired on the civil inhabitants of that place. Thirteen of said individuals were seen by me in that place, and I believe there is actually an insurrection in that place.

"HENRY ROOT.

"Subscribed and sworn to this 3rd day of October, 1838.

"WILLIAM B. MORTON, J. P."

In consequence of which information, and belief of an attack being made on said place, I have ordered out the two companies raised by your order, to be held in readiness under the commands of Captains Bogart and Houston, to march for De Witt, in Carroll county, by eight o'clock tomorrow morning, armed and equipped as the law directs, with six days' provisions and fifty rounds of powder and ball. I will proceed with these troops in person, leaving Colonel Thomas in command of Grand river. As soon as I reach De Witt, I will advise you of the state of affairs more fully. I will use all due precaution in the affair, and deeply regret the necessity of this recourse.

H. G. PARKS,
Brigadier-General 2nd Brigade, 3rd Division.

Thursday, October 4.—I spent most of this day with my family.

The mob again fired upon the Saints at De Witt, who were compelled to return the fire in self-defense.

Scattering Firebrands.

To show how firebrands, arrows and death were scattered through the State, and that too by men high in authority, and who were sworn to preserve the public peace, I quote the following from a communication of General Lucas to the governor dated Boonville, Missouri, October 4, 1838:

Letter of General Lucas to Governor Boggs.

DEAR SIR:—As we passed down the Missouri river, on Monday last, we saw a large force of Mormons at De Witt, in Carroll county, under arms. Their commander, Colonel Hinkle, formerly of Caldwell county, informed me that there were two hundred, and that they were hourly expecting an attack from the citizens of Carroll county, who he said were then encamped only six miles from there, waiting for a reinforcement from Saline county. Hinkle said they had determined to fight. News had just been received at this place, through Dr. Scott of Fayette, that a fight took place on yesterday, and that several persons were killed. Dr. Scott informed me that he got his information from a gentleman of respectability, who had heard the firing of their guns as he passed down. If a fight has actually taken place, of which I have no doubt, it will create excitement in the whole of upper Missouri, and those base and degraded beings will be exterminated from the face of the earth. If one of the citizens of Carroll should be killed, before five days I believe that there will be from four to five thousand volunteers in the field against the Mormons, and nothing but their blood will satisfy them. It is an unpleasant state of affairs. The remedy I do not pretend to suggest to your Excellency. My troops of the Fourth Division were only dismissed subject to further orders, and can be called into the field at an hour's warning.

SAMUEL D. LUCAS.

"*Base and degraded beings!*" Whoever heard before of high-minded and honorable men condescending to sacrifice their honor, by stooping to wage war, without cause or provocation, against "base and degraded beings." But General Lucas is ready with his whole Division, at "an hour's warning," to enter the field of battle on such degraded terms, if his own statement is true. But General Lucas knew better. He knew the Saints were an innocent, unoffending people, and would not fight, only in self-defense, and why write such a letter to the governor to influence his mind? Why not keep to truth and justice? Poor Lucas! The annals of eternity will unfold to you who are the "base beings," and what it will take to "satisfy" for the shedding of "Mormon blood."

The Prophet's Comment.

Friday, October 5.—Report of the committee of Chariton county:

The undersigned committee were appointed at a public meeting by the citizens of Chariton county, on the 3rd day of October for the purpose of repairing to De Witt, in Carroll county, to inquire into the nature of the difficulties between the citizens of Carroll and the Mormons. We arrived at the place of difficulties on the 4th of October, and found a large portion of the citizens of Carroll and the adjoining counties assembled near De Witt, well armed. We inquired into the nature of the difficulties. They said that there was a large portion of the people called Mormons embodied in De Witt, from different parts of the world. They were unwilling for them to remain there, which is the cause of their waging war against them. To use the gentlemen's language, "they were waging a war of extermination, or to remove them from the said county." We also went into De Witt, to see the situation of the Mormons. We found them in the act of defense, begging for peace, and wishing for the civil authorities to repair there as early as possible, to settle the difficulties between the parties. Hostilities have commenced and will continue until they are stopped by the civil authorities. This we believe to be a correct statement of both parties. This the 5th day of October, 1838.

JOHN W. PRICE,
WM. H. LOGAN.

Subscribed to and sworn before me, the undersigned, one of the

Justices of the Peace within and for Chariton county, and State of Missouri, the 5th day of October, 1838.

JOHN MORSE, J. P.

This day also [October 5] General Atchison wrote the governor from Boonville, that in Carroll county the citizens were in arms for the purpose of driving the "Mormons" from that county.

The third Quarterly Conference of the Church in Caldwell county was held at Far West, President Brigham Young presiding. As there was not a sufficient number of members present to form a quorum for business, after singing and prayer, conference adjourned till 2 p. m., when they met and opened as usual, Presidents Marsh and Young presiding. There was not a sufficient number of the members of the High Council or any other quorum to do business as a quarterly Conference. They voted to ordain a few Elders, appointed a few missions, and adjourned till tomorrow at ten o'clock a. m.

Conference at Far West.

About this time I took a journey in company with some others, to the lower part of the county of Caldwell, for the purpose of selecting a location for a town. While on my journey, I was met by one of the brethren from De Witt, in Carroll county, who stated that our people who had settled in that place were and had been some time, surrounded by a mob, who had threatened their lives, and had shot at them several times; and that he was on his way to Far West, to inform the brethren there of the facts.

News of Mob Violence from De Witt.

I was surprised on receiving this intelligence, although there had, previous to this time, been some manifestations of mobs, but I had hoped that the good sense of the majority of the people, and their respect for the Constitution, would have put down any spirit of persecution which might have been manifested in that neighborhood.

The Prophet's Hopes of Peace Disappointed.

Immediately on receiving this intelligence I made preparations to go to that place, and endeavor, if possible, to allay the feelings of the citizens, and save the lives of my brethren who were thus exposed to their wrath.

The Prophet Arrives at De Witt.

Saturday, October 6.—I arrived at De Witt, and found that the accounts of the situation of that place were correct; for it was with much difficulty, and by traveling unfrequented roads, that I was able to get there, all the principal roads being strongly guarded by the mob, who refused all ingress as well as egress. I found my brethren, who were only a handful in comparison to the mob by which they were surrounded, in this situation, and their provisions nearly exhausted, and no prospect of obtaining any more. We thought it necessary to send immediately to the governor, to inform him of the circumstances, hoping to receive from the executive the protection which we needed; and which was guaranteed to us in common with other citizens. Several gentlemen of standing and respectability, who lived in the immediate vicinity who were not in any way connected with the Church of Latter-day Saints, who had witnessed the proceedings of our enemies, came forward and made affidavits to the treatment we had received, and concerning our perilous situation; and offered their services to go and present the case to the governor themselves.

Continuance of Far West Conference.

The Quarterly Conference convened at Far West this day [October 6th] at ten o'clock according to adjournment, Presidents Marsh and Young presiding. Elder Benjamin L. Clapp* said he had just returned from Kentucky, where he had been laboring, and that many doors were open there. A call was made for volunteers to go into the vineyard and preach, when Elders James Carroll, James Galliher, Lu-

* Benjamin L. Clapp, who afterwards became one of the First Council of Seventy, was born in the state of Alabama, August 19, 1814. He had joined the Church in an early day, and had already performed successful missions in the South, especially in the state of Kentucky.

man A. Shurtliff, James Dana, Ahaz Cook, Isaac Decker, Cornelius P. Lott and Alpheus Gifford offered themselves. President Marsh instructed them not to go forth boasting of their faith, or of the judgments of the Lord, but to go in the spirit of meekness, and preach repentance.*

John Taylor Sustained to be an Apostle.

Elder John Taylor† from Canada, by request, gave a statement of his feelings respecting his having been appointed as one of the Twelve, saying that he was willing to do anything that God would require of him; whereupon it was voted that Brother John

* This missionary movement at a time when it may be said that the whole country was "up in arms" against the Church, and its fortunes were apparently desperate, is truly an astonishing thing. And yet such missionary movements have become quite characteristic of the Church of Jesus Christ of Latter-day Saints. Its fortunes have never been at so low an ebb but what it could always undertake some great missionary enterprise. For example, when apostasy was rife in Kirtland, and the powers of darkness seemed massed for its overthrow, the Prophet, "to save the Church," organized and sent forth a mission to Great Britain; and now from upper Missouri, when the whole organization seemed to be in danger of disintegration, a mission is nevertheless organized to go into the Southern States to preach the Gospel. In later volumes of this work we shall also see that in 1850, when the whole body of the Mormon people had been expatriated from their country and fled into the desert wilderness of the Rocky mountain region, and when it was generally supposed that the world had practically seen the last of Mormonism, and when the Saints still had before them the task of subduing a wilderness, and many thousands of their people yet to gather from the East, where they were in a scattered condition, and the very existence of the people to human eyes seemed precarious, lo! a world-wide mission was organized and members of the quorum of Apostles were sent from the Church in the wilderness, into Scandinavia, France, Germany, Italy and Switzerland. This missionary spirit so characteristic of the Church, and to which it so staunchly adheres in all its fortunes, proclaims the genius of the work. The primary purpose of the Church's existence is to proclaim the truth of which it is the sacred depository, and after that to perfect the lives of those who receive its message. In proportion to its devotion to these two grand objects of its existence, has been and always will be the measure of its success.

† John Taylor was born November 1st, 1808, in Milnthorp, a small town near the head of Morecombe bay, and not far from Windemere, the "Queen of English Lakes," in the county of Westmoreland, England. His father's name was James Taylor, whose forefathers for many generations had lived on an estate known as Craig Gate, in Ackenthwaite. John Taylor's mother's name was Agnes; her maiden name was also Taylor. Her grandfather, Christopher Taylor, lived to be ninety-seven years of age. His son John, father of Agnes, held an office in the excise under the government from his first setting out in life to the age of about sixty. The maiden name of Agnes Taylor's mother was Whittington, a descendant of the family made famous by Richard Whittington, the younger son of Sir William Whittington.

Taylor fill one of the vacancies in the quorum of the Twelve. Stephen Chase was ordained president of the Elders' quorum in Far West. Isaac Laney, Horace Alexander and Albert Sloan were ordained Elders under the hands of the presidents. Samuel Bent and Isaac Higbee were appointed to fill the places of John Murdock and George M. Hinkle in the High Council, the two last named brethren having removed to De Witt. Conference adjourned to the first Friday and Saturday in January next, at ten a. m.

EBENEZER ROBINSON, Clerk.

England.

There were seven cut off from the Church in Preston, England, this day.

De Witt.

General Parks wrote General Atchison from Brigade Headquarters, five miles from De Witt, Carroll county:

Communication of Clark to Atchison on Affairs at De Witt.

SIR:—Immediately after my express to you by Mr. Warder was sent, I proceeded to this place, which I reached yesterday with two companies of mounted men from Ray county. I ordered Colonel Jones to call out three companies from this county, to hold themselves in readiness to join me at Carrolton on the fifth instant, which order has not been carried into effect. None of Carroll county regiment is with me.

At the age of seventeen Elder Taylor was made a Methodist exhorter or local preacher, and was very active and earnest in his ministerial labors. In 1832 he removed with his family to Toronto, upper Canada, and here engaged in preaching under the auspices of the Methodist church. Within a year after his arrival in Canada he married Leonora Cannon, daughter of Captain George Cannon (grandfather of the late George Q. Cannon). Leonora Cannon had come to Canada as the companion of the wife of Mr. Mason, the private secretary of Lord Aylmer, Governor-General of Canada. She was a devout Methodist, and through attendance upon church became acquainted with Mr. Taylor. While living in Toronto Elder Taylor associated himself with a number of gentlemen of education and refinement who were not quite satisfied with the doctrines of their respective churches, as those doctrines did not agree with the teachings of the Bible. Through this organization, they were seeking for greater religious light, and it was under these circumstances that Elder Parley P. Pratt arrived in Toronto with a letter of introduction to Elder Taylor, and several times addressed this association of gentlemen who were seeking the truth. The end of the matter was that John Taylor accepted the Gospel under the ministration of Elder Pratt; and was soon afterwards ordained an Elder in the Church, and commenced his missionary labors. Of his journey to Kirtland and defense of the Prophet against the fulminations of apostates we have already spoken. [See vol. II, p. 488—Note]. Elder Taylor had come to Missouri in response to the notification he had received that he was chosen an Apostle of the Lord Jesus Christ by revelation. (See revelation of 8th of July, 1838, pp. 46, 47).

On arriving in the vicinity of De Witt, I found a body of armed men under the command of Dr. Austin, encamped near De Witt, besieging that place, to the number of two or three hundred, with a piece of artillery ready to attack the town of De Witt. On the other side, Hinkle has in that place three or four hundred Mormons to defend it, and says he will die before he will be driven from thence.

On the 4th instant they had a skirmish—fifteen or thirty guns fired on both sides, one man from Saline county wounded in the hip.

The Mormons are at this time too strong, and no attack is expected before Wednesday or Thursday next, at which time Dr. Austin hopes his forces will amount to five hundred men, when he will make a second attempt on the town of De Witt, with small arms and cannon. In this posture of affairs, I can do nothing but negotiate between the parties until further aid is sent me.

I received your friendly letter of the 5th instant, by Mr. Warder, authorizing me to call on General Doniphan, which call I have made on him for five companies from Platte, Clay and Clinton counties, with two companies I ordered from Livingston, of which I doubt whether these last will come; if they do, I think I will have a force sufficient to manage these belligerents. Should these troops arrive here in time, I hope to be able to prevent bloodshed. Nothing seems so much in demand here (to hear the Carroll county men talk) as Mormon scalps; as yet they are scarce. I believe Hinkle, with the present force and position, will beat Austin with five hundred of his troops. The Mormons say they will die before they will be driven out, etc. As yet they have acted on the defensive, as far as I can learn. It is my settled opinion, the Mormons will have no rest until they leave; whether they will or not, time only can tell.

H. G. PARKS.

TheMob's Appeal to Howard County for Help.

Under the same date, [October 6th] from the mob camp near De Witt, eleven blood-thirsty fellows, viz., Congrave Jackson, Larkin H. Woods, Thomas Jackson, Rolla M. Daviess, James Jackson, Jun., Johnson Jackson, John L. Tomlin, Sidney S. Woods, Geo. Crigler. William L. Banks, and Whitfield Dicken, wrote a most inflammatory, lying and murderous communication to the citizens of Howard county, calling upon them as friends and fellow citizens, to come to their immediate rescue, as the "Mormons" were then firing upon them and they would have to act on the defensive until they could procure more assistance.

A. C. Woods, a citizen of Howard county, made a certificate to the same lies, which he gathered in the mob camp; he did not go into De Witt, or take any trouble to learn the truth of what he certified. While the people will lie and the authorities will uphold them, what justice can honest men expect?

Tuesday, October 9.—General Clark wrote the governor from Boonville, that the names subscribed to the paper named above, are worthy, prudent and patriotic citizens of Howard county, yet these men would leave their families and everything dear, and go to a neighboring county to seek the blood of innocent men, women and children! If this constitutes "worth, prudence and patriotism," let me be worthless, imprudent and unpatriotic.

General Clark's Endorsement of the Mob.

The messenger, Mr. Caldwell, who had been dispatched to the governor for assistance, returned, but instead of receiving any aid or even sympathy from his Excellency, we were told that "the quarrel was between the Mormons and the mob," and that "we might fight it out."

The Governor's Answer to the Saints.

About this time a mob, commanded by Hyrum Standly, took Smith Humphrey's goods out of his house, and said Standly set fire to Humphrey's house and burned it before his eyes, and ordered him to leave the place forthwith, which he did by fleeing from De Witt to Caldwell county. The mob had sent to Jackson county and got a cannon, powder and balls, and bodies of armed men had gathered in, to aid them, from Ray, Saline, Howard, Livingston, Clinton, Clay, Platte counties and other parts of the state, and a man by the name of Jackson, from Howard county, was appointed their leader.

House Burning and Robbing.

The Saints were forbidden to go out of the town under pain of death, and were shot at when they attempted to go out to get food, of which they were destitute. As fast as their cattle or horses got where the mob could get hold of them, they were taken as spoil, as also other kinds of property. By these outrages the brethren were obliged, most of them, to live in wagons or tents.

Application had been made to the judge of the Circuit Court for protection, and he ordered out two companies of militia, one commanded by Captain Samuel Bogart, a Methodist minister, and one of the worst of the mobocrats. The whole force was placed under the command of General Parks, another mobber, if his letter speaks his feelings, and his actions do not belie him, for he never made the first attempt to disperse the mob, and when asked the reason of his conduct, he always replied that Bogart and his company were mutinous and mobocratic, that he dare not attempt a dispersion of the mob. Two other principal men of the mob were Major Ashly, member of the Legislature, and Sashiel Woods, a Presbyterian clergyman.

Mob Leaders Made Commanders of Militia.

General Parks informed us that a greater part of his men under Captain Bogart had mutinied, and that he would be obliged to draw them off from the place, for fear they would join the mob; consequently he could offer us no assistance.

We had now no hopes whatever of successfully resisting the mob, who kept constantly increasing; our provisions were entirely exhausted, and we were worn out by continually standing on guard, and watching the movements of our enemies, who, during the time I was there, fired at us a great many times. Some of the brethren perished from starvation; and for once in my life, I had the pain of beholding some of my fellow creatures fall victims to the spirit of persecution, which did then, and has since, prevailed to such an extent in Upper Missouri. They were men, too, who were virtuous and against whom no legal process could for one moment be sustained, but who, in consequence of their love of God, attachment to His cause, and their determination to

Hardships of the Saints.

keep the faith, were thus brought to an untimely grave.

In the meantime Henry Root and David Thomas, who had been the soul cause of the settlement of our people in De Witt, solicited the Saints to leave the place. Thomas said he had assurances from the mob, that if they would leave the place they would not be hurt, and that they would be paid for all losses which they had sustained, and that they had come as mediators to accomplish this object, and that persons should be appointed to set a value on the property which they had to leave, and that they should be paid for it. The Saints finally, through necessity, had to comply, and leave the place. Accordingly the committee was appointed—Judge Erickson was one of the committee, and Major Florey, of Rutsville, another, the names of others are not remembered. They appraised the real estate, that was all.

Proposals for the Departure of the Saints.

When the people came to start, many of their horses, oxen and cows were gone, and could not be found. It was known at the time, and the mob boasted of it, that they had killed the oxen and lived on them. Many houses belonging to my brethren were burned, their cattle driven away, and a great quantity of their property was destroyed by the mob. The people of De Witt utterly failed to fulfill their pledge to pay the Saints for the losses they sustained. The governor having turned a deaf ear to our entreaties, the militia having mutinied, the greater part of them being ready to join the mob, the brethren, seeing no prospect of relief, came to the conclusion to leave that place, and seek a shelter elsewhere. Gathering up as many wagons as could be got ready, which was about seventy, with a remnant of the property they had been able to save from their ruthless foes, they left De Witt and started for Caldwell county on the afternoon of Thursday, October 11, 1838. They traveled that day about twelve miles, and encamped in a grove of timber near the road.

A Sad Journey.

That evening a woman, of the name of Jensen, who

had some short time before given birth to a child, died in consequence of the exposure occasioned by the operations of the mob, and having to move before her strength would properly admit of it. She was buried in the grove, without a coffin.

During our journey we were continually harassed and threatened by the mob, who shot at us several times, whilst several of our brethren died from the fatigue and privation which they had to endure, and we had to inter them by the wayside, without a coffin, and under circumstances the most distressing. We arrived in Caldwell on the twelfth of October.

CHAPTER XII.

MOVEMENTS OF THE MOB UPON DE WITT—BATTLE OF CROOKED RIVER—EXTERMINATING ORDER OF GOVERNOR BOGGS.

No sooner had the brethren left De Witt than Sashiel Woods called the mob together, and made a speech to them to the effect that they must hasten to assist their friends in Daviess county. The land sales, he said, were coming on, and if they could get the "Mormons" driven out, they could get all the lands entitled to pre-emptions, and that they must hasten to Daviess county in order to accomplish their object; that if they would join and drive out the Saints, the old settlers could get all the lands back again, as well as all the pay they had received for them. He assured the mob that they had nothing to fear from the state authorities in so doing, for they had now full proof that those authorities would not assist the "Mormons," and that they [the mob] might as well take their property from them as not. His proposition was agreed to, and accordingly the whole banditti started for Daviess county, taking with them their cannon.

Plan of the Mob to Dispossess the Saints.

In the meantime, Cornelius Gilliam was busily engaged in raising a mob in Platte and Clinton counties, to aid Woods in his effort to drive peaceable citizens from their homes and take their property.

On my arrival in Caldwell, I was informed by General Doniphan, of Clay county, that a company of mobbers, eight hundred strong, were marching toward a settlement of our people in Daviess county. He ordered out one of the officers to raise a force and march immediately to what he called Wight's

Plans of Doniphan to Protect the Saints

Town [Adam-ondi-Ahman], and defend our people from the attacks of the mob, until he should raise the militia in his [Clay] and the adjoining counties to put them down. A small company of militia, who were on their way to Daviess county, and who had passed through Far West, he ordered back again, stating that they were not to be depended upon, as many of them were disposed to join the mob, and to use his own expression, were "damned rotten hearted."

Sunday, October 14.—I preached to the brethren at Far West from the saying of the Savior: "Greater love hath no man than this, that he lay down his life for his brethren." At the close I called upon all that would stand by me to meet me on the public square the next day.

There were seven cut off from the Church in Preston, England, this day. It was a general time of pruning in England. The powers of darkness raged, and it seemed as though Satan was fully determined to make an end of the work in that kingdom. Elders Joseph Fielding and Willard Richards had as much as they could do for some time, to see to the branches already planted, without planting new ones.

State of Affairs in England.

Monday, October 15.—The brethren assembled on the public square of Far West and formed a company of about one hundred, who took up a line of march for Adam-ondi-Ahman. Here let it be distinctly understood that this company were militia of the county of Caldwell, acting under Lieutenant-Colonel George M. Hinkle, agreeable to the order of General Doniphan, and the brethren were very careful in all their movements to act in strict accordance with the constitutional laws of the land.

Organization for Defense.

The special object of this march was to protect Adam-ondi-Ahman, and repel the attacks of the mob in Daviess county. Having some property in that county, and having a house building there, I went up at the same time. While I was there a number of houses belonging to our people were burned by the

Mob Depredations at "Diahman."

mob, who committed many other depredations, such as driving off horses, sheep, cattle, hogs, etc. A number of those whose houses were burned down, as well as those who lived in scattered and lonely situations, fled into the town for safety, and for shelter from the inclemency of the weather, as a considerable snowstorm took place on the 17th and 18th. Women and children, some in the most delicate condition, were thus obliged to leave their homes and travel several miles in order to effect their escape. My feelings were such as I cannot describe when I saw them flock into the village, almost entirely destitute of clothes, and only escaping with their lives.

Affairs at Millport.

During this state of affairs, General Parks arrived in Daviess county, and was at the house of Colonel Lyman Wight on the 18th, when the intelligence was brought that the mob were burning houses; and also when women and children were fleeing for safety, among whom was Agnes M. Smith, wife of my brother, Don Carlos Smith, who was absent on a mission in Tennessee. Her house had been plundered and burned by the mob, and she had traveled nearly three miles, carrying her two helpless babes, and had to wade Grand river.

Parks' Order to Wight to Disperse the Mob.

Colonel Wight, who held a commission in the 59th regiment under his (General Parks') command, asked what was to be done. Parks told him that he must immediately call out his men and go and put the mob down. Accordingly a force was immediately raised for the purpose of quelling the mob, and in a short time was on its march, with a determination to disperse the mob, or die in the attempt; as the people could bear such treatment as was being inflicted upon them no longer.

Strategem of the Mob.

The mob, having learned the orders of General Parks, and likewise being aware of the determination of the oppressed, broke up their encampment and fled. The mob seeing that they could not succeed by force, now resorted to strategem; and after removing their property out of their houses, which were nothing but log cabins, they fired them, and then reported to the authorities of the state that the "Mormons" were burning and destroying all before them.*

Beginning of Wm. Clayton's Ministry

Friday, October 19.—Elder William Clayton quitted his temporal business in England, and gave himself wholly to the ministry, and soon commenced preaching and baptizing in Manchester.

Vindication of the Prophet's Business Course in Kirtland.

As I was driven away from Kirtland without the privilege of settling my business, I had, previous to this, employed Colonel Oliver Granger as my agent, to close all my affairs in the east; and as I have been accused of "running away, cheating my creditors, etc., I will insert one of the many cards and letters I have received from gentlemen who have had the best opportunity of knowing my busi-

* It was a cunning piece of diabolism which prompted the mob of Daviess county to set fire to their own log cabins, destroy some of their own property and then charge the crime to the Saints. But it was not without a precedent in Missouri. Two years before that, something very similar occurred in Mercer county, just northeast of Daviess. In June of the year 1836, the Iowa Indians, then living near St. Joseph, made a friendly hunting excursion through the northern part of the state, and their line of travel led them through what was known as the "Heatherly settlement," in Mercer county. The Heatherlys, who were ruffians of the lowest type, took advantage of the excitement produced by the incursion of the Indians, and circulated a report that they were robbing and killing the whites. During the excitement these Heatherlys murdered a man by the name of Dunbar, and another man against whom they had a grudge, and then fled to the settlements along the Missouri river, representing that they were fleeing from the Indians for their lives. This produced great excitement in the settlements in the surrounding counties; the people not knowing at what hour the Indians might be upon them. The militia was called out for their protection; but it was soon ascertained that the alarm was a false one. The Heatherlys were arrested, tried for murder, and some of them sent to the penitentiary This circumstance occurring only two years before the action of the mob about Millport, and in a county adjacent to Daviess county, doubtless suggested the course pursued by the mob in burning their own houses and fleeing to all parts of the state with the report that the "Mormons" had done it, and were murdering and plundering the old settlers. These false rumors spread by the mob, were strengthened in the public ear by such men as Adam Black, Judge King of Richmond, and other prominent men who were continually writing inflammatory communications to the governor.—For the Heatherly incident, see "History of Livingston County, Missouri," written and compiled by the National Historical Company (1886), chapter 3, pp. 710, 713.

ness transactions, and whose testimony comes unsolicited:

A Card.

PAINSVILLE, October 19, 1838.

We, the undersigned, being personal acquaintances of Oliver Granger, firmly believe that the course which he has pursued in settling the claims, accounts, etc., against the former citizens of Kirtland township, has done much credit to himself, and all others that committed to him the care of adjusting their business with this community, which also furnishes evidence that there was no intention on their part of defrauding their creditors.

[Signed] THOMAS GRIFFITH,
JOHN S. SEYMOUR.

Crimes of the Mob Charged to the Saints.

About this time William Morgan, sheriff of Daviess county, Samuel Bogart, Colonel William P. Penniston, Doctor Samuel Venable, Jonathan J. Dryden, James Stone and Thomas J. Martin, made communications or affidavits of the most inflammatory kind, charging upon the "Mormons" those depredations which had been committed by the mob, endeavoring thereby to raise the anger of those in authority, rallying a sufficient force around their standard, and produce a total overthrow, massacre, or banishment of the "Mormons" from the state. These and their associates were the ones who fired their own houses and then fled the country crying "fire and murder."

Departure of Orson Hyde from Far West.

It was reported in Far West today [October 19th] that Orson Hyde had left that place, the night previous, leaving a letter for one of the brethren, which would develop the secret.

Return of the Prophet to Far West.

Monday, *22*.—On the retreat of the mob from Daviess county, I returned to Caldwell, with a company of the brethren, and arrived at Far West about seven in the evening, where I had hoped to enjoy some respite from our enemies, at least for a short time; but upon my arrival there, I was informed that a mob had commenced hostilities on the borders of Caldwell county, adjoining Ray county, and that they had taken some of our brethren prisoners, burned some houses, and had committed depredations on the peaceable inhabitants.

Tuesday, *23*.—News came to Far West, this morning, that the brethren had found the cannon, which the mob brought from Independence, buried in the earth, and had secured it by order of General Parks. The word of the Lord was given several months since, for the Saints to gather into the cities, but they have been slow to obey until the judgments were upon them, and now they are gathering by flight and haste, leaving all their effects, and are glad to get off at that. The city of Far West is literally crowded, and the brethren are gathering from all quarters.

The Saints Flock into Far West.

Fourteen citizens of Ray county, one of whom was a Mr. Hudgins, a postmaster, wrote the governor an inflammatory epistle. Thomas C. Burch, of Richmond, wrote a similar communication. Also the citizens of Ray county, in public meeting, appealed to the governor of the state, to give the people of Upper Missouri protection from the fearful body of "thieves and robbers;" while the fact is the Saints were minding their own business, only as they were driven from it by those who were crying thieves and robbers.

Inflammatory Letters to the Governor.

The mail came in this evening, but not a single letter to anybody, from which it is evident there is no deposit sacred to those marauders who are infesting the country and trying to destroy the Saints.

The Mail Robbed.

Wednesday, *24*.—Austin A. King and Adam Black renewed their inflammatory communications to the governor, as did other citizens of Richmond, viz., C. R. Morehead, William Thornton, and Jacob Gudgel, who scrupled at no falsehood or exaggeration, to raise the governor's anger against us.

The Course of King and Black.

Thomas B. Marsh, formerly president of the Twelve,

having apostatized, repaired to Richmond and made affidavit before Henry Jacobs, justice of the peace, to all the vilest slanders, aspersions, lies and calumnies towards myself and the Church, that his wicked heart could invent. He had been lifted up in pride by his exaltation to office and the revelations of heaven concerning him, until he was ready to be overthrown by the first adverse wind that should cross his track, and now he has fallen, lied and sworn falsely, and is ready to take the lives of his best friends. Let all men take warning by him, and learn that he who exalteth himself, God will abase. Orson Hyde was also at Richmond and testified to most of Marsh's statements.*

The Apostasy of Thomas B. Marsh.

* The chief points in the affidavit of Thomas B. Marsh, referred to in the text, are as follows: "They have among them a company, considered true Mormons, called the Danites, who have taken an oath to support the heads of the Church in all things that they say or do, *whether right or wrong*. Many, however, of this band are much dissatisfied with this oath, as being against moral and religious principles. On Saturday last, I am informed by the Mormons, that they had a meeting at Far West, at which they appointed a company of twelve, by the name of the 'Destruction Company,' for the purpose of burning and destroying, and that if the people of Buncombe came to do mischief upon the people of Caldwell, and committed depredations upon the Mormons, they were to burn Buncombe; and if the people of Clay and Ray made any movement against them, this destroying company were to burn Liberty and Richmond. * * * * The Prophet inculcates the notion, and it is believed by every true Mormon, that Smith's prophecies are superior to the laws of the land. I have heard the Prophet say that he would yet tread down his enemies, and walk over their dead bodies; and if he was not let alone, he would be a second Mohammed to this generation, and that he would make it one gore of blood from the Rocky mountains to the Atlantic ocean; that like Mohammed, whose motto in treating for peace was, 'the Alcoran or the Sword.' So should it be eventually with us, 'Joseph Smith or the Sword.' These last statements were made during the last summer. The number of armed men at Adam-ondi-Ahman was between three and four hundred.

"THOMAS B. MARSH.

"Sworn to and subscribed before me, the day herein written.

"HENRY JACOBS,
"J. P. Ray county, Missouri.

"Richmond, Missouri, October 24, 1838."

"AFFIDAVIT OF ORSON HYDE.

"The most of the statements in the foregoing disclosure I know to be true; the remainder I believe to be true.

"ORSON HYDE.

"Richmond, October 24, 1838.

"Sworn to and subscribed before me, on the day above written.

"HENRY JACOBS, J. P."

Of this testimony and the action of Marsh and Hyde the late President Taylor in

The following letter, being a fair specimen of the "truth and honesty" of many others which I shall notice, I give it in full:

Communication of Woods and Dickson to Governor Boggs.

CARROLTON, MISSOURI, October 24, 1838.

SIR:—We were informed, last night, by an express from Ray county, that Captain Bogart and all his company, amounting to between fifty and sixty men were massacred by the Mormons at Buncombe, twelve miles north of Richmond, except three. This statement you may rely on as being true, and last night they expected Richmond to be laid in ashes this morning. We could distinctly hear cannon, and we know the Mormons had one in their possession. Richmond is about twenty-five

his discourse on Succession in the Presidency, makes these pertinent remarks: "Testimonies from these sources are not always reliable, and it is to be hoped, for the sake of the two brethren, that some things were added by our enemies that they did not assert, but enough was said to make this default and apostasy very terrible. I will here state that I was in Far West at the time these affidavits were made, and was mixed up with all prominent Church affairs. I was there when Thomas B. Marsh and Orson Hyde left there; and there are others present who were there at the same time. And I know that these things, referred to in the affidavits, are not true. I have heard a good deal about Danites, but I never heard of them among the Latter-day Saints. If there was such an organization, I never was made acquainted with it * * * * * * Thomas B. Marsh was unquestionably instigated by the devil when he made this statement, which has been read in your hearing [the foregoing affidavit]. The consequence was, he was cut off from the Church. * * * * * * It would be here proper to state, however, that Orson Hyde had been sick with a violent fever for some time, and had not yet fully recovered therefrom, which, with the circumstances with which we were surrounded, and the influence of Thomas B. Marsh, may be offered as a slight palliation for his default. * * * * * * It may be proper here again to say a few words with regard to Brother Orson Hyde, whose endorsement of the terrible charges made by Thomas B. Marsh in his affidavit, has already been read. Suffice it to say, in addition to what has previously been stated, he was cut off from the Church, and of course lost his apostleship; and when he subsequently returned, and made all the satisfaction that was within his power, he was forgiven by the authorities and the people and was again re-instated in the quorum."

Schuyler Colfax, vice-president of the United States, in his discussion with the late President John Taylor on the "Mormon Question," quoted this Marsh-Hyde affidavit, and Elder Taylor in reply said: "I am sorry to say that Thomas B. Marsh did make that affidavit, and that Orson Hyde stated that he knew part of it and believed the other; and it would be disingenuous in me to deny it; but it is not true that these things existed, for I was there and knew to the contrary; and so did the people of Missouri, and so did the governor of Missouri. How do you account for their acts? Only on the score of the weakness of our common humanity. We were living in troublous times, and all men's nerves are not proof against such shocks as we then had to endure."

miles west of this place, on a straight line. We know not the hour or minute we will be laid in ashes—our country is ruined—for God's sake give us assistance as quick as possible.

Yours, etc.,
SASHIEL WOODS,
JOSEPH DICKSON.

The Prophet's Statement of the Buncombe Affair.

These mobbers must have had very accute ears to hear cannon, (a six pounder) thirty-seven miles! So much for the lies of a priest of this world. Now for the truth of the case. This day about noon, Captain Bogart, with some thirty or forty men called on Brother Thoret Parsons, at the head of the east branch of Log creek, where he was living, and warned him to be gone before next day at ten in the morning, declaring also that he would give Far West thunder and lightning before next day at noon, if he had good luck in meetin Neil Gillum, (Cornelius Gilliam) who would camp about six miles west of Far West that night, and that he should camp on Crooked creek. He then departed towards Crooked creek.

Raid on the Pinkham Residence.

Brother Parsons dispatched a messenger with this news to Far West, and followed after Bogart to watch his movements. Brothers Joseph Holbrook and David Juda, who went out this morning to watch the movements of the enemy, saw eight armed mobbers call at the house of Brother Pinkham, where they took three prisoners, Nathan Pinkham, Brothers William Seely and Addison Green, and four horses, arms, etc. When departing they threatened Father Pinkham that if he did not leave the state immediately they "would have his damned old scalp." Having learned of Bogart's movements the brethren returned to Far West near midnight, and reported their proceedings and those of the mob.

On hearing the report, Judge Elias Higbee, the first judge of the county, ordered Lieutenant Colonel Hinkle, the highest officer in command in Far West, to send out a company to disperse the mob and retake their prisoners, whom, it was reported, they intended to murder that night. The trumpet sounded, and the brethren were assembled on the public square about midnight, when the facts were stated, and about seventy-five volunteered to obey the judge's order, under command of Captain David W. Patten, who immediately commenced their march on horseback, hoping without the loss of blood to surprise and scatter the camp, retake the prisoners and prevent the attack threatening Far West.

Crooked River Battle.

Thursday, *25*.—Fifteen of the company were detached from the main body while sixty continued their march till they arrived near the ford of Crooked river, (or creek) where they dismounted, tied their horses, and leaving four or five men to guard them, proceeded towards the ford, not knowing the location of the encampment. It was just at the dawning of light in the east, when they were marching quietly along the road, and near the top of the hill which descends to the river that the report of a gun was heard, and young Patrick O'Banion reeled out of the ranks and fell mortally wounded. Thus the work of death commenced, when Captain Patten ordered a charge and rushed down the hill on a fast trot, and when within about fifty yards of the camp formed a line. The mob formed a line under the bank of the river, below their tents. It was yet so dark that little could be seen by looking at the west, while the mob looking towards the dawning light, could see Patten and his men, when they fired a broadside, and three or four of the brethren fell. Captain Patten ordered the fire returned, which was instantly obeyed, to great disadvantage in the darkness which yet continued. The fire was repeated by the mob, and returned by Captain Patten's company, who gave the watchword "God and Liberty." Captain Patten then ordered a charge, which was instantly obeyed. The parties immediately came in contact, with their swords, and the mob were soon put to flight, crossing the river at the ford and such places as they could get a chance. In the pursuit, one of the mob fled from behind a tree, wheeled, and shot Captain Patten, who instantly fell, mortally wounded, having received a large ball in his bowels.

The ground was soon cleared, and the brethren gathered up a wagon or two, and making beds therein of tents, etc, took their wounded and retreated towards Far West. Three brethren were wounded in the bowels, one in the neck, one in the shoulder, one through the hips, one through both thighs, one in the arms, all by musket shot. One had his arm broken by a sword. Brother Gideon Carter was shot in the head, and left dead on the ground so defaced that the brethren did not know him. Bogart reported that he had lost one man. The three prisoners were released and returned with the brethren to Far West. Captain Patten was carried some of the way in a litter, but it caused so much distress that he begged to be left by the way side. He was carried into Brother Winchester's, three miles from the city of Far West, where he died that night. Patrick O'Banion died soon after, and Brother Carter's body was also brought from Crooked river, when it was discovered who he was.

List of Casualties. Death of Patten and O'Banion.

I went with my brother Hyrum and Lyman Wight to meet the brethren on their return, near Log creek, where I saw Captain Patten in a most distressing condition. His wound was incurable.

Brother David Patten was a very worthy man, beloved by all good men who knew him. He was one of the Twelve Apostles, and died as he had lived, a man of God, and strong in the faith of a glorious resurrection, in a world where mobs will have no power or place. One of his last expressions to his wife was—"Whatever you do else, O! do not deny the faith."

The Prophet's Reflections on the Death of David W. Patten.

How different his fate to that of the apostate, Thomas

B. Marsh, who this day vented all the lying spleen and malice of his heart towards the work of God, in a letter to Brother and Sister Abbot, to which was annexed an addenda by Orson Hyde.

The following letter will show the state of public feeling in the country at this time:

E. M. Ryland's Letter to Messrs. Rees and Williams.

LEXINGTON, six o'clock p. m.
October 25, 1838.

To Messrs. Amos Rees and Wiley C. Williams:

GENTLEMEN:—This letter is sent on after you on express by Mr. Bryant, of Ray county, since you left this morning. Mr. C. R. Morehead came here on express for men to assist in repelling a threatened attack upon Richmond tonight. He brought news that the Mormon armed force had attacked Captain Bogart this morning at daylight, and had cut off his whole company of fifty men. Since Mr. Morehead left Richmond, one of the company (Bogart's) has come in and reported that there were ten of his comrades killed and the remainder were taken prisoners, after many of them had been severely wounded; he stated further that Richmond would be sacked and burned by the Mormon banditti tonight. Nothing can exceed the consternation which this news gave rise to. The women and children are flying from Richmond in every direction. A number of them have repaired to Lexington, amongst whom is Mrs. Rees. We will have sent from this county since one o'clock this evening about one hundred well-armed and daring men, perhaps the most effective our county can boast of. They will certainly give them (the Mormons) a warm reception at Richmond tonight. You will see the necessity of hurrying on to the City of Jefferson, and also of imparting correct information to the public as you go along. My impression is, that you had better send one of your number to Howard, Cooper and Boone counties, in order that volunteers may be getting ready and flocking to the scene of trouble as fast as possible. They must make haste and put a stop to the devastation which is menaced by these infuriated fanatics, and they must go prepared and with the full determination to exterminate or expel them from the state *en masse.* Nothing but this can give tranquility to the public mind, and re-establish the supremacy of the laws. There must be no further delaying with this question any where. The Mormons must leave the state, or we will, one and all, and to this complexion it must come at last. We have great reliance upon your ability, discretion and fitness for the task you have undertaken, and we have only time to say, God speed you.

Yours truly,
E. M. RYLAND, Judge.

The brethren had *not thought* of going to Richmond—it was a lie out of whole cloth.

Governor Boggs' Order to General John B. Clark.

FRIDAY, HEADQUARTERS OF THE MILITIA,
CITY OF JEFFERSON October 26, 1838.

General John B. Clark, 1st Division Missouri Militia:

SIR:—Application has been made to the commander-in-chief, by the citizens of Daviess county, in this state, for protection, and to be restored to their homes and property, with intelligence that the Mormons, with an armed force, have expelled the inhabitants of that county from their homes, have pillaged and burnt their dwellings, driven off their stock, and were destroying their crops; that they (the Mormons) have burnt to ashes the towns of Gallatin and Millport in said county; the former being the county seat of said county, and including the clerk's office and all the public records of the county, and that there is not now a civil officer within said county. The commander-in-chief therefore orders that there be raised, from the 1st, 4th, 5th, 6th and 12th Divisions of the militia of this state, four hundred men each, to be mounted and armed as Infantry or Riflemen, each man to furnish himself with at least fifty rounds of ammunition, and at least fifteen days provisions. The troops from the 1st, 5th, 6th and 12th, will rendezvous at Fayette, in Howard county, on Saturday, the 3rd day of next month (November) at which point they will receive further instructions as to their line of march. You will therefore cause to be raised the quota of men required of your division (four hundred men) without delay, either by volunteer or drafts, and rendezvous at Fayette, in Howard county, on Saturday, the third day of next month (November) and there join the troops from the 5th, 6th and 12th divisions. The troops from the 4th division will join you at Richmond in Ray county. You will cause the troops raised in your division, to be formed into companies according to law, and placed under officers already in commission. If volunteer companies are raised, they shall elect their own officers. The preference should always be given to volunteer companies already organized and commissioned. You will also detail the necessary field and staff officers. For the convenience of transporting the camp equipage, provisions and hospital stores for the troops under your command, you are authorized to employ two or three baggage wagons.

By order of the Commander-in-Chief,

B. M. LISLE, Adj.-General.

Letters of Horace Kingsbury and John W. Hawden on the Business Integrity of the Prophet and his Agents in Kirtland.

To all persons that are or may be interested. I, Horace Kingsbury, of Painsville township, Geauga county, and state of Ohio, feeling the importance of recommending to remembrance every worthy citizen who has by his conduct commended himself to personal acquaintance by his course of strict integrity, and desire for truth and common justice, feel it my duty to state that Oliver Granger's management in the arrangement of the unfinished business of people that have moved to the Far West, in redeeming their pledges and thereby sustaining their integrity, has been truly praiseworthy, and has entitled him to my highest esteem, and ever grateful recollection.

HORACE KINGSBURY.

Painesville, October 26, 1838.

To whom it may concern. This may certify that during the year of eighteen hundred and thirty-seven, I had dealings with Messrs. Joseph Smith, Junior, and Sidney Rigdon, together with other members of the [Mormon] society, to the amount of about three thousand dollars, and during the spring of eighteen hundred and thirty-eight, I have received my pay in full of Colonel Oliver Granger to my satisfaction. And I would here remark that it is due Messrs. Smith and Rigdon, and the [Mormon] society generally, to say that they have ever dealt honorably and fair with me: and I have received as good treatment from them as I have received from any other society in this vicinity; and so far as I have been correctly informed and made acquainted with their business transactions generally, they have, so far as I can judge, been honorable and honest, and have made every exertion to arrange and settle their affairs. And I would further state, that the closing up of my business with said society has been with their agent, Colonel Granger, appointed by them for that purpose; and I consider it highly due Colonel Granger from me, here to state that he has acted truly and honestly in all his business with me, and has accomplished more than I could reasonably have expected. And I have also been made acquainted with his business in that section; and wherever he has been called upon to act, he has done so and with good management he has accomplished and effected the close of a large amount of business for said society,and as I believe, to the entire satisfaction of all concerned.

JOHN W. HAWDEN.

Painesville, Geauga county, Ohio, October 27, 1838.

Saturday, 27.—Brother Patten was buried this day at Far West, and before the funeral, I called at Brother Patten's house, and while meditating on the scene before me in presence of his friends, I could not help pointing to his lifeless body and testifying, "There lies a man that has done just as he said he would—he has laid down his life for his friends."

Funeral of David W. Patten.

Governor Boggs' Exterminating Order.

HEADQUARTERS MILITIA, CITY OF JEFFERSON,
October 27, 1838.

SIR:—Since the order of the morning to you, directing you to cause four hundred mounted men to be raised within your division, I have received by Amos Rees, Esq., and Wiley C. Williams, Esq., one of my aids, information of the most appalling character, which changes the whole face of things, and places the Mormons in the attitude of open and avowed defiance of the laws, and of having made open war upon the people of this state. Your orders are, therefore, to hasten your operations and endeavor to reach Richmond, in Ray county, with all possible speed. The Mormons must be treated as enemies and *must be exterminated* or driven from the state, if necessary for the public good. Their outrages are beyond all description. If you can increase your force, you are authorized to do so, to any extent you may think necessary. I have just issued orders to Major-General Wallock, of Marion county, to raise five hundred men, and to march them to the northern part of Daviess and there to unite with General Doniphan, of Clay, who has been ordered with five hundred men to proceed to the same point for the purpose of intercepting the retreat of the Mormons to the north. They have been directed to communicate with you by express; and you can also communicate with them if you find it necessary. Instead, therefore, of proceeding as at first directed, to reinstate the citizens of Daviess in their homes, you will proceed immediately to Richmond, and there operate against the Mormons. Brigadier-General Parks, of Ray, has been ordered to have four hundred men of his brigade in readiness to join you at Richmond. The whole force will be placed under your command.

L. W. BOGGS,
Governor and Commander-inChief.

To General Clark.

Great excitemet now prevailed, and mobs were heard

of in every direction, who seemed determined on our destruction. They burned the houses in the country, and took off all the cattle they could find. They destroyed corn fields, took many prisoners, and threatened death to all the Mormons.

Excitement in Upper Missouri.

The Appeal of Atchison and Lucas to Governor Boggs, Asking his Presence at the seat of War.

HEADQUARTERS OF THE 3RD AND 4TH DIVISION, MISSOURI MILITIA, RICHMOND, October 28, 1838.

To the Commander-in-Chief, Missouri Militia:

SIR:—From late outrages committed by the *Mormons*, *civil war* is inevitable. They have set the laws of the country at defiance, and are in open rebellion. We have about two thousand men under arms to keep them in check. The presence of the commander-in-chief is deemed absolutely necessary, and we most respectfully urge that your excellency be at the seat of *war* as soon as possible.

Your most obedient servants,

DAVID R. ATCHISON, M. G. 3rd Div.*

SAMUEL D. LUCAS, M. G. 4th Div.

* It is to be regretted that General David R. Atchison joined with General Lucas in signing the above communication. Up to this time Major General Atchison had apparently exercised his influence counseling moderation in dealing with the "Mormons." He was a resident of Clay county when the Saints were driven into that county from Jackson. He, with General Doniphan and Amos Rees, had acted as counsel for the exiles, and had seen the doors of the temple of justice closed in their faces by mob violence, and all redress denied them. He was acquainted with the circumstances which led to their removal from Clay county, to the unsettled prairies of what afterwards became Caldwell county. He knew how deep and unreasonable the prejudices were against the Saints. Can it be possible that he did not know how utterly unjustifiable the present movement against them was? Whether he was blinded by the false reports about Millport and Gallatin and Crooked river, or whether his courage faltered, and he became afraid longer to defend a people against whom every man's hand was raised, I cannot now determine, but one or the other must have been the case. General Atchison, however, was afterwards "dismounted," to use a word of General Doniphan's in relating the incident, and sent back to Liberty in Clay county by special order of Governor Boggs, on the ground that he was inclined to be too merciful to the "Mormons," so that he was not active in the operations about Far West. But how he could consent to join with Lucas in sending such an untruthful and infamous report to the governor about the situation in Upper Missouri, is difficult to determine. The Saints had not set the laws at defiance, nor were they in open rebellion. But when all the officers of the law refused to hear their complaints, and both civil and military authority delivered them into the hands of merciless mobs to be plundered and outraged at their brutal pleasure, and all petitions for protection at the hands of the governor had been answered with: "It is a quarrel be-

tween the Mormons and the mob, and they must fight it out," what was left for them to do but to arm themselves and stand in defense of their homes and families? The movement on Gallatin by Captain Patten and that on Millport by Colonel Wight was ordered by General Parks, who called upon Colonel Wight to take command of his company of men, when the militia under Parks' command mutinied, and dispersed all mobs wherever he found them. Gallatin was not burned, nor were the records of the county court, if they were destroyed at all, destroyed by the Saints. What houses were burned in Millport had been set on fire by the mob. The expedition to Crooked river was ordered by Judge Higbee, the first judge in Caldwell county and the highest civil authority in Far West, and was undertaken for the purpose of dispersing a mob which had entered the house of a peaceable citizen—one Pinkham—and carried off three people prisoners, four horses and other property, and who had threatened to "give Far West hell before noon the next day." So that in their operations the acts of the Saints had been strictly within the law, and only in self defense.

CHAPTER XIII.

MOB MOVEMENTS ON FAR WEST—TREACHERY OF COLONEL HINKLE—SORROWFUL SCENES.

The Prophet's Comment on Governor Boggs.

LILBURN W. BOGGS had become so hardened by mobbing the Saints in Jackson county, and his conscience so "seared as with a hot iron," that he was considered a fit subject for the gubernatorial chair; and it was probably his hatred to truth and the "Mormons," and his blood-thirsty, murderous disposition, that raised him to the station he occupied. His *exterminating order* of the twenty-seventh aroused every spirit in the state, of the like stamp of his own; and the Missouri mobocrats were flocking to the standard of General Clark from almost every quarter.

General Clark

Clark, although not the ranking officer, was selected by Governor Boggs as the most fit instrument to carry out his murderous designs; for bad as they were in Missouri, very few commanding officers were yet sufficiently hardened to go all lengths with Boggs in this contemplated inhuman butchery, and expulsion from one of the should-be free and independent states of the Republic of North America, where the Constitution declares, that "*every man shall have the privilege of worshiping God according to the dictates of his own conscience;*" and this was all the offense the Saints had been guilty of.

Doctor Sampson Avard.

And here I would state, that while the evil spirits were raging up and down in the state to raise mobs against the "Mormons," Satan himself was no less busy in striving to stir up mischief in the camp of the Saints: and among the most conspicuous of his willing devotees was one Doctor Sampson Avard, who had been in the Church but a short time, and who, although he had generally behaved with a tolerable degree of external decorum, was secretly aspiring to be the greatest of the great, and become the leader of the people. This was his pride and his folly, but as he had no hopes of accomplishing it by gaining the hearts of the people openly he watched his opportunity with the brethren—at a time when mobs oppressed, robbed, whipped, burned, plundered and slew, till forbearance seemed no longer a virtue, and nothing but the grace of God without measure could support men under such trials—to form a secret combination by which he might rise a mighty conqueror, at the *expense and the overthrow of the Church.* This he tried to accomplish by his smooth, flattering, and winning speeches, which he frequently made to his associates, while his room was well guarded by some of his followers, ready to give him the signal on the approach of anyone who would not approve of his measures.

Avard's Danites.

In these proceedings he stated that he had the sanction of the heads of the Church for what he was about to do; and by his smiles and flattery, persuaded them to believe it, and proceeded to administer to the few under his control, an oath, binding them to everlasting secrecy to everything which should be communicated to them by himself. Thus Avard initiated members into his band, firmly binding them, by all that was sacred, in the protecting of each other in all things that were lawful; and was careful to picture out a great glory that was then hovering over the Church, and would soon burst upon the Saints as a cloud by day, and a pillar of fire by night, and would soon unveil the slumbering mysteries of heaven, which would gladden the hearts and arouse the stupid spirits of the Saints of the latter-day, and fill their hearts with that love which is unspeakable and full of glory, and arm them with power, that the gates of hell could not prevail against them; and would often affirm to his company that the principal men of the Church had put him forward as a spokesman, and a leader of this band, which *he* named *Danites*.

Thus he duped many, which gave him the opportunity of figuring as a person of importance. He held his meetings daily, and carried on his crafty work in great haste, to prevent mature reflection upon the matter by his followers, until he had them bound under the penalties of death to keep the secrets and certain signs of the organization by which they were to know each other by day or night.

Avard's Manner of Proceeding.

After those performances, he held meetings to organize his men into companies of tens and fifties, appointing a captain over each company. After completing this organization, he went on to teach the members of it their duty under the orders of their captains; he then called his captains together and taught them in a secluded place, as follows:

Avard's Instructions to His Captains.

My brethren, as you have been chosen to be our leading men, our captains to rule over this last kingdom of Jesus Christ—and you have been organized after the ancient order—I have called upon you here today to teach you, and instruct you in the things that pertain to your duty, and to show you what your privileges are, and what they soon will be. Know ye not, brethren, that it soon will be your privilege to take your respective companies and go out on a scout on the borders of the settlements, and take to yourselves spoils of the goods of the ungodly Gentiles? for it is written, the riches of the Gentiles shall be consecrated to my people, the house of Israel; and thus you will waste away the Gentiles by robbing and plundering them of their property; and in this way we will build up the kingdom of God, and roll forth the little stone that Daniel saw cut out of the mountain without hands, and roll forth until it filled the whole earth. For this is the very way that God destines to build up His kingdom in the last days. If any of us should be recognized, who can harm us? for we will stand by each other and defend one another in all things. If our enemies swear against us, we can swear also. [The captains were confounded at this, but Avard continued]. Why do you startle at this, brethren? As the Lord liveth, I would swear to a lie to clear any of you; and if this would not do, I would put them or him under the sand as Moses did the Egyptian; and in this way we will consecrate much unto the Lord, and

build up His kingdom; and who can stand against us? And if any of us transgress, we will deal with him amongst ourselves. And if any one of this Danite society reveals any of these things, I will put him where the dogs *cannot bite him.*

At this lecture all of the officers revolted, and said it would not do, they would not go into any such measures, and it would not do to name any such thing; "such proceedings would be in open violation of the laws of our country, would be robbing our fellow citizens of their rights, and are not according to the language and doctrine of Christ, or of the Church of Latter-day Saints."

Revolt of Avard's Officers.

Avard replied, and said there was no laws that were executed in justice, and he cared not for them, this being a different dispensation, a dispensation of the fullness of times; in this dispensation he learned from the Scriptures that the kingdom of God was to put down all other kingdoms, and the Lord Himself was to reign, and His laws alone were the laws that would exist.

Avard's teachings were still manfully rejected by all. Avard then said that they had better drop the subject, although he had received his authority from Sidney Rigdon the evening before. The meeting then broke up; the eyes of those present were opened, Avard's craft was no longer in the dark, and but very little confidence was placed in him, even by the warmest of the members of his Danite scheme.

Avard's Teachings Rejected.

When a knowledge of Avard's rascality came to the Presidency of the Church, he was cut off from the Church, and every means proper used to destroy his influence, at which he was highly incensed, and went about whispering his evil insinuations, but finding every effort unavailing, he again turned conspirator, and sought to make friends with the mob.

Avard Excommunicated.

And here let it be distinctly understood, that these companies of tens and fifties got up by Avard, were altogether separate and distinct from those companies of tens and fifties organized by the brethren for self defense, in case of an attack from the mob. This latter organization was called into existence more particularly that in this time of alarm no family or person might be neglected; therefore, one company would be engaged in drawing wood, another in cutting it, another in gathering corn, another in grinding, another in butchering, another in distributing meat, etc., etc., so that all should be employed in turn, and no one lack the necessaries of life. Therefore, let no one hereafter, by mistake or design, confound this organization of the Church for good and righteous purposes, with the organization of the "Danites," of the apostate Avard, which died almost before it had existed.

Distinction in Organization Pointed Out.

The mob began to encamp at Richmond on the twenty-sixth, and by this time amounted to about two thousand men, all ready to fulfill the exterminating order, and join the standard of the governor. They took up a line of march for Far West, traveling but part way, where they encamped for the night.

Gathering of the Mob at Richmond.

Tuesday, *October 30*.—The advance guard of the mob were patrolling the country and taking many prisoners, among whom were Brother Stephen Winchester, and Brother Carey, whose skull they laid open by a blow from a rifle barrel. In this mangled condition, the mob laid him in their wagon and went on their way, denying him every comfort, and thus he remained that afternoon and night.

General Clark was in camp at Chariton under a forced march to Richmond, with about a thousand men, and the governor's exterminating order.

Gen. Clark's Movements.

For the history of this day at Haun's Mills, on Shoal creek, I quote the following affidavit of Elder Joseph Young, First President of the Seventies:

Joseph Young's Narrative of the Massacre at Haun's Mills.

On the sixth day of July last, I started with my family from Kirtland, Ohio, for the state of Missouri, the county of Caldwell, in the upper part of the state, being the place of my destination.

On the thirteenth day of October I crossed the Mississippi at Louisiana, at which place I heard vague reports of the disturbances in the upper country, but nothing that could be relied upon. I continued my course westward till I crossed Grand river, at a place called Compton's Ferry, at which place I heard, for the first time, that if I proceeded any farther on my journey, I would be in danger of being stopped by a body of armed men. I was not willing, however, while treading my native soil, and breathing republican air, to abandon my object, which was to locate myself and family in a fine, healthy country, where we could enjoy the society of our friends and connections. Consequently, I prosecuted my journey till I came to Whitney's Mills, situated on Shoal creek, in the eastern part of Caldwell county.

After crossing the creek and going about three miles, we met a party of the mob, about forty in number, armed with rifles, and mounted on horses, who informed us that we could go no farther west, threatening us with instant death if we proceeded any farther. I asked them the reason of this prohibition; to which they replied, that we were "Mormons;" that everyone who adhered to our religious faith, would have to leave the state in ten days, or *renounce* their religion. Accordingly they drove us back to the mills above mentioned.

Here we tarried three days; and, on Friday, the twenty-sixth, we recrossed the creek, and following up its banks, we succeeded in eluding the mob for the time being, and gained the residence of a friend in Myer's settlement.

On Sunday, twenty-eighth October, we arrived about twelve o'clock, at Haun's Mills, where we found a number of our friends collected together, who were holding a council, and deliberating on the best course for them to pursue, to defend themselves against the mob, who were collecting in the neighborhood under the command of Colonel Jennings, of Livingston county, and threatening them with house burning and killing. The decision of the council was, that our friends there should place themselves in an attitude of self defense. Accordingly about twenty-eight of our men armed themselves, and were in constant readiness for an attack of any small body of men that might come down upon them.

The same evening, for some reason best known to themselves, the mob sent one of their number to enter into a treaty with our friends, which was accepted, on the condition of mutual forbearance on both sides, and that each party, as far as their influence extended, should exert themselves to prevent any further hostilities upon either party.

At this time, however, there was another mob collecting on Grand river, at William Mann's, who were threatening us, consequently we remained under arms.

Monday passed away without molestation from any quarter.

On Tuesday, the 30th, that bloody tragedy was acted, the scene of which I shall never forget. More than three-fourths of the day had passed in tranquility, as smiling as the preceding one. I think there was no individual of our company that was apprised of the sudden and awful fate that hung over our heads like an overwhelming torrent, which was to change the prospects, the feelings and the circumstances of about thirty families. The banks of Shoal creek on either side teemed with children sporting and playing, while their mothers were engaged in domestic employments, and their fathers employed in guarding the mills and other property, while others were engaged in gathering in their crops for their winter consumption. The weather was very pleasant, the sun shone clear, all was tranquil, and no one expressed any apprehension of the awful crisis that was near us—even at our doors.

It was about four o'clock, while sitting in my cabin with my babe in my arms, and my wife standing by my side, the door being open, I cast my eyes on the opposite bank of Shoal creek and saw a large company of armed men, on horses, directing their course towards the mills with all possible speed. As they advanced through the scattering trees that stood on the edge of the prairie they seemed to form themselves into a three square position, forming a vanguard in front.

At this moment, David Evans, seeing the superiority of their numbers, (there being two hundred and forty of them, according to their own account), swung his hat, and cried for peace. This not being heeded, they continued to advance, and their leader, Mr. Nehemiah Comstock, fired a gun, which was followed by a solemn pause of ten or twelve seconds, when, all at once, they discharged about one hundred rifles, aiming at a blacksmith shop into which our friends had fled for safety; and charged up to the shop, the cracks of which between the logs were sufficiently large to enable them to aim directly at the bodies of those who had there fled for refuge from the fire of their murderers. There were several families tented in the rear of the shop, whose lives were exposed, and amidst a shower of bullets fled to the woods in different directions.

After standing and gazing on this bloody scene for a few minutes, and finding myself in the uttermost danger, the bullets having reached the house where I was living, I committed my family to the protection of heaven, and leaving the house on the opposite side, I took a path which led up the hill, following in the trail of three of my brethren that had fled from the shop. While ascending the hill we were discovered by the mob, who immediately fired at us, and continued so to do till we reached the summit. In descending the hill, I secreted myself in a thicket of bushes, where I lay till eight o'clock in the evening, at which time I heard a female voice calling my name in an under tone, telling me that the mob had gone and there was no danger. I immediately left the thicket, and went to the house of Benjamin Lewis, where I found my family (who had fled there) in safety, and two of my friends mortally wounded, one of whom died before morning. Here we passed the painful night in deep and awful reflections on the scenes of the preceding evening.

After daylight appeared, some four or five men, who with myself, had escaped with our lives from the horrid massacre, and who repaired as soon as possible to the mills, to learn the condition of our friends, whose fate we had but too truly anticipated. When we arrived at the house of Mr. Haun, we found Mr. Merrick's body lying in the rear of the house, Mr. McBride's in front, literally mangled from head to foot. We were informed by Miss Rebecca Judd, who was an eye witness, that he was shot with his own gun, after he had given it up, and then cut to pieces with a corn cutter by a Mr. Rogers of Daviess county, who keeps a ferry on Grand river, and who has since repeatedly boasted of this act of savage barbarity. Mr. York's body we found in the house, and after viewing these corpses, we immediately went to the blacksmith's shop, where we found nine of our friends, eight of whom were already dead; the other, Mr. Cox, of Indiana, struggling in the agonies of death and soon expired. We immediately prepared and carried them to the place of interment. The last office of kindness due to the remains of departed friends, was not attended with the customary ceremonies or decency, for we were in jeopardy, every moment expecting to be fired upon by the mob, who, we supposed, were lying in ambush, waiting for the first opportunity to despatch the remaining few who were providentially preserved from the slaughter of the preceding day. However, we accomplished without molestation this painful task. The place of burying was a vault in the ground, formerly intended for a well, into which we threw the bodies of our friends promiscuously. Among those slain I will mention Sardius Smith, son of Warren Smith, about nine years old, who, through fear, had crawled under the bellows in the shop, where he remained till the massacre was over, when he was discovered by a Mr. Glaze, of Carroll county, who presented his rifle near the boy's head, and literally blowed off the upper part of it. Mr. Stanley, of Carroll, told me afterwards that Glaze boasted of this fiend-like murder and heroic deed all over the country.

The number killed and mortally wounded in this wanton slaughter was eighteen or nineteen, whose names as far as I recollect were as follows: Thomas McBride, Levi N. Merrick, Elias Benner, Josiah Fuller, Benjamin Lewis, Alexander Campbell, Warren Smith, Sardius Smith, George S. Richards, Mr. William Napier, Augustine Harmer, Simon Cox, Mr. [Hiram] Abbott, John York, Charles Merrick, (a boy eight or nine nears old), [John Lee, John Byers], and three or four others, whose names I do not recollect, as they were strangers, to me. Among the wounded who recovered were Isaac Laney, Nathan K. Knight, Mr. [William] Yokum, two brothers by the name of [Jacob and George] Myers, Tarlton Lewis, Mr. [Jacob] Haun, and several others, [Jacob Foutz, Jacob Potts, Charles Jimison, John Walker, Alma Smith, aged about nine years]. Miss Mary Stedwell, while fleeing, was shot through the hand, and, fainting, fell over a log, into which they shot upwards of twenty balls.

To finish their work of destruction, this band of murderers, composed of men from Daviess, Livingston, Ray, Carroll, and Chariton counties, led by some of the principal men of that section of the upper country, (among whom I am informed were Mr. Ashby, of Chariton, member of the state legislature; Colonel Jennings, of Livingston county, Thomas O. Bryon, clerk of Livingston county; Mr. Whitney, Dr. Randall, and many others), proceeded to rob the houses, wagons, and tents, of bedding and clothing; drove off horses and wagons, leaving widows and orphans destitute of the necessaries of life; and even stripped the clothing from the bodies of the slain. According to their own account, they *fired seven* rounds in this awful butchery, making upwards of sixteen hundred shots at a little company of men, about thirty in number. I hereby certify the above to be a true statement of facts, according to the best of my knowledge.

JOSEPH YOUNG.

STATE OF ILLINOIS, } ss.
COUNTY OF ADAMS. }

I hereby certify that Joseph Young this day came before me, and made oath in due form of law, that the statements contained in the foregoing sheet are true, according to the best of his knowledge and belief. In testimony whereof I have hereunto set my hand and affixed the seal of the Circuit Court at Quincy, this fourth day of June, in the year of our Lord one thousand eight hundred and thirty-nine.

C. M. WOODS,
Clerk Circuit Court, Adams Co., Ill.

A younger brother of the boy here killed, aged eight, was shot through the hip. The little fellow himself states that seeing his father and brother both killed, he thought they would shoot him again if he stirred, and so feigned himself dead, and lay perfectly still, till he heard his mother call him after dark.

Additional Events of the Massacre.

Nathan K. Knight saw a Missourian cut down Father McBride with a corn-cutter, and also saw them stripping the dying, and heard the boys crying for mercy. Brother Knight made his escape across the mill-dam, after receiving wounds through his lungs and finger. After the massacre was over, he was led to a house by a woman, and whilst lying there wounded he heard Mr. Jesse Maupin say that he blew one of the boys' brains out. Some time later whilst walking the streets of Far West Brother Knight was met by three Missourians who threatened to butcher him, and one of them by the name of Rogers drew a butcher knife, and said that he had not got his corn-cutter with him, that he cut down McBride with, "but by —— I have got something that will do as well:" but by a great chance Brother Knight made his escape from the ruffian.

General Atchison withdrew from the army at Richmond as soon as the governor's extermination order was received. Up to this time we were ignorant at Far West of the movements of the mob at Richmond, and the governor's order of extermination.

Atchison Withdraws from "Militia."

On the 30th of October a large company of armed soldiers were seen approaching Far West. They came up near to the town, and then drew back about a mile, and encamped for the night. We were informed that they were militia, ordered out by the governor for the purpose of stopping our proceedings, it having been represented to his excellency, by wicked and designing men from Daviess that we were the aggressors, and had committed outrages in Daviess county. They had not yet got the governor's order of

Arrival of more Mob-Militia.

extermination, which I believe did not arrive till the next day.

Wednesday, October 31.—The militia of Far West guarded the city the past night, and arranged a temporary fortification of wagons, timber, etc., on the south. The sisters, many of them, were engaged in gathering up their most valuable effects, fearing a terrible battle in the morning, and that the houses might be fired and they obliged to flee. The enemy was five to one against us.

Prepartions for a Battle.

About eight o'clock a flag of truce was sent from the enemy, which was met by several of our people, and it was hoped that matters would be satisfactorily arranged after the officers had heard a true statement of all the circumstances. Colonel Hinkle went to meet the flag, and secretly made the following engagement: First, to give up their [the Church's] leaders to be tried and punished; second, to make an appropriation of the property of all who had taken up arms, for the payment of their debts, and indemnify for the damage done by them; third, that the remainder of the Saints should leave the state, and be protected while doing so by the militia; but they were to be permitted to remain under protection until further orders were received from the commander-in-chief; fourth, to give up their arms of every description, which would be receipted for.

Col. Hinkle's Treachery.

The enemy was reinforced by about one thousand five hundred men today, and news of the destruction of property by the mob reached us from every quarter.

Reinforcement of the Mob.

Towards evening I was waited upon by Colonel Hinkle, who stated that the officers of the militia desired to have an interview with me and some others, hoping that the difficulties might be settled without having occasion to carry into effect the exterminating orders which they had received from the governor. I immediately complied with the request, and in

Betrayal of the Prophet *et al.*

company with Elders Sidney Rigdon and Parley P. Pratt, Colonel Wight and George W. Robinson, went into the camp of the militia. But judge of my surprise, when, instead of being treated with that respect which is due from one citizen to another, we were taken as prisoners of war, and treated with the utmost contempt.* The officers would not converse with us, and the soldiers, almost to a man, insulted us as much as they felt disposed, breathing out threats against me and my companions. I

* Elder Parley P. Pratt in his Autobiography referring to this betrayal cf the brethren on the part of Hinkle and their reception and treatment by the mob, says: "Colonel George M. Hinkle, who was at that time the highest officer of the militia assembled for the defense of Far West, waited on Messrs. Joseph Smith, Sidney Rigdon, Hyrum Smith, Lyman Wight, George W. Robinson and myself, with a request from General Lucas that we would repair to his camp, with the assurance that as soon as peaceable arrangements could be entered into we should be released. We had no confidence in the word of a murderer and robber, but there was no alternative but to put ourselves into the hands of such monsters, or to have the city attacked, and men, women and children massacred. We, therefore, commended ourselves to the Lord, and voluntarily surrendered as sheep into the hands of wolves. As we approached the camp of the enemy General Lucas rode out to meet us with a guard of several hundred men. The haughty general rode up, and, without speaking to us, instantly ordered his guards to surround us. They did so very abruptly, and we were marched into camp surrounded by thousands of savage looking beings, many of whom were dressed and painted like Indian warriors. These all set up a constant yell, like so many bloodhounds let loose upon their prey, as if they had achieved one of the most miraculous victories that ever graced the annals of the world. If the vision of the infernal regions could suddenly open to the mind, with thousands of malicious fiends, all clamoring, exulting, deriding, blaspheming, mocking, railing, raging and foaming like a troubled sea, then could some idea be formed of the hell which we had entered.

In camp we were placed under a strong guard, and were without shelter during the night, lying on the ground in the open air, in the midst of a great rain. The guards during the whole night kept up a constant tirade of mockery, and the most obscene blackguardism and abuse. They blasphemed God; mocked Jesus Christ; swore the most dreadful oaths; taunted Brother Joseph and others; demanded miracles; wanted signs, such as 'Come, Mr. Smith, show us an angel.' 'Give us one of your revelations.' 'Show us a miracle.' 'Come, there is one of your brethren here in camp whom we took prisoner yesterday in his own house, and knocked his brains out with his own rifle, which we found hanging over his fireplace; he lays speechless and dying; speak the word and heal him, and then we will all believe ' 'Or, if you are Apostles or men of God, deliver yourselves, and then we will be Mormons'' Next would be a volley of oaths and blasphemies; then a tumultuous tirade of lewd boastings of having defiled virgins and wives by force, etc., much of which I dare not write; and, indeed, language would fail me to attempt more than a faint description. Thus passed this dreadful night, and before morning several other captives were added to our number, among whom was Brother Amasa Lyman."—Autobiography of Parley P. Pratt, pp. 203-205.

cannot begin to tell the scene which I there witnessed. The loud cries and yells of more than one thousand voices, which rent the air and could be heard for miles, and the horrid and blasphemous threats and curses which were poured upon us in torrents, were enough to appall the stoutest heart. In the evening we had to lie down on the cold ground, surrounded by a strong guard, who were only kept back by the power of God from depriving us of life. We petitioned the officers to know why we were thus treated, but they utterly refused to give us any answer, or to converse with us. After we arrived in the camp, Brother Stephen Winchester and eleven other brethren who were prisoners, volunteered, with permission of the officers, to carry Brother Carey into the city to his family, he having lain exposed to the weather for a show to the inhuman wretches, without having his wound dressed or being nourished in any manner. He died soon after he reached home.

The Prophet and Companions Condemned to be Shot.

Thursday, November 1.—Brothers Hyrum Smith and Amasa Lyman were brought prisoners into camp. The officers of the militia held a court martial, and sentenced us to be shot, on Friday morning, on the public square of Far West as a warning to the "Mormons."* However, notwithstanding their sentence and determination, they were

* This incident of sentencing the Prophet and his companion prisoners to be shot on the public square at Far West is also referred to in the History of Caldwell county, compiled by the St. Louis National Historical Company, and the formal orders of General Lucas to Brigadier-General Doniphan and also Doniphan's reply are given. I quote the following: "Yielding to the pressure upon him, it is alleged that General Lucas, at about midnight, issued the following order to General Doniphan, in whose keeping the hostages were:

" '*Brigadier-General Doniphan:*

" 'SIR:—You will take Joseph Smith and the other prisoners into the public square of Far West, and shoot them at 9 o'clock to-morow morning.

" 'SAMUEL D. LUCAS,
" 'Major-General Commanding.'

But General Doniphan, in great and righteous indignation, promptly returned the following reply to his superior:

" 'It is cold-blooded murder. I will not obey your order. My brigade shall march not permitted to carry their murderous sentence into execution. Having an opportunity of speaking to General Wilson, I inquired of him why I was thus treated. I told him I was not aware of having done anything worthy of such treatment; that I had always been a supporter of the Constitution and of democracy. His answer was, "I know it, and that is the reason why I want to kill you, or have you killed."

Robbings of the Militia.

The militia went into the town, and without any restraint whatever, plundered the houses, and abused the innocent and unoffending inhabitants and left many destitute. They went to my house, drove my family out of doors, carried away most of my property. General Doniphan declared he would have nothing to do with such cold-blooded murder, and that he would withdraw his brigade in the morning.

Governor Boggs wrote General Clark from Jefferson City, that he considered full and ample powers were

for Liberty tomorrow morning, at 8 o'clock; and if you execute these men, I will hold you responsible before an earthly tribunal, so help me God.

" 'A. W. Doniphan,
" 'Brigadier-General.'

"The prisoners somehow heard of the order, and kneeled in prayer, and prayed fervently that it might not be executed. And it was not. Flagrantly insubordinate as was General Doniphan's refusal, he was never called to account for it. The 'Mormons' have always remembered General Doniphan's humanity on this occasion, as well as on others, and when, in 1873, he went to Salt Lake City, he was received with much feeling, and shown every regard and attention by Brigham Young and the other authorities of the Church and city, and by even the masses of the people."—(History of Caldwell County, p. 137).

Parley P. Pratt, referring to this incident, says: "We were informed that the general officers held a secret council during most of the night, which was dignified by the name of court martial; in which, without a hearing, or, without even being brought before it, we were all sentenced to be shot. The day and hour was also appointed for the execution of this sentence, viz., next morning at 8 o'clock, in the public square at Far West. Of this we were informed by Brigadier-General Doniphan, who was one of the council, but who was so violently opposed to this cold-blooded murder that he assured the council that he would revolt and withdraw his whole brigade, and march them back to Clay county as soon as it was light, if they persisted in so dreadful an undertaking. Said he, 'It is cold-blooded murder, and I wash my hands of it.' His firm remonstrance, and that of a few others, so alarmed the haughty murderer and his accomplices that they dare not put the decree in execution."

vested in him [Clark] to carry into effect the former orders; says Boggs:

Excerpt from Governor Boggs' Communication to General Lucas.

The case is now a very plain one—the "Mormons" must be subdued; and peace restored to the community; you will therefore proceed without delay to execute the former orders. Full confidence is reposed in your ability to do so; your force will be amply sufficient to accomplish the object. Should you need the aid of artillery, I would suggest that an application be made to the commanding officer of Fort Leavenworth, for such as you may need. You are authorized to request the loan of it in the name of the state of Missouri. The ringleaders of this rebellion should be made an example of; and if it should become necessary for the public peace, the "Mormons" should be exterminated, or expelled from the state.

Citizens of Far West Disarmed.

This morning General Lucas ordered the Caldwell militia to give up their arms. Hinkle, having made a treaty with the mob on his own responsibility, to carry out his treachery, marched the troops out of the city, and the brethren gave up their arms, their own property, which no government on earth had a right to require.

High Handed Procedure of the Mob.

The mob (called Governor's troops) then marched into town, and under pretense of searching for arms, tore up floors, upset haystacks, plundered the most valuable effects they could lay their hands on, wantonly wasted and destroyed a great amount of property, compelled the brethren at the point of the bayonet to sign deeds of trust to pay the expenses of the mob, even while the place was desecrated by the chastity of women being violated. About eighty men were taken prisoners, the remainder were ordered to leave the state, and were forbidden, under threat of being shot by the mob to assemble more than three in a place.

Avard's Treachery.

Friday, *November* 2.—About this time Sampson Avard was found by the mob secreted in the hazel brush some miles from Far West, and brought into camp, where he and they were "hail fellows well met;" for Avard told them that Daniteism was an order of the Church, and by his lying tried to make the Church a scape-goat for his sins.

Myself and fellow prisoners were taken to the town, into the public square, and before our departure we, after much entreaty, were suffered to see our families, being attended all the while by a strong guard. I found my wife and children in tears, who feared we had been shot by those who had sworn to take our lives, and that they would see me no more. When I entered my house, they clung to my garments, their eyes streaming with tears, while mingled emotions of joy and sorrow were manifested in their countenances. I requested to have a private interview with them a few minutes, but this privilege was denied me by the guard. I was then obliged to take my departure. Who can realize the feelings which I experienced at that time, to be thus torn from my companion, and leave her surrounded with monsters in the shape of men, and my children, too, not knowing how their wants would be supplied; while I was to be taken far from them in order that my enemies might destroy me when they thought proper to do so. My partner wept, my children clung to me, until they were thrust from me by the swords of the guards. I felt overwhelmed while I witnessed the scene, and could only recommend them to the care of that God whose kindness had followed me to the present time, and who alone could protect them, and deliver me from the hands of my enemies, and restore me to my family.*

*Of these scenes connected with the separation of the prisoners from their families, Parley P. Pratt writes as follows: "We were now marched to Far West, under the conduct of the whole army; and while they halted in the public square, we were permitted to go with a guard for a change of linen, and to take final leave of our families, in order to depart as prisoners to Jackson county, a distance of sixty miles.

"This was the most trying scene of all. I went to my house, being guarded by two or three soldiers, the cold rain was pouring down without, and on entering my little cottage, there lay my wife sick of a fever, with which she had been for some time confined. At her breast was our son Nathan, an infant of three months, and

After this painful scene I was taken back to the camp, and with the rest of my brethren, namely, Sidney Rigdon, Hyrum Smith, Parley P. Pratt, Lyman Wight, Amasa Lyman, and George W. Robinson, started off for

by her side a little girl of five years. On the foot of the same bed lay a woman in travail, who had been driven from her house in the night, and had taken momentary shelter in my hut of ten feet square—my larger house having been torn down. I stepped to the bed; my wife burst into tears; I spoke a few words of comfort, telling her to try to live for my sake and the children's; and expressing a hope that we should meet again though years might separate us. She promised to try to live. I then embraced and kissed the little babies and departed. Till now I had refrained from weeping; but, to be forced from so helpless a family, who were destitute of provisions and fuel, and deprived almost of shelter in a bleak prairie, with none to assist them, exposed to a lawless banditti who were utter strangers to humanity, and this at the approach of winter, was more than nature could well endure. I went to General Moses Wilson in tears, and stated the circumstances of my sick, heart-broken and destitute family in tears which would have moved any heart that had a latent spark of humanity yet remaining. But I was only answered with an exultant laugh, and a taunt of reproach by this hardened murderer. As I returned from my house towards the troops in the square, I halted with the guard at the door of Hyrum Smith, and heard the sobs and groans of his wife, at his parting words. She was then near confinement; and needed more than ever the comfort and consolation of a husband's presence. As we returned to the wagon we saw Sidney Rigdon taking leave of his wife and daughters, who stood at a little distance, in tears of anguish indescribable. In the wagon sat Joseph Smith, while his aged father and venerable mother came up overwhelmed with tears, and took each of the prisoners by the hand with a silence of grief too great for utterance. In the meantime hundreds of the brethren crowded around us, anxious to take a parting look, or a silent shake of the hand; for feelings were too intense to allow of speech. In the midst of these scenes orders were given and we moved slowly away, under the conduct of General Wilson and his whole brigade."—Autobiography of Parley P. Pratt, pp. 207, 208.

The Prophet's mother describes these scenes of sorrow and parting in the following vivid manner:

"At the time when Joseph went into the enemy's camp, Mr. Smith and myself stood in the door of the house in which we were then living, and could distinctly hear their horrid yellings. Not knowing the cause, we supposed they were murdering him. Soon after the screaming commenced, five or six guns were discharged. At this, Mr. Smith, folding his arms tight across his heart, cried out, 'Oh, my God! my God! they have killed my son! they have murdered him! and I must die, for I cannot live without him?'

"I had no word of consolation to give him, for my heart was broken within me—my agony was unutterable. I assisted him to the bed and he fell back upon it helpless as a child, for he had not strength to stand upon his feet. The shrieking continued; no tongue can describe the sound which was conveyed to our ears; no heart can imagine the sensation of our breasts, as we listened to those awful screams. Had the army been composed of so many bloodhounds, wolves, and panthers, they could not have made a sound more terrible. * * * *

"When they [the division of the mob in charge of the prisoners] were about starting from Far West, a messenger came and told us that if we ever saw our sons alive, we must go immediately to them, for they were in a wagon that would

Independence, Jackson county, and encamped at night on Crooked river, under a strong guard commanded by Generals Lucas and Wilson.

The following letter gives the particulars relating to the movements of the governor's troops in conjunction with the mob:

Report of General S. D. Lucas to Governor Boggs.

HEADQUARTERS, CAMP NEAR FAR WEST,
November 2, 1838.

To His Excellency, L. W. Boggs, Commander-in-Chief, Missouri Militia:

SIR:—On Monday, October 29th, the troops ordered out by Major-General Atchison and myself (as per our report to you of said date), took up their line of march from camp near Richmond, for Far West. We encamped on the night of the 29th at Linville's creek (a short distance from the road), about sixteen miles from Far West, at which point we received an express from Brigadier-General Doniphan, informing us that he was then encamped on Log creek with a force of five hundred men, and that he would join us at the crossing of said creek, on the road from Richmond to Far West, by ten o'clock the next morning.

start in a few minutes for Independence, and in all probability they would never return alive. Receiving this intimation, Lucy and myself set out directly for the place. On coming within about a hundred yards of the wagon, we were compelled to stop, for we could press no further through the crowd. I therefore appealed to those around me, exclaiming, 'I am the mother of the Prophet—is there not a gentleman here who will assist me to that wagon, that I may take a last look at my children, and speak to them once more before I die?' Upon this, one individual volunteered to make a pathway through the army, and we passed on, threatened with death at every step, till at length we arrived at the wagon. The man who led us through the crowd spoke to Hyrum, who was sitting in front, and, telling him that his mother had come to see him, requested that he should reach his hand to me. He did so, but I was not allowed to see him; the cover was of strong cloth, and nailed down so close that he could hardly get his hand through. We had merely shaken hands with him, when we were ordered away by the mob, who forbade any conversation between us, and, threatening to shoot us, they ordered the teamster to drive over us. Our friend then conducted us to the back part of the wagon, where Joseph sat, and said, 'Mr. Smith, your mother and sister are here, and wish to shake hands with you.' Joseph crowded his hand through between the cover and wagon, and we caught hold of it; but he spoke not to either of us, until I said, 'Joseph, do speak to your poor mother once more—I cannot bear to go till I hear your voice.' 'God bless you, mother!' he sobbed out. Then a cry was raised, and the wagon dashed off, tearing him from us just as Lucy pressed his hand to her lips, to bestow upon it a sister's last kiss—for he was then sentenced to be shot."—History of the Prophet Joseph by his Mother, Lucy Smith, pp. 249, 250.

On the 30th of October, the troops got together at the last named point, when we mustered about eighteen hundred men. Whilst at this place we received your orders of the 26th ultimo, and I received an order of the 27th ultimo, and a letter from you of the same date. At this point Major-General Atchison left me for Liberty, when I was left in sole command. I then took up my line of march for Goose creek, one mile south of Far West, which point we reached about one hour by sun in the evening. Just as the troops were encamping, I received intelligence from General Doniphan, from his position on the right, that he had discovered a party of mounted Mormons approaching Far West from the east, and requested permission to intercept them, if possible. Leave was granted, and his brigade started off at nearly full speed to accomplish the order, but the Mormons succeeded in reaching the fort. General Doniphan approached within two hundred yards of their fortress, when they displayed a force of about eight hundred [150] men. At this juncture, I ordered General Graham's brigade (holding General Parks' and part of General Wilson's mounted in reserve) to march full speed to the relief of the First Brigade, Third Division, but from the inequality of the force of the first detachment, (being only two hundred and fifty strong at that time, and the "Mormons eight hundred [150] it was considered prudent to withdraw the troops, and march against them in the morning, which was accordingly done, and they all returned, as dark set in, to camp. At this place I established my headquarters, and continued there during the expedition against the Mormons. The detachment under General Wilson returned about nine o'clock p. m.

The next morning, 31st of October, I received a message from Colonel Hinkle, the commander of the Mormon forces [Caldwell militia], requesting an interview with me on an eminence near Far West, which he would designate by hoisting a white flag. I sent him word I would meet him at two o'clock p. m., being so much engaged in receiving and encamping fresh troops, who were hourly coming in, that I could not attend before. Accordingly at that time, I started with my staff officers and Brigadier-Generals Wilson, Doniphan and Graham, General Parks being left in command. We met him and some other Mormons at the point before mentioned. He stated that his object in asking me to meet him there, was to know if there could not be some compromise or settlement of the difficulty without a resort to arms.

After giving him to understand the nature of your orders, I made him the following propositions, which I furnished him a copy of, also a copy of your order, viz.:

"First—To give up their [the Church's] leaders to be tried and punished.

"Second—To make an appropriation of their property, all who have taken up arms, to the payment of their debts, and indemnify for damages done by them.

"Third—That the balance should leave the state, and be protected out by the militia, but to be permitted to remain under protection until further orders were received from the commander-in-chief.

"Fourth—To give up the arms of every description, to be receipted for."

Colonel Hinkle agreed to the proposition readily, but wished to postpone the matter until morning. I then told him that I would require Joseph Smith, Jun., Sidney Rigdon, Lyman Wight, Parley P. Pratt, and George W. Robinson, as hostage for his faithful compliance with the terms, and would pledge myself and each one of the officers present, that in case he, after reflecting and consulting upon the proposition during the night, declined acceding to them, that the hostages should be returned to him in the morning, at the same point they were received, but it was understood in case they did comply, they were to be held for trial as part of the leaders called for by the first stipulation; I then gave him until one hour by sun in the evening to produce and deliver them. We then returned to camp, and I directed the troops to make preparations to march to Far West by an hour and a half by the sun, with a determination in case the hostages were not produced to make an attack upon the town forthwith.

I directed General Parks' brigade to be mounted, and to form on the right of the division, to act as flankers if necessary, and if required to pass entirely around the town, and form on the north side, with instructions to make the attack at the report of the cannon, which was to be the signal for the general attack. General Graham's brigade was mounted, and formed on the extreme left to act as flankers, and if required to form the line on the west side, with similar instructions as to the commencement of the attack.

General Doniphan's brigade was ordered to parade on foot, and to form on the left of General Parks, with instructions to form the line of battle on the south side, with the same instructions as to commencement of attack.

The artillery company, with one piece of ordnance, was placed at the head of General Doniphan's and General Wilson's brigade, with instructions to occupy an eminence within three hundred yards of the town.

The army being disposed of in this manner, at the appointed time I took up the line of march in direction of Far West. When the troops got within about six hundred yards, I discovered the flag and the hostages advancing. I immediately halted the army, and rode out and met them, received the hostages, and placed a guard over them for their safety and protection, and ordered the forces back to our encampment. I cannot forbear, at this point, expressing my gratification and approbation of the good conduct and gallant bravery* evinced by all the officers and men under my command. They marched up with as much determination and deliberation as old veterans—not knowing but that the charge would be sounded every moment for surrounding the town.† There was no noise or confusion, nothing but an eager anxiety upon the countenance of every man to get at the work.

When the hostages were received, the troops, with some slight exceptions, marched back‡ in profound silence.

November 1st. I ordered the whole forces, amounting to two thousand five hundred men, to parade at nine o'clock a. m., and to take up the line of march for Far West at half-past nine o'clock, to receive the prisoners and their arms.

The troops marched out and formed in the prairie about two hundred yards southeast of the town. General Wilson's brigade formed the west line, General Doniphan's the east line, General Graham and General Parks the south line, with the artillery company and the cannon in the center of the two latter, leaving one side of the square open.

The "Mormon" army, reduced to about six hundred men by desertion and otherwise, under their commander, Colonel Hinkle marched out of their town through the space into our square, formed a hollow square, and grounded their arms. Colonel Hinkle then rode forward and delivered up to me his sword and pistols.

I then directed a company from the respective brigades to form a front, rear, right and left flank guards, and to march the prisoners back to Far West, and protect and take charge of them until the next morning. I then detailed a company from General Doniphan's command to take charge of the arms. Then, in order to gratify the army and to let the "Mormons" see our forces, marched around the town, and through the principal streets and back to headquarters.

*On this passage the Prophet makes the following comments:

"Gallant bravery," that some thousands of men should be so anxious to wash their hands in the blood of five hundred poor Saints? I claim not the honor of commanding such a brave army.

†Again the Prophet comments:

"The wicked flee when no man pursueth " This saying was truly verified in the first retreat of this army—they fled precipitately through fear and a great proportion of the men were anxious to get back to the creek, where they could dispense with some of their clothing and wash themselves in the water.

‡"Profound silence." It might have been silence to the general for aught I know; for the shoutings, bellowings and yells of this army of mobocrats was sufficient to deafen anyone, not guarded by some higher spirit, and could only be equalled in the savage war whoop, and the yells of the damned.

Considering the war at an end in this place I issued orders for General Doniphan's brigade, with the exception of one company, and General Graham's brigade, to take up their line of march for their respective headquarters and dismiss their men, and directed General Wilson to take charge of the prisoners (demanded for trial) and arms, and to march them to my headquarters at Independence, to await further orders, and to dismiss all except a guard for the prisoners and arms.

November 2nd. I relieved the guard placed over the prisoners at Far West by four companies of General Parks' brigade, and placed them under the command of Colonel Thompson, Second brigade, Third division, with instructions to report to General Clark. The balance of General Parks' brigade, with Captain Gillium's company of General Doniphan's brigade, under the command of General Parks, I ordered to Adam-ondi-Ahman, a Mormon town in Daviess county, with instructions to disarm the Mormon forces at that place and to leave a guard of fifty men for the protection of prisoners, and to report to General Clark.

In order to carry the treaty and stipulations into effect I have required your aid-de-camp, Colonel Williams, together with Colonel Burch, and Major A. Rees, of Ray, to attend to drawing up the papers legally, and directed Colonel Thompson to wait on them with a portion of his command, and to cause all their orders and requirements, consistent with the stipulations, to be carried into effect.

This day, about twelve o'clock, there was a battalion of one hundred men from Platte arrived at Far West, which I ordered back, having understood that Major-General Clark would be on in a day or two with sufficient force to operate in Daviess and Livingston, and for any service that may be required.

SAMUEL D. LUCAS,
Major-General Commanding.

CHAPTER XIV.

RIVALRY AMONG THE MILITIA GENERALS FOR POSSESSION OF THE PRISONERS—"TRIAL" AT RICHMOND.

Saturday, *3.*—We continued our march and arrived at the Missouri river, which separated us from Jackson county, where we were hurried across the ferry when but few troops had passed.* The truth was, General Clark had sent an express from Richmond to General Lucas, to have the prisoners sent to him, and thus prevent our going to Jackson county, both armies being competitors for the honor of possessing "the royal prisoners." Clark wanted the privilege of putting us to death himself, and Lucas and his troops were desirous of exhibiting us in the streets of Independence.†

Rival Efforts for Possession of the Prisoners.

Sunday, *4.*—We were visited by some ladies and gentlemen. One of the women came up, and very candidly inquired of the troops which of the prisoners was the Lord

* It was during this march between Crooked river and the Missouri that the Prophet predicted that none of the prisoners would lose their lives during their captivity. The incident is thus related by Parley P. Pratt: "As we arose and commenced our march on the morning of the 3rd of November, Joseph Smith spoke to me and the other prisoners, in a low, but cheerful and confidential tone; said he: *'Be of good cheer, brethren; the word of the Lord came to me last night that our lives should be given us, and that whatever we may suffer during this captivity, not one of our lives shall be taken.'* Of this prophecy I testify in the name of the Lord, and, though spoken in secret, its public fulfillment and the miraculous escape of each one of us is too notorious to need my testimony."—Autobiography of Parley P. Pratt, p. 210.

† On this matter of competition for possession of the prisoners Parley P. Pratt, one of the prisoners, repeats a statement made by General Wilson as follows: "It was repeatedly insinuated, by the other officers and troops that we should hang you prisoners on the first tree we came to on the way to Independence. But I'll be d——d if anybody shall hurt you. We just intend to exhibit you in Independence, let the people look at you, and see what a d——d set of fine fellows you are. And, more particularly, to keep you from that old bigot of a General Clark and his troops, from down country who are so stuffed with lies and prejudice that they would shoot you down in a moment."—Autobiography of Parley P. Pratt, p. 209.

whom the "Mormons" worshiped? One of the guard pointed to me with a significant smile, and said, "This is he." The woman then turning to me inquired whether I professed to be the Lord and Savior? I replied, that I professed to be nothing but a man, and a minister of salvation, sent by Jesus Christ to preach the Gospel.

Prophet's Interview with a Lady,

This answer so surprised the woman that she began to inquire into our doctrine, and I preached a discourse, both to her and her companions, and to the wondering soldiers, who listened with almost breathless attention while I set forth the doctrine of faith in Jesus Christ, and repentance, and baptism for remission of sins, with the promise of the Holy Ghost, as recorded in the second chapter of the Acts of the Apostles.

The woman was satisfied, and praised God in the hearing of the soldiers, and went away, praying that God would protect and deliver us. Thus was fulfilled a prophecy which had been spoken publicly by me, a few months previous—that a sermon should be preached in Jackson county by one of our Elders, before the close of 1838.

The troops having crossed the river about ten o'clock, we proceeded on and arrived at Independence, past noon, in the midst of a great rain, and a multitude of spectators who had assembled to see us, and hear the bugles sound a blast of triumphant joy, which echoed through the camp. We were ushered into a vacant house prepared for our reception, with a floor for our beds and blocks of wood for our pillows.

Arrival of the Prisoners in Independence

General Clark arrived at Far West with one thousand six hundred men, and five hundred more were within eight miles of the city.

Thus, Far West has been visited by six thousand men in one week, when the militia of the city (before any were taken prisoners) amounted only to about five hundred. After depriving these of their arms the mob continued to hunt the brethren like wild beasts, and shot several, ravished the women, and killed one near the city. No Saint was permitted to go in or out of the city; and meantime the Saints lived on parched corn.

Overwhelming Numbers of Mob Militia.

General Clark ordered General Lucas, who had previously gone to Adam-ondi-Aham with his troops, "to take the whole of the men of the 'Mormons' prisoners, and place such a guard around them and the town as will protect the prisoners and secure them until they can be dealt with properly," and secure all their property, till the best means could be adopted for paying the damages the citizens had sustained.

Monday, 5.—We were kept under a small guard, and were treated with some degree of hospitality and politeness, while many flocked to see us. We spent most of our time in preaching and conversation, explanatory of our doctrines and practice, which removed mountains of prejudice, and enlisted the populace in our favor, notwithstanding their old hatred and wickedness towards our society.

Severity in the Treatment of Prisoners Modified.

The brethren at Far West were ordered by General Clark to form a line, when the names of fifty-six present were called and made prisoners to await their trial for something they knew not what. They were kept under a close guard.

Fifty-six Additional Prisoners.

Tuesday, 6.—General Clark paraded the brethren at Far West, and then addressed them as follows.

General Clark's Harrangue to the Brethren.

Gentlemen, you whose names are not attached to this list of names, will now have the privilege of going to your fields and providing corn, wood, etc., for your families. Those who are now taken will go from this to prison, be tried, and receive the due demerit of their crimes. But you (except such as charges may hereafter be preferred against) are now at liberty, as soon as the troops are removed that now guard the place, which I shall cause to be done immediately. It now devolves upon you to fulfill the treaty that you have entered into, the leading items of which I shall now lay before you:

The first requires that your leading men be given up to be tried according to law; this you have already complied with.

The second is, that you deliver up your arms; this has been attended to.

The third stipulation is, that you sign over your properties to defray the expenses of the war; this you have also done.

Another article yet remains for you to comply with, and that is, that you leave the state forthwith; and whatever may be your feelings concerning this, or whatever your innocence, it is nothing to me; General Lucas, who is equal in authority with me, has made this treaty with you—I approve of it—I should have done the same had I been here—I am therefore determined to see it fulfilled. The character of this state has suffered almost beyond redemption, from the character, conduct and influence that you have exerted, and we deem it an act of justice to restore her character to its former standing among the states, by every proper means.

The orders of the governor to me were, that you should be exterminated, and not allowed to remain in the state, and had your leaders not been given up, and the terms of the treaty complied with, before this, you and your families would have been destroyed and your houses in ashes.

There is a discretionary power vested in my hands which I shall exercise in your favor for a season; for *this* lenity you are indebted to *my* clemency. I do not say that you shall go now, but you must not think of staying here another season, or of putting in crops, for the moment you do this the citizens will be upon you. If I am called here again, in case of a non-compliance of a treaty made, do not think that I shall act any more as I have done—you need not expect any mercy, but extermination, for I am determined the governor's order shall be executed. As for your leaders, do not once think—do not imagine for a moment—do not let it enter your mind that they will be delivered, or that you will see their faces again, for their *fate is fixed—their die is cast—their doom is sealed.*

I am sorry, gentlemen, to see so great a number of apparently intelligent men found in the situation that you are; and oh! that I could invoke that *Great Spirit, the unknown God*, to rest upon you, and make you sufficiently intelligent to break that chain of superstition, and liberate you from those fetters of fanaticism with which you are bound—that you no longer worship a man.

I would advise you to scatter abroad, and never again organize yourselves with Bishops, Presidents, etc., lest you excite the jealousies of the people, and subject yourselves to the same calamities that have now come upon you.

You have always been the aggressors—you have brought upon yourselves these difficulties by being disaffected and not being subject to rule—and my advice is, that you become as other citizens, lest by a recurrence of these events you bring upon yourselves irretrievable ruin.*

The governor wrote General Clark as follows:

It will also be necessary that you hold a military court of inquiry in Daviess county, and arrest the Mormons who have been guilty of the late outrages, committed towards the inhabitants of said county. My instructions to you are to settle this whole matter completely, if possible, before you disband your forces; if the Mormons are disposed voluntarily to leave the state, of course it would be advisable in you to promote that object, in any way deemed proper. The *ringleaders of this rebellion, though, ought by no means to be permitted to escape the punishment they merit.*

The prisoners at Far West were started off for Richmond, under a strong guard.

Wednesday, 7.—The following order was issued at Far West by General Clark:

Brigadier-General Robert Wilson will take up the line of march with his brigade on this morning for Adam-ondi-Ahman, in Daviess county, and take possession of the prisoners at that place, and proceed to ascertain those who committed crimes, and when done, to put them under close guard, and when he moves, take them to Keytesville, after having them recognized by the proper authority.

Thursday, 8.—There was a severe snowstorm yesterday and today. General Wilson arrived at Adam-ondi-Ahman; he placed guards around the town so that no persons

* This speech of General Clark's is to be found in the "History of Caldwell and Livingston counties, Missouri, written and compiled by the St. Louis National Historical Company," 1886, and is introduced as follows: "A few days after his arrival General Clark removed a portion of the restraint he had imposed upon the Mormons' allowing them to go out for wood, provisions, etc. He assembled the multitude on the temple square and delivered to them a written speech, a copy of which is here given. It goes far to prove that General Clark was ordered to 'exterminate' the Mormons, not excepting the women and children, and burn their houses and otherwise destroy their property."—History of Caldwell and Livington Counties, p. 140.

might pass out or in without permission. All the men in town were then taken and put under guard, and a court of inquiry was instituted, with Adam Black on the bench; the said Adam Black belonged to the mob, and was one of the leaders of it from the time mobbing first commenced in Daviess county. The attorney belonged to General Clark's army.

Progress of Affairs at Diahman.

Shortly after our arrival in Jackson county, Colonel Sterling Price, from the army of General Clark, came with orders from General Clark, who was commander-in-chief of the expedition, to have us forwarded forthwith to Richmond. Accordingly, on Thursday morning, we started with three guards only, and they had been obtained with great difficulty, after laboring all the previous day to get them. Between Independence and Roy's Ferry, on the Missouri river, they all got drunk, and we got possession of their arms and horses.

The Prophet and his Fellow Prisoners Sent to Richmond.

It was late in the afternoon, near the setting of the sun. We traveled about half a mile after we crossed the river, and put up for the night.

Friday, 9.—This morning there came a number of men, some of them armed. Their threatenings and savage appearance were such as to make us afraid to proceed without more guards. A messenger was therefore dispatched to Richmond to obtain them. We started before their arrival, but had not gone far before we met Colonel Price with a guard of about seventy-four men, and were conducted by them to Richmond, and put into an old vacant house, and a guard set.

Prisoners not Sufficiently Protected by Guards.

Some time through the course of that day General Clark came in, and we were introduced to him. We inquired of him the reason why we had been thus carried from our homes, and what were the charges against us. He said that he was not then able to determine, but would be in a short time; and with very little more conversation withdrew.

Meeting of the Prophet and Gen. Clark.

Some short time after he had withdrawn Colonel Price came in with two chains in his hands, and a number of padlocks. The two chains he fastened together. He had with him ten men, armed, who stood at the time of these operations with a thumb upon the cock of their guns. They first nailed down the windows, then came and ordered a man by the name of John Fulkerson, whom he had with him, to chain us together with chains and padlocks, being seven in number. After that he searched us, examining our pockets to see if we had any arms. He found nothing but pocket knives, but these he took away with him.

The Prisoners Chained.

Saturday, November 10.—The following is a true specimen of Missouri liberty.

Form of Permit.

I permit David Holman to remove from Daviess to Caldwell county, there to remain during the winter, or to pass out of the state.

R. WILSON, Brigadier-General.
By F. G. COCKNU, Aid.

November 10, 1838.

General Clark had spent his time since our arrival at Richmond in searching the laws to find authority for trying us by court martial. Had he not been a lawyer of eminence, I should have supposed it no very difficult task to decide that quiet, peaceful unoffending, and private citizens too, except as ministers of the Gospel, were not amenable to a *military tribunal*, in a country governed by *civil laws.* But be this as it may, General Clark wrote the governor that he had—

General Clark Desires to Try the Prophet by Court Martial.

General Clark's Report to Governor Boggs.

Detained General White and his field offices here a day or two for the purpose of holding a court martial, if necessary. I this day made out charges against the prisoners, and called on Judge King to try them as a committing court; and I am now busily engaged in procuring witnesses and submitting facts. There being no civil officers in Caldwell,

I have to use the military to get witnesses from there, which I do without reserve. The most of the prisoners here I consider guilty of *treason;* and I believe will be convicted; and the only difficulty in law is, can they be tried in any county but Caldwell? If not, they cannot be there indicted, until a change of population. In the event the latter view is taken by the civil courts, I suggest the propriety of trying Jo Smith and those leaders taken by General Lucas, by a court martial, for mutiny. This I am in favor of only as *dernier resort.* I would have taken this course with Smith at any rate; but it being doubtful whether a court martial has jurisdiction or not in the present case—that is, whether these people are to be treated as in time of war, and the mutineers as having mutinied in time of war—and I would here ask you to forward to me the attorney-general's opinion on this point. It will not do to allow these leaders to return to their treasonable work again, on account of their not being indicted in Caldwell. They have committed *treason, murder, arson, burglary, robbery, larceny, and perjury.*

The three days' investigation having closed at Adam-ondi-Ahman, every man was honorably acquitted, Adam Black being judge.

General Wilson tnen ordered every family to be out of Diahman in ten days, with permission to go to Caldwell, and there tarry until spring, and then leave the state under pain of extermination. The weather is very cold, more so than usual for this season of the year.

Hardships Inflicted on the "Diahman" Saints.

In keeping the order of General Wilson the Saints had to leave their crops and houses, and to live in tents and wagons, in this inclement season of the year. As for their flocks and herds, the mob had relieved them from the trouble of taking care of them, or from the pain of seeing them starve to death—by stealing them.

An arrangement was made in which it was stipulated that a committee of twelve, which had been previously appointed, should have the privilege of going from Far West to Daviess county, for the term of four weeks, for the purpose of conveying their crops from Daviess to Caldwell. The committee were to wear white badges on their hats for protection.

Casualties of the Mobbing.

About thirty of the brethren have been killed, many wounded, about a hundred are missing, and about sixty at Richmond awaiting their trial—for what they know not.

Sunday, *11*.—While in Richmond we were under the charge of Colonel Price from Chariton county, who allowed all manner of abuses to be heaped upon us. During this time my afflictions were great, and our situation was truly painful.*

* It was during this time that the very remarkable circumstance of the Prophet rebuking the prison guards occurred. The matter is related by Elder Parley P. Pratt in his Autobiography. It appears that during the imprisonment at Richmond Elder Rigdon was taken very ill from the hardships and exposure he had to endure. He was chained next to his son-in-law, George W. Robinson, and compelled to sleep on the hard floor notwithstanding his delirium, the result of fever. Mrs. Robinson, the daughter of Elder Rigdon, had accompanied her husband and father into the prison for the purpose of caring for the latter during his illness. She is represented as being a very delicate woman with an infant at the breast. She continued by the side of her father until he recovered from his illness notwithstanding the loathsomeness of the prison and the vileness of the guards. And now the story of the rebuke as related by Elder Pratt: "In one of those tedious nights we had lain as if in sleep till the hour of midnight had passed, and our ears and hearts had been pained, while we had listened for hours to the obscene jests, the horrid oaths, the dreadful blasphemies and filthy language of our guards, Colonel Price at their head, as they recounted to each other their deeds of rapine, murder, robbery, etc., which they had committed among the "Mormons" while at Far West and vicinity. They even boasted of defiling by force wives, daughters and virgins, and of shooting or dashing out the brains of men, women and children. I had listened till I became so disgusted, shocked, horrified, and so filled with the spirit of indignant justice that I could scarcely refrain from rising upon my feet and rebuking the guards; but had said nothing to Joseph, or anyone else, although I lay next to him and knew he was awake. On a sudden he arose to his feet, and spoke in a voice of thunder, or as the roaring lion, uttering, as nearly as I can recollect, the following words:

" '*Silence*, ye fiends of the infernal pit! In the name of Jesus Christ I rebuke you, and command you to be still; I will not live another minute and hear such language. Cease such talk, or you or I die *this instant!*'

He ceased to speak. He stood erect in terrible majesty. Chained, and without a weapon; calm, unruffled and dignified as an angel, he looked upon the quailing guards, whose weapons were lowered or dropped to the ground; whose knees smote together, and who, shrinking into a corner, or crouching at his feet, begged his pardon, and remained quiet till a change of guards.

"I have seen the ministers of justice, clothed in magisterial robes, and criminals arraigned before them, while life was suspended on a breath, in the courts of England; I have witnessed a Congress in solemn session to give laws to nations; I have tried to conceive of kings, of royal courts, of thrones and crowns; and of emperors assembled to decide the fate of kingdoms; but dignity and majesty have I seen but once, as it stood in chains, at midnight in a dungeon, in an obscure village in Missouri."—Autobiography of Parley P. Pratt, pp. 228-230.

General Clark informed us that he would turn us over to the civil authorities for trial. Joseph Smith, Jun., Hyrum Smith, Sidney Rigdon, Parley P. Pratt, Lyman Wight, Amasa Lyman, George W. Robinson, Caleb Baldwin, Alanson Ripley, Washington Voorhees, Sidney Turner, John Buchanan, Jacob Gates, Chandler Holbrook, George W. Harris, Jesse D. Hunter, Andrew Whitlock, Martin C. Allred, William Allred, George D. Grant, Darwin Chase, Elijah Newman, Alvin G. Tippets, Zedekiah Owens, Isaac Morley, Thomas Beck, Moses Clawson, John J. Tanner, Daniel Shearer, Daniel S. Thomas, Alexander McRae, Elisha Edwards, John S. Higbee, Ebenezer Page, Benjamin Covey, Ebenezer Robinson, Luman Gibbs, James M. Henderson, David Pettegrew, Edward Partridge, Francis Higbee, David Frampton, George Kimball, Joseph W. Younger, Henry Zobriskie, Allen J. Stout, Sheffield Daniels, Silas Maynard, Anthony Head, Benjamin Jones, Daniel Garn, John T. Earl, and Norman Shearer, were brought before Austin A. King, at Richmond, for trial, charged with the several crimes of high treason against the state, murder, burglary, arson, robbery, and larceny.

List of the Prisoners.

Monday, 12.—The first act of the court was to send out a body of armed men, without a civil process, to obtain witnesses.

Tuesday, 13.—We were placed at the bar, Austin A. King presiding, and Thomas C. Burch, the state's attorney. Witnesses were called and sworn at the point of the bayonet.

The Villainy of Avard.

Dr. Sampson Avard was the first brought before the court. He had previously told Mr. Oliver Olney that if he [Olney] wished to save himself, he must swear hard against the heads of the Church, as they were the ones the court wanted to criminate; and if he could swear hard against them, they would not (that is, neither court nor mob) disturb him. "I intend to do it," said he, "in order to escape, for if I do not, they will take my life."

This introduction is sufficient to show the character of his testimony, and he swore just according to the statement he had made, doubtless thinking it a wise course to ingratiate himself into the good graces of the mob.

List of Witnesses against the Saints

The following witnesses were examined in behalf of the state, many of whom, if we may judge from their testimony, swore upon the same principle as Avard, they were: Wyatt Cravens, Nehemiah Odle, Captain Samuel Bogart, Morris Phelps, John Corrill, Robert Snodgrass, George Walton, George M. Hinkle, James C. Owens, Nathaniel Carr, Abner Scovil, John Cleminson, Reed Peck, James C. Owens (re-examined), William Splawn, Thomas M. Odle, John Raglin, Allen Rathbun, Jeremiah Myers, Andrew J. Job, Freeburn H. Gardner, Burr Riggs, Elisha Camron, Charles Bleckley, James Cobb, Jesse Kelly, Addison Price, Samuel Kimball, William W. Phelps, John Whitmer, James B. Turner, George W. Worthington, Joseph H. McGee, John Lockhart, Porter Yale, Benjamin Slade, Ezra Williams, Addison Green, John Taylor, Timothy Lewis, and Patrich Lynch.

Sunday, 18.—While our suit was going forward General Wilson gave the following permit, in Daviess county:

Permit.

I permit the following persons, as a committee on the part of the Mormons, to pass and re-pass in and through the county of Daviess during the winter, to-wit.: William Huntington, John Reed, Benjamin S. Wilbur, Mayhew Hillman, Z. Wilson, E. B. Gaylord, Henry Herriman, Daniel Stanton, Oliver Snow, William Earl, Jonathan H. Hale, Henry Humphrey—upon all lawful business.

R. Wilson, Brig.-Gen. Commanding.
By F. G. Cocknu, Aid.

November 18, 1838.

We were called upon for our witnesses, and we gave the names of some forty or fifty. Captain Bogart was despatched with a company of militia to procure them. He arrested all he could find, thrust them into prison, and we were not allowed to see them.

Treatment of Witnesses for the Defense.

During the week we were again called upon most tauntingly for witnesses; we gave the names of some others, and they were thrust into prison, so many as were to be found.

In the meantime Malinda Porter, Delia F. Pine, Nancy Rigdon, Jonathan W. Barlow, Thoret Parsons, Ezra Chipman, and Arza Judd, Jun., volunteered, and were sworn, on the defense, but were prevented as much as possible by threats from telling the truth. We saw a man at the window by the name of Allen, and beckoned him to come in, and had him sworn, but when he did not testify to please the court, several rushed upon him with their bayonets, and he fled the place; three men took after him with loaded guns, and he barely escaped with his life. It was of no use to get any more witnesses, even if we could have done so.

Thus this mock investigation continued from day to day, till Saturday, when several of the brethren were discharged by Judge King, as follows—

Some Prisoners Discharged.

Defendants against whom nothing is proven, viz., Amasa Lyman, John Buchanan, Andrew Whitlock, Alvah L. Tippets, Jedediah Owens, Isaac Morley, John J. Tanner, Daniel S. Thomas, Elisha Edwards, Benjamin Covey, David Frampton, Henry Zobriskie, Allen J. Stout, Sheffield Daniels, Silas Maynard, Anthony Head, John T. Earl, Ebenezer Brown, James Newberry, Sylvester Hulett, Chandler Holbrook, Martin C. Allred, William Allred. The above defendants have been discharged by me, there being no evidence against them.

AUSTIN A. KING, Judge, etc.

November 24, 1838.

Our Church organization was converted, by the testimony of the apostates, into a temporal kingdom, which was to fill the whole earth, and subdue all other kingdoms.

Misconception of the Church Organization.

The judge, who by the by was a Methodist, asked much concerning our views of the prophecy of Daniel: "In the days of these kings shall the God of heaven set up a kingdom which shall break in pieces all other kingdoms, and stand forever," * * * * "and the kingdom and the greatness of the kingdom, under the whole heaven, shall be given to the Saints of the Most High." As if it were treason to believe the Bible.*

Ashby's Report of Haun's Mills Massacre.

Wednesday, *28*.—Daniel Ashby, a member of the state senate, wrote General Clark that he was in the battle [massacre] at Haun's Mills, that thirty-one "Mormons" were killed, and seven of his party wounded.

Prisoners Discharged and Retained.

The remaining prisoners were all released or admitted to bail, except Lyman Wight, Caleb Baldwin, Hyrum Smith, Alexander McRae, Sidney Rigdon, and myself, who were sent to Liberty, Clay county, to jail, to stand our trial for treason and murder. Our treason consisted of having whipped the mob out of Daviess county, and taking their cannon from them; the murder, of killing the man in the Bogart battle; also Parley P. Pratt, Morris Phelps, Luman Gibbs, Darwin Chase, and Norman Shearer, who were put into Richmond jail to stand their trial for the same "crimes."

Legal Advice to Cease Defense.

During the investigation we were confined in chains and received much abuse. The matter of driving away witnesses or casting them into prison, or chasing them out of the county, was carried to such length that our lawyers, General Doniphan and Amos Rees, told us not to bring our witnesses

* Respecting this inquiry concerning the passage in Daniel's prophecy, Elder Parley P. Pratt writes: "This court of inquisition inquired diligently into our belief of the seventh chapter of Daniel concerning the kingdom of God, which should subdue all other kingdoms and stand forever. And when told that we believed in that prophecy, the court turned to the clerk and said: 'Write that down; it is a strong point for treason.' Our lawyer observed as follows: 'Judge, you had better make the Bible treason.' The court made no reply."—Autobiography of Parley P. Pratt, p. 230.

there at all; for if we did, there would not be one of them left for final trial; for no sooner would Bogart and his men know who they were, than they would put them out of the country.

As to making any impression on King, Doniphan said, if a cohort of angels were to come down, and declare we were innocent, it would all be the same; for he (King) had determined from the beginning to cast us into prison. We never got the privilege of introducing our witnesses at all; if we had, we could have disproved all the evidence of our enemies.

M. Arthur, Esq., to the Representatives from Clay County.

LIBERTY, November 29, 1838.

RESPECTED FRIENDS:—Humanity to an injured people prompts me at present to address you thus: You were aware of the treatment (to some extent before you left home) received by that unfortunate race of beings called the Mormons, from Daviess, in the form of human beings inhabiting Daviess, Livingston, and part of Ray counties; not being satisfied with the relinquishment of all their rights as citizens and human beings, in the treaty forced upon them by General Lucas, by giving up their arms, and throwing themselves upon the mercy of the state, and their fellow citizens generally, hoping thereby protection of their lives and property, they are now receiving treatment from those demons, that makes humanity shudder, and the cold chills run over any man, not entirely destitute of the feelings of humanity. These demons are now constantly strolling up and down Caldwell county, in small companies armed, insulting the women in any way and every way, and plundering the poor devils of all the means of subsistence (scanty as it was) left them, and driving off their horses, cattle, hogs, etc., and rifling their houses and farms of everything therein, taking beds, bedding, wardrobes, and such things as they see they want, leaving the poor Mormons in a starving and naked condition.

These are facts I have from authority that cannot be questioned, and can be maintained and substantiated at any time. There is now a petition afloat in our town, signed by the citizens of all parties and grades, which will be sent you in a few days, praying the legislature to make some speedy enactment applicable to their case. They are entirely willing to leave our state, so soon as this inclement season is over; and a number have already left, and are leaving daily, scattering themselves to the four winds of the earth.

Now, sirs, I do not want by any means to dictate to you the course to be pursued, but one fact I will merely suggest. I this day was conversing with Mr. George M. Pryer, who is just from Far West, relating the outrages there committed daily. I suggested to him the propriety of the legislature's placing a guard to patrol on the lines of Caldwell county, say, of about twenty-five men, and give them, say, about one dollar or one and a half per day, each man, and find their provisions, etc., until, say, the first day of June next; these men rendering that protection necessary to the Mormons, and allowing them to follow and bring to justice any individuals who have heretofore or will hereafter be guilty of plundering or any violation of the laws. I would suggest that George M. Pryer be appointed captain of said guard, and that he be allowed to raise his own men, if he is willing thus to act. He is a man of correct habits, and will do justice to all sides, and render due satisfaction.

Should this course not be approved of, I would recommend the restoration of their [the Mormons'] arms for their own protection. One or the other of these suggestions is certainly due the Mormons from the state. She has now their leaders prisoners, to the number of fifty or sixty, and I apprehend no danger from the remainder in any way until they will leave the state.

M. ARTHUR.

Mr. Arthur is not a "Mormon," but a friend of man.

Attested Copy of the Mittimus under which Joseph Smith, Jun., and Others, were sent from Judge King to the Jailer of Liberty Prison, in Clay County, Missouri.

STATE OF MISSOURI,
RAY COUNTY. }

To the Keeper of the Jail of Clay County:

GREETING:—Whereas, Joseph Smith, Jun., Hyrum Smith, Lyman Wight, Alexander McRae, and Caleb Baldwin, as also Sidney Rigdon, have been brought before me, Austin A. King, judge of the fifth judicial circuit in the state of Missouri, and charged with the offense of treason against the state of Missouri, and the said defendants, on their examination before me, being held to answer further to said charge, the said Joseph Smith, Jun., Hyrum Smith, Lyman Wight, Alexander McRae, and Caleb Buldwin, to answer in the county of Daviess, and the said Sidney Rigdon to answer further in the county of Caldwell, for said charge of treason, and there being no jail in said counties; these are therefore to command that you receive the said Joseph Smith, Jun., Hyrum Smith, Lyman Wight, Alexander

McRae, Caleb Baldwin, and Sidney Rigdon into your custody in the jail of the said county of Clay, there to remain until they be delivered therefrom by due course of law.

Given under my hand and seal the 29th day of November, 1838.

AUSTIN A. KING.

State of Missouri, County of Clay.

I, Samuel Hadley, sheriff of Clay county, do hereby certify that the above is a true copy of the mittimus to me, directed in the cases therein named.

SAMUEL HADLEY, Jailer.
By SAMUEL TILLERY, Deputy Jailer.

Clay County, Missouri.

Friday, *30*.—About this time those of us who had been sentenced thereto, were conveyed to Liberty jail, put in close confinement, and all communication with our friends cut off.

In Liberty Prison.

During our trial William E. McLellin, accompanied by Burr Riggs and others, at times were busy in plundering and robbing the houses of Sidney Rigdon, George Morey, the widow Phebe Ann Patten, and others, under pretense or color of law, on an order from General Clark, as testified to by the members of the different families robbed.*

Course of Wm. E. McLellin and Burr Riggs.

Saturday, *December 1*, *1838*.—A committee on the part

* Further concerning the apostasy and conduct of William E. McLellin, soon after the Prophet and his associates were taken prisoners at Far West, Parley P. Pratt says: "While thus confined, William E. McLellin, once my fellow laborer in the Gospel, but now a Judas, with hostile weapon in hand to destroy the Saints, came to me and observed: 'Well, Parley, you have now got where you are certain never to escape; how do you feel as to the course you have taken in religion?' I answered, that I had taken the course which I should take if I had my life to live over again. He seemed thoughtful for a moment, and then replied: 'Well, I think, if I were you, I should die as I had lived; at any rate, I see no possibility of escape for you and your friends.' "—Autobiography of Parley P. Pratt, p. 206.

While the brethren were imprisoned at Richmond it is said that "McLellin, who was a large and active man, went to the sheriff and asked for the privilege of flogging the Prophet. Permission was granted on condition that Joseph would fight. The sheriff made known to Joseph McLellin's earnest request, to which Joseph consented, if his irons were taken off. McLellin then refused to fight unless he could have a club, to which Joseph was perfectly willing; but the sheriff would not allow them to fight on such unequal terms. McLellin was a man of superficial education, though he had a good flow of language. He adopted the profession of medicine."—Mill. Star, vol, xxxvi: pp. 808, 809.

of the "Mormons" and a like committee on the part of the citizens of Daviess county, met at Adam-ondi-Ahman, on the first of December, 1838, the following propositions by the "Mormon" committee were made and agreed to by the Daviess county committee:

First—That the Mormon committee be allowed to employ, say twenty teamsters for the purpose of hauling off their property.

Second—That the Mormon committee collect whatever stock they may have in Daviess county at some point, and some two or three of the Daviess county committee be notified to attend for the purpose of examining said stock, and convey or attend the Mormon committee out of the limits of the county; and it is further understood, that the Mormon committee is not to drive or take from this county any stock of any description, at any other time, nor under any other circumstances, than these mentioned.

As witness our hands,

William P. Peniston,
Dr. K. Kerr,
Adam Black,
Committee.

The above propositions were made and agreed to by the undersigned committee on the part of the Mormons.

William Huntington,
B. S. Wilbur,
J. H. Hale,
Henry Herriman,
Z. Wilson.

CHAPTER XV.

THE CASE OF THE SAINTS PRESENTED TO THE MISSOURI LEGISLATURE—THE PROPHET'S COMMUNICATION TO THE SAINTS FROM LIBERTY PRISON.

Wednesday, December 5.—The Missouri Legislature having assembled, Governor Boggs laid before the House of Representatives all the information in his possession relative to the difficulties between the mob and the "Mormons."

Report of Governor Boggs to the Legislature.

Monday, December 10.—

Memorial of a Committee to the State Legislature of Missouri in Behalf of the Citizens of Caldwell County.

To the Honorable Legislature of the State of Missouri in Senate and House of Representatives convened:

We, the undersigned petitioners and inhabitants of Caldwell county, Missouri, in consequence of the late calamity that has come upon us taken in connection with former afflictions, feel it a duty we owe to ourselves and our country to lay our case before your honorable body for consideration. It is a well known fact, that a society of our people commenced settling in Jackson county, Missouri, in the summer of 1831, where they, according to their ability, purchased lands, and settled upon them, with the intention and expectation of becoming permanent citizens in common with others.

Soon after the settlement began, persecution commenced; and as the society increased, persecution also increased, until the society at last was compelled to leave the county; and although an account of these persecutions has been published to the world, yet we feel that it will not be improper to notice a few of the most prominent items in this memorial.

On the 20th of July, 1833, a mob convened at Independence—a committee of which called upon a few of the men of our Church there, and stated to them that the store, printing office, and indeed all other mechanic shops must be closed forthwith, and the society leave the county immediately.

These propositions were so unexpected, that a certain time was asked for to consider on the subject, before an answer should be returned, which was refused, and our men being individually interrogated, each one answered that he could not consent to comply with their propositions. One of the mob replied that he was sorry, for the work of destruction would commence immediately.

In a short time the printing-office, which was a two story brick building, was assailed by the mob and soon thrown down, and with it much valuable property destroyed. Next they went to the store for the same purpose; but Mr. Gilbert, one of the owners, agreeing to close it, they abandoned their design. Their next move was the dragging of Bishop Partridge from his house and family to the public square, where, surrounded by hundreds, they partially stripped him of his clothes, and tarred and feathered him from head to foot. A man by the name of Allen was also tarred at the same time. This was Saturday, and the mob agreed to meet the following Tuesday, to accomplish their purpose of driving or massacring the society.

Tuesday came, and the mob came also, bearing with them a red flag in token of blood. Some two or three of the principal men of the society offered their lives, if that would appease the wrath of the mob, so that the rest of the society might dwell in peace upon their lands. The answer was, that unless the society would leave *en masse*, every man should die for himself. Being in a defenseless situation, to save a general massacre, it was agreed that one half of the society should leave the county by the first of the next January, and the remainder by the first of the following April. A treaty was entered into and ratified, and all things went on smoothly for awhile. But sometime in October, the wrath of the mob began again to be kindled, insomuch that they shot at some of our people, whipped others, and threw down their houses, and committed many other depredations; indeed the society of Saints were harassed for some time both day and night; their houses were brick-batted and broken open and women and children insulted. The store-house of A. S. Gilbert and Company was broken open, ransacked, and some of the goods strewed in the streets.

These abuses, with many others of a very aggravated nature, so stirred up the indignant feelings of our people, that when a party of them, say about thirty, met a company of the mob of about double their number, a skirmish took place, in which some two or three of the mob, and one of our people, were killed. This raised, as it were, the whole county in arms, and nothing would satisfy the mob but an im mediate surrender of the arms of our people, who forthwith were to leave the county. Fifty-one guns were given up, which have never been returned, or paid for, to this day. The next day, parties of the mob, from fifty to seventy, headed by priests, went from house to house, threatening women and children with death if they were not gone before they returned. This so alarmed our people that they fled in different directions; some took shelter in the woods, while others wandered in the prairies till their feet bled; and the weather being very cold, their sufferings in other respects were great.

The society made their escape to Clay county as fast as they possibly could, where the people received them kindly, and administered to their wants. After the society had left Jackson county, their buildings, amounting to about two hundred, were either burned or otherwise destroyed, and much of their crops, as well as furniture and stock; which if properly estimated would make a large sum, for the loss of which they have not as yet received any remuneration.

The society remained in Clay county nearly three years; when, at the suggestion of the people there, they removed to that section of the state known as Caldwell county. Here the people bought out most of the former inhabitants, and also entered much of the wild land. Many soon owned a number of eighties [eighty acres] while there was scarcely a man who did not secure to himself at least a forty [forty acres]. Here we were permitted to enjoy peace for a season; but as our society increased in numbers, and settlements were made in Daviess and Carroll counties, the mob spirit spread itself again. For months previous to our giving up our arms to General Lucas' army, we heard little else than rumors of mobs collecting in different places and threatening our people. It is well known that the people of our Church, who had located themselves at De Witt, had to give up to a mob, and leave the place, notwithstanding the militia were called out for their protection.

From De Witt the mob went towards Daviess county, and while on their way there they took two of our men prisoners, and made them ride upon the cannon, and told them that they would drive the "Mormons" from Daviess to Caldwell, and from Caldwell to hell; and that they would give them no quarter, only at the cannon's mouth. The threats of the mob induced some of our people to go to Daviess to help to protect their brethren who had settled at Adam-ondi-Ahman, on Grand river. The mob soon fled from Daviess county; and after they were dispersed and the cannon taken, during which time no blood was shed, the people of Caldwell returned to their homes, in hopes of enjoying peace and quiet; but in this they were disappointed; for a large mob was soon found to be collecting on the Grindstone fork of Grand river from ten to fifteen miles off, under the command of Cornelius Gillium, a scouting party of which came within four miles of Far West, in open daylight, and drove off stock belonging to our people.

About this time, word came to Far West that a party of the mob had come into Caldwell county to the south of Far West; that they were taking horses and cattle, burning houses and ordering the inhabitants to leave their homes immediately; and that they had then actually in their possession three men prisoners. This report reached Far West in the evening, and was confirmed about midnight. A company of about sixty men went forth under the command of David W. Patten to disperse the mob, as they supposed. A battle was the result, in which Captain Patten and three of his men were killed, and others wounded. Bogart, it appears, had but one killed and others wounded. Notwithstanding the unlawful acts committed by Captain Bogart's men previous to the battle, it is now asserted and claimed that he was regularly ordered out as a militia captain, to preserve the peace along the line of Ray and Caldwell counties. The battle was fought four or five days previous to the arrival of General Lucas and his army. About the time of the battle with Captain Bogart, a number of our people who were living near Haun's mill, on Shoal creek, about twenty miles below Far West, together with a number of emigrants who had been stopped there in consequence of the excitement, made an agreement with the mob in that vicinity that neither party should molest the other, but dwell in peace. Shortly after this agreement was made, a mob party of from two to three hundred, many of whom are supposed to be from Chariton county, some from Daviess, and also those who had agreed to dwell in peace, came upon our people there, whose number in men was about forty, at a time they little expected any such thing, and without any ceremony, notwithstanding they begged for quarter, shot them down as they would tigers or panthers. Some few made their escape by fleeing. Eighteen were killed and a number more were severely wounded.

This tragedy was conducted in the most brutal and savage manner. An old man [Father Thomas McBride] after the massacre was partially over, threw himself into their hands and begged for quarter, when he was instantly shot down; that not killing him. they took an old corn cutter and literally mangled him to pieces.* A lad of ten years of age, after being shot down, also begged to be spared, when one of the mob placed the muzzle of his gun to the boy's head and blew out his brains.

* This barbarous deed is vividly described by President John Taylor in his controversy with Mr. Schuyler Colfax, Vice-President of the United States, 1870: "My mind wanders back upwards of thirty years ago, when, in the state of Missouri, Mr. McBride, an old, grey-haired, venerable veteran of the Revolution, with

The slaughter of these not satisfying the mob, they then proceeded to rob and plunder. The scene that presented itself after the massacre, to the widows and orphans of the killed, is beyond description. It was truly a time of weeping, mourning and lamentation.

As yet we have not heard of any one being arrested for these murders, notwithstanding there are men boasting about the country that they did kill on that occasion more than one "Mormon;" whereas all our people who were in the battle with Captain Patten against Bogart, that can be found, have been arrested, and are now confined in jail to await their trial for murder.

When General Lucas arrived near Far West, and presented the Governor's order, we were greatly surprised; yet we felt willing to submit to the authorities of the state. We gave up our arms without reluctance. We were then made prisoners, and confined to the limits of the town for about a week, during which time the men from the country were not permitted to go to their families, many of whom were in a suffering condition for want of food and firewood, the weather being very cold and stormy.

Much property was destroyed by the troops in town during their stay there, such as burning house logs, rails, corn-cribs, boards; the using of corn and hay, the plundering of houses, the killing of cattle, sheep and hogs, and also the taking of horses not their own; and all this without regard to owners, or asking leave of any one. In the meantime men were abused, women insulted and abused by the troops; and all this while we were kept prisoners.

Whilst the town was guarded, we were called together by the order of General Lucas, and a guard placed close around us, and in that situation we were compelled to sign a deed of trust for the purpose of making our individual property, all holden, as they said, to pay all the debts of every individual belonging to the Church, and also to pay for all damages the old inhabitants of Daviess may have sustained in consequence of the late difficulties in that county.

General Clark had now arrived, and the first important move made by him was the collecting of our men together on the square and selecting about fifty of them, whom he immediately marched into a house, and placed in close confinement. This was done without the aid of the

feeble frame and tottering steps, cried to a Missouri patriot: 'Spare my life, I am a Revolutionary soldier, I fought for liberty. Would you murder me? What is my offense, I believe in God and revelation?' This frenzied disciple of misplaced faith said: 'Take that, you —— —— Mormon,' and with the butt of his gun he dashed his brains out, and he lay quivering there,—his white locks clotted with his own brains and gore, on that soil that he had heretofore shed his blood to redeem—a sacrifice at the shrine of liberty! Shades of Franklin, Jefferson and Washington, were you there? Did you gaze on this deed of blood? Did you see your companion in arms thus massacred?"

sheriff, or any legal process. The next day forty-six of those taken, were driven off to Richmond, like a parcel of menial slaves, not knowing why they were taken, or what they were taken for. After being confined in Richmond more than two weeks, about one half were liberated; the rest, after another week's confinement, were required to appear at court, and have since been let to bail. Since General Clark withdrew his troops from Far West, parties of armed men have gone through the country, driving off horses, sheep and cattle,and also plundering houses; the barbarity of General Lucas' troops ought not to be passed over in silence. They shot our cattle and hogs merely for the sake of destroying them,leaving them for the ravens to eat. They took prisoner an aged man by the name of John Tanner, and without any reason for it, he was struck over the head with a gun, which laid his skull bare. Another man by the name of Carey was also taken prisoner by them, and without any provocation had his brains dashed out by a gun. He was laid in a wagon and there permitted to remain for the space of twenty-four hours; during which time no one was permitted to administer to him comfort or consolation; and after he was removed from that situation, he lived but a few hours.

The destruction of property at and about Far West is very great. Many are stripped bare, as it were, and others partially so; indeed take us as a body at this time, we are a poor and afflicted people; and if we are compelled to leave the state in the Spring, many, yes a large portion of our society, will have to be removed at the expense of the state; as those who might have helped them are now debarred that privilege in consequence of the deed of trust we were compelled to sign; which deed so operated upon our real estate, that it will sell for but little or nothing at this time.

We have now made a brief statement of some of the most prominent features of the troubles that have befallen our people since our first settlement in this state; and we believe that these persecutions have come in consequence of our religious faith, and not for any immorality on our part. That instances have been, of late, where individuals have trespassed upon the rights of others, and thereby broken the laws of the land, we will not pretend to deny; but yet we do believe that no crime can be substantiated against any of the people who have a standing in our Church of an earlier date than the difficulties in Daviess county. And when it is considered that the rights of this people have been trampled upon from time to time with impunity, and abuses almost innumerable heaped upon them it ought in some degree to palliate for any infraction of the law which may have been made on the part of our people.

The late order of Governor Boggs to drive us from the state, or exterminate us, is a thing so novel, unlawful, tyrannical, and oppressive, that we have been induced to draw up this memorial, and present this statement of our case to your honorable body, praying that a law may be passed, rescinding the order of the governor to drive us from the state, and also giving us the sanction of the legislature to possess our lands in peace. We ask an expression of the legislature, disapproving the conduct of those who compelled us to sign a deed of trust, and also disapproving of any man or set of men taking our property in consequence of that deed of trust, and appropriating it to the payment of debts not contracted by us or for the payment of damages sustained in consequence of trespasses committed by others.

We have no common stock; our property is individual property, and we feel willing to pay our debts as other individuals do; but we are not willing to be bound for other people's debts. The arms which were taken from us here, which we understand to be about six hundred and thirty, besides swords and pistols, we care not so much about, as we do the pay for them; only we are bound to do military duty, which we are willing to do, and which we think was sufficiently manifested by the raising of a volunteer company last fall at Far West when called upon by General Parks to raise troops for the frontier.

The arms given up by us, we consider were worth between twelve and fifteen thousand dollars; but we understand they have been greatly damaged since taken, and at this time probably would not bring near their former value. And as they were, both here and in Jackson county, taken by the militia, and consequently by the authority of the state, we therefore ask your honorable body to cause an appropriation to be made by law, whereby we may be paid for them, or otherwise have them returned to us, and the damages made good.

The losses sustained by our people in leaving Jackson county are such that it is impossible to obtain any compensation for them by law, because those who have sustained them are unable to prove those trespasses upon individuals. That the facts do exist that the buildings, crops, stock, furniture, rails, timber, etc., of the society have been destroyed in Jackson county, is not doubted by those who are acquainted in this upper country [the part of the state north of the Missouri river was so called]; and since these trespasses cannot be proven upon individuals, we ask your honorable body to consider this case; and if in your liberality and wisdom you can conceive it to be proper to make an appropriation by law to these sufferers, many of whom are still pressed down with poverty in consequence of their losses, they would be able to pay their debts, and also in some degree be relieved from poverty and woe; whilst the widow's heart would be made to rejoice, and the orphan's tear measurably dried up, and the prayers of a grateful people ascend on high, with thanksgiving and praise to the Author of our existence for such beneficent act.

In laying our case before your honorable body, we say that we are willing, and ever have been, to conform to the Constitution and laws of the United States, and of this state. We ask, in common with others, the protection of the laws. We ask for the privilege guaranteed to all free citizens of the United States, and of this state, to be extended to us that we may be permitted to settle and live where we please, and worship God according to the dictates of our conscience without molestation. And while we ask for ourselves this privilege, we are willing all others should enjoy the same.

We now lay our case at the feet of you legislators, and ask your honorable body to consider it, and do for us, after mature deliberation, that which your wisdom, patriotism and philanthropy may dictate. And we, as in duty bound, will ever pray.

EDWARD PARTRIDGE,
HEBER C. KIMBALL,
JOHN TAYLOR,
THEODORE TURLEY,
BRIGHAM YOUNG,
ISAAC MORLEY,
GEORGE W. HARRIS,
JOHN MURDOCK,
JOHN M. BURK.

A committee appointed by the citizens of Caldwell county, to draft the memorial and sign it in their behalf.

Far West, Caldwell county, Missouri, December 10, 1838.

Minutes of a High Council Held at Far West, Thursday, December 13, 1838.

Agreeable to appointment, the standing High Council met, when it was found that several were absent, who, (some of them) have had to flee for their lives; therefore it being necessary that those vacancies be filled, the meeting was called for that purpose, and also to express each other's feelings respecting the word of the Lord; President Brigham Young presiding.

The council was opened by prayer by Elder Kimball. After prayer, President Young made a few remarks, saying he thought it all important to have the Council reorganized, and prepared to do business. He advised the councilors to be wise and judicious in all their movements, and not hasty in their transactions. As for his faith, it was the same as ever; and he fellowshiped all such as loved the Gospel of our Lord and Savior Jesus Christ, in act as well as word.

Elder Kimball arose and said he felt as formerly, for he had endeavored to keep a straightforward course; but wherein he had been out of the way in any manner, he meant to mend in that thing; and he was determined, as far as possible, to do as he would be done by; and his faith was as good as ever; he was in fellowship with all who wanted to do right.

Simeon Carter said, as to his faith in the work it was the same as ever; he did not think that Joseph was a fallen Prophet, but he believed in every revelation that had come through him; still he thought that perhaps Joseph had not acted in all things according to the best wisdom; yet how far he had been unwise he could not say. He did not think that Joseph would be removed and another planted in his stead; but he believed that he would still perform his work. He was still determined to persevere and act in righteousness in all things, so that he might at last gain a crown of glory, and reign in the kingdom of God.

Jared Carter, responded to President Brigham Young's feelings, and wished all to walk with the brethren.

Thomas Grover said he was firm in the faith, and he believed the time would come when Joseph would stand before kings, and speak marvelous words.

David Dort expressed his feelings in a similar manner.

Levi Jackman says his faith is the same as ever, and he has confidence in Brother Joseph, as ever.

Solomon Hancock says he is a firm believer in the Book of Mormon and Doctrine and Covenants, and that Brother Joseph is not a fallen prophet, but will yet be exalted and become very high.

John Badger says his confidence in the work is the same as ever, and his faith, if possible, is stronger than ever. He believes that it was necessary that these scourges should come.

George W. Harris says that, as it respects the scourges which have come upon us, the hand of God was in it.

Samuel Bent says that his faith is as it ever was, and that he feels to praise God in prisons and in dungeons, and in all circumstances.

After some consultation it was thought expedient to nominate High Priests to fill the vacancies.

The Council was organized as follows: Simeon Carter, No. 1; Jared Carter, 2; Thomas Grover 3; David Dort, 4; Levi Jackman, 5; Solomon Hancock, 6; John Badger, 7; John Murdock, 8; John E. Page, 9; George W. Harris, 10; John Taylor, 11; Samuel Bent, 12.

Voted that John Murdock fill the vacancy of John P. Greene, No. 4, and David Dort the place of Elias Higbee, No. 11, and John Badger the place of George Morey, No. 7, and Lyman Sherman the place of Newel Knight, until he returns.

Council adjourned until Friday evening, six o'clock. Closed by prayer by President Brigham Young.

E. ROBINSON, Clerk.

Isaac Russell, who had become connected with a small camp of the Saints, of about thirty families, going west, turned from his course at Louisiana, and led them north ten miles on the Spanish claims, where they built huts or lived in tents through the winter in great suffering. Russell turned prophet (apostate). He said Joseph had fallen and he was appointed to lead the people.

Chandler Rogers, who was moving west, was met by a mob at Huntsville, and compelled to turn back, and fell in with Russell's camp. Russell said he was "the chosen of the Lord;" and when they left the place, they would have to go on foot, and take nothing with them, and they must sell their teams. Some would not sell and he cursed them.

Sunday, December 16.—I wrote the following letter:

The Prophet's Letter to the Church.

LIBERTY JAIL, MISSOURI,
December 16, 1838.

To the Church of Jesus Christ of Latter-day Saints in Caldwell county, and all the Saints who are scattered abroad, who are persecuted, and made desolate, and who are afflicted in divers manners for Christ's sake and the Gospel's, by the hands of a cruel mob and the tyrannical disposition of the authorities of this state; and whose perils are greatly augmented by the wickedness and corruption of false brethren, greeting:

May grace, mercy, and the peace of God be and abide with you; and notwithstanding all your sufferings, we assure you that you have our prayers and fervent desires for your welfare, day and night. We believe that that God who seeth us in this solitary place, will hear our prayers, and reward you openly.

Know assuredly, dear brethren, that it is for the testimony of Jesus that we are in bonds and in prison. But we say unto you, that we consider that our condition is better (notwithstanding our sufferings) than that of those who have persecuted us, and smitten us, and borne false witness against us; and we most assuredly believe that those who do bear false witness against us, do seem to have a great triumph over us for the present. But we want you to remember Haman and Mordecai: you know that Haman could not be satisfied so long as he saw Mordecai at the king's gate, and he sought the life of Mordecai and the destruction of the people of the Jews. But the Lord so ordered it, that Haman was hanged upon his own gallows.

So shall it come to pass with poor Haman in the last days, and those who have sought by unbelief and wickedness and by the principle of mobocracy to destroy us and the people of God, by killing and scattering them abroad, and wilfully and maliciously delivering us into the hands of murderers, desiring us to be put to death, thereby having us dragged about in chains and cast into prison. And for what cause? It is because we were honest men, and were determined to defend the lives of the Saints at the expense of our own. I say unto you, that those who have thus vilely treated us, like Haman, shall be hanged upon their own gallows; or, in other words, shall fall into their own gin, and snare, and ditch, and trap, which they have prepared for us, and shall go backwards and stumble and fall, and their name shall be blotted out, and God shall reward them according to all their abominations.

Dear brethren, do not think that our hearts faint, as though some strange thing had happened unto us, for we have seen and been assured of all these things beforehand, and have an assurance of a better hope than that of our persecutors. Therefore God hath made broad our shoulders for the burden. We glory in our tribulation, because we know that God is with us, that He is our friend, and that He will save our souls. We do not care for them that can kill the body; they cannot harm our souls. We ask no favors at the hands of mobs, nor of the world, nor of the devil, nor of his emissaries the dissenters, and those who love, and make, and swear falsehoods, to take away our lives. We have never dissembled, nor will we for the sake of our lives.

Forasmuch, then, as we know that we have been endeavoring with all our mind, might, and strength, to do the will of God, and all things whatsoever He has commanded us; and as to our light speeches, which may have escaped our lips from time to time, they have nothing to do with the fixed purposes of our hearts; therefore it sufficeth us to say, that our souls were vexed from day to day. We refer you to Isaiah, who considers those who make a man an offender for a word, and lay a snare for him that reproveth in the gate. We believe that the old Prophet verily told the truth: and we have no retraction to make. We have reproved in the gate, and men have laid snares for us. We have spoken words, and men have made us offenders. And notwithstanding all this, our minds are not yet darkened, but feel strong in the

Lord. But behold the words of the Savior: "If the light which is in you become darkness, behold how great is that darkness." Look at the dissenters. Again, "If you were of the world the world would love its own." Look at Mr. Hinkle—a wolf in sheep's clothing. Look at his brother John Corrill. Look at the beloved brother Reed Peck, who aided him in leading us, as the Savior was led, into the camp of His enemies, as a lamb prepared for the slaughter, as a sheep dumb before his shearers; so we opened not our mouths.

But these men, like Balaam, being greedy for reward, sold us into the hands of those who loved them, for the world loves his own. I would remember William E. McLellin, who comes up to us as one of Job's comforters. God suffered such kind of beings to afflict Job—but it never entered into their hearts that Job would get out of it all. This poor man who professes to be much of a prophet, has no other dumb ass to ride but David Whitmer,* to forbid his madness when he goes up to curse Israel; and this ass not being of the same kind as Balaam's, therefore, the angel notwithstanding appeared unto him, yet he could not penetrate his understanding sufficiently, but that he brays out cursings instead of blessings. Poor ass! Whoever lives to see it, will see him and his rider perish like those who perished in the gain-saying of Korah, or after the same condemnation. Now as for these and the rest of their company, we will not presume to say that the world loves them; but we presume to say they love the world, and we classify them in the error of Balaam, and in the gain-sayings of Korah, and with the company of Korah, Dathan, and Abiram.

Perhaps our brethren will say, because we thus write, that we are offended at these characters. If we are, it is not for a word, neither because they reproved in the gate—but because they have been the means of shedding innocent blood. Are they not murderers then at heart? Are not their consciences seared as with a hot iron? We confess that we are offended; but the Savior said, "It must needs be that offenses come, but woe unto them by whom they come." And again, "Blessed are ye when men shall revile you, and persecute you, and shall say all manner of evil against you falsely for my sake; rejoice and be exceeding glad, for great is your reward in heaven, for so persecuted they the Prophets which were before you."

Now, dear brethren, if any men ever had reason to claim this promise, we are the men; for we know that the world not only hate us,

*In order to appreciate the allusions here made to David Whitmer it will be necessary to remember that William E. M'Lellin claimed that President Joseph Smith was a fallen prophet and himself sought to bring into existence a re-organized church with David Whitmer as the president thereof. See foot note in this volume at pages 31, 32.

but they speak all manner of evil of us falsely, for no other reason than that we have been endeavoring to teach the fullness of the Gospel of Jesus Christ.

After we were bartered away by Hinkle, and were taken into the militia camp, we had all the evidence we could have asked for that the world hated us. If there were priests among them of all the different sects, they hated us, and that most cordially too. If there were generals, they hated us; if there were colonels, they hated us; and the soldiers, and officers of every kind, hated us; and the most profane, blasphemous, and drunkards; and whoremongers, hated us—they all hated us, most cordially. And now what did they hate us for? Purely because of the testimony of Jesus Christ. Was it because we were liars? We know that it has been so reported by some, but it has been reported falsely. Was it because we have committed treason against the government in Daviess county, or burglary, or larceny, or arson, or any other unlawful act in Daviess county? We know that we have been so reported by priests, and certain lawyers, and certain judges, who are the instigators, aiders, and abettors of a certain gang of murderers and robbers, who have been carrying on a scheme of mobocracy to uphold their priestcraft, against the Saints of the last days; and for a number of years have tried, by a well contemplated and premeditated scheme, to put down by physical power a system of religion that all the world, by their mutual attainments, and by any fair means whatever, were not able to resist.

Hence mobbers were encouraged by priests and Levites, by the Pharisees, by the Sadducees, and Essenes, and Herodians, and the most worthless, abandoned, and debauched, lawless, and inhuman, and the most beastly set of men that the earth can boast of—and indeed a parallel cannot be found anywhere else—to gather together to steal, to plunder, to starve, and to exterminate, and burn the houses of the "Mormons."

These are characters that, by their treasonable and overt acts, have desolated and laid waste Daviess county. These are the characters that would fain make all the world believe that we are guilty of the above named acts. But they represent us falsely; we stood in our own defense, and we believe that no man of us acted only in a just, a lawful, and a righteous retaliation against such marauders.

We say unto you, that we have not committed treason, nor any other unlawful act in Daviess county. Was it for murder in Ray county, against mob-militia; who was as a wolf in the first instance, hide and hair, teeth, legs and tail, who afterwards put on a militia sheep skin with the wool on; who could sally forth, in the day time, into the flock, and snarl, and show his teeth, and scatter and devour the flock, and satiate himself upon his prey, and then sneak back into the bramble in order that he might conceal himself in his well tried skin with the wool on?

We are well aware that there is a certain set of priests and satellites, and mobbers that would fain make all the world believe that we were guilty of the doings of this howling wolf that made such havoc among the sheep, who, when he retreated, howled and bleated at such a desperate rate, that if one could have been there, he would have thought that all the wolves, whether wrapped up in sheep skins or in goat skins, or in some other skins, and in fine all the beasts of the forest, were awfully alarmed, and catching the scent of innocent blood, they sallied forth with one tremendous howl and crying of all sorts; and such a howling, and such a tremendous havoc never was known before; such inhumanity, and relentless cruelty and barbarity as were practiced against the Saints in Missouri can scarcely be found in the annals of history.

Now those characters if allowed to would make the world believe that we had committed murder, by making an attack upon this howling wolf, while the fact is we were at home and in our bed, and asleep, and knew nothing of that transaction any more than we know what is going on in China while we are within these walls. Therefore we say again unto you, we are innocent of these things, and they have represented us falsely.

Was it for committing adultery that we were assailed? We are aware that that false slander has gone abroad, for it has been reiterated in our ears. These are falsehoods also. Renegade "Mormon" dissenters are running through the world and spreading various foul and libelous reports against us, thinking thereby to gain the friendship of the world, because they know that we are not of the world, and that the world hates us; therefore they [the world] make a tool of these fellows [the dissenters]; and by them try to do all the injury they can, and after that they hate them worse than they do us, because they find them to be base traitors and sycophants.

Such characters God hates; we cannot love them. The world hates them, and we sometimes think that the devil ought to be ashamed of them.

We have heard that it is reported by some, that some of us should have said, that we not only dedicated our property, but our families also to the Lord; and Satan, taking advantage of this, has perverted it into licentiousness, such as a community of wives, which is an abomination in the sight of God.

When we consecrate our property to the Lord it is to administer to the wants of the poor and needy, for this is the law of God; it is not for the benefit of the rich, those who have no need; and when a man consecrates or dedicates his wife and children, he does not give them to his brother, or to his neighbor, for there is no such law: for the law of God is, Thou shalt not commit adultery. Thou shalt not covet thy neighbor's wife. He that looketh upon a woman to lust after her, has committed adultery already in his heart. Now for a man to consecrate his property, wife and children, to the Lord, is nothing more nor less than to feed the hungry, clothe the naked, visit the widow and fatherless, the sick and afflicted, and do all he can to administer to their relief in their afflictions, and for him and his house to serve the Lord. In order to do this, he and all his house must be virtuous, and must shun the very appearance of evil.

Now if any person has represented anything otherwise than what we now write, he or she is a liar, and has represented us falsely—and this is another manner of evil which is spoken against us falsely.

We have learned also since we have been prisoners, that many false and pernicious things, which were calculated to lead the Saints far astray and to do great injury, have been taught by Dr. Avard as coming from the Presidency, and we have reason to fear that many other designing and corrupt characters like unto himself, have been teaching many things which the Presidency never knew were being taught in the Church by anybody until after they were made prisoners. Had they known of such things they would have spurned them and their authors as they would the gates of hell. Thus we find that there have been frauds and secret abominations and evil works of darkness going on, leading the minds of the weak and unwary into confusion and distraction, and all the time palming it off upon the Presidency, while the Presidency were ignorant as well as innocent of those things which those persons were practicing in the Church in their name. Meantime the Presidency were attending to their own secular and family concerns, weighed down with sorrow, in debt, in poverty, in hunger, essaying to be fed, yet finding [*i. e.* supporting] themselves. They occasionally received deeds of charity, it is true; but these were inadequate to their subsistence; and because they received those deeds, they were envied and hated by those who professed to be their friends.

But notwithstanding we thus speak, we honor the Church, when we speak of the Church as a Church, for their liberality, kindness, patience, and long suffering, and their continual kindness towards us.

And now, brethren, we say unto you—what more can we enumerate? Is not all manner of evil of every description spoken of us falsely, yea, we say unto you falsely. We have been misrepresented and misunderstood, and belied, and the purity and integrity and uprightness of our hearts have not been known—and it is through ignorance—yea, the very depths of ignorance is the cause of it; and not only ignorance, but on the part of some, gross wickedness and hypocrisy also; for some, by a long face and sanctimonious prayers, and very pious sermons, had power to lead the minds of the ignorant and unwary, and thereby obtain such influence that when we approached their iniquities the devil gained great advantage—would bring great trouble and sorrow upon our heads; and, in fine, we have waded through an ocean of tribulation and mean abuse, practiced upon us by the ill bred and the ignorant, such as Hinkle, Corrill, Phelps, Avard, Reed Peck, Cleminson, and various others, who are so very ignorant that they cannot appear respectable in any decent and civilized society, and whose eyes are full of adultery, and cannot cease from sin. Such characters as McLellin, John Whitmer, David Whitmer, Oliver Cowdery, and Martin Harris, are too mean to mention; and we had liked to have forgotten them. Marsh and "another," whose hearts are full of corruption, whose cloak of hypocrisy was not sufficient to shield them or to hold them up in the hour of trouble, who after having escaped the pollutions of the world through the knowledge of their Lord and Savior Jesus Christ, became again entangled and overcome—their latter end is worse than the first. But it has happened unto them according to the word of the Scripture: "The dog has returned to his vomit, and the sow that was washed to her wallowing in the mire."

Again, if men sin wilfully after they have received the knowledge of the truth, there remaineth no more sacrifice for sin, but a certain fearful looking for of judgment and fiery indignation to come, which shall devour these adversaries. For he who despised Moses' law died without mercy under two or three witnesses. Of how much more severe punishment suppose ye, shall he be thought worthy, who hath sold his brother, and denied the new and everlasting covenant by which he was sanctified, calling it an unholy thing, and doing despite to the Spirit of grace.

And again we say unto you, that inasmuch as there is virtue in us, and the Holy Priesthood has been conferred upon us—and the keys of the kingdom have not been taken from us, for verily thus saith the Lord, "Be of good cheer, for the keys that I gave unto you are yet with you"—therefore we say unto you, dear brethren, in the name of the Lord Jesus Christ, we deliver these characters unto the buffetings of Satan until the day of redemption, that they may be dealt with according to their works; and from henceforth their works shall be made manifest.

And now dear and well beloved brethren—and when we say brethren, we mean those who have continued faithful in Christ, men, women and children—we feel to exhort you in the name of the Lord Jesus, to be

strong in the faith in the new and everlasting covenant, and nothing frightened at your enemies. For what has happened unto us is an evident token to them of damnation; but unto us, of salvation, and that of God. Therefore hold on even unto death; for "he that seeks to save his life shall lose it; and he that loses his life for my sake, and the Gospel's, shall find it," saith Jesus Christ.

Brethren, from henceforth, let truth and righteousness prevail and abound in you; and in all things be temperate; abstain from drunkenness, and from swearing, and from all profane language, and from everything which is unrighteous or unholy; also from enmity, and hatred, and covetousness, and from every unholy desire. Be honest one with another, for it seems that some have come short of these things, and some have been uncharitable, and have manifested greediness because of their debts towards those who have been persecuted and dragged about with chains without cause, and imprisoned. Such characters God hates—and they shall have their turn of sorrow in the rolling of the great wheel, for it rolleth and none can hinder. Zion shall yet live, though she seem to be dead.

Remember that whatsoever measure you mete out to others, it shall be measured to you again. We say unto you, brethren, be not afraid of your adversaries; contend earnestly against mobs, and the unlawful works of dissenters and of darkness.

And the very God of peace shall be with you, and make a way for your escape from the adversary of your souls. We commend you to God and the word of His grace, which is able to make us wise unto salvation. Amen.

JOSEPH SMITH, JUN.

CHAPTER XVI.

CASE OF THE "MORMONS" BEFORE THE MISSOURI LEGISLATURE—CLOSE OF THE YEAR 1838.

Varied Reports as to the Intentions of the Saints.

THIS day [16th December] Elder David H. Redfield arrived in Jefferson City, and on Monday, 17th, presented the petition of the brethren to General David R. Atchison and others, who were very anxious to hear from Caldwell, as there were many reports in circulation, such as "the Mormons kept up the Danite system," "were going to build the Lord's house," and "more blood would be spilled before they left the state," which created a hardness in the minds of the people.

Interview Beween David H. Redfield and Governor Boggs.

In the afternoon Brother Redfield had an interview with Governor Boggs, who inquired about our people and property with as much apparent interest as though his whole soul was engaged for our welfare; and said that he had heard that "the citizens were committing depredations on the 'Mormons,' and driving off their stock."

Brother Redfield informed him that armed forces came in the place and abused men, women and children, stole horses, drove off cattle, and plundered houses of everything that pleased their fancy.

Governor Boggs said that he would write Judge King and Colonel Price, to go to Far West, and put down every hostile appearance. He also stated that "the stipulations entered into by the 'Mormons' to leave the state, and to sign the deed of trust, were unconstitutional, and not valid."

Brother Redfield replied, "We want the legislature pass a law to that effect, showing that the stipulati

and deeds of trust are not valid and are unconstitutional; and unless you do pass such a law, we shall not consider ourselves safe in the state. You say there has been a stain upon the character of the state, and now is the time to pass some law to that effect; and unless you do, farewell to the virtue of the state; farewell to her honor and good name; farewell to her Christian virtue, until she shall be peopled by a different race of men; farewell to every name that binds man to man; farewell to a fine soil and a glorious home; they are gone, they are rent from us by a lawless banditti."

Tuesday, *December 18*.—Mr. Turner, from the joint committee on the "Mormon" investigation, submitted a report, preamble and resolutions, as follows:

The Turner Committee Report to the Missouri Legislature,*

In Senate, Tuesday, December 18, 1838.

Mr. Turner, from the joint committee on the Mormon investigation, submitted the following report, preamble and resolutions:

The joint committee to whom was referred so much of the governor's message as relates to the recent difficulties between the people called Mormons, and a part of the people of this state, with instructions to inquire into the causes of said disturbances, and the conduct of the military operations in suppressing them, have taken the same under consideration, and would respectfully submit the following report and resolutions:

They have thought it unwise and injudicious under all the existing circumstances of this case, to predicate a report upon the papers, documents, etc., purporting to be copies of the evidence taken before an examining court, held in Richmond, in Ray county, for the purpose of inquiring into the charges alleged against the people called Mormons, growing out of the late difficulties between that people and other citizens of this state.

They consider the evidence adduced in the examination there held, in a great degree, *exparte*, and not of the character which should be desired for the basis of a fair and candid investigation. Moreover, the papers, documents, etc., have not been certified in such manner as to satisfy the committee of their authenticity.

* In the previous publication of this history only part of this report is given, but here the whole document is inserted.

It has been represented to them that the examining court has sent on for further trial, many of that class of citizens called Mormons, charged with various crimes and offenses; under the charge of treason, six; for murder and as accessories thereto, before and after the fact, eight; and for other felonies, twenty-seven. Special terms of the circuit court are expected to be held in the several counties, in which the above mentioned crimes are represented to have been committed. Grand juries will then have these charges against said people before them, and must act upon the same documentary evidence which the committee would necessarily be compelled to examine, by which circumstance two co-ordinate branches of this government may be brought into collision—a contingency that should be studiously avoided and cautiously guarded against.

Another insuperable objection that has presented itself to the mind of the committee, and which would induce them to suspend an investigation, under present and existing circumstances, would be the consequences likely to result from a publication of their report. Those persons who have been sent on for further trial, have guaranteed to them the sacred and constitutional right of "a speedy trial by an impartial jury of the vicinage," and if the guilt of the accused should be confirmed by the report of the committee, it would so prejudice public sentiment against them, as to deprive them of that right, which should not be taken away by any consideration involved in this inquiry.

If the committee were to find it necessary in the prosecution of their object, to have access to the papers, documents, etc., connected with this difficulty, the probable interference of the several courts being in session, might seriously interrupt their views. It might reasonably be expected that all the evidence of every description, would be in the possession of the courts, to be used on the final trial, and by that means the investigation would be protracted to a much greater length than would be necessary under different circumstances. They would therefore recommend, in order to avoid all the difficulties that have been presented, that a committee, after the adjournment of the general assembly, go into the vicinity of the scene of difficulties, and make their investigation, and report at such time, and in such manner, as the legislature may direct. If this course should be adopted, the committee believe that the session would be much shortened, and heavy expenses saved to the state, which otherwise would necessarily be incurred in sending for witnesses, and bringing them from so great a distance. By a resolution of both houses, the special message of the governor in relation to the subject of inquiry, with the accompanying documents, was referred to the committee, with instructions to select such documents as in their opinion ought to be published with the message, and report to their respective houses. The committee after a full consideration of the subject, with due regard to its importance, are of opinion that it is inexpedient at this time, to publish any of the documents, under the authority of the general assembly, and submit to the two houses the leading reasons for that opinion.

The documents may be divided into several classes:

First—The affidavits and correspondence preceding each series of authorized military operations.

Second—The orders issued upon such evidence.

Third—The military operations and correspondence consequent thereon; and

Fourth—The evidence taken before a court of inquiry, held for the investigation of criminal charges against individuals.

It was found by the joint committee, at an early period after their organization, that, in order to a full and satisfactory investigation of the subjects referred to them, a mass of additional testimony, oral and written, would be required. This becomes apparent to the committee, from the contents of the documents referred to them. These documents, although they are serviceable in giving direction to the courts of inquiry, are none of them, except the official orders and correspondence, such as ought to be received as conclusive evidence of the facts stated; nor are their contents such as would, without the aid of further evidence, enable the committee to form a satisfactory opinion in relation to the material points of the inquiry.

The copy of the examination taken before the criminal court of inquiry, is manifestly not such evidence as ought to be received by the committee:

First—Because it is not authenticated; and

Second—It is confined chiefly to the object of that inquiry; namely: the investigation of criminal charges against individuals under arrest; for these reasons, but above all, for the reason that it would be a direct interference with the administration of justice, this document ought not to be published, with the sanction of the legislature.

The committee conclude, that it would not be proper to publish the official orders and correspondence between the officers in command, and the executive, without the evidence on which they were founded; and that evidence is not sufficiently full and satisfactory to authorize its publication. To publish the whole together might tend to give a direction to the public mind, prejudicial to an impartial administration of justice in pending cases, while it will not afford the means of forming any satisfactory conclusion as to the cause of the late disturbances, or the conduct of the military operations in suppressing them.

The committee therefore recommend to each house to adopt the following resolutions:

Resolved, That it is inexpedient at this time, to prosecute further the inquiry into the causes of the late disturbances and the conduct of the military operations in suppressing them.

Resolved, That it is inexpedient to publish at this time, any of the documents accompanying the governor's message in relation to the late disturbances.

Resolved, That it is expedient to appoint a joint committee, composed of —— senators, and —— representatives, to investigate the cause of said disturbances, and the conduct of the military operations in suppressing them, to meet at such time, and to be invested with such powers as may be prescribed by law.*

Wednesday, December 19.—Mr. John Corrill presented the petition† to the house. While it was reading the members were silent as the house of death; after which the debate commenced, and excitement increased till the house was in an uproar; their faces turned red; their eyes flashed fire, and their countenances spoke volumes.

The Debate on the Petition.

Mr. Childs, of Jackson county, said, there was not one word of truth in it, so far as he had heard, and that it ought never to have been presented to that body. Not long ago we appropriated two thousand dollars to their relief, and now they have petitioned for the pay for their lands, which we took away from them. We got rid of a great evil when we drove them from Jackson county, and we have had peace there ever since; and the state will always be in difficulty so long as they suffer them to live in the state; and the

*The above report is taken from a book containing the documents, the correspondence, orders, etc., in relation to the disturbances with the "Mormons;" and the evidence given before the Hon. Austin A. King, judge of the Fifth Judicial Circuit of the state of Missouri, at the courthouse in Richmond, in a criminal court of inquiry, begun November 12, 1838, on the trial of Joseph Smith, Jun., and others, for high treason and other crimes against the state, pp. 1-4. The book is published by order of the general assembly.

†This was the petition of the 10th of December, signed by Edward Partridge, Heber C. Kimball, John Taylor *et al.* in behalf of the citizens of Caldwell county, which petition appears in chapter xv. of this volume. Subsequently, viz., in 1841, when the Missouri legislature published, by order of the general assembly, what is alleged to be the documents in relation to the disturbances with the "Mormons," etc., neither this document nor any account of the debate which followed its introduction, as here referred to appears.

quicker they get that petition from before this body the better.

Mr. Ashley, from Livingston, said the petition was false from beginning to end, and that himself and the "Mormons" could not live together, for he would always be found fighting against them, and one or the other must leave the state. He gave a history of the Haun's Mill massacre, and said he saw Jack Rogers cut up McBride with a corn-cutter.

Mr. Corrill corrected Mr. Childs, and stated facts in the petition which he was acquainted with, and that Mr. Childs ought to know that there could not be the first crime established against the "Mormons" while in Jackson county.

One member hoped the matter would not be looked over in silence, for his constituents required of him to know the cause of the late disturbances.

Mr. Young, of Lafayette, spoke very bitterly against the petition and the "Mormons."

An aged member from St. Charles moved a reference of the bill to a select committee; and, continued he, "as the gentleman that just spoke, and other gentlemen, want the petition ruled out of the house for fear their evil doings will be brought to light; this goes to prove to me and others, that the petition is true."

Mr. Redman, of Howard county, made a long speech in favor of a speedy investigation of the whole matter; said he, "The governor's order has gone forth, and the Mormons are leaving; hundreds are waiting to cross the Mississippi river, and by and by they are gone, and our state is blasted; her character is gone; we gave them no chance for a fair investigation. The state demands of us that we give them a speedy investigation."

Nature of the Testimony.

Mr. Gyer, from St. Louis, agreed with the gentleman from Howard county, that the committee should have power to call witnesses from any part of the state, and defend them; and unless the governor's order was rescinded, he for one would leave the state. Other gentlemen made similar remarks.

The testimony presented the committee of investigation, before referred to, was the governor's orders, General Clark's reports, the report of the *ex parte* trial at Richmond, and a lot of papers signed by nobody, given to nobody, and directed to nobody, containing anything our enemies were disposed to write.

Minutes of the High Council at Far West.

The High council of Zion met in Far West, Wednesday, December 19, 1838.

The Council was organized as follows: Ebenezer Robinson, No. 1; Jared Carter, No. 2; Thomas Grover, 3; Reynolds Cahoon, 4; Theodore Turley, 5; Solomon Hancock, 6; John Badger, 7; John Murdock, 8; Harlow Redfield, 9; George W. Harris, 10; David Dort, 11; Samuel Bent 12. The Council was opened by prayer by President Brigham Young, who presided.

Harlow Redfield gave a statement of his feelings. He said his faith was as good as it ever was, notwithstanding he did not feel to fellowship all the proceedings of his brethren in Daviess county; he thought they did not act as wisely as they might have done.

Voted by the Council that John E. Page and John Taylor* be or-

* Of John Taylor a biographical note has already been given. See page 154. The following facts concerning John E. Page are given by himself:

The subscriber was born of Ebenezer and Rachael Page, their first child, February 25th, A. D. 1799. My father was of pure English extraction; my mother of English, Irish, and Welsh extraction. My place of birth was Trenton Township, Oneida county, State of New York. I embraced the faith of the Church of Jesus Christ of Latter-day Saints, and was baptized August the 18th, 1833, by the hands of Elder Emer Harris (own brother to Martin Harris, one of the Three Witnesses to the divinity of the Book of Mormon). I was ordained an Elder under the hands of Elders Nelson Higgins, Ebenezer Page, Jun., and others. My baptism took place in Brownhelm, Lorain county, Ohio; my ordination in Florence, Huron county, of the same state, on the 12th of September, 1833.

I moved to Kirtland, Geauga county Ohio, in the fall of 1835.

On the 31st day of May, 1836, I started on a mission to Canada West, Leeds county. I was gone from my family seven months and twenty days.

On the 16th day of February, 1837, I again left Kirtland with my family, a wife and two small children, taking with me all the earthly goods I possessed, which consisted of one bed and our wearing apparel of the plainest kind, to continue my mission in the same region of country as before.

In July following the commandment came forth for me to occupy a place in the quorum of the Twelve.

dained to the Apostleship, to fill vacancies in the quorum of the Twelve. They came forward and received their ordination under the hands of Brigham Young and Heber C. Kimball.

Voted that we send a petition to the general government, and send it by mail.

Voted that Edward Partridge and John Taylor be a committee to draft the above-mentioned petition; also it is their privilege to choose another person to assist them.

Council adjourned until next Wednesday at one o'clock, at same place.

E. ROBINSON, Clerk.

Return of Don Carlos Smith and George A. Smith.

Tuesday, December 25.—My brother, Don Carlos, and my cousin George A. Smith returned, [from missions through Kentucky and Tennessee], having traveled fifteen hundred miles—nine hundred on foot, and the remainder by steamboat and otherwise. They visited several branches, and would have accomplished the object of their mission, had it not been for the troubles at Far West.

When nearly home they were known and pursued by the mob, which compelled them to travel one hundred miles in two days and nights. The ground at the time was slippery, and a severe northwest wind was blowing in their faces; they had but little to eat, and narrowly escaped freezing both nights.

On the 14th day of May, 1838, I started with a company of Saints, made up of men, women and their children, for the state of Missouri, where we landed with a company occupying thirty wagons, in the first week of October, at a place called De Witt, some six miles above the outlet of Grand river, on the north side of the Missouri river, where we were attacked by an armed mob, and by them barbarously treated for nearly two weeks. We then went to Far West, Caldwell county, where we united with the general body of the Church, and with them participated in all the grievous persecutions practiced on the Church by means of a furious mob, by which means I buried one wife and two children as martyrs to our holy religion, since they died through extreme suffering for the want of the common comforts of life—which I was not allowed to provide even with my money.

On the 19th of December, 1838, at Far West, Elder John Taylor and myself were ordained as Apostles under the hands of Elders Brigham Young and Heber C. Kimball, in the quorum of the Twelve, to fill some vacancies in the quorum, which had occurred by apostasies. In two year's time I had baptized upwards of six hundred persons, and traveled more than five thousand miles, principally on foot and under the most extreme poverty, relative to earthly means, being sustained alone by the power of God and not of man, or the wisdom of the world.—JOHN E. PAGE.

Wednesday, December 26.—David H. Redfield having returned to Far West, made his report, and the High Council voted that they were satisfied with his proceedings.*

Redfield's Report.

Thursday, December 27.—Anson Call went to Ray county, near Elk Horn, to sell some property, and was taken by ten of the mob and one old negro. Some of the mob were two of Judge Dickey's sons, a Mr. Adams, and a constable. They ordered him to disarm himself. He told them he had no arms about his person. They ordered him to turn his pockets wrong side out. They then said they would peel off his naked back before morning, with a hickory gad. They beat him with their naked hands times without number; they struck him in the face with a bowie knife, and severely hurt him a number of times.

Experience of Anson Call.

After abusing him about four hours, saying he was a —— "Mormon," and they would serve him as they had others, tie him with a hickory withe and gad him, and keep him till morning, they then started off and came to a hazel grove; while consulting together what course to pursue with him, he leaped into the bush, when they pursued him, but he made his escape and returned to Far West.

After much controversy and angry disputation, as the papers of Missouri, published at the time, abundantly testify, our petition and memorial was laid on the table until the 4th of July following; thus utterly refusing to grant the request of the memorialists to investigate the subject.†

Action of Missouri Legislature.

After we were cast into prison, we heard nothing but

*David H. Redfield, it will be remembered, was the messenger from the citizens of Caldwell county to the Missouri state legislature, bearing with him the petition of the 10th of December, and it is, of course, from his report of the manner in which the petition was received and the report of the debate thereon that the Prophet makes up his account of that affair.

†The bill providing for an investigation of the "Mormon" difficulties was finally laid upon the table until the 4th of July in the house by a vote of 48 in favor of such action and 37 against such procedure. Seven members were absent. The matter was not again taken up until the legislature of 1840, of which more later.

threatenings, that, if any judge or jury, or court of any kind, should clear any of us, we should never get out of the state alive.

The state appropriated two thousand dollars to be distributed among the people of Daviess and Caldwell counties, the "Mormons" of Caldwell not excepted. The people of Daviess thought they could live on "Mormon" property, and did not want their thousand, consequently it was pretended to be given to those of Caldwell. Judge Cameron, Mr. McHenry, and others attended to the distribution. Judge Cameron would drive in the brethren's hogs (many of which were identified) and shoot them down in the streets; and without further bleeding, and half dressing, they were cut up and distributed by McHenry to the poor, at a charge of four and five cents per pound; which, together with a few pieces of refuse goods, such as calicoes at double and treble prices soon consumed the two thousand dollars; doing the brethren very little good, or in reality none, as the property destroyed by them, [i. e. the distributing commission] was equal to what they gave the Saints.*

State Appropriation of $2,000.

The proceedings of the legislature were warmly opposed by a minority of the house—among whom were David R. Atchison, of Clay county, and all the members from St. Louis, and Messrs. Rollins and Gordon, from Boone county, and by various other members from other counties; but the mob majority carried the day, for the guilty wretches feared an investigation—knowing that it would endanger their lives and liberties. Some time during this

Course of the Minority in the Legislature.

*Of this matter of distributing the legislature's appropriation the late President John Taylor in his discussion with Schuyler Colfax, Vice-President of the United States, 1870, says: "The legislature of Missouri, to cover their infamy, appropriated the munificent (?) sum of $2,000 to help the suffering 'Mormons.' Their agent took a few miserable traps, the sweepings of an old store; for the balance of the patrimony he sent into Daviess county and killed our hogs, which we were then prevented from doing, and brought them to feed the poor 'Mormons' as part of the legislative appropriation. This I saw."

session the legislature appropriated two hundred thousand dollars to pay the troops for driving the Saints out of the state.

Course of the State Press.

Many of the state journals tried to hide the iniquity of the state by throwing a covering of lies over her atrocious deeds. But can they hide the govenor's cruel order for banishment or extermination? Can they conceal the facts of the disgraceful treaty of the generals with their own officers and men at the city of Far West? Can they conceal the fact that twelve or fifteen thousand men, women and children, have been banished from the state without trial or condemnation? And this at an expense of two hundred thousand dollars—and this sum appropriated by the state legislature, in order to pay the troops for this act of lawless outrage? Can they conceal the fact that we have been imprisoned for many months, while our families, friends and witnesses have been driven away? Can they conceal the blood of the murdered husbands and fathers, or stifle the cries of the widows and the fatherless? Nay! The rocks and mountains may cover them in unknown depths, the awful abyss of the fathomless deep may swallow them up, and still their horrid deeds will stand forth in the broad light of day, for the wondering gaze of angels and of men! They cannot be hid.

Some time in December Heber C. Kimball and Alanson Ripley were appointed, by the brethren in Far West, to visit us at Liberty jail as often as circumstances would permit, or occasion required, which duty they faithfully performed. We were sometimes visited by our friends, whose kindness and attention I shall ever remember with feelings of lively gratitude; but frequently we were not suffered to have that privilege. Our food was of the coarsest kind, and served up in a manner which was disgusting.

Thus, in a land of liberty, in the town of Liberty, Clay county, Missouri, my fellow prisoners and I in chains, and dungeons, saw the close of 1838.

CHAPTER XVII.

PREPARATIONS FOR LEAVING MISSOURI—ACTION OF THE STATE LEGISLATURE.

Tuesday, January 1, 1839.—The day dawned upon us as prisoners of hope, but not as sons of liberty. O Columbia, Columbia! How thou art fallen! "The land of the free, the home of the brave!" "The asylum of the oppressed"—oppressing thy noblest sons, in a loathsome dungeon, without any provocation, only that they have claimed to worship the God of their fathers according to His own word, and the dictates of their own consciences. Elder Parley P. Pratt and his companions in tribulation were still held in bondage in their doleful prison in Richmond.

Reflections on the Opening Year.

Monday, January 7.—Anson Call returned to his farm on the three forks of Grand river, to see if he could secure any of the property he had left in his flight to Adam-ondi-Ahman, and was there met by the mob, and beaten with a hoop pole about his limbs, body and head; the man that used the pole about his person was George W. O'Neal. With much difficulty Brother Call returned to Far West, with his person much bruised, and from that time gave up all hopes of securing any of his property.

Anson Call Beaten.

Tuesday, January 8.—About this time England and Ireland were visited by a tremendous storm of wind from the northwest, which unroofed and blew down many houses in the cities and in the country, doing much damage to the shipping; many hundreds of persons were turned out of doors, many lives lost on the land and sea, and an immense amount of property was destroyed.

Storm in England.

Such a wind had not been witnessed by any one living; and some began to think that the judgments were about to follow the Elders' preaching.

Thursday, January 10.—

Missouri State Senate Resolutions on Mormon Difficulties.

Resolved by the Senate, the House of Representatives concurring therein, that the three resolutions of the 18th of December be referred to a joint committee of the two Houses, heretofore raised, on the subject of the Mormon difficulties, with the instructions to report a bill in conformity thereto, as soon as they can conveniently prepare the same; which was agreed to.*

Wednesday, January 16.—Mr. Turner, from the joint select committee, introduced to the Senate, "*A Bill to provide for the investigation of the late disturbances in this state.*" This bill consists of twenty-three sections, of which the following is the first:

1st. A joint committee shall be appointed to investigate the causes of the late disturbances between the people called Mormons and other inhabitants of this state, and the conduct of the military operations in repressing them; which committee shall consist of two senators, to be elected by the Senate and three representatives, to be elected by the House of Representatives.

Other Provisions of the Bill.

The bill further provided that the committee should meet at Richmond, Ray county, on the first Monday in May, and thereafter at such times and places as they should appoint; that they should choose a chairman, clerk, sergeant-at-arms and assistants; issue subpœnas and other processes; admin-

* The above resolutin was offered by Mr. William M. Campbell in the Senate, and the three resolutions of the 18th of December were in Mr. Turner's report to the Senate of that date, and are as follows:

Resolved, That it is inexpedient at this time,to prosecute further the inquiry into the causes of the late disturbances and the conduct of the military operations in suppressing them.

Resolved, That it is inexpedient to publish at this time. any of the documents accompanying the governor's message in relation to the late disturbances.

Resolved, That it is expedient to appoint a joint committee composed of —— Senators, and —— Representatives to investigate the cause of said disturbances, and the conduct of the military operations in suppressing them, to meet at such time, and to be invested with such powers as may be prescribed by law." See the whole report of Mr. Turner's, at pp. 235-8.

ister oaths; keep a record; furnish rooms; pay witnesses one dollar and fifty cents per day out of the treasury; receive their pay as members of the legislature; clerk four dollars per day, and one dollar and fifty cents for each arrest. In short, all parties concerned were to be paid the highest price—and this committee were to be clothed with all the powers of the highest courts of record. This bill did not concern the "Mormons," as the exterminating order of Governor Boggs, and the action of General Clark thereon, would compel all the Saints to be out of the state before the court would sit, so that they would have no testimony but from mobbers and worse, apostates; and this was evidently their object in postponing the time so long.

Proposition to Help the Poor.

About this time President Brigham Young proposed to Bishop Partridge to help the poor out of the state. The Bishop replied, "The poor may take care of themselves, and I will take care of myself." President Brigham Young replied, "If you will not help them out, I will."

Thursday, January 24.—I wrote as follows from Liberty jail:

The Prophet's Petition to the Missouri Legislature.

To the Honorable Legislature of Missouri:

Your memorialists, having a few days since solicited your attention to the same subject,* would now respectfully submit to your honorable body a few additional facts in support of their prayer.

They are now imprisoned under a charge of treason against the state of Missouri, and their lives, and fortunes, and characters, are suspended upon the result of the trial on the criminal charges preferred against them. Therefore your honorable body will excuse them for manifesting the deep concern they feel in relation to their trial for a crime so enormous as that of treason.

It is not our object to complain—to asperse any one. All we ask is a fair and impartial trial. We ask the sympathies of no one. We ask sheer justice; 'tis all we expect, and all we merit, but we merit that. We know the people of no county in this state to which we would ask our final trial to be sent, who are prejudiced in our favor. But we be-

* The previous document here referred to, does not appear in this history as heretofore published, nor is it to be found in any of the manuscrips in the historian's office.

lieve that the state of excitement existing in most of the upper counties is such that a jury would be improperly influenced by it. But that excitement, and the prejudice against us in the counties comprising the fifth Judicial Circuit, are not the only obstacles we are compelled to meet. We know that much of that prejudice against us is not so much to be attributed to a want of honest motives amongst the citizens as it is to misrepresentation.

It is a difficult task to change opinions once formed. The other obstacle which we candidly consider one of the most weighty, is the feeling which we believe is entertained by Hon. Austin A. King against us, and his consequent inability to do us impartial justice. It is from no disposition to speak disrespectfully of that high officer, that we lay before your honorable body the facts we do; but simply that the legislature may be apprised of our real condition. We look upon Judge King as like all other mere men, liable to be influenced by his feelings, his prejudices, and his previously formed opinions. From his reputation we consider him as being partially, if not entirely, committed against us. He has written much upon the subject of our late difficulties, in which he has placed us in the wrong. These letters have been published to the world. He has also presided at an excited public meeting as chairman, and no doubt sanctioned all the proceedings. We do not complain of the citizens who held that meeting, they were entitled to that privilege. But for the judge before whom the very men were to be tried for a capital offense to participate in an expression of condemnation of these same individuals, is to us, at least,apparently wrong;and we cannot think that we should, after such a course on the part of the judge, have the same chance of a fair and impartial trial as all admit we ought to have.

We believe that the foundation of the feeling against us, which we have reason to think Judge King entertains, may be traced to the unfortunate troubles which occurred in Jackson county some few years ago; in a battle between the "Mormons" and a portion of the citizens of that county, Mr. Brazeale, the brother-in-law of Judge King, was killed. It is natural that the judge should have some feelings against us, whether we were right or wrong in that controversy.

We mention these facts, not to disparage Judge King; we believe that from the relation he bears to us, he would himself prefer that our trials should be had in a different circuit, and before a different court. Many other reasons and facts we might mention, but we forebear.

Postscript to the Petition.

This letter was directed to James M. Hughes, Esq., member of the House of Representatives, Jefferson City, with the following request:

Will you be so kind as to present this to the House. The community here would, I believe, have no objection for the trial of these men being transferred to St. Louis.

P. H. B.*

Saturday, 26.—

Minutes of a Public Meeting at Far West.

A meeting of a respectable number of the citizens of Caldwell county, members of the Church of Jesus Christ of Latter-day Saints, was held in Far West, according to previous notice, to devise and take into consideration such measures as might be thought necessary in order to comply with the orders of the Executive to remove from the state of Missouri immediately, as made known by General Clark to the citizens of said county, in the month of November last.

The meeting was called to order by Don C. Smith; and on motion, John Smith was unanimously called to the chair, and Elias Smith appointed secretary.

The object of the meeting was then stated by the chairman, who briefly adverted to the causes which had brought about the present state of affairs, and called for an expression of sentiment on the best course to be pursued in the present emergency.

Several gentlemen addressed the meeting on the subject of our removal from the state and the seeming impossibility of complying with the orders of the governor of Missouri, in consequence of the extreme poverty of many, which had come upon them by being driven from place to place, deprived of their constitutional rights and privileges, as citizens of this, and the United States, and were of the opinion that an appeal to the citizens of Upper Missouri ought to be made, setting forth our condition, and claiming their assistance towards furnishing means for the removal of the poor of this county out of the state, as being our right and our due in the present case.

On motion, resolved: That a committee of seven be appointed to make a draft of a preamble and resolutions in accordance with the foregoing sentiments to be presented to a future meeting for their consideration.

The following were then appointed. viz.,—John Taylor, Alanson Ripley, Brigham Young, Theodore Turley, Heber C. Kimball, John Smith and Don C. Smith.

Resolved: That the committee be further instructed to ascertain the

* Whom these initials represent cannot be ascertained, or whether they represent one person or three They evidently represent secret friends or a friend of the Prophet at Liberty, Clay county, willing to urge this matter upon the attention of Mr. Hughes and also upon the House.

number of families who are actually destitute of means for their removal, and report at the next meeting.

Resolved: That it is the opinion of this meeting that an exertion should be made to ascertain how much can be obtained from individuals of the society [the Church], and that it is the duty of those who have, to assist those who have not, that thereby we may, as far as possible, within and of ourselves, comply with the demands of the Executive.

Adjourned to meet again on Tuesday, the 29th instant, at twelve o'clock, m.

JOHN SMITH, Chairman.
ELIAS SMITH, Secretary.

Tuesday, 29.—

Minutes of the Second Meeting at Far West.

The brethren met again according to adjournment. John Smith was again called to the chair, and Elias Smith appointed secretary.

The committee appointed to draw up a preamble and resolutions to be presented to the meeting for consideration, presented by their chairman, John Taylor, a memorial of the transactions of the people of Missouri towards us since our first settlement in this state, in which was contained some of our sentiments and feelings on the subject of our persecutions by the authority of the state, and our deprivation of the rights of citizenship guaranteed to us by the Constitution. The document under preparation by the committee was yet in an unfinished state, owing to causes which were stated by the committee; and they further apologized for not drawing it up in the form of resolutions, agreeable to the vote of the former meeting.

The report was accepted as far as completed, and by a vote of the meeting, the same committee were directed to finish it, and prepare it for and send it to the press for publication, and they were instructed to dwell minutely on the subject relating to our arms, and the fiend-like conduct of the officers of the militia in sequestering all the best of them after their surrender on condition of being returned to us again, or suffering them to be exchanged for others, not worth half their value, in violation of their bond, and of the honor of the commander of the forces sent against us by the state.

On motion of President Brigham Young, it was resolved that we this day enter into a covenant to stand by and assist each other to the utmost of our abilities in removing from this state, and that we will never desert the poor who are worthy, till they shall be out of the reach of the exterminating order of General Clark, acting for and in the name of the state.

After an expression of sentiments by several who addressed the meeting on the propriety of taking efficient measures to remove the poor from the state, it was resolved, that a committee of seven be appointed to superintend the business of our removal, and to provide for those who have not the means of moving, till the work shall be completed.

The following were then appointed, viz., William Huntington, Charles Bird, Alanson Ripley, Theodore Turley, Daniel Shearer, Shadrach Roundy, and Jonathan H. Hale.

Resolved: That the secretary draft an instrument expressive of the sense of the covenant entered into this day, by those present, and that those who were willing to subscribe to the covenant should do it, that their names might be known, which would enable the committee more expeditiously to carry their business into effect.

The instrument was accordingly drawn, and by vote of the meeting the secretary attached the names of those who were willing to subscribe to it.

Adjourned to meet again on Friday, the 1st of February next, at twelve o'clock, m.

JOHN SMITH, Chairman.
ELIAS SMITH, Secretary.

The following is the covenant referred to in the preceding minutes, with the names which were then and afterwards attached to it, as far as they have been preserved:

We, whose names are hereunder written, do for ourselves individually hereby covenant to stand by and assist one another, to the utmost of our abilities, in removing from this state in compliance with the authority of the state; and we do hereby acknowledge ourselves firmly bound to the extent of all our available property, to be disposed of by a committee who shall be appointed for the purpose of providing means for the removing from this state of the poor and destitute who shall be considered worthy, till there shall not be one left who desires to remove from the state: with this proviso, that no individual shall be deprived of the right of the disposal of his own property for the above purpose, or of having the control of it, or so much of it as shall be necessary for the removing of his own family, and to be entitled to the over-plus, after the work is effected; and furthermore, said committee shall give receipts for all property, and an account of the expenditure of the same.

Far West, Missouri, January 29, 1839.

List of Names Subscribed to the Foregoing.

John Smith,	James McMillan,
Wm. Huntington,	Chandler Holbrook,

Charles Bird,
Alanson Ripley,
Theodore Turley,
Daniel Shearer,
Shadrach Roundy,
Jonathan H. Hale,
Elias Smith,
Brigham Young,
James Burnham,
Leicester Gaylord,
Samuel Williams,
John Miller,
Aaron M. York,
George A. Smith,
Daniel Howe,
James Bradin,
Jonathan Beckelshimer
David Jones,
Wm. M. Fossett,
Charles N. Baldwin,
Jesse N. Reed,
Benjamin Johnson,
Jonathan Hampton,
Anson Call,
Peter Dopp,
Samuel Rolph,
Abel Lamb,
Daniel McArthur,
William Gregory,
Zenas Curtis,
John Reed,
William R. Orton,
Samuel D. Tyler,
John H. Goff,
Thomas Butterfield,
Dwight Hardin,
Norvil M. Head,
Stephen V. Foot,
Jacob G. Bigler,
Eli Bagley,
William Milam,
Lorenzo Clark,
William Allred,
Alexander Wright,
William Taylor,
John Taylor,
Reuben P. Hartwell,
John Lowry,
Welcome Chapman,
Solomon Hancock,
Arza Adams,
Henry Jacobs,
James Carroll,
David Lyons,
John Taylor,
Don Carlos Smith,
William J. Stewart,
Isaac B. Chapman,
Roswell Stephens,
Reuben Headlock,
David Holman,
Joel Goddard,
Phineas R. Bird,
Duncan McArthur,
Allen Talley,
James Hampton,
Sherman A. Gilbert,
James S. Holman,
Andrew Lytle,
Aaron Johnson,
Heber C. Kimball,
George W. Harris,
George W. Davidson,
Harvey Strong,
Elizabeth Mackley,
Sarah Mackley,
Andrew More,
Harvey Downey,
John Maba,
Lucy Wheeler,
John Turpin,
William Earl,
Zenos H. Gurley,
Joseph W. Coolidge.
Anthony Head,
S. A. P. Kelsey,

Wm. Van Ausdall,
Nathan K. Knight,
John Thorp,
Andrew Rose,
John S. Martin,
Albert Sloan,
John D. Lee,
Eliphas Marsh,
Joseph Wright,
John Badger,
Levi Richards.
Erastus Bingham,
Elisha Everett,
John Lytle,
Levi Jackman,
Thomas Guyman,
Nahum Curtis,
Lyman Curtis,
Philip Ballard,
William Gould,
Reuben Middleton,
William Harper,
Seba Joes,
Charles Butler,
Richard Walton,
Isaac Kerron,
Joseph Rose,
David Foot,
L. S. Nickerson,
Moses Daley,
David Sessions,
Perrigrine Sessions,
Alford P. Childs,
James Daley,
Noah T. Guyman,
David Winters,
John Pack,
Sylvanus Hicks,
Horatio N. Kent,
Joseph W. Pierce,
Thomas Gates,
Squire Bozarth,
Nathan Lewis,
Moses Evord,
Ophelia Harris,
Zuba McDonald,
Mary Goff,
Harvey J. Moore,
Francis Chase,
Stephen Markham,
John Outhouse,
Wm. F. Leavens,
Daniel Tyler,
Noah Rogers,
Stephen N. St. John,
Francis Lee,
Eli Lee,
Benjamin Covey,
Michel Borkdull,
Miles Randall,
Horace Evans,
David Dort,
Levi Hancock,
Edwin Whiting,
William Barton,
Elisha Smith,
James Gallaher,
Robert Jackson,
Lemuel Merrick,
James Dunn,
Orin Hartshorn,
Nathan Hawke,
Pierce Hawley,
Thomas J. Fisher,
James Leithead,
Alfred Lee,
Stephen Jones,
Eleazer Harris,
Elijah B. Gaylord,
Thomas Grover,
Alexander Badlam,
Phebe Kellog,
Albert Miner,
William Woodland,
Martin C. Allred,
Jedediah Owen,

Philander Avery,
Benjamin F. Bird,
Charles Squire,
Jacob Curtis,
Rachel Medfo,
Lyman Stevens,
Roswell Evans,
Leonard Clark,
Nehemiah Harmon,
Daniel Cathcart,
Gershom Stokes,
Rachel Page,
Barnet Cole,
William Thompson,
Nathan Cheney,
James Sherry,
David Frampton,
Elizabeth Pettigrew,
Charles Thompson,
Orin P. Rockwell,
Nathan B. Baldwin,
Truman Brace,
Sarah Wixom,
Lewis Zobriski,
Henry Zobriski,
Morris Harris,
Absolom Tidwell,
Alvin Winegar,
Samuel T. Winegar,
John E. Page,
Levi Gifford,
Edmund Durfee,
Josiah Butterfield,
John Killion,
John Patten,
John Wilkins,
Abram Allen,
William Felshaw.

Activity of the Committee on Removal.

The committee who had been appointed for removing the poor from the state of Missouri, viz.: William Huntington, Charles Bird, Alanson Ripley, Theodore Turley, Daniel Shearer, Shadrach Roundy, and Jonathan H. Hale, met in the evening of that day [January 29, 1839], at the house of Theodore Turley, and organized by appointing William Huntington chairman, Daniel Shearer treasurer, and Alanson Ripley clerk, and made some arrangements for carrying into operation the business of removing the poor. President Brigham Young got eighty subscribers to the covenant the first day, and three hundred the second day.

Investigation Ordered.

Thursday, *31*.—Mr. Turner's bill of the 16th instant passed the senate. I sent the poor brethren a hundred dollar bill from jail, to assist them in their distressed situation.

Friday, *February 1:*

Minutes of a Meeting of the Cammittee on Removal.

The committee met according to adjournment, at the house of Theodore Turley; John Smith was present and acted as chairman, and Elias Smith as secretary. The meeting was called to order by the chairman.

On motion, Resolved: That the covenant entered into at the last meeting be read by the Secretary, which was done accordingly.

The chairman then called for the expression of sentiments on the subject of the covenant.

Resolved, That the committee be increased to eleven.

The following were then appointed: Elias Smith, Erastus Bingham, Stephen Markham, and James Newberry.

Several of the committee addressed the meeting on the arduous task before them, and exhorted all to exert themselves to relieve and assist them in the discharge of the duties of their office, to the utmost of their abilities.

Elders Taylor and Young, in the most forcible manner addressed the assembly on the propriety of union in order to carry our resolutions into effect, and exhorted the brethren to use wisdom in the sale of their property.

JOHN SMITH, Chairman,
ELIAS SMITH, Secretary.

The committee met again in the evening at Theodore Turley's. Alanson Ripley declined acting as clerk, and Elias Smith was appointed in his stead.

Resolved, That exertions be made to remove the families of the Presidency and the other prisoners first.

Several of the committee made report of what had been done by them towards carrying the business of the committee into operation. Elder John Taylor had also been appointed to visit the branches of the Church on Log and Upper Goose creeks, and made a report of his proceedings.

Resolved, That Charles Bird be appointed to go down towards the Mississippi river and establish deposits of corn for the brethren on the road, and make contracts for ferriage, etc.

Monday, February 4.—Mr. Turner's bill of 16th January came up for the first reading, "when Mr Wright moved that the bill be laid on the table until the 4th day of July next; and upon this question Mr. Primm desired the yeas and nays, which were ordered, and the decision was in the affirmative" by eleven majority, which by many was considered an approval of all the wrongs the Saints had sustained in the state.*

6th and 7th.† The committee on the removal of the Saints from Missouri were in session. Stephen Markham started for Illinois, with my wife and children, and Jonathan Holmes and wife.

* At any rate Mr. Turner's bill providing for an elaborate investigation was never taken from the table. In the legislature, however, which convened in 1840-41, the subject of the "Mormon" difficulties was again taken up on recommendation of Governor Boggs, who concludes what he had to say in his message in this language. "To explain the attitude which we have been made to assume I would recommend the publication of all the events relating to the occurrence, and distributing the same to the chief authorities of each state." In pursuance of this recommendation the joint committee appointed from the senate and house made a collection of documents on the subject covering 162 pages. In the collection, however, there are none of the statements, petitions, or representations made to the public or the legislature by the Saints. The documents consist in part of the action of the respective houses in the appointment of committees and reports of those committees recommending investigations, etc.; of the reports and military orders of the militia generals; while the remainder of the pamphlet is made up of the *ex parte* testimony taken before Judge King at Richmond, concerning which testimony the Turner senate committee in reporting to the senate, under date of December 18, 1838, said: It "is manifestly not such evidence as ought to be received by the committee:

"First, *because it is not authenticated;* and,

"Second, it is confined chiefly to the object of the inquiry, namely, the investigation of criminal charges against individuals under arrest."

The action of the legislature in the matter was a "white-washing affair," to use a phrase common in such cases. It was an attempt to vindicate the state of Missouri in her treatment of the Latter-day Saints. The effort, however, was in vain. The truths in relation to those transactions, in spite of all the efforts of the legislature, were known, and the state's attempt to deny them by a publication of documents giving a hearing to but one side of the case, only emphasized the crime.

† February 7th. An event occurred on this date which ought not to be omitted from this history, as it throws great light upon the prison life of the Prophet and his associates, upon the character of the Prophet himself, and the great faith his associates had in his prophetic powers. This event, and some others of equal interest were related by Alexander McRae, one of the fellow prisoners of the Prophet, in two communications to the *Deseret News*, under the dates of October 9th, and November 1st, respectively, of the year 1854. At that time "The History of Joseph Smith" was being published in current numbers of the *News*, and Brother McRae, then Bishop of the Eleventh Ward of Salt Lake City, being surprised at the omission in the narrative of the Prophet of many items of interest concerning their prison life, wrote the two following letters to the *News:*

Letter of Alexander McRae to the Deseret News.

SALT LAKE CITY, UTAH, Oct. 9, 1854.

Mr. Editor:—In reading the History of Joseph Smith as published in the *News* last winter, and especially that part of it which relates to his imprisonment in

Liberty jail, Missouri, I see there are many interesting facts which are omitted; and as I had the honor of being a fellow prisoner with him, I thought I would write some of those incidents for the satisfaction of any of your readers who may feel interested in them.

During our imprisonment, we had many visitors, both friends and enemies. Among the latter, many were angry with Brother Joseph, and accused him of killing a son, a brother, or some relative of theirs, at what was called the Crooked River Battle. This looked rather strange to me, that so many should claim a son, or a brother killed there, *when they reported only one man killed.*

Among our friends who visited us, were Presidents Brigham Young and Heber C. Kimball [now—i. e. at the time this letter was written, 1854], of the First Presidency—the latter several times; George A. Smith, of the quorum of the Twelve; Don C. Smith, brother of Joseph, came several times, and brought some of our families to see us. Benjamin Covey, Bishop of the Twelfth Ward of this city, brought each of us a new pair of boots, and made us a present of them. James Sloan, his wife and daughter, came several times. Alanson Ripley also visited us, and many others, whom to name would be too tedious. Orin P. Rockwell brought us refreshments many times; and Jane Bleven and her daughter brought cakes, pies, etc., and handed them in at the window. These things helped us much, as our food was very coarse, and so filthy that we could not eat it until we were driven to it by hunger.

After we had been there some time, and had tried every means we could to obtain our liberty by the law, without effect (except Sidney Rigdon who was bailed out), and also having heard, from a reliable source, that it had been stated in the public street, by the most influential men in that part of the country, that "the Mormon prisoners would have to be condemned or the character of the state would have to go down," we came to the conclusion that we would try other means to effect it.

Accordingly, on the 7th day of February, 1839, after counseling together on the subject, we concluded to try to go that evening when the jailor came with our supper; but Brother Hyrum, before deciding fully, and to make it more sure, asked Brother Joseph to inquire of the Lord as to the propriety of the move. He did so, and received answer to this effect—that if we were all agreed, we could go clear that evening; and if we would ask, we should have a testimony for ourselves. I immediately asked, and had not no more than asked, until I received as clear a testimony as ever I did of anything in my life, that it was true. Brother Hyrum Smith and Caleb Baldwin bore testimony to the same: but Lyman Wight said we might go if we chose, but he would not. After talking with him for some time, he said, "if we would wait until the next day, he would go with us." Without thinking we had no promise of success on any other day than the one above stated, we agreed to wait.

When night came, the jailor came alone with our supper, threw the door wide open, put our supper on the table, and went to the back part of the room, where a pile of books lay, took up a book, and went to reading, leaving us between him and the door, thereby giving us every chance to go if we had been ready. As the next day was agreed upon, we made no attempt to go that evening.

When the next evening came, the case was very different; the jailer brought a double guard with him, and with them six of our brethren, to-wit.: Erastus Snow, William D. Huntington, Cyrus Daniels, David Holeman, Alanson Ripley and Watson Barlow. I was afterwards informed that they were sent by the Church. The jailer seemed to be badly scared; he had the door locked and everything made secure. It looked like a bad chance to get away, but we were determined to try it; so when the jailer started out, we started too Brother Hyrum took hold of the door, and the rest followed; but before we were able to render him the assistance he needed, the jailer and guard succeeded in closing the door, shutting the brethren in with us, except Cyrus Daniels, who was on the outside.

As soon as the attempt was made inside, he took two of the guards, one under each arm, and ran down the stairs that led to the door, it being in the second story. When he reached the ground they got away from him; and seeing we had failed to get out, he started to run, but put his foot in a hole and fell, a bullet from one of the guards passed very close to his head, and he thinks the fall saved his life.

The scene that followed this defies description. I should judge, from the number, that all the town, and many from the country, gathered around the jail, and every mode of torture and death that their imagination could fancy, was proposed for us, such as blowing up the jail, taking us out and whipping us to death, shooting us, burning us to death, tearing us to pieces with horses, etc. But they were so divided among themselves that they could not carry out any of their plans, and we escaped unhurt.

During this time, some of our brethren spoke of our being in great danger; and I confess I felt that we were. But Brother Joseph told them "not to fear, that not a hair of their heads should be hurt, and that they should not lose any of their things, even to a bridle, saddle, or blanket; that everything should be restored to them; they had offered their lives for us and the Gospel; that it was necessary the Church should offer a sacrifice, and the Lord accepted the offering."

The brethren had next to undergo a trial, but the excitement was so great that they [the officers] dare not take them out until it abated a little. While they were waiting for their trial, some of the brethren employed lawyers to defend them. Brother [Erastus] Snow asked Brother Joseph whether he had better employ a lawyer or not. Brother Joseph told him to plead his own case. "But," said Brother Snow, "I do not understand the law." Brother Joseph asked him if he did not understand justice; he thought he did. "Well," said Brother Joseph, "go and plead for justice as hard as you can, and quote Blackstone and other authors now and then, and they will take it all for law."

He did as he was told, and the result was as Joseph had said it would be; for when he got through his plea, the lawyers flocked around him, and asked him where he had studied law, and said they had never heard a better plea. When the trial was over Brother Snow was discharged, and all the rest were held to bail, and were allowed to bail each other, by Brother Snow going bail with them; and they said they got everything that was taken from them, and nothing was lost, although no two articles were in one place. More anon.

Yours respectfully,

ALEXANDER MCRAE.

Second Letter of Alexander McRae to the Deseret News.

SALT LAKE CITY, UTAH, Nov. 1, 1854.

Mr. Editor:—Sometime during our stay in Liberty jail an attempt was made to destroy us by poison. I supposed it was administered in either tea or coffee, but as I did not use either, I escaped unhurt, while all who did were sorely afflicted, some being blind two or three days, and it was only by much faith and prayer that the effect was overcome.

We never suffered ourselves to go into any important measure without asking Brother Joseph to inquire of the Lord in relation to it. Such was our confidence in him as a Prophet, that when he said "Thus saith the Lord," we were confident it would be as he said; and the more we tried it, the more confidence we had, for we never found his word fail in a single instance.

A short time before we were to go to Daviess county for trial, word came to us that either General Atchison or Doniphan, would raise a military force, and go with us to protect us from the wrath of that people. The matter was discussed by the brethren (except Brother Joseph), and they naturally enough concluded it would be best; and although I had nothing to say, I concurred with them in my feelings. Brother Hyrum asked Brother Joseph what he thought of it. Brother Joseph hung his head a few moments, and seemed in a deep study, and then raised up and said, "Brother Hyrum, it will not do; we must trust in the Lord; if we take a guard with us we shall be destroyed."

This was very unexpected to us, but Brother Hyrum remarked, "If you say it in the name of the Lord, we will rely on it." Said Brother Joseph, "In the name of the Lord, if we take a guard with us, we will be destroyed; but if we put our trust in the Lord, we shall be safe, and no harm shall befall us, and we shall be better treated than we have ever been since we have been prisoners."

This settled the question, and all seemed satisfied, and it was decided that we should have no extra guard, and they had only such a guard as they chose for our safe keeping. When we arrived at the place where the court was held, I began to think he was mistaken for once, for the people rushed upon us *en masse*, crying, "Kill them: ——— them, kill them." I could see no chance for escape, unless we could fight our way through, and we had nothing to do it with. At this, Brother Joseph, at whom all seemed to rush, rose up and said, "We are in your hands; if we are guilty, we refuse not to be punished by the law." Hearing these words, two of the most bitter mobocrats in the country—one by the name of William Peniston and the other Kinney, or McKinney, I do not remember which—got up on benches and began to speak to the people, saying, "Yes, gentlemen, these men are in our hands; let us not use violence, but let the law have its course; the law will condemn them, and they will be punished by it. We do not want the disgrace of taking the law into our own hands."

In a verv few minutes they were quieted, and they seemed now as friendly as they had a few minutes before been enraged. Liquor was procured, and we all had to drink in token of friendship. This took place in the court-room (a small log cabin about twelve feet square), during the adjournment of the court; and from that time until we got away, they could not put a guard over us who would not become so friendly that they dare not trust them, and the guard was very frequently changed. We were seated at the first table with the judge, lawyers, etc., and had the best the country afforded, with feather beds to sleep on—a privilege we had not before enjoyed in all our imprisonment.

On one occasion, while we were there, the above-named William Peniston, partly in joke and partly in earnest, threw out a rather hard insinuation against some of the brethren This touched Joseph's feelings, and he retorted a good deal in the same way, only with such power that the earth seemed to tremble under his feet, and said, "Your heart is as black as your whiskers," which were as black as any crow. He seemed to quake under it and left the room.

The guards, who had become friendly, were alarmed for our safety, and exclaimed, "O, Mr. Smith, do not talk so; you will bring trouble upon yourself and companions." Brother Joseph replied, "Do not be alarmed; I know what I am about." He always took up for the brethren, when their characters were assailed, sooner than for himself, no matter how unpopular it was to speak in their favor.

Yours as ever,

ALEXANDER MCRAE.

CHAPTER XVIII.

THE EXILED SAINTS GATHER AT QUINCY, ILLINOIS—PROPOSITION TO SETTLE AT COMMERCE.

SOME time this month there was a conference of the Church at Quincy, a report of which is as follows:

Minutes of a Conference of the Church Held at Quincy.

At a meeting of the Church of Jesus Christ of Latter-day Saints, held in the town of Quincy, February —, 1839, to take into consideration the expediency of locating the Church in some place, Brother William Marks was chosen president and Robert B. Thompson, clerk.

Elder John P. Greene, by request, then stated the object of the meeting, and stated that a liberal offer had been made by a gentleman, of about twenty thousand acres, lying between the Mississippi and Des Moines rivers, at two dollars per acre, to be paid in twenty annual installments, without interest; that a committee had examined the land and reported very favorably respecting it, and thought it every way suited for a location for the Church.

Brother Rogers then made some statements, and gave information respecting the land, being one of the committee appointed to examine it.

President William Marks observed that he was altogether in favor of making the purchase, providing that it was the will of the Lord that we should again gather together; but from the circumstances of being driven from the other places, he almost was led to the conclusion that it was not wisdom that we should do so, but hoped that the brethren would speak their minds; the Lord would undoubtedly manifest His will by His Spirit.

Brother Israel Barlow thought that it might be in consequence of not building according to the pattern, that we had thus been scattered.

Brother Mace spoke in favor of an immediate gathering.

Bishop Partridge then spoke on the subject, and thought it was not expedient under the present circumstances to collect together, but thought it was better to scatter into different parts and provide for the poor, which would be acceptable to God.

Judge Higbee said that he had been very favorable to the proposition of purchasing the land and gathering upon it, but since the Bishop had expressed his opinion, he was willing to give up the idea.

Several of the brethren then spoke on the subject, after which it was moved and seconded, and unanimously agreed upon, that it would not be deemed advisable to locate on the lands for the present.

A committee was appointed to draft a petition to the General government, stating our grievances, and one likewise to be presented to the citizens [of the United States] for the same object.

Tuesday, February 12.—The committee [on removal] sent a delegation to Sister Murie to ascertain her necessities. Daniel Shearer and Erastus Bingham went.

Applications for Assistance.

Applications for assistance were made from Sister Morgan L. Gardner, Jeremiah Mackley's family, Brother Forbush, Echoed Cheney, T. D. Tyler, D. McArthur and others.

Wednesday, February 13.—Voted that Theodore Turley be appointed to superintend the management of the teams provided for removing the poor, and see that they are furnished for the journey.

Persecution of Brigham Young.

Thursday, February 14.—The persecution was so bitter against Elder Brigham Young (on whom devolved the presidency of the Twelve by age,* Thomas B. Marsh having apostatized) and his life was so diligently sought for, that he was compelled to flee; and he left Far West on this day for Illinois.

Petition to Help the Smith Family From Mo.

My brother Don Carlos Smith had carried a petition to the mob, to get assistance to help our father's family out of Missouri. I know not how much he obtained, but my father and mother started this day for Quincy, with an ox team.

The committee on removal discussed the propriety of paying the debts of the Saints in Clay county. Alanson

* It will be remembered that when the first quorum of the Twelve was organized the Prophet arranged the members in the order of their standing according to their age. Thereafter and now they hold their places in the quorum according to seniority of ordination. A full explanation of this matter is given in the HISTORY OF THE CHURCH, volume II, pp. 219-20. See foot notes.

Ripley was requested to call on lawyer Barnet, who was in town, and make arrangements concerning the matter. A letter of attorney was drawn up for the brethren to sign, who felt willing to dispose of their real estate to discharge their debts, appointing Alanson Ripley their attorney for that purpose. This was not exactly according to the minds of the committee, for they only directed Brother Ripley to confer with the person above named, for the purpose of obtaining information without reference to his being appointed an attorney for that purpose, independent of any other person or persons.

Arrangements for paying the Debts of the Saints.

Friday, February 15.—My family arrived at the Mississippi, opposite Quincy, after a journey of almost insupportable hardships, and Elder Markham returned immediately to Far West.

Monday, 18.—

The Governor's Order to Return the Arms Belonging to the Saints.

EXECUTIVE DEPARTMENT, CITY OF JEFFERSON,
February 18, 1839.

To Colonel Wiley C. Williams, Aid to the Commander-in-Chief:

SIR:—You will take the measures as soon as practicable, to cause the arms surrendered by the Mormons, to be delivered to the proper owners upon their producing satisfactory evidence of their claims. If in any case you think an improper use would be made of them, you can retain such, using a sound discretion in the matter. You will call upon Captain Pollard or any other person who may have arms in possession, and take charge of them; and this will be your authority for so doing.

I am respectfully,
Your obedient servant,
LILBURN W. BOGGS.

Little benefit would have resulted from this order, even if it had been promptly executed, as many of the brethren who owned the arms had left the state and it would be very difficult to decide what would be satisfactory evidence of claims.

Tuesday, February 19.—The committee on removal appointed Charles Bird to visit the several parts of Caldwell county, and William Huntington the town of Far West, to ascertain the number of families that would have to be assisted in removing, and solicit means from those who are able to give for the assistance of the needy, and make report as soon as possible.

Labors in the Interests of the Poor.

Thursday, February 21—Elder Markham arrived at Far West, and in the evening the committee on removal were in council. Elders Bingham, Turley, and Shearer, were appointed to sell the house of Joseph Smith, Sen., to a gentleman from Clay county.

Charles Bird was sent to Liberty relative to a power of attorney.

Committee Resolutions.

Resolved: To send Stephen Markham to Illinois, to visit the brethren there and obtain a power of attorney from such as had left their lands without selling them. A report of the committee appointed to visit the different parts of the country to ascertain the number of families who were destitute of teams for their removal, was made. William Huntington reported thirty-two families, and Charles Bird seven, as far as they had prosecuted their labors.

Resolved: To send Erastus Bingham to visit the north-west part of Caldwell county for the same purpose, and then adjourned till Monday next.

Saturday, February 25.—At a meeting of the Democratic Association, held this evening at Quincy, Adams county, Illinois, Mr. Lindsay introduced a resolution setting forth that the people called "Latter-day Saints" were many of them in a situation requiring the aid of the citizens of Quincy, and recommending that measures be adopted for their relief, which resolution was adopted, and a committee consisting of eight persons appointed by the chair; of which committee J. W. Whitney was chairman. The association then adjourned to meet on Wednesday evening next after instructing the committee to procure the Congregational church as a place of meeting, and to invite as many of

Action of the Democratic Committee of Quincy.

our people to attend as should choose to do so; for it was in their behalf that the meeting was to be held. Also all other citizens of the town who felt to do so were invited to attend. The committee not being able to obtain the meeting house, procured the Court House for that purpose.

Determination of the Prisoners to Escape.

After we were cast into prison, we heard nothing but threatenings, that if any judge or jury, or court of any kind, should clear any of us, we should never get out of the state alive.

This soon determined our course, and that was to escape out of their hands as soon as we could, and by any means we could. After we had been some length of time in prison, we demanded a habeas corpus of Judge Turnham, one of the county judges, which with some considerable reluctance, was granted. Great threatenings were made at this time, by the mob, that if any of us were liberated, we should never get out of the county alive.

Sidney Rigdon's Departure from Prison.

After the investigation, Sidney Rigdon was released from prison by the decision of the judge; the remainder were committed to jail; he, however, returned with us until a favorable opportunity offered for his departure. Through the friendship of the sheriff, Mr. Samuel Hadley, and the jailor, Mr. Samuel Tillery, he was let out of the jail secretly in the night, after having declared in prison, that the sufferings of Jesus Christ were a fool to his; and being solemnly warned by them to be out of the state with as little delay as possible, he made his escape. Being pursued by a body of armed men, it was through the direction of a kind Providence that he escaped out of their hands, and safely arrived in Quincy, Illinois.

Importunities for the Release of the Prisoners.

About this time, Elders Heber C. Kimball and Alanson Ripley were at Liberty, where they had been almost weekly importuning at the feet of the judges; and while performing this duty on a certain occasion, Judge Hughes stared them full in the face, and observed to one of his associates, that "by the look of these men's eyes, they are whipped, but not conquered; and let us beware how we treat these men; for their looks bespeak innocence;" and at that time he entreated his associates to admit of bail for all the prisoners; but the hardness of their hearts would not admit of so charitable a deed. But the brethren continued to importune at the feet of the judges, and also to visit the prisoners. No one of the ruling part of the community disputed the innocence of the prisoners, but said, in consequence of the fury of the mob, that even-handed justice could not be administered; Elders Kimball and Ripley were therefore compelled to abandon the idea of importuning at the feet of the judges, and leave the prisoners in the hands of God.

Meeting of Elder Israel Barlow and Isaac Galland.

When Elder Israel Barlow left Missouri in the fall of 1838, either by missing his way, or some other cause, he struck the Des Moines river some distance above its mouth. He was in a destitute situation; and making his wants known, found friends who assisted him, and gave him introductions to several gentlemen, among whom was Dr. Isaac Galland, to whom he communicated the situation of the Saints; the relation of which enlisted Mr. Galland's sympathies, or interest, or both united, and hence a providential introduction of the Church to Commerce [the place of residence of Mr. Galland] and its vicinity; for Brother Barlow went direct to Quincy, the place of his destination, and made known his interview with Dr. Galland to the Church.

Communication of Isaac Galland.

COMMERCE, ILLINOIS, February 26, 1839.

Mr. D. W. Rogers:

DEAR SIR:—Yours of the 11th instant was received yesterday. I perceive that it had been written before your brethren visited my house. I had also written to Mr. Barlow before I received yours, and which is herewith also sent. I wish here to remark that about ten or fifteen houses or cabins can be had in this neighborhood, and several farms may be rented here, on the half breed lands. I think that more than fifty families can be accommodated with places to dwell in, but not a great quantity of cultivated land, as the improvements on that tract are generally new; there are, however, several farms which can also be rented.

Since writing to Mr. Barlow, I have conversed with a friend of mine, who has also conversed with Governor Lucas, of Iowa territory, in relation to your Church and people. Governor Lucas says that the people called Mormons were good citizens in the state of Ohio, and that he respects them now as good and virtuous citizens, and feels disposed to treat them as such.

I wish also to say, through you, to your people, that Isaac Van Allen, Esq., the attorney-general of Iowa territory, is a personal and tried friend of mine; and I feel fully authorized, from a conversation which I have had with him on the subject, to say that I can assure you of his utmost endeavors to protect you from insult or violence.

I will here repeat what I have written to Mr. Barlow, that I do believe that under a territorial form of government which is directly connected with the general government of the United States, your Church will be better secured against the capriciousness of public opinion, than under a state government, where murder, rapine and robbery are admirable (!) traits in the character of a demagogue; and where the greatest villains often reach the highest offices. I have written to Governor Lucas on the subject; and when I receive his answer, I will communicate it to your Church.

I desire very much to know how your captive brethren in Missouri are faring. I should like to know if Joseph Smith, Jun., is at liberty or not, and what his prospects are. I shall be at Carthage, our county seat, during the fore part of next week, and soon after that, (perhaps the next week following) I expect to go to Burlington, Iowa territory, when I expect to see the governor and converse with him on the subject. I will probably be at home from the 6th until the 12th of March. I shall be pleased to see you or any of your people at my house at any time when you can make it convenient. It is now necessary that something definite should be done in relation to renting farms, as the season for commencing such operations is fast approaching us. A Mr. Whitney, a merchant in Quincy, is owner and proprietor of several farms in this vicinity, and it might be well to see him on the subject.

I wish to serve your cause in any matter which Providence may afford me the opportunity of doing, and I therefore request that you feel no hesitancy or reluctance in communicating to me your wishes, at all times and on any subject. I should be much gratified if it could be convenient for Mr. Rigdon, or some one or more of the leading members of your Church to spend some time with me in traveling through the tract, and in hearing and learning the state of the public mind, and feelings of the community, in relation to the location of the Church.

I feel that I am assuming a very great responsibility in this undertaking, and I wish to be governed by the dictates of wisdom and discretion, while at the same time I am aware that we are often disposed to view things as we would wish to have them, rather than as they really are; and our great anxiety to accomplish an object may sometimes diminish the obstacles below their real measure.

The little knowledge which I have as yet of the doctrine, order or practice of the Church, leaves me under the necessity of acting in all this matter as a stranger, though, as I sincerely hope, as a friend, for such, I assure you I feel myself to be, both towards you collectively, as a people, and individually as sufferers. If it should not be convenient for any one to come up about the 7th or 8th of March, please write me by the mail. Say to Mr. Rigdon, that I regret that I was absent when he was at my house. I cannot visit Quincy until after my return from Burlington, when, I think if it is thought necessary, I can.

Accept, dear sir, for yourself and in behalf of the Church and people, assurance of my sincere sympathy in your sufferings and wrongs, and deep solicitude for your immediate relief from present distress, and future triumphant conquest over every enemy.

Yours truly,

ISAAC GALLAND.

Minutes of the Meeting of the Democratic Association of Quincy.

Wednesday, February 27, 1839, six o'clock p. m.

The members of the Democratic Association and the citizens of Quincy generally, assembled in the court house, to take into consideration the state and condition of the people called the "Latter-day Saints," and organized the meeting by appointing General Leach chairman, and James D. Morgan secretary. Mr. Whitney, from the committee appointed at a former meeting, submitted the following:

The select committee to whom the subject was referred of inquiring into and reporting the situation of the persons who have recently arrived here from Missouri, and whether their circumstances are such as that they would need the aid of the citizens of Quincy and its vicinity, to be guided by what they might deem the principles of an expanded benevolence, have attended to the duties assigned them, and have concluded on the following:

REPORT.

"The first idea that occurred to your committee was, to obtain correctly the facts of the case, for without them the committee could come to no conclusion as to what it might be proper for us to do. Without the facts they could form no basis upon which the committee might recommend to this association what would be proper for us to do, or what measures to adopt. The committee, soon after their appointment, sent invitations to Mr. Rigdon and several others to meet the committee and give them a statement of the facts, and to disclose their situation. Those individuals accordingly met the committe and entered into a free conversation and disclosure of the facts of their situation; and after some time spent therein, the committee concluded to adjourn and report to this meeting, but not without first requesting those individuals to draw up and send us in writing, a condensed statement of the facts relative to the subject in charge of your committee, which those individuals engaged to do, and which the committee request may be taken as part of their report.

"That statement is herewith lettered A.

"The committee believe that our duties at this time, and on this occasion, are all included within the limits of an expanded benevolence and humanity, and which are guided and directed by that charity which never faileth.

"From the facts already disclosed, independent of the statement furnished to the committee, we feel it our duty to recommend to this association that they adopt the following resolutions:

"Resolved, That the strangers recently arrived here from the state of Missouri, known by the name of the 'Latter-day Saints,' are entitled to our sympathy and kindest regard, and that we recommend to the citizens of Quincy to extend all the kindness in their power to bestow on the persons who are in affliction.

"Resolved, That a numerous committee be raised, composed of some individuals in every quarter of the town and its vicinity, whose duty it shall be to explain to our misguided fellow citizens, if any such there be, who are disposed to excite prejudices and circulate unfounded rumors; and particularly to explain to them that these people have no design to lower the wages of the laboring class, but to procure something to save them from starving.

"Resolved, That a standing committee be raised and be composed of individuals who shall immediately inform Mr. Rigdon and others, as many as they may think proper, of their appointment, and who shall be authorized to obtain information from time to time; and should they [the committee] be of opinion that any individuals, either from destitution or sickness, or if they find them houseless, that they appeal directly and promptly to the citizens of Quincy to furnish them with the means to relieve all such cases.

"Resolved, That the committee last aforesaid be instructed to use their utmost endeavors to obtain employment for all these people, who are able and willing to labor; and also to afford them all needful, suitable and proper encouragement.

"Resolved, That we recommend to all the citizens of Quincy, that in all their intercourse with the strangers, they use and observe a becoming decorum and delicacy, and be particularly careful not to indulge in any conversation or expressions calculated to wound their feelings, or in any way to reflect upon those, who by every law of humanity, are entitled to our sympathy and commiseration.

"All which is submitted,

"J. W. WHITNEY, Chairman.

"QUINCY, February 27, 1839."

Document A.

"This, gentlemen, is a brief outline of the difficulties that we have labored under, in consequence of the repeated persecutions that have been heaped upon us; and as the governor's exterminating order has not been rescinded, we as a people were obliged to leave the state of Missouri, and with it our lands, corn, wheat, pork, etc., that we had provided for ourselves and families, together with our fodder, which we have collected for our cattle, horses, etc., those of them that we have been able to preserve from the wreck of that desolation which has spread itself over Daviess and Caldwell counties. In consequence of our brethren being obliged to leave the state, and as a sympathy and friendly spirit has been manifested by the citizens of Quincy, numbers of our brethren, glad to obtain an asylum from the hand of persecution, have come to this place.

"We cannot but express our feelings of gratitude to the inhabitants of this place, for the friendly feelings which have been manifested, and the benevolent hand which has been stretched out to a poor, oppressed, injured, and persecuted people. And as you, gentlemen of the Democratic Association, have felt interested in our welfare, and have desired to be put in possession of a knowledge of our situation, our present wants, and what would be most conducive to our present good, together with what led to those difficulties, we thought that those documents [Memorial, Order of Extermination, and General Clark's Address] would furnish you with as correct information of our difficulties, and what led to them, as anything we are in possession of.

"If we should say what our present wants are, it would be beyond all calculation; as we have been robbed of our corn, wheat, horses, cattle, cows, hogs, wearing apparel, houses and homes, and, indeed, of all that renders life tolerable. We do not, we cannot expect to be placed in the situation that we once were in; nor are we capable of ourselves of supplying the many wants of those of our poor brethren, who are daily crowding here and looking to us for relief, in consequence of our property, as well as theirs, being in the hands of a ruthless and desolating mob.

"It is impossible to give an exact account of the widows, and those that are entirely destitute, as there are so many coming here daily; but from inquiry, the probable amount will be something near twenty; besides numbers of others who are able bodied men, both able and willing to work, to obtain a subsistence: yet owing to their peculiar situation, are destitute of means to supply the immediate wants that the necesssities of their families call for.

"We would not propose, gentlemen, what you shall do; but after making these statements, shall leave it to your own judgment and generosity. As to what we think would be the best means to promote our permanent good, we think that to give us employment, rent us farms, and allow us the protection and privileges of other citizens, would raise us from a state of dependence, liberate us from the iron grasp of poverty, put us in possession of a competency, and deliver us from the ruinous effects of persecution, despotism, and tyranny.

"Written in behalf of a committee of the Latter-day Saints.

"ELIAS HIGBEE, President,
"JOHN P. GREENE, Clerk.

"To the Quincy Democratic Association."

Statement of Sidney Rigdon.

Mr. Rigdon then made a statement of the wrongs received by the Mormons, from a portion of the people of Missouri, and of their present suffering condition.

On motion of Mr. Bushnell, the report and resolutions were laid upon the table until tomorrow evening.

On motion of Mr. Bushnell, the meeting adjourned to meet at this place tomorrow evening at seven o'clock.

Stephen Markham left Far West [on the 27th of February] for Illinois, to fulfill his appointment of the 21st instant.

Minutes of the Adjourned Meeting of the Democratic Association of Quincy.

Thursday evening, February 28th. Met pursuant to adjournment. The meeting was called to order by the chairman.

On motion of Mr. Morris, a committee of three was appointed to take up a collection; Messrs. J. T. Holmes, Whitney and Morris were appointed. The committee subsequently reported that $48.25 had been collected. On motion the amount was paid over to the committee on behalf of the Mormons. On motion of Mr. Holmes, a committee of three, consisting of S. Holmes, Bushnell and Morris, was appointed to draw up subscription papers and circulate them among the citizens, for the purpose of receiving contributions in clothing and provisions. On motion six were added to that committee.

On motion of J. T. Holmes, J. D. Morgan was appointed a committee to wait upon the Quincy Grays [militia company] for the purpose of receiving subscriptions. Mr. Morgan subsequently reported that twenty dollars had been subscribed by that company.

The following resolutions were then offered by Mr. J. T. Holmes:

Resolved, That we regard the rights of conscience as natural and inalienable, and the most sacred guaranteed by the Constitution of our free government.

Resolved, That we regard the acts of all mobs as flagrant violations of law; and those who compose them, individually responsible, both to the laws of God and man, for every depredation committed upon the property, rights, or life of any citizen.

Resolved, that the inhabitants upon the western frontier of the state of Missouri, in their late persecutions of the class of people denominated Mormons, have violated the sacred rights of conscience, and every law of justice and humanity.

Resolved, That the governor of Missouri, in refusing protection to this class of people, when pressed upon by a heartless mob, and turning upon them a band of unprincipled militia, with orders encouraging their extermination, has brought a lasting disgrace upon the state over which he presides.

The resolutions were supported in a spirited manner by Messrs. Holmes, Morris and Whitney.

On motion, the resolutions were adopted.

On motion the meeting then adjourned.

Samuel Leach, Chairman,
J. D. Morgan, Secretary.

CHAPTER XIX.

LETTERS TO THE PROPHET—AFFAIRS IN ENGLAND—PETITIONS.

Tuesday, March 5.—

Edward Partridge's Letter to Joseph Smith, Jun., and Others, Confined in Liberty Jail, Missouri.

QUINCY, ILLINOIS.

BELOVED BRETHREN:—Having an opportunity to send direct to you by Brother Rogers, I feel to write a few lines to you.

President Rigdon, Judge Higbee, Israel Barlow, and myself went to see Dr. Isaac Galland week before last. Brothers Rigdon, Higbee and myself are of the opinion that it is not wisdom to make a trade with the Doctor at present; possibly it may be wisdom to effect a trade hereafter.

The people here receive us kindly; they have contributed near $100 cash, besides other property, for the relief of the suffering among our people. Brother Joseph's wife lives at Judge Cleveland's; I have not seen her, but I sent her word of this opportunity to send to you. Brother Hyrum's wife lives not far from me. I have been to see her a number of times; her health was very poor when she arrived, but she has been getting better; she knows of this opportunity to send. I saw Sister Wight soon after her arrival here; all were well; I understand she has moved about two miles with father and John Higbee, who are fishing this spring. Sister McRae is here, living with Brother Henderson, and is well; I believe she knows of this opportunity to send. Brother Baldwin's family I have not seen, and do not know that she has got here as yet. She, however, may be upon the other side of the river; the ice has run these three days past, so that there has been no crossing; the weather is now moderating, and the crossing will soon commence again.

This place is full of our people, yet they are scattering off nearly all the while. I expect to start tomorrow for Pittsfield, Pike county, Illinois, about forty-five miles southeast from this place. Brother George W. Robinson told me this morning that he expected that his father-in-law, Judge Higbee, and himself would go on a farm about twenty miles northeast from this place. Some of the leading men have given us [that is the Saints] an invitation to settle in and about this place. Many no doubt will stay here.

Brethren, I hope that you will bear patiently the privations that you are called to endure; the Lord will deliver you in His own due time.

Your letter respecting the trade with Galland was not received here until after our return from his residence, at the head of the shoals or rapids. If Brother Rigdon were not here, we might, after receiving your letter, come to a different conclusion respecting that trade. There are some here that are sanguine that we ought to trade with the Doctor. Bishops Whitney and Knight are not here, and have not been, as I know of. Brothers Morley and Billings have settled some twenty or twenty-five miles north of this place, for the present. A Brother Lee, who lived near Haun's Mill, died on the opposite side of the river a few days since. Brother Rigdon preached his funeral sermon in the court-house. It is a general time of health here.

We greatly desire to see you and to have you enjoy your freedom. The citizens here are willing that we should enjoy the privileges guaranteed to all civil people without molestation.

I remain your brother in the Lord,

EDWARD PARTRIDGE.

Don Carlos Smith to Joseph Smith, Jun., and Others Confined in Liberty Jail, Missouri.

QUINCY, ILLINOIS, March 6, 1839.

BROTHERS HYRUM AND JOSEPH:—Having an opportunity to send a line to you, I do not feel disposed to let it slip unnoticed. Father's family have all arrived in this state except you two; and could I but see your faces this side of the Mississippi, and know and realize that you had been delivered from your enemies, it would certainly light up a new gleam of hope in our bosoms; nothing could be more satisfactory, nothing could give us more joy.

Emma and the children are well; they live three miles from here, and have a tolerably good place. Hyrum's children and mother Grinold's are living at present with father; they are all well. Mary [wife of Hyrum Smith] has not got her health yet, but I think it increases slowly. She lives in the house with old Father Dixon; likewise Brother Robert T. Thompson and family; they are probably a half mile from father's. We are trying to get a house, and to get the family together; we shall do the best we can for them, and that which we consider to be most in accordance with Hyrum's feelings.

Father and mother stood their journey remarkably well. They are in tolerable health. Samuel's wife has been sick ever since they arrived. William has removed forty miles from here, but is here now, and says he is anxious to have you liberated, and see you enjoy liberty once more. My family is well; my health has not been good for about two weeks; and for two or three days the toothache has been my tormentor. It all originated with a severe cold.

Dear brethren, we just heard that the governor says that he is going to set you all at liberty; I hope it is true; other letters that you will probably receive will give you information concerning the warm feeling of the people here towards us.

After writing these hurried lines in misery, I close by leaving the blessings of God with you, and praying for your health, prosperity and restitution to liberty.

This from a true friend and brother,

DON C. SMITH.

William Smith to Joseph and Hyrum Smith.

BROTHERS HYRUM AND JOSEPH:—I should have called down to Liberty to have seen you had it not been for the multiplicity of business that was on my hands; and again, I thought that perhaps the people might think that the "Mormons" would rise up to liberate you; consequently too many going to see you might make it worse for you; but we all long to see you and have you come out of that lonesome place. I hope you will be permitted to come to your families before long. Do not worry about them, for they will be taken care of. All we can do will be done; further than this, we can only wish, hope, desire, and pray for your deliverance.

WILLIAM SMITH.

To Joseph Smith, Jun., and Hyrum Smith.

Friday, March 8.—

Minutes of a Meeting of the Committee on Removal.

The committee met at Theodore Turley's, William Huntington in the chair.

Alanson Ripley made a report of his journey to Liberty, and said that President Joseph Smith, Jun., counseled to sell all the land in Jackson county, and all other lands in the state whatsoever.

Resolved, That the names of those of the brethren who have subscribed to our covenant and have done nothing, be sought for, and a record made of them, that they may be had in remembrance.

Resolved, That an extra exertion be made to procure money for removing the poor, by visiting those who have money, and laying the necessities of the committee, in their business of removing the poor out of the state, before them, and solicit their assistance.

Voted that the clerk write a letter to Bishop Partridge, laying before him the advice of President Joseph Smith, Jun., concerning selling the Jackson county lands, and requesting a power of attorney to sell them.

Saturday, 9.—

Minutes of the Adjourned Meeting of the Democratic Association of Quincy.

At a meeting held at the committee room in the city of Quincy, Illinois, at two o'clock, p. m., on the 9th March, 1839, pursuant to previous appointment, it was moved by President Rigdon, and seconded, that Judge Elias Higbee be called to the chair, and he was unanimously appointed. James Sloan was then appointed clerk by vote.

President Rigdon spoke as to the members of the committee being absent who had called the meeting, and proposed that other business be proceeded with in the meantime, and left it to the chair to decide on the propriety thereof. The chair assented to the suggestion of President Rigdon.

President Rigdon then applied for a paper which had been prepared, and signed by several of the citizens of Quincy, describing our situation as a people and calling upon the humane in St. Louis and elsewhere to assist them in affording us relief. The paper, being presented by Brother Ephraim Owen, was then read, and President Rigdon spoke at length upon the subject, and proposed that a committee of two of the brethren be appointed by the voice of the meeting to go to St. Louis on such business. The motion was then put and carried, and Brother Mace was appointed as one of said committee, and Brother Ephraim Owen the other. It was proposed that Brother Orson Pratt (who is now in St. Louis) be appointed an assistant.

After the motion was made, and before it was seconded, President Rigdon spoke of its inconsistency, and stated, as a better mode, that all the Saints in St. Louis, or such of them as the committee may think proper, be called upon to assist them. The motion was withdrawn, and this business closed.

Some of the committee who called this meeting, being now present, President Rigdon spoke of two letters which had been received here by the brethren, from Iowa Territory, respecting lands in said place, and containing sentiments of sympathy on occount of our grievances and distressed situation. One of these letters has been mislaid, and the other, from Isaac Galland to Brother Rogers, was read. It was then proposed that a committee be appointed to visit the lands, and confer with the gentlemen who had so written, and declared themselves interested for our welfare.

Elder John P. Greene moved that a committee be appointed for that purpose, which was seconded, and adopted unanimously President

Rigdon moved that the committe shall select the land, if it can be safely occupied. Seconded by Elder Greene, and carried that the committee be composed of five, viz.: President Rigdon, Elder Greene, Judge Higbee, Brother Benson and Brother Israel Barlow.

It was moved, seconded and adopted, that if any one or more of the committee be unable to go, the remainder of the committee are to appoint others in their stead.

The chairman now produced a power of attorney, sent here from the committee at Far West, to be executed by such of the brethren here who had lands in Caldwell county, and were willing to have them sold, to enable the families who are in distress at that place to get here, say about one hundred families.

Power of attorney was read. Moved, seconded and adopted, that the clerk of this meeting do make out a copy of the minutes of this meeting, to be sent to the committee at Far West.

JAMES SLOAN, Clerk.

Condition of Affairs in England.

While the persecutions were progressing against us in Missouri, the enemy of all righteousness was no less busy with the Saints in England, according to the length of time the Gospel had been preached in that kingdom. Temptation followed temptation, and being young in the cause, the Saints suffered themselves to be buffeted by their adversary. From the time that Elder Willard Richards was called to the apostleship, in July, 1838, the devil seemed to take a great dislike to him, and strove to stir up the minds of many against him. Elder Richards was afflicted with sickness, and several times was brought to the borders of the grave, and many were tempted to believe that he was under transgression, or he would not be thus afflicted. Some were tried and tempted because Elder Richards took to himself a wife; they thought he should have given himself wholly to the ministry, and followed Paul's advice to the letter. Some were tried because his wife wore a veil, and others because she carried a muff to keep herself warm when she walked out in cold weather; and even the President of the Church [Joseph Fielding] there, thought "she had better done without it;" she had nothing ever purchased by the Church; and to gratify their feelings, wore the poorest clothes she had, and they were too good, so hard was it to buffet the storm of feeling that arose from such foolish causes. Sister Richards was very sick for some time, and some were dissatisfied because her husband did not neglect her entirely and go out preaching; and others, that she did not go to meeting when she was not able to go so far.

From such little things arose a spirit of jealousy, tattling, evil speaking, surmising, covetousness, and rebellion, until the Church but too generally harbored more or less of those unpleasant feelings: and this evening [March 9th] Elder Halsal came out openly in council against Elder Richards, and preferred some heavy charges, none of which he was able to substantiate. Most of the Elders in Preston were against Elder Richards for a season, except James Whitehead, who proved himself true in the hour of trial.

Charges of Elder Halsal Against Elder Willard Richards.

Sunday, 10.—When Elder Richards made proclamation from the pulpit, that if anyone had aught against him, or his wife Jennetta, he wished they would come to him and state their grievances, and if he had erred in anything, he would acknowledge his fault, one only of the brethren came to him, and that to acknowledge his own fault to Elder Richards in harboring unpleasant feelings without a cause.

The Cause of Elder Richards' Troubles.

Sister Richards bore all these trials and persecutions with patience. Elder Richards knew the cause of these unpleasantries, his call [to the apostolate] having been made known to him by revelation; but he told no one of it. The work continued to spread in Manchester and vicinity, among the Staffordshire potteries, and other places in England.

Friday, 15.—I made the following petition:

The Petition of the Prophet et al. to Judge Tompkins et al.

To the Honorable Judge Tompkins, or either of the Judges of the Supreme Court of the State of Missouri:

Your petitioners, Alanson Ripley, Heber C. Kimball, Joseph B. Noble,

William Huntington, and Joseph Smith, Jun., beg leave respectfully to represent to your honor, that Joseph Smith, Jun., is now unlawfully confined and restrained of his liberty in Liberty jail, Clay county, Missouri; that he has been restrained of his liberty nearly five months. Your petitioners claim that the whole transaction which has been the cause of his confinement, is unlawful from the first to the last. He was taken from his house by a fraud being practiced upon him by a man of the name of George M. Hinkle, and one or two others; thereby your petitioners respectfully show, that he was forced, contrary to his wishes, and without knowing the cause, into the camp, which was commanded by General Lucas of Jackson county, and thence sent to Ray county, sleeping on the ground, and suffering many insults and injuries, and deprivations, which were calculated in their nature to break down the spirit and constitution of the most robust and hardy of mankind.

He was put in chains immediately on his being landed at Richmond, and there underwent a long and tedious *ex parte* examination.

Your petitioners show that the said Joseph Smith, Jun., was deprived of the privileges of being examined before the court as the law directs; that the witnesses on the part of the state were taken by force of arms, threatened with extermination or immediate death, and were brought without subpoena or warrant, under the awful and glaring anticipation of being exterminated if they did not swear something against him to please the mob or his persecutors; and those witnesses were compelled to swear at the muzzle of the gun, and some of them have acknowledged since, which your petitioners do testify, and are able to prove, that they did swear falsely, and that they did it in order to save their lives.

And your petitioners testify that all the testimony that had any tendency or bearing of criminality against said Joseph Smith, Jun., is false. We are personally acquainted with the circumstances, and being with him most of the time, and being present at the time spoken of by them, therefore we know that their testimony was false; and if he could have had a fair trial, and impartial, and lawful examination before the court, and could have been allowed the privilege of introducing his witnesses, he could have disproved everything that was against him; but the court suffered them to be intimidated, some of them in the presence of the court, and they were driven also and hunted, and some of them driven entirely out of the state.

And thus he was not able to have a fair trial; that the spirit of the court was tyrannical and overbearing, and the whole transaction of his treatment during the examination was calculated to convince your petitioners that it was a religious persecution, proscribing him in the liberty of conscience which is guaranteed to him by the Constitution of the

United States, and the state of Missouri; that a long catalogue of garbled testimony was permitted by the court, purporting to be the religious sentiment of the said Joseph Smith, Jun., which testimony was false, and your petitioners know that it was false, and can prove that it was false; because the witnesses testified that those sentiments were promulgated on certain days, and in the presence of large congregations; and your petitioners can prove, by those congregations, that the said Joseph Smith, Jun., did not promulgate such ridiculous and absurd sentiments for his religion as were testified of and admitted before the Honorable Austin A. King; and at the same time those things had no bearing on the offenses that the said Joseph Smith, Jun., was charged with; and after the examination the said prisoner was committed to the jail for treason against the state of Missouri; whereas the said Joseph Smith, Jun., did not levy war against the state of Missouri; neither did he commit any overt acts; neither did he aid or abet an enemy against the state of Missouri during the time he is charged with having done so.

And further, your petitioners have yet to learn that the state has an enemy; neither is the proof evident, nor the presumption great, in its most malignant form, upon the testimony on the part of the state, exparte as it is in its nature, that the said prisoner has committed the slightest degree of treason, or any other act of transgression against the laws of the state of Missouri; and yet said prisoner has been committed to Liberty jail, Clay county, Missouri, for treason. He has continually offered bail to any amount that could be required, notwithstanding your petitioners allege that he ought to have been acquitted.

Your petitioners also allege, that the commitment was an illegal commitment, for the law requires that a copy of the testimony should be put in the hands of the jailer, which was not done.

Your petitioners allege, that the prisoner has been denied the privilege of the law in a writ of habeas corpus, by the judge of this county. Whether they have prejudged the case of the prisoner, or whether they are not willing to administer law and justice to the prisoner, or that they are intimidated by the high office of Judge King, who only acted in the case of the prisoner as a committing magistrate, a conservator of the peace, or by the threats of a lawless mob, your petitioners are not able to say; but it is a fact that they do not come forward boldly and administer the law to the relief of the prisoner.

And further, your petitioners allege that immediately after the prisoner was taken, his family were frightened and driven out of their house, and that too, by the witnesses on the part of the state, and plundered of their goods; that the prisoner was robbed of a very fine horse, saddle and bridle, and other property of considerable amount;

that they (the witnesses) in connection with the mob, have finally succeeded, by vile threatening and foul abuse, in driving the family of the prisoner out of the state, with little or no means; and without a protector, and their very subsistence depends upon the liberty of the prisoner. And your petitioners allege, that he is not guilty of any crime, whereby he should be restrained of his liberty, from a personal knowledge, having been with him, and being personally acquainted with the whole of the difficulties between the "Mormons" and their persecutors; and that he has never acted at any time, only in his own defense, and that too on his own ground, property and possessions. That the prisoner has never commanded any military company, nor held any military authority, neither any other office, real or pretended in the state of Missouri, except that of a religious instructor; that he never has borne arms in the military rank; and in all such cases has acted as a private character and as an individual.

How, then, your petitioners would ask, can it be possible that the prisoner has committed treason? The prisoner has had nothing to do in Daviess county, only on his own business as an individual.

The testimony of Dr. Avard concerning a council held at James Sloan's was false. Your petitioners do solemnly declare, that there was no such council; that your petitioners were with the prisoner, and there was no such vote or conversation as Dr. Avard swore to. That Dr. Avard also swore falsely concerning a constitution, as he said was introduced among the Danites; that the prisoner had nothing to do with burning in Daviess county; that the prisoner made public proclamation against such things; that the prisoner did oppose Dr. Avard and George M. Hinkle against vile measures with the mob, but was threatened by them if he did not let them alone. That the prisoner did not have anything to do with what is called Bogart's battle, for he knew nothing of it until it was over; that he was at home, in the bosom of his own family, during the time of that whole transaction.

And, in fine, your petitioners allege, that he is held in confinement without cause, and under an unlawful and tyrannical oppression, and that his health, and constitution, and life depend on being liberated from his confinement.

Your petitioners aver that they can disprove every item of testimony that has any tendency of criminality against the prisoner; for they know the facts themselves, and can bring many others also to prove the same.

Therefore your petitioners pray your honor to grant to him the state's writ of habeas corpus, directed to the jailer of Clay county, Missouri, commanding him forthwith to bring before you the body of the prisoner, so that his case may be heard before your honor, and the situation of the prisoner be considered and adjusted according to law and justice, as it shall be presented before your honor, and, as in duty bound, your petitioners will ever pray.

And further, your petitioners testify that the said Joseph Smith, Jun., did make a public proclamation in Far West, in favor of the militia of the state of Missouri, and of its laws and also of the Constitution of the United States; and that he has ever been a warm friend to his country, and did use all his influence for peace; that he is a peaceable and quiet citizen, and is not worthy of death, of stripes, bond, or imprisonment.

The above mentioned speech was delivered on the day before the surrender of Far West,

ALANSON RIPLEY,
HEBER C. KIMBALL,
WILLIAM HUNTINGTON,
JOSEPH B. NOBLE,
JOSEPH SMITH, JUN.

STATE OF MISSOURI, } ss.
COUNTY OF CLAY. }

This day personally appeared before me, Abraham Shafer, a justic of the peace within and for the aforesaid county, Alanson Ripley, Heber C. Kimball, William Huntington, Joseph B. Noble and Joseph Smith, Jun., who being duly sworn, do depose and say that the matters and things set forth in the foregoing petition, upon their own knowledge, are true in substance and in fact; and so far as set forth upon the information of others, they believe to be true.

ALANSON RIPLEY,
HEBER C. KIMBALL,
WILLIAM HUNTINGTON,
JOSEPH B. NOBLE,
JOSEPH SMITH, JUN.

Sworn and subscribed to before me, this 15th day of March, 1839.

ABRHAM SHAFER, J. P.

We, the undersigned, being many of us personally acquainted with the said Joseph Smith, Jun., and the circumstances connected with his imprisonment, do concur in the petition and testimony of the above-named individuals, as most of the transactions therein mentioned we know from personal knowledge to be correctly set forth; and from information of others, believe the remainder to be true.

AMASA LYMAN,
H. G. SHERWOOD,
JAMES NEWBERRY,
CYRUS DANIELS,
ERASTUS SNOW,
ELIAS SMITH.

The same day Caleb Baldwin, Lyman Wight, Alexander McRae, and Hyrum Smith, my fellow prisoners, made each a similar petition.

CHAPTER XX.

SUNDRY MOVEMENTS IN THE INTEREST OF THE EXILED SAINTS—PROPHET'S LETTERS FROM LIBERTY PRISON.

Sunday, *17*.—I here give an extract from the minutes of a conference of the Church of Jesus Christ of Latter-day Saints, held this day in Quincy; Brigham Young by a unanimous vote was called to the chair, and Robert B. Thompson chosen clerk.

Minutes of the Conference at Quincy, Illinois.

Elder Young arose and gave a statement of the circumstances of the Church at Far West, and his feelings in regard to the scattering of the brethren, believing it to be wisdom to unite together as much as possible in extending the hand of charity for the relief of the poor, who were suffering for the Gospel's sake, under the hand of persecution in Missouri, and to pursue that course which would prove for the general good of the whole Church. He would advise the Saints to settle (if possible) in companies, or in a situation so as to be organized into branches of the Church, that they might be nourished and fed by the shepherds; for without, the sheep would be scattered; and he also impressed it upon the minds of the Saints to give heed to the revelations of God; the Elders especially should be careful to depart from all iniquity, and to remember the counsel given by those whom God hath placed as counselors in His Church; that they may become as wise stewards in the vineyard of the Lord, that every man may know and act in his own place; for there is order in the kingdom of God, and we must regard that order if we expect to be blessed.

Elder Young also stated that Elder Jonathan Dunham had received previous instructions not to call any conferences in this state, or elsewhere; but to go forth and preach repentance, this was his calling; but contrary to those instructions, he called a conference in Springfield, Illinois, and presided there, and brought forth the business which he had to transact; and his proceeding in many respects during the conference was contrary to the feelings of Elder Wilford Woodruff and other official members who were present. They considered his proceedings contrary to the will and order of God.

The conference then voted that Elder Dunham be reproved for his improper course, and that he be advised to adhere to the counsel given him.

After the conference had transacted various other business, Elder George W. Harris made some remarks relative to those who had left us in the time of our perils, persecutions and dangers, and were acting against the interests of the Church; he said that the Church could no longer hold them in fellowship unless they repented of their sins, and turned unto God.

After the conference had fully expressed their feelings upon the subject it was unanimously voted that the following persons be excommunicated from the Church of Jesus Christ of Latter-day Saints, viz.: George M. Hinkle, Sampson Avard, John Corrill, Reed Peck, William W. Phelps, Frederick G. Williams, Thomas B. Marsh, Burr Riggs, and several others. After which the conference closed by prayer.

BRIGHAM YOUNG, President.
ROBERT B. THOMPSON, Clerk.

Departure of Mrs. Pratt.

This day, 17th of March, Parley P. Pratt's wife left the prison house, where she had voluntarily been with her husband most of the winter, and returned to Far West, to get passage with some of the brethren for Illinois.

Action of the Committee of Removal.

The committee met at the house of Daniel Shearer, Far West, William Huntington in the chair.

Present—Brother Daniel W. Rogers, from Quincy, Illinois. Brother Rogers made known the proceedings of the brethren in Quincy, in relation to locating in the Iowa territory, and read a private letter from Dr. Isaac Galland to him on the same subject, and presented a power of attorney from Bishop Partridge to dispose of the lands of the Church in Jackson county, and also some lots in Far West. He then presented a copy of the proceedings of a council held in Quincy on the 9th instant, which was read; after which Brother Rogers explained some things relative to said meeting, and the proceedings thereof.

A bill of articles wanted by the prisoners in Liberty jail, was presented by Elder Heber C. Kimball, and accepted. Charles Bird was appointed to accompany Brother Rogers to Jackson county to assist him in the sale of the Jackson county lands.

On motion, resolved: That we will not patronize Brother Lamb in his market shaving [extortion] shop, or any other of the kind in this place.

A petition of Alanson Ripley and others to the Honorable Judge Thompkins, of the Supreme Court of the State of Missouri, praying for a writ of habeas corpus for Joseph, Smith, Jun., was read by Elder Ripley.

Monday, *18.*—The committee met in the course of the day, and appointed Theodore Turley to go to Jefferson City with Elder Heber C. Kimball to carry the petitions of the prisoners in Liberty and Richmond jails.

*Letter of the Prophet to Mrs. Norman Bull.**

LIBERTY JAIL, March 15, 1839.

Dear Sister:

My heart rejoices at the friendship you manifest in requesting to have a conversation with us, but the jailer is a very jealous man, fearing some one will leave tools for us to get out with. He is under the eye of the mob continually, and his life is at stake if he grants us any privileges. He will not let us converse with any one alone. Oh, what joy it would be to us to see our friends! It would have gladdened my heart to have had the privilege of conversing with you, but the hand of tyranny is upon us; thanks be to God, it cannot last always; and He that sitteth in the heaven will laugh at their calamity, and mock when their fear cometh. We feel, dear sister, that our bondage is not of long duration. I trust that I shall have the chance to give such instructions as are communicated to us before long. I suppose you want some instruction for yourself, and also to give us some information and administer consolation to us, and to find out what is best for you to do. I think that many of the brethren, if they will be pretty still, can stay in this country until the indignation is over and past; but I think it would be better for Brother Bull to leave and go with the rest of the brethren, if he keep the faith, and at any rate, thus speaketh the Spirit concerning him. I want him and you to know that I am your true friend. I was glad to see you. No tongue can tell what inexpressible

*Among others who called to see the Prophet in prison about this time was Mrs. Norman Bull; but apparently she was not allowed to have the coveted interview, and hence the prophet wrote to her. The letter here inserted appears in the manuscript history of the Church, but not until now has it been published. It is important as showing the frame of mind the Prophet was in, and his anxiety to administer comfort, and give helpful counsel to the Saints.

joy it gives a man, after having been enclosed in the walls of a prison for five months, to see the face of one who has been a friend. It seems to me that my heart will always be more tender after this than ever it was before. My heart bleeds continually when I contemplate the distress of the Church. O, that I could be with them! I would not shrink at toil and hardship to render them comfort and consolation. I want the blessing once more of lifting my voice in the midst of the Saints. I would pour out my soul to God for their instruction. It has been the plan of the devil to hamper me and distress me from the beginning, to keep me from explaining myself to them; and I never have had opportunity to give them the plan that God has revealed to me; for many have run without being sent, crying "Tidings, my Lord," and have done much injury to the Church, giving the devil more power over those that walk by sight and not by faith. But trials will only give us the knowledge necessary to understand the minds of the ancients. For my part, I think I never could have felt as I now do, if I had not suffered the wrongs that I have suffered. All things shall work together for good to them that love God. Beloved sister, we see that perilous times have truly come, and the things which we have so long expected have at last began to usher in; but when you see the fig tree begin to put forth its leaves, you may know that the summer is nigh at hand. There will be a short work on the earth. It has now commenced. I suppose there will soon be perplexity all over the earth. Do not let our hearts faint when these things come upon us, for they must come, or the word cannot be fulfilled. I know that something will soon take place to stir up this generation to see what they have been doing, and that their fathers have inherited lies and they have been led captive by the devil, to no profit; but they know not what they do. Do not have any feelings of enmity towards any son or daughter of Adam. I believe I shall be let out of their hands some way or another, and shall see good days. We cannot do anything only stand still and see the salvation of God. He must do His own work, or it must fall to the ground. We must not take it in our hands to avenge our wrongs. Vengeance is mine, saith the Lord, and I will repay. I have no fears. I shall stand unto death, God being my helper. I wanted to communicate something, and I wrote this.

Write to us if you can.

(Signed) JOSEPH SMITH, JUN.

To Mrs. Norman Bull, Clay Co., Mo.

While I was in jail, the following statements were made by the witnesses, and sent to Colonel Price, namely:

William E. McLellin is guilty of entering the house of Joseph Smith,

Jun., in the city of Far West, and plundering it of the following articles, viz.—one roll of linen cloth, a quantity of valuable buttons, one piece of cashmere, a number of very valuable books of great variety, a number of vestings, with various other articles of value.

Said McLellin was aided and assisted in the above transactions by Harvey Green, Burr Riggs and Harlow Redfield.*

The above mentioned William E. McLellin also came to and took away from the stable of the said above mentioned Joseph Smith, Jun.,

*When the History of Joseph Smith was being published in the *Deseret News*, and the above part of the History was reached, Harlow Redfield sent the following communications to the Editors vindicating himself from the charge of aiding McLellin in his robberies. It appears in the *News* of March 16, 1854.

To the Editor of The Deseret News:

SIR—In the History of Joseph Smith, published February 2, *News* No. 5, I find my name associated with others, as aiding McLellin and others in plundering the house of Joseph Smith while in prison. This is incorrect. The excitement of those times was sufficient reason for the rumor going abroad incorrectly:

I was at Hyrum Smith's house, rather by accident than design, in company with McLellin and Burr Riggs, at a time when they took some books, etc., but was not with them when they went to Joseph's. Soon after the rumor got afloat; I explained the matter before the Council in Missouri satisfactorily, as I supposed, but some time after, an enemy, in my absence, again agitated the subject before the Conference in Nauvoo, which led to an inquiry before the High Council in presence of Joseph and Hyrum, and the subject appearing in its true light, Joseph instructed the Council to give me a certificate of acquittal, that would close every man's mouth.

The following is the certificate, viz:—

"The High Council of the Church of Jesus Christ of Latter-day Saints met at Nauvoo, 20th October, 1840, to consider the case of Harlow Redfield, against whom certain accusations were brought at our last conference, in consequence of which, he was suspended, and his case referred to the High Council for decision. We being organized to investigate his case, when no charge was brought against him, nor did an implication appear, nor do we believe that a charge could be sustained against Elder Redfield. He volunteered confession of certain inadvertent, imprudent, [but] no evil meaning acts, that he greatly sorrowed for, and asked forgiveness for his folly in such acts. This Council voted that Elder Redfield be forgiven, and restored to his former official state and standing, and to be in full fellowship, the same as if no evil insinuation had ever been brought against him; and that he take a transcript of these proceedings, to be signed by the Clerk of this meeting.

"I hereby certify that the above is a true transcript of the proceedings and decision of the aforesaid case.

"H. G. SHERWOOD."

I will only add that I had before heard how that "poor Tray" got whipped for being in bad company, and it ought to have been a sufficient warning for me, and I trust it will be for the future.

I remain your humble servant,

HARLOW REDFIELD.

Provo, Feb. 7. 1854.

one gig and harness, with some other articles which cannot now be called to mind, aided and assisted by Burr Riggs—which can be proven by the following witnesses—

CAROLINE CLARK,
JAMES MULHOLLAND,
MRS. SALLY HINKLE,
JOANNA CARTER.

J. Stollins is guilty of entering the house of Joseph Smith, Jun., in the city of Far West, in company with Sashiel Woods and another man not known, and taking from a trunk, the property of James Mulholland, an inmate of said house, one gold ring, which they carried away; also of breaking open a sealed letter, which was in said trunk inside a pocket book, in which was the ring above mentioned; besides tossing and abusing the rest of the contents of said trunk; which can be proven by the following persons—

MRS. EMMA SMITH,
MRS. SALLY HINKLE,
CAROLINE CLARK,
JAMES MULHOLLAND.

Monday, March 25.—About this time, Elders Kimball and Turley started on their mission to see the governor. They called on the sheriff of Ray county and the jailer for a copy of the mittimus, by which the prisoners were held in custody, but they confessed they had none. They went to Judge King, and he made out a kind of mittimus. At this time we had been in prison several months without even a mittimus; and that too for crimes said to have been committed in another county.

The Mission of Kimball and Turley to Governor Boggs.

Elders Kimball and Turley took all the papers by which we were held, or which were then made out for them, with our petition to the supreme judges, and went to Jefferson City.

The governor was absent. The secretary of state treated them very kindly; and when he saw the papers, could hardly believe those were all the documents by which the prisoners were held in custody, for they were illegal.

Lawyer Doniphan had also deceived them in his papers and sent them off with such documents, that a change of venue could not be effected in time. The secretary was astonished at Judge King acting as he did, but said he could do nothing in the premises, and if the governor were present, he could do nothing. But the secretary wrote a letter to Judge King.

The Faulty Mittimus.

The brethren then started to find the supreme judges, and get writs of habeas corpus; and after riding hundreds of miles to effect this object, returned to Liberty on the 30th of March, having seen Matthias McGirk, George Thompkins and John C. Edwards, the supreme judges, but did not obtain the writ of habeas corpus in consequence of a lack in the order of commitment, although the judges seemed to be friendly.

We were informed that Judge King said, that there was nothing against my brother Hyrum, only that he was a friend to the Prophet. He also said there was nothing against Caleb Baldwin, and Alexander McRae.

Brother Horace Cowan was put into Liberty jail today for debt, in consequence of the persecution of the mob.

*The Prophet's Epistle to the Church, Written in Liberty Prison.**

LIBERTY JAIL, CLAY COUNTY, MISSOURI,
March 25, 1839.

To the Church of Latter-day Saints at Quincy, Illinois, and Scattered Abroad, and to Bishop Partridge in Particular:

Your humble servant, Joseph Smith, Jun., prisoner for the Lord Jesus Christ's sake, and for the Saints, taken and held by the power of mobocracy, under the exterminating reign of his excellency, the governor, Lilburn W. Boggs, in company with his fellow prisoners and be-

* The following important communication of the Prophet and his fellow prisoners to the Church at large, and to Bishop Edward Partridge in particular, was written between the 20th and 25th of March. In the Prophet's history as published many years ago in current issues of the *Deseret News* and *Millennial Star* the communication is divided near the middle of it by reciting the few incidents happening between the 20th and 25th of March—the former being the date on which the letter was begun, the latter the date on which it was completed; but in this publication it is thought desirable that the letter be given without this division, and hence it appears under the date on which it was completed, *viz*, the 25th of March, 1839. The parts of the communication enclosed in brackets and double leaded were regarded of such special value that they were taken from this communication and placed in the Doctrine and Covenants and comprise sections cxxi, cxxii, cxxiii of that work.

loved brethren, Caleb Baldwin, Lyman Wight, Hyrum Smith, and Alexander McRae, send unto you all greeting. May the grace of God the Father, and of our Lord and Savior Jesus Christ, rest upon you all, and abide with you forever. May knowledge be multiplied unto you by the mercy of God. And may faith and virtue, and knowledge and temperance, and patience and godliness, and brotherly kindness and charity be in you and abound, that you may not be barren in anything, nor unfruitful.

For inasmuch as we know that the most of you are well acquainted with the wrongs and the high-handed injustice and cruelty that are practiced upon us; whereas we have been taken prisoners charged falsely with every kind of evil, and thrown into prison, enclosed with strong walls, surrounded with a strong guard, who continually watch day and night as indefatigable as the devil does in tempting and laying snares for the people of God:

Therefore, dearly beloved brethren, we are the more ready and willing to lay claim to your fellowship and love. For our circumstances are calculated to awaken our spirits to a sacred remembrance of everything, and we think that yours are also, and that nothing therefore can separate us from the love of God and fellowship one with another; and that every species of wickedness and cruelty practiced upon us will only tend to bind our hearts together and seal them together in love. We have no need to say to you that we are held in bonds without cause, neither is it needful that you say unto us, We are driven from our homes and smitten without cause. We mutually understand that if the inhabitants of the state of Missouri had let the Saints alone, and had been as desirable of peace as they were, there would have been nothing but peace and quietude in the state unto this day; we should not have been in this hell, surrounded with demons (if not those who are damned, they are those who shall be damned) and where we are compelled to hear nothing but blasphemous oaths, and witness a scene of blasphemy, and drunkenness and hypocrisy, and debaucheries of every description.

And again, the cries of orphans and widows would not have ascended up to God against them. Nor would innocent blood have stained the soil of Missouri. But oh! the unrelenting hand! The inhumanity and murderous disposition of this people! It shocks all nature; it beggars and defies all description; it is a tale of woe; a lamentable tale; yea a sorrowful tale; too much to tell; too much for contemplation; too much for human beings; it cannot be found among the heathens; it cannot be found among the nations where kings and tyrants are enthroned; it cannot be found among the savages of the wilderness; yea, and I think it cannot be found among the wild and ferocious beasts of the forest—

that a man should be mangled for sport! women be robbed of all that they have—their last morsel for subsistence, and then be violated to gratify the hellish desires of the mob, and finally left to perish with their helpless offspring clinging around their necks.

But this is not all. After a man is dead, he must be dug up from his grave and mangled to pieces, for no other purpose than to gratify their spleen against the religion of God.

They practice these things upon the Saints, who have done them no wrong, who are innocent and virtuous; who loved the Lord their God, and were willing to forsake all things for Christ's sake. These things are awful to relate, but they are verily true. It must needs be that offenses come, but woe unto them by whom they come.

[Oh God! where art Thou? And where is the pavilion that covereth Thy hiding place? How long shall Thy hand be stayed, and Thine eye, yea Thy pure eye, behold from the eternal heavens, the wrongs of Thy people, and of Thy servants, and Thy ear be penetrated with their cries? Yea, O Lord, how long shall they suffer these wrongs and unlawful oppressions, before Thine heart shall be softened towards them, and Thy bowels be moved with compassion towards them?

O Lord God Almighty, Maker of Heaven, Earth and Seas, and of all things that in them are, and who controllest and subjectest the devil, and the dark and benighted dominion of Sheol! Stretch forth Thy hand, let Thine eye pierce; let Thy pavilion be taken up; let Thy hiding place no longer be covered; let Thine ear be inclined; let Thine heart be softened,and Thy bowels moved with compassion towards us, Let Thine anger be kindled against our enemies; and in the fury of Thine heart, with Thy sword avenge us of our wrongs; remember Thy suffering Saints, O our God! and Thy servants will rejoice in Thy name forever.]

Dearly and beloved brethren, we see that perilous times have come, as was testified of. We may look, then, with most perfect assurance, for the fulfillment of all those things that have been written, and with more confidence than ever before, lift up our eyes to the luminary of day, and say in our hearts, Soon thou wilt veil thy blushing face. He that said "Let there be light," and there was light, hath spoken this word. And again, Thou moon, thou dimmer light, thou luminary of night, shalt turn to blood.

We see that everything is being fulfilled; and that the time shall soon come when the Son of Man shall descend in the clouds of heaven. Our hearts do not shrink, neither are our spirits altogether broken by the grievous yoke which is put upon us. We know that God will have our oppressors in derision; that He will laugh at their calamity, and mock when their fear cometh.

O that we could be with you, brethren, and unbosom our feelings to you! We would tell, that we should have been liberated at the time Elder Rigdon was, on the writ of habeas corpus, had not our own lawyers interpreted the law, contrary to what it reads, against us; which prevented us from introducing our evidence before the mock court.

They have done us much harm from the beginning. They have of late acknowledged that the law was misconstrued, and tantalized our feelings with it, and have entirely forsaken us, and have forfeited their oaths and their bonds; and we have a come-back on them, for they are co-workers with the mob.

As nigh as we can learn, the public mind has been for a long time turning in our favor, and the majority is now friendly; and the lawyers can no longer browbeat us by saying that this or that is a matter of public opinion, for public opinion is not willing to brook it; for it is beginning to look with feelings of indignation against our oppressors, and to say that the "Mormons" were not in the fault in the least. We think that truth, honor, virtue and innocence will eventually come out triumphant. We should have taken a habeas corpus before the high judge and escaped the mob in a summary way; but unfortunately for us, the timber of the wall being very hard, our auger handles gave out, and hindered us longer than we expected; we applied to a friend, and a very slight incautious act gave rise to some suspicions, and before we could fully succeed, our plan was discovered; we had everything in readiness, but the last stone, and we could have made our escape in one minute, and should have succeeded admirably, had it not been for a little imprudence or over-anxiety on the part of our friend.*

The sheriff and jailer did not blame us for our attempt; it was a fine breach, and cost the county a round sum; but public opinion says that we ought to have been permitted to have made our escape; that then the disgrace would have been on us, but now it must come on the state; that there cannot be any charge sustained against us; and that the conduct of the mob, the murders committed at Haun's Mills, and the exterminating order of the governor, and the one-sided, rascally proceedings of the legislature, have damned the state of Missouai to all eternity. I would just name also that General Atchison has proved himself as contemptible as any of them.

We have tried for a long time to get our lawyers to draw us some

This alludes to another effort to escape from prison besides the one related by Alexander McRae at pp. 257-8.

petitions to the supreme judges of this state. but they utterly refused. We have examined the law, and drawn the petitions ourselves, and have obtained abundance of proof to counteract all the testimony that was against us, so that if the supreme judge does not grant us our liberty, he has to act without cause, contrary to honor, evidence, law or justice, sheerly to please the devil, but we hope better things and trust before many days God will so order our case, that we shall be set at liberty and take up our habitation with the Saints.

We received some letters last evening—one from Emma, one from Don C. Smith, and one from Bishop Partridge—all breathing a kind and consoling spirit. We were much gratified with their contents. We had been a long time without information; and when we read those letters they were to our souls as the gentle air is refreshing, but our joy was mingled with grief, because of the sufferings of the poor and much injured Saints. And we need not say to you that the floodgates of our hearts were lifted and our eyes were a fountain of tears, but those who have not been enclosed in the walls of prison without cause or provocation, can have but little idea how sweet the voice of a friend is; one token of friendship from any source whatever awakens and calls into action every sympathetic feeling; it brings up in an instant everything that is passed; it seizes the present with the avidity of lightning; it grasps after the future with the fierceness of a tiger; it moves the mind backwark and forward, from one thing to another, until finally all enmity, malice and hatred, and past differences, misunderstandings and mismanagements are slain victorious at the feet of hope; and when the heart is sufficiently contrite, then the voice of inspiration steals along and whispers, [My son, peace be unto thy soul; thine adversity and thine afflictions shall be but a small moment; and then if thou endure it well, God shall exalt thee on high; thou shalt triumph over all thy foes; thy friends do stand by thee, and they shall hail thee again, with warm hearts and friendly hands; thou art not yet as Job; thy friends do not contend against thee, neither charge thee with transgression, as they did Job; and they who do charge thee with transgression, their hope shall be blasted and their prospects shall melt away as the hoar frost melteth before the burning rays of the rising sun; and also that God hath set His hand and seal to change the times and seasons, and to blind their minds, that they may not understand His marvelous workings, that He may prove them also and take them in their own craftiness; also because their hearts are corrupted, and the things which they are willing to bring upon others, and love to have others suffer, may come upon themselves to the very uttermost; that they may be disappointed also, and their hopes may be cut off; and not many years hence, that they and their posterity shall be swept from under heaven, saith God, that not one of them is left to stand by the wall. Cursed are all those that shall lift up the heel against mine anointed, saith the Lord, and cry they have sinned when they have not sinned before me, saith the Lord, but have done that which was meet in mine eyes, and which I commanded them; but those who cry transgression do it because they are the servants of sin and are the children of disobedience themselves; and those who swear falsely against my servants, that they might bring them into bondage and death; wo unto them; because they have offended my little ones; they shall be severed from the ordinances of mine house; their basket shall not be full, and their houses and their barns shall perish, and they themselves shall be despised by those that flattered them; they shall not have right to the Priesthood, nor their posterity after them, from generation to generation; it had been better for them that a millstone had been hanged about their necks, and they drowned in the depth of the sea.

Wo unto all those that discomfort my people, and drive and murder, and testify against them, saith the Lord of Hosts: a generation of vipers shall not escape the damnation of hell. Behold mine eyes see and know all their works, and I have in reserve a swift judgment in the season thereof, for them all; for there is a time appointed for every man according as his work shall be.]

And now, beloved brethren, we say unto you, that inasmuch as God hath said that He would have a tried people, that He would purge them as gold, now we think that this time He has chosen His own crucible, wherein we have been tried; and we think if we get through with any degree of safety, and shall have kept the faith, that it will be a sign to this generation, altogether sufficient to leave them without excuse; and we think also, it will be a trial of our faith equal to that of Abraham, and that the ancients will not have whereof to boast over us in the day of judgment, as being called to pass through heavier afflictions; that we may hold an even weight in the balance with them; but now, after having suffered so great sacrifice and having passed through so great a season of sorrow, we trust that a ram may be caught in the thicket speedily, to relieve the sons and daughters of Abraham from their great anxiety, and to light up the lamp of salvation upon their countenances, that they may hold on now, after having gone so far unto everlasting life.

Now, brethren, concerning the places for the location of the Saints, we cannot counsel you as we could if we were present with you; and as to the things that were written heretofore, we did not consider them anything very binding, therefore we now say once for all, that we think it most proper that the general affairs of the Church, which are necessary to be considered, while your humble servant remains in bondage, should be transacted by a general conference of the most faithful and the most respectable of the authorities of the Church, and a minute of those transactions may be kept, and forwarded from time to time. to your humble servant; and if there should be any corrections by the word of the Lord, they shall be freely transmitted. and your humble servant will approve all things whatsoever is acceptable unto God. If anything should have been suggested by us, or any names mentioned, except by commandment, or thus saith the Lord, we do not consider it binding; therefore our hearts shall not be grieved if different arrangements should be entered into. Nevertheless we would suggest the propriety of being aware of an aspiring spirit, which spirit has oftentimes urged men forward to make foul speeches, and influence the Church to reject milder counsels, and has eventually been the means of bringing much death and sorrow upon the Church.

We would say, beware of pride also; for well and truly hath the wise man said, that pride goeth before destruction, and a haughty spirit before a fall. And again, outward appearance is not always a criterion by which to judge our fellow man; but the lips betray the haughty and overbearing imaginations of the heart; by his words and his deeds let him be judged. Flattery also is a deadly poison. A frank and open rebuke provoketh a good man to emulation; and in the hour of trouble he will be your best friend; but on the other hand, it will draw out all the corruptions of corrupt hearts, and lying and the poison of asps is under their tongues; and they do cause the pure in heart to be cast into prison, because they want them out of their way.

A fanciful and flowery and heated imagination beware of; because the things of God are of deep import; and time, and experience, and careful and ponderous and solemn thoughts can only find them out. Thy mind, O man! if thou wilt lead a soul unto salvation, must stretch as high as the utmost heavens, and search into and contemplate the darkest abyss, and the broad expanse of eternity—thou must commune with God. How much more dignified and noble are the thoughts of God, than the vain imaginations of the human heart! None but fools will trifle with the souls of men.

How vain and trifling have been our spirits, our conferences, our councils, our meetings, our private as well as public conversations—too low, too mean, too vulgar, too condescending for the dignified characters of the called and chosen of God, according to the purposes of His will, from before the foundation of the world! We are called to hold the keys of the mysteries of those things that have been kept hid from the foundation of the world until now. Some have tasted a little of these things, many of which are to be poured down from heaven upon the heads of babes; yea, upon the weak, obscure and despised ones of the earth. Therefore we beseech of you,brethren, that you bear with those who do not feel themselves more worthy than yourselves, while we exhort one another to a reformation with one and all, both old and young, teachers and taught, both high and low, rich and poor, bond and free, male and female; let honesty, and sobriety, and candor, and solemnity, and virtue, and pureness, and meekness, and simplicity crown our heads in every place; and in fine, become as little children, without malice, guile or hypocrisy.

And now, brethren, after your tribulations, if you do these things, and exercise fervent prayer and faith in the sight of God always, [He shall give unto you knowledge by His Holy Spirit, yea by the unspeakable gift of the Holy Ghost, that has not been revealed since the world was until now; which our forefathers have waited with anxious expectation to be revealed in the last times, which their minds were pointed to by the angels, as held in reserve for the fullness of their glory; a time to come in the which nothing shall be withheld, whether there be one God or many Gods, they shall be manifest; all thrones and dominions, principalities and powers, shall be revealed and set forth upon all who have endured valiantly for the Gospel of Jesus Christ; and also if there be bounds set to the heavens, or to the seas; or to the dry land, or to the sun, moon or stars; all the times of their revolutions; all the appointed days, months and years, and all the days of their days, months and years, and all their glories, laws, and set times, shall be revealed, in the days of the dispensation of the fullness of times, according to that which was ordained in the midst of the Council of the Eternal God of all other Gods, before this world was, that should be reserved unto the finishing and the end thereof, when every man shall enter into His eternal presence, and into His immortal rest].

But I beg leave to say unto you, brethren, that ignorance, superstition and bigotry placing itself where it ought not, is oftentimes in the way of the prosperity of this Church; like the torrent of rain from the mountains, that floods the most pure and crystal stream with mire, and dirt, and filthiness, and obscures everything that was clear before, and all rushes along in one general deluge; but time weathers tide; and notwithstanding we are rolled in the mire of the flood for the time being, the next surge peradventure, as time rolls on, may bring to us the fountain as clear as crystal, and as pure as snow; while the filthiness, flood-wood and rubbish is left and purged out by the way.

[How long can rolling water remain impure? What power shall stay the heavens? As well might man stretch forth his puny arm to stop the Missouri river in its decreed course, or to turn it up stream, as to hinder the Almighty from pouring down knowledge from heaven, upon the heads of the Latter-day Saints].

What is Boggs or his murderous party, but wimbling willows upon the shore to catch the flood-wood? As well might we argue that water is not water, because the mountain torrents send down mire and roil the crystal stream, although afterwards render it more pure than before; or that fire is not fire, because it is of a quenchable nature, by pouring on the flood; as to say that our cause is down because renegados, liars, priests, thieves and murderers, who are all alike tenacious of their crafts and creeds, have poured down, from their spiritual wickedness in high places, and from their strongholds of the devil, a flood of dirt and mire and filthiness and vomit upon our heads.

No! God forbid. Hell may pour forth its rage like the burning lava of mount Vesuvius, or of Etna, or of the most terrible of the burning mountains; and yet shall "Mormonism" stand. Water, fire, truth and God are all realities. Truth is "Mormonism." God is the author of it. He is our shield. It is by Him we received our birth. It was by His voice that we were called to a dispensation of His Gospel in the beginning of the fullness of times. It was by Him we received the Book of Mormon; and it is by Him that we remain unto this day; and by Him we shall remain, if it shall be for our glory; and in His Almighty name we are determined to endure tribulation as good soldiers unto the end.

But, brethren, we shall continue to offer further reflections in our next epistle. You will learn by the time you have read this, and if you do not learn it, you may learn it, that walls and irons, doors and creaking hinges, and half-scared-to-death guards and jailers, grinning like some damned spirits, lest an innocent man should make his escape to bring to light the damnable deeds of a murderous mob, are calculated in their very nature to make the soul of an honest man feel stronger than the powers of hell.

But we must bring our epistle to a close. We send our respects to fathers, mothers, wives and children, brothers and sisters; we hold them in the most sacred remembrance.

We feel to inquire after Elder Rigdon; if he has not forgotten us, it has not been signified to us by his writing. Brother George W. Robinson also; and Elder Cahoon, we remember him, but would like to jog his memory a little on the fable of the bear and the two friends who mutually agreed to stand by each other. And perhaps it would not be amiss to mention uncle John [Smith], and various others. A word of consolation and a blessing would not come amiss from anybody, while we are being so closely whispered by the bear. But we feel to excuse everybody and everything, yea the more readily when we contemplate that we are in the hands of persons worse that a bear, for the bear would not prey upon a dead carcass.

Our respects and love and fellowship to all the virtuous Saints. We are your brethren and fellow-sufferers, and prisoners of Jesus Christ for the Gospel's sake, and for the hope of glory which is in us. Amen.

We continue to offer further reflections to Bishop Partridge, and to the Church of Jesus Christ of Latter-day Saints, whom we love with a fervent love, and do always bear them in mind in all our prayers to the throne of God.

It still seems to bear heavily on our minds that the Church would do well to secure to themselves the contract of the land which is proposed to them by Mr. Isaac Galland, and to cultivate the friendly feelings of that gentleman, inasmuch as he shall prove himself to be a man of honor and a friend to humanity; also Isaac Van Allen, Esq., the attorney-general of Iowa Territory, and Governor Lucas, that peradventure such men may be wrought upon by the providence of God, to do good unto His people. We really think that Mr. Galland's letter breathes that kind of a spirit, if we may judge correctly. Governor Lucas also. We suggest the idea of praying fervently for all men who manifest any degree of sympathy for the suffering children of God.

We think that the United States Surveyor of the Iowa Territory may be of great benefit to the Church, if it be the will of God to this end; and righteousness should be manifested as the girdle of our loins.

It seems to be deeply impressed upon our minds that the Saints ought to lay hold of every door that shall seem to be opened unto them, to obtain foothold on the earth, and be making all the preparation that is within their power for the terrible storms that are now gathering in the heavens, "a day of clouds, with darkness and gloominess, and of thick darkness," as spoken of by the Prophets, which cannot be now of a long time lingering, for there seems to be a whispering that the angels of heaven who have been entrusted with the counsel of these matters for the last days, have taken counsel together; and among the rest of the general affairs that have to be transacted in their honorable council, they have taken cognizance of the testimony of those who were murdered at Haun's Mills, and also those who were martyred with David W. Patten. and elsewhere, and have passed some decisions peradventure in favor of the Saints, and those who were called to suffer without cause.

These decisions will be made known in their time; and the council will take into consideration all those things that offend.

We have a fervent desire that in your general conferences everything should be discussed with a great deal of care and propriety, lest you grieve the Holy Spirit, which shall be poured out at all times upon your heads, when you are exercised with those principles of righteousness that are agreeable to the mind of God, and are properly affected one toward another, and are careful by all means to remember, those who are in bondage, and in heaviness, and in deep affliction far your sakes. And if there are any among you who aspire after their own aggrandizement, and seek their own opulence, while their brethren are groaning in poverty, and are under sore trials and temptations, they cannot be benefited by the intercession of the Holy Spirit, which maketh intercession for us day and night with groanings that cannot be uttered.

We ought at all times to be very careful that such high-mindedness shall never have place in our hearts; but condescend to men of low estate, and with all long-suffering bear the infirmities of the weak.

[Behold, there are many called, but few are chosen. And why are they not chosen? Because their hearts are set so much upon the things of this world, and aspire to the honors of men, that they do not learn this one lesson—that the rights of the Priesthood are inseparably connected with the powers of heaven, and that the powers of heaven cannot be controlled nor handled only upon the principles of righteousness. That they may be conferred upon us, it is true; but when we undertake to cover our sins, or to gratify our pride, our vain ambition, or to exercise control, or dominion, or compulsion, upon the souls of the children of men, in any degree of unrighteousness, behold, the heavens withdraw themselves; the Spirit of the Lord is grieved; and when it is withdrawn, *Amen to the Priesthood*, or the authority of that man. Behold! ere he is aware, he is left unto himself, to kick against the pricks; to persecute the Saints, and to fight against God.

We have learned by sad experience that it is the nature and disposition of almost all men, as soon as they get a little authority, as they suppose, they will immediately begin to exercise unrighteous dominion. Hence many are called, but few are chosen.

No power or influence can or ought to be maintained by virtue of the Priesthood, only by persuasion, by long-suffering, by gentleness, and meekness, and by love unfeigned; by kindness, and pure knowledge, which shall greatly enlarge the soul without hypocrisy, and without guile, reproving betimes with sharpness, when moved upon by the Holy Ghost, and then showing forth afterwards an increase of love toward him whom thou hast reproved, lest he esteem thee to be his enemy; that he may know that thy faithfulness is stronger than the cords of death; let thy bowels also be full of charity towards all men, and to the household of faith, and virtue garnish thy thoughts unceasingly, then shall thy confidence wax strong in the presence of God, and the doctrine of the Priesthood shall distill upon thy soul as the dews from heaven. The Holy Ghost shall be thy constant companion, and thy sceptre an unchanging sceptre of righteousness and truth, and thy dominion shall be an everlasting dominion, and without compulsory means it shall flow unto thee forever and ever].

[The ends of the earth shall inquire after thy name, and fools shall have thee in derision, and hell shall rage against thee, while the pure in heart, and the wise, and the noble, and the virtuous, shall seek counsel, and authority and blessings constantly from under thy hand, and thy people shall never be turned against thee by the testimony of traitors; and although their influence shall cast thee into trouble, and into bars and walls, thou shalt be had in honor, and but for a small moment and thy voice shall be more terrible in the midst of thine enemies, than the fierce lion, because of thy righteousness; and thy God shall stand by thee forever and ever.

If thou art called to pass through tribulations; if thou art in perils among false brethren; if thou art in perils among robbers; if thou art in perils by land or by sea; if thou art accused with all manner of false accusations; if thine enemies fall upon thee; if they tear thee from the society of thy father and mother and brethren and sisters; and if with a drawn sword thine enemies tear thee from the bosom of thy wife, and of thine offspring, and thine elder son, although but six years of age, shall cling to thy garments, and shall say, My father, my father, why can't you stay with us? O, my father, what are the men going to do with you? and if then he shall be thrust from thee by the sword, and thou be dragged to prison, and thine enemies prowl around thee like wolves for the blood of the lamb; and if thou shouldst be cast into the pit, or into the hands of murderers, and the sentence of death passed upon thee; if thou be cast into the deep; if the billowing surge conspire against thee; if fierce winds become thine enemy; if the heavens gather blackness, and all the elements combine to hedge up the way; and above all, if the very jaws of hell shall gape open the mouth wide after thee, know thou, my son, that all these things shall give thee experience, and shall be for thy good. The Son of Man hath descended below them all; art thou greater than he?

Therefore, hold on thy way, and the Priesthood shall remain with thee, for their bounds are set, they cannot pass. Thy days are known, and thy years shall not be numbered less; therefore, fear not what man can do, for God shall be with you forever and ever].

Now, brethren, I would suggest for the consideration of the conference, its being carefully and wisely understoood by the council or conferences that our brethren scattered abroad, who understand the spirit of the gathering, that they fall into the places and refuge of safety that God shall open unto them, between Kirtland and Far West. Those from the east and from the west, and from far countries, let them fall in somewhere between those two boundaries, in the most safe and quiet places they can find; and let this be the present understanding, until God shall open a more effectual door for us for further considerations.

And again, we further suggest for the considerations of the Council, that there be no organization of large bodies upon common stock principles, in property, or of large companies of firms, until the Lord shall signify it in a proper manner, as it opens such a dreadful field for the avaricious, the indolent, and the corrupt hearted to prey upon the innocent and virtuous, and honest.

We have reason to believe that many things were introduced among the Saints before God had signified the times; and notwithstanding the principles and plans may have been good, yet aspiring men, or in other words, men who had not the substance of godliness about them, perhaps undertook to handle edged tools. Children, you know, are fond of tools, while they are not yet able to use them.

Time and experience, however, are the only safe remedies against such evils. There are many teachers, but, perhaps, not many fathers. There are times coming when God will signify many things which are expedient for the well-being of the Saints; but the times have not yet come, but will come, as fast as there can be found place and reception for them.

[And again, we would suggest for your consideration the propriety of all the Saints gathering up a knowledge of all the facts and sufferings and abuses put upon them by the people of this state; and also of all the property and amount of damages which they have sustained, both of character and personal injuries, as well as real property; and also the names of all persons that have had a hand in their oppressions, as far as they can get hold of them and find them out; and perhaps a committee can be appointed to find out these things, and to take statements, and affidavits, and also to gather up the libelous publications that are afloat, and all that are in the magazines, and in the encyclopædias, and all the libelous histories that are published, and are writing, and by whom, and present the whole concatenation of diabolical rascality, and nefarious and murderous impositions that have been practiced upon this people, that we may not only publish to all the world, but present them to the heads of government in all their dark and hellish hue, as the last effort which is enjoined on us by our Heavenly Father, before we can fully and completely claim that promise which shall call Him forth from His hiding place, and also that the whole nation may be left without excuse before He can send forth the power of His mighty arm.

It is an imperative duty that we owe to God, to angels, with whom we shall be brought to stand, and also to ourselves, to our wives and children, who have been made to bow down with grief, sorrow, and care, under the most damning hand of murder, tyranny, and oppression, supported and urged on and upheld by the influence of that spirit which hath so strongly riveted the creeds of the fathers, who have inherited lies, upon the hearts of the children, and filled the world with confusion, and has been growing stronger and stronger, and is now the very main-spring of all corruption, and the whole earth groans under the weight of its iniquity.

It is an iron yoke, it is a strong band; they are the very hand-cuffs, and chains, and shackles, and fetters of hell.

Therefore it is an imperative duty that we owe, not only to our own wives and children, but to the widows and fatherless, whose husbands and fathers have been murdered under its iron hand; which dark and blackening deeds are enough to make hell itself shudder, and to stand aghast and pale, and the hands of the very devil to tremble and palsy. And also it is an imperative duty that we owe to all the rising generation, and to all the pure in heart, (for there are many yet on the earth among all sects, parties, denominations, who are blinded by the subtle craftiness of men, whereby they lie in wait to deceive, and who are only kept from the truth because they know not where to find it); therefore, that we should waste and wear out our lives in bringing to light all the hidden things of darkness, wherein we know them; and they are truly manifest from heaven.

These should then be attended to with great earnestness. Let no man count them as small things; for there is much which lieth in futurity, pertaining to the Saints, which depends upon these things. You know, brethren, that a very large ship is benefited very much by a very small helm in the time of a storm, by being kept workways with the wind and the waves.

Therefore, dearly beloved brethren, let us cheerfully do all things that lie in our power, and then may we stand still with the utmost assurance, to see the salvation of God, and for His arm to be revealed].

And again, I would further suggest the impropriety of the organization of bands or companies, by covenant or oaths, by penalties or secrecies; but let the time past of our experience and sufferings by the wickedness of Doctor Avard suffice and let our covenant be that of the Everlasting Covenant, as is contained in the Holy Writ and the things that God hath revealed unto us. Pure friendship always becomes weakened the very moment you undertake to make it stronger by penal oaths and secrecy.

Your humble servant or servants, intend from henceforth to disapprobate everything that is not in accordance with the fullness of the Gospel of Jesus Christ, and is not of a bold, and frank, and upright nature. They will not hold their peace—as in times past when they see iniquity beginning to rear its head—for fear of traitors, or the consequences that shall follow by reproving those who creep in unawares, that they may get something with which to destroy the flock. We believe that the experience of the Saints in times past has been sufficient, that they will from henceforth be always ready to obey the truth without having men's persons in admiration because of advantage. It is expedient that we should be aware of such things; and we ought always to be aware of those prejudices which sometimes so strangely present themselves, and are so congenial to human nature, against our friends, neighbors, and brethren of the world, who choose to differ from us in opinion and in matters of faith. Our religion is between us and our God. Their religion is between them and their God.

There is a love from God that should be exercised toward those of our faith, who walk uprightly, which is peculiar to itself, but it is without prejudice; it also gives scope to the mind, which enables us to conduct ourselves with greater liberality towards all that are not of our faith, than what they exercise towards one another. These principles approximate nearer to the mind of God, because it is like God, or Godlike.

Here is a principle also, which we are bound to be exercised with, that is, in common with all men, such as governments, and laws, and regulations in the civil concerns of life. This principle guarantees to all parties, sects, and denominations, and classes of religion, equal, coherent, and indefeasible rights; they are things that pertain to this life; therefore all are alike interested; they make our responsibilities one towards another in matters of corruptible things, while the former principles do not destroy the latter, but bind us stronger, and make our responsibilities not only one to another, but unto God also. Hence we say, that the Constitution of the United States is a glorious standard; it is founded in the wisdom of God. It is a heavenly banner; it is to all those who are privileged with the sweets of its liberty, like the cooling shades and refreshing waters of a great rock in a thirsty and weary land. It is like a great tree under whose branches men from every clime can be shielded from the burning rays of the sun.

We, brethren, are deprived of the protection of its glorious principles, by the cruelty of the cruel, by those who only look for the time being, for pasturage like the beasts of the field, only to fill themselves; and forget that the "Mormons," as well as the Presbyterians, and those of every other class and description, have equal rights to partake of the fruits of the great tree of our national liberty. But notwithstanding we see what we see, and feel what we feel, and know what we know, yet that fruit is no less precious and delicious to our taste; we cannot be weaned from the milk, neither can we be driven from the breast; neither will we deny our religion because of the hand of oppression; but we will hold on until death.

We say that God is true; that the Constitution of the United States is true; that the Bible is true; that the Book of Mormon is true; that the Book of Covenants is true; that Christ is true; that the ministering angels sent forth from God are true, and that we know that we have an house not made with hands eternal in the heavens, whose builder and maker is God; a consolation which our oppressors cannot feel, when fortune, or fate, shall lay its iron hand on them as it has on us. Now, we ask, what is man? Remember, brethren, that time and chance happen to all men.

We shall continue our reflections in our next.

We subscribe ourselves, your sincere friends and brethren in the bonds of the everlasting Gospel, prisoners of Jesus Christ, for the sake of the Gospel and the Saints.

We pronounce the blessings of heaven upon the heads of the Saints who seek to serve God with undivided hearts, in the name of Jesus Christ. Amen.

JOSEPH SMITH, JUN.,
HYRUM SMITH,
LYMAN WIGHT,
CALEB BALDWIN,
ALEXANDER MCRAE.

CHAPTER XXI.

STIRRING SCENES ABOUT FAR WEST—THE ESCAPE OF THE PROPHET AND HIS FELLOW PRISONERS.

Thursday, April 4.—Brothers Kimball and Turley called on Judge King, who was angry at their having reported the case to the governor, and, said he, "I could have done all the business for you properly, if you had come to me; and I would have signed the petition for all except Joe, and he is not fit to live." I bid Brothers Kimball and Turley to be of good cheer, "for we shall be delivered; but no arm but God's can deliver us now. Tell the brethren to be of good cheer and get the Saints away as fast as possible."

Judge King's Anger.

Brothers Kimball and Turley were not permitted to enter the prison, and all the communication we had with them was through the grate of the dungeon. The brethren left Liberty on their return to Far West.

Friday, April 5.—Brothers Kimball and Turley arrived at Far West.

This day a company of about fifty men in Daviess county swore that they would never eat or drink, until they had murdered "Joe Smith." Their captain, William Bowman, swore, in the presence of Theodore Turley, that he would "never eat or drink, after he had seen Joe Smith, until he had murdered him."

Plot Against the Prophet's Life.

Also eight men—Captain Bogart, who was the county judge, Dr. Laffity, John Whitmer, and five others—came into the committee's room [i.e. the room or office of the committee on removal] and presented to Theodore Turley the paper containing the revelation of July 8, 1838,* to Joseph Smith, directing the Twelve to take their leave of the Saints in

The Truth of a Revelation Questioned.

*See Doctrine and Covenants, sec. cxviii.

Far West on the building site of the Lords House on the 26th of April, to go to the isles of the sea, and then asked him to read it. Turley said, "Gentlemen, I am well acquainted with it." They said, "Then you, as a rational man, will give up Joseph Smith's being a prophet and an inspired man? He and the Twelve are now scattered all over creation; let them come here if they dare; if they do, they will be murdered. As that revelation cannot be fulfilled, you will now give up your faith."

Turley jumped up and said, "In the name of God that revelation will be fulfilled." They laughed him to scorn. John Whitmer hung down his head. They said, "If they (the Twelve) come, they will get murdered; they dare not come to take their leave here; that is like all the rest of Joe Smith's d——n prophecies." They commenced on Turley and said, he had better do as John Corrill had done; "he is going to publish a book called 'Mormonism Fairly Delineated;' he is a sensible man, and you had better assist him."

Turley's Defense of the Prophet.

Turley said, "Gentlemen, I presume there are men here who have heard Corrill say, that 'Mormonism' was true, that Joseph Smith was a prophet, and inspired of God. I now call upon you, John Whitmer: you say Corrill is a moral and a good man; do you believe him when he says the Book of Mormon is true, or when he says it is not true? There are many things published that they say are true, and again turn around and say they are false?" Whitmer asked, "Do you hint at me?" Turley replied, "If the cap fits you, wear it; all I know is that you have published to the world that an angel did present those plates to Joseph Smith." Whitmer replied: "I now say, I handled those plates; there were fine engravings on both sides. I handled them;" and he described how they were hung, and "they were shown to me by a supernatural power;" he acknowledged all.

Colloquy between Turley and John Whitmer.

Turley asked him, "Why is not the translation now

true?" He said, "I could not read it [in the original] and I do not know whether it [i. e., the translation] is true or not." Whitmer testified all this in the presence of eight men.

The committee [on removal of the Saints from Missouri] met, and Brother William Huntington made report of his journey to Liberty on business of the committee.

Land Sales and the Clothing of Prisoners.

The subject of providing some clothing for the prisoners at Richmond was discussed, and the propriety of sending two brethren to Liberty, to make sales of some lands, was taken up, and Elders H. G. Sherwood and Theodore Turley were appointed.

A bill of clothing for the Richmond prisoners having been made up, was presented and given to those appointed to go to Liberty, that they might procure the goods on the sales of land.

The Prisoners Hurried into Daviess County.

Saturday, April 6.—Judge King evidently fearing a change of venue, or some movement on our part to escape his unhallowed persecution (and most probably expecting that we would be murdered on the way) hurried myself and fellow prisoners off to Daviess county, under a guard of about ten men, commanded by Samuel Tillery, deputy jailer of Clay county. We were promised that we should go through Far West, which was directly on our route, which our friends at that place knew, and expected us; but instead of fulfilling their promise, they took us around the city, and out of the direct course some eighteen miles; far from habitations, where every opportunity presented for a general massacre.

Peremptory Orders Considered.

This evening the committee (i. e. on removal) met in council. Prayer by Elder Kimball. The business of the council was the consideration of the order of the leaders of the Daviess mob, delivered this day to the Saints in Caldwell county, to leave before Friday next.

Resolved: To hire all teams that can be hired, to move the families of the Saints out of the county, to Tenny's Grove.

Resolved: To send Henry G. Sherwood immediately to Illinois for assistance, in teams from the Saints there.

The mission of Elders Sherwood and Turley to Liberty was deferred for the present.

Sunday, April 7.—The committee met in council at Brother Turley's. Brother Erastus Snow made a report of his visit to the judges at Jefferson city. A letter from the prisoners at Liberty was read and Daniel Shearer and Heber C. Kimball were appointed to see Mr. Hughes and get him to go to Daviess county and attend the sitting of the court there.

Actions of the Committee.

We continued our travels across the prairie, while the brethren at Far West, anxious for our welfare, gave a man thirty dollars to convey a letter to us in Daviess county, and return an answer.

Monday, April 8.—After a tedious journey—for our long confinement had enfeebled our bodily powers—we arrived in Daviess county, about a mile from Gallatin, where we were delivered into the hands of William Morgan, sheriff of Daviess county, with his guard, William Bowman, John Brassfield and John Pogue. The Liberty guard returned immediately, but became divided, or got lost on their way; a part of them arrived in Far West after dark, and got caught in the fence; and calling for help, Elder Markham went to their assistance and took them to the tavern. From them he got a letter I had written to the committee, informing them of our arrival in Daviess county.

Arrival of the Prisoners in Daviess County.

Tuesday, April 9.—Our trial commenced before a drunken grand jury, Austin A. King, presiding judge, as drunk as the jury; for they were all drunk together. Elder Stephen Markham had been dispatched by the committee to visit us, and bring a hundred dollars that was sent by Elder Kimball, as we were destitute of means at that time. He left Far

Arrival of Stephen Markham in Gallatin.

West this morning, and swimming several streams he arrived among us in the afternoon, and spent the evening in our company. Brother Markham brought us a written copy of a statute which had passed the legislature, giving us the privilege of a change of venue on our own affidavit.

Judge Morin arrived from Mill Port, and was favorable to our escape from the persecution we were enduring, and spent the evening with us in prison, and we had as pleasant a time as such circumstances would permit, for we were as happy as the happiest; the Spirit buoyed us above our trials, and we rejoiced in each other's society.

Judge Morin Favors the Prophet's Escape.

Wednesday, April 10.—The day was spent in the examination of witnesses before the grand jury. Dr. Sampson Avard was one of the witnesses. Brother Markham was not permitted to give his testimony.

The Examination of Witnesses.

Our guard went home, and Colonel William P. Peniston, Blakely, and others took their place.

Letter of Sidney Rigdon to the Prophet. Rigdon's Plans for the Impeachment of Missouri.

QUINCY, ILLINOIS, April 10, 1839.

To the Saints in Prison, Greeting:

In the midst of a crowd of business, I haste to send a few lines by the hand of Brother Mace, our messenger. We wish you to know that our friendship is unabating, and our exertions for your delivery, and that of the Church unceasing. For this purpose we have labored to secure the friendship of the governor of this state, with all the principal men in this place. In this we have succeeded beyond our highest anticipations. Governor Carlin assured us last evening, that he would lay our case before the legislature of this state, and have the action of that body upon it; and he would use all his influence to have an action which should be favorable to our people. He is also getting papers prepared signed by all the noted men in this part of the country, to give us a favorable reception at Washington, whither we shall repair forthwith, after having visited the Governor of Iowa, of whose frienship we have the strongest testimonies. We leave Quincy this day to visit him. Our plan of operation is to impeach the state of Missouri on an item of the Constitution of the United States; that the general government shall give to each state a Republican form of government. Such a form of government does not exist in Missouri, and we can prove it.

Governor Carlin and his lady enter with all the enthusiasm of their natures into this work, having no doubt but that we can accomplish this object.

Our plan of operation in this work is, to get all the governors, in their next messages, to have the subject brought before the legislatures; and we will have a man at the capital of each state to furnish them with the testimony on the subject; and we design to be at Washington to wait upon Congress, and have the action of that body on it also; all this going on at the same time, and have the action of the whole during one session.

Brother George W. Robinson will be engaged all the time between this and the next sitting of the legislatures, in taking affidavits, and preparing for the tug of war; while we will be going from state to state, visiting the respective governors, to get the case mentioned in their respective messages to legislatures, so as to have the whole going on at once. You will see by this that our time is engrossed to overflowing.

The Bishops of the Church are required to ride and visit all scattered abroad, and to collect money to carry on this great work.

Be assured, brethren, that operations of an all-important character are under motion, and will come to an issue as soon as possible. Be assured that our friendship is unabated for you, and our desires for your deliverance intense. May God hasten it speedily, is our prayer day and night.

Yours in the bonds of affliction,

SIDNEY RIGDON.

To Joseph Smith, Jun., Hyrum Smith, Caleb Baldwin, Lyman Wight, Alexander McRae.

*Letter of Alanson Ripley to the Prophet.**

QUINCY, ILLINOIS, April 10, 1839.

Dear Brethren in Christ Jesus:

It is with feelings of no small moment that I take pen in hand to address you, the prisoners of Jesus Christ, and in the same faith of the

*It must be remembered that this letter was written under very great stress of feeling, and that accounts for its general harshness. It should also be remembered that as Edmund Burke said a long while ago—and it is now accepted as a trueism—"It is not fair to judge of the temper or disposition of any man, or any set of men when they are composed and at rest, from their conduct or their expressions in a state of disturbance and irritation."

Gospel with myself—who are holden by the cords of malice and of hellish plottings against the just, and through the lifting up the heel against the Lord's anointed; but they shall soon fall and not rise again, for their destruction is sure; and no power beneath the heavens can save them.

President Rigdon is wielding a mighty shaft against the whole host of foul calumniators and mobocrats of Missouri. Yesterday he spent a part of the day with Governor Carlin of this state. President Rigdon told him that he was informed that Governor Boggs was calculating to take out a bench warrant for himself and others, and then make a demand of his excellency for them to be given up, to be taken back to Missouri for trial; and he was assured by that noble-minded hero, that if Mr. Boggs undertook the thing, he would get himself insulted. He also assured him that the people called "Mormons" should find a permanent protection in this state. He also solicited our people, one and all, to settle in this state, and if there could be a tract of country that would suit our convenience, he would use his influence for Congress to make a grant of it to us, to redress our wrongs, and make up our losses.

We met last night in council of the whole, and passed some resolutions with respect to sending to the city of Washington. We are making every exertion possible that lies in our power, to accomplish that grand object upon which hangs our temporal salvation; and interwoven with this, our eternal salvation; and so closely allied to each other are they, that I want to see the head connected with the body again; and while we are enjoying one, let us be ripening for the other. But my heart says, Where is he whose lips used to whisper the words of life to us? Alas! he is in the hands of Zion's enemies. O Lord! crieth my heart, will not heaven hear our prayers, and witness our tears! Yes, saith the the Spirit, thy tears are all remembered, and shall speedily be rewarded with the deliverance of thy dearly beloved brethren.

But when I see the fearful apprehensions of some of our brethren, it causes me to mourn. One instance I will mention. When I arrived at Far West I made my mind known to some of the community, and told them that I wanted they should send a messenger to the jail to communicate with you; but my request was denied. They said that the Presidency was so anxious to be free once more, that they would not consider the danger the Church was in.

They met in council and passed resolutions that myself, Amasa Lyman, and Watson Barlow, should leave Far West for Quincy forthwith. My spirit has been grieved ever since, so that I can hardly hold my peace; but there is a God in Israel that can blast the hellish desires and designs of that infernal banditti, whose hands have been imbrued in the blood of the martyrs and Saints. They wish to destroy the Church of

God; but their chain is short; there is just enough left to bind their own hands with.

Dear brethren, I am at your service, and I await your counsel at Quincy, and shall be happy to grant you the desire of your hearts. I am ready to act. Please to give me all the intelligence that is in your power. If you take a change of venue, let me know what county you will come to, and when, as near as possible, and what road you will come; for I shall be an adder in the path.

Yes, my dear brethren, God Almighty will deliver you. Fear not, for your redemption draweth near; the day of your deliverance is at hand.

Dear brethren, I have it in my heart to lay my body in the sand, or deliver you from your bonds; and my mind is intensely fixed on the latter.

Dear brethren, you will be able to judge of the spirit that actuates my breast; for when I realize your sufferings, my heart is like wax before the fire; but when I reflect upon the cause of your afflictions, it is like fire in my bones, and burns against your enemies, and I never can be satisfied, while there is one of them to stand against a wall, or draw a sword, or pull a trigger. My sword has never been sheathed in peace, for the blood of David W. Patten and those who were butchered at Haun's Mill, crieth for vengeance from the ground.

Therefore, hear O ye heavens! and write it, O ye recording angels! bear the tidings ye flaming seraphs! that I from this day declare myself the avenger of the blood of those innocent men, and of the innocent cause of Zion, and of her prisoners; and I will not rest until they are as free, who are in prison, as I am.

Your families are all well and in good spirits. May the Lord bless you all. Amen.

Brother Amasa Lyman and Watson Barlow join in saying, Our hearts are as thy heart. Brother Joseph, if my spirit is wrong, for God's sake correct it. Brethren, be of good cheer, for we are determined, as God liveth, to rescue you from that hellish crowd, or die in the furrow. We shall come face foremost.

ALANSON RIPLEY.

N. B.—S. B. Crockett says he has been once driven but not whipped; Brother Brigham Young sends his best respects to you all.

A. R.

Thursday April 11.—

Letter of Don Carlos Smith to His Brother, Hyrum Smith.

Brother Hyrum:

After reading a line from you to myself, and one to father, which awakens all the feelings of tenderness and brotherly affection that one heart is capable of containing, I sit down in haste to answer it. My health and that of my family is good; mother and Lucy have been very sick, but are getting better. Your families are in better health now than at any other period since your confinement.

Brother Hyrum, I am in hopes that my letter did not increase your trouble, for I know that your affliction is too great for human nature to bear; and if I did not know that there was a God in heaven, and that His promises are sure and faithful, and that He is your friend in the midst of all your trouble, I would fly to your relief, and either be with you in prison, or see you breathe free air—air too that had not been inhaled and corrupted by a pack of ruffians, who trample upon virtue and innocence with impunity; and are not even satisfied with the property and blood of the Saints, but must exult over the dead. You both have my prayers, my influence and warmest feelings, with a *fixed determination*, if it should so be that you should be destroyed, to *avenge* your blood four fold.

Joseph must excuse me for not writing to him at this time. Give my love to all the prisoners. Write to me as often as you can, and do not be worried about your families. Yours in affliction as well as in peace.

DON C. SMITH.

Letter of Agnes Smith to Hyrum and Joseph Smith.

Beloved Brothers, Hyrum and Joseph:

By the permit of my companion, I write a line to show that I have not forgotten you; neither do I forget you; for my prayer is to my Heavenly Father for your deliverance. It seems as though the Lord is slow to hear the prayers of the Saints. But the Lord's ways are not like our ways; therefore He can do better than we ourselves. You must be comforted, Brothers Hyrum and Joseph, and look forward for better days. Your little ones are as playful as little lambs; be comforted concerning them, for they are not cast down and sorrowful as we are; their sorrows are only momentary but ours continual.

May the Lord bless, protect, and deliver you from all your enemies and restore you to the bosom of your families, is the prayer of

AGNES M. SMITH.

To Hyrum and Joseph Smith, Liberty, Missouri.

The examination of witnesses was continued, and Elder Markham was permitted to give his testimony. After he had closed, Blakely, one of the guard, came in and said to Markham, that he wanted to speak to him. Brother

Markham walked out with him, and around the end of the house when Blakely called out, "—— —— you —— old Mormon; I'll kill you;" and struck at Markham with his fist and then with a club. Markham took the club from him and threw it over the fence.

Attempt upon the Life of Stephen Markham.

There were ten of the mob who immediately rushed upon Markham to kill him, Colonel William P. Peniston, captain of the guard, being one of the number. But Markham told them he could kill the whole of them at one blow apiece, and drove them off. The court and grand jury stood and saw the affray, and heard the mob threaten Markham's life, by all the oaths they could invent, but they took no cognizance of it.

The ten mobbers went home after their guns to shoot Markham, and the grand jury brought in a bill for "murder, treason, burglary, arson, larceny, theft, and stealing," against Lyman Wight, Alexander McRae, Caleb Baldwin, Hyrum Smith and myself.

A "True Bill" Found against the Prisoners.

This evening the committee [on removal] assembled at Daniel Shearer's. After prayer by Brother James Newberry, he was ordained an Elder on the recommendation of Elder Heber C. Kimball, under the hands of Hiram Clark and William Huntington.

Meeting of the Committee on Removal.

Elder Kimball reported that Jessie P. Maupin, the thirty-dollar messenger they had sent to us, had returned; that the prisoners were well and in good spirits.

Brother Rogers who had returned from Jackson county, reported that he had sold all the lands in Jackson. Elder Kimball was requested to attend a meeting of the Daviess county officials tomorrow, and as an individual, mention the case of the committee [on removal] and the brethren generally, and learn their feelings, whether they would protect the brethren from the abuse of the mob, in case they came im-

Sale of Jackson County Lands.

mediately to drive them out, as they had recently threatened.

During this night the visions of the future were opened to my understanding; when I saw the ways and means and near approach of my escape from imprisonment, and the danger that my beloved Brother Markham was in. I awoke Brother Markham, and told him if he would rise very early and not wait for the judge and lawyers, as he had contemplated doing, but rise briskly, he would get safe home, almost before he was aware of it; and if he did not the mob would shoot him on the way; and I told him to tell the brethren to be of good cheer, but lose no time in removing from the country.

Vision of the Prophet for Markham's safety

Friday, April 12.—This morning Brother Markham arose at dawn of day, and rode rapidly towards Far West, where he arrived before nine a. m. The mobbers pursued to shoot him, but did not overtake him.

Escape of Markham.

This day I received the following letter:

Jacob Stollings' Communication to the Prophet.

DEAR SIR:—Enclosed I send you the receipt which I promised; and if you will pay the necessary attention to it, it will be a benefit to the Church and to me; and I think with a little attention on your part, they can be produced; and any person who will deliver them at any point in the state, so I can get them, I will compensate them well, as I know you feel deeply interested in the welfare of the Church; and when you consider it will add to their character, and look upon it in a proper light, you will spare no pains in assisting me in the recovery of those books.

Yours, etc., in haste,

JACOB STOLLINGS.

To Joseph Smith, Jun., Diahman.

GALLATIN, DAVIESS COUNTY, MISSOURI,
April 12, 1839.

Know all men by these presents—That I, Jacob Stollings, have this day agreed with Joseph Smith, Jun., to release all members of the Mormon Church, from any and all debts due to me from them for goods sold to them by me at Gallatin during the year 1838, on the following condition, viz.: That said Joseph Smith, Jun., return or cause to be returned to me the following books—one ledger, three day books, and one day book of groceries, which was taken from my store in Gallatin when said store was burned. And if said books are returned to me within four months, this shall be a receipt in full, to all intents and purposes, against any debt or debts due from said Mormons to me on said books; but if not returned, this is to be null and void.

Given under my hand this day and date before written.

JACOB STOLLINGS.

Attest, J. Lynch.

The Prophet's Comments.

A curious idea, that I who had been a prisoner many months should be called upon to hunt up lost property, or property most likely destroyed by the mob; but it is no more curious than a thousand other things that have happened; and I feel to do all I can to oblige any of my fellow creatures.

Isaac Galland's Communication to the Quincy Argus.

COMMERCE, ILLINOIS, April 12, 1839.

MESSRS. EDITORS:—Enclosed I send you a communication from Governor Lucas of Iowa territory. If you think the publication thereof will in any way promote the cause of justice, by vindicating the slandered reputation of the people called "Mormons," from the ridiculous falsehoods which the malice, cupidity and envy of their murderers in Missouri have endeavored to heap upon them, you are respectfully solicited to publish it in the *Argus*. The testimony of Governor Lucas as to the good moral character of these people, I think will have its deserved influence upon the people of Illinois, in encouraging our citizens in their humane and benevolent exertions to relieve this distressed people, who are now wandering in our neighborhoods without comfortable food, raiment, or a shelter from the pelting storm.

I am, gentlemen, very respectfully,
Your obedient servant,
ISAAC GALLAND.

Letter of Robert Lucas, Governor of the Territory of Iowa, Respecting the Manner in Which the Saints Might Hope to be Received and Treated in Iowa.

EXECUTIVE OFFICE, IOWA, BURLINGTON,
March, 1839.

DEAR SIR:—On my return to this city, after a few weeks' absence in the interior of the territory, I received your letter of the 25th ultimo, in which you give a short account of the sufferings of the people called Mormons and ask "whether they could be permitted to purchase lands and settle upon them, in the territory of Iowa, and there worship Almighty God according to the dictates of their own consciences, secure from oppression," etc.

In answer to your inquiry, I would say that I know of no authority that can constitutionally deprive them of this right. They are citizens of the United States, and are entitled to all the rights and privileges of other citizens. The 2nd section of the 4th Article of the Constitution of the United States (which all are solemnly bound to support) declares that "the citizens of each state shall be entitled to all the privileges and immunities of citizens of the several states." This privilege extends in full force to the territories of the United States. The first amendment to the Constitution of the United States, declares that "Congress shall make no law respecting an establishment of religion, or prohibiting the free exercise thereof."

The ordinance of Congress of the 13th July, 1787, for the government of the territory northwest of the river Ohio, secures to the citizens of said territory, and the citizens of the states thereafter to be formed therein, certain privileges which were by the late Act of Congress organizing the territory of Iowa, extended to the citizens of this territory.

The first fundamental Article in the Ordinance, which is declared to be forever unalterable, except by common consent, reads as follows, to wit: "No person demeaning himself in a peaceable and orderly manner, shall ever be molested on account of his mode of worship or religious sentiment in said territory."

These principles I trust will ever be adhered to in the territory of Iowa. They make no distinction between religious sects. They extend equal privileges and protection to all; each must rest upon its own merits, and will prosper in proportion to the purity of its principles, and the fruit of holiness and piety produced thereby.

With regard to the peculiar people mentioned in your letter, I know but little. They had a community in the northern part of Ohio for several years; and I have no recollection of ever having heard in that state of any complaints against them for violating the laws of the country. Their religious opinions I consider have nothing to do with our political transactions. They are citizens of the United States, and are entitled to the same political rights and legal protection that other citizens are entitled to.

The foregoing are briefly my views on the subject of your inquiries.

With sincere respect,

I am your obedient servant,

ROBERT LUCAS.

To Isaac Galland, Esq., Commerce, Illinois.

Saturday, April 13.—Elder Markham went to Independence to close the business of the Church in that region.

Sunday, April 14.—The committee [on removal] in council resolved to send Sisters Fosdick and Meeks, and Brother William Monjar and another family, with Brothers Jones, Burton, and Barlow's teams. which had recently arrived at Quincy.

Activity of the Committee on Removal.

The committee moved thirty-six families into Tenney's Grove, about twenty-five miles from Far West; and a few men were appointed to chop wood for them, while Brother Turley was to furnish them with meal and meat, until they could be removed to Quincy. The corn was ground at the committee's horse mill, in Far West. Elder Kimball was obliged to secrete himself in the cornfields during the day, and was in at night counseling the committee and brethren.

Monday, April 15.—Having procured a change of venue we started for Boone county, and were conducted to that place by a strong guard.

The Prophet and Fellow Prisoners Start for Boone county.

This evening the committee [on removal] met to make arrangements concerning teams and the moving of the few families who yet remained at Far West.

Letter of Elias Higbee to Joseph Smith, Jun., and Fellow Prisoners.

TUESDAY, QUINCY, April 16, 1839.

To Joseph Smith, Jun., and others, Prisoners in Liberty or Elsewhere, Greeting:

DEAR BRETHREN IN AFFLICTION:—Through the mercy and providence of God, I am here alive, and in tolerable health, as also are all of your families, as far as I know, having heard from them lately, and having seen Sister Emma yesterday.

Brethren, I have sorrow of heart when I think of your great sufferings by that ungodly mob which has spread such desolation and caused so much suffering among us. I often reflect on the scenes which we passed through together; the course we pursued; the counselings we had; the results which followed, when harassed, pressed on every side insulted and abused by that lawless banditti; and I am decidedly of opinion that the hand of the Great God hath controlled the whole business for purposes of His own, which will eventually work out good for the Saints (I mean those who are worthy of the name). I know that your intentions, and the intentions of all the worthy Saints, have been pure, and tending to do good to all men, and to injure no man in person or property, except we were forced to it in defense of our lives.

Brethren, I am aware that I cannot wholly realize your sufferings; neither can any other person who has not experienced the like afflictions; but I doubt not for a moment, neither have I ever doubted for a moment, that the same God which delivered me from their grasp (though narrowly) will deliver you. I staid near Far West for about three weeks, being hunted by them almost every day; and as I learned, they did not intend to give me the chance of a trial, but put an end to me forthwith, I went for my horse and left the wicked clan and came off. Francis* is with his uncle in Ohio. I received a letter lately from him; he is strong in the faith. I now live in the Big-Neck-Prairie, on the same farm with President Rigdon, who is here with me and waiting for me with his riding dress on, to go home. So I must necessarily close, praying God to speedily deliver you, and bless you.

From yours in the bonds of the everlasting love,

ELIAS HIGBEE.

The Prophet's Reasons for Escaping from the Officers of the Law.

This evening our guard got intoxicated. We thought it a favorable opportunity to make our escape; knowing that the only object of our enemies was our destruction; and likewise knowing that a number of our brethren had been massacred by them on Shoal Creek, amongst whom were two children; and that they sought every opportunity to abuse others who were left in that state; and that they were never brought to an account for their barbarous proceedings, which were winked at and encouraged by those in authority. We thought that it was necessary for us, inasmuch as we loved our lives, and did not wish to die by the hand of murderers and assassins; and inasmuch as we loved our families and friends, to deliver ourselves from our enemies, and from that land of tyranny and oppression, and again take our stand among a people

*This refers to Francis M. Higbee, son of Elias Higbee

in whose bosoms dwell those feelings of republicanism and liberty which gave rise to our nation: feelings which the inhabitants of the State of Missouri were strangers to. Accordingly, we took advantage of the situation of our guard and departed, and that night we traveled a considerable distance.*

* Undoubtedly the guards, and for matter of that Judge Birch himself, and also the ex-sheriff of Daviess county, William Bowman, connived at the escape of the prisoners. The story of the escape was afterwards told in detail by Hyrum Smith, as follows: "They got us a change of venue from Daviess to Boone county, and a mittimus was made out by the pretended Judge Birch, without date, name, or place. They [the court officials at Gallatin] fitted us out with a two horse wagon, a horse and four men, besides the sheriff, to be our guard. There were five of us that started from Gallatin, the sun about two hours high, and went as far as Diahman that evening, and stayed till morning. There we bought two horses of the guard. and paid for one of them in our clothing which we had with us, and for the other we gave our note. We went down that day as far as Judge Morin's, a distance of some four or five miles. There we stayed until the next morning, when we started on our journey to Boone county, and traveled on the road about twenty miles distance. There we bought a jug of whisky, with which we treated the company, and while there the sheriff showed us the mittimus before referred to, without date or signature, and said that Judge Birch told him never to carry us to Boone county, and never to show the mittimus; and, said he, I shall take a good drink of grog, and go to bed, and you may do as you have a mind to. Three others of the guards drank pretty freely of the whisky, sweetened with honey. They also went to bed, and were soon asleep and the other guard went along with us, and helped to saddle the horses. Two of us mounted the horses, and the other three started on foot, and we took our change of venue for the State of Illinois; and in the course of nine or ten days arrived safely at Quincy, Adams county, where we found our families in a state of poverty, although in good health." (From the affidavit of Hyrum Smith before the municipal court of Nauvoo, given July 1, 1843.)

The name of the sheriff in charge of the prisoners was William Morgan, and upon his return to Gallatin both he and the ex-sheriff, William Bowman, who was suspected of complicity in the escape of the prisoners, received harsh treatment at the hands of the citizens of that place. The story is told in the "History of Daviess County," published by Birdsall & Dean, 1882, as follows: "The prisoners took change of venue to Boone county, and the Daviess county officers started with the prisoners to their destination in Boone county. Some of the prisoners having no horses, William Bowman, the first sheriff of Daviess county, [and now ex-sheriff], furnished the prisoners three horses, and they left in charge of William Morgan, the sheriff of the county. The sheriff alone returned on horseback, the guard who accompanied him returning on foot, or riding and tying by turns. The sheriff reported that the prisoners had all escaped in the night, taking the horses with them, and that a search made for them proved unavailing. The people of Gallatin were greatly exercised, and they disgraced themselves by very ruffianly conduct. They rode the sheriff on a rail, and Bowman was dragged over the square by the hair of the head. The men guilty of these dastardly acts, accused sheriff Morgan and ex-Sheriff Bowman of complicity in the escape of the Mormon leaders; that Bowman furnished the horses, and that Morgan allowed them to escape, and both got well paid for their treachery. The truth of history compels us

Wednesday, April 17.—We prosecuted our journey towards Illinois, keeping off from the main road as much as possible, which impeded our progress.

Elder Kimball's Warning to the Committee.

Thursday, April 18.—This morning Elder Kimball went into the committee room and told the committee [on removal] to wind up their affairs and be off, or their lives would be taken. Stephen Markham had gone over the Missouri river on business. Elders Turley and Shearer were at Far West.

Attack on Theodore Turley.

Twelve men went to Elder Turley's with loaded rifles to shoot him. They broke seventeen clocks into match wood. They broke tables, smashed in the windows; while Bogart (the county judge) looked on and laughed. One Whitaker threw iron pots at Turley, one of which hit him on the shoulder, at which Whitaker jumped and laughed like a madman. The mob shot down cows while the girls were milking them. The mob threatened to send the committee "to hell jumping," and "put daylight through them."

The Mob's Assault on Elder Kimball.

The same day, previous to the breaking of the clocks, some of the same company met Elder Kimball on the public square in Far West, and asked him if he was a "—— Mormon;" he replied, "I am a Mormon." "Well, —— —— you, we'll blow your brains out, you —— —— Mormon," and tried to ride over him with their horses. This was in the presence of Elias Smith, Theodore Turley, and others of the committee.

The Mob Loots Far West.

The brethren gathered up what they could and left Far West in one hour; and the mob staid until they left, then plundered thousands of dollars' worth of property which had been left by the exiled brethren and sisters to help the poor to remove.

One mobber rode up, and finding no convenient place

to state that the charges were never sustained by any evidence adduced by the persons who committed this flagrant act of mob law."—See above named history, page 206.

to fasten his horse, shot a cow that was standing near, and while the poor animal was yet struggling in death, he cut a strip of her hide from her nose to the tip of her tail, this he tied round a stump, to which he fastened his halter.

During the commotion this day, a great portion of the records of the committee, accounts, history, etc., were destroyed or lost, so that but few definite items can be registered in their place.

The Loss of Records, Accounts, etc.

When the Saints commenced removing from Far West they shipped as many families and goods as possible at Richmond to go down the Missouri river to Quincy, Illinois. This mission was in charge of Elder Levi Richards and Reuben Hedlock, who were appointed by the committee.

Flight of the Saints *via* Missouri River.

I continued on my journey with my brethren towards Quincy.

Elder David W. Rogers made a donation of money to remove the poor from Missouri.

Assistance for the Poor.

The brethren and sisters who had arrived in Illinois were beginning to write of their sufferings and losses in Missouri. The statement of Sister Amanda Smith, written by her own hand, I will here insert:

Narrative of Amanda Smith Respecting the Massacre at Haun's Mills.

To whom this may come:

I do hereby certify that my husband, Warren Smith,in company with several other families,was moving [in 1838]from Ohio to Missouri. We came to Caldwell county. Whilst we were traveling, minding our own business, we were stopped by a mob; they told us that if we went another step, they would kill us all. They took our guns from us (as we were going into a new country, we took guns along with us); they took us back five miles, placed a guard around us, kept us three days, and then let us go.

I thought—Is this our boasted land of liberty? for some said we must deny our faith, or they would kill us; others said, we should die at any rate.

The names of this mob, or the heads, were Thomas O'Brien, county clerk; Jefferson Brien, William Ewell, Esq., and James Austin, all of Livingston county. After they let us go we traveled ten miles, came to a small town composed of one grist mill, one saw mill, and eight or ten houses belonging to our brethren; there we stopped for the night.

A little before sunset a mob of three hundred came upon us. The men hallooed for the women and children to run for the woods; and they ran into an old blacksmith's shop, for they feared, if we all ran together, they would rush upon us and kill the women and children. The mob fired before we had time to start from our camp. Our men took off their hats and swung them, and cried "quarters" until they were shot. The mob paid no attention to their cries nor entreaties, but fired alternately.

I took my little girls, my boy I could not find, and started for the woods. The mob encircled us on all sides but the brook. I ran down the bank, across the mill-pond on a plank, up the hill into the bushes. The bullets whistled around me all the way like hail, and cut down the bushes on all sides of us. One girl was wounded by my side, and fell over a log, and her clothes hung across the log; and they shot at them, expecting they were hitting her; and our people afterwards cut out of that log twenty bullets.

I sat down and witnessed the dreadful scene. When they had done firing, they began to howl, and one would have thought that all the infernals had come from the lower regions. They plundered the principal part of our goods, took our horses and wagons, and ran off howling like demons.

I came down to view the awful sight. Oh horrible! My husband, and one son ten years old, lay lifeless upon the ground, and one son seven years old, wounded very badly. The ground was covered with the dead. These little boys crept under the bellows in the shop; one little boy of ten years had three wounds in him; he lived five weeks and died; he was not mine.

Realize for a moment the scene! It was sunset; nothing but horror and distress; the dogs filled with rage, howling over their dead masters; the cattle caught the scent of the innocent blood, and bellowed; a dozen helpless widows, thirty or forty fatherless children, crying and moaning for the loss of their fathers and husbands; the groans of the wounded and dying were enough to have melted the heart of anything but a Missouri mob.

There were fifteen dead, and ten wounded; two died the next day. There were no men, or not enough to bury the dead; so they were thrown into a dry well and covered with dirt. The next day the mob came back. They told us we must leave the state forthwith, or be killed. It was cold weather, and they had our teams and clothes, our husbands were dead or wounded. I told them they might kill me and my children, and welcome. They sent word to us from time to time that if we did not leave the state, they would come and kill us. We had little prayer meetings. They said if we did not stop them they would kill every man, woman and child. We had spelling schools for our little children; they said if we did not stop them they would kill every man, woman and child. We did our own milking, got our own wood; no man to help us.

I started the first of February for Illinois, without money, (mob all the way), drove my own team, slept out of doors. I had five small children; we suffered hunger, fatigue and cold; for what? For our religion, where, in a boasted land of liberty, "Deny your faith or die," was the cry.

I will mention some of the names of the heads of the mob: two brothers by the name of Comstock, William Mann, Benjamin Ashley, Robert White, one by the name of Rogers, who took an old scythe and cut an old white-headed man all to pieces. [Thomas McBride.]

I wish further also to state, that when the mob came upon us (as I was told by one of them afterwards), their intention was to kill everything belonging to us, that had life; and that after our men were shot down by them, they went around and shot all the dead men over again, to make sure of their death.

I now leave it with this Honorable Government [the United States] to say what my damages may be, or what they would be willing to see their wives and children slaughtered for, as I have seen my husband, son and others.

I lost in property by the mob—to goods stolen, fifty dollars; one pocketbook, and fifty dollars cash notes; damage of horses and time, one hundred dollars; one gun, ten dollars; in short, my all. Whole damages are more than the State of Missouri is worth.

Written by my own hand, this 18th day of April, 1839.

AMANDA SMITH.

Quincy, Adams County, Illinois.

Thus are the cries of the widows and the fatherless ascending to heaven. How long, O Lord, wilt thou not avenge the blood of the Saints?*

Friday, April 19.—Elders Turley and Clark had traveled but a few miles from Far West when an axle-tree broke,

* The number of killed and wounded in the tragedy at Haun's Mills, [according to information supplied by the late Church Historian, Franklin D. Richards, to the "National Historical Company," St. Louis, Missouri, which issued a history of

and Brother Clark had to go to Richmond after some boxes, which delayed them some days.

Saturday, April 20.—The last of the Saints left Far West.

Sunday, April 21.—I had still continued my journey.

Caldwell and Livingston counties, in 1886], are seventeen of the former and thirteen of the latter; and their names are given as follows:

KILLED.

Thomas McBride,	Simon Cox,
Levi N. Merrick,	Hiram Abbott,
Elias Benner,	John York,
Josiah Fuller,	John Lee,
Benjamin Lewis,	John Myers,
Alexander Campbell,	Warren Smith,
George S. Richards,	Sardius Smith, aged 10,
William Napier,	Charles Merrick, aged 9.
Augustine Harner,	

WOUNDED.

Isaac Laney,	Jacob Haun, (founder of the Mills),
Nathan K. Knight,	Jacob Foutz,
Jacob Myers,	Jacob Potts,
George Myers,	Charles Jimison,
William Yokum,	John Walker,
Tarlton Lewis,	Alma Smith, aged 7 years.

A young Mormon woman, Miss Mary Stedwell, was shot through the hand, as she was running to the woods.

Following this statement concerning the killed and wounded among the Saints, the history above referred to, also says: "The militia, or Jennings' men, had but three men wounded, and none killed. John Renfrow, now [1886] living in Ray county, had a thumb shot off. Allen England, a Daviess county man, was severely wounded in the thigh, and the other wounded man was named Hart.

"*Dies irae!* What a woeful day this had been to Haun's Mills! What a pitiful scene was there when the militia rode away upon the conclusion of their bloody work! The wounded men had been given no attention, and the bodies of the slain were left to fester and putrify in the Indian summer temperature, warm and mellowing. The widows and orphans of the dead came timidly and warily forth from their hiding places as soon as the troops left, and as they recognized one a husband, another a father, another a son, another a brother among the bloody corpses, the wailings of grief and terror that went up were pitiful and agonizing. All that night they were alone with their dead. A return visit of Jennings' men to complete the work of 'extermination' had been threatened and was expected. Verily, the experience of the poor survivors of the Haun's Mills affair was terrible; no wonder that they long remember it."—History of Caldwell and Livingston Counties, Missouri. National Historical Company, 1886.

CHAPTER XXII.

THE PROPHET'S ACCOUNT OF HIS EXPERIENCES IN MISSOURI —FULFILLMENT OF A PROPHETIC REVELATION—COMPLETE EXODUS OF THE SAINTS FROM MISSOURI.

Monday, April 22.—We continued on our journey, both by night and by day; and after suffering much fatigue and hunger, I arrived in Quincy, Illinois, amidst the congratulations of my friends, and the embraces of my family, whom I found as well as could be expected, considering what they had been called to endure. Before leaving Missouri I had paid the lawyers at Richmond thirty-four thousand dollars in cash, lands, etc.; one lot which I let them have, in Jackson county, for seven thousand dollars, they were soon offered ten thousand dollars for it, but would not accept it. For other vexatious suits which I had to contend against the few months I was in this state, I paid lawyers' fees to the amount of about sixteen thousand dollars, making in all about fifty thousand dollars, for which I received very little in return; for sometimes they were afraid to act on account of the mob, and sometimes they were so drunk as to incapacitate them for business. But there were a few honorable exceptions.

The Prophet and Companions Continue their Flight.

Among those who have been the chief instruments and leading characters in the cruel persecutions against the Church of Latter-day Saints, the following stand conspicuous, viz.: Generals Clark, Wilson and Lucas, Colonel Price, and Cornelius Gillium; Captain Bogart also, whose zeal in the cause of oppression and injustice was unequalled, and whose delight has been to rob, murder, and

The Leading Characters in the Persecutions of the Saints.

spread devastation among the Saints. He stole a valuable horse, saddle, and bridle from me, which cost two hundred dollars, and then sold the same to General Wilson. On understanding this, I applied to General Wilson for the horse, who assured me, upon the honor of a gentleman and an officer, that I should have the horse returned to me; but this promise has not been fulfilled.

All the threats, murders, and robberies, which these officers have been guilty of, are entirely overlooked by the executive of the state; who, to hide his own iniquity, must of course shield and protect those whom he employed to carry into effect his murderous purposes.

Part of Governor Boggs in the Persecutions.

I was in their hands, as a prisoner, about six months; but notwithstanding their determination to destroy me, with the rest of my brethren who were with me, and although at three different times (as I was informed) we were sentenced to be shot, without the least shadow of law (as we were not military men), and had the time and place appointed for that purpose, yet through the mercy of God, in answer to the prayers of the Saints, I have been preserved and delivered out of their hands, and can again enjoy the society of my friends and brethren, whom I love, and to whom I feel united in bonds that are stronger than death; and in a state where I believe the laws are respected, and whose citizens are humane and charitable.

Treatment of the Prophet by the Mob.

During the time I was in the hands of my enemies, I must say, that although I felt great anxiety respecting my family and friends, who were so inhumanly treated and abused, and who had to mourn the loss of their husbands and children who had been slain, and, after having been robbed of nearly all that they possessed, were driven from their homes, and forced to wander as strangers in a strange country, in order that they might save themselves and their little ones from the destruction they were threatened

Calm Assurance of the Prophet Respecting his own Safety.

with in Missouri, yet as far as I was concerned, I felt perfectly calm, and resigned to the will of my Heavenly Father. I knew my innocence as well as that of the Saints, and that we had done nothing to deserve such treatment from the hands of our oppressors. Consequently, I could look to that God who has the lives of all men in His hands, and who had saved me frequently from the gates of death, for deliverance; and notwithstanding that every avenue of escape seemed to be entirely closed, and death stared me in the face, and that my destruction was determined upon, as far as man was concerned, yet, from my first entrance into the camp, I felt an assurance that I, with my brethren and our families, should be delivered. Yes, that still small voice, which has so often whispered consolation to my soul, in the depths of sorrow and distress, bade me be of good cheer, and promised deliverance, which gave me great comfort.* And although the heathen raged, and the people imagined vain things, yet the Lord of Hosts, the God of Jacob was my refuge; and when I cried unto Him in the day of trouble, He de livered me; for which I call upon my soul, and all that is within me, to bless and praise His holy name. For although I was "troubled on every side, yet not distressed; perplexed, but not in despair; persecuted, but not forsaken; cast down, but not destroyed."

Deportment of the Saints.

The conduct of the Saints, under their accumulated wrongs and sufferings, has been praiseworthy; their courage in defending their brethren from the ravages of the mobs; their attachment to the cause of truth, under circumstances the most trying and distressing which humanity can possibly endure; their love to each other; their readiness to afford assistance to me and my brethren who were confined in a dungeon; their sacrifices in leaving Missouri, and assisting the poor widows and orphans, and securing them houses in a more hospitable

*See the prediction of the Prophet on the safety of himself and fellow prisoners, this volume, p. 200, note.

land; all conspire to raise them in the estimation of all good and virtuous men, and has secured them the favor and approbation of Jehovah, and a name as imperishable as eternity. And their virtuous deeds and heroic actions, while in defense of truth and their brethren, will be fresh and blooming when the names of their oppressors shall be either entirely forgotten, or only remembered for their barbarity and cruelty.

Their attention and affection to me, while in prison, will ever be remembered by me; and when I have seen them thrust away and abused by the jailer and guard, when they came to do any kind offices, and to cheer our minds while we were in the gloomy prison-house, gave me feelings which I cannot describe; while those who wished to insult and abuse us by their threats and blasphemous language, were applauded, and had every encouragement given them.

Sure Reward of the Faithful Saints.

However, thank God, we have been delivered. And although some of our beloved brethren have had to seal their testimony with their blood, and have died martyrs to the cause of truth—

> Short though bitter was their pain,
> Everlasting is their joy.

Let us not sorrow as "those without hope;" the time is fast approaching when we shall see them again and rejoice together, without being afraid of wicked men. Yes, those who have slept in Christ, shall He bring with Him, when He shall come to be glorified in His Saints, and admired by all those who believe, but to take vengeance upon His enemies and all those who obey not the Gospel.

At that time the hearts of the widows and fatherless shall be comforted, and every tear shall be wiped from their faces. The trials they have had to pass through shall work together for their good, and prepare them for the society of those who have come up out of great tribulation, and have washed their robes and made them white in the blood of the Lamb.

The Saints not to Marvel at Persecution.

Marvel not, then, if you are persecuted; but remember the words of the Savior: "The servant is not above his Lord; if they have persecuted me, they will persecute you also;" and that all the afflictions through which the Saints have to pass, are the fulfillment of the words of the Prophets which have spoken since the world began.

We shall therefore do well to discern the signs of the times as we pass along, that the day of the Lord may not "overtake us as a thief in the night." Afflictions, persecutions, imprisonments, and death, we must expect, according to the scriptures, which tell us that the blood of those whose souls were under the altar could not be avenged on them that dwell on the earth, until their brethren should be slain as they were.

The Crime of Missouri to be Viewed in the Light of the Civilized Age in which it was Committed.

If these transactions had taken place among barbarians, under the authority of a despot, or in a nation where a certain religion is established according to law, and all others proscribed, then there might have been some shadow of defense offered. But can we realize that in a land which is the cradle of liberty and equal rights, and where the voice of the conquerors who had vanquished our foes had scarcely died away upon our ears, where we frequently mingled with those who had stood amidst "the battle and the breeze," and whose arms have been nerved in the defense of their country and liberty, whose institutions are the theme of philosophers and poets, and held up to the admiration of the whole civilized world—in the midst of all these scenes, with which we were surrounded, a persecution the most unwarrantable was commenced, and a tragedy the most dreadful was enacted, by a large portion of the inhabitants of one of those free and sovereign states which comprise this vast Republic; and a deadly blow was struck at the institutions for which our fathers had fought many a hard battle, and for which many a patriot had shed his blood. Suddenly was heard, amidst the voice of joy and gratitude for our national liberty, the voice of mourning, lamentation and woe. Yes! in this land, a mob, regardless of those laws for which so much blood had been spilled, dead to every feeling of virtue and patriotism which animated the bosom of freemen, fell upon a people whose religious faith was different from their own, and not only destroyed their homes, drove them away, and carried off their property, but murdered many a free-born son of America—a tragedy which has no parallel in modern, and hardly in ancient, times; even the face of the red man would be ready to turn pale at the recital of it. It would have been some consolation, if the authorities of the state had been innocent in this affair; but they are involved in the guilt thereof, and the blood of innocence, even of children, cry for vengeance upon them.

The Appeal of the Prophet to the People of the United States.

I ask the citizens of this Republic whether such a state of things is to be suffered to pass unnoticed, and the hearts of widows, orphans, and patriots to be broken, and their wrongs left without redress? No! I invoke the genius of our Constitution. I appeal to the patriotism of Americans to stop this unlawful and unholy procedure; and pray that God may defend this nation from the dreadful effects of such outrages.

Is there no virtue in the body politic? Will not the people rise up in their majesty, and with that promptitude and zeal which are so characteristic of them, discountenance such proceedings, by bringing the offenders to that punishment which they so richly deserve, and save the nation from that disgrace and ultimate ruin, which otherwise must inevitably fall upon it?

Pursuit of Elder Markham.

Elder Markham had closed his business in Jackson county and returned to Far West, having been chased as far as the river by the mob on horses at full speed, for the purpose of shooting him. Brother Markham tarried in and near Far West until the 24th of April.

On my arrival at Quincy I found the brethren had been diligent in preparing for an investigation of their wrongs in Missouri, as the following letters will show.

Letter of Governor Lucas of Iowa to Elder Rigdon.

BURLINGTON, IOWA TERRITORY,
April 22, 1839.

DEAR SIR:—I herewith enclose two letters, one addressed to the President of the United States, and one to Governor Shannon, of Ohio. As the object sought by you is an investigation into the facts connected with your misfortunes, I have thought it the most prudent course to refrain from an expression of an individual opinion in the matter, relative to the merits or demerits of the controversy. I sincerely hope that you may succeed in obtaining a general investigation into the cause and extent of your sufferings, and that you may obtain from the government that attention which is your due as citizens of the United States.

Very respectfully your obedient servant,
ROBERT LUCAS.

Doctor Sidney Rigdon.

Letter of Governor Lucas to President Martin Van Buren, Respecting the Latter-day Saints.

BURLINGTON, IOWA TERRITORY,
April 22, 1839.

To His Excellency, Martin Van Buren, President of the United States:

SIR:—I have the honor to introduce to your acquaintance, the bearer, Doctor Sidney Rigdon, who was for many years a citizen of the State of Ohio, and a firm supporter of the administration of the General Government.

Doctor Rigdon visits Washington (as I am informed) as the representative of a community of people called Mormons, to solicit from the Government of the United States, an investigation into the cause that led to their expulsion from the State of Missouri: together with the various circumstances connected with that extraordinary affair.

I think it due to that people to state, that they had for a number of years a community established in Ohio, and that while in that state they were (as far as I ever heard) believed to be an industrious, inoffensive people; and I have no recollection of having ever heard of any of them being charged in that state as violators of the laws.

With sincere respect, I am your obedient servant,

ROBERT LUCAS.

Letter of Governor Lucas to the Governor of Ohio Introducing President Rigdon.

BURLINGTON, IOWA TERRITORY,
April 22, 1839.

To His Excellency Wilson Shannon, Governor of the State of Ohio:

SIR:—I have the honor to introduce to your acquaintance, Doctor Sidney Rigdon, who was for many years a citizen of Ohio. Doctor Rigdon wishes to obtain from the General Government of the United States, an investigation into the causes that led to the expulsion of the people called Mormons from the State of Missouri; together with all the facts connected with that extraordinary affair. This investigation, it appears to me, is due them as citizens of the United States, as well as to the nation at large.

Any assistance that you can render the Doctor, towards accomplishing that desirable object, will be gratefully received and duly appreciated by your sincere friend and humble servant,

ROBERT LUCAS.

Letter of W. W. Phelps to John P. Greene.

FAR WEST, MISSOURI, April 23, 1839.

SIR:—The summit end of Mr. Benson's mill-dam was carried away by the late freshet, and, unless repaired, it will all go the next.

The committee have gone, and if Father Smith would send me a power of attorney, in connection with Mr. Benson's and Corrill's, I have a chance to sell it before it is all lost. Maybe I might save the old gentleman something, which I promised Hyrum I would do if possible, because they have now need. Will you have them do so?

W. W. PHELPS.

To John P. Greene, Quincy, Illinois.

All this day I spent in greeting and receiving visits from my brethren and friends, and truly it was a joyful time.

Wednesday, April 24.—Elder Parley P. Pratt and his fellow prisoners were brought before the grand jury of Ray county at Richmond, and Darwin Chase and Norman

Shearer were dismissed, after being imprisoned about six months. Mrs. Morris Phelps, who had been with her husband in prison some days, hoping he would be released, now parted from him, and, with her little infant, started for Illinois. The number of prisoners at Richmond was now reduced to four. King Follett having been added about the middle of April: he was dragged from his distressed family just as they were leaving the state. Thus of all the prisoners which were taken at an expense of two hundred thousand dollars, only two of the original ones who belonged to the Church, now remained (Luman Gibbs having denied the faith to try to save his life); these were Morris Phelps and Parley P. Pratt. All who were let to bail were banished from the state, together with those who bailed them.

Parley P. Pratt *et al.* Before the Grand Jury at Richmond.

Thus none are like to have a trial by law but Brothers Pratt and Phelps, and they are without friends or witnesses in the state.

Elders Clark and Turley met Alpheus Cutler, Brigham Young, Orson Pratt, George A. Smith, John Taylor, Wilford Woodruff, John E. Page, Daniel Shearer, and others, going up from Quincy to Far West, to fulfill the revelation on the 26th of April, and Clark and Turley turned and went back with them.

The Twelve en route for Far West,

Elder Markham visited at Tenney's Grove.

This evening I met the Church in council.

Minutes of a Council Meeting Held at Quincy, Illinois.

Minutes of a council held in Quincy on the 24th day of April, A. D. 1839, when President Joseph Smith, Jun., was called to the chair, and Brother Alanson Ripley chosen Clerk.

After prayer by the chairman, Elder John P. Greene arose and explained the object of the meeting. A document intended for publication was handed in, touching certain things relative to disorderly persons, who have represented or may represent themselves as belonging to our Church; which document was approved by the council. After which it was

Resolved first: That President Joseph Smith, Jun., Bishop Knight, and Brother Alanson Ripley, visit Iowa Territory immediately, for the purpose of making a location for the Church.

Resolved second: That the advice of the conference to the brethren in general is, that as many of them as are able, move north to Commerce, as soon as they possibly can.

Resolved third: That all the prisoners be received into fellowship.

Resolved fourth: That Brother Mulholland be appointed clerk *pro tem.*

Resolved fifth: That Father Smith's case relative to his circumstances, be referred to the Bishops.

Resolved sixth: That Brother Rogers receive some money to remunerate him for his services in transacting business for the Church in Missouri.

ALANSON RIPLEY, Clerk.

Seeking a New Location

Thursday, *April 25.*—I accompanied the committee to Iowa to select a location for the Saints. Elder Markham returned from Tenney's Grove to Far West, waiting the arrival of the brethren from Quincy.

Arrival of the Twelve at Far West.

Friday, *April 26.*—Early this morning, soon after midnight, the brethren arrived at Far West, and proceeded to transact the business of their mission according to the following minutes:

Minutes of the Meeting of the Twelve Apostles at Far West, April 26, 1839.

At a conference held at Far West by the Twelve, High Priests, Elders, and Priests, on the 26th day of April, 1839, the following resolution was adopted:

Resolved: That the following persons be no more fellowshiped in the Church of Jesus Christ of Latter-day Saints, but excommunicated from the same, viz.: Isaac Russell, Mary Russell, John Goodson and wife, Jacob Scott, Sen., and wife, Isaac Scott, Jacob Scott, Jun., Ann Scott, Sister Walton, Robert Walton, Sister Cavanaugh, Ann Wanlass, William Dawson, Jun., and wife, William Dawson, Sen., and wife, George Nelson, Joseph Nelson and wife and mother, William Warnock and wife, Jonathan Maynard, Nelson Maynard, George Miller, John Grigg and wife, Luman Gibbs, Simeon Gardner, and Freeborn Gardner.

The council then proceeded to the building spot of the Lord's House; when the following business was transacted: Part of a hymn was sung, on the mission of the Twelve.

Elder Alpheus Cutler, the master workman of the house, then recommenced laying the foundation of the Lord's House, agreeably to revelation, by rolling up a large stone near the southeast corner.

The following of the Twelve were present: Brigham Young, Heber C. Kimball, Orson Pratt, John E. Page, and John Taylor, who proceeded to ordain Wilford Woodruff,* and George A. Smith, (who had

* Wilford Woodruff was born March 1, 1807, at Farmington (now called Avon), Hartford County, Connecticut. He was the son of Aphek and Beulah Thompson Woodruff. His father, his grandfather, Eldad Woodruff, and his great-grandfather, Josiah Woodruff, were men of strong constitutions, and were noted for their arduous manual labors. His great-grandfather was nearly one hundred years old when he died, and was able to work until shortly before his decease. At an early age Wilford assisted his father on the Farmington mills, and when 20 years of age, took charge of a flouring mill belonging to his aunt, Helen Wheeler, holding the position of manager for three years, when he was placed in charge of the Collins flouring mills at South Canton, Connecticut, and subsequently of the flouring mill owned by Richard B. Cowles, of New Hartford, Connecticut. In the spring of 1832 in company with his brother Azmon Woodruff, he went to Richland, Oswego county, New York, purchased a farm and sawmill, and settled down to business on his own account. On December 29, 1833, he and his brother Azmon heard the Gospel preached by Elders Zera Pulsipher and Elijah Cheney, and they both believed at once, entertained the Elders, offered themselves for baptism, read the Book of Mormon, and received the divine testimony of its truth. He was baptized and confirmed by Elder Zera Pulsipher, December 31, 1833. At a very early age Wilford Woodruff was imbued with religious sentiments, but never allied himself with any of the various sects. He received much information from Robert Mason, who resided at Simsbury, Connecticut, and was called "the old Prophet Mason." He taught that no man had authority to administer in the things of God without revelation from God; that the modern religious societies were without that authority; that the time would come when the true Church would be established with all its gifts and graces and manifestations, and that the same blessings enjoyed in the early Christian Church could be obtained in this age through faith. This led the youthful Wilford to hold aloof from the churches of the day, and to desire and pray for the coming of an Apostle or other inspired man to show the way of life. For three years previous to receiving the everlasting Gospel, he was impressed with the conviction that God was about to set up His Church and kingdom on the earth in the last days, and for the last time, hence, he was prepared to receive the truth when it was presented to him by the Elders. On January 2, 1834, he was ordained a Teacher, and on February 1st, being visited by Elder Parley P. Pratt, he was instructed to prepare himself to join the body of the Church at Kirtland. He immediately commenced to settle up his business, and started with wagon and horses, and arrived in Kirtland April 25, 1834. There he met with the Prophet Joseph Smith, and many leading Elders, and received much light and knowledge. A week later he went to New Portage, where he joined the company of volunteers which was organized by the Prophet Joseph Smith, and known as "Zion's Camp," to go into Missouri for the relief of the suffering Saints in that state. He remained with the camp through all its travels and trials, until it was dispersed in Clay county, Missouri. * * * At a meeting of the High Council in Lyman Wight's house, November 5, 1834, Brother Woodruff was ordained a Priest by Elder Simeon Carter, and was shortly afterwards sent on a mission to the Southern States. * * * On April 13, 1837. he married Phebe W. Carter.

been previously nominated by the First Presidency, accepted by the Twelve, and acknowledged by the Church), to the office of Apostles and members of the quorum of the Twelve, to fill the places of those who are fallen. Darwin Chase and Norman Shearer (who had just been liberated from the Richmond prison, where they had been confined for the cause of Jesus Christ) were then ordained to the office of the Seventies.

The Twelve then offered up vocal prayer in the following order: Brigham Young, Heber C. Kimball, Orson Pratt, John E. Page, John Taylor, Wilford Woodruff, and George A. Smith.* After which we

* * * In July of the same year, when enroute for a mission to the Fox Islands, he preached at Farmington, Connecticut, and converted several members of his father's house. In August he arrived in Fox Islands. (For an account of his success in that mission see volume 2, page 507, and note). In July, 1838, he again visited Farmington, Connecticut, and resumed his labors in the ministry, succeeding in converting his father and step-mother; his sister Eunice, and several other relatives. Meantime, he had been called by revelation (see Doctrine and Covenants, section cxviii) to fill a vacancy in the quorum of the Twelve Apostles, and was ordained under the circumstances given in the minutes of the meeting of the Twelve Apostles at Far West, April 26, 1839. (The foregoing account of Wilford Woodruff's life is taken mainly from a sketch written by Franklin D. Richards, historian of the Church, at the request of Wilford Woodruff.)

* Following is the prophet's account of George A. Smith:—

"George A. Smith, son of John and Clarissa Smith, was born June 26, 1817, in Potsdam, St. Lawrence county, New York. When nine years old he received a blow on the head which deprived him of his senses about three weeks. Five noted physicians decided that he must be trepanned, or he would not recover. His father dismissed them on this decision, believing that God would heal his son; and he firmly believes that He did heal him in answer to the prayer of faith. He was early trained by his parents, who were Presbyterians, to religious habits, and to a regular attendance in the Sabbath school. Hence he had early and anxious desires to know the way of life; but was not satisfied with the sects.

"In the summer of 1830, when my father and my brother Don Carlos visited relatives in St. Lawrence county, George A. became convinced of the truth of the Book of Mormon, and from that time defended the cause against those who opposed it.

"His mother was baptized in August, 1831. His father was baptized on the ninth of January, 1832, and ordained an Elder. He had been given up by the doctors to die of consumption. The weather was extremely cold, and the ice had to be cut. From that time he gained health and strength. George A. was baptized on the 10th of September, 1832, and on the 1st of May, 1833, his father and family took leave of their old home and removed to Kirtland, Ohio. George A. spent the season in laboring on the Temple, although much afflicted with inflammation of the eyes.

"On the 5th of May, 1834, he started for Zion, in the camp, and acted his part well as my armor-bearer although still much afflicted with sore eyes. On the twenty-eighth he was attacked by the cholera, but was delivered by faith. He was ordained into the first Seventy under my hands on the 1st of March, 1835, being seventeen years old. He left on the 5th of June, in company with Lyman Smith, for the State of New York, to preach the Gospel without purse or scrip. Traveled two thousand miles, baptized eight, held eighty meetings, and returned on the sung Adam-ondi-Ahman, and then the Twelve took their leave of the following Saints, agreeable to the revelation, viz.: Alpheus Cutler, Elias Smith, Norman Shearer, William Burton, Stephen Markham, Shadrach Roundy, William O. Clark, John W. Clark, Hezekiah Peck, Darwin Chase, Richard Howard, Mary Ann Peck, Artimesa Grainger, Martha Peck, Sarah Grainger, Theodore Turley, Hyrum Clark, and Daniel Shearer.

Elder Alpheus Cutler then placed the stone before alluded to in its regular position, after which, in consequence of the peculiar situation of the Saints, he thought it wisdom to adjourn until some future time, when the Lord shall open the way; expressing his determination then to proceed with the building; whereupon the conference adjourned.

BRIGHAM YOUNG, President.
JOHN TAYLOR, Clerk.

Thus was fulfilled a revelation of July 8, 1838, which our enemies had said could not be fulfilled, as no "Mormon" would be permitted to be in the state.

The Revelation of April 8, 1838, Fulfilled.

As the Saints were passing away from the meeting, Brother Turley said to Elders Page and Woodruff, "Stop a bit, while I bid Isaac Russell good bye;" and knocking at the door, called Brother Russell. His wife answered, "Come in, it is Brother Turley." Russell replied, "It is not; he left here two weeks ago;" and appeared quite alarmed; but on finding it was Brother Turley, asked him to sit down; but the latter replied, "I cannot, I shall lose my company." "Who is your company?" enquired Russell. "The Twelve." "*The Twelve!*" "Yes, don't you know that this is the twenty-sixth, and

2nd of November. Spent the winter in school, much afflicted with the rheumatism. In the spring, summer, and fall of 1836, he preached in different parts of Ohio with good success. Returned and went to school in the winter. On the 6th of June, 1837, he took leave of me and started with my blessing for the South. After a successful mission of ten months, mostly in Virginia, he returned and assisted his father in moving to Far West, Missouri. He was ordained a High Councilor at Adam-ondi-Ahman, and sent on a mission to the South in company with Don Carlos Smith; returned about the 25th of December.

"He visited me while in Liberty jail, when I made known to him that he was appointed to fill the place of Thomas B. Marsh in the quorum of the Twelve Apostles. He assisted in moving the Saints out of Far West, and returned with the twelve to fulfill the revelation concerning the Twelve taking their leave of the Saints on the building site of the Temple at Far West."

the day the Twelve were to take leave of their friends on the foundation of the Lord's House, to go to the islands of the sea? The revelation is now fulfilled, and I am going with them." Russell was speechless, and Turley bid him farewell.

The brethren immediately returned to Quincy, taking with them the families from Tenney's Grove.

CHAPTER XXIII.

SETTLEMENT AT COMMERCE, ILLINOIS.

THE committee continued to look at the different locations which were presented in Lee county, Iowa, and about Commerce, in Hancock county, Illinois.

Seeking a New Location.

Wednesday, May 1.—The following letter was communicated to the *Quincy Argus*, a weekly newspaper, published at Quincy:

Elder Taylor's Warning to the People of Quincy Against Impostors.

To the Editor of the Argus:

SIR:—In consequence of so great an influx of strangers arriving in this place daily, owing to their late expulsion from the State of Missouri, there must of necessity be, and we wish to state to the citizens of Quincy and the vicinity, through the medium of your columns, that there are many individuals amongst the number who have already arrived, as well as among those who are now on their way here, who never did belong to our Church, and others who once did, but who, for various reasons, have been expelled from our fellowship. Amongst these there are some who have contracted habits which are at variance with the principles of moral rectitude, (such as swearing, dram-drinking, etc.,) which immoralities the Church of Latter-day Saints is liable to be charged with, owing to our amalgamation [with them] under our late existing circumstances. And as we as a people do not wish to lie under any such imputation, we would also state, that such individuals do not hold a name nor a place amongst us; that we altogether discountenance everything of the kind; that every person belonging to our community, contracting or persisting in such immoral habits, has hitherto been expelled from our society; and that we will hold no communion with all such as we may hereafter be informed of, but will withdraw our fellowship from them.

We wish further to state, that we feel ourselves laid under peculiar obligations to the citizens of this place, for the patriotic feeling which has been manifested, and for the hand of liberality and friendship which has been extended to us in our late difficulties; and should feel sorry to see that philanthropy and benevolence abused by wicked and designing people, who under pretense of poverty and distress, would try to work upon the feelings of the charitable and humane, get into their debt without any prospect or intention of paying, and finally, perhaps, we as a people be charged with dishonesty.

We say that we altogether disapprove of such practices, and we warn the citizens of Quincy against such individuals, who may pretend to belong to our community.

By inserting this in your columns, you, sir, will confer upon us a very peculiar favor.

Written and signed in behalf of the Church of Latter-day Saints, by your very humble servant,

JOHN TAYLOR.

Land Purchases.

I this day purchased, in connection with others of the committee, a farm of Hugh White, consisting of one hundred and thirty-five acres, for the sum of five thousand dollars; also a farm of Dr. Isaac Galland, lying west of the White purchase, for the sum of nine thousand dollars; both of which were to be deeded to Alanson Ripley, according to the counsel of the committee; but Sidney Rigdon declared that "no committee should control any property which he had anything to do with;" consequently the Galland purchase was deeded to George W. Robinson, Rigdon's son-in-law, with the express understanding that he should deed it to the Church, when the Church had paid for it according to their obligation in the contract.

The English Saints Warned against Isaac Russell.

A letter was received by the Presidency of the Church in England, then at Preston, from President Heber C. Kimball, stating that Isaac Russell had apostatized, and styled himself the Prophet; and that Joseph had fallen. Elder Kimball said the Spirit signified to him that Russell was secretly trying to lead away the Church at Alston, England, and wished the Elders to see to it. The Spirit had manifested the same thing to Elder Richards, and he was deputed by a council of the Presidency to visit the Alston branch.

Friday, 3.—I returned to Quincy.

Elder Richards left Preston for Alston.

Saturday, 4.—Elder Richards arrived at Alston and discovered by stratagem that a letter had been received from Isaac Russell, as follows:

Isaac Russell's Letter to the Saints in England.

FAR WEST, January 30, 1839.

To the Faithful Brethren and Sisters of the Church of Latter-day Saints in Alston:

DEAR BRETHREN:—Inasmuch as wisdom is only to be spoken amongst those who are wise, I charge you to read this letter to none but those who enter into a covenant with you to keep those things that are revealed in this letter from all the world, and from all the churches, except the churches to whom I myself have ministered, viz.—the church in Alston and the branches round about, to whom I ministered, and to none else; and to none but the faithful amongst you; and wo be to the man or woman that breaketh this covenant.

Now the Indians, who are the children of the Nephites and the Lamanites, who are spoken of in the Book of Mormon, have all been driven to the western boundaries of the States of America, by the Gentiles, as I told you; they have now to be visited by the gospel, for the day of their redemption is come, and the Gentiles have now well nigh filled up the measure of their wickedness, and will soon be cut off, for they have slain many of the people of the Lord, and scattered the rest; and for the sins of God's people, the Gentiles will now be suffered to scourge them from city to city, and from place to place, and few of all the thousands of the Church of Latter-day Saints will stand to receive an inheritance in the land of promise, which is now in the hands of our enemies. But a few will remain and be purified as gold seven times refined; and they will return to Zion with songs of everlasting joy, to build up the old waste places that are now left desolate.

Now the thing that I have to reveal to you is sacred, and must be kept with care; for I am not suffered to reveal it at all to the churches in this land, because of their wickedness and unbelief—for they have almost cast me out from amongst them, because I have testified of their sins to them, and warned them of the judgments that have yet to come upon them; and this thing that I now tell you, will not come to the knowledge of the churches until they are purified.

Now the thing is as follows—The Lord has directed me, with a few others, whose hearts the Lord has touched, to go into the wilderness, where we shall be fed and directed by the hand of the Lord until we are purified and prepared to minister to the Lamanites, and with us the Lord will send those three who are spoken of in the Book of Mormon, who were with Jesus after His resurrection, and have tarried on the earth to minister to their brethren in the last days.

Thus God is sending us before to prepare a place for you and for the remnant who will survive the judgments which are now coming on the Church of Latter-day Saints, to purify them, for we are sent to prepare a Zion, (as Joseph was before sent into Egypt), a city of Peace, a place of Refuge, that you may hide yourselves with us and all the Saints in the due time of the Lord, before His indignation shall sweep away the nations.

These things are marvelous in our eyes, for great is the work of the Lord that He is going to accomplish. All this land will be redeemed by the hands of the Lamanites, and room made for you, when you hear again from me. Abide where you are, and be subject to the powers that be amongst you in the church. Keep diligently the things I taught you, and when you read this, be comforted concerning me, for though you may not see me for some few years, yet as many of you as continue faithful, will see me again, and it will be in the day of your deliverance. Pray for me always, and be assured that I will not forget you. To the grace of God I commend you in Christ. Amen.

ISAAC RUSSELL.

P. S.—We have not yet gone in the wilderness, but we shall go when the Lord appoints the time. If you should hear that I have apostatized, believe it not, for I am doing the work of the Lord. I. R.

Russell's Efforts Counteracted.

Elder Richards being led by the Spirit of God, soon unfolded the sophistry and falsehood of this letter to the convincing of the Saints at Alston and Brampton, so as to entirely destroy their confidence in the apostate Russell, although they had loved him as a father.

Minutes of a General Conference of the Church Held near Quincy, Illinois, May 4th, 5th and 6th, 1839.

Minutes of a general conference held by the Church of Latter-day Saints at the Presbyterian camp ground, near Quincy, Adams county, Illinois, on Saturday, the 4th of May, 1839.

At a quarter past eleven o'clock meeting was called to order and President Joseph Smith, Jun., appointed chairman.

A hymn was then sung, when President Smith made a few observations on the state of his peculiar feelings, after having been separated from the brethren so long, etc., and then proceeded to open the meeting by prayer.

After some preliminary observations by Elder J. P. Greene and President Rigdon, concerning a certain purchase of land in the Iowa Territory, made for the Church by the Presidency, the following resolutions were unanimously adopted:

Resolved 1st: That Almon W. Babbitt, Erastus Snow and Robert B. Thompson be appointed a traveling committee to gather up and obtain all the libelous reports and publications which have been circulated against our Church, as well as other historical matter connected with said Church, that they possibly can obtain.

Resolved 2nd: That Bishop Vinson Knight be appointed, or received into the Church in full bishopric.

Resolved 3rd: That this conference do entirely sanction the purchase lately made for the Church in the Iowa Territory, and also the agency thereof.

Resolved 4th: That Elder Grainger be appointed to go to Kirtland and take the charge and oversight of the House of the Lord, and preside over the general affairs of the Church in that place.

Resolved 5th: That the advice of this conference to the brethren living in the Eastern States is, for them to move to Kirtland and the vicinity thereof, and again settle that place as a Stake of Zion; provided they feel so inclined, in preference to their moving farther west.

Resolved 6th: That George A. Smith be acknowledged one of the Twelve Apostles.

Resolved 7th: That this conference are entirely satisfied with, and give their sanction to the proceedings of the conference of the Twelve and their friends, held on the Temple site at Far West, Missouri, on Friday, the 26th of April last.

Resolved 8th: That they also sanction the act of the council held the same date and same place, in cutting off from the communion of said Church, certain persons mentioned in the minutes thereof.

Resolved 9th: That Elders Orson Hyde and William Smith be allowed the privilege of appearing personally before the next general conference of the Church, to give an account of their conduct; and that in the meantime they be both suspended from exercising the functions of their office.

Resolved 10th: That the conference do sanction the mission intended for the Twelve to Europe, and that they will do all in their power to enable them to go.

Resolved 11th: That the subject of Elder Rigdon's going to Washington be adjourned until tomorrow.

Resolved 12th: That the next general conference be held on the first Saturday in October next, at Commerce, at the house of Elder Rigdon.

Resolved 13th: That we now adjourn until tomorrow at ten o'clock a. m.

JOSEPH SMITH, JUN., President.
J. MULHOLLAND, Clerk.

Certificate of Appointment.

This is to certify that at a general conference held at Quincy, Adams county, Illinois, by the Church of Jesus Christ of Latter-day Saints, on Saturday, the 4th day of May, 1839, President Joseph Smith, Jun., presiding, it was resolved: That Almon W. Babbitt, Erastus Snow, and Robert B. Thompson be appointed a traveling committee to gather up and obtain all the libelous reports and publications which have been circulated against the Church of Jesus Christ of Latter-day Saints, as well as other historical matter connected with said Church, which they can possibly obtain.

JOSEPH SMITH, JUN., President.
JAMES MULHOLLAND, Clerk.

Minutes of the 5th.

Sunday, 5th, 10 a. m.—Conference opened pursuant to adjournment as usual, by prayer and singing; when it was unanimously resolved: That this conference send a delegate to the City of Washington, to lay our case before the General Government; and that President Rigdon be the delegate.

Resolved 2nd: That Almon W. Babbitt be sent to Springfield, Illinois, clothed with authority, and required to set to rights the Church in that place in every way which may become necessary according to the order of the Church of Jesus Christ.

Resolved 3rd: That Colonel Lyman Wight be appointed to receive the affidavits which are to be sent to the City of Washington; after which the afternoon was spent in receiving instructions from the Presidency and those of the Twelve who were present.

At 5 o'clock p. m. conference adjourned.

JOSEPH SMITH, JUN., President.
JAMES MULHOLLAND, Clerk.

Minutes of the 6th.

Monday, 6th.—At a conference held at Quincy, Illinois, on the 6th of

May, 1839, President Joseph Smith, Jun., presiding, the following resolutions were unanimously agreed to:

Resolved 1st: That the families of Elder Marks, Elder Grainger, and Bishop N. K. Whitney, be kept here amongst us for the time being.

Resolved 2nd: That Elder Marks be hereby appointed to preside over the Church at Commerce, Illinois.

Resolved 3rd: That Bishop Whitney also go to Commerce, and there act in unison with the other Bishops of the Church.

Resolved 4th: That Brother Turley's gunsmith tools shall remain for the general use of the Church, until his return from Europe.

Resolved 5th: That the following of the Seventies have the sanction of this council that they accompany the Twelve to Europe, namely. Theodore Turley, George Pitkin, Joseph Bates Noble, Charles Hubbard, John Scott, Lorenzo D. Young, Samuel Mulliner, Willard Snow, John Snider, William Burton, Lorenzo D. Barnes, Milton Holmes, Abram O. Smoot, Elias Smith; also the following High Priests: Henry G. Sherwood, John Murdock, Winslow Farr, William Snow, Hiram Clark.

Resolved 6th: That it be observed as a general rule, that those of the Seventies who have not yet preached, shall not for the future be sent on foreign missions.

Resolved 7th: That Elder John P. Greene be appointed to go to the City of New York and preside over the churches there and in the regions round about.

I also gave the following letter to John P. Greene:

John P. Greene's Letter of Appointment.

At a conference meeting held by the Church of Jesus Christ of Latter-day Saints, in the town of Quincy, Adams county, Illinois, on Monday, the 6th day of May, 1839, Joseph Smith, Jun., presiding, it was unanimously resolved: That Elder John P. Greene be appointed to go to the City of New York, and preside over the Saints in that place and in the regions round about, and regulate the affairs of the Church according to the laws and doctrines of said Church; and he is fully authorized to receive donations by the liberality of the Saints for the assistance of the poor among us. who have been persecuted and driven from their homes in the State of Missouri; and from our long acquaintance with Elder Greene, and with his experience and knowledge of the laws of the Kingdom of God, we do not hesitate to recommend him to the Saints as one in whom they may place the fullest confidence, both as to their spiritual welfare, as well as to the strictest integrity in all temporal concerns with which he may be entrusted.

And we beseech the brethren, in the name of the Lord Jesus, to receive this brother in behalf of the poor with readiness, and to abound unto him in a liberal manner; for "inasmuch as ye have done it unto the least of these, ye have done it unto me."

Yours in the bonds of the everlasting Gospel, though no longer a prisoner in the hands of the Missourians, and still faithful with the Saints.

JOSEPH SMITH, JUN., Chairman.

Tuesday, 7.—I was in council with the Twelve and others at Quincy.

Wednesday, 8.—I was preparing to remove to Commerce, and engaged in counseling the brethren, etc.

Letter of Recommendation to Elder John P. Greene from Certain Citizens of Quincy.

QUINCY, ILLINOIS, May 8, 1839.

To All Whom it May Concern:

The undersigned citizens of Quincy, Illinois, take great pleasure in recommending to the favorable notice of the public, the bearer of this, John P. Greene. Mr. Greene is connected with the Church of "Mormons" or "Latter-day Saints," and makes a tour to the east for the purpose of raising means to relieve the sufferings of this unfortunate people, stripped as they have been of their all, and now scattered throughout this part of the state.

We say to the charitable and benevolent, you need have no fear but your contributions in aid of humanity will be properly applied if entrusted to the hands of Mr. Greene. He is authorized by his Church to act in the premises; and we most cordially bear testimony to his piety and worth as a citizen.

Very respectfully yours,

SAMUEL HOLMES, Merchant.
I. N. MORRIS, Attorney at Law, and Editor of *Argus*.
THOMAS CARLIN, Governor State of Illinois.
RICHARD M. YOUNG, U. S. Senator.
L. V. RALSTON, M. D.
SAMUEL LEACH, Receiver of Public Moneys
HIRAM ROGERS, M. D.
J. T. HOLMES, Merchant.
NICHOLAS WREN, County Clerk.
C. M. WOODS, Clerk of Circuit Court, Adams Co., Ill.

Sidney Rigdon's Letter of Introduction to the President of the United States, et al.

QUINCY, ILLINOIS, May 8, 1839.

To His Excellency the President of the United States, the Heads of Departments, and all to whom this may be shown:

The undersigned citizens of Quincy, Illinois, beg leave to introduce to you the bearer, Rev. Sidney Rigdon. Mr. Rigdon is a divine, connected with the Church of Latter-day Saints, and having enjoyed his acquaintance for some time past, we take great pleasure in recommending him to your favorable notice as a man of piety and a valuable citizen.

Any representation he may make, touching the object of his mission to your city, may be implicitly relied on.

Very respectfully yours,

SAMUEL HOLMES,
THOMAS CARLIN,
RICHARD M. YOUNG,
I. N. MORRIS,
HIRAM ROGERS,
J. T. HOLMES,
NICHOLAS WREN,
C. M. WOODS.

The Prophet Settles at Commerce.

Thursday, 9.—I started with my family for Commerce, Hancock county, and stayed this night at Uncle John Smith's, at Green Plains, where we were most cordially received.

Friday, 10.—I arrived with my family at the White purchase and took up my residence in a small log house on the bank of the river, about one mile south of Commerce City, hoping that I and my friends may here find a resting place for a little season at least.

Sidney Rigdon's General Letter of Introduction.

QUINCY, ILLINOIS, 10th May, 1839.

The bearer, Rev. Sidney Rigdon, is a member of a society of people called "Mormons," or "Latter-day Saints," who have been driven from the State of Missouri, by order of the executive of that state, and who have taken up their residence in and about this place in large numbers. I have no hesitation in saying that this people have been most shamefully persecuted and cruelly treated by the people of Missouri.

Mr. Rigdon has resided in and near this place for three or four months, during which time his conduct has been that of a gentleman and a moral and worthy citizen.

SAMUEL LEECH.

Monday, May 13.—I was engaged in general business at home and in transacting a variety of business with Brother Oliver Granger, and gave him the following letter:

A Letter of Recommendation to Oliver Granger from the First Presidency.

COMMERCE, ILLINOIS, 13th May, 1839.

Joseph Smith, Jun., Sidney Rigdon, and Hyrum Smith, presiding Elders of the Church of Jesus Christ of Latter-day Saints, do hereby certify and solemnly declare unto all the Saints scattered abroad, and send unto them greeting: That we have always found President Oliver Granger to be a man of the most strict integrity and moral virtue; and in fine, to be a man of God.

We have had long experience and acquaintance with Brother Granger. We have entrusted vast business concerns to him, which have been managed skilfully to the support of our characters and interest as well as that of the Church; and he is now authorized by a general conference to go forth and engage in vast and important concerns as an agent for the Church, that he may fill a station of usefulness in obedience to the commandment of God, which was given unto him July 8, 1838, which says, "Let him (meaning Brother Granger) contend earnestly for the redemption of the First Presidency of my Church, saith the Lord."

We earnestly solicit the Saints scattered abroad to strengthen his hands with all their might, and to put such means into his hands as shall enable him to accomplish his lawful designs and purposes, according to the commandments, and according to the instructions which he shall give unto them. And that they entrust him with moneys, lands, chattels, and goods, to assist him in this work; and it shall redound greatly to the interest and welfare, peace and satisfaction of my Saints, saith the Lord God, for this is an honorable agency which I have appointed unto him, saith the Lord. And again, verily, thus saith the Lord, I will lift up my servant Oliver, and beget for him a great name on the earth, and among my people, because of the integrity of his soul: therefore, let all my Saints abound unto him, with all liberality and long suffering, and it shall be a blessing on their heads.

We would say unto the Saints abroad, let our hearts abound with grateful acknowledgements unto God our Heavenly Father, who hath called us unto His holy calling by the revelation of Jesus Christ, in these last days, and has so mercifully stood by us, and delivered us out of the seventh trouble, which happened unto us in the State of Missouri. May God reward our enemies according to their works. We request the prayers of all the Saints, subscribing ourselves their humble brethren in tribulations, in the bonds of the everlasting Gospel.

JOSEPH SMITH, JUN.,
SIDNEY RIGDON,
HYRUM SMITH.

Letter of R. B. Thompson to the First Presidency Complaining of the Conduct of Lyman Wight.

To the Presidency of the Church of Jesus Christ of Latter-day Saints, Greeting:

I beg leave to call your attention to a subject of considerable importance to our Church, and which if not attended to is calculated (in my humble opinion) to raise a prejudice in a considerable portion of the community, and destroy those benevolent and philanthropic feelings which have been manifested towards us as a people by a large portion of this community: I have reference to the letters of Brother Lyman Wight, which have been inserted in the *Quincy Whig*. I am aware that upon a cursory view of these, nothing very objectionable may appear; yet, if they are attentively considered, there will be found very great objections to them indeed; for instance, in condemning the Democracy of Missouri, why condemn that of the whole Union? and why use such epithets as "Demagogue" to Thomas H. Benton, for not answering his letter, when it is very probable that he had not received it?

Yesterday I was waited on by Mr. Morris, who asked me what was intended by such publications, and why we should come out against the Democracy of the nation, when they were doing all in their power to assist us; it was something which he could not understand, and wished to know if we as a people countenanced such proceedings. I told him for my part I was sorry that these letters had ever made their appearance, and believed that such a course was at variance with the sentiments of the greater part of our people.

Yesterday I brought the subject before the authorities of the Church who are here, where it was manifest that his conduct was not fellowshiped, and the brethren wished to disavow all connection with such proceedings, and appointed a committee to wait on Brother Wight, to beg of him not to persist in the course, which, if not nipped in the bud, will probably bring persecution with all its horrors upon an innocent people, by the folly and imprudence of one individual.

From information I understand that the feelings of the governor are very much hurt by the course which is pursued. I think we ought to correct the public mind on this subject, and, as a Church; disavow all connection with politics. By such a procedure we may in some measure counteract the baneful influence which his letters have occasioned. But if such a course which he (Brother Wight) has adopted, be continued, (as I understand that he intends to do), it will block up our way, and we can have no reasonable prospect of obtaining justice from the authorities of the Union, whom we wantonly condemn before we have made application. The same feelings are beginning to be manifested in Springfield by those who have been our friends there.

The Whigs are glad of such weapons, and make the most of them. You will probably think I am a little too officious, but I feel impressed with the subject; I feel for my brethren. The tears of widows, the cries of orphans, and the moans of the distressed, are continually present in my mind; and I want to adopt and continue a course which shall be beneficial to us; but if through the imprudence and conduct of isolated individuals, three, four, or five years hence, our altars should be thrown down, our houses destroyed, our brethren slain, our wives widowed, and our children made orphans, your unworthy brother wishes to lift up his hands before God and appeal to Him and say, Thou who knowest all things, knowest that I am innocent in this matter.

I am with great respect, gentlemen, yours in the bonds of Christ,

R. B. Thompson.

P. S.—If you do not intend to be in Quincy this week, would you favor us with your opinion on this subject?

R. B. Thompson

Quincy, Monday morning, 13th May, 1839.

Letter of Elder Parley P. Pratt to Judge Austin A. King.

State of Missouri, Richmond,
Ray County, May 13, 1839.

To the Honorable Austin A. King, Judge of the Court of this and the adjoining counties:

Honorable Sir:—Having been confined in prison near seven months, and the time having now arrived when a change of venue can be taken in order for the further prosecution of our trials, and the time having come when I can speak my mind freely, without endangering the lives of any but myself, I now take the liberty of seriously objecting to a trial anywhere within the bounds of the state, and of earnestly praying to your honor and to all the authorities, civil and military, that my case may come within the law of banishment, which has been so rigorously enforced upon near ten thousand of our society, including my wife and little ones, with all my witnesses and friends.

My reasons are obvious, and founded upon notorious facts, which are known to you, sir, and to the people in general of this Republic, and therefore need no proof. They are as follows: First, I have never received any protection by law, either of my person, property, or family, while residing in this state, to which I first emigrated in 1831. Secondly, I was driven by force of arms from Jackson county, wounded and bleeding, in 1833, while my house was burned, my crops and provision, robbed from me or destroyed, and my land kept from me until now, while my family was driven out without shelter, at the approach of winter. Thirdly, these crimes still go unpunished, notwithstanding I made oath before the Honorable Judge Ryland, then Circuit Judge of that district, to the foregoing outrages; and I also applied in person to His Excellency Daniel Dunklin, then Governor of the state, for redress and protection, and a restoration of myself and about 1,200 of my fellow-sufferers, to our rights—but all in vain.

Fourthly, my wife and children have now been driven from our home and improvements in Caldwell county, and banished from the state on pain of death, together with about ten thousand of our society, including all my friends and witnesses; and this by the express orders of His Excellency Lilburn W. Boggs, Governor of the state of Missouri, and by the vigorous execution of his order, by Generals Lucas and Clark, and followed up by murders, rapes, plunderings, thefts and robberies of the most inhuman character by a lawless mob, who have from time to time for more than five years past, trampled upon all law and authority, and upon all the rights of man.

Fifthly, all these inhuman outrages and crimes go unpunished, and are unnoticed by you, sir, and by all the authorities of the state.

Sixthly, the legislature of the state has approved of and sanctioned this act of banishment, with all the crimes connected with it, by voting some two hundred thousand dollars for the payment of troops engaged in this unlawful, unconstitutional, and treasonable enterprise. In monarchial governments the banishment of criminals after their trial and legal condemnation, has been frequently resorted to—but the banishment of innocent women and children from house and home and country, to wander in a land of strangers, unprotected and unprovided for, while their husbands and fathers are retained in dungeons, to be tried by some other law, is an act unknown in the annals of history, except in this single instance in the nineteenth century, when it has actually transpired in a republican state, where the Constitution guarantees to every man the protection of life and property, and the rights of trial by jury. These are outrages which would put monarchy to the blush, and from which the most despotic tyrants of the dark ages would turn away with shame and disgust. In these proceedings, Missouri has enrolled her name on the list of immortal fame—her transactions will be handed down the stream of time to the latest posterity, who will read with wonder and astonishment the history of proceedings which are without a parallel in the annals of time. Why should the authorities of the state strain at a gnat and swallow a camel? Why be so strictly legal as to compel me to go through all the forms of a slow and legal prosecution previous to my enlargement, [being set free] out of a pretense of respect to laws of the state, which have been openly trampled upon and disregarded towards us from the first to the last? Why not include me in the general wholesale banishment of our society, that I may support my family which are now reduced to beggary, in a land of strangers? But when the authorities of the state shall redress all these wrongs; shall punish the guilty according to law; and shall restore my family and friends to all the rights of which we have been unlawfully deprived, both in Jackson and all other counties; and shall pay all the damages which we as a people have sustained; then I shall believe them sincere in their professed zeal for law and justice; then shall I be convinced that I can have a fair trial in the state. But until then, I hereby solemnly protest against being tried in this state, with the full and conscientious conviction that I have no just grounds to expect a fair and impartial trial.

I therefore most sincerely pray your honor, and all the authorities of the state, to either banish me without further prosecution; or I freely consent to a trial before a judiciary of the United States.

With sentiments of high consideration and due respect, I have the honor to subscribe myself, your honor's most humble and obedient; etc.

PARLEY P. PRATT.

To Austin A. King.

Tuesday, May 14.—I returned to Quincy.

Wednesday and Thursday, 15th and 16th. Was engaged in a variety of business relating to the general welfare of the Church.

Letter of the First Presidency to the Quincy Whig, Disclaiming the Attitude of Lyman Wight.

COMMERCE, May 17, 1839.

To the Editors of the Quincy Whig:

GENTLEMEN:—Some letters in your paper have appeared over the signature of Lyman Wight in relation to our affairs with Missouri. We consider it is Mr. Wight's privilege to express his opinion in relation to political or religious matters, and we profess no authority in the case whatever, but we have thought, and do still think, that it is not doing our cause justice to make a political question of it in any manner whatever.

We have not at any time thought there was any political party, as such, chargeable with the Missouri barbarities, neither any religious society, as such. They were committed by a mob composed of all parties, regardless of all differences of opinion either political or religious.

The determined stand in this state, and by the people of Quincy in particular, made against the lawless outrages of the Missouri mobbers by all parties in politics and religion, have entitled them equally to our thanks and our profoundest regards, and such, gentlemen, we hope they will always receive from us. Favors of this kind ought to be engraven on the rock, to last forever.

We wish to say to the public, through your paper, that we disclaim any intention of making a political question of our difficulties with Missouri, believing that we are not justified in so doing.

We ask the aid of all parties, both in politics and religion, to have justice done us and obtain redress. We think, gentlemen, in so saying, we have the feelings of [i. e. represent] our people generally, however, individuals may differ; and we wish you to consider the letters of Lyman Wight as the feelings and views of an individual, but not of the society as such. We are satisfied that our people as a body disclaim all such sentiments and feel themselves equally bound to both parties in this state, as far as kindness is concerned, and good will; and also believe that all political parties in Missouri are equally guilty.

Should this note meet the public eye through the medium of your paper, it will much oblige your humble servants.

JOSEPH SMITH, JUN.,
SIDNEY RIGDON,
HYRUM SMITH.

CHAPTER XXIV.

ADVENTURES OF THE PRISONERS REMAINING IN MISSOURI—THE PROPHET'S NARRATIVE OF PERSONAL EXPERIENCES IN MISSOURI.

Saturday, May 18.—Finished my business at Quincy for the present.

Sunday, 19.—I arrived at home [Commerce] this evening.

Monday 20.—At home attending to a variety of business.

Tuesday, 21.—To show the feelings of that long scattered branch of the house of Israel, the Jews, I here quote a letter written by one of their number, on hearing that his son had embraced Christianity:

Rabbi Landau's Letter to his Son.

BRESLAU, May 21st, 1839.

My Dear Son—I received the letter of the Berlin Rabbi, and when I read it there ran tears out of my eyes in torrents; my inward parts shook, my heart became as a stone! Now do you not know that the Lord sent me already many hard tribulations? That many sorrows do vex me? But this new harm which you are about to inflict, makes me forget all the former, does horribly surpass them; as well respecting its sharpness, as its stings! I write you this lying on my bed, because my body is afflicted not less than my soul, at the report that you were about to do something which I had not expected from you. I fainted; my nerves and feelings sank, and only by the help of a physician, for whom I sent immediately, I am able to write these lines to you with a trembling hand.

Alas! you, my son, whom I have bred, nourished and fostered; whom I have strengthened spiritually as well as bodily, you will commit a crime on me! Do not shed the innocent blood of your parents for no harm have we inflicted upon you; we are not conscious of any guilt against you, but at all times we thought it our duty to show to you, our first born, all love and goodness. I thought I should have some cheering account of you, but, alas! how terribly I have been disappointed!

But to be short; your outward circumstances are such that you may finish your study or [suffer] pain. Do you think that the Christians, to whom you will go over by changing your religion, will support you and fill up the place of our fellow believers? Do not imagine that your outward reasons, therefore, if you have any, are nothing. But out of true persuasion, you will, as I think, not change our true and holy doctrine, for that deceitful, untrue and perverse doctrine of Christianity.

What! will you give up a pearl for that which is nothing, which is of no value in itself? But you are light-minded; think of the last judgment; of that day when the books will be opened and hidden things will be made manifest; of that day when death will approach you in a narrow pass; when you cannot go out of the way! Think of your death bed, from which you will not rise any more, but from which you will be called before the judgment seat of the Lord!

Do you not know, have you not heard, that there is over you an all-hearing ear and an all-seeing eye? That all your deeds will be written in a book and judged hereafter? Who shall then assist you when the Lord will ask you with a thundering voice, Why hast thou forsaken that holy law which shall have an eternal value; which was given by my servant Moses, and no man shall change it? Why hast thou forsaken that law, and accepted instead of it lying and vanity?

Come, therefore, again to yourself, my son! remove your bad and wicked counselors; follow my advice, and the Lord will be with you! Your tender father must conclude because of weeping.

A. L. LANDAU, Rabbi.*

*This letter was written, it will be observed in 1839. It cannot fail to be of interest to all to see the marked change which in more recent years has come over Jewish thought concerning Jesus of Nazareth. Nephi prophesied over five hundred years B.C. that in the latter days the Jews would begin to believe in Christ, and should begin to gather in upon the face of the land given to their fathers. In the year 1901 Dr. Isaac K. Funk, for Funk and Wagnalls, published an editon of Dr. George Croly's work entitled, "Salathiel the Immortal," or "The Wandering Jew." This work was first published in 1827. Dr. Funk gave the book the title, "Tarry Thou Till I Come," and in the appendix of the work he published some twenty-seven letters received from distinguished Jews in response to his question, "What is the Jewish thought today of Jesus of Nazareth?" From this great number of answers to this question, the following represent the general trend of the whole collection.

"I regard Jesus of Nazareth as a Jew of the Jews, one whom all Jewish people are learning to love. His teaching has been an immense service to the world in bringing Israel's God to the knowledge of hundreds of millions of mankind. The great change in Jewish thought concerning Jesus of Nazareth, I cannot better illustrate than by this fact:

"When I was a boy, had my father, who was a very pious man, heard the name of Jesus uttered from the pulpit of our synagogue, he and every other man in the congregation would have left the building, and the rabbi would have been dismissed at once.

The Prophet's Letter to W. W Phelps.

COMMERCE, ILLINOIS, May 22, 1839.

Sir:—In answer to yours of the 23rd of April, to John P. Greene, we have to say that we shall feel obliged by your not making yourself officious concerning any part of our business in future. We shall be glad if you can make a living by minding your own affairs; and we desire (so far as you are concerned) to be left to manage ours as well as we can. We would much rather lose our properties than to be molested by

"Now, it is not strange in many synagogues, to hear sermons preached eulogistic of this Jesus, and nobody thinks of protesting—in fact, we are all glad to claim Jesus as one of our people."

"ISADORE SINGER."

New York, March 25, 1901.

"The Jew of today beholds in Jesus an inspiring ideal of matchless beauty. While He lacks the element of stern justice expressed so forcibly in the law and in the Old Testament characters, the firmness of self-assertion so necessary to the full development of manhood, all those social qualities which build up the home and society, industry and worldly progress, He is the unique exponent of the principle of redeeming love. His name as helper of the poor, as sympathizing friend of the fallen, as brother of every fellow sufferer, as lover of man and redeemer of woman, has become the inspiration, the symbol and the watchword for the world's greatest achievements in the field of benevolence. While continuing the work of the synagogue, the Christian Church with the larger means at her disposal created those institutions of charity and redeeming love that accomplished wondrous things. The very sign of the cross has lent a new meaning, a holier pathos to suffering, sickness and sin, so as to offer new practical solutions for the great problems of evil which fill the human heart with new joys of self-sacrificing love."

KAUFMAN KOHLER, Ph. D.,
Rabbi of Temple Beth-El.

New York, August 23, 1904.

"If the Jews up to the present time have not publicly rendered homage to the sublime beauty of the figure of Jesus, it is because their tormentors have always persecuted, tortured, assassinated them in His name. The Jews have drawn their conclusions from the disciples as to the Master, which was wrong, a wrong pardonable in the eternal victims of the implacable, cruel hatred of those who called themselves Christians. Every time that a Jew mounted to the sources and contemplated Christ alone, without His pretended faithful, he cried, with tenderness and admiration: "Putting aside the Messianic mission, this man is ours. He honors our race and we claim Him as we claim the gospels—flowers of Jewish literature and only Jewish."

MAX NORDAU, M. D.,
Critic and Philosopher.

Paris, France.

"The Jews of every shade of religious belief do not regard Jesus in the light of Paul's theology. But the gospel of Jesus, the Jesus who teaches so superbly the principles of Jewish ethics, is revered by all the expounders of Judaism. His words are studied; the New Testament forms a part of Jewish literature. Among the great preceptors that have worded the truths of which Judaism is the historical such interference; and, as we consider that we have already experienced much over-officiousness at your hands, concerning men and things pertaining to our concerns, we now request, once for all, that you will avoid all interference in our business or affairs from this time henceforth and forever. Amen.*

JOSEPH SMITH, JUN,

guardian, none in our estimation and esteem, takes precedence of the rabbi of Nazareth. To impute to us suspicious sentiments concerning Him does us gross injustice. We know Him to be among our greatest and purest.

EMIL G. HIRSCH, Ph. D., LL. D., L. H. D.,
Rabbi of Sinai Congregation, Professor of Rabbinical Literature in Chicago University, Chicago, Ill., January 26, 1901.

Again, in 1905, the New York *Sun* published a symposium compiled by Dr. Isadore Singer, editor of the "Jewish Encyclopedia," on the same subject, in which he quotes some of the most eminent contemporary Jewish theologians, historians and orientalists. The following is typical of the whole collection.

"If He has added to their [the Jewish prophet's] spiritual bequests new jewels of religious truth, and spoken words which are words of life because they touch the deepest springs of the human heart, why should we Jews not glory in Him? The crown of thorns on His head makes Him only the more our brother, for to this day it is borne by His people. Were He alive today who, think you, would be nearer His heart,—the persecuted or the persecutors?"

DR. GUSTAV GOTTHELL.

* It will be remembered that William W. Phelps, with Oliver Cowdery and the Whitmers, left the Church in 1838, and was among the most bitter enemies of the Prophet; he was also among those who testified against the Prophet and his fellow prisoners before Judge Austin A. King at Richmond. (See report of Missouri Legislature on Mormon Difficulties. pp. 120-5). He also joined with others in whitewashing the proceedings of General Clark and his troops in their treatment of the citizens of Far West. Following is the document as it appears in the report of the Missouri Legislature p. 87:

"*Certificate of Mormons as to the conduct of Gen. Clark and his troops.*

"Richmond, November 23, 1838.

"Understanding that Maj. Gen. Clark is about to return with the whole of his command from the scene of difficulty, we avail ourselves of this occasion to state that we were present when the "Mormons" surrendered to Maj. Gen. Lucas at Far West, and remained there until Maj. Gen. Clark arrived; and we are happy to have an opportunity as well as the satisfaction of stating that the course of him [Clark] and his troops while at Far West was of the most respectful kind and obliging character towards the said Mormons; and that the destitute among that people are much indebted to him for sustenance during his stay. The modification of the terms upon which the "Mormons" surrendered, by permitting them to remain until they could safely go in the spring, was also an act that gave general satisfaction to the Mormons. We have no hesitation in saying that the course taken by Gen. Clark with the Mormons was necessary for the public peace, and that the "Mormons" are generally satisfied with his course, and feel in duty bound to say that the conduct of the General, his staff officers and troops, was highly honorable as soldiers and citizens, so far as our knowledge extends; and

A bill of indictment having been found by a grand jury of the mob in Ray county, against Parley P. Pratt, Morris Phelps and Luman Gibbs, for murder, and against King Follet for robbery, and having obtained a change of venue to Boone county, they were handcuffed together two by two on the morning of the twenty-second, [of May] with irons around the wrists of each, and in this condition they were taken from prison and placed in a carriage. The people of Richmond gathered around them to see them depart, but none seemed to feel for them except two persons. One of these (General Parks' lady) bowed to them through the window, and looked as if touched with pity. The other was a Mr. Hugins, merchant of Richmond, who bowed with some feeling as they passed.

Indictment of Parley P. Pratt *et al.*

They then took leave of Richmond, accompanied by Sheriff Brown, and four guards with drawn pistols, and moved towards Columbia. It had been thundering and raining for some days, and the thunder storm lasted with but short cessations from the time they started till they arrived at the place of destination, which took five days. The small streams were swollen, making it very difficult to cross them.

Thursday, *May 23.*—The prisoners came to a creek which was several rods across, with a strong current and very deep. It was towards evening, and far from any house, and they had received no refreshments through the day. Here the company halted, and knew not what to do; they waited awhile for the water

An Adventure by the Way.

we have heard nothing derogatory to the dignity of the state in the treatment of the prisoners."

Respectfully, &c.

[Signed] W. W. PHELPS,
GEO WALTER,
JOHN CLEMINSON,
G. M. HINKLE,
JOHN CORRILL.

In view of these proceedings on the part of W. W. Phelps it is no matter of astonishment, when he began to show activity respecting the affairs of the Saints, that the Prophet wrote him the curt letter of the text.

to fall, but it fell slowly. All hands were hungry and impatient, and a lowery night seemed to threaten that the creek would rise before morning by the falling of additional rains.

In this dilemma some counseled one thing and some another. At last Mr. Pratt proposed to the sheriff, that if he would take off his irons, he would go into the water to bathe, and by that means ascertain the depths and bottom. This the sheriff consented to after some hesitation. Brother Pratt then plunged into the stream and swam across, and attempted to wade back; he found it to be a hard bottom, and the water about up to his chin, but a very stiff current.

After this, Mr. Brown, the sheriff, undertook to cross on his horse, but was thrown off and buried in the stream. This accident decided the fate of the day Being now completely wet, the sheriff resolved to effect the crossing of the whole company bag and baggage. Accordingly several stripped off their clothes and mounted on the bare backs of the horses, and taking their clothing, saddles and arms, together with one trunk, and bedding, upon their shoulders, they bore them across in safety, without wetting. This was done by riding backwards and forwards across the stream several times. In this sport and labor prisoners, guards and all mingled in mutual exertion All was now safe but the carriage. Brother Phelps then proposed to swim that across, by hitching two horses before it; and he mounted on one of their backs, while Brother Pratt and one of the guards swam by the side of the carriage to keep it from upsetting by the force of the current; and thus they all got safe to land. Everything was soon replaced; prisoners in the carriage and the suite on horseback, moving swiftly on, and at dark arrived at a house of entertainment, amid a terrible thunder storm.

I was busy in counseling, writing letters and attending to general business of the Church this week.

The Prophet's Letter to E. W. Harris.

COMMERCE, ILLINOIS, May 24, 1839.

Dear Sir:—I write you to say that I have selected a town lot for you just across the street from my own, and immediately beside yours, one for Mr. Cleveland. As to getting the temporary house erected which you desired, I have not been able to find any person willing to take hold of the job, and have thought that perhaps you may meet with some person at Quincy who could take it in hand.

Business goes on with us in quite a lively manner, and we hope soon to have Brother Harris and family, with other friends, to assist us in our arduous, but glorious undertaking.

Our families are all well, as far as we have knowledge, all things are going on quietly and smoothly.

Yours, etc.
JOSEPH SMITH, JUN.

Letter of The Prophet and Emma Smith to Judge Cleveland.

COMMERCE, ILLINOIS, May 24th, 1839.

Dear Mr. and Mrs. Cleveland:—We write you in order to redeem our pledge, which we would have done before now, but that we have been in the midst of the bustle of business of various kinds ever since our arrival here. We, however, beg to assure you and your family that we have not forgotten you, but remember you all, as well as the great kindness and friendship which we have experienced at your hands.

We have selected a lot for you, just across the street from our own, beside Mr. Harris; and in the orchard, according to the desire of Sister Cleveland, and also on the river, adapted to Mr. Cleveland's trade.

The various [lines of] business attendant on settling a new place, go on here at present briskly; while all around and concerning us, goes on quietly and smoothly, as far as we have knowledge. It would give us great pleasure to have you all here along with us, and this we hope to enjoy in a short time. I have also remembered Rufus Cleveland to the surveyor, and am happy to be able to say that the land in Iowa far exceeds my expectations both as to richness of soil, and beauty of location, more so than any part of Missouri which I have seen.

We desire to have Mr. Cleveland and his brother come up here as soon as convenient, and see our situation, when they can judge for themselves, and we shall be happy to see them and give them all information in our power. Father Smith and family arrived here yesterday; his health rather improves. We all join in sending our sincere respects to each and every one of you, and remain your very sincere friends,

JOSEPH SMITH, JUN.,
EMMA SMITH.

Addressed to Judge Cleveland and Lady, Quincy, Illinois.

The Prophet's letter to Bishop Whitney, Asking him to Settle at Commerce.

COMMERCE, ILLINOIS, 24th May, 1839.

DEAR SIR:—This is to inform you that Elder Granger has succeeded in obtaining the house which he had in contemplation when he left here; and as we feel very anxious to have the society of Bishop Whitney and his family here, we hope that he will use every exertion consistent with his own business and convenience to come up to us at Commerce as soon as it is in his power.

JOSEPH SMITH, JUN.

Bishop N. K. Whitney.

The Twelve to go to England.

Friday, May 24.—The Twelve made a report of the proceedings of the Seventies, which I sanctioned. I also approved of the Twelve going to England.

Cruel Treatment of Parley P. Pratt and Companions.

This day the Missouri prisoners crossed the Missouri river at "Arrow Rock," so called from the Lamanites coming from all quarters to get a hard rock from the bluff out of which to make arrow points. During this journey the prisoners had slept each night on their backs on the floor; being all four of them ironed together with hand and ankle irons made for the purpose. This being done the windows and doors were all fastened, and then five guards with their loaded pistols staid in the room, and one at a time sat up and watched during the night. This cruelty was inflicted on them more to gratify a wicked disposition than anything else: for it was vain for them to have tried to escape, without any irons being put on them; and had they wished to escape, they had a tolerably good opportunity at the creek.

Answer of the First Presidency to R. B. Thompson on the Lyman Wight Affair.

COMMERCE, HANCOCK CO., ILLINOIS, 25th May, 1839.

DEAR SIR:—In answer to yours of the 13th instant, to us, concerning the writings of Colonel Lyman Wight, on the subject of our late sufferings in the state of Missouri, we wish to say, that as to a statement of our persecutions being brought before the world as a political question, we entirely disapprove of it. Having, however, great confidence in Colonel Wight's good intentions, and considering it to be the indefeasible right of every free man to hold his own opinion in politics as well as religion, we will only say that we consider it to be unwise, as it is unfair, to charge any one party in politics or any sect of religionists with having been our oppressors, since we so well know that our persecutors in the state of Missouri were of every sect, and of all parties, both religious and political; and as Brother Wight disclaims having spoken evil of any administration, save that of Missouri, we presume that it need not be feared that men of sense will now suppose him wishful to implicate any other.

We consider that in making these remarks we express the sentiments of the Church in general,as well as our own individually,and also when we say in conclusion, that we feel the fullest confidence, that when the subject of our wrongs has been fully investigated by the authorities of the United States,we shall receive the most perfect justice at their hands; whilst our unfeeling oppressors shall be brought to condign punishment, with the approbation of a free and enlightened people, without respect to sect or party.

We desire that you may make whatever use you may think proper of this letter, and remain your sincere friends and brethren.

JOSEPH SMITH, JUN.,
HYRUM SMITH,
SYDNEY RIGDON.

Elder Robert B. Thompson.

Case of Wm. Smith.

Saturday, *May 25*.—This day I met the Twelve in council. The case of Brother William Smith came up for investigation and was disposed of.*

Sunday, *26*.—I spent the day at home. Elders Orson Pratt and John Taylor preached.

Parley P. Pratt and Fellow Prisoners Arrive at Columbia.

As the prisoners in Missouri arrived at their new house in Boone county, I will give a sketch of their experience from Elder Pratt's testimony:

When we arrived within four miles of Columbia the bridge had been destroyed from over a large and rapid

* That is, Elder Smith who had been guilty of some wilful and irregular conduct while in the state of Missouri, was permitted to retain his standing in the quorum of the Twelve.

river; and here we were some hours in crossing over in a tottlish canoe having to leave our carriage, together with our bedding, clothing, our trunk of clothing, books, papers, etc.; but all came to us in safety after two days. After we had crossed the river, our guards having swam their horses, mounted them, and we proceeded towards Columbia, the prisoners walking on foot, being fastened together two by two by the wrists. After walking two or three miles, Mr. Brown hired a carriage and we rode into Columbia. It was about sunset on Sunday evening, and as the carriage and our armed attendants drove through the streets we were gazed upon with astonishment by hundreds of spectators, who thronged the streets and looked out at the windows, doors, etc., anxious to get a glimpse of the strange beings called "Mormons."

On our arrival we were immediately hurried to the prison, without going to a tavern for refreshment, although we had traveled a long summer day without anything to eat. When unloosed from our fetters we were ushered immediately into the jail, and next moment a huge trap door was opened and down we went into a most dismal dungeon, which was full of cobwebs and filth above, below, and all around the walls, having stood empty for nearly two years. Here was neither beds, nor chairs, nor water, nor food, nor friends, nor any one on whom we might call, even for a drink of cold water; for Brown and all the others had withdrawn to go where they could refresh themselves. When thrust into this dungeon, we were nearly ready to faint of hunger and thirst and weariness.

We walked the room for a few moments, and then sank down upon the floor in despondency and wished to die; for like Elijah of old, if the Lord had enquired "What dost thou here?" we could have replied, "Lord, they have killed thy prophets, and thrown down thine altars and have driven out all Thy Saints from the land, and we only are left to tell Thee; and they seek our lives, to take them away; and now, therefore, let us die."

When we had been in the dungeon some time, our new jailer handed down some provisions, but by this time I was too faint to eat; I tasted a few mouthfulls, and then suddenly the trap door opened, and some chairs were handed to us, and the new sheriff, Mr. Martin, and his deputy, Mr. Hamilton, entered our dungeon and talked so kindly to us, that our spirits again revived in some measure. This night we slept cold and uncomfortable, having but little bedding. Next morning we were suffered to come out of the dungeon, and the liberty of the upper room was given us through the day ever afterwards.

We now began to receive kind treatment from our jailer and from our new sheriff; for it was Mr. Brown that had caused all our neglect and sufferings the previous evening. Our jail in Columbia was a large wooden block building with two apartments; one was occupied by the jailer and his family and the other by the prisoners.

Monday, 27.—I was at home.

The Prophet and Vinson Knight's Letter to Mark Bigler.

COMMERCE, HANCOCK COUNTY, ILLINOIS, May 27, 1839.

Father Bigler:

DEAR SIR:—We have thought well to write you by Brother Markham on the subject of our purchase of lands here, in order to stir up your pure mind to a remembrance of the situation in which we have been placed by the act of the councils of the Church having appointed us a committee to transact business here for the Church. We have, as is known to the Church in general, made purchases and entered into contracts and promised payments of moneys, for all of which we now stand responsible.

Now as money seems to come in too slowly, in order that we may be able to meet our engagements, we have determined to call upon the liberality of Father Bigler, through the agency of Brother Markham, and request that he will place in his hands for us, the sum of five or six hundred dollars, for which he shall have the security of said committee, also through the agency of Brother Markham, and the thanks of the Church besides.

JOSEPH SMITH, JUN.,
VINSON KNIGHT.

To Mark Bigler, Quincy, Illinois.

The Prophet's Letter to Lyman Wight, on the Matter of R. B. Thompson's Complaint.

COMMERCE, ILLINOIS, MAY 27, 1839.

DEAR SIR:—Having last week received a letter from Brother Robert B. Thompson, concerning your late writings in the *Quincy Whig*, and understanding thereby that the Church in general in Quincy were rather uneasy concerning these matters, we have thought best to consider the matter, of course, and accordingly being in council on Saturday last, the subject was introduced, and discussed at some length, when an answer to Brother Thompson's letter was agreed to and sanctioned by the Council, which answer I expect will be published, and of course you will have an opportunity to see it.

It will be seen by that letter that we do not at all approve of the course which you have thought proper to take, in making the subject of our sufferings a political question. At the same time you will perceive that we there express what we really feel: that is, a confidence in your good intentions. And (as I took occasion to state to the Council) knowing your integrity of principle, and steadfastness in the cause of Christ, I feel not to exercise even the privilege of counsel on the subject, save only to request that you will endeavor to bear in mind the importance of the subject, and how easy it might be to get into a misunderstanding with the brethren concerning it; and though last, not least, that whilst you continue to go upon your own credit you will also steer clear of making the Church appear as either supporting or opposing you in your politics lest such a course may have a tendency to bring about persecution on the Church, where a little wisdom and caution may avoid it.

I do not know that there is any occasion for my thus cautioning you in this thing, but having done so, I hope it will be well taken, and that all things shall eventually be found to work together for the good of the Saints.

I should be happy to have you here to dwell amongst us and am in hopes soon to have that pleasure. I was happy to receive your favor of the 20th instant, and to observe the contents; and beg to say in reply that I shall attend to what you therein suggest, and shall feel pleasure at all times to answer any requests of yours, and attend to them also in the best manner possible.

With every possible feeling of love and friendship, for an old fellow prisoner and brother in the Lord, I remain, sir, your sincere friend,

JOSEPH SMITH, JUN.

To Lyman Wight, Quincy, Illinois.

Letter of Appointment to Stephen Markham.

To the Church of Jesus Christ of Latter-day Saints, Greeting:

From our knowledge of the good sacrifices made by the bearer, Brother Stephen Markham, in behalf of the welfare of us, and the Church generally, and from the great trust which we have oftentimes reposed in him, and as often found him trustworthy, not seeking his own aggrandizement, but rather that of the community, we feel warranted in commissioning him to go forth among the faithful, as our agent to gather up and receive such means in money or otherwise, as shall enable us to meet our engagements which are now about to devolve upon us in consequence of our purchases here for the Church; and we humbly trust that our brethren generally will enable him to come to our assistance before our credit shall suffer on this account.

JOSEPH SMITH, JUN., Presiding Elder.

Thursday, May 28.—I was at home.

Parley P. Pratt *et al* Seek a Trial.

When the Missouri prisoners arrived at Columbia they applied to Judge Reynolds for a special term of court to be holden for their trials. The petition was granted and July 1st was appointed for the sitting of the court.

Monday May 29.—I was about home until the latter part of the week, when I went to Quincy in company with my Counselors. I continued to assist in making preparations to lay our grievances before the general government, and many of the brethren were making their reports of damages sustained in Missouri. I wrote as follows:

June 4, 1839.

The Prophet's Narration of his Personal Experiences in Missouri 1838-9, Which he Calls "A Bill of Damages Against the State of Missouri on Account of the Suffering and Losses Sustained Therein."

March 12, 1838. With my family I arrived at Far West, Caldwell county, after a journey of one thousand miles, being eight weeks on my journey, enduring great affliction in consequence of persecution and expending two or three hundred dollars.

Soon after my arrival at that place, I was informed that a number of men living in Daviess county (on the Grinstone Forks) had offered the sum of one thousand dollars for my scalp: persons to whom I was an entire stranger, and of whom I had no knowledge. In order to attain their end, the roads were frequently waylaid for me. At one time in particular, when watering my horse on Shoal Creek, I distinctly heard three or four guns snapped at me. I was credibly informed also, that Judge King, of the Fifth Judicial Circuit, gave encouragement to individuals to carry into effect their diabolical designs, and has frequently stated that I ought to be beheaded on account of my religion.

In consequence of such expressions from Judge King and others in authority, my enemies endeavored to take every advantage of me, and heaping up abuse, getting up vexatious lawsuits, and stirring up the minds of the people against me and the people with whom I was connected, although we had done nothing [on our part] to deserve such treatment, but were busily engaged in our several vocations, and desirous to live on peaceable and friendly terms with all men. In consequence of such threats and abuse which I was continually subject to, my family were kept in a continual state of alarm, not knowing any morning what would befall me from day to day, particularly when I went from home.

In the latter part of September, 1838, I went to the lower part of the county of Caldwell for the purpose of selecting a location for a town. When on my journey I was met by one of our friends with a message from De Witt, in Carrol county, stating that our brethren who had settled in that place, were, and had for some time been, surrounded by a mob, who had threatened their lives, and had shot several times at them. Immediately on hearing this strange intelligence, I made preparations to start, in order if possible to allay the feeling of opposition, if not to make arrangements with those individuals of whom we had made purchases, and to whom I was responsible and holden for part of the purchase money.

I arrived there on the — day of September, and found the account which I heard was correct. Our people were surrounded by a mob, and their provisions nearly exhausted. Messengers were immediately sent to the Governor, requesting protection; but instead of lending any assistance to the oppressed, he stated that the quarrel was between the "Mormons" and the mob, and they must fight it out.

Being now almost destitute of provisions, and having suffered great distress, and some of the brethren having died in consequence of their privations and sufferings—I had then the pain of beholding some of my fellow-creatures perish in a strange land, from the cruelty of a mob—and seeing no prospect of relief, the brethren agreed to leave that place and seek a shelter elsewhere, after having their houses burnt down, their cattle driven away, and much of their property destroyed.

Judge King was also petitioned to afford us some assistance. He sent a company of about one hundred men; but instead of affording us any relief, we were told by General Parks [who commanded them] that he could afford none, in consequence of the greater part of his company, under their officer, Captain Samuel Bogart, having mutinied. About seventy wagons left De Witt for Caldwell, and during their journey were continually insulted by the mob, who threatened to destroy us, and shot at us. In our journey several of our friends died and had to be interred without a coffin, and under such circumstances, this was extremely distressing. Immediately on my arrival at Caldwell, I was informed by General Doniphan, of Clay county, that a company of about eight hundred were marching towards a settlement of our brethren in Daviess county, and he advised one of the officers that we should immediately go to protect our brethren in Daviess county, (in what he called Whit's Town,) until he should get the militia to put them down. A company of militia, to the number of sixty, who were on their route to that place, he ordered back, believing, as he said, that they were not to be depended upon; and to use his own language were "damned rotten hearted."

Lieut.-Colonel Hinkle, agreeably to the advice of General Doniphan, and a number of our brethren, volunteered to go to Daviess county to render what assistance they could. My labors having been principally expended in Daviess county, where I intended to take up my residence; and having a house in building, and having other property there, I hastened up to that place; and while I was there, a number of houses belonging to the brethren were burnt, and depredations were continually committed, such as driving off horses, cattle, sheep, etc., etc.

Being deprived of shelter, and others having no safety in their houses—because of their being scattered—and being alarmed at the approach of the mob, they had to flock together; their sufferings were very great in consequence of their defenseless situation—being exposed to the weather, which was extremely cold, a large snow storm having just fallen.

In this state of affairs, General Parks arrived in Daviess county, and was at the house of Colonel Wight when the intelligence was brought that the mob were burning houses, etc.; and also that men, women, and children were flocking into the village for safety. Colonel Wight, who held a commission in the fifty-ninth regiment under his [Parks] command, asked him what steps should be taken. General Parks told him that he must immediately call out his men, and go and put the mob down.

Preparations were made at once to raise a force to quell the mob, who, on ascertaining that we were determined to bear such treatment no longer, but to make a vigorous effort to subdue them, and likewise being informed of the orders of General Parks, broke up their encampment and fled.

Some of the inhabitants in the immediate neighborhood, who seeing no prospects of driving us by force, resorted to stratagem, and actually set fire to their own houses (miserable log houses, after having removed their property and effects) and then sent information to the Governor, stating that our brethren were committing depredations and destroying their property, burning houses, etc.

On the retreat of the mob from Daviess county, I returned home to Caldwell. On my arrival there, I understood that a mob had commenced hostilities in the borders of Caldwell; had taken some of our people prisoners; burnt some houses, and had done considerable damage. Immediately Captain Patten was ordered out by Lieut.-Col. Hinkle to go against them, and about daylight next morning came up with them. Upon the approach of our people the mob fired upon them, and after discharging their pieces, fled with great precipitation.

In this affray, Captain Patten, along with two others, fell a victim to that spirit of mobocracy which has prevailed to such an extent; others were severely wounded. On the day after this affray, Captain Patten sent for me to pray for him, which request I complied with, and then returned to my home.

There continued to be great commotion in the county, caused by the conduct of the mob, who were continually burning houses, driving off horses, cattle, etc., and taking prisoners, and threatening death to all the "Mormons." Amongst the cattle driven off were two cows of mine.

On the 28th of October, a large company of armed soldiers were seen approaching Far West, and encamped about one mile from the town. The next day I was waited upon by Lieutenant-Colonel Hinkle, who stated that the officers of the militia requested an interview with us in order to come to some amicable settlement of the difficulties which then existed; they, the officers, not wishing, under the present circumstances, to carry into effect the exterminating orders they had received. I immediately complied with the request, and in company with Messieurs Rigdon, Robinson, Wight, and Pratt, proceeded to meet the officers of the militia, but instead of treating us with respect, and as persons desirous to accommodate matters, to our astonishment we were delivered up as prisoners of war, and taken into their camp as such. It would be in vain for me to give any idea of the scene which now presented itself in the camp. The hideous yells of more than a thousand infuriated beings, whose desire was to wreak their vengeance upon me and the rest of my friends, was truly awful, and enough to appall the stoutest heart.

In the evening we had to lie down on the cold ground, surrounded by a strong guard. We petitioned the officers to know why we were thus treated; but they utterly refused to hold any conversation with us. The next day they held a court martial upon us and sentenced me, with the rest of the prisoners, to be shot; which sentence was to be carried into effect on Friday morning in the public square, as they said as an ensample to the rest of the members; but through the kind providence of God, their murderous sentence was not carried into execution. The militia then went to my house and drove my family out of doors under sanction of General Lucas, and carried away all my property.

I had an opportunity of speaking to General Wilson, and on asking him the cause of such strange proceedings, I told him that I was a democrat, and had always been a supporter of the Constitution. He answered, "I know that, and that is the reason why I want to kill you, or have you killed."

We were led into the public square, and after considerable entreaty, we were permitted to see our families, being attended by a strong guard. I found my family in tears, they having believed that the mob had carried into effect their sentence; they clung to my garments weeping. I requested to have a private interview with my wife in an adjoining room, but was refused; when taking my departure from my family, it was almost too painful for me. My children clung to me, and were thrust away at the point of the swords of the soldiery. We were then removed to Jackson county, under the care of General Wilson; and during our stay there, we had to sleep on the floor, with nothing but a mantle for our covering, and a stick of wood for our pillow, and had to pay for our own board.

While we were in Jackson county, General Clark with his troops arrived in Caldwell, and sent an order for our return, holding out the inducement that we were to be reinstated to our former privileges; but instead of being taken to Caldwell county, we were taken to Richmond, Ray county, where we were immured in prison and bound in chains. After we were thus situated, we were under the charge of Colonel Price, of Chariton county, who suffered us to be abused in every manner which the people thought proper.

Our situation at this time was truly painful. We were taken before a court of inquiry; but in consequence of the proceedings of the mob, and their threats, we were not able to get such witnesses as would have been serviceable; even those we had were abused by the State's Attorney, and the court, and were not permitted to be examined by the court as the law directs. We were committed to Liberty jail, and petitioned Judge Turnham for a writ of habeas corpus; but owing to the prejudice of the jailer, all communication was entirely cut off. However, at length we succeeded in getting a petition conveyed to the judge, but he neglected to pay any attention to it for fourteen days, and kept us in suspense. He then ordered us to appear before him; but he utterly refused to hear any of our witnesses, which we had been at a great trouble in providing. Our lawyer also refused to act, being afraid of the people.

We likewise petitioned Judge King and the judges of the Supreme Court, but they utterly refused. Our victuals were of the coarsest kind, and served up in a manner which was disgusting. After bearing up under repeated injuries, we were moved to Daviess county under a strong guard. We were then arraigned before the Grand Jury, who were mostly intoxicated, who indicted me and the rest of my companions for treason. We then got a change of venue to Boone county,and when on our way to that place, on the second evening after our departure, our guards getting intoxicated, I thought it a favorable time to effect our escape from such men, whose aim was only to destroy our life and to abuse us in every manner that wicked men could invent. Accordingly we took advantage of their situation, and made our escape; and after enduring considerable fatigue, and suffering hunger and weariness, expecting that our enemies would be in pursuit, we arrived in the town of Quincy, Illinois, amidst the congratulations of our friends, and the joy of our families. I have been here for several weeks, as it is known to the people of the state of Missouri; but they, knowing they had no justice in their crusade against me, have not to my knowledge taken the first step to have me arrested.

The loss of property which I have sustained is as follows:—Losses sustained in Jackson county, Daviess county, Caldwell county, including lands, houses, harness, hogs, cattle, etc.; books and store goods, expenses while in bonds, of moneys paid out, expenses of moving out of the State, and damages sustained by false imprisonments, threatenings, intimidations, exposure, etc., etc., one hundred thousand dollars.

My brother Hyrum Smith wrote the following—

Hyrum Smith's Statement of sufferings and damages sustained in Missouri, and of being driven therefrom.

I left Kirtland, Ohio, in the spring of 1838, having the charge of a family of ten individuals; the weather was very unfavorable, and the roads worse than I had ever seen, which materially increased my expenses, on account of such long delays upon the road. However, after suffering many privations, I reached my destination in safety, and intended to make my permanent residence in the state of Missouri. I sent on by water all my household furniture and a number of farming implements, amounting to several hundred dollars, having made purchases of lands of several hundreds of acres, upon which I intended to settle.

In the meantime, I took a house in Far West, until I could make further arrangements. I had not been there but a few weeks, before the report of mobs, whose intention was to drive us from our homes, was heard from every quarter. I thought that the reports were false, inasmuch as I know that as a people we had done nothing to merit any such treatment as was threatened. However, at length, from false and wicked reports, circulated for the worst of purposes, the inhabitants of the upper counties of Missouri commenced hostilities, threatened to burn our dwellings, and even menaced the lives of our people, if we did not move away; and afterwards, horrid to relate, they put their threats into execution.

Our people endeavored to calm the fury of our enemies, but in vain; for they carried on their depredations to a greater extent than ever, until most of our people who lived in places at a distance from the towns had collected together, so that they might be the better able to escape from the fury of our enemies, and be in better condition to defend their lives and the little property they had been able to save. It is probable that our persecutors might have been deterred from their purposes, had not wicked and shameful reports been sent to the Governor of the state, who ordered out a very large force to exterminate us. When they arrived at Far West, we were told what were their orders. However, they did not fall upon us, but took several of my friends and made them prisoners; and the day after, a company of the militia came to my house and ordered me to go with them into the camp. My family at that time particularly needed my assistance, being much afflicted. I told them my situation, but remonstrance was in vain, and I was hurried into the camp, and was subject to the most cruel treatment.

Along with the rest of the prisoners, I was ordered to be shot; but it was providentially overruled. We were then ordered to Jackson county, where our bitterest persecutors resided. Before we started, after much entreaty, I was privileged to visit my family, accompanied with a strong guard. I had only time to get a change of linen, &c., and was hurried to where the teams were waiting to convey us to the city of Independence, in Jackson county. While there I was subjected to continued insult from the people who visited us. I had likewise to lie on the floor, and had to cover myself with my mantle; after remaining there for some time we were ordered to Richmond, in Ray county, where our enemies expected to shoot us; but finding no law to support them in carrying into effect so strange an act, we were delivered up to the civil law. As soon as we were so, we were thrust into a dungeon, and our legs were chained together. In this situation we remained until called before the court, who ordered us to be sent to Liberty in Clay county, where I was confined for more than four months, and endured almost everything but death, from the nauseous cell, and the wretched food we were obliged to eat.

In the meantime, my family were suffering every privation. Our enemies carried off nearly everything of value, until my family were left almost destitute. My wife had been but recently confined and had to suffer more than tongue can describe; and then in common with the rest of the people, had to move, in the month of February, a distance of two hundred miles, in order to escape further persecutions and injury.

Since I have obtained my liberty, I feel my body broken down and my health very much impaired, from the fatigue and afflictions which I have undergone, so that I have not been able to perform any labor since I have escaped from my oppressors. The loss of property which I sustained in the state of Missouri would amount to several thousand dollars; and one hundred thousand dollars would be no consideration for what I have suffered from privations—from my life being continually sought—and all the accumulated sufferings I have been subjected to.

HYRUM SMITH.

CHAPTER XXV.

COMMERCE—THE PROPHET'S HISTORY—DOCTRINAL DEVELOPMENT.

Wednesday, June 5.—I returnd to Commerce and spent the remainder of the week at home.

Sunday, 9.—I attended meeting with my wife and family at Brother Bosiers. Elder John E. Page preached.

Monday, 10.—Elder Page baptized one woman. I was engaged in study preparatory to writing my history.

Tuesday, 11.—I commenced dictating my history for my clerk, James Mulholland, to write. About this time Elder Theodore Turley raised the first house built by the Saints in this place [Commerce]; it was built of logs, about twenty-five or thirty rods north north-east of my dwelling, on the north-east corner of lot 4, block 147, of the White purchase.

First House Built by the Saints at Commerce.

When I made the purchase of White and Galland, there were one stone house, three frame houses, and two block houses, which constituted the whole city of Commerce. Between Commerce and Mr. Davidson Hibbard's, there was one stone house and three log houses, including the one that I live in, and these were all the houses in this vicinity, and the place was literally a wilderness. The land was mostly covered with trees and bushes, and much of it so wet that it was with the utmost difficulty a footman could get through, and totally impossible for teams. Commerce was so unhealthful, very few could live there; but believing that it might become a healthful place by the blessing of heaven to the Saints, and no more eligible place presenting itself, I considered it wisdom to make an attempt to build up a city.

Description of Commerce.

Wednesday and Thusday, 12 and 13.—I continued to dictate my history.

Letter of Edward Partridge to the Prophet.

QUINCY, June 13, 1839.

President Smith:

SIR:—Your letter in answer to my note to Bishop Knight, I received by the hand of Brother Harris. Respecting the cattle, I had promised three or four yoke to Father Myers. I did expect Brother Shearer would have sent the cattle down immediately, or I should not have been quite so willing to accommodate him with some to move with.

Some of our poor brethren wished me to furnish them teams to move up to town with, and I promised them that when the teams returned, I would. They were very anxious to get up in time to get in a little garden; and were not my plans frustrated, I could have accommodated them greatly to their satisfaction.

The brethren that I allude to are the blind brethren, who say that they had as lief live in tents there as here. It is now too late to think of making gardens, and what is best for them to do, I know not. I had promised some money as soon as I could sell a yoke of cattle. I know of nothing else I have that I can raise money with at this time; and they are getting to be dull sale to what they were.

Sister Meeks has been quite sick, but she is getting better. She has nothing to eat only what she is helped to. A number of other poor here, I think, need assistance; widow Sherman for one; but if you think that all the means should be kept up there [at Commerce], I have nothing to say, only that I do not believe it to be my duty to stay here living on expense, where I can earn nothing for myself, nor do anything to benefit others.

As I before stated, I have promised some money as soon as I can raise it. I have not at this time two dollars in the world, one dollar and forty-four cents is all. I owe for my rent, and for making clothes for some of the poor, and some other things. I am going into the room Brother Harris leaves, to save rent. What is best for me to do, I hardly know. Hard labor I cannot perform; light labor I can; but I know of no chance to earn anything, at anything that I can stand to do. It is quite sickly here. Five were buried in four days—Brother Moses' child, Sister Louisa P. and Brother Pettigrew's son Hiram, eighteen or nineteen years of age; the other two were children of the world.

I spoke to Brother Isaac Higbee about his seine; he said that he would speak to his brother about it. He said he thought they would sell it, or they would come up in the fall and fish a while, but to lend it, he thought it would not be best, as those unaccustomed to fish in the rivers would be apt to tear it to pieces. You perceive that I have not means to get you twine at present; therefore I presume that you will not blame me for not doing it.

Were I well, I would go up to Commerce with Brother Whitney and settle with the committee and Brother Rogers, and see what is best to do; probably may come next week. If Brother Markham could sell one yoke of cattle and let me have the avails of them, I should be glad; and I think it best to let two yoke, that are up there, go to Father Myers. As to teams to move up some of the poor, do as you think best.

EDWARD PARTRIDGE.

President Joseph Smith, Jun., Commerce.

Friday, *14*.—Continued writing history. This evening there was a great excitement about the jail of Columbia, Missouri. Several individuals went and called for the jailer, but he was absent. They next called for the jailer's wife, and offered her money to let the prisoners go, which she declined, and becoming alarmed, raised a cry which brought the whole village together, armed with bowie knives, guns, pistols, etc.; but finding no one there, they soon returned home, except a few to guard the prison. This now brought different individuals to see the prisoners, and by acquaintance those feelings were softened towards the Saints.

Excitement at Columbia Prison, Mo.

Saturday, *15*.—I started with my family to visit Brother Don Carlos Smith. We met Brother William on the prairie, about four miles west of Carthage; found him in good spirits, and went with him to his house in Plymouth; found his family well. Staid over night, and had a very satisfactory visit.

Visit of the Prophet with Wm. Smith.

Sunday, *16*.—We went to Brother Don Carlos Smith's, in McDonough county, near the village of Macombe, where we spent the remainder of the day.

Visit with Don Carlos.

Monday, *17*.—Bishops Whitney and Knight arrived at Commerce. I staid at Brother Don Carlos' this day, and my brother Samuel H. Smith came in; I had not seen him before, since my deliverance from prison. Bishop Knight returned to Quincy.

Tuesday, *18*.—I went to the house of a man by the name of Matthews. During the evening the neighbors came in and I gave them a short discourse.

Thursday, *20*.—Visited at Elder Zebedee Coltrin's. From thence we were invited to visit at Brother Vance's, which we did, and there gave to the brethren and friends of the neighborhood a brief history of the coming forth of the Book of Mormon.

Ministry of the Prophet.

Saturday, *22*.—We returned to Brother Don Carlos' place.

Sunday, *23*.—Went to Brother Wilcox's and preached to a very crowded congregation; and so eager were they to hear, that a part of them stood out in the rain during the sermon. In general they expressed good satisfaction as to what they heard.

Monday, *24*.—We started for home, and went to Brother Perkins, near Fountain Green, in Hancock county, where they insisted we should tarry, and we complied. This day the Church purchased the town of Nashville, in Lee county, Iowa Territory, together with twenty thousand acres of land adjoining it.

Purchase of Lands in Iowa.

Tuesday, *25*.—We held a meeting, at which I spoke with considerable liberty to a large congregation.

Wednesday, *26*.—I with my family returned to our home at Commerce.

Return of the Prophet to Commerce.

Thursday, *27*.—

The Prophet's Answer to Jacob Stollings.

COMMERCE, ILLINOIS, June 27, 1839.

SIR:—In answer to yours concerning those books, I have to say that I have made inquiry concerning them, as far as I consider there is any prospect of obtaining them for you; and not having been able to trace them in the least degree, I have determined to give up the pursuit. I would recommend you to inquire after them of Dr. Avard, as the only chance I know of at present.

Yours, etc.,

JOSEPH SMITH, JUN.

P. S.—Since writing the above, I have ascertained of one man (who told me) that he saw Dr. Avard have the books; but what he did with them, he knows not.

J. S.

To Mr. Jacob Stollings.

I attended a conference of the Twelve, at which time Brother Orson Hyde made his confession, and was restored to the Priesthood again.

Restoration of Orson Hyde.

At this time I taught the brethren at considerable length on the following subjects:

The Prophet's Instruction on Various Doctrines.

FAITH comes by hearing the word of God, through the testimony of the servants of God; that testimony is always attended by the Spirit of prophecy and revelation.

REPENTANCE is a thing that cannot be trifled with every day. Daily transgression and daily repentance is not that which is pleasing in the sight of God.

BAPTISM is a holy ordinance preparatory to the reception of the Holy Ghost; it is the channel and key by which the Holy Ghost will be administered.

THE GIFT OF THE HOLY GHOST by the laying on of hands, cannot be received through the medium of any other principle than the principle of righteousness, for if the proposals are not complied with, it is of no use, but withdraws.

TONGUES were given for the purpose of preaching among those whose language is not understood; as on the day of Pentecost, etc., and it is not necessary for tongues to be taught to the Church particularly, for any man that has the Holy Ghost, can speak of the things of God in his own tongue as well as to speak in another; for faith comes not by signs, but by hearing the word of God.

THE DOCTRINE OF THE RESURRECTION OF THE DEAD AND THE ETERNAL JUDGMENT are necessary to preach among the first principles of the Gospel of Jesus Christ.

THE DOCTRINE OF ELECTION. St. Paul exhorts us to make our calling and election sure. This is the sealing power spoken of by Paul in other places.

"13. In whom ye also trusted, that after ye heard the word of truth, the

Gospel of your salvation: in whom also after that ye believed, ye were sealed with that Holy Spirit of promise,

"14. Which is the earnest of our inheritance until the redemption of the purchased possession, unto the praise of His glory, that we may be sealed up unto the day of redemption."—Ephesians, 1st chapter.

This principle ought (in its proper place) to be taught, for God hath not revealed anything to Joseph, but what He will make known unto the Twelve, and even the least Saint may know all things as fast as he is able to bear them, for the day must come when no man need say to his neighbor, Know ye the Lord; for all shall know Him (*who remain*) from the least to the greatest. How is this to be done? It is to be done by this sealing power, and the other Comforter spoken of, which will be manifest by revelation.

There are two Comforters spoken of. One is the Holy Ghost, the same as given on the day of Pentecost, and that all Saints receive after faith, repentance, and baptism. This first Comforter or Holy Ghost has no other effect than pure intelligence. It is more powerful in expanding the mind, enlightening the understanding, and storing the intellect with present knowledge, of a man who is of the literal seed of Abraham, than one that is a Gentile, though it may not have half as much visible effect upon the body; for as the Holy Ghost falls upon one of the literal seed of Abraham, it is calm and serene; and his whole soul and body are only exercised by the pure spirit of intelligence; while the effect of the Holy Ghost upon a Gentile, is to purge out the old blood, and make him actually of the seed of Abraham. That man that has none of the blood of Abraham (naturally) must have a new creation by the Holy Ghost. In such a case, there may be more of a powerful effect upon the body, and visible to the eye, than upon an Israelite, while the Israelite at first might be far before the Gentile in pure intelligence.

The other Comforter spoken of is a subject of great interest, and perhaps understood by few of this generation. After a person has faith in Christ, repents of his sins, and is baptized for the remission of his sins and receives the Holy Ghost, (by the laying on of hands), which is the first Comforter, then let him continue to humble himself before God, hungering and thirsting after righteousness, and living by every word of God, and the Lord will soon say unto him, Son, thou shalt be exalted. When the Lord has thoroughly proved him, and finds that the man is determined to serve Him at all hazards, then the man will find his calling and his election made sure, then it will be his privilege to receive the other Comforter, which the Lord hath promised the Saints, as is recorded in the testimony of St. John, in the 14th chapter, from the 12th to the 27th verses.

Note the 16, 17, 18, 21, 23 verses:

"16. And I will pray the Father, and He shall give you another Comforter, that he may abide with you forever;

"17. Even the Spirit of Truth; whom the world cannot receive, because it seeth him not, neither knoweth him; but ye know him; for he dwelleth with you, and shall be in you.

"18. I will not leave you comfortless: I will come to you. * * *

"21. He that hath my commandments, and keepeth them, he it is that loveth me: and he that loveth me shall be loved of my Father, and I will love him, and will manifest myself to him.

"23. If a man love me, he will keep my words: and my Father will love him, and we will come unto him, and make our abode with him."

Now what is this other Comforter? It is no more nor less that the Lord Jesus Christ Himself; and this is the sum and substance of the whole matter; that when any man obtains this last Comforter, he will have the personage of Jesus Christ to attend him, or appear unto him from time to time, and even He will manifest the Father unto him, and they will take up their abode with him, and the visions of the heavens will be opened unto him, and the Lord will teach him face to face, and he may have a perfect knowledge of the mysteries of the Kingdom of God; and this is the state and place the ancient Saints arrived at when they had such glorious visions—Isaiah, Ezekiel, John upon the Isle of Patmos, St. Paul in the three heavens, and all the Saints who held communion with the general assembly and Church of the First Born.

THE SPIRIT OF REVELATION is in connection with these blessings. A person may profit by noticing the first intimation of the spirit of revelation; for instance, when you feel pure intelligence flowing into you, it may give you sudden strokes of ideas, so that by noticing it, you may find it fulfilled the same day or soon; (i. e.) those things that were presented unto your minds by the Spirit of God, will come to pass; and thus by learning the Spirit of God and understanding it, you may grow into the principle of revelation, until you become perfect in Christ Jesus.

AN EVENGELIST is a Patriarch, even the oldest man of the blood of Joseph or of the seed of Abraham. Wherever the Church of Christ is established in the earth, there should be a Patriarch for the benefit of the posterity of the Saints, as it was with Jacob in giving his patriarchal blessing unto his sons, etc.

CHAPTER XXVI.

THE PROPHET'S MINISTRY IN THE VICINITY OF COMMERCE—ADDRESS TO THE TWELVE.

Friday, 28.—I was transacting business of various kinds; counseling, consulting the brethren, etc., etc.

Saturday 29.—I was mostly at home.

Sunday 30.—I attended meeting at Brother Bosier's. There was a crowded audience, and I bore testimony concerning the truth of the work, and also of the truth of the Book of Mormon.

The Prophet Testifies to the Book of Mormon.

This day Sister Morris Phelps, who had traveled one hundred and fifty miles, in company with her brother, John W. Clark, to see her husband, arrived at Columbia jail.

Monday, July 1, 1839.—I spent the day principally in counseling the brethren.

The Missouri Prisoners.

This day also the court was called for the trial of Parley P. Pratt, and brethren in prison in Boone county; but as they were not ready for trial, (all their witnesses had been banished the state), the court was adjourned to the 23rd of September.

Tuesday 2.—Spent the forenoon of this day on the Iowa side of the river. Went, in company with Elders Sidney Rigdon, Hyrum Smith, and Bishops Whitney and Knight, and others, to visit a purchase lately made by Bishop Knight as a location for a town, and advised that a town be built there, and called Zarahemla.

Founding of Zarahemla.

In the afternoon met with the Twelve and some of the Seventies who are about to proceed on their mission to Europe, and the nations of the earth, and islands of the sea.

The Prophet with the Twelve and the Seventies.

The meeting was opened by singing and prayer, after which the Presidency proceeded to bless two of the Twelve who had lately been ordained into the quorum, namely, Wilford Woodruff and George A. Smith; and one of the Seventies, namely, Theodore Turley; after which, blessings were also pronounced by them [the Presidency] on the heads of the wives of some of those about to go abroad.

Hyrum Smith's Admonition to the Twelve.

The meeting was then addressed by President Hyrum Smith, by way of advice to the Twelve, chiefly concerning the nature of their mission; their practicing prudence and humility in their plans or subjects for preaching; necessity of their not trifling with their office, and of holding on strictly to the importance of their mission, and the authority of the Priesthood.

I then addressed them and gave much instruction calculated to guard them against self-sufficiency, self-righteousness, and self-importance; touching upon many subjects of importance and value to all who wish to walk humbly before the Lord, and especially teaching them to observe charity, wisdom and fellow-feeling, with love one towards another in all things, and under all circumstances, in substance as follows:

The Prophet's Address to the Twelve.

Mercy and Forgiveness.

Ever keep in exercise the principle of mercy, and be ready to forgive our brother on the first intimations of repentance, and asking forgiveness; and should we even forgive our brother, or even our enemy, before he repent or ask forgiveness, our heavenly Father would be equally as merciful unto us.

Humility and Brotherhood of the Twelve.

Again, let the Twelve and all Saints be willing to confess all their sins, and not keep back a part; and let the Twelve be humble, and not be exalted, and beware of pride, and not seek to excel one above another, but act for each other's good, and pray for one another, and honor our brother or make honorable mention of his name, and not backbite and devour our brother. Why will not man learn wisdom by precept at this late age of the world, when we have such a cloud of witnesses and examples before us, and not be obliged to learn by sad experience everything we know? Must the new ones that are chosen to fill the places of those that are fallen, of the quorum of the Twelve, begin to exalt themselves, until they exalt themselves so high that they will soon tumble over and have a great fall, and go wallowing through the mud and mire and darkness, Judas like, to the buffetings of Satan, as several of the quorum have done, or will they learn wisdom and be wise? O God! give them wisdom, and keep them humble, I pray.

Avoid Vain-glory.

When the Twelve or any other witnesses stand before the congregations of the earth, and they preach in the power and demonstration of the Spirit of God, and the people are astonished and confounded at the doctrine, and say, "That man has preached a powerful discourse, a great sermon," then let that man or those men take care that they do not ascribe the glory unto themselves, but be careful that they are humble, and ascribe the praise and glory to God and the Lamb; for it is by the power of the Holy Priesthood and the Holy Ghost that they have power thus to speak. What art thou, O man, but dust? And from whom receivest thou thy power and blessings, but from God?

Be Honest, Sober, Vigilant.

Then, O ye Twelve! notice this *Key*, and be wise for Christ's sake, and your own soul's sake. Ye are not sent out to be taught, but to teach. Let every word be seasoned with grace. Be vigilant; be sober. It is a day of warning, and not of many words. Act honestly before God and man. Beware of Gentile sophistry; such as bowing and scraping unto men in whom you have no confidence. Be honest, open, and frank in all your intercourse with mankind.

O ye Twelve! and all Saints! profit by this important *Key*—that in all your trials, troubles, temptations, afflictions, bonds, imprisonments and death, see to it, that you do not betray heaven; that you do not betray Jesus Christ; that you do not betray the brethren; that you do not betray the revelations of God, whether in the Bible, Book of Mormon, or Doctrine and Covenants, or any other that ever was or ever will be given and revealed unto man in this world or that which is to come. Yea, in all your kicking and flounderings, see to it that you do not this thing, lest innocent blood be found upon your skirts, and you go down to hell. All other sins are not to be compared to sinning against the Holy Ghost, and proving a traitor to the brethren.

Beware of Treason.

I will give you one of the *Keys* of the mysteries of the Kingdom. It is an eternal principle, that has existed with God from all eternity: That man who rises up to condemn others, finding fault with the Church, saying that they are out of the way, while he himself is righteous, then know assuredly, that that man is in the high road to apostasy; and if he does not repent, will apostatize, as God lives. The principle is as correct as the one that Jesus put forth in saying that he who seeketh a sign is an adulterous person; and that principle is eternal, undeviating, and firm as the pillars of heaven; for whenever you see a man seeking after a sign, you may set it down that he is an adulterous man.

The sign of Apostasy.

About this time, in reply to many inquiries, I also gave an explanation of the Priesthood, and many principles connected therewith, of which the following is a brief synopsis:

The Prophet on Priesthood.

The Priesthood was first given to Adam; he obtained the First Presidency, and held the keys of it from generation to generation. He obtained it in the Creation, before the world was formed, as in Gen. i: 26, 27, 28.* He had dominon given him over every living creature. He is Michael the Archangel, spoken of in the Scriptures. Then to Noah, who is Gabriel; he stands next in authority to Adam in the Priesthood; he was called of God to this office, and was the father of all living in his day, and to him was given the dominion. These men held keys first on earth, and then in heaven.

Adam and the Presidency of the Priesthood.

The Priesthood is an everlasting principle, and existed with God from eternity, and will to eternity, without beginning of days or end of years. The keys have to be brought from heaven whenever the Gospel is sent. When they are revealed from heaven, it is by Adam's authority.

Eternity of the Priesthood.

Daniel in his seventh chapter speaks of the Ancient of Days; he means the oldest man, our Father Adam, Michael,† he will call his children together and hold a council with them to prepare them for the coming of the Son of Man. He (Adam) is the

Adam's Place in the Order of the Worthies.

"* And God said, Let us make man in our image, after our likeness: and let them have dominion over the fish of the sea, and over the fowl of the air, and over the cattle, and over all the earth, and over every creeping thing that creepeth upon the earth. So God created man in his own image, in the image of God created he him; male and female created he them. And God blessed them, and God said unto them, Be fruitful, and multiply, and replenish the earth, and subdue it: and have dominion over the fish of the sea, and over the fowl of the air, and over every living thing that moveth upon the earth.—Gen. I: 26-28.

† The reader will better understand the Prophet's exposition of the 7th chapter of Daniel if those parts of it with which he deals are before him, hence the following quotation:

"I beheld till the thrones were cast down, and the Ancient of Days did sit, whose garment was white as snow, and the hair of his head like the pure wool: his throne was like the fiery flame, and his wheels as burning fire. A fiery stream issued and came forth from before him: thousand thousands ministered unto him and ten thousand times ten thousand stood before him: the judgment was set, and the books were opened. * * * * I saw in the night visions, and, behold, one like the Son of Man came with the clouds of heaven, and came to the Ancient of Days, and they brought him near before him. And there was given him dominion, and glory, and a kingdom, that all people, nations, and languages, should serve him: his dominion is an everlasting dominion, which shall not pass away, and his kingdom that which shall not be destroyed."

The Prophet Daniel saw an earth-power arise and make war upon the Saints and prevail against them until—

father of the human family, and presides over the spirits of all men, and all that have had the keys must stand before him in this grand council. This may take place before some of us leave this stage of action. The Son of Man stands before him, and there is given him glory and dominion. Adam delivers up his stewardship to Christ, that which was delivered to him as holding the keys of the universe, but retains his standing as head of the human family.

The Spirit of Man Eternal.

The spirit of man is not a created being; it existed from eternity, and will exist to eternity. Anything created cannot be eternal; and earth, water, etc., had their existence in an elementary state, from eternity. Our Savior speaks of children and says, Their angels always stand before my Father. The Father called all spirits before Him at the creation of man, and organized them. He (Adam) is the head, and was told to multiply. The keys were first given to him, and by him to others. He will have to give an account of his stewardship, and they to him.

The Nature of the Priesthood.

The Priesthood is everlasting. The Savior, Moses, and Elias, gave the keys to Peter, James, and John, on the mount, when they were transfigured before him. The Priesthood is everlasting—without beginning of days or end of years; without father, mother, etc. If there is no change of ordinances, there is no change of Priesthood. Wherever the ordinances of the Gospel are administered, there is the Priesthood.

The Restoration of the Priesthood.

How have we come at the Priesthood in the last days? It came down, down, in regular succession. Peter, James, and John had it given to them and they gave it to others. Christ is the

"The Ancient of Days came, and judgment was given to the Saints of the Most High; and the time came that the Saints possessed the kingdom. * * * * And the kingdom and dominion, and the greatness of the kingdom under the whole heavens, shall be given to the people of the Saints of the Most High, whose kingdom is an everlasting kingdom, and all dominions shall serve and obey him."

Great High Priest; Adam next.* Paul speaks of the Church coming to an innumerable company of angels—to God the Judge of all—the spirits of just men made perfect; to Jesus the Mediator of the new covenant.—Heb. xii: 23.

Adam in the Valley of Adam-ondi-Ahman.

I saw Adam in the valley of Adam-ondi-Ahman. He called together his children and blessed them with a patriarchal blessing. The Lord appeared in their midst, and he (Adam) blessed them all, and foretold what should befall them to the latest generation.†

Labors of the Patriarchs and Moses.

This is why Adam blessed his posterity; he wanted to bring them into the presence of God. They looked for a city, etc., ["whose builder and maker is God."—Heb. xi: 10]. Moses sought to bring the children of Israel into the presence of God, through the power of the Priesthood, but he could not. In the first ages of the world they tried to establish the same thing; and there were Eliases raised up who tried to restore these very glories, but did not obtain them; but they prophesied of a day when this glory would be revealed. Paul spoke of the dispensation of the fullness of times, when God would gather together all things in one, etc.; and those men to whom these keys have been given,

* This is in keeping with the word of the Lord in a revelation given March, 1832, where the Lord, in speaking to the Saints, said that it was His desire—

"That you may come up unto the crown prepared for you, and be made rulers over many kingdoms, saith the Lord God, the Holy One of Zion, who hath established the foundations of Adam-ondi-Ahman; who hath appointed Michael [Adam] your prince, and established his feet, and set him upon high, and given unto him the keys of salvation under the counsel and direction of the Holy One, who is without beginning of days or end of life."

It is generally supposed that Brigham Young was the author of the doctrine which places Adam as the patriarchal head of the human race, and ascribes to him the dignity of future presidency over this earth and its inhabitants, when the work of redemption shall have been completed. Those who read the Prophet's treatise on the Priesthood in the text above will have their opinions corrected upon this subject; for clearly it is the word of the Lord through the Prophet Joseph Smith which established that docrine. The utterances of President Brigham Young but repeat and expound the doctrine which the Prophet here sets forth.

†Doctrine and Covenants, sec. cvii: 53-57.

will have to be there; and they without us cannot be made perfect.

Angels to Have Part in the Work.

These men are in heaven, but their children are on the earth. Their bowels yearn over us. God sends down men for this reason. "And the Son of Man shall send forth His angels, and they shall gather out of His kingdom all things that give offense and them that do iniquity."—(Matt. xiii: 41). All these authoritative characters will come down and join hand in hand in bringing about this work.

The Kingdom of Heaven.

The Kingdom of Heaven is like a grain of mustard seed. The mustard seed is small, but brings forth a large tree, and the fowls lodge in the branches. The fowls are the angels. Thus angels come down, combine together to gather their children, and gather them. We cannot be made perfect without them, nor they without us; when these things are done, the Son of Man will descend, the Ancient of Days sit; we may come to an innumerable company of angels, have communion with and receive instructions from them. Paul told about Moses' proceedings; spoke of the children of Israel being baptized.—(I Cor. x: 1-4). He knew this, and that all the ordinances and blessings were in the Church. Paul had these things, and we may have the fowls of heaven lodge in the branches, etc.

Future Deliverance of the Saints.

The "Horn" made war with the Saints and overcame them, until the Ancient of Days came; judgment was given to the Saints of the Most High from the Ancient of Days; the time came that the Saints possessed the Kingdom. This not only makes us ministers here, but in eternity.

Importance of Revelation.

Salvation cannot come without revelation; it is in vain for anyone to minister without it. No man is a minister of Jesus Christ without being a Prophet. No man can be a minister of Jesus Christ except he has the testimony of Jesus; and this is the spirit of prophecy. Whenever salvation has been administered, it has been by testimony. Men of the present time testify of heaven and hell, and have never seen either; and I will say that no man knows these things without this.

A Vision and Prophecy.

Men profess to prophesy. I will prophesy that the signs of the coming of the Son of Man are already commenced. One pestilence will desolate after another. We shall soon have war and bloodshed. The moon will be turned into blood. I testify of these things, and that the coming of the Son of Man is nigh, even at your doors. If our souls and our bodies are not looking forth for the coming of the Son of Man; and after we are dead, if we are not looking forth, we shall be among those who are calling for the rocks to fall upon them.

The Mission of Elijah.

The hearts of the children of men will have to be turned to the fathers, and the fathers to the children, living or dead, to prepare them for the coming of the Son of Man. If Elijah did not come, the whole earth would be smitten.

Blessings for the Saints in Stakes of Zion.

There will be here and there a Stake [of Zion] for the gathering of the Saints. Some may have cried peace, but the Saints and the world will have little peace from henceforth. Let this not hinder us from going to the Stakes; for God has told us to flee, not dallying, or we shall be scattered, one here, and another there. There your children shall be blessed, and you in the midst of friends where you may be blessed. The Gospel net gathers of every kind.

Haste to Build up Zion.

I prophesy, that that man who tarries after he has an opportunity of going, will be afflicted by the devil. Wars are at hand; we must not delay; but are not required to sacrifice. We ought to have the building up of Zion as our greatest object. When wars come, we shall have to flee to Zion. The cry is to make haste. The last revelation says, Ye shall not have time to have gone over the earth, until these things come. It will come as did the cholera, war, fires, and earthquakes;

one pestilence after another, until the Ancient of Days comes, then judgment will be given to the Saints.

Peace in Zion and Her Stakes.

Whatever you may hear about me or Kirtland, take no notice of it; for if it be a place of refuge, the devil will use his greatest efforts to trap the Saints. You must make yourselves acquainted with those men who like Daniel pray three times a day toward the House of the Lord. Look to the Presidency and receive instruction. Every man who is afraid, covetous, will be taken in a snare. The time is soon coming, when no man will have any peace but in Zion and her stakes.

The Prophet's Vision of Judgment.

I saw men hunting the lives of their own sons, and brother murdering brother, women killing their own daughters, and daughters seeking the lives of their mothers. I saw armies arrayed against armies. I saw blood, desolation, fires. The Son of Man has said that the mother shall be against the daughter, and the daughter against the mother. These things are at our doors. They will follow the Saints of God from city to city. Satan will rage, and the spirit of the devil is now enraged. I know not how soon these things will take place; but with a view of them, shall I cry peace? No! I will lift up my voice and testify of them. How long you will have good crops, and the famine be kept off, I do not know; when the fig tree leaves, know then that the summer is nigh at hand.

Visions.

We may look for angels and receive their ministrations, but we are to try the spirits and prove them, for it is often the case that men make a mistake in regard to these things. God has so ordained that when He has communicated, no vision is to be taken but what you see by the seeing of the eye, or what you hear by the hearing of the ear. When you see a vision, pray for the interpretation; if you get not this, shut it up; there must be certainty in this matter. An open vision will manifest that which is more important. Lying spirits are going forth in the earth. There will be great manifestations of spirits, both false and true.

Being born again, comes by the Spirit of God through ordinances. An angel of God never has wings. Some will say that they have seen a spirit; that he offered them his hand, but they did not touch it. This is a lie. First, it is contrary to the plan of God: a spirit cannot come but in glory; an angel has flesh and bones; we see not their glory. The devil may appear as an angel of light. Ask God to reveal it; if it be of the devil, he will flee from you; if of God, He will manifest Himself, or make it manifest. We may come to Jesus and ask Him; He will know all about it; if He comes to a little child, He will adapt himself to the language and capacity of a little child.

Angels.

Every spirit, or vision, or singing, is not of God. The devil is an orator; he is powerful; he took our Savior on to a pinnacle of the Temple, and kept Him in the wilderness for forty days. The gift of discerning spirits will be given to the Presiding Elder. Pray for him that he may have this gift. Speak not in the gift of tongues without understanding it, or without interpretation. The devil can speak in tongues; the adversary will come with his work; he can tempt all classes; can speak in English or Dutch. Let no one speak in tongues unless he interpret, except by the consent of the one who is placed to preside; then he may discern or interpret, or another may. Let us seek for the glory of Abraham, Noah, Adam, the Apostles, who have communion with [knowledge of] these things, and then we shall be among that number when Christ comes.

Powers of the Devil.

The Gift of Tongues.

CHAPTER XXVII.

BAPTISM OF ISAAC GALLAND—EPISTLE OF THE TWELVE TO THE CHURCH.

Wednesday, July 3, 1839.—I baptized Dr. Isaac Galland, and confirmed him at the water's edge; and about two hours afterwards I ordained him to the office of an Elder.

Afternoon. I was engaged in dictating my history.

About this time the Twelve wrote the following epistle:

Epistle of the Twelve.

To the Elders of the Church of Jesus Christ of Latter-day Saints, to the Churches Scattered Abroad and to All the Saints:

We, the undersigned, feeling deeply interested in the welfare of Zion, the upbuilding of the Church of Christ, and the welfare of the Saints in general, send unto you greeting, and pray that "grace, mercy and peace may rest upon you from God our Father and the Lord Jesus Christ." But, brethren, the situation of things as they have of late existed has been to us of a peculiarly trying nature.

Many of you have been driven from your homes, robbed of your possessions, and deprived of the liberty of conscience. You have been stripped of your clothing, plundered of your furniture, robbed of your horses, your cattle, your sheep, your hogs, and refused the protection of law; you have been subject to insult and abuse, from a set of lawless miscreants; you have had to endure cold, nakedness, peril and sword; your wives and your children have been deprived of the comforts ot life; you have been subject to bonds, to imprisonment, to banishment, and many to death, "for the testimony of Jesus, and for the word of God." Many of your brethren, with those whose souls are now under the altar, are crying for the vengeance of heaven to rest upon the heads of their devoted murderers, and saying, "How long, O Lord, holy and true, dost Thou not judge and avenge our blood on them that dwell on the earth?" But it was said to them, that they should rest yet for a little season, until their fellow servants also and their brethren that should be killed, as *they were*, should be fulfilled.

Dear brethren, we would remind you of this thing; and although you have had indignities, insults and injuries heaped upon you till further suffering would seem to be no longer a virtue; we would say, be patient, dear brethren, for as saith the apostle, "Ye have need of patience, that after being tried, ye may inherit the promise." You have been tried in the furnace of affliction; the time to exercise patience is now come; and we shall reap, brethren, in due time, if we faint not. Do not breathe vengeance upon your oppressors, but leave the case in the hands of God; "for vengeance is mine, saith the Lord, and I will repay."

We would say to the widow and the orphan, to the destitute and to the diseased, who have been made so through persecution, be patient; you are not forgotten; the God of Jacob has His eye upon you; the heavens have been witness to your sufferings, and these are registered on high; angels have gazed upon the scene, and your tears, your groans, your sorrows, and anguish of heart, are had in remembrance before God; they have entered into the sympathies of one whose bosom is "touched with the feelings of our infirmities," and who was "tempted in all points like unto you;" they have entered into the ears of the Lord of Sabaoth; be patient, then, until the words of God be fulfilled and His design accomplished; and then shall He pour out His vengeance upon the devoted heads of your murderers; and then shall they know that He is God, and that you are His people.

And we would say to all the Saints who have made a covenant with the Lord by sacrifice, that, inasmuch as you are faithful, you shall not lose your reward, although not numbered among those who were in the late difficulties in the west.

We wish to stimulate all the brethren to faithfulness; you have been tried, you are now being tried; and those trials, if you are not watchful, will corrode the mind, and produce unpleasant feelings; but recollect that now is the time of trial; soon the victory will be ours; now may be a day of lamentation—then will be a day of rejoicing; now may be a day of sorrow—but by and by we shall see the Lord; our sorrow will be turned into joy, and our joy no man taketh from us. Be honest; be men of truth and integrity; let your word be your bond; be diligent, be prayerful; pray for and with your families; train up your children in the fear of the Lord; cultivate a meek, a quiet spirit; clothe the naked, feed the hungry, help the destitute, be merciful to the widow and orphan, be merciful to your brethren, and to all men; bear with one another's infirmities, considering your own weakness; bring no railing accusations against your brethren, especially take care that you do not against the authorities or Elders of the Church, for that principle is of the devil; he is called the accuser of the brethren; and Michael, the archangel, dared not bring a railing accusation against the devil, but said, "The Lord rebuke thee, Satan;" and any man who pursues this course of accusation and murmuring, will fall into the snare of the devil, and apostatize, except he repent.

Jude, in the eighth verse, says, "These filthy dreamers defile the flesh, despise dominion, and speak evil of dignities;" and, says he, "Behold, the Lord cometh with ten thousands of His Saints, to execute judgment upon all, and to convince all that are ungodly among them of all their ungodly deeds which they have ungodly committed, and of all their hard speeches which ungodly sinners have spoken against him."

Peter, speaking on the same principle, says: "The Lord knoweth how to deliver the godly out of temptations, and to reserve the unjust unto the day of judgment to be punished: but chiefly them that walk after the flesh in the lust of uncleanness, and despise government. Presumptuous are they, self-willed, they are not afraid to speak evil of dignities. Whereas angels, which are greater in power and might, bring not railing accusation against them before the Lord."

If a man sin, let him be dealt with according to the law of God in the Bible, the Book of Mormon and Doctrine and Covenants; and then leave him in the hands of God to rebuke, as Michael left the devil. Gird yourselves with righteousness, and let truth, eternal truth, be written indelibly on your hearts. Pray for the prosperity of Zion, for the Prophet and his counselors, for the Twelve, the High Council, the High Priests, the Seventies, the Elders, the Bishops, and all Saints—that God may bless them, and preserve His people in righteousness, and grant unto them wisdom and intelligence; that His kingdom may roll forth.

We would say to the Elders, that God has called you to an important office; He has laid upon you an onerous duty; He has called you to an holy calling, even to be the priests of the Most High God, messengers to the nations of the earth; and upon your diligence, your perseverance and faithfulness, the soundness of the doctrines which you preach, the moral precepts that you advance and practice, and upon the sound principles that you inculcate, while you hold that priesthood, hang the destinies of the human family. You are the men that God has called to spread forth His kingdom; He has committed the care of souls to your charge, and when you received this priesthood, you became the legates of heaven; and the Great God demands it of you, that you should be faithful; and inasmuch as you are not, you will not be chosen; but it will be said unto you, "Stand by and let a more honorable man than thou art take thy place, and receive thy crown."

Be careful that you teach not for the word of God the commandments of men, nor the doctrines of men, nor the ordinances of men, inasmuch as you are God's messengers. Study the word of God, and preach it and not your opinions, for no man's opinion is worth a straw. Advance no principle but what you can prove, for one scriptural proof is worth ten thousand opinions. We would moreover say, abide by that revelation which says "Preach nothing but repentance to this generation," and leave the further mysteries of the kingdom till God shall tell you to preach them, which is not now.

The horns of the beast, the toes of the image, the frogs, and the beast mentioned by John, are not going to save this generation; for if a man does not become acquainted with the first principles of the Gospel, how shall he understand those greater mysteries, which the most wise cannot understand without revelation? These things, therefore, have nothing to do with your mission.

We have heard of some foolish vagaries, and wild speculations, originating only in a disordered imagination, which are set forth by some, telling what occupation they had before they came into this world, and what they would be employed with after they leave this state of existence; those and other vain imaginations we would warn the Elders against, because if they listen to such things, they will fall into the snare of the devil; and when the trying time comes, they will be overthrown.

We would also warn the Elders, according to previous counsel, not to go on to another's ground without invitation, to interfere with an other's privilege, for your mission is to the world, and not to the churches.

We would also remark, that no man has a right to usurp authority or power over any church, nor has any man power to preside over any church, unless he is solicited and received by the voice of that church to preside.

Preach the first principles of the doctrine of Christ—faith in the Lord Jesus Christ, repentance towards God, baptism in the name of Jesus for the remission of sins, laying on of hands for the gift of the Holy Ghost, the resurrection of the dead, and eternal judgment.

When you go forth to preach, and the Spirit of God rests upon you, giving you wisdom and utterance, and enlightening your understanding, be careful that you ascribe the glory to God, and not to yourselves. Boast not of intelligence, of wisdom, or of power; for it is only that which God has imparted unto you; but be humble, be meek, be patient and give glory to God.

We would counsel all who have not received a recommend since the difficulties in Missouri, to obtain one from the authorities of the Church if they wish to be accounted as wise stewards.

We are glad, dear brethren, to see that spirit of enterprise and perseverance which is manifested by you in regard to preaching the Gospel;

and rejoice to know that neither bonds nor imprisonment, banishment nor exile, poverty or contempt, nor all the combined powers of earth and hell, hinder you from delivering your testimony to the world, and publishing those glad tidings which have been revealed from heaven by the ministering of angels, by the gift of the Holy Ghost, and by the power of God, for the salvation of the world in these last days. And we would say to you that the hearts of the Twelve are with you, and they, with you, are determined to fulfill their mission, to clear their garments of the blood of this generation, to introduce the Gospel to foreign nations, and to make known to the world these great things which God has developed. They are now on the eve of their departure for England, and will start in a few days. They feel to pray for you and to solicit an interest in your prayers and in the prayers of the Church, that God may sustain them in their arduous undertaking, grant them success in their mission, deliver them from the powers of darkness, and stratagem of wicked men, and all the combined powers of earth and hell. And if you unitedly seek after unity of purpose and design: if you are men of humility and of faithfulness, of integrity and perseverance; if you submit yourselves to the teachings of heaven, and are guided by the Spirit of God; if you at all times seek the glory of God and the salvation of men, and lay your honor prostrate in the dust, if need be, and are willing to fulfill the purposes of God in all things, the power of the Priesthood will rest upon you, and you will become mighty in testimony; the widow and the orphan will be made glad and the poor among men rejoice in the Holy One of Israel. Princes will listen to the things that you proclaim, and the nobles of the earth will attend with deference to your words; queens will rejoice in the glad tidings of salvation, and kings bow to the sceptre of Immanuel; light will burst forth as the morning, and intelligence spread itself as the rays of the sun; the cringing sycophant will be ashamed, and the traitor flee from your presence; superstition will hide its hoary head, and infidelity be ashamed. And amid the clamor of men, the din of war, the rage of pestilence, the commotion of nations, the overthrow of kingdoms, and the dissolution of empires, Truth shall walk forth with mighty power, guided by the arm of Omnipotence, and lay hold of the honest in heart among all nations; Zion shall blossom as a rose, and the nations flock to her standard, and the kingdoms of this world shall soon become the kingdoms of our God and of His Christ, and He shall reign for ever and ever. Amen.

Brigham Young,
Heber C. Kimball,
John E. Page,
Wilford Woodruff,
John Taylor,
Geo. A. Smith.

N. B.—We have heard that a man by the name of John M. Hinkle is preaching in the Iowa territory. We would remark to the public, that we have withdrawn our fellowship from him, and will not stand accountable for any doctrines held forth by him; nor will we be amenable for his conduct. The minutes of a conference will be published, mentioning the names of others from whom we have withdrawn our fellowship.

CHAPTER XXVIII.

THE ESCAPE OF PARLEY P. PRATT AND HIS FELLOW PRISONERS FROM MISSOURI—THE CLOSE OF AN EPOCH.

Thursday, July 4, 1839.—I dictated history.

To show the situation of the prisoners at Columbia, Missouri, I quote from Elder Pratt's "Persecution of the Saints"—

Parley P. Pratt's Account of His Escape from Missouri.

Sister Phelps, Orson Pratt, and Sister Phelps' brother came from Illinois on horseback and visited with us for several days.* On the fourth of July we felt desirous as usual to celebrate the anniversary of American liberty; we accordingly manufactured a white flag, consisting of the half of a shirt, on which was inscribed the word "Liberty," in large letters, and also a large American eagle was put on in red; we then obtained a pole from our jailer, and on the morning of the fourth, this flag was suspended from the front window of our prison, overhanging the public square, and floating triumphantly in the air to the full view of the citizens who assembled by hundreds to celebrate the National Jubilee.

With this the citizens seemed highly pleased, and sent a portion of

* This was really a rescuing party as the subsequent events clearly disclose. The plan of escape was as follows: Orson Pratt waited on the district judge and district attorney and obtained various papers and arranged for summoning witnesses from Illinois to attend a trial which had just been adjourned for some months. He was to procure an order from the court to take affidavits in Illinois in case the witnesses should object to come to the state from which they had been banished to attend the trial. This activity on the part of the prisoners for a trial, and their engaging a lawyer or two and paying part of their fees in advance to defend their case, served as a sufficient covering for the real intentions of the rescuing party. The papers were all prepared and placed in the hands of Orson Pratt, but the company of visitors were to remain until after the 4th of July celebration. Arrangements were also made by which Mrs. Phelps was to stay with her husband a few weeks in prison, engaging her board in the meantime in the family of the jailer who occupied part of the prison as a residence. When Orson Pratt and Mr. Clark, brother of Mrs. Phelps, departed, apparently on their mission to secure witnesses, they took Sister Phelps' horse with them as if to take it back to Illinois, all of which, of course, served stillmore to conceal the real plot that was laid for the escape of the prisoners. (See Autobiography of Parley P. Pratt p. 268).

the public dinner to us and our friends, who partook with us in prison with merry hearts, as we intended to gain our liberties or be in paradise before the close of that eventful day.

While we were thus employed in prison, the town was alive with troops parading, guns firing, music sounding, and shouts of joy resounding on every side. In the meantime we wrote the following toast, which was read at their public dinner, with many and long cheers—

"The patriotic and hospitable citizens of Boone county: opposed to tyranny and oppression, and firm to the original principles of republican liberty; may they, in common with every part of our wide spreading country, long enjoy the blessings which flow from the fountain of American Independence."

Our dinner being ended, our two brethren took leave of us and started for Illinois, (leaving Mrs. Phelps to still visit with her husband;) they had proceeded a mile or two on the road and then took into the woods, and finally placed their three horses in a thicket within one-third of a mile of the prison, and there they waited in anxious suspense until sundown. In the meantime we put on our coats and hats and waited for the setting sun.

With prayer and supplication for deliverance from this long and tedious bondage, and for a restoration to the society of our friends and families, we then sung the following lines—

Lord cause their foolish plans to fail,
And let them faint or die;
Our souls would quit this loathsome jail,
And fly to Illinois.

To join with the embodied Saints,
Who are with freedom blessed—
That only bliss for which we pant—
With them a while to rest.

Give joy for grief—give ease for pain;
Take all our foes away;
But let us find our friends again,
In this eventful day.

Thus ended the celebration of our National Liberty; but the gaining of our own was the grand achievement now before us. In the meantime, the sun was setting; the moment arrived—the footsteps of the jailer were heard on the stairs; every man flew to his feet, and stood near the door. The great door was opened, and our supper handed in through a small hole in the inner door, which still remained locked; but at length the key was turned in order to hand in the pot of coffee. No sooner was the key turned than the door was jerked open, and in a moment all three of us were out—and rushing down the stairs, through the entry, and out into the door yard, when Phelps cleared himself without injuring the jailor, and all of us leaped several fences, ran through the fields towards the thicket, where we expected to find our friends and horses.

In the meantime the town was alarmed; and many were seen rushing after us, some on horseback, and some on foot, prepared with dogs, guns, and whatever came to hand. But the flag of Liberty, with its eagle, still floated on high in the distance: and under that banner, our nerves seemed to strengthen at every step.

We gained the horses, mounted, and dashed into the wilderness, each his own way. After a few jumps of my horse, I was hailed by an armed man at pistol shot distance, crying, "d—— you, stop, or I'll shoot you!" I rushed onward deeper into the forest, while the cry was repeated in close pursuit, "d—— you, stop, or I'll shoot you," at every step, till at length it died away in the distance. I plunged a mile into the forest—came to a halt—tied my horse in a thicket—went a distance, and climbed a tree, to await the approaching darkness.

Being so little used to exercise, I fainted through over-exertion, and remained so faint for nearly an hour that I could not get down from the tree; but calling on the Lord, He strengthened me, and I came down from the tree. But my horse had got loose and gone. I then made my way on foot for several days and nights, principally without food, and scarcely suffering myself to be seen.

After five days of dreadful suffering, with fatigue and hunger, I crossed the Mississippi, and found myself once more in a land of freedom. Mr. Phelps made his escape also;* but King Follet was retaken

* The account of Phelp's escape is thus given by Parley P. Pratt: "Mr. Phelps made his escape much in the same manner as myself. He was at first closely pursued, but at length he out-distanced them all, and, once out of their sight, he struck directly into the road, and rode on toward Illinois. He had proceeded but a few miles on his way, when he was suddenly surrounded in the darkness of the night by a company of horsemen who were out in pursuit of the prisoners. They immediately hailed him, and cried out, 'Say, stranger, G—d d—— you, what is your name?' He replied in the same rough and careless manner, 'You d——d rascals, what is yours?' On finding that he could 'damn' as well as themselves, they concluded he could not be a Mormon, while his bold and fearless manner convinced them that he was not a man who was fleeing for his life. They then begged his pardon for the rough manner in which they had accosted him, 'Oh, you are one of the real breed. By G—d, no d——d Mormon could counterfeit that language, you swear real natteral; hurrah for old Kentuck. But whar mout you live, stranger?" He replied, "just up here; you mout a kno'd me, and then agin you moun't. I think I've seed you all a heap o' times, but I've been so d——d drunk at the fourth of Independence, I hardly know myself or anybody else, but hurrah for old Kentuck; and what about the d——d Mormons?' 'What about

and carried back.* Luman Gibbs continued in the prison; he had apostatized and turned traitor to the others."

'em? egad, you'd a know'd that without axin', if you'd a seed 'em run.' 'What! they are not out of prison, are they?' 'Out of prison! yes, the d——d rascals raised a flag of liberty in open day, and burst out, and down stairs right into the midst of the public celebration, out-wrestling the d——d jailer, and outrunning the whole town in a fair foot race. They reached the timber jist as they war overtaken, but afore we could cotch 'em they mounted their nags, and the way they cleared was a caution to Crockett. We tuk one on 'em, and seed the other two a few feet distant, rushin' their nags at full speed, but we couldn't cotch 'em nor shoot 'em either; I raised my new Kentucky rifle, fresh loaded and primed, with a good percussion, and taking fair aim at one of their heads only a few yards distant, I fired, but the d——d cap burst, and the powder wouldn't burn.' 'Well, now, stranger, that's a mighty big story, and seems enemost impossible. Did you say you cotched one on 'em? Why I'd a tho't you'd a kilt him on the spot; what have you done with him?' 'They tuk him back to prison, I suppose, but it was only the old one. If it had been one o' them tother chaps we would a skinn'd 'em as quick as Crockett would a coon, and then eat 'em alive without leaving a grease spot.'

"This interview over, the horsemen withdrew and left Phelps to pursue his way in peace; * * * * and he finally arrived in Illinois in safety, having reached the ferry before his pursuers, and before the news of the escape had spread so far." (Autobiography of Parley P. Pratt pp. 282-4).

* What befell Brother King Follet after he was captured, and his final escape from Missouri is thus related by Parley P. Pratt:

"He had been surrounded, overpowered and taken at the time we were each separated from the others. He was finally rescued from the mob, and thrust alive into the lower dungeon and chained down to the floor. He remained in this doleful situation for a few days, till the wrath of the multitude had time to cool a little, and then he was unchained by the Sheriff and again brought into the upper apartment and treated with some degree of kindness. They now laughed with him about his adventure, praised him for his bravery, and called him a good fellow. The truth of the matter was, they had no great desire to take the lives of any but those whom they had considered leaders; and since they had discovered that Mr. Follett and Mr. Phelps were not considered religious leaders among our society, they were in no great danger, except they should happen to be killed in the heat of excitement or passion. * * * * * Mr. Follet remained in confinement for several months, and finally was dismissed and sent home to Illinois, where he met his family, who had been expelled from the State of Missouri, in common with others, during his confinement." (Autobiography of Parley P. Pratt, pp. 288-9).

The escape of these prisoners from Missouri completed the expulsion of the Latter-day Saints from that state, and closed a great epoch in the history of the Church.

APPENDIX TO VOLUME III.

AFFIDAVITS OF HYRUM SMITH *et al.* ON AFFAIRS IN MISSOURI, 1831-39; OFFICIALLY SUBSCRIBED TO BEFORE THE MUNICIPAL COURT OF NAUVOO THE FIRST DAY OF JULY, 1843.

Explanatory Note.

[In the month of June, 1843, a desperate effort was made to drag the Prophet Joseph Smith back to the state of Missouri, on a charge of treason against that state; and also alleging that because of his escape from Liberty prison in Clay county, Missouri, he had become a fugitive from justice. A process was issued by Thomas Reynolds, governor of the state of Missouri, and placed in the hands of Joseph H. Reynolds, appointed the agent of that state to receive the Prophet from the hands of the Illinois authorities who were to make the arrest. Thomas Ford, governor of Illinois, issued the necessary papers for the arrest, and placed them in the hands of Harmon T. Wilson, who, in company with Reynolds, the Missouri agent, arrested the Prophet near Dixon in Lee county, Illinois, something more than two hundred miles north and east of Nauvoo. The Prophet managed with the assistance of his friends in Illinois, to be returned to Nauvoo, where he succeeded in getting out a writ of *habeas corpus* before the municipal court of that place, by which he was delivered from the hands of the Missouri agent. In the course of the *ex parte* hearing the following witnesses were examined, *viz.*, Hyrum Smith, Parley P. Pratt, Brigham Young, George W. Pitkin, Lyman Wight, and Sidney Rigdon. In the course of the examination of these witnesses by affidavit the story of the persecutions of the Latter-day Saints is related at length. It cannot be said that anything new is added to the Missouri period of the Church history by these affidavits, but they are statements made officially before a court of inquiry and therefore have a value of their own on that account, and as this is a documentary history of the Church, these volumes would be incomplete without them. A desire to group all events closelyrelated has in duced the Editors to take these affidavits out of the place where they were given, in 1843, and place them in this volume, which is so largely devoted to the Missouri period of the Church history.

The municipal court of Nauvoo sat on the first day of July, 1843, at eight o'clock a. m., William Marks acting as chief justice, Daniel H. Wells, Newel K. Whitney,George W. Harris,Gustavus Hills and Hiram Kimball associate justices and the witnesses were examined in the order in which their affidavits are here published.

I.

THE TESTIMONY OF HYRUM SMITH.

Hyrum Smith sworn, said that the defendant now in court is his brother, and that his name is not Joseph Smith, Jun., but Joseph Smith, Sen., and has been for more than two years past.* I have been acquainted with him ever since he was born, which was thirty-seven years in December last; and I have not been absent from him at any one time not even for the space of six months, since his birth, to my recollection, and have been intimately acquainted with all his sayings, doings, business transactions and movements, as much as any one man could be acquainted with another man's business, up to the present time, and do know that he has not committed treason against any state in the Union, by any overt act, or by levying war, or by aiding, abetting or assisting an enemy in any state in the Union; and that the said Joseph Smith, Sen.,has not committed treason in the state of Missouri, or violated any law or rule of said state; I being personally acquainted with the transactions and doings of said Smith whilst he resided in said state, which was for about six months in the year 1838; I being also a resident in said state during the same period of time; and I do know that said Joseph Smith, Sen., never was subject to military duty in any state, neither was he in the state of Missouri, he being exempt by the amputation or extraction of a bone from his leg, and by having a license to preach the Gospel, or being, in other words, a minister of the Gospel; and I do know that said Smith never bore arms, as a military man, in any capacity whatever, whilst in the state of Missouri, or previous to that time; neither has he given any orders or assumed any command in any capacity whatever. But I do know that whilst he was in the state of Missouri, the people commonly called "Mormons" were threatened with violence and extermination; and on or about the first

* Joseph Smith, the father of the prophet, died on September 14th, 1840, and hence at the time these warrants were issued against the prophet in June, 1843, he was no longer Joseph Smith, Junior, but Joseph Smith, Senior.

Monday in August, 1838, at the election in Gallatin, the county seat in Daviess county, the citizens who were commonly called "Mormons" were forbidden to exercise the rights of franchise; and from that circumstance an affray commenced and a fight ensued among the citizens of that place; and from that time a mob commenced gathering in that county, threatening the extermination of the "Mormons." The said Smith and myself, upon hearing the mobs were collecting together, and that they also murdered two of the citizens of the same place, [Gallatin] and would not suffer them to be buried, the said Smith and myself went over to Daviess county to learn the particulars of the affray; but upon our arrival at Diahman we learned that none was killed, but several were wounded. We tarried all night at Colonel Lyman Wight's. The next morning, the weather being very warm, and having been very dry, for some time previously, the springs and wells in the region were dried up. On mounting our horses to return, we rode up to Mr. Black's who was then an acting justice of the peace, to obtain some water for ourselves and horses. Some few of the citizens accompanied us there; and, after obtaining water, Mr. Black was asked by said Joseph Smith, Sen., if he would use his influence to see that the laws were faithfully executed, and to put down mob violence; and he gave us a paper written by his own hand, stating that he would do so. He [Joseph Smith, Sen.] also requested him to call together the most influential men of the county on the next day, that we might have an interview with them. To this he acquiesced, and, accordingly, the next day they assembled at the house of Colonel Wight, and entered into a mutual covenant of peace to put down mob violence and protect each other in the enjoyment of their rights. After this, we all parted with the best of feelings, and each man returned to his own home.

This mutual agreement of peace, however, did not last long; for, but a few days afterwards, the mob began to collect again, until several hundreds rendezvoused at Millport, a few miles distant from Diahman. They immediately commenced making aggressions upon the citizens called "Mormons," taking away their hogs and cattle and threatening them with extermination or utter extinction, saying that they had a cannon, and there should be no compromise only at its mouth. They frequently took men, women and children prisoners, whipping them and lacerating their bodies with hickory withes, and tying them to trees and depriving them of food until they were compelled to gnaw the bark from the trees to which they were bound, in order to sustain life; treating them in the most cruel manner they could invent or think of, and doing everything they could to excite the indignation of the "Mormon" people to rescue them, in order that they might make that a pretext for an accusation for the breach of the law, and that they might the better excite the prejudice of the populace, and thereby get aid and assistance to carry out their hellish purposes of extermination.

Immediately on the authentication of these facts, messengers were despatched from Far West to Austin A. King, judge of the fifth judicial district of the state of Missouri, and also to Major-General Atchison, commander-in-chief of that division, and Brigadier-General Doniphan, giving them information of the existing facts, and demanding immediate assistance.

General Atchison returned with the messengers, and went immediately to Diahman, and from thence to Millport, and he found that the facts were true as reported to him—that the citizens of that county were assembled together in a hostile attitude, to the number of two or three hundred men, threatening the utter extermination of the "Mormons." He at once returned to Clay county, and ordered out a sufficient military force to quell the mob.

Immediately after, they were dispersed, and the army returned. The mob commenced collecting again soon after. We again applied for military aid, when General Doniphan came out with a force of sixty armed men to Far West; but they were in such a state of insubordination that he said he could not control them, and it was thought advisable by Col. Hinkle, Mr. Rigdon and others, that they should return home. General Doniphan ordered Colonel Hinkle to call out the militia of Caldwell and defend the town against the mob; for, said he, you have great reason to be alarmed. He said Neil Gillium, from the Platte county, had come down with two hundred armed men, and had taken up their station at Hunter's Mill, a place distant about seventeen or eighteen miles northwest of the town of Far West, and also that an armed force had collected again at Millport, in Daviess county, consisting of several hundred men; and that another armed force had collected at De Witt, in Carroll county, about fifty miles southeast of Far West, where about seventy families of the "Mormon" people had settled upon the banks of the Missouri river, at a little town called De Witt.

Immediately, whilst he was yet talking, a messenger came in from De Witt, stating that three or four hundred men had assembled together at that place, armed *cap-a-pie*, and that they had threatened the utter extinction of the citizens of De Witt, if they did not leave the place immediately; and that they had also surrounded the town and cut off all supplies of food, so that many of the inhabitants were suffering from hunger.

General Doniphan seemed to be very much alarmed, and appeared to be willing to do all he could to assist and to relieve the sufferings of the "Mormon" people. He advised that a petition be gotten up at once and sent to the Governor. A petition was accordingly prepared, and a messenger despatched to the governor, and another petition was sent to Judge King.

The "Mormon" people throughout the country were in a great state of alarm and also in great distress. They saw themselves completely surrounded by armed forces on the north, and on the northwest and on the south. Bogart, who was a Methodist preacher and a captain over a militia company of fifty soldiers, but who had added to this number out of the surrounding counties about one hundred more, which made his force about one hundred and fifty strong, was stationed at Crooked creek, sending out his scouting parties, taking men, women and children prisoners, driving off cattle, hogs and horses, entering into every house on Log and Long creeks, rifling their houses of their most precious articles, such as money, bedding and clothing, taking all their old muskets and their rifles, or military implements, threatening the people with instant death, if they did not deliver up all their precious things and enter into a covenant to leave the state or go into the city of Far West by the next morning, saying that they "calculated to drive the people into Far West, and then drive them to hell." Gillium also was doing the same on the northwest side of Far West; and Sashiel Woods, a Presbyterian minister, was the leader of the mob in Daviess county; and a very noted man of the same society was the leader of the mob in Carroll county. And they were also sending out their scouting parties, robbing and pillaging houses, driving away hogs, horses and cattle, taking men, women and children and carrying them off, threatening their lives, and subjecting them to all manner of abuses that they could invent or think of.

Under this state of alarm, excitement and distress, the messengers returned from the governor and from the other authorities, bringing the startling news that the "Mormons" could have no assistance. They stated that the governor said the "Mormons" had got into a difficulty with the citizens, and they might fight it out, for all he cared. He could not render them any assistance.

The people of De Wit were obliged to leave their homes and go into Far West, but did not do so until after many of them had starved to death for want of proper sustenance, and several died on the road there, and were buried by the wayside, without a coffin or a funeral ceremony; and the distress, sufferings, and privations of the people cannot be expressed.

All the scattered families of the "Mormon" people, with but few exceptions, in all the counties, except Daviess, were driven into Far West.

This only increased their distress, for many thousands who were driven there had no habitations or houses to shelter them, and were huddled together, some in tents and others under blankets, while others had no shelter from the inclemency of the weather. Nearly two months the people had been in this awful state of consternation; many of them had been killed, whilst others had been whipped until they had to swathe up their bowels to prevent them from falling out.

About this time General Parks came out from Richmond, Ray county. He was one of the commissioned officers sent out at the time the mob was first quelled, and went out to Diahman. My brother, Joseph Smith, Sen., and I went out at the same time.

On the evening that General Parks arrived at Diahman, the wife of my brother, the late Don Carlos Smith, came into Colonel Wight's about 11 o'clock at night, bringing her two children along with her, one about two and a half years old, the other a babe in her arms.

She came on foot, a distance of three miles, and waded Grand river. The water was then waist deep, and the snow three inches deep. She stated that a party of the mob—a gang of ruffians—had turned her out of doors and taken her household goods, and had burnt up her house, and she had escaped by the skin of her teeth. Her husband at that time was in Tennessee, [on a mission] and she was living alone.

This cruel transaction excited the feelings of the people of Diahman, especially of Colonel Wight and he asked General Parks in my hearing *how long we had got to suffer such base treatment.* General Parks said he did not know how long.

Colonel Wight then asked him what should be done? General Parks told him "he should take a company of men, well armed, and go and disperse the mob wherever he should find any collected together, and take away their arms." Colonel Wight did so precisely according to the orders of General Parks. And my brother, Joseph Smith, Sen., made no order about it.

And after Col. Wight had dispersed the mob, and put a stop to their burning houses belonging to the "Mormon" people, and turning women and children out of doors, which they had done up to that time to the number of eight or ten houses, which houses were consumed to ashes. After being cut short in their intended designs, the mob started up a new plan. They went to work and moved their families out of the county and set fire to their houses; and not being able to incense the "Mormons" to commit crimes, they had recourse to this stratagem to set their houses on fire, and send runners into all the counties adjacent to declare to the people that the "Mormons" had burnt up their houses and destroyed their fields; and if the people would not believe them, they would tell them to go and see if what they had said was not true.

Many people came to see. They saw the houses burning; and, being filled with prejudice, they could not be made to believe but that the

"Mormons" set them on fire; which deed was most diabolical and of the blackest kind; for indeed the "Mormons" did not set them on fire, nor meddle with their houses or their fields.

And the houses that were burnt, had all been previously purchased by the "Mormons" of the people, together with the pre-emption rights and the corn in the fields, and paid for in money, and with wagons and horses, and with other property, about two weeks before; but they had not taken possession of the premises. This wicked transaction was for the purpose of clandestinely exciting the minds of a prejudiced populace and the executive, that they might get an order that they could the more easily carry out their hellish purposes, in expulsion, or extermination, or utter extinction of the "Mormon" people.

After witnessing the distressed situation of the people in Diahman, my brother, Joseph Smith, Sen., and myself returned to the city of Far West, and immediately dispatched a messenger, with written documents, to General Atchison, stating the facts as they did then exist, praying for assistance, if possible, and requesting the editor of the *Far West* to insert the same in his newspaper. But he utterly refused to do so.

We still believed that we should get assistance from the Governor, and again petitioned him, praying for assistance, setting forth our distressed situation. And in the meantime the presiding judge of the county court issued orders, upon affidavits made to him by the citizens, to the sheriff of the county, to order out the militia of the county to stand in constant readiness, night and day, to prevent the citizens from being massacred, which fearful situation they were in every moment.

Everything was very portentous and alarming. Notwithstanding all this, there was a ray of hope yet existing in the minds of the people that the governor would render us assistance; and whilst the people were waiting anxiously for deliverance—men, women, and children frightened, praying, and weeping, we beheld at a distance, crossing the prairies and approaching the town, a large army in military array, brandishing their glittering swords in the sunshine; and we could not but feel joyful for a moment, thinking that probably the governor had sent an armed force to our relief, notwithstanding the awful forebodings that pervaded our breasts.

But, to our great surprise, when the army arrived, they came up and formed a line in double file within one-half mile on the south of the city of Far West, and despatched three messengers with a white flag to the city. They were met by Captain Morey, with a few other individuals, whose names I do not now recollect. I was myself standing close by, and could very distinctly hear every word they said.

Being filled with anxiety, I rushed forward to the spot, expecting to hear good news. But, alas! and heart-thrilling to every soul that heard them, they demanded three persons to be brought out of the city before they should massacre the rest.

The names of the persons they demanded were Adam Lightner, John Cleminson, and his wife. Immediately the three persons were brought forth to hold an interview with the officers who had made the demand, and the officers told them they had now a chance to save their lives, for they intended to destroy the people and lay the city in ashes. They replied to the officers, if the people must be destroyed and the city burned to ashes, they would remain in the city and die with them.

The officers immediately returned, and the army retreated and encamped about a mile and a half from the city.

A messenger was at once dispatched with a white flag from the colonel of the militia of Far West, requesting an interview with General Atchison and General Doniphan; but as the messenger approached the camp, he was shot at by Bogart, the Methodist preacher.

The name of the messenger was Charles C. Rich, who is now [1843] Brigadier-General in the Nauvoo Legion. However, he gained permission to see General Doniphan; he also requested an interview with General Atchison.

General Doniphan said that General Atchison had been dismounted a few miles back, by a special order of the Governor, and had been sent back to Liberty, Clay county. He also stated that the reason was, that he (Atchison) was too merciful unto the "Mormons," and Boggs would not let him have the command, but had given it to General Lucas, who was from Jackson county, and whose heart had become hardened by his former acts of rapine and bloodshed, he being one of the leaders in murdering, driving, and plundering the "Mormon" people in that county, and burning some two or three hundred of their houses, in the years 1833 and 1834.

Mr. Rich requested General Doniphan to spare the people, and not suffer them to be massacred until the next morning, it then being evening. He coolly agreed that he would not, and also said that he had not as yet received the Governor's order, but expected it every hour, and should not make any further move until he had received it; but he would not make any promises so far as regarded Neil Gillium's army, it having arrived a few minutes previously and joined the main body of the army, he [Gillium] knowing well at what hour to form a junction with the main body.

Mr. Rich then returned to the city, giving this information. The Colonel [G. M. Hinkle] immediately dispatched a second messenger with a white flag, to request another interview with General Doniphan, in order to touch his sympathy and compassion, and, if it were possible for him to use his best endeavors to preserve the lives of the people.

On the return of this messenger. we learned that several persons had been killed by some of the soldiers who were under the command of General Lucas.

One Mr. Carey had his brains knocked out by the breech of a gun, and he lay bleeding several hours; but his family were not permitted to approach him, nor any one else allowed to administer relief to him whilst he lay upon the ground in the agonies of death.

Mr. Carey had just arrived in the country, from the State of Ohio, only a few hours previous to the arrival of the army. He had a family, consisting of a wife and several small children. He was buried by Lucius N. Scovil, who is now [1843] the senior Warden of the Nauvoo [Masonic] lodge.

Another man, of the name of John Tanner, was knocked on the head at the same time, and his skull laid bare to the width of a man's hand; and he lay, to all appearances, in the agonies of death for several hours; but by the permission of General Doniphan, his friends brought him out of the camp; and with good nursing, he slowly recovered, and is now living.

There was another man, whose name is Powell, who was beat on the head with the breech of a gun until his skull was fractured, and his brains ran out in two or three places. He is now alive and resides in this [Hancock] county, but has lost the use of his senses. Several persons of his family were also left for dead, but have since recovered.

These acts of barbarity were also committed by the soldiers under the command of General Lucas, previous to having received the Governor's order of extermination.

It was on the evening of the 30th October, according to the best of my recollections, that the army arrived at Far West, the sun about half-an-hour high. In a few moments afterwards, Cornelius Gillium arrived with his army and formed a junction.

This Gillium had been stationed at Hunter's Mills for about two months previous to that time, committing depredations upon the inhabitants, capturing men, women, and children carrying them off as prisoners and lacerating their bodies with hickory withes.

The army of Gillium were painted like Indians: some, more conspicuous than others, were designated by red spots; and he also was painted in a similar manner with red spots marked on his face, and styled himself the "DELAWARE CHIEF." They would whoop and halloo, and yell as nearly like Indians as they could, and continued to do so all that night.

In the morning, early, the colonel of militia [G. M, Hinkle] sent a messenger into the camp with a white flag, to have another interview with General Doniphan. On his return, he informed us that the governor's order had arrived.

General Doniphan said that the order of the governor was, to exterminate the Mormons, by God; but *he* would be *damned* if *he* obeyed *that order*, but General Lucas might do what he pleased.

We immediately learned from General Doniphan, that "the Governor's order that had arrived was only a copy of the original, and that the original order was in the hands of Major-General Clark, who was on his way to Far West with an additional army of 6,000 men."

Immediately after this, there came into the city a messenger from Haun's Mills, bringing the intelligence of an awful massacre of the people who were residing in that place, and that a force of two or three hundred detached from the main body of the army, under the superior command of Colonel Ashley, but under the immediate command of Captain Nehemiah Comstock, who, the day previous, had promised them peace and protection; but on receiving a copy of the Governor's order "to *exterminate or to expel*" from the hands of Colonel Ashley, he returned upon them the following day and surprised and massacred nearly the whole population of the place, and then came on to the town of Far West, and entered into conjunction with the main body of the army.

The messenger informed us that he himself, with a few others, fled into the thickets, which preserved them from the massacre; and on the following morning they returned and collected the dead bodies of the people, and cast them into a well; and there were upwards of 20 who were dead or mortally wounded; and there are several of the wounded now [1843] living in this city [Nauvoo].

One, of the name of Yocum, has lately had his leg amputated, in consequence of wounds he then received. He had a ball shot through his head, which entered near his eye and came out at the back part of his head, and another ball passed through one of his arms.

The army, during all the while they had been encamped at Far West, continued to lay waste fields of corn, making hogs, sheep, and cattle common plunder, and shooting them down for sport.

One man shot a cow and took a strip of her skin, the width of his hand, from her head to her tail, and tied it around a tree to slip his halter into to tie his horse with.

The city was surrounded with a strong guard; and no man, woman or child was permitted to go out or to come in, under penalty of death. Many of the citizens were shot at in attempting to go out to obtain sustenance for themselves and families.

There was one field fenced in, consisting of 1,200 acres, mostly covered with corn. It was entirely laid waste by the hands of the army. The next day after the arrival of the army, towards evening, Colonel Hinkle came up from the camp, requesting to see my brother Joseph, Parley P. Pratt, Sidney Rigdon, Lyman Wight, and George W. Robinson, stating that the officers of the army wanted a mutual consultation with those men; Hinkle also assured them that these generals—Doniphan, Lucas, Wilson, and Graham—(however, General Graham is an honorable exception; he did all he could to preserve the lives of the people, contrary to the order of the governor);—had pledged their sacred honor that they should not be abused or insulted, but should be guarded back in safety in the morning, or as soon as the consultation was over.

My brother Joseph replied that he did not know what good he could do in any consultation, as he was only a private individual. However, he said he was always willing to do all the good he could, and would obey every law of the land, and then leave the event with God.

They immediately started with Colonel Hinkle to go down into the camp. As they were going down, about half way to the camp, they met General Lucas with a phalanx of men, with a wing to the right and to the left, and a four-pounder [cannon] in the center. They supposed he was coming with this strong force to guard them into the camp in safety; but, to their surprise, when they came up to General Lucas, he ordered his men to surround them, and Hinkle stepped up to the general and said, "These are the prisoners I agreed to deliver up." General Lucas drew his sword and said, "Gentlemen, you are my prisoners," and about that time the main army were on their march to meet them.

They came up in two divisions, and opened to the right and left, and my brother and his friends were marched down through their lines, with a strong guard in front, and the cannon in the rear, to the camp, amidst the whoopings, howlings, yellings, and shoutings of the army, which were so horrid and terrific that it frightened the inhabitants of the city.

It is impossible to describe the feelings of horror and distress of the people.

After being thus betrayed, they [the prisoners] were placed under a strong guard of thirty men, armed *cap-a-pie*, who were relieved every two hours. They were compelled to lie on the cold ground that night, and were told in plain language that they need never to expect their liberties again. So far for their honor pledged! However, this was as much as could be expected from a mob under the garb of military and executive authority in the state of Missouri.

On the next day, the soldiers were permitted to patrol the streets, of Far West to abuse and insult the people at their leisure, and enter into houses and pillage them, and ravish the women, taking away every gun and every other kind of arms or military implements. About twelve o'clock on that day, Colonel Hinkle came to my house with an armed force, opened the door, and called me out of doors and delivered me up as a prisoner unto that force. They surrounded me and commanded me to march into the camp. I told them that I could not go; my family were sick, and I was sick myself, and could not leave home. They said they did not care for that—I must and should go. I asked when they would permit me to return. They made me no answer, but forced me along with the point of the bayonent into the camp, and put me under the same guard with my brother Joseph; and within about half an hour afterwards, Amasa Lyman was also brought and placed under the same guard. There we were compelled to stay all that night and lie on the ground. But some time in the same night, Colonel Hinkle came to me and told me that he had been pleading my case before the court-martial, but he was afraid he would not succeed.

He said there was a court-martial then in session, consisting of thirteen or fourteen officers; Circuit Judge Austin A. King, and Mr. Birch, district attorney; also Sashiel Woods, Presbyterian priest, and about twenty other priests of the different religious denominations in that country. He said they were determined to shoot us on the next morning in the public square in Far West. I made him no reply.

On the next morning, about sunrise, General Doniphan ordered his brigade to take up the line of march and leave the camp. He came to us where we were under guard, to shake hands with us, and bid us farewell. His first salutation was, "By God, you have been sentenced by the court-martial to be shot this morning; but I will be damned if I will have any of the honor of it, or any of the disgrace of it; therefore I have ordered my brigade to take up the line of march and to leave the camp, for I consider it to be cold-blooded murder, and I bid you farewell;" and he went away.

This movement of Colonel Doniphan made considerable excitement in the army, and there was considerable whisperings amongst the officers. We listened very attentively, and frequently heard it mentioned by the guard that "the damned Mormons would not be shot this time."

In a few moments the guard was relieved by a new set. One of those new guards said that "the damned Mormons would not be shot this time," for the movement of General Doniphan had frustrated the whole plan, and that the officers had called another court-martial, and had ordered us to be taken to Jackson county, and there to be executed; and in a few moments two large wagons drove up, and we were ordered to get into them; and while we were getting into them, there came up four or five men armed with guns, who drew up and snapped their guns at us, in order to kill us; some flashed in the pan, and others only snapped, but none of their guns went off. They were immediately arrested by several officers, and their guns taken from them, and the drivers drove off.

We requested General Lucas to let us go to our houses and get some clothing. In order to do this, we had to be driven up into the city. It was with much difficulty that we could get his permission to go and see our families and get some clothing; but, after considerable consultation, we were permitted to go under a strong guard of five or six men to each of us, and we were not permitted to speak to any one of our families, under the pain of death. The guard that went with me ordered my wife to get me some clothes immediately, within two minutes; and if she did not do it, I should go off without them.

I was obliged to submit to their tyrannical orders, however painful it was, with my wife and children clinging to my arms and to the skirts of my garments, and was not permitted to utter to them a word of consolation, and in a moment was hurried away from them at the point of the bayonet.

We were hurried back into the wagons and ordered into them, all in about the same space of time. In the meanwhile our father and mother and sisters had forced their way to the wagons to get permission to see us, but were forbidden to speak to us; and they [the guard] immediately drove off for Jackson county. We traveled about twelve miles that evening, and encamped for the night.

The same strong guard was kept around us, and were relieved every two hours, and we were permitted to sleep on the ground. The nights were then cold, with considerable snow on the ground; and for want of covering and clothing, we suffered extremely with the cold. That night was the commencement of a fit of sickness, from which I have not wholly recovered unto this day, in consequence of my exposure to the inclemency of the weather.

Our provision was fresh beef roasted in the fire on a stick, the army having no bread, in consequence of the want of mills to grind the grain.

In the morning, at the dawn of day, we were forced on our journey, and were exhibited to the inhabitants along the road, the same as they exhibit a caravan of elephants and camels. We were examined from head to foot by men, women and children, only I believe they did not make us open our mouths to look at our teeth. This treatment was continued incessantly until we arrived at Independence, in Jackson county.

After our arrival at Independence, we were driven all through the town for inspection, and then we were ordered into an old log house, and there kept under guard as usual, until supper, which was served up to us as we sat upon the floor, or on billets of wood, and we were compelled to stay in that house all that night and the next day.

They continued to exhibit us to the public, by letting the people come in and examine us, and then go away and give place for others, alternately, all that day and the next night. But on the morning of the following day, we were all permitted to go to the tavern to eat and to sleep; but afterward they made us pay our own expenses for board, lodging, and attendance, and for which they made a most exorbitant charge.

We remained in the tavern about two days and two nights, when an officer arrived with authority from General Clark to take us back to Richmond, Ray county, where the general had arrived with his army to await our arrival. But on the morning of our start for Richmond, we were informed, by General Wilson, that it was expected by the soldiers that we would be hung up by the necks on the road, while on the march to that place, and that it was prevented by a demand made for us by General Clark, who had the command in consequence of seniority; and that it was his prerogative to execute us himself; and he should give us up into the hands of the officer, who would take us to General Clark, and he might do with us as he pleased.

During our stay at Independence, the officers informed us that there were eight or ten horses in that place belonging to the Mormon people, which had been stolen by the soldiers, and that we might have two of them to ride upon, if we would cause them to be sent back to the owners after our arrival at Richmond.

We accepted them, and they were ridden to Richmond, and the owners came there and got them.

We started in the morning under our new officer, Colonel Price, of Keytsville, Chariton county, with several other men to guard us.

We arrived there on Friday evening, the 9th day of November, and were thrust into an old log house, with a strong guard placed over us.

After we had been there for the space of half an hour, there came in a man who was said to have some notoriety in the penitentiary, bringing in his hands a quantity of chains and padlocks. He said he was commanded by General Clark to put us in chains.

Immediately the soldiers rose up, and pointing their guns at us, placed their thumb on the cock, and their finger on the trigger; and the state's prison-keeper went to work, putting a chain around the leg of each man, and fastening it on with a padlock, until we were all chained together—seven of us.

In a few moments General Clark came in. We requested to know of him what was the cause of all this harsh and cruel treatment. He refused to give us any information at that time, but said he would in a few days; so we were compelled to continue in that situation camping on the floor, all chained together, without any chance or means to be made comfortable, having to eat our victuals as it was served up to us, using our fingers and teeth instead of knives and forks.

Whilst we were in this situation, a young man of the name of Jedediah M. Grant, brother-in-law to my brother William Smith, came to see us, and put up at the tavern where General Clark made his quarters. He happened to come in time to see General Clark make choice of his men to shoot us on Monday morning, the 12th day of November. He saw them make choice of their rifles, and load them with two balls in each; and after they had prepared their guns, General Clark saluted them by saying, "*Gentlemen, you shall have the honor of shooting the Mormon leaders on Monday morning at eight o'clock!*"

But in consequence of the influence of our friend, the inhuman general was intimidated, so that he dared not carry his murderous designs into execution, and sent a messenger immediately to Fort Leavenworth to obtain the military code of laws.

After the messenger's return the general was employed nearly a whole week examining the laws; so Monday passed away without our being shot. However, it seemed like foolishness to me that so great a man as General Clark pretended to be should have to search the military law to find out whether preachers of the Gospel, who never did military duty, could be subject to court-martial.

However, the general seemed to learn that fact after searching the military code, and came into the old log cabin where we were under guard and in chains, and told us he had concluded to deliver us over to the civil authorities as persons guilty of "treason, murder, arson, larceny, theft, and stealing." The poor deluded general did not know the difference between theft, larceny, and stealing.

Accordingly, we were handed over to the pretended civil authorities, and the next morning our chains were taken off, and we were guarded to the court-house, where there was a pretended court in session, Austin A. King being the judge, and Mr. Birch the district attorney—the two extremely and very honorable gentlemen who sat on the court-martial when we were sentenced to be shot!

Witnesses were called up and sworn at the point of the bayonet; and if they would not swear to the things they were told to do, they were threatened with instant death; and I do know positively that the evidence given in by those men whilst under duress was false.

This state of things continued twelve or fourteen days; and after that time, we were ordered by the judge to introduce some rebutting evidence--saying that, if we did not do it, we should be thrust into prison.

I could hardly understand what the judge meant, for I considered we were in prison already, and could not think of anything but the persecutions of the days of Nero, knowing that it was a religious persecution, and the court an inquisition. However, we gave him the names of forty persons who were acquainted with all the persecutions and sufferings of the people.

The judge made out a subpoena and inserted the names of those men, and caused it to be placed in the hands of Bogart, the notorious Methodist minister; and he took fifty armed soldiers and started for Far West. I saw the subpoenas given to him and his company, when they started.

In the course of a few days they returned with almost all those forty men whose names were inserted in the subpoenas, and thrust them into jail, and we were not permitted to bring one of them before the court. But the judge turned upon us with an air of indignation and said, "Gentlemen, you must get your witnesses, or you shall be committed to jail immediately; for we are not going to hold the court open on expense much longer for you anyhow."

We felt very much distressed and oppressed at that time. Colonel Wight said, "What shall we do? Our witnesses are all thrust into prison, and probably will be; and we have no power to do anything. Of course, we must submit to this tyranny and oppression: we cannot help ourselves."

Several others made similar expressions in the agony of their souls; but my brother Joseph did not say anything, he being sick at that time with the toothache and pain in his face, in consequence of a severe cold brought on by being exposed to the severity of the weather.

However, it was considered best by General Doniphan and lawyer Rees that we should try to get some witnesses before the pretended court.

Accordingly, I gave the names of about twenty other persons. The Judge inserted them in a subpœna, and caused it to be placed into the hands of Bogart, the Methodist priest; and he again started off with his fifty soldiers to take those men prisoners, as he had done the forty others.

The Judge sat and laughed at the good opportunity of getting the names, that they might the more easily capture them, and so bring them down to be thrust into prison, in order to prevent us from getting the truth before the pretended court, of which he was the chief inquisitor or conspirator. Bogart returned from his second expedition with one witness only, whom he also thrust into prison.

The people at Far West had learned the intrigue, and had left the state, having been made acquainted with the treatment of the former witnesses.

But we, on learning that we could not obtain witnesses, whilst privately consulting with each other what we should do, discovered a Mr. Allen standing by the window on the outside of the house. We beckoned to him as though we would have him come in. He immediately came in.

At that time Judge King retorted upon us again, saying, "Gentlemen, are you not going to introduce some witnesses?"—also saying it was the last day he should hold court open for us; and that if we did not rebutt the testimony that had been given against us, he should have to commit us to jail.

I had then got Mr. Allen into the house and before the court (so called). I told the Judge we had one witness, if he would be so good as to put him under oath. He seemed unwilling to do so; but after a few moments consultation, the State's Attorney arose and said he should object to that witness being sworn, and that he should object to that witness giving in his evidence at all, stating that this was not a court to try the case, but only a court of investigation on the part of the state.

Upon this, General Doniphan arose and said, "He would be —— —— if the witness should not be sworn, and that it was a damned shame that these defendants should be treated in this manner,—that they could not be permitted to get one witness before the court, whilst all their witnesses, even forty at a time, have been taken by force of arms and thrust into that damned 'bull pen,' in order to prevent them from giving their testimony."

After Doniphan sat down, the Judge permitted the witness to be sworn and enter upon his testimony, but as soon as he began to speak, a man by the name of Cook, who was a brother-in-law to priest Bogart, the Methodist, and who was a lieutenant, [in the state militia] and whose duty at that time was to superintend the guard, stepped in before the pretended court, and took him by the nape of his neck and jammed his head down under the pole, or log of wood, that was around the place where the inquisition was sitting to keep the bystanders from intruding upon the majesty of the inquisitors, and jammed him along to the door, and kicked him out of doors. He instantly turned to some soldiers who were standing by him, and said to them, "Go and shoot him, damn him; shoot him, damn him."

The soldiers ran after the man to shoot him. He fled for his life, and with great difficulty made his escape. The pretended court immediately arose, and we were ordered to be carried to Liberty, Clay county, and there to be thrust into jail. We endeavored to find out for what cause; but all we could learn was, that it was because we were "Mormons."

The next morning a large wagon drove up to the door, and a blacksmith came into the house with some chains and handcuffs. He said his orders were from the Judge to handcuff us and chain us together. He informed us that the Judge had made out a mittimus and sentenced us to jail for treason. He also said the Judge had done this that we might not get bail. He also said the Judge declared his intention to keep us in jail until all the "Mormons" were driven out of the state. He also said that the Judge had further declared that if he let us out before the "Mormons" had left the state, we would not let them leave, and there would be another damned fuss kicked up. I also heard the Judge say, whilst he was sitting in his pretended court, that there was no law for us, nor for the "Mormons" in the state of Missouri; that he had sworn to see them exterminated and to see the Governor's order executed to the very letter; and that he would do so. However, the blacksmith proceeded and put the irons upon us, and we were ordered into the wagon, and they drove off for Clay county. As we journeyed along on the road, we were exhibited to the inhabitants, and this course was adopted all the way, thus making a public exhibition of us, until we arrived at Liberty, Clay county.

There we were thrust into prison again, and locked up, and were held there in close confinement for the space of six months; and our place of lodging [bed] was the square side of a hewed white oak log, and our food was anything but good and decent. Poison was administered to us three or four times. The effect it had upon our system was, that it vomited us almost to death; and then we would lie some two or three days in a torpid, stupid state, not even caring or wishing for life,—the poison being administered in too large doses, or it would inevitably have proved fatal, had not the power of Jehovah interposed in our behalf, to save us from their wicked purpose.

We were also subjected to the necessity of eating human flesh for the space of five days or go without food, except a little coffee or a little corn-bread. The latter I chose in preference to the former. We none of us partook of the flesh, except Lyman Wight. We also heard the guard which was placed over us making sport of us, saying they had fed us on "Mormon" beef. I have described the appearance of this flesh to several experienced physicians and they have decided that it was human flesh. We learned afterwards, by one of the guard, that it was supposed that that act of savage cannibalism in feeding us with human flesh would be considered a popular deed of notoriety: but the people, on learning that it would not take, tried to keep it secret; but the fact was noised abroad before they took that precaution.

Whilst we were incarcerated in prison we petitioned the Supreme Court of the state of Missouri for [a writ of] habeas corpus twice but were refused both times by Judge Reynolds, who is now [1843] the Governor of that state. We also petitioned one of the county Judges for a writ of habeas corpus, which was granted in about three weeks afterwards, but were not permitted to have any trial. We were only taken out of jail and kept out for a few hours, and then remanded back again.

In the course of three or four days after that time, Judge Turnham came into the jail in the evening, and said he had permitted Mr. Rigdon to get bail, but said he had to do it in the night, and had also to get away in the night and unknown to any of the citizens, or they would kill him; for they had sworn to kill him, if they could find him. And as to the rest of us, he dared not let us go, for fear of his own life as well as ours. He said it was damned hard to be confined under such circumstances, for he knew we were innocent men; and he said *the people also knew it*; and that it was only a persecution, and treachery, and the scenes of Jackson county acted over again, for fear that we should become too numerous in that upper country. He said that the plan was concocted from the governor down to the lowest judge and that damned Baptist priest, Riley, who was riding into town every day to watch the people, stirring up the minds of the people against us all he could, exciting them and stirring up their religious prejudices against us, for fear they would let us go. Mr. Rigdon, however, got bail and made his escape into Illinois.

The jailer, Samuel Tillery, Esq., told us also that the whole plan was concocted by the governor down to the lowest judge in that upper country early in the previous spring, and that the plan was more fully carried out at the time that General Atchison went down to Jefferson city with Generals Wilson, Lucas, and Gillium, the self-styled Delaware Chief. This was sometime in the month of September, when the mob were collected at De Witt, in Carroll county. He also told us that the governor was now ashamed enough of the whole transaction, and would be glad to set us at liberty, if he dared do it. "But," said he, "you need not be concerned, for the governor has laid a plan for your release." He also said that Squire Birch, the state's attorney, was appointed to be circuit judge on the circuit passing through Daviess county, and that he (Birch) was instructed to fix the papers, so that we should be sure to be clear from any incumbrance in a very short time.

Some time in April we were taken to Daviess county, as they said, to have a trial. But when we arrived at that place, instead of finding a court or jury, we found another inquisition; and Birch, who was the district attorney, the same man who had been one of the court-martial when we were sentenced to death, was now the circuit judge of that pretended court; and the grand jury that were empannelled were all at the massacre at Haun's Mills and lively actors in that awful, solemn, disgraceful, cool-blooded murder; and all the pretense they made of excuse was, they had done it because the governor ordered them to do it.

The same men sat as a jury in the day time, and were placed over us as a guard in the night time. They tantalized us and boasted of their great achievments at Haun's Mills and at other places, telling us how many houses they had burned, and how many sheep, cattle, and hogs they had driven off belonging to the "Mormons," and how many rapes they had committed, and what squealing and kicking there was among the d—— b——s, saying that they lashed one woman upon one of the damned "Mormon" meeting benches, tying her hands and her feet fast, and sixteen of them abused her as much as they had a mind to, and then left her bound and exposed in that distressed condition. These fiends of the lower regions boasted of these acts of barbarity, and tantalized our feelings with them for ten days. We had heard of these acts of cruelty previous to this time, but we were slow to believe that such acts had been perpetrated. The lady who was the subject of this brutality did not recover her health to be able to help herself for more than three months afterwards.

This grand jury constantly celebrated their achievements with grog and glass in hand, like the Indian warriors at their war dances, singing and telling each other of their exploits in murdering the "Mormons," in plundering their houses and carrying off their property. At the end of every song they would bring in the chorus, "G— d—, G— d—, G — d—, Jesus Christ, G— d— the Presbyterians, G— d— the Baptists, G— d— the Methodists," reitering one sect after another in the same manner, until they came to the "Mormons." To them it was, G— d— the G— d— Mormons, we have sent them to hell." Then they would slap their hands and shout, Hosanna! Hosanna! Glory to God! and fall down on their backs and kick with their feet a few moments. Then they would pretend to have swooned away into a glorious trance, in order to imitate some of the transactions at camp meetings. Then they would pretend to come out of the trance, and would shout and again slap their hands and jump up, while one would take a bottle of whisky and a tumbler, and turn it out full of whisky, and pour down each other's necks, crying, "Damn it, take it; you must take it!" And if anyone refused to drink the whisky, others would clinch him and hold him, whilst another poured it down his neck; and what did not go down the inside went down the outside. This is a part of the farce acted out by the grand jury of Daviess county, whilst they stood over us as guards for ten nights successively. And all this in the presence of the *great Judge Birch*, who had previously said, in our hearing, that there was no law for the "Mormons" in the state of Missouri. His brother was there acting as district attorney in that circuit, and, if anything, was a greater ruffian than the judge.

After all their ten days of drunkenness, we were informed that we were indicted for "*treason, murder, arson, larceny, theft, and stealing.*" We asked for a change of venue from that county to Marion county; they would not grant it; but they gave us a change of venue from Daviess to Boone county, and a mittimus was made out by Judge Birch, without date, name, or place.

They fitted us out with a two-horse wagon, and horses, and four men, besides the sheriff, to be our guard. There were five of us. We started from Gallatin in the afternoon, the sun about two hours high, and went as far as Diahman that evening and stayed till morning. There we bought two horses of the guard, and paid for one of them in clothing, which we had with us; and for the other we gave our note.

We went down that day as far as Judge Morin's—a distance of some four or five miles. There we stayed until the next morning, when we started on our journey to Boone county, and traveled on the road about twenty miles distance. There we bought a jug of whisky, with which we treated the company; and while there the sheriff showed us the mittimus before referred to, without date or signature, and said that Judge Birch told him never to carry us to Boone county, and never to show the mittimus; and, said he, I shall take a good drink of grog and go to bed, and you may do as you have a mind to.

Three others of the guard drank pretty freely of whisky, sweetened with honey. They also went to bed, and were soon asleep, and the other guard went along with us, and helped to saddle the horses.

Two of us mounted the horses, and the other three started on foot, and we took our change of venue for the state of Illinois, and in the course of nine or ten days arrived safe at Quincy, Adams county, where we found our families in a state of poverty, although in good health, they having been driven out of the state previously by the murderous militia, under the exterminating order of the executive of Missouri; and now [1843] the people of that state, a portion of them, would be glad to make the people of this state [Illinois] believe that my brother Joseph had committed treason, for the purpose of keeping up their murderous and hellish persecution; and they seem to be unrelenting and thirsting for the blood of innocence; for I do know most positively that my brother Joseph has not committed treason, nor violated one solitary item of law or rule in the state of Missouri.

But I do know that the "Mormon" people, *en masse*, were driven out of that state, after being robbed of all they had; and they barely escaped with their lives, as also my brother Joseph, who barely escaped with his life. His family also were robbed of all they had, and barely escaped with the skin of their teeth, and all this in consequence of the exterminating order of Governor Boggs, the same being sanctioned by the legislature of the state.

And I do know, so does this court, and every rational man who is acquainted with the circumstances, and every man who shall hereafter become acquainted with the particulars thereof, will know that Governor Boggs and Generals Clark, Lucas, Wilson, and Gillium, also Austin A. King, have committed treason upon the citizens of Missouri, and did violate the Constitution of the United States, and also the constitution and laws of the state of Missouri, and did exile and expel, at the point of the bayonet, some twelve or fourteen thousand inhabitants from the state, and did murder a large number of men, women and children in cold blood, and in the most horrid and cruel manner possible; and the whole of it was caused by religious bigotry and persecution, because the "Mormons" dared to worship Almighty God according to the dictates of their own consciences, and agreeable to His divine will as revealed in the scriptures of eternal truth, and had turned away from following the vain traditions of their fathers, and would not worship according to the dogmas and commandments of those men who preach for hire and divine for money, and teach for doctrine the precepts of men; the Saints expecting that the Constitution of the United States would have protected them therein.

But notwithstanding the "Mormon" people had purchased upwards of *two hundred thousand dollars' worth of land*, most of which was entered and paid for at the land office of the United States, in the state of Missouri; and although the President of the United States has been made acquainted with these facts and the particulars of our persecutions and oppressions, by petition to him and to Congress, yet they have not even attempted to restore the "Mormons" to their rights, or given any assurance that we may hereafter expect redress from them. And I do also know most positively and assuredly that my brother Joseph Smith, Sen., has not been in the state of Missouri since the spring of the year 1839. And further this deponent saith not.

[Signed] Hyrum Smith.

II

TESTIMONY OF PARLEY P. PRATT.

Parley P. Pratt, sworn, says that he fully concurs in the testimony of the preceding witness, so far as he is acquainted with the same; and that Joseph Smith has not been known as Joseph Smith, Jun., for the time stated by Hyrum Smith. He was an eye-witness of most of the scenes testified to by said Hyrum Smith, during the persecutions of our people in Missouri. That during the latter part of summer and fall of the year 1838, there were large bodies of the mob assembled in various places for the avowed object of driving, robbing, plundering, killing, and exterminating the "Mormons," and they actually committed many murders and other depredations, as related by the preceding witness.

The Governor was frequently petitioned, as also the other authorities, for redress and protection. At length, Austin A. King, the Judge of the Circuit court of the Fifth Judicial District, ordered out somewhere near a thousand men, for the avowed purpose of quelling the mob and protecting the "Mormons." These being under arms for several weeks, did in some measure prevent the mob's proceedings for some time. After which, Judge King* withdrew the force, refusing to put the State to further expense for our protection without orders from the Governor.

The mobs then again collected in great numbers, in Carroll, Daviess, and Caldwell counties, and expressed their determination to drive the "Mormons" from the State or kill them. They did actually drive them from De Witt, firing upon some, and taking other prisoners.

They turned a man by the name of Smith Humphrey and family out of doors, when sick, and plundered his house and burned it before his eyes. They also plundered the citizens generally, taking their lands, houses, and property.

Those whose lives were spared, precipitately fled to Far West in the utmost distress and consternation. Some of them actually died on the way, through exposure, suffering and destitution. Other parties of the mob were plundering and burning houses in Daviess county, and another party of the mob were ravaging the south part of Caldwell county in a similar manner.

The Governor was again and again petitioned for redress and protection, but utterly refused to render us any assistance whatever. Under these painful and distressing circumstances, we had the advice of Generals Atchison, Doniphan and Parks to call out the militia of Caldwell and Daviess counties, which was mostly composed of "Mormons" and to make a general defense.

The presiding Judge of Caldwell county, Elias Higbee, gave orders to the sheriff of said county to call out the militia. They were called out under the command of Colonel Hinkle, who held a commission from the Governor, and was the highest military officer in the county. This force effectually dispersed the mob in several places, and a portion of

* For explanation of how it was that the militia was under direction of the Judge, a civil officer, see testimony of Sidney Rigdon.

them were so organized in the city of Far West, that they could assemble themselves upon the shortest notice, and were frequently ordered to assemble in the public square of said city, in cases of emergency.

These proceedings against the mob being misrepresented by designing men, both to the Governor and other authorities and people of the State, caused great excitement against the "Mormons." Many tried to have it understood that the "Mormons" were in open rebellion, and making war upon the State.

With these pretenses, Governor Boggs issued the following:—

Exterminating Order.

HEADQUARTERS OF THE MILITIA,
CITY OF JEFFERSON, October 27, 1838.

Gen. John B. Clark.

SIR:—Since the order of the morning to you, directing you to come with 400 mounted men to be raised within your division, I have received, by Amos Rees, Esq., of Ray county, and Wiley C. Williams, Esq., one of my aides, information of the most appalling character, which entirely changes the face of things, and places the "Mormons" in the attitude of an open and avowed defiance of the laws, and of having made war upon the people of this State.

Your orders are, therefore, to hasten your operations with all possible speed. The "Mormons" must be treated as enemies, and must be exterminated or driven from the State, if necessary, for the public peace.

Their outrages are beyond all descriptions. If you can increase your force, you are authorized to do so to any extent you may consider necessary. I have just issued orders to Major-General Willock, of Marion county, to raise 500 men, and to march them to the northern part of Daviess [county], and there unite with General Doniphan, of Clay, who has been ordered with 500 men to proceed to the same point for the purpose of intercepting the retreat of the "Mormons" to the north. They have been directed to communicate with you by express. You can also communicate with them, if you find it necessary.

Instead, therefore, of proceeding as at first directed, to reinstate the citizens of Daviess, in their homes, you will proceed immediately to Richmond, and there operate against the "Mormons."

Brigadier General Parks, of Ray, has been ordered to have 400 of his brigade in readiness to join you at Richmond. The whole force will be placed under your command.

I am very respectfully your ob't Serv't,
L. W. BOGGS,
Commander-in-chief.*

* The above now celebrated "*Exterminating order*" is copied from the collection of Documents published by order of the "General Assembly" of Missouri (the state legislature), 1841.

In the meantime Major-General Lucas and Brigadier-General Wilson, both of Jackson county, (who had, five years previously, assisted in driving about 1,200 "Mormon" citizens from that county, besides burning 203 houses, and assisted in murdering several, and plundering the rest), raised forces to the amount of several thousand men, and appeared before the city of Far West in battle array.

A few of the militia then paraded in front of the city, which caused the cowardly assailants to come to a halt at about a mile distant, in full view of the town.

A messenger arrived from them and demanded three persons before they massacred the rest and laid the town in ashes. The names of the persons demanded were Adam Lightner, John Clemenson, and his wife. They gave no information who this army were, nor by what authority they came; neither had we at that time any knowledge of the governor's order, nor any of these movements, the mail having been designedly stopped by our enemies for three weeks previously. We had supposed, on their first appearance, that they were friendly troops sent for our protection; but on receiving this alarming information of their wicked intentions, we were much surprised, and sent a messenger with a white flag to inquire of them who they were, and what they wanted of us, and by whose authority they came.

This flag was fired upon by Captain Bogart, the Methodist priest, who afterwards told me the same with his own mouth. After several attempts, however, we got an interview, by which we learned who they were, and that they pretended to have been sent by the governor to exterminate our people.

Upon learning this fact no resistance was offered to their will or wishes. They demanded the arms of the militia, and forcibly took them away. They requested that Mr. Joseph Smith and other leaders of the Church should come into their camp for consultation, giving them a sacred promise of protection and safe return. Accordingly, Messrs. Joseph Smith, Sidney Rigdon, Lyman Wight, George W. Robinson, and myself started in company with Colonel Hinkle to their camp when we were soon abruptly met by General Lucas with several hundred of his soldiers, in a hostile manner, who immediately surrounded us, and set up the most hideous yells that might have been supposed to have proceeded from the mouths of demons, and marched us as prisoners within their lines.

There we were detained for two days and nights, and had to sleep on the ground, in the cold month of November, in the midst of rain and mud, and were continually surrounded with a strong guard, whose mouths were filled with cursing and bitterness, blackguardism and blasphemy—who offered us every abuse and insult in their power, both by night and day; and many individuals of the army cocked their rifles and, taking deadly aim at our heads, swore they would shoot us.

While under these circumstances, our ears were continually shocked with the relation of the horrid deeds they had committed and which they boasted of. They related the circumstance in detail of having, the previous day, disarmed a certain man in his own house, and took him prisoner, and afterwards *beat out his brains with his own gun*, in presence of their officers. They told of other individuals lying here and there in the brush, whom they had shot down without resistance, and who were lying unburied for the hogs to feed upon.

They also named one or two individual females of our society, whom they had forcibly bound, and twenty or thirty of them, one after another, committed rape upon them. One of these females was a daughter of a respectable family with whom I have been long acquainted, and with whom I have since conversed and learned that it was truly the case. Delicacy at present forbids my mentioning the names. I also heard several of the soldiers acknowledge and boast of having stolen money in one place, clothing and bedding in another, and horses in another, whilst corn, pork, and beef were taken by the whole army to support the men and horses; and in many cases cattle, hogs, and sheep were shot down, and only a small portion of them used—the rest left to waste. Of these crimes, of which the soldiers boasted, the general officers freely conversed and corroborated the same. And even General Doniphan, who professed to be opposed to such proceedings, acknowledged the truth of them, and gave us several particulars in detail.

I believe the name of the man whose brains they knocked out was Carey, Another individual had his money chest broken open and several hundred dollars in specie taken out. He was the same Smith Humphrey whose house the mob burned at De Witt.

After the "Mormons" were all disarmed, General Lucas gave a compulsory order for men, women, and children to leave the state forthwith, without any exceptions, counting it a mercy to spare their lives on these conditions. Whilst these things were proceeding, instead of releasing us from confinement, Hyrum Smith and Amasa Lyman were forcibly added to our number as prisoners; and under a large military escort, commanded by General Wilson before mentioned, we were all marched to Jackson county, a distance of between fifty and sixty miles, leaving our families and our friends at the mob's mercy, in a destitute condition, to prepare for a journey of more than two hundred miles, at the approach of winter, without our protection, and every moment exposed to robbery, ravishment, and other insults, their personal property robbed and their houses and lands already wrested from them.

We were exhibited like a caravan of wild animals on the way and in the streets of Independence, and were also kept prisoners for a show for several days.

In the meantime, General Clark had been sent by Governor Boggs with an additional force of 6,000 men from the lower country, to join General Lucas in his operations against the "Mormons." He soon arrived before Far West with his army, and confirmed all Lucas had done, and highly commended them for their virtue, forbearance, and other deeds in *bringing about so peaceable and amicable an adjustment of affairs.* He kept up the same scene of ravage, plunder, ravishment, and depredation, for the support and enrichment of his army, even burning the houses and fences for fuel.

He also insisted that every man, woman, and child of the "Mormon" society should leave the state, except such as he detained as prisoners, stating that *the governor had sent him to exterminate them*, but that *he* would, as a *mercy*, *spare* their *lives*, and gave them until the first of April following to get out of the state.

He also compelled them, at the point of the bayonet, to sign a deed of trust of all their real estate, to defray the expenses of what *he* called "*The Mormon War.*"

After arranging all these matters to *his* satisfaction, he returned to Richmond, thirty miles distant, taking about sixty men, heads of families, with him, and marching them through a severe snowstorm on foot, as prisoners, leaving their families in a perishing condition.

Having established his headquarters at Richmond, Ray county, he sent to General Lucas and demanded us to be given up to him. We were accordingly transported some thirty or forty miles, delivered over to him, and put in close confinement in chains, under a strong guard.

At length we obtained an interview with him, and inquired why we were detained as prisoners. I said to him, "Sir, we have now been prisoners, under the most aggravating circumstances, for two or three weeks, during which time we have received no information as to why we are prisoners, or for what object, and no writ has been served upon us. We are not detained by the civil law; and as ministers of the Gospel in time of peace, *who never bear arms*, we cannot be considered prisoners of war, especially as there has been no war; and from present appearances, we can hardly be considered prisoners of hope. Why, then, these bonds?"

Said he, "You were taken to be tried." "Tried by what authority?" said I. "By court-martial," replied he. "By court-martial?" said I. "Yes," said he. "How," said I, "can men who are not military men, but ministers of the Gospel, be tried by court-martial in this country, where every man has a right to be tried by a jury?" He replied, it was according to the treaty with General Lucas, on the part of the state of Missouri, and Colonel Hinkle, the commanding officer of the fortress of Far West, on the part of the "Mormons," and in accordance with the governor's order. "And," said he, "I approve of all that Lucas has done, and am determined to see it fulfilled." Said I, "Colonel Hinkle was but a colonel of the Caldwell county militia, and commissioned by the governor, and the 'Mormons' had no fortress, but were, in common with others, citizens of Missouri; and therefore we recognize no authority in Colonel Hinkle to sell our liberties or make treaties for us."

Several days afterwards, General Clark again entered our prison, and said he had concluded to deliver us over to the civil authorities. Accordingly, we were soon brought before Austin A. King, judge of the Fifth Judicial Circuit, where an examination was commenced, and witnesses sworn, at the point of the bayonet, and threatened on pain of death, if they did not swear to that which would suit the court.

During this examination, I heard Judge King ask one of the witnesses, who was a "Mormon," if he and his friends intended to live on their lands any longer than April, and to plant crops? Witness replied, "Why not?" The judge replied, "If you once think to plant crops or to occupy your lands any longer than the first of April, the citizens will be upon you; they will kill you every one—men, women and children, and leave you to manure the ground without a burial. They have been mercifully withheld from doing this on the present occasion, but will not be restrained for the future."

On examining a "Mormon" witness, for the purpose of substantiating the charge of treason against Mr. Joseph Smith, he questioned him concerning our religious faith:—1st. Do the Mormons send missionaries to foreign nations? The witness answered in the affirmative. 2nd. Do the Mormons believe in a certain passage in the Book of Daniel (naming the passage) which reads as follows:—"And the kingdom and dominion, and the greatness of the kingdom under the whole heaven, shall be given to the people of the Saints of the Most High, whose kingdom is an everlasting kingdom, and all dominions shall serve and obey him?" (Dan. 7: 27.) On being answered in the affirmative, the judge ordered the scribe to put it down as a strong point for treason; but this was *too* much for even a Missouri lawyer to bear. He remonstrated against such a course of procedure, but in vain. Said he, "Judge, you had better make the Bible treason."

After an examination of this kind for many days, some were set at liberty, others [were] admitted to bail, and themselves and [those who went their] bail [were] expelled from the state forthwith, with the rest of the "Mormon" citizens, and Joseph Smith, Hyrum Smith, Sidney

Rigdon, Lyman Wight, and others, were committed to the Clay county jail for further trial. Two or three others and myself were put into the jail at Ray county for the same purpose.

The "Mormon" people now began to leave the state, agreeably to the exterminating order of Governor Boggs. Ten or twelve thousand left the state during the winter, and fled to the state of Illinois.

A small number of the widows and the poor, together with my family and some of the friends of the other prisoners, still lingered in Far West, when a small band of armed men entered the town and committed many depredations and threatened life; and swore that if my wife and children, and others whom they named, were not out of the state in so many days, they would kill them, as the time now drew near for the completion of the exterminating order of Governor Boggs.

Accordingly, my wife and children and others left the state as best they could, wandered to the state of Illinois, there to get a living among strangers, without a husband, father or protector. Myself and party still remained in prison, after all the other "Mormons" had left the state; and even Mr. Smith and his party had escaped.

In June, by change of venue, we were removed from Ray county to Columbia, Boone county, upwards of one hundred miles towards the state of Illinois; and by our request a special court was called for final trial. But notwithstanding we were removed more than one hundred miles from the scenes of the depredations of the mob, yet such was the fact, that neither our friends nor witnesses dare come into that state to attend our trial, as they had been banished from the state by the governor's order of extermination, executed to the very letter by the principal officers of the state, civil and military.

On these grounds, and having had all these opportunities to know, I testify that neither Mr. Smith nor any other "Mormon" has the least prospect for justice, or to receive a fair and impartial trial in the state of Missouri.

If tried at all, they must be tried by authorities who have trampled all law under their feet, and who have assisted in committing murder, robbery, treason, arson, rape, burglary and felony, and who have made a law of banishment, contrary to the laws of all nations, and executed this barbarous law with the utmost rigor and severity.

Therefore, Mr. Smith, and the "Mormons" generally, having suffered without regard to law, having been expelled from the state, Missouri has no further claims whatever upon any of them.

I furthermore testify that the authorities of other states who would assist Missouri to wreak further vengeance upon any individual of the persecuted "Mormons," are either ignorantly or willfully aiding and abetting in all these crimes.

Cross-examined he stated that he was very intimate with Mr. Smith all the time he resided in the state of Missouri, and was with him almost daily; and that he knows positively that Mr. Smith held no office, either civil or military, either real or pretended, in that state; and that he never bore arms or did military duty, not even in self-defense; but that he was a peaceable, law-abiding and faithful citizen, and a preacher of the Gospel, and exhorted all the citizens to be peaceable, long-suffering and slow to act even in self-defense.

He further stated that there was no fortress in Far West, but a temporary fence made of rails, house logs, floor planks, wagons, carts, etc., hastily thrown together, after being told by General Lucas that they were to be massacred the following morning, and the town burnt to ashes, without giving any information by what authority. And he further states that he only escaped himself from that state by walking out of the jail when the door was open to put in food, and came out in obedience to the governor's order of banishment, and to fulfill the same.

PARLEY P. PRATT.

III.

TESTIMONY OF GEORGE W. PITKIN.

George W. Pitkin sworn. Says that he concurs with the preceding witnesses, Hyrum Smith and Parley P. Pratt, in all the facts with which he is acquainted; that in the summer of 1838 he was elected Sheriff of the county of Caldwell and State of Missouri. That in the fall of the same year, while the county was threatened and infested with mobs, he received an order from Judge Higbee, the presiding Judge of said county, to call out the Militia, and he executed the same.

The said order was presented by Joseph Smith, Sen., who showed the witness a letter from General Atchison, giving such advice as was necessary for the protection of the citizens of said county. Reports of the mobs destroying property were daily received. Has no knowledge that Joseph Smith was concerned in organizing or commanding said Militia in any capacity whatever.

About this time he received information that about forty or fifty "Yauger rifles" and a quantity of ammunition were being conveyed through Caldwell to Daviess county, for the use of the mob, upon which he deputized William Allred to go with a company of men and intercept them, if possible. He did so, and brought the said arms and ammunition into Far West, which were afterwards delivered up to the order of Austin A. King, Judge of the Fifth, Circuit in Missouri.

It was generally understood at that time that said arms had been stolen by Neil Gillum and his company of volunteers, who had been upon a six months' tour of service in the war between the United States and the Florida Indians. They were supposed to have been taken from the Fort at Tampa Bay, and brought to Richmond, Clay county, and that Captain Pollard or some other person loaned them to the mob.

He further says that whilst in office as Sheriff, he was forcibly and illegally compelled by Lieutenant Cook, the son-in-law or brother-in-law of Bogart, the Methodist priest, to start for Richmond; and when he demanded of him by what authority he acted, he was shown a bowie-knife and a brace of pistols; and when he asked what they wanted of him, he said they would let him know when he got to Richmond. Many of the citizens of Caldwell county were taken in the same manner, without any legal process whatever, and thrust into prison.

GEORGE W. PITKIN.

IV.

TESTIMONY OF BRIGHAM YOUNG.

Brigham Young sworn. Says that so far as he was acquainted with the facts stated by the previous witnesses, he concurs with them, and that he accompanied Mr. Joseph Smith, Sen., into the State of Missouri, and arrived at Far West on the 14th day of March, 1838, and was neighbor to Mr. Smith until he was taken by Governor Boggs' Militia a prisoner of war, as they said, and that he was knowing to his character whilst in the State of Missouri; and that he, Mr. Smith, was in no way connected with the Militia of that state, neither did he bear arms at all, nor give advice, but was a peaceable, law-abiding, good citizen, and a true Republican in every sense of the word.

He was with Mr. Smith a great share of the time, until driven out of Missouri by an armed force, under the exterminating order of Governor Boggs.

He heard the most of Mr. Smith's public addresses, and never did he hear him give advice or encourage anything contrary to the laws of the State of Missouri; but, to the contrary, always instructing the people to be peaceable, quiet, and law-abiding; and if necessity should compel them to withstand their enemies, by whom they were daily threatened in mobs at various points, that they, the "Mormons," should attend to their business strictly, and not regard reports; and if the mob did come upon them, to contend with them by the strong arm of the law; and if that should fail, our only relief would be self-defense; and be sure and act only upon the defensive. And there were no operations against the mob by the Militia of Caldwell county, only by the advice of Generals Atchison, Doniphan, and Parks.

At the time that the army came in sight of Far West, he observed their approach, and thought some of the Militia of the state had come to the relief of the citizens; but, to his great surprise, he found that they were come to strengthen the hands of the mobs that were around and which immediately joined the army.

A part of these mobs were painted like Indians; and Gillum, their leader, was also painted in a similar manner, and styled himself the "Delaware Chief;" and afterwards he and the rest of the mob claimed and obtained pay as Militia from the state for all the time they were engaged as a mob, as will be seen by reference to the acts of the Legislature.

That there were "Mormon" citizens wounded and murdered by the army under the command of General Lucas; and he verily believes that several women were ravished to death by the soldiery of Lucas and Clark.

He also stated that he saw Joseph Smith, Sidney Rigdon, Parley P. Pratt, Lyman Wight, and George W. Robinson delivered up by Colonel Hinkle to General Lucas, but expected that they would have returned to the city that evening or the next morning, according to agreement, and the pledge of the sacred honor of the officers that they should be allowed to do so; but they did not return at all.

The next morning, General Lucas demanded and took away the arms of the Militia of Caldwell county, (which arms have never been returned), assuring them that they should be protected. But as soon as they obtained possession of the arms, they commenced their ravages by plundering the citizens of their bedding, clothing, money, wearing apparel, and everything of value they could lay their hands upon; and also attempting to violate the chastity of the women in sight of their husbands and friends, under the pretence of hunting for prisoners and arms.

The soldiers shot down our oxen, cows, hogs, and fowls at our own doors, taking part away and leaving the rest to rot in the streets. The soldiers also turned their horses into our fields of corn.

Here the witness was shown General Clark's speech, which is as follows, viz.:—

"Gentlemen,—You, whose names are not attached to this list of names, will now have the privilege of going to your fields, and of providing corn, wood, etc., for your families.

"Those that are now taken will go from this to prison, be tried, and receive the due demerit of their crimes; but you (except such as charges may hereafter be preferred against,) are at liberty as soon as the troops are removed that now guard the place, which I shall cause to be done immediately.

"It now devolves upon you to fulfill the treaty that you have entered into, the leading items of which I shall now lay before you.

"The first requires that your leading men be given up to be tried according to law. This you have complied with. The second is, that you deliver up your arms. This has also been attended to. The third stipulation is, that you sign over your properties to defray the expenses that have been incurred on your account. This you have also done.

"Another article yet remains for you to comply with, and that is, that you leave the State forthwith. And whatever may be your feelings concerning this, or whatever your innocence is, it is nothing to me.

"General Lucas (whose military rank is equal with mine,) has made this treaty with you. I approve of it. I should have done the same, had I been here, and am therefore determined to see it executed.

"The character of this state has suffered almost beyond redemption, from the character, conduct, and influence that you have exerted; and we deem it an act of justice to restore her character by every proper means.

"The order of the Governor to me was, that you should be exterminated, and not allowed to remain in the state. And had not your leaders been given up and the terms of the treaty complied with before this time, your families would have been *destroyed* and your houses in *ashes.*

"There is a discretionary power vested in my hands, which, considering your circumstances, I shall exercise for a season. You are indebted to me for this clemency.

"I do not say that you shall go now, but you must not think of staying here another season, or of putting in crops; for the moment you do this, the citizens will be upon you. And if I am called here again, in case of non-compliance with the treaty made, do not think that I shall act as I have done now.

"You need not expect any mercy, but *extermination;* for I am determined the Governor's order shall be executed.

"As for your leaders, do not think—do not imagine for a moment—do not let it enter into your minds that they will be delivered and restored to you again; for their *fate* is fixed—the DIE is cast—their doom is *sealed.*

"I am sorry, gentlemen, to see so many apparently intelligent men found in the situation that you are; and oh! if I could invoke that great Spirit of the unknown God to rest upon and deliver you from that awful chain of superstition and liberate you from those fetters of fanaticism with which you are bound—that you no longer do homage to a man! I would advise you to scatter abroad, and never again organize yourselves with Bishops, Priests, etc., lest you excite the jealousies of the people and subject yourselves to the same calamities that have now come upon you.

"You have always been the aggressors. You have brought upon yourselves these difficulties by being disaffected, and not being subject to rule. And my advice is, that you become as other citizens, lest by a recurrence of these events you bring upon yourselves irretrievable ruin."

When asked by the Court if it was correct, and after reading it, he [Brigham Young] replied:—

Yes, as far as it goes; for, continued he, I was present when that speech was delivered, and when fifty-seven of our brethren were betrayed into the hands of our enemies, as prisoners, which was done at the instigation of our open and avowed enemies, such as William E. M'Lellin and others, and the treachery of Colonel Hinkle. In addition to the speech referred to, General Clark said that we must not be seen as many as five together. If you are, said he, the citizens will be upon you and destroy you, but flee immediately out of the state. There was no alternative for them but to flee; that they need not expect any redress, for there was none for them.

With respect to the treaty, the witness further says that there never was any treaty proposed or entered into on the part of the "Mormons," or even thought of. As to the leaders being given up, there was no such contract entered into or thought of by the "Mormons," or any one called a "Mormon," except by Colonel Hinkle. And with respect to the trial of the prisoners at Richmond, I do not consider that tribunal a legal court, but an inquisition, for the following reasons: That Mr. Smith was not allowed any evidence whatever on his part; for the conduct of the Court, as well as the Judge's own words, affirmed that there was no law for "Mormons" in the state of Missouri. He also knew that when Mr. Smith left the state of Missouri, he did not flee from justice, for the plain reason that the officers and the people manifested by their works and their words that there was *no law nor justice* for the people called "Mormons." And further, he knows that Mr. Smith has ever been a strong advocate for the laws and constitutions of his country, and that there was no act of his life while in the state of Missouri, according to his knowledge, that could be implied or construed in any way whatever to prove him a fugitive from justice, or that he has been guilty of "murder, treason, arson, larceny, theft, and stealing,"—the crimes he was charged with by General Clark, when he delivered him over to the civil authorities; and he supposes that the learned General did not know but that there was a difference between "larceny, theft, and stealing."

The witness also says that they compelled the brethren to sign away their property by executing a Deed of Trust at the point of the bayonet; and that Judge Cameron stood and saw the "Mormons" sign away their property; and then he and others would run and kick up their heels, and said they were glad of it, and "we have nothing to trouble us now." This Judge also said, "G—— d—— them, see how well they feel now." General Clark also said he had authority to make what treaties he pleased, and the Governor would sanction it.

The witness also stated that he never transgressed any of the laws of Missouri, and he never knew a Latter-day Saint break a law while there. He also said that if they would search the records of Clay, Caldwell, or Daviess counties, they could not find one record of crime against a Latter-day Saint, or even in Jackson county, so far as witness knew.

BRIGHAM YOUNG.

V.

TESTIMONY OF LYMAN WIGHT.

Lyman Wight sworn, saith that he has been acquainted with Joseph Smith, Sen., for the last twelve years, and that he removed to the state of Missouri in the year 1831, when the Church of Jesus Christ of Latter-day Saints was organized agreeable to the law of the land. No particular difficulty took place until after some hundreds had assembled in that land who believed in the Book of Mormon and revelations which were given through said Joseph Smith, Sen. After nearly two years of peace had elapsed, a strong prejudice among the various sects arose, declaring that Joseph Smith was a false prophet, and ought to die; and I heard hundreds say they had never known the man; but, if they could come across him, they would kill him as soon as they would a rattlesnake. Frequently heard them say of those who believed in the doctrine he promulgated, that, if they did not renounce it, they would exterminate or drive them from the county in which they lived. On inquiring of them if they had any prejudice against us, they said "No: but Joe Smith ought to die; and if ever he comes to this county we will kill him, G— d— him."

Matters went on thus until some time in the summer of 1833, when mobs assembled in considerable bodies, frequently visiting private houses, threatening the inmates with death and destruction instantly, if they did not renounce Joe Smith as a prophet, and the Book of Mormon. Sometime towards the last of the summer of 1833, they commenced their operations of mobocracy. On account of their priests, by uniting in their prejudices against Joseph Smith, Sen., as I believe, gangs of them thirty to sixty, visited the house of George Bebee, called him out of his house at the hour of midnight, with many guns and pistols pointed at his breast, beat him most inhumanly with clubs and whips; and the same night or night afterwards, this gang unroofed thirteen houses in what was called the Whitmer Branch of the Church in Jackson county. These scenes of mobocracy continued to exist with unabated fury.

Mobs went from house to house, thrusting poles and rails in at the windows and doors of the houses of the Saints, tearing down a number of houses, turning hogs and horses into corn fields, and burning fences. Some time in the month of October they broke into the store of A. S. Gilbert & Co., and I marched up with thirty or forty men to witness the scene, and found a man by the name of McCarty, brickbatting the store door with all fury, the silks, calicos, and other fine goods entwined about his feet, reaching within the door of the store-house. McCarty was arrested and taken before Squire Weston; and although seven persons testified against him, he was acquitted without delay. The next day the witnesses were taken before the same man for false imprisonment, and by the testimony of this one burglar were found guilty and committed to jail.

This so exasperated my feelings that I went with 200 men to inquire into the affair, when I was promptly met by the colonel of the militia, who stated to me that the whole had been a religious farce, and had grown out of a prejudice they had imbibed against said Joseph Smith —a man with whom they were not acquainted. I here agreed that the Church would give up their arms, provided the said Colonel Pitcher would take the arms from the mob. To this the colonel cheerfully agreed, and pledged his honor with that of Lieutenant-Governor Boggs, Samuel C. Owen, and others. This treaty entered into, we returned home, resting assured on their honor that we should not be farther molested. But this solemn contract was violated in every sense of the word.

The arms of the mob were never taken away, and the majority of the militia, to my certain knowledge, were engaged the next day with the mob, (Colonel Pitcher and Boggs not excepted), going from house to house in gangs from sixty to seventy in number, threatening the lives of women and children, if they did not leave forthwith. In this diabolical scene men were chased from their houses and homes without any preparation for themselves or families. I was chased by one of these gangs across an open prairie five miles, without being overtaken, and lay three weeks in the woods, and was three days and three nights without food.

In the meantime my wife and three small children, in a skiff, passed down Big Blue river, a distance of fourteen miles, and crossed over the Missouri river, and there borrowed a rag carpet of one of her friends and made a tent of the same, which was the only shield from the inclemency of the weather during the three weeks of my expulsion from home. Having found my family in this situation, and making some inquiry, I was informed I had been hunted throughout Jackson,

Lafayette, and Clay counties, and also the Indian Territory. Having made the inquiry of my family why it was they had so much against me, the answer was, "He believes in Joe Smith and the Book of Mormon, G— d— him; and we believe Joe Smith to be a —— rascal!"

Here, on the banks of the Missouri river, were eight families, exiled from plenteous homes, without one particle of provisions or any other means under the heavens to get any, only by hunting in the forest.

I here built a camp, twelve feet square, against a sycamore log, in which my wife bore me a fine son on the 27th of December. The camp having neither chimney nor floor, nor covering sufficient to shield them from the inclemency of the weather, rendered it intolerable.

In this doleful condition I left my family for the express purpose of making an appeal to the American people to know something of the toleration of such vile and inhuman conduct, and traveled one thousand and three hundred miles through the interior of the United States, and was frequently answered, "that such conduct was not justifiable in a Republican government; yet we feel to say that we fear that Joe Smith is a very bad man, and circumstances alter cases. We would not wish to prejudice a man, but in some circumstances the voice of the people ought to rule."

The most of these expressions were from professors of religion; and in the aforesaid persecution, I saw one hundred and ninety women and children driven thirty miles across the prairie, with three decrepit men only in their company, in the month of November, the ground thinly crusted with sleet; and I could easily follow on their trail by the *blood that flowed from their lacerated feet* on the stubble of the burnt prairie!

This company, not knowing the situation of the country or the extent of Jackson county, built quite a number of cabins, that proved to be in the borders of Jackson county. The mob, infuriated at this, rushed on them in the month of January, 1834, burned these scanty cabins, and scattered the inhabitants to the four winds; from which cause many were taken suddenly ill, and of this illness died. In the meantime, they burned two hundred and three houses and one grist mill, these being the only residences of the Saints in Jackson county.

The most part of one thousand and two hundred Saints who resided in Jackson county, made their escape to Clay county. I would here remark that among one of the companies that went to Clay county was a woman named Sarah Ann Higbee, who had been sick of chills and fever for many months, and another of the name of Keziah Higbee, who, under the most delicate circumstances, lay on the banks of the river, without shelter, during one of the most stormy nights I ever witnessed, while torrents of rain poured down during the whole night, and streams of the smallest size were magnified into rivers. The former was carried across the river, apparently a lifeless corpse. The latter was delivered of a fine son on the banks, within twenty minutes after being carried across the river, under the open conopy of heaven; and from which cause I have every reason to believe she died a premature death.

The only consolation they received from the mob, under these circumstances, was, "G— d— you, do you believe in Joe Smith now?" During this whole time, the said Joseph Smith, Sen., lived in Ohio, in the town of Kirtland, according to the best of my knowledge and belief, a distance of eleven hundred miles from Jackson county, and I think that the Church in Missouri had but little correspondence with him during that time.

We now found ourselves mostly in Clay county—some in negro cabins, some in gentlemen's kitchens, some in old cabins that had been out of use for years, and others in the open air, without anything to shelter them from the dreary storms of a cold and severe winter.

Thus, like men of servitude, we went to work to obtain a scanty living among the inhabitants of Clay county. Every advantage which could be taken of a people under these circumstances was not neglected by the people of Clay county. A great degree of friendship prevailed between the Saints and the people, under these circumstances, for the space of two years, when the Saints commenced purchasing some small possessions for themselves. This, together with the immigration, created a jealousy on the part of the old citizens that we were to be their servants no longer.

This raised an apparent indignation, and the first thing expressed in this excitement was, "You believe too much in Joe Smith." Consequently, they commenced catching the Saints in the streets, whipping some of them until their bowels gushed out, and leaving others for dead in the streets.

This so exasperated the Saints that they mutually agreed with the citizens of Clay county that they would purchase an entire new county north of Ray and cornering on Clay. There being not more than forty or fifty inhabitants in this new county, they frankly sold out their possessions to the Saints, who immediately set in to enter the entire county from the general government.

The county having been settled, the governor issued an order for the organization of the county and of a regiment of militia; and an election being called for a colonel of said regiment, I was elected unanimously, receiving 236 votes in August, 1837; we then organized with subaltern officers, according to the statutes of the state, and received legal and lawful commissions from Governor Boggs for the same.

I think, some time in the latter part of the winter, said Joseph Smith moved to the district of country the Saints had purchased, and he settled down like other citizens of a new county, and was appointed the first Elder in the Church of Jesus Christ of Latter-day Saints, holding no office in the county, either civil or military. I declare that I never knew said Joseph Smith to dictate, by his influence or otherwise, any of the officers, either civil or military; he himself being exempt from military duty from the amputation, from his leg, of a part of a bone, on account of a fever sore.

I removed from Caldwell to Daviess county, purchased a pre-emption right, for which I gave seven hundred and fifty dollars, gained another by the side thereof, put in a large crop, and became acquainted with the citizens of Daviess, who appeared very friendly.

In the month of June or July there was a town laid off, partly on my pre-emption and partly on lands belonging to government. The immigration commenced flowing to this newly laid off town very rapidly. This excited a prejudice in the minds of some of the old citizens, who were an ignorant set, and not very far advanced before the aborigines of the country in civilization or cultivated minds. They feared that this rapid tide of immigration should deprive them of office, of which they were dear lovers. This was more plainly exhibited at the August election in the year 1838. The old settlers then swore that not one "Mormon" should vote at that election; accordingly they commenced operations by fist and skull. This terminated in the loss of some teeth, some flesh, and some blood. The combat being very strongly contested on both sides, many Mormons were deprived of their votes, and I was followed to the polls by three ruffians with stones in their hands, swearing they would kill me if I voted.

A false rumor was immediately sent to Far West, such as that two or three "Mormons" were killed and were not suffered to be buried. The next day a considerable number of the Saints came out to my house. Said Joseph Smith came with them. He inquired of me concerning the difficulty. The answer was, political difficulties. He then asked if there was anything serious. The answer was, No, I think not. We then all mounted our horses and rode on to the prairie, a short distance from my house, to a cool spring near the house of Esquire Black, where the greater number stopped for refreshments, whilst a few waited on Esquire Black. He was interrogated to know whether he justified the course of conduct at the late election, or not. He said he did not, and was willing to give his protest in writing; which he did, and also desired that there should be a public meeting called; which, I think, was done on the next day.

Said Joseph Smith was not addressed on the subject, but I was, who, in behalf of the Saints, entered into an agreement with the other citizens of the county that we would live in peace, enjoying those blessings fought for by our forefathers. But while some of their leading men were entering into this contract, others were raising mobs; and in a short time the mob increased to two hundred and five, rank and file, and they encamped within six miles of Adam-ondi-Ahman.

In the meantime, Joseph Smith and those who came with him from Far West returned to their homes in peace, suspecting nothing. But I, seeing the rage of the mob and their full determination to drive the Church from Daviess county, sent to General Atchison (major-general of the division in which we lived). He immediately sent Brigadier-General Doniphan with between two and three hundred men. General Doniphan moved his troops near the mob force, and came up and conversed with me on the subject. After conversing some time on the subject, Major Hughes came and informed General Doniphan that his men were mutinying, and the mob were determined to fall on the Saints in Adam-ondi-Ahman. Having a colonel's commission under Doniphan I was commanded to call out my troops forthwith, and, to use Doniphan's own language, "kill every G— d—— mobocrat you can find in the county, or make them prisoners; and if they come upon you give them hell." He then returned to his troops and gave them an address, stating the interview he had with me; and he also said to the mob, that if they were so disposed, they could go on with their measures; that he considered that Colonel Wight, with the militia under his command all sufficient to quell every G— d—— mobocrat in the county; and if they did not feel disposed so to do, to go home or G— d—— them, he would kill every one of them. The mob then dispersed.

During these movements, neither Joseph Smith nor any of those of Far West were at Adam-ondi-Ahman, only those who were settlers and legal citizens of the place.

The mob again assembled and went to De Witt, Carroll county, there being a small branch of the Church at that place. But of the transactions at this place I have no personal knowledge. They succeded in driving the Church twice from that place, some to the east and some to the west. This increased their ardor, and, with redoubled forces from several counties of the state, they returned to Daviess county to renew the attack. Many wanton attacks and violations of the rights of citizens took place at this time from the hands of this hellish band.

Believing forbearance no longer to be a virtue I again sent to the Major-General for military aid, who ordered out Brigadier-General Parks. Parks came part of the way, but fearing his men would mutiny and join the mob, he came on ahead and conversed with me a considerable time.

The night previous to his arrival, the wife of Don Carlos Smith was driven from her house by this ruthless mob, and came into Adam-ondi-Ahman—a distance of three miles, carrying her two children on her hips, one of which was then rising of two years old, the other six or eight months old, the snow being over shoemouth deep, and she having to wade Grand river, which was at this time waist deep. The mob burnt the house and everything they had in it. General Parks passing the ruins thereof seemed fired with indignation at their hellish conduct and said he had hitherto thought it imprudent to call upon the militia under my command, in consequence of popular opinion; but he now considered it no more than justice that I should have command of my own troops, and said to me, "I therefore command you forthwith to raise your companies immediately, and take such course as you may deem best in order to disperse the mob from this county."

I then called out sixty men, and placed them under the command of Captain David W. Patten, and I also took about the same number. Captain Patten was ordered to Gallatin, where a party of the mob was located, and I went to Millport where another party was located. Captain Patten and I formed the troops under our command and General Parks addressed them as follows:

"Gentlemen, I deplore your situation. I regret that transactions of this nature should have transpired in our once happy state. Your condition is certainly not an enviable one, surrounded by mobs on one side and popular opinion and prejudice on the other. Gladly would I fly to your relief with my troops, but I fear it would be worse for you. Most of them have relations living in this county, and will not fight against them.

"One of my principal captains (namely Samuel Bogart) and his men have already mutinied and have refused to obey my command.

"I can only say to you, gentlemen, follow the command of Colonel Wight, whom I have commanded to disperse all mobs found in Daviess county, or to make them prisoners and bring them before the civil authorities forthwith.

"I wish to be distinctly understood that Colonel Wight is vested with power and authority from me to disperse from your midst all who may be found on the side of mobocracy in the county of Daviess.

"I deeply regret, gentlemen, (knowing as I do, the vigilance and perseverance of Colonel Wight in the cause of freedom and rights of man) that I could not even be a soldier under his command in quelling the hellish outrages I have witnessed.

"In conclusion, gentlemen, be vigilant, and persevere, and allay every excitement of mobocracy. I have visited your place frequently, find you to be an industrious and thriving people, willing to abide the laws of the land; and I deeply regret that you could not live in peace and enjoy the privileges of freedom. I shall now, gentlemen, return and dismiss my troops, and put Captain Bogart under arrest, leave the sole charge with Colonel Wight, whom I deem sufficiently qualified to perform according to law, in all military operations necessary."

Captain Patten then went to Gallatin. When coming in sight of Gallatin, he discovered about one hundred of the mob holding some of the Saints in bondage, and tantalizing others in the most scandalous manner. At the sight of Captain Patten and company the mob took fright and such was their hurry to get away, some cut their bridle reins, and some pulled the bridles from their horses' heads and went off with all speed.

I went to Millport, and on my way discovered the inhabitants had become enraged at the orders of Generals Doniphan and Parks, and that they had sworn vengeance, not only against the Church, but also against the two generals, together with General Atchison; and to carry out their plans, they entered into one of the most diabolical schemes ever entered into by man, and these hellish schemes were ingeniously carried out.

Namely, by loading their families and goods in covered wagons, setting fire to their houses, moving into the midst of the mob, and crying out, "The Mormons have driven us and burnt our houses." In this situation I found the country between my house and Millport, and also found Millport evacuated and burnt.

Runners were immediately sent to the governor with the news that the "Mormons" were killing and burning everything before them, and that great fears were entertained that they would reach Jefferson City before the runners could bring the news.

This was not known by the Church of Latter-day Saints until two thousand two hundred of the militia had arrived within half a mile of Far West; and they then supposed the militia to be a mob.

I was sent for from Adam-ondi-Ahman to Far West; reached there, the sun about one hour high, in the morning of the 29th of October, 1838; called upon Joseph Smith, and inquired the cause of the great uproar. He declared he did not know, but feared the mob had increased their numbers, and were endeavoring to destroy us.

I inquired of him if he had had any conversation with any one concerning the matter. He said he had not, as he was only a private citizen of the county—that he did not interfere with any such matters.

He told me there had been an order, either from General Atchison or Doniphan, to the sheriff to call out the militia in order to quell the riots, and to go to him; he could give me any information on this subject. On inquiring for the sheriff, I found him not. That between three and four p. m. George M. Hinkle, colonel of the militia in that place, called on me, in company with Joseph Smith, and said Hinkle said he had been in the camp in order to learn the intention of the same. He said they greatly desired to see Joseph Smith, Lyman Wight, Sidney Rigdon, Parley P. Pratt, and George, W. Robinson.

Joseph Smith first inquired why they should desire to see him, as he held no office, either civil or military. I next inquired why it was they should desire to see a man out of his own county.

Colonel Hinkle here observed, There is no time for controversy. If you go not into the camp immediately, they are determined to come upon Far West before the setting of the sun; and said they did not consider us as military leaders, but religious leaders. He said that if the aforesaid persons went into the camp, they would be liberated that night or very early next morning; that there should be no harm done.

We consulted together and agreed to go down. On going about half the distance from the camp, I observed it would be well for Generals Lucas, Doniphan and others, to meet us, and not have us go in so large a crowd of soldiers. Accordingly, the generals moved onwards, followed by fifty artillerymen, with a four-pounder. The whole twenty-two hundred moved in steady pace on the right and left, keeping about even with the former.

General Lucas approached the aforesaid designated persons with a vile, base and treacherous look in his countenance. I shook hands with him and saluted him thus: "We understand, general, you wish to confer with us a few moments. Will not tomorrow morning do as well."

At this moment George M. Hinkle spake and said, "Here, general are the prisoners I agreed to deliver to you." General Lucas then brandished his sword with a most hideous look and said, "You are my prisoners, and there is no time for talking at the present. You will march into the camp."

At this moment I believe that there were five hundred guns cocked, and not less than twenty caps bursted; and more hideous yells were never heard, even if the description of the yells of the damned in hell is true, as given by the modern sects of the day.

The aforesaid designated persons were then introduced into the midst of twenty-two hundred mob militia. They then called out a guard of ninety men, placing thirty around the prisoners, who were on duty two hours and off four. The prisoners were placed on the ground, with nothing to cover them but the heavens, and they were over-shadowed by clouds that moistened them before morning.

Sidney Rigdon, who was of a delicate constitution, received a slight shock of apoplectic fits, which excited great laughter and much ridicule in the guard and mob militia. Thus the prisoners spent a doleful night in the midst of a prejudiced and diabolical community.

Next day Hyrum Smith and Amasa Lyman were dragged from their families and brought prisoners into the camp, they alleging no other reason for taking Hyrum Smith than that he was a brother to Joe Smith the Prophet, and one of his counselors as President of the Church.

The prisoners spent this day as comfortably as could be expected under the existing circumstances. Night came on, and under the dark shadows of the night, General Wilson, subaltern of General Lucas, took me on one side and said; "We do not wish to hurt you nor kill you, neither shall you be, by G——; but we have one thing against you, and that is, you are too friendly to Joe Smith, and we believe him to be a G—— d—— rascal, and, Wight, you know all about his character." I said, "I do, sir." "Will you swear all you know concerning him?" said Wilson. "I will, sir" was the answer I gave. "Give us the outlines," said Wilson. I then told Wilson I believed said Joseph Smith to be the most philanthropic man he ever saw, and possessed of the most pure and republican principles—a friend to mankind, a maker of peace; "and sir, had it not been that I had given heed to his counsel, I would have given you hell before this time, with all your mob forces."

He then observed, "Wight, I fear your life is in danger, for there is no end to the prejudice against Joe Smith." "Kill and be damned sir," was my answer. He answered and said "There is to be a court-martial held this night; and will you attend, sir." "I will not, unless compelled by force," was my reply.

He returned about eleven o'clock that night, and took me aside and said: "I regret to tell you your die is cast; your doom is fixed; you are sentenced to be shot tomorrow morning on the public square in Far West, at eight o'clock." I answered, "Shoot, and be damned."

"We were in hopes," said he, "you would come out against Joe Smith; but as you have not, you will have to share the same fate with him." I answered "You may thank Joe Smith that you are not in hell this night; for, had it not been for him, I would have put you there." Somewhere about this time General Doniphan came up, and said to me, "Colonel the decision is a d—— hard one, and I have washed my hands against such cool and deliberate murder." He further told me that General Graham and several others (names not recollected) were with him in the decision and opposed it with all their power; and he should move his soldiers away by daylight in the morning, that they should not witness a heartless murder. "Colonel, I wish you well."

I then returned to my fellow-prisoners, to spend another night on the cold, damp earth, and the canopy of heaven to cover us. The night again proved a damp one.

At the removal of General Doniphan's part of the army, the camp was thrown into the utmost confusion and consternation. General Lucas, fearing the consequence of such hasty and inconsiderate measures, revoked the decree of shooting the prisoners, and determined to take them to Jackson county. Consequently, he delivered the prisoners over to General Wilson, ordering him to see them safe to Independence, Jackson county.

About the hour the prisoners were to have been shot on the public square in Far West, they were exhibited in a wagon in the town, all of them having families there but myself; and it would have broken the heart of any person possessing an ordinary share of humanity to have seen the separation. The aged father and mother of Joseph Smith were not permitted to see his face, but to reach their hands through the cover of the wagon, and thus take leave of him. When passing his own house, he was taken out of the wagon and permitted to go into the house, but not without a strong guard, and not permitted to speak with his family but in the presence of his guard; and his eldest son, Joseph, about six or eight years old, hanging to the tail of his coat, crying, "Father, is the mob going to kill you?" The guard said to him, "You d—— little brat, go back; you will see your father no more."

The prisoners then set out for Jackson county, accompanied by Generals Lucas and Wilson, and about three hundred troops for a guard. We remained in Jackson county three or four days and nights, during most of which time the prisoners were treated in a gentlemanly manner and boarded at a hotel, for which they had afterwards, when confined in Liberty jail, to pay the most extravagant price, or have their property, if any they had, attached for the same.

At this time General Clark had arrived at Richmond, and, by orders from the Governor, took on himself the command of the whole of the militia, notwithstanding General Atchison's commission was the oldest; but he was supposed to be too friendly to the "Mormons," and therefore dismounted; and General Clark sanctioned the measures of General Lucas, however cruel, and said he should have done the same, had he been there himself.

Accordingly, he remanded the prisoners from Jackson county, and they were taken and escorted by a strong guard to Richmond; threatened several times on the way with violence and death. They were met five miles before they reached Richmond by about one hundred armed men; and when they arrived in town, they were thrust into an old cabin under a strong guard. I was informed by one of the guards that, two nights previous to their arrival, General Clark held a court-martial, and the prisoners were again sentenced to be shot; but he being a little doubtful of his authority, sent immediately to Fort Leavenworth for the military law and a decision from the United States' officers, where he was duly informed that any such proceedings would be a cool-blooded and heartless murder. On the arrival of the prisoners at Richmond, Joseph Smith and myself sent for General Clark, to be informed by him what crimes were alleged against us. He came in and said he would see us again in a few minutes. Shortly he returned and said he would inform us of the crimes alleged against us by the state of Missouri.

"Gentlemen, you are charged with treason, murder, arson, burglary, larceny, theft, and stealing, and various other charges too tedious to mention at this time;" and he immediately left the room. In about twenty minutes, there came in a strong guard, together with the keeper of the penitentiary of the state, who brought with him three common trace chains, noozed together by putting the small end through the ring, and commenced chaining us up, one by one, and fastening us with padlocks about two feet apart.

In this uncomfortable situation the prisoners remained fifteen days, and in this situation General Clark delivered us to the professed civil authorities of the state, without any legal process being served on us at all during the whole time we were kept in chains, with nothing but *ex parte* evidence, and that given either by the vilest apostates or by the mob who had committed murder in the state of Missouri. Notwithstanding all this *ex parte* evidence, Judge King did inform our lawyer, ten days previous to the termination of the trial, whom he should commit and whom he should not; and I heard Judge King say on his bench, in the presence of hundreds of witnesses, that there was no law for the "Mormons," and they need not expect any. Said he, "If the Governor's exterminating order had been directed to me, I would have seen it fulfilled to the very letter ere this time."

After a tedious trial of fifteen days, with no other witnesses but *ex parte* ones, the witnesses for the prisoners were either kicked out of doors or put on trial themselves. The prisoners were now committed to Liberty jail, under the care and direction of Samuel Tillery, jailer. Here we were received with a shout of indignation and scorn by the prejudiced populace.

Prisoners were here thrust into jail without a regular mittimus, the jailer having to send for one some days after. The mercies of the jailer were intolerable, feeding us with a scanty allowance on the dregs of coffee and tea from his own table, and fetching the provisions in a basket, without being cleaned, on which the chickens had roosted the night before. Five days he fed the prisoners on human flesh, and from extreme hunger I was compelled to eat it. In this situation we were kept until about the month of April, when we were remanded to Daviess county for trial before the grand jury. We were kept under the most loathsome and despotic guard they could produce in that county of lawless mobs. After six or eight days, the grand jury (most of whom, by-the-bye, were so drunk that they had to be carried out and into their rooms as though they were lifeless.) formed a fictitious indictment, which was sanctioned by Judge Birch, who was the State's Attorney under Judge King at our *ex parte* trial, and who at that time stated that the "Mormons" ought to be hung without judge or jury. He, the said Judge, made out a mittimus, without day or date, ordering the Sheriff to take us to Columbia. The Sheriff selected four men to guard five of us.

We then took a circuitous route, crossing prairies sixteen miles without houses; and after traveling three days, the Sheriff and I were together by ourselves five miles from any of the rest of the company for sixteen miles at a stretch. The Sheriff here observed to me that he wished to God he was at home, and your friends and you also. The Sheriff then showed me the mittimus, and he found it had neither day nor date to it, and said the inhabitants of Daviess county would be surprised that the prisoners had not left them sooner; and, said he, "By G——, I shall not go much further."

We were then near Yellow Creek, and there were no houses nearer than sixteen miles one way, and eleven another way, except right on the creek. Here a part of the guard took a spree, while the balance helped us to mount our horses, which we purchased of them, and for which they were paid. Here we took a change of venue, and went to Quincy without difficulty, where we found our families, who had been driven out of the State under the exterminating order of Governor Boggs. I never knew of Joseph Smith's holding any office, civil or military, or using any undue influence in religious matters during the whole time of which I have been speaking.

LYMAN WIGHT.

VI.

TESTIMONY OF SIDNEY RIGDON.

Sidney Rigdon sworn, says I arrived in Far West, Caldwell county, Missouri, on the 4th of April, 1838, and enjoyed peace and quietness, in common with the rest of the citizens, until the August following, when great excitement was created by the office-seekers. Attempts were made to prevent the citizens of Daviess from voting. Soon after the election, which took place in the early part of August, the citizens of Caldwell were threatened with violence from those of Daviess county and other counties adjacent to Caldwell.

This, the August of 1838, I may date as the time of the beginning of all the troubles of our people in Caldwell county and in all the counties in the state where our people were living. We had lived in peace from the April previous until this time; but from this time till we were all out of the state, it was one scene of violence following another in quick succession.

There were at this time settlements in Clay, Ray, Carroll, Caldwell, and Daviess counties, as well as some families living in other counties. A simultaneous movement was made in all the counties and in every part of the state, where settlements were made, this soon became violent; and threatenings were heard from every quarter. Public meetings were held, and the most inflammatory speeches made, and resolutions passed, which denounced all the "Mormons" in the most bitter and rancorous manner. These resolutions were published in the papers, and the most extensive circulation given to them that the press of the country was capable of giving.

The first regular mob that assembled was in Daviess county, and their efforts were directed against the settlements made in that county, declaring their determination to drive out of the county all the citizens who were of our religion, and that indiscriminately, without regard to anything else but their religion.

The only evidence necessary to dispossess any individual or family, or all the evidence required, would be that they were "Mormons," as we were called, or rather that they were of the "Mormon" religion. This was considered of itself crime enough to cause any individual or family to be driven from their homes, and their property made common plunder. Resolutions to this effect were made at public meetings held for the purpose, and made public through the papers of the state, in the face of all law and all authority.

I will now give a history of the settlement in Carroll county. In the preceding April, as myself and family were on our way to Far West, we put up at a house in Carroll county, on a stream called Turkey Creek, to tarry for the night. Soon after we stopped, a young man came riding up, who also stopped and stayed through the night. Hearing my name mentioned, he introduced himself to me as Henry Root; said he lived in that county at a little town called De Witt, on the Missouri river, and had been at Far West to get some of those who were coming into that place to form a settlement at De Witt. Speaking highly of the advantages of the situation, and soliciting my interference in his behalf to obtain a number of families to commence at that place, as he was a large proprietor in the town plat, he offered a liberal share in all the profits which might arise from the sale of property there to those who would aid him in getting the place settled. In the morning we proceeded on our journey.

Some few weeks after my arrival, the said Henry Root, in company with a man by the name of David Thomas, came to Far West on the same business; and after much solicitation on their part, it was agreed that a settlement should be made in that place; and in the July following the first families removed there, and the settlement soon increased, until in the October following it consisted of some seventy families. By this time a regular mob had collected, strongly armed, and had obtained possession of a cannon, and stationed themselves a mile or two from the town. The citizens, being nearly all new comers, had to live in their tents and wagons, and were exerting themselves to the uttermost to get houses for the approaching winter. The mob commenced committing their depredations on the citizens, by not suffering them to procure the materials for building, keeping them shut up in the town, not allowing them to go out to get provisions, driving off their cattle, and preventing the owners from going in search of them. In this way the citizens were driven to the greatest extremities, actually suffering for food and every comfort of life; in consequence of which, there was much sickness, and many died. Females gave birth to children, without a house to shelter them; and in consequence of the exposure, many suffered great afflictions, and many died.

Hearing of their great sufferings, a number of the men of Far West determined on going to see what was doing there. Accordingly we started, eluded the vigilance of the mob, and, notwithstanding they had sentinels placed on all the principal roads, to prevent relief from being sent to the citizens, we safely arrived in De Witt, and found the people as above stated.

During the time we were there, every effort that could be was made to get the authorities of the county to interfere and scatter the mob. The judge of the circuit court was petitioned, but without success; and after that, the governor of the state, who returned for answer that the citizens of De Witt had got into a difficulty with the surrounding country, and they might get out of it, for he would have nothing to do with it; or this was the answer the messenger brought, when he returned.

The messenger was a Mr. Caldwell, who owned a ferry on Grand river, about three miles from De Witt, and was an old settler in the place.

The citizens were completely besieged by the mob: no man was at liberty to go out, nor any to come in. The extremities to which the people were driven were very great, suffering with much sickness, without shelter, and deprived of all aid, either medical or any other kind, and being without food or the privilege of getting it, and betrayed by every man who made the least pretension to friendship; a notable instance of which I will here give as a sample of many others of a similar kind.

There was neither bread nor flour to be had in the place. A steamboat landed there, and application was made to get flour; but the captain said there was none on board.

A man then offered his services to get flour for the place, knowing, he said, where there was a quantity. Money was given to him for that purpose. He got on the boat and went off, and that was the last we heard of the man or the money. This was a man who had been frequently in De Witt during the siege, and professed great friendship.

In this time of extremity, a man who had a short time before moved into De Witt, bringing with him a fine yoke of cattle, started out to hunt his cattle, in order to butcher them, to keep the citizens from actual starvation; but before he got far from the town, he was fired upon by the mob, and narrowly escaped with his life, and had to return; or, at least, such was his report when he returned.

Being now completely enclosed on every side, we could plainly see many men on the opposite side of the river, and it was supposed that they were there to prevent the citizens from crossing; and, indeed, a small craft crossed from them, and three men in it, who said that that was the object for which they had assembled.

At this critical moment, with death staring us in the face, in its worst form, cut off from all communication with the surrounding country, and all our provisions exhausted, we were sustained as the children of Israel in the desert, only by different animals,—they by quails, and we by cattle and hogs, which came walking into the camp; for such it truly was, as the people were living in tents and wagons, not being privileged with building houses.

What was to be done in this extremity? Why, recourse was had to the only means of subsistence left, and that was to butcher the cattle and hogs which came into the place, without asking who was the owner, or without knowing; and what to me is remarkable is, that a sufficient number of animals came into the camp to sustain life during the time in which the citizens were besieged by the mob. This, indeed, was but coarse living; but such as it was, it sustained life.

From this circumstance the cry went out that the citizens of De Witt were thieves and plunderers, and were stealing cattle and hogs. During this time, the mob of Carroll county said that all they wanted was that the citizens of De Witt should leave Carroll county and go to Caldwell and Daviess counties.

The citizens, finding that they must leave De Witt or eventually starve, finally agreed to leave; and accordingly preparations were made, and De Witt was vacated.

The first evening after we left, we put up for the night in a grove of timber. Soon after our arrival in the grove, a female who a short time before had given birth to a child, in consequence of exposure, died.

A grave was dug in the grove, and the next morning the body was deposited in it without a coffin, and the company proceeded on their journey, part of them going to Daviess county, and part into Caldwell. This was in the month of October, 1838.

In a short time after their arrival in Daviess and Caldwell counties, messengers arrived, informing the new citizens of Caldwell and Daviess that the mob, with their cannon, was marching to Daviess county, threatening death to the citizens, or else that they should all leave Daviess county. This caused other efforts to be made to get the authorities to interfere. I wrote two memorials, one to the governor and one to Austin A. King, circuit judge, imploring their assistance and intervention to protect the citizens of Daviess against the threatened violence of the mob.

These memorials were accompanied with affidavits, which could leave no doubt on the mind of the governor or judge that the citizens before mentioned were in imminent danger.

At this time things began to assume an alarming aspect both to the citizens of Daviess and Caldwell counties. Mobs were forming all around the country, declaring that they would drive the people out of the state.

This made our appeals to the authorities more deeply solicitous as the danger increased, and very soon after this the mobs commenced their depredations, which was a general system of plunder, tearing down fences, exposing all within the field to destruction, and driving off every animal they could find.

Some time previous to this, in consequence of the threatenings which were made by mobs, or those who were being formed into mobs, and the abuses committed by them on the persons and property of the citizens, an association was formed, called the Danite Band.

This, as far as I was acquainted with it, (not being myself one of the number, neither was Joseph Smith, Sen.,) was for mutual protection against the bands that were forming and threatened to be formed for the professed object of committing violence on the property and persons of the citizens of Daviess and Caldwell counties. They had certain signs and words by which they could know one another, either by day or night. They were bound to keep these signs and words secret, so that no other person or persons than themselves could know them. When any of these persons were assailed by any lawless band, he would make it known to others, who would flee to his relief at the risk of life.

In this way they sought to defend each other's lives and property; but they were strictly enjoined not to touch any person, only those who were engaged in acts of violence against the persons or property of one of their own number, or one of those whose life and property they had bound themselves to defend.

This organization was in existence when the mobs commenced their most violent attempts upon the citizens of the before-mentioned counties; and from this association arose all the horror afterwards expressed by the mob at some secret clan known as Danites.

The efforts made to get the authorities to interfere at this time was attended with some success. The militia was ordered out under the command of Major-General Atchison of Clay county, Brigadier-Generals Doniphan of Clay, and Parks of Ray county, who marched their troops to Daviess county, where they found a large mob; and General Atchison said, in my presence, that he took the following singular method to disperse them.

He organized them with his troops as part of the militia called out to suppress and arrest the mob. After having thus organized them, he discharged them and all the rest of the troops, as having no further need for their services, and all returned home.

This, however, only seemed to give the mob more courage to increase their exertion with redoubled vigor. They boasted, after that, that the authorities would not punish them, and they would do as they pleased.

In a very short time their efforts were renewed with a determination not to cease until they had driven the citizens of Caldwell, and such of the citizens of Daviess as they had marked out as victims, from the state.

A man by the name of Cornelius Gillum, who resided in Clay county, and formerly sheriff of said county, organized a band, who painted themselves like Indians, and had a place of rendezvous at Hunter's Mills, on a stream called Grindstone. I think it was in Clinton county, the county west of Caldwell, and between it and the west line of the state.

From this place they would sally out and commit their depredations. Efforts were again made to get the authorities to put a stop to these renewed outrages, and again General Doniphan and General Parks were called out with such portions of their respective brigades as they might deem necessary to suppress the mob, or rather mobs, for by this time there were a number of them.

General Doniphan came to Far West; and, while there, recommended to the authorities of Caldwell to have the militia of said county called out as a necessary measure of defense, assuring us that Gillum had a large mob on Grindstone Creek, and his object was to make a descent upon Far West, burn the town and kill or disperse the inhabitants; and that it was very necessary that an effective force should be ready to oppose him, or he would accomplish his object.

The militia were accordingly called out. He also said that there had better be a strong force sent to Daviess county to guard the citizens there. He recommended that, to avoid any difficulties which might arise, they had better go in very small parties without arms, so that no legal advantage could be taken of them. I will here give a short account of the courts and internal affairs of Missouri, for the information of those who are not acquainted with the same.

Missouri has three courts of law peculiar to that state—the supreme court, the circuit court, and the county court; the two former about the same as in many other states of the Union. The county court is composed of three judges, elected by the people of the respective counties. This court is in some respects like the court of probate in Illinois, or the surrogate's court of New York; but the powers of this court are more extensive than the courts of Illinois or New York.

The judges (or any one of them of the county court of Missouri) have the power of issuing habeas corpus in all cases where arrests are made within the county where they preside. They have also all power of justices of the peace in civil as well as criminal cases. For instance, a warrant may be obtained from one of these judges by affidavit, and a person arrested under such warrant.

From another of these judges, a habeas corpus may issue, and the person arrested be ordered before him, and the character of the arrest be inquired into; and if, in the opinion of the judge, the person ought not to be holden by virtue of said process, he has power to discharge him. They are considered conservators of the peace, and act as such.

In the internal regulations of the affairs of Missouri, the counties in some respects are nearly as independent of each other as the several states of the Union. No considerable number of men armed can pass out of one county into or through another county, without first obtaining the permission of the judges of the county court, or some one of them; otherwise they are liable to be arrested by the order of said judges; and if in their judgment they ought not thus to pass, they are ordered back from whence they came; and, in case of refusal, are subject to be arrested or even shot down in case of resistance.

The judges of the county court (or any one of them) have the power to call out the militia of said county, upon affidavit being made to them for that purpose by any of the citizens of said county, showing it just, in the judgment of such judge or judges, why said militia should be called out to defend any portion of the citizens of said county.

The following is the course of procedure: Affidavit is made before one or any number of the judges, setting forth that the county (or any particular portion of it) is either invaded or threatened with invasion by some unlawful assembly, whereby the liberties, lives, or property of the citizens may be unlawfully taken.

When such affidavit is made to any one of the judges, or all of them, it is the duty of him or them before whom such affidavit is made to issue an order to the sheriff of the county, to make requisition upon the commanding officer of the militia of said county to have immediately put under military order such portion of the militia under his command as may be necessary for the defense of the citizens of said county.

In this way the militia of any county may be called out at any time deemed necessary by the county judges, independently of any other civil authority of the state.

In case that the militia of the county is insufficient to quell the rioters and secure the citizens against the invaders, then recourse can be had to the judge of the circuit court, who has the same power over the militia of his judicial district as the county judges have over the militia of the county. And in case of insufficiency in the militia of the judicial district of the circuit judge, recourse can be had to the Governor of the state, and all the militia of the state called out; and if this should fail, then the Governor can call on the President of the United States.

I have given this explanation of the internal regulation of the affairs of Missouri, in order that the court may clearly understand what I have before said on this subject, and what I may hereafter say on it.

It was in view of this order of things that General Doniphan, who is a lawyer of some celebrity in Missouri, gave the recommendation he did at Far West, when passing into Daviess county with his troops, for the defense of the citizens of said county.

It was in consequence of this that he said that those of Caldwell county who went into Daviess county should go in small parties and unarmed; in which condition they were not subject to any arrest from any authority whatever.

In obedience to these recommendations the militia of Caldwell county was called out, affidavits having been made to one of the judges of the county, setting forth the danger which it was believed the citizens were in from a large marauding party assembled under the command of one Cornelius Gillum, on a stream called Grindstone.

When affidavit was made to this effect, the judge issued his order to the sheriff of the county, and the sheriff to the commanding officer, who was Colonel George M. Hinkle; and thus were the militia of the county of Caldwell put under orders.

General Doniphan, however, instead of going into Daviess county, soon after he left Far West returned to Clay county with all his troops, giving as his reason the mutinous character of his troops, who he believed would join the mob, instead of acting against them, and that he had not power to restrain them.

In a day or two afterwards, General Parks, of Ray county, also came to Far West, and said that he had sent on a number of troops to Daviess county, to act in concert with General Doniphan. He also made the same complaint concerning the troops that Doniphan had, doubting greatly whether they would render any service to those in

Daviess, who were threatened with violence by the mobs assembling; but on hearing that Doniphan, instead of going to Daviess county, had returned to Clay, followed his example and ordered his troops back to Ray county; and thus were the citizens of Caldwell county and those of Daviess county, who were marked out as victims by the mob, left to defend themselves the best way they could.

What I have here stated in relation to Generals Doniphan and Parks, was learned in conversations had between myself and them, about which I cannot be mistaken, unless my memory has betrayed me.

The militia of the county of Caldwell were now all under requisition, armed and equipped according to law. The mob, after all the authority of the state had been recalled except from the force of Caldwell county, commenced the work of destruction in earnest, showing a determination to accomplish their object.

Far West, where I resided, which was the shire town of Caldwell county, was placed under the charge of a captain by the name of John Killian, who made my house his headquarters. Other portions of the troops were distributed in different portions of the county, wherever danger was apprehended. In consequence of Captain Killian making my house his headquarters, I was put in possession of all that was going on, as all intelligence in relation to the operations of the mob was communicated to him. Intelligence was received daily of depredations being committed not only against the property of the citizens, but their persons; many of whom, when attending to their business, would be surprised and taken by marauding parties, tied up, and whipped in a most desperate manner.

Such outrages were common during the progress of these extraordinary scenes, and all kinds of depredations were committed. Men driving their teams to and from the mills where they got their grinding done, would be surprised and taken, their persons abused, and their teams, wagons and loading all taken as booty by the plunderers. Fields were thrown open, and all within exposed to the destruction of such animals as chose to enter. Cattle, horses, hogs and sheep were driven off, and a general system of plunder and destruction of all kinds of property carried on, to the great annoyance of the citizens of Caldwell and that portion of the citizens of Daviess marked as victims by the mob.

One afternoon a messenger arrived at Far West calling for help, saying that a banditti had crossed the south line of Caldwell and were engaged in threatening the citizens with death, if they did not leave their homes and go out of the state within a very short time—the time not precisely recollected; but I think it was the next day by ten o'clock, but of this I am not certain. He said they were setting fire to the prairies, in view of burning houses and desolating farms; that they had set fire to a wagon loaded with goods, and they were all consumed; that they had also set fire to a house, and when he left it was burning down.

Such was the situation of affairs at Far West at that time, that Captain Killian could not spare any of his forces, as an attack was hourly expected at Far West.

The messenger went off, and I heard no more about it till some time the night following, when I was awakened from sleep by the voice of some man apparently giving command to a military body. Being somewhat unwell, I did not get up. Some time after I got up in the morning the sheriff of the county stopped at the door and said that David W. Patten had had a battle with the mob last night at Crooked River, and that several were killed and a number wounded; that Patten was among the number of the wounded, and his wound supposed to be mortal. After I had taken breakfast, another gentleman called, giving me the same account, and asking me if I would not take my horse and ride out with him and see what was done. I agreed to do so, and we started, and after going three or four miles, met a company coming into Far West. We turned and went back with them.

The mob proved to be that headed by the Reverend Samuel Bogart, a Methodist preacher; and the battle was called the Bogart Battle. After this battle there was a short season of quiet; the mobs disappeared, and the militia returned to Far West, though they were not discharged, but remained under orders until it should be known how the matter would turn.

In the space of a few days, it was said that a large body of armed men were entering the south part of Caldwell county. The county court ordered the militia to go and inquire what was their object in thus coming into the county without permission.

The militia started as commanded, and little or no information was received at Far West about their movements until late the next afternoon, when a large army was descried making their way towards Far West. Far West being an elevated situation, the army was discovered while a number of miles from the place.

Their object was entirely unknown to the citizens as far as I had any knowledge on the subject; and every man I heard speak of their object expressed as great ignorance as myself. They reached a small stream on the south side of the town, which was studded with timber on its banks, and for perhaps from half a mile to a mile on the south side of the stream, an hour before sundown.

There the main body halted; and soon after a detachment under the command of Brigadier-General Doniphan, marched towards the town in line of battle. This body was preceded probably three-fourths of a mile in advance of them by a man carrying a white flag, who approached within a few rods of the eastern boundary of the town and demanded three persons who were in the town, to be sent to their camp; after which, the whole town, he said, would be massacred. When the persons who were inquired for were informed, they refused to go, determined to share the common fate of the citizens. One of those persons did not belong to the Church of Latter-day Saints. His name is Adam Lightner, a merchant in that city.

The white flag returned to the camp. To the force of General Doniphan was opposed the small force of Caldwell militia, under Colonel Hinkle, who also marched in line of battle to the southern line of the town. The whole force of Colonel Hinkle did not exceed three hundred men; that of Doniphan perhaps three times that number. I was in no way connected with the militia, being over age, neither was Joseph Smith, Sen.

I went into the line formed by Colonel Hinkle, though unarmed, and stood among the rest to await the result, and had a full view of both forces. The armies were within rifle shot of each other.

About the setting of the sun, Doniphan ordered his army to return to the camp at the creek. They wheeled and marched off. After they had retired a consultation was held as to what was best to do. By what authority the army was there, no one could tell, as far as I knew. It was agreed to build, through the night, a sort of fortification, and, if we must fight, sell our lives as dearly as we could. Accordingly, all hands went to work; rails, house-logs and wagons were all put in requisition, and the south line of the town as well secured as could be done by the men and means, and the short time allowed; we expected an attack in the morning.

The morning at length came, and that day passed away, and still nothing was done but plundering the cornfields, shooting cattle and hogs, stealing horses and robbing houses, and carrying off potatoes, turnips, and all such things as the army of General Lucas could get, for such they proved to be; for the main body was commanded by Samuel D. Lucas, a deacon in the Presbyterian church. The next day came, and then it was ascertained that they were there by order of the governor.

A demand was made for Joseph Smith, Sen., Lyman Wight, George W. Robinson, Parley P. Pratt and myself to go into their camp. With this command we instantly complied, and accordingly started.

When we came in sight of their camp, the whole army was on parade marching towards the town. We approached and met them, and were informed by Lucas that we were prisoners of war. A scene followed that would defy any mortal to describe; a howling was set up that would put anything I ever heard before or since at defiance. I thought at the time it had no parallel except it might be the perdition of ungodly men. They had a cannon.

I could distinctly hear the guns as the locks were sprung, which appeared, from the sound, to be in every part of the army. General Doniphan came riding up where we were, and swore by his Maker that he would hew the first man down that cocked a gun. One or two other officers on horseback also rode up, ordering those who had cocked their guns to uncock them, or they would be hewed down with their swords. We ware conducted into their camp and made to lie on the ground through the night.

This was late in October. We were kept here for two days and two nights. It commenced raining and snowing until we were completely drenched; and being compelled to lie on the ground, which had become very wet, the water was running around us and under us. What consultation the officers and others had in relation to the disposition that was to be made of us, I am entirely indebted to the report made to me by General Doniphan, as none of us was put on any trial.

General Doniphan gave an account, of which the following is the substance, as far as my memory serves me: That they held a court-martial and sentenced us to be shot at eight o'clock the next morning, after the court-martial was holden, in the public square in the presence of our families; that this court-martial was composed of seventeen preachers and some of the principal officers of the army. Samuel D. Lucas presided. Doniphan arose and said that neither himself nor his brigade should have any hand in the shooting, that it was nothing short of cold-blooded murder; and left the court-martial and ordered his brigade to prepare and march off the ground.

This was probably the reason why they did not carry the decision of the court-martial into effect. It was finally agreed that we should be carried into Jackson county. Accordingly, on the third day after our arrest, the army was all paraded; we were put into wagons and taken into the town, our families having heard that we were to be brought to town that morning to be shot. When we arrived a scene ensued such as might be expected under the circumstances.

I was permitted to go alone with my family into the house. There I found my family so completely plundered of all kinds of food, that they had nothing to eat but parched corn, which they ground with a handmill and thus were they sustaining life.

I soon pacified my family and allayed their feelings by assuring them that the ruffians dared not kill me. I gave them strong assurances that they dared not do it, and that I would return to them again. After this interview I took my leave of them and returned to the wagons, got in, and we were all started off to Jackson county.

Before we reached the Missouri river, a man came riding along the line apparently in great haste. I did not know his business. When we got to the river, Lucas came to me and told me that he wanted us to hurry, as Jacob Stolling had arrived from Far West with a message from General John C. Clark, ordering him to return with us to Far West, as he was there with a large army. He said he would not comply with the demand, but did not know but Clark might send an army to take us by force. We were hurried over the river as fast as possible, with as many of Lucas' army as could be sent over at one time, and sent hastily on, and thus we were taken to Independence, the shire town of Jackson county, and put into an old house, and a strong guard placed over us.

In a day or two they relaxed their severity. We were taken to the best tavern in town, and there boarded and treated with kindness. We were permitted to go and come at our pleasure without any guard. After some days Colonel Sterling G. Price arrived from Clark's army with a demand to have us taken to Richmond, Ray county. It was difficult to get a guard to go with us. Indeed, we solicited them to send one with us, and finally got a few men to go, and we started. After we had crossed the Missouri, on our way to Richmond, we met a number of very rough-looking fellows, and as rough-acting as they were looking. They threatened our lives. We solicited our guard to send to Richmond for a stronger force to guard us there, as we considered our lives in danger. Sterling G. Price met us with a strong force, and conducted us to Richmond, where we were put in close confinement.

One thing I will here mention, which I forgot. While we were at Independence, I was introduced to Burrell Hicks, a lawyer of some note in the country. In speaking on the subject of our arrest and being torn from our families, he said he presumed it was another Jackson county scrape. He said the Mormons had been driven from that county and that without any offense on their part. He said he knew all about it; they were driven off because the people feared their political influence. And what was said about the Mormons was only to justify the mob in the eyes of the world for the course they had taken. He said this was another scrape of the same kind.

This Burrell Hicks, by his own confession, was one of the principal leaders in the Jackson county mob.

After this digression, I will resume. The same day that we arrived at Richmond, Price came into the place where we were, with a number of armed men, who immediately on entering the room cocked their guns; another followed with chains in his hands, and we were ordered to be chained together. A strong guard was placed in and around the house, and thus we were secured. The next day General Clark came in, and we were introduced to him. The awkward manner in which he entered and his apparent embarrassment were such as to force a smile from me.

He was then asked for what he had thus cast us into prison? To this question he could not or did not give a direct answer. He said he would let us know in a few days; and after a few more awkward and uncouth movements he withdrew. After he went out, I asked some of the guard what was the matter with General Clark, that made him appear so ridiculous? They said he was near-sighted. I replied that I was mistaken if he were not as near-witted as he was near-sighted.

We were now left with our guards, without knowing for what we had been arrested, as no civil process had issued against us. For what followed until General Clark came in again to tell us that we were to be delivered into the hands of the civil authorities, I am entirely indebted to what I heard the guards say. I heard them say that General Clark had promised them before leaving Coles county, that they should have the privilege of shooting Joseph Smith, Jun., and myself; and that General Clark was engaged in searching the military law to find authority for so doing, but found it difficult, as we were not military men and did not belong to the militia; but he had sent to Fort Leavenworth for the military code of law, to find law to justify him in shooting us.

I must here again digress to relate a circumstance which I forgot in its place. I had heard that Clark had given a military order to some persons who had applied to him for it, to go to my house and take such goods as they claimed. The goods claimed were goods sold by the sheriff of Caldwell county on an execution, which I had purchased at the sale.

The man against whom the execution was issued availed himself of that time of trouble to go and take the goods wherever he could find them.

I asked General Clark if he had given any such authority. He said that an application had been made to him for such an order, but he said, "Your lady wrote me a letter requesting me not to do it, telling me that the goods had been purchased at the sheriff's sale; and I would not grant the order."

I did not, at the time, suppose that Clark in this had barefacedly lied; but the sequel proved he had; for, some time afterwards, behold there comes a man to Richmond with the order, and showed it to me, signed by Clark. The man said he had been at our house and taken all the goods he could find. So much for a lawyer, a Methodist, and a very pious man at that time in religion, and a major-general of Missouri.

During the time that Clark was examining the military law, there was something took place which may be proper to relate in this place. I heard a plan laying among a number of those who belonged to Clark's army, and some of them officers of high rank, to go to Far West and commit violence on the persons of Joseph Smith, Sen's wife and my wife and daughter.

This gave me some uneasiness. I got an opportunity to send my family word of their design and to make such arrangements as they could to guard against their vile purpose. The time at last arrived, and the party started for Far West. I waited with painful anxiety for their return. After a number of days, they returned. I listened to all they said, to find out, if possible, what they had done. One night—I think the very night after their return—I heard them relating to some of those who had not been with them the events of their adventure. Inquiry was made about their success in the particular object of their visit to Far West. The substance of what they said in answer was that they had passed and repassed both houses, and saw the females; but there were so many men about the town, that they dare not venture, for fear of being detected; and their numbers were not sufficient to acomplish anything, if they made the attempt; and they came off without trying.

No civil process of any kind had been issued against us. We were then held in duress, without knowing what for or what charges were to be preferred against us. At last, after long suspense, General Clark came into the prison, presenting himself about as awkwardly as at the first, and informed us that we would be put into the hands of the civil authorities. He said he did not know precisely what crimes would be charged against us, but they would be within the range of treason, murder, burglary, arson, larceny, theft, and stealing. Here, again, another smile was forced, and I could not refrain from smiling at the expense of this would-be great man, in whom, he said, "the faith of Missouri was pledged." After long and awful suspense, the notable Austin A. King, judge of the circuit court, took the seat, and we were ordered before him for trial; Thomas Birch, Esq., prosecuting attorney. All things being arranged, the trial opened. No papers were read to us, no charges of any kind preferred, nor did we know against what we had to plead. Our crimes had yet to be found out.

At the commencement we requested that we might be tried separately; but this was refused, and we were all put on our trial together. Witnesses appeared, and the swearing commenced. It was so plainly manifested by the judge that he wanted the witnesses to prove us guilty of treason, that no person could avoid seeing it. The same feelings were also visible in the state's attorney. Judge King made an observation something to this effect, as he was giving directions to the scribe who was employed to write down the testimony, that he wanted all the testimony directed to certain points. Being taken sick at an early stage of the trial, I had not the opportunity of hearing but a small part of the testimony when it was delivered before the court.

During the progress of the trial, after the adjournment of the court in the evening, our lawyers would come into the prison, and there the matters would be talked over.

The propriety of our sending for witnesses was also discussed. Our attorneys said that they would recommend us not to introduce any evidence at that trial. Doniphan said it would avail us nothing, for the judge would put us in prison, if a cohort of angels were to come and swear we were innocent. And besides that, he said that if we were to give the court the names of our witnesses, there was a band there ready to go, and they would go and drive them out of the country, or arrest them and have them cast into prison, or else kill them, to prevent them from swearing. It was finally concluded to let the matter be so for the present.

During the progress of the trial, and while I was lying sick in prison, I had an opportunity of hearing a great deal said by those who would come in. The subject was the all-absorbing one. I heard them say that we must be put to death—that the character of the state required it; the state must justify herself in the course she had taken, and nothing but punishing us with death could save the credit of the state; and it must therefore be done.

I heard a party of them, one night, telling about some female whose person they had violated; and this language was used by one of them: "The d— b—, how she yelled!" Who this person was, I did not know; but before I got out of prison I heard that a widow, whose husband had died some few months before, with consumption, had been brutally violated by a gang of them, and died in their hands, leaving three little children, in whose presence the scene of brutality took place.

After I got out of prison and had arrived in Quincy, Illinois, I met a strange man in the street who inquired of me respecting a circumstance of this kind, saying that he had heard of it, and was on his way going to Missouri to get the children if he could find them. He said the woman thus murdered was his sister, or his wife's sister, I am not positive which. The man was in great agitation. What success he had, I know not.

The trial at last ended, and Lyman Wight, Joseph Smith, Sen., Hyrum Smith, Caleb Baldwin, Alexander McRae, and myself were sent to jail in the village of Liberty, Clay county, Missouri.

We were kept there from three to four months; after which time we were brought out on habeas corpus before one of the county judges. During the hearing under the habeas corpus, I had, for the first time, an opportunity of hearing the evidence, as it was all written and read before the court.

It appeared from the evidence that they attempted to prove us guilty of treason in consequence of the militia of Caldwell county being under arms at the time that General Lucas' army came to Far West. This calling out of the militia was what they founded the charge of treason upon, an account of which I have given above. The charge of murder was founded on the fact that a man of their number, they said, had been killed in the Bogart battle.

The other charges were founded on things which took place in Daviess county. As I was not in Daviess county at that time, I cannot testify anything about them.

A few words about this written testimony:

I do not now recollect one single point about which testimony was given, with which I was acquainted, but was misrepresented, nor one solitary witness whose testimony was there written, that did not swear falsely; and in many instances I cannot see how it could avoid being intentional on the part of those who testified, for all of them did swear to things that I am satisfied they knew to be false at the time, and it would be hard to persuade me to the contrary.

There were things there said so utterly without foundation in truth—so much so, that the persons swearing must at the time of swearing have known it. The best construction I can ever put upon it is that they swore things to be true which they did not know to be so; and this, to me, is wilful perjury.

This trial lasted for a long time, the result of which was that I was ordered to be discharged from prison, and the rest remanded back. But I was told by those who professed to be my friends that it would not do for me to go out of jail at that time, as the mob were watching and would most certainly take my life; and when I got out, that I must leave the state, for the mob, availing themselves of the exterminating order of Governor Boggs, would, if I were found in the state, surely take my life; that I had no way to escape them but to flee with all speed from the state. It was some ten days after this before I dared leave the jail. At last, the evening came in which I was to leave the jail. Every preparation was made that could be made for my escape. There was a carriage ready to take me in and carry me off with all speed. A pilot was ready—one who was well acquainted with the country—to pilot me through the country, so that I might not go on any of the public roads. My wife came to the jail to accompany me, of whose society I had been deprived for four months. Just at dark, the sheriff and jailer came to the jail with our supper. I sat down and ate. There were a number watching. After I had supped, I whispered to the jailer to blow out all the candles but one, and step away from the door with that one. All this was done. The sheriff then took me by the arm, and an apparent scuffle ensued,—so much so, that those who were watching did not know who it was the sheriff was scuffling with. The sheriff kept pushing me towards the door, and I apparently resisting until we reached the door, which was quickly opened, and we both reached the street. He took me by the hand and bade me farewell, telling me to make my escape, which I did with all possible speed. The night was dark. After I had gone probably one hundred rods, I heard some person coming after me. I drew a pistol and cocked it, determined not to be taken alive. When the person approaching me spoke, I knew his voice, and he speedily came to me. In a few moments I heard a horse coming. I again sprung my pistol cock. Again a voice saluted my ears that I was acquainted with. The man came speedily up and said he had come to pilot me through the country. I now recollected I had left my wife in jail. I mentioned it to them, and one of them returned, and the other and myself pursued our journey as swiftly as we could. After I had gone about three miles, my wife overtook me in a carriage, into which I got and rode all night. It was an open carriage, and in the month of February, 1839. We got to the house of an acquaintance just as day appeared. There I put up until the next morning, when I started again and reached a place called Tenney's Grove; and, to my great surprise, I here found my family, and was again united with them, after an absence of four months, under the most painful circumstances. From thence I made my way to Illinois, where I now am. My wife, after I left her, went directly to Far West and got the family under way, and all unexpectedly met at Tenney's Grove.

SIDNEY RIGDON.

[END OF VOLUME III.]

INDEX TO VOLUME III.

C

D

I

J

K

L

M

Q

R

T

V

W

Y